DIFFERENTIAL EQUATIONS

(Including Calculus of Variations)

Salient features of the present edition :

- ★ It has **detailed theory** supplemented with well explained **examples.**
- ★ It has **adequate number of unsolved problems** of all types in exercises.
- ★ It has **Working rules for solving problems** before exercises.
- ★ It has **Hints of tricky problems** after relevant exercises.
- ★ It has **questions** appeared in examinations of **MDU** and **KU**.

Other books by the same author :

1. **Comprehensive Mathematics XI** (*Part A*)
2. **Comprehensive Mathematics XI** (*Part B*)
3. **Comprehensive Mathematics XI** (*Part C*)
4. **Comprehensive Mathematics XII** (*Part A*)
5. **Comprehensive Mathematics XII** (*Part B*)
6. **Comprehensive Mathematics XII** (*Part C*)
7. **Comprehensive IIT-JEE Screening Model Test Papers**
8. **Comprehensive Objective Mathematics** (*For Engg. Entrance Tests*)
9. **Comprehensive Applied Mathematics** (*For Diploma Students*)
10. **Comprehensive Mathematics** (*For Indian Civil Services Exam.*)
11. **Comprehensive Algebra and Trigonometry** (*For B.A./B.Sc. I*)
12. **Comprehensive Calculus** (*For B.A./B.Sc. I*)
13. **Comprehensive Abstract Algebra** (*For B.A./B.Sc. III*)
14. **Comprehensive Discrete Mathematics** (*For B.A./B.Sc. III*)
15. **Comprehensive Business Mathematics** (*For B.Com. I*)
16. **Comprehensive Business Statistics** (*For B.Com. II*)
17. **An Introduction to Computer**

Comprehensive

DIFFERENTIAL EQUATIONS

(Including Calculus of Variations)

(B.A./B.Sc. IInd Year)

PAPER II

(Strictly According to KU and UGC Syllabus)

By

PARMANAND GUPTA

M.Sc., M.Phil. (Maths)

M.A. (Economics)

Head, Deptt. of Mathematics

Indira Gandhi National College, Ladwa

KURUKSHETRA UNIVERSITY

UNIVERSITY SCIENCE PRESS

(An Imprint of Laxmi Publications Pvt. Ltd.)

An ISO 9001:2015 Company

BENGALURU • CHENNAI • GUWAHATI • HYDERABAD

KOCHI • KOLKATA • LUCKNOW • RANCHI

NEW DELHI

Printed and bound in India
First Edition : 2007, *Reprint:* 2009, 2012, *New Edition :* 2016, *Edition* : 2025
ISBN : 978-81-318-0673-9

Branches

✆	Bengaluru	080-26 75 69 30
✆	Chennai	044-24 34 47 26
✆	Guwahati	0361-254 36 69
✆	Hyderabad	040-27 55 53 83
✆	Kochi	0484-405 13 03
✆	Kolkata	033-40 04 77 79
✆	Lucknow	0522-430 36 13
✆	Ranchi	0651-224 24 64

Published in India by

UNIVERSITY SCIENCE PRESS
(An Imprint of Laxmi Publications Pvt. Ltd.)

An ISO 9001:2015 Company
113, GOLDEN HOUSE, GURUDWARA ROAD, DARYAGANJ,
NEW DELHI - 110002, INDIA

Corporate Office : B-33, Sector-5, Noida,
Gautambuddha Nagar (U.P.) - 201 301, INDIA
Telephone : +91-120-44 46 900
www.laxmipublications.com
info@laxmipublications.com

PREFACE TO THE FOURTH EDITION

It is a great pleasure for me to write the preface for the revised fourth edition of this book. I express my heartfelt thanks to my worthy colleagues for conveying their suggestions during the writing work of this book.

The following are some of the salient features of the present edition :

★ **The present edition is in strict confirmity with the U.G.C. Model Curriculum for the new session.**

★ **A new feature "Working Rules for Solving Problems" has been introduced. This would help the students to tackle various types of problems more confidently.**

★ **Questions appeared in latest MDU and KU examinations have also been included in the book.**

★ **The problems, which are comparatively harder, are provided with suitable hints. The author has not desired to dishearten the students by incorporating very tedious problems, which are not expected from the students of average calibre.**

I firmly believe that there is always scope for improvement. Suggestions and comments from worthy teachers would be gratefully received and acknowledged.

—**Author**

SYLLABUS

BM 202 DIFFERENTIAL EQUATIONS AND CALCULUS OF VARIATIONS

Section I (2 Questions)

Series solutions of differential equations—Power series method, Bessel, Legendre and Hypergeometric equations. Bessel, Legendre and Hypergeometric functions and their properties—convergence, recurrence and generating relations. Orthogonality of functions. Sturm-Liouville problem. Orthogonality of eigen-functions. Reality of eigenvalues. Orthogonality of Bessel functions and Legendre polynomials.

Section II (2 Questions)

Laplace Transformation—Linearity of the Laplace transformation. Existence theorem for Laplace transforms. Laplace transforms of derivatives and integrals. Shifting theorems. Differentiation and integration of transforms. Convolution theorem. Solution of integral equations and systems of differential equations using the Laplace transformation.

Section III (3 Questions)

Partial differential equations of the first order. Lagrange's solution. Some special types of equations which can be solved easily by methods other than the general method. Charpit's general method of solution.

Partial differential equations of second and higher orders. Classification of linear partial differential equations of second order. Homogeneous and non-homogeneous equations with constant coefficients. Partial differential equation reducible to equations with constant coefficients. Monge's methods.

Section IV (3 Questions)

Calculus of Variations—Variational problems with fixed boundaries—Euler's equation for functionals containing first order derivative and one independent variable. Extremals. Functionals dependent on higher order derivatives. Functionals dependent on more than one independent variable. Variational problems in parametric form. Invariance of Euler's equation under coordinates transformation.

Variational Problems with Moving Boundaries—Functionals dependent on one and two functions. One sided variations.

Sufficient conditions for an Extremum—Jacobi and Legendre conditions. Second Variation. Variational principle of least action.

Note. The examiner is requested to set ten questions in all selecting questions sectionwise as indicated in the syllabus. The candidate is required to attempt five questions selecting at least one question from each section.

Dedicated to my teachers whose teachings have made me able to grasp some of the fundamentals of Mathematics

CONTENTS

Chapter *Pages*

SECTION II

SECTION III

SECTION IV

SECTION I

SERIES SOLUTION OF DIFFERENTIAL EQUATIONS

1

Series Solution of Differential Equations

1. INTRODUCTION

We know that linear differential equations with constant coefficients can be solved and their solutions are elementary functions.* There also exists some methods in which linear differential equations (with some specific types of variable coefficients) can be solved and their solutions are elementary functions. In general, a linear differential equation with variable coefficients may not admit of any solution which is expressible in terms of elementary functions. In the present chapter, we shall learn the method of solving linear differential equations and obtaining solutions in the form of an infinite series.

2. POWER SERIES

An infinite series of the form $\sum_{m=0}^{\infty} a_m (x - x_0)^m = a_0 + a_1 (x - x_0) + a_2 (x - x_0)^2 + \ldots\ldots$ is called a **power series** in $x - x_0$. Here $a_0, a_1, a_2, \ldots\ldots$ are constants, called the **coefficients** of the power series. The constant x_0 is called the **centre** of the power series. In the above power series, x is a variable.

In particular, if $x_0 = 0$, then the power series in x is $\sum_{m=0}^{\infty} a_m x^m = a_0 + a_1 x + a_2 x^2 + \ldots\ldots$.

For example, $1 + (x-2) + \frac{(x-2)^2}{2!} + \frac{(x-2)^3}{3!} + \ldots\ldots$ is a power series in $x - 2$.

The centre of this power series is 2.

3. CONVERGENCE OF POWER SERIES

Let $$\sum_{m=0}^{\infty} a_m (x - x_0)^m = a_0 + a_1 (x - x_0) + a_2 (x - x_0)^2 + \ldots\ldots \qquad \ldots(1)$$

be a power series in $x - x_0$ with centre x_0 and real coefficients $a_0, a_1, a_2, \ldots\ldots$.

*The *elementary functions* consists of algebraic functions, trigonometric functions, inverse trigonometric functions, exponential functions, logarithmic functions and all others that can be constructed from these by adding, subtracting, multiplying, dividing or forming a function of a function. For example, $\sin x + \tan x^2$, $e^{\cot x} + \sqrt{\log x}$, $\frac{x + x^2 e^{x^3} + \sec x}{\log(1 + x^2)}$ are elementary functions.

This power series is said to be convergent at $x = x_1$, if

$$\lim_{n \to \infty} \sum_{m=0}^{n} a_m (x_1 - x_0)^m$$

exists finitely and in this case the sum of the power series $\sum_{m=0}^{\infty} a_0 (x_1 - x_0)^m$ is the value of this limit.

The power series (1) is always convergent at $x = x_0$ because in this case the power series (1) becomes $a_0 + 0 + 0 + \ldots\ldots$ If there are other values of x for which (1) is convergent, then these values form an interval, called the **convergence interval**. If the convergence interval is finite then it is of the form $|x - x_0| < R$. The constant R is called the **radius of convergence** of (1).

The radius of convergence of the series $\sum_{m=0}^{\infty} a_m (x - x_0)^m$ can be found by using either of the following formulae :

$$(i)\ R = \frac{1}{\lim\limits_{m \to \infty} \sqrt[m]{|a_m|}} \qquad (ii)\ R = \frac{1}{\lim\limits_{m \to \infty} \left| \frac{a_{m+1}}{a_m} \right|}.$$

In this case, the above limits are non-zero finite numbers.

In case, $\lim\limits_{m \to \infty} \sqrt[m]{|a_m|} \left(\text{or } \lim\limits_{m \to \infty} \left| \frac{a_{m+1}}{a_m} \right| \right)$ is zero, then the power series (1) converges for all x and its convergence interval is infinite and radius of convergence, $R = \infty$.

If the power series (1) converges only at its centre x_0, then its radius of convergence, R is defined to be zero.

Thus, we see that radius of convergence exists for each type of power series. If the radius of convergence R is finite and non-zero, then the power series is convergent inside the interval $|x - x_0| < R$ *i.e.*, $x_0 - R < x < x_0 + R$ and divergent outside this interval. A power series may or may not converge at the end points of its interval of convergence.

4. OPERATIONS ON POWER SERIES

(*i*) **Termwise differentiation.** Let $\sum_{m=0}^{\infty} a_0 (x - x_0)^m$ be a power series in $x - x_0$ with centre x_0 and real coefficients $a_0, a_1, a_2, \ldots\ldots$. Let R (> 0) be the radius of convergence of this power series.

$\therefore$ This power series converges in the interval of convergence $|x - x_0| < R$. Let its sum be deonoted by $f(x)$.

$$\therefore \qquad f(x) = \sum_{m=0}^{\infty} a_0 (x - x_0)^m = a_0 + a_1 (x - x_0) + a_2 (x - x_0)^2 + \ldots \text{ for } |x - x_0| < R.$$

It can be proved that the power series on the right side can be differentiated term by term and we have

$$f'(x) = a_1 + 2a_2(x - x_0) + 3a_3(x - x_0)^2 + \ldots\ldots \text{ for } | x - x_0 | < R.$$

Similarly, $f''(x) = 2a_2 + 6a_3(x - x_0) + 12a_4(x - x_0)^2 + \ldots\ldots$ for $| x - x_0 | < R$ etc.

In compact form, we can write :

$$f'(x) = \sum_{m=1}^{\infty} m a_m (x - x_0)^{m-1} \quad \text{and} \quad f''(x) = \sum_{m=2}^{\infty} m(m-1)\, a_m (x - x_0)^{m-2}.$$

(*ii*) **Termwise addition and multiplication.** Let $\sum_{m=0}^{\infty} a_m (x - x_0)^m$ and $\sum_{m=0}^{\infty} b_m (x - x_0)^m$ be two power series with each centre x_0 and sums $f(x)$ and $g(x)$ with radii of convergence R_1 and R_2 respectively.

$$\therefore \qquad f(x) = \sum_{m=0}^{\infty} a_m (x - x_0)^m = a_0 + a_1(x - x_0) + a_2(x - x_0)^2 + \ldots\ldots \text{ for } | x - x_0 | < R_1$$

and

$$g(x) = \sum_{m=0}^{\infty} b_m (x - x_0)^m = b_0 + b_1(x - x_1) + b_2(x - x_2)^2 + \ldots\ldots \text{ for } | x - x_0 | < R_2$$

If $R = \min \{R_1, R_2\}$, then

$$f(x) + g(x) = \sum_{m=0}^{\infty} (a_m + b_m)(x - x_0)^m = (a_0 + b_0) + (a_1 + b_1)(x - x_0) + (a_2 + b_2)(x - x_0)^2 + \ldots\ldots \text{ for } |x - x_0| < R$$

Also $f(x)\, g(x) = \sum_{m=0}^{\infty} c_m (x - x_0)^m$ for $| x - x_0 | < R$,

where $\quad c_m = a_0 b_m + a_1 b_{m-1} + \ldots\ldots + a_m b_0 \quad \forall\ m.$

5. SHIFTING OF SUMMATION INDEX

The shifting of summation index is generally needed in finding the series solution of a differential equation. The summation letter in a sum is a dummy index and any letter can do this job.

For example, $\sum_{m=0}^{\infty} \frac{1}{m!} x^m = \sum_{n=0}^{\infty} \frac{1}{n!} x^n = \sum_{k=0}^{\infty} \frac{1}{k!} x^k$

and each sum is equal to $1 + x + \frac{x^2}{2!} + \frac{x^3}{3!} + \ldots\ldots$

Let the sum $s = \sum_{m=0}^{\infty} m(m+2)\, x^{m+3}$ is to be written in terms of x^m.

We put $m + 3 = k$.

$$\therefore \qquad s = \sum_{k=3}^{\infty} (k-3)(k-1)\, x^k.$$

Since the summation letter is immaterial, we replace k by m and get

$$s = \sum_{m=3}^{\infty} (m-3)(m-1)\, x^m.$$

Example 1. *Express the following sums in terms of x^m and verify the result :*

(i) $\sum_{m=0}^{\infty} \frac{(m+3)^3}{(m+2)!} x^{m+1}$ (ii) $\sum_{m=3}^{\infty} \frac{m!}{(m+4)^2} x^{m-2}$.

Sol. (i) Let $$s = \sum_{m=0}^{\infty} \frac{(m+3)^3}{(m+2)!} x^{m+1}.$$

Let $m + 1 = k$. $\therefore$ $m = k - 1$. Also, $m = 0 \Rightarrow k = 1$

$$\therefore \quad s = \sum_{k=1}^{\infty} \frac{(k+2)^3}{(k+1)!} x^k$$

Replacing k by m, we get

$$s = \sum_{m=1}^{\infty} \frac{(m+2)^3}{(m+1)!} x^m.$$

Verification : $$\sum_{m=0}^{\infty} \frac{(m+3)^3}{(m+2)!} x^{m+1} = \frac{(3)^3}{2!} x + \frac{(4)^3}{3!} x^2 + \frac{(5)^3}{4!} x^3 + \ldots\ldots$$

and $$\sum_{m=1}^{\infty} \frac{(m+2)^3}{(m+1)!} x^m = \frac{(3)^3}{2!} x + \frac{(4)^3}{3!} x^2 + \frac{(5)^3}{4!} x^3 + \ldots\ldots$$

$\therefore$ We get the same power series.

(ii) Let $s = \sum_{m=3}^{\infty} \frac{m!}{(m+4)^2} x^{m-2}$.

Let $m - 2 = k$. $\therefore$ $m = k + 2$. Also, $m = 3 \Rightarrow k = 3 - 2 = 1$

$$\therefore \quad s = \sum_{k=1}^{\infty} \frac{(k+2)!}{(k+6)^2} x^k$$

Replacing k by m, we get, $s = \sum_{m=1}^{\infty} \frac{(m+2)!}{(m+6)^2} x^m$.

Verification : $$\sum_{m=3}^{\infty} \frac{m!}{(m+4)^2} x^{m-2} = \frac{3!}{(7)^2} \quad \frac{4!}{8)^2} x^2 + \frac{5!}{(9)^2} x^3 + \ldots\ldots$$

and $$\sum_{m=1}^{\infty} \frac{(m+2)!}{(m+6)^2} x^m = \frac{3!}{(7)^2} x + \frac{4!}{(8)^2} x^2 + \frac{5!}{(9)^2} x^3 + \ldots\ldots$$

$\therefore$ We get the same power series.

Example 2. *Find the radius of convergence of the following series :*

(i) $\sum_{m=0}^{\infty} \frac{(x-1)^m}{(m+1)!}$ (ii) $\sum_{m=0}^{\infty} (m+2)(m+3)\, x^{m+1}$

(iii) $\sum_{m=0}^{\infty} \frac{x^m}{2^m}$ (iv) $\sum_{m=2}^{\infty} m^m (x - x_0)^m$.

Sol. (*i*) Comparing $\sum_{m=0}^{\infty} \frac{(x-1)^m}{(m+1)!}$ with $\sum_{m=0}^{\infty} a_m (x-1)^m$, we get

$$a_m = \frac{1}{(m+1)!}.$$

$$\therefore \quad \frac{a_{m+1}}{a_m} = \frac{1}{(m+2)!} \div \frac{1}{(m+1)!} = \frac{(m+1)!}{(m+2)!} = \frac{1}{m+2}$$

$$\therefore \quad \lim_{m \to \infty} \left| \frac{a_{m+1}}{a_m} \right| = \lim_{m \to \infty} \left| \frac{1}{m+2} \right| = \lim_{m \to \infty} \frac{1}{m+2} = 0.$$

$\therefore$ Radius of convergence, $R = \infty$.

(*ii*) Let $m + 1 = k$.

$$\therefore \quad \sum_{m=0}^{\infty} (m+2)(m+3)\, x^{m+1} = \sum_{k=1}^{\infty} (k+1)(k+2)\, x^k$$

Replacing k by m, the given series reduces to $\sum_{m=1}^{\infty} (m+1)(m+2)\, x^m$.

Comparing $\sum_{m=1}^{\infty} (m+1)(m+2)\, x^m$ by $\sum_{m=1}^{\infty} a_m x^m$, we get

$$a_m = (m+1)(m+2).$$

$$\therefore \quad \frac{a_{m+1}}{a_m} = \frac{(m+2)(m+3)}{(m+1)(m+2)} = \frac{m+3}{m+1}$$

$$\therefore \quad \lim_{m \to \infty} \left| \frac{a_{m+1}}{a_m} \right| = \lim_{m \to \infty} \left| \frac{m+3}{m+1} \right| = \lim_{m \to \infty} \frac{m+3}{m+1} = \lim_{m \to \infty} \frac{1+\frac{3}{m}}{1+\frac{1}{m}} = \frac{1+0}{1+0} = 1.$$

$\therefore$ Radius of convergence, $R = \frac{1}{1} = \mathbf{1}$.

(*iii*) Comparing $\sum_{m=0}^{\infty} \frac{x^m}{2^m}$ with $\sum_{m=0}^{\infty} a_m x^m$, we get $a_m = \frac{1}{2^m}$.

$$\therefore \quad \frac{a_{m+1}}{a_m} = \frac{2^m}{2^{m+1}} = \frac{1}{2}$$

$$\therefore \quad \lim_{m \to \infty} \left| \frac{a_{m+1}}{a_m} \right| = \lim_{m \to \infty} \left| \frac{1}{2} \right| = \frac{1}{2}$$

$\therefore$ Radius of convergence, $R = \frac{1}{1/2} = \mathbf{2}$.

(*iv*) Comparing $\sum_{m=2}^{\infty} m^m (x - x_0)^m$ with $\sum_{m=2}^{\infty} a_m (x - x_0)^m$, we get $a_m = m^m$.

$$\therefore \qquad \sqrt[m]{|a_m|} = \sqrt[m]{|m^m|} = (m^m)^{1/m} = m$$

$$\therefore \qquad \lim_{m \to \infty} \sqrt[m]{|a_m|} = \lim_{m \to \infty} m = \infty$$

$\therefore$ Radius of convergence, R = **0**.

WORKING RULES FOR FINDING RADIUS OF CONVERGENCE

Step I. Express the given series in the form $\sum_{m=\lambda} a_m (x - x_0)^m$ where x_0 may or may not be zero and λ is a non-negative integer.

Step II. Find $\left|\dfrac{a_{m+1}}{a_m}\right|$ and simplify it.

Step III. Find $\lim_{m \to \infty} \left|\dfrac{a_{m+1}}{a_m}\right|$ and let it be l.

Step IV. (*i*) If $l = 0$, then $R = \infty$.
(*ii*) If $l > 0$ is finite, then $R = 1/l$.
(*iii*) If $l = \infty$, then $R = 0$.

Note. In case a_m contains m as index, then we use $R = \dfrac{1}{\lim_{m \to \infty} \sqrt[m]{|a_m|}}$

EXERCISE 1

1. Express ᵗʰe following sums in terms of x^m and verify the result :

(*i*) $\sum_{m=1}^{\infty} m a_m x^{m-1}$ (*ii*) $\sum_{m=2}^{\infty} m(m-1)\, a_m\, x^{m-2}$ (*iii*) $\sum_{m=0}^{\infty} (m+2)^3\, x^{m+2}$

(*iv*) $\sum_{m=0}^{\infty} \dfrac{(m+1)}{(m+2)} x^{m+3}$ (*v*) $\sum_{m=0}^{\infty} \dfrac{(2m+3)!}{(2m-1)^2}\, x^{m+2}$ (*vi*) $\sum_{m=3}^{\infty} \dfrac{(m+1)^2}{(m-2)^3}\, x^{m-2}$

2. Find the radius of convergence of the following series :

(*i*) $\sum_{m=0}^{\infty} (m+1)!\,(x -$ [illegible] (*ii*) $\sum_{m=0}^{\infty} (2m-1)!\, x^m$ (*iii*) $\sum_{m=0}^{\infty} \dfrac{1}{(m+2)!} (x-3)^m$

(*iv*) $\sum_{m=0}^{\infty} (m+1)^2\, x^m$ (*v*) $\sum_{m=0}^{\infty} \dfrac{(-1)^m}{8^m} (x+2)^m$ (*vi*) $\sum_{m=0}^{\infty} \dfrac{(3m)!}{(m!)^3}\, x^m$

$$f'(x) = a_1 + 2a_2(x - x_0) + 3a_3(x - x_0)^2 + \ldots\ldots \text{ for } |x - x_0| < R.$$

Similarly, $f''(x) = 2a_2 + 6a_3(x - x_0) + 12a_4(x - x_0)^2 + \ldots\ldots$ for $|x - x_0| < R$ etc.

In compact form, we can write :

$$f'(x) = \sum_{m=1}^{\infty} m a_m (x - x_0)^{m-1} \quad \text{and} \quad f''(x) = \sum_{m=2}^{\infty} m(m-1)\, a_m (x - x_0)^{m-2}.$$

(*ii*) **Termwise addition and multiplication.** Let $\sum_{m=0}^{\infty} a_m (x - x_0)^m$ and $\sum_{m=0}^{\infty} b_m (x - x_0)^m$ be two power series with each centre x_0 and sums $f(x)$ and $g(x)$ with radii of convergence R_1 and R_2 respectively.

$$\therefore \quad f(x) = \sum_{m=0}^{\infty} a_m (x - x_0)^m = a_0 + a_1(x - x_0) + a_2(x - x_0)^2 + \ldots\ldots \text{ for } |x - x_0| < R_1$$

and
$$g(x) = \sum_{m=0}^{\infty} b_m (x - x_0)^m = b_0 + b_1(x - x_1) + b_2(x - x_2)^2 + \ldots\ldots \text{ for } |x - x_0| < R_2$$

If $R = \min\{R_1, R_2\}$, then

$$f(x) + g(x) = \sum_{m=0}^{\infty} (a_m + b_m)(x - x_0)^m = (a_0 + b_0) + (a_1 + b_1)(x - x_0) + (a_2 + b_2)(x - x_0)^2 + \ldots\ldots \text{ for } |x - x_0| < R$$

Also $f(x)\, g(x) = \sum_{m=0}^{\infty} c_m (x - x_0)^m$ for $|x - x_0| < R$,

where
$$c_m = a_0 b_m + a_1 b_{m-1} + \ldots\ldots + a_m b_0 \quad \forall\ m.$$

5. SHIFTING OF SUMMATION INDEX

The shifting of summation index is generally needed in finding the series solution of a differential equation. The summation letter in a sum is a dummy index and any letter can do this job.

For example, $\sum_{m=0}^{\infty} \frac{1}{m!} x^m = \sum_{n=0}^{\infty} \frac{1}{n!} x^n = \sum_{k=0}^{\infty} \frac{1}{k!} x^k$

and each sum is equal to $1 + x + \frac{x^2}{2!} + \frac{x^3}{3!} + \ldots\ldots$

Let the sum $s = \sum_{m=0}^{\infty} m(m+2)\, x^{m+3}$ is to be written in terms of x^m.

We put $m + 3 = k$.

$$\therefore \quad s = \sum_{k=3}^{\infty} (k-3)(k-1)\, x^k.$$

Since the summation letter is immaterial, we replace k by m and get

$$s = \sum_{m=3}^{\infty} (m-3)(m-1)\, x^m.$$

Example 1. *Express the following sums in terms of x^m and verify the result :*

(*i*) $\sum_{m=0}^{\infty} \frac{(m+3)^3}{(m+2)!} x^{m+1}$ (*ii*) $\sum_{m=3}^{\infty} \frac{m!}{(m+4)^2} x^{m-2}$.

Sol. (*i*) Let $s = \sum_{m=0}^{\infty} \frac{(m+3)^3}{(m+2)!} x^{m+1}$.

Let $m + 1 = k$. $\therefore$ $m = k - 1$. Also, $m = 0 \Rightarrow k = 1$

$$\therefore \quad s = \sum_{k=1}^{\infty} \frac{(k+2)^3}{(k+1)!} x^k$$

Replacing k by m, we get

$$s = \sum_{m=1}^{\infty} \frac{(m+2)^3}{(m+1)!} x^m.$$

Verification :

$$\sum_{m=0}^{\infty} \frac{(m+3)^3}{(m+2)!} x^{m+1} = \frac{(3)^3}{2!} x + \frac{(4)^3}{3!} x^2 + \frac{(5)^3}{4!} x^3 + \ldots\ldots$$

and

$$\sum_{m=1}^{\infty} \frac{(m+2)^3}{(m+1)!} x^m = \frac{(3)^3}{2!} x + \frac{(4)^3}{3!} x^2 + \frac{(5)^3}{4!} x^3 + \ldots\ldots$$

$\therefore$ We get the same power series.

(*ii*) Let $s = \sum_{m=3}^{\infty} \frac{m!}{(m+4)^2} x^{m-2}$.

Let $m - 2 = k$. $\therefore$ $m = k + 2$. Also, $m = 3 \Rightarrow k = 3 - 2 = 1$

$$\therefore \quad s = \sum_{k=1}^{\infty} \frac{(k+2)!}{(k+6)^2} x^k$$

Replacing k by m, we get, $s = \sum_{m=1}^{\infty} \frac{(m+2)!}{(m+6)^2} x^m$.

Verification :

$$\sum_{m=3}^{\infty} \frac{m!}{(m+4)^2} x^{m-2} = \frac{3!}{(7)^2} \quad \frac{4!}{8)^2} x^2 + \frac{5!}{(9)^2} x^3 + \ldots\ldots$$

and

$$\sum_{m=1}^{\infty} \frac{(m+2)!}{(m+6)^2} x^m = \frac{3!}{(7)^2} x + \frac{4!}{(8)^2} x^2 + \frac{5!}{(9)^2} x^3 + \ldots\ldots$$

$\therefore$ We get the same power series.

Example 2. *Find the radius of convergence of the following series :*

(*i*) $\sum_{m=0}^{\infty} \frac{(x-1)^m}{(m+1)!}$ (*ii*) $\sum_{m=0}^{\infty} (m+2)(m+3)\, x^{m+1}$

(*iii*) $\sum_{m=0}^{\infty} \frac{x^m}{2^m}$ (*iv*) $\sum_{m=2}^{\infty} m^m (x - x_0)^m$.

SECTION IV

Chapter		*Pages*

SECTION I

SERIES SOLUTION OF DIFFERENTIAL EQUATIONS

1

Series Solution of Differential Equations

1. INTRODUCTION

We know that linear differential equations with constant coefficients can be solved and their solutions are elementary functions.* There also exists some methods in which linear differential equations (with some specific types of variable coefficients) can be solved and their solutions are elementary functions. In general, a linear differential equation with variable coefficients may not admit of any solution which is expressible in terms of elementary functions. In the present chapter, we shall learn the method of solving linear differential equations and obtaining solutions in the form of an infinite series.

2. POWER SERIES

An infinite series of the form $\sum_{m=0}^{\infty} a_m (x - x_0)^m = a_0 + a_1 (x - x_0) + a_2 (x - x_0)^2 + \ldots\ldots$ is called a **power series** in $x - x_0$. Here $a_0, a_1, a_2, \ldots\ldots$ are constants, called the **coefficients** of the power series. The constant x_0 is called the **centre** of the power series. In the above power series, x is a variable.

In particular, if $x_0 = 0$, then the power series in x is $\sum_{m=0}^{\infty} a_m x^m = a_0 + a_1 x + a_2 x^2 + \ldots\ldots$.

For example, $1 + (x - 2) + \dfrac{(x-2)^2}{2!} + \dfrac{(x-2)^3}{3!} + \ldots\ldots$ is a power series in $x - 2$.

The centre of this power series is 2.

3. CONVERGENCE OF POWER SERIES

Let $$\sum_{m=0}^{\infty} a_m (x - x_0)^m = a_0 + a_1 (x - x_0) + a_2 (x - x_0)^2 + \ldots\ldots \qquad \ldots(1)$$

be a power series in $x - x_0$ with centre x_0 and real coefficients $a_0, a_1, a_2, \ldots\ldots$.

---

*The *elementary functions* consists of algebraic functions, trigonometric functions, inverse trigonometric functions, exponential functions, logarithmic functions and all others that can be constructed from these by adding, subtracting, multiplying, dividing or forming a function of a function. For example, $\sin x + \tan x^2$, $e^{\cot x} + \sqrt{\log x}$, $\dfrac{x + x^2 e^{x^3} + \sec x}{\log(1 + x^2)}$ are elementary functions.

This power series is said to be convergent at $x = x_1$, if

$$\lim_{n \to \infty} \sum_{m=0}^{n} a_m (x_1 - x_0)^m$$

exists finitely and in this case the sum of the power series $\sum_{m=0}^{\infty} a_0 (x_1 - x_0)^m$ is the value of this limit.

The power series (1) is always convergent at $x = x_0$ because in this case the power series (1) becomes $a_0 + 0 + 0 + \ldots\ldots$ If there are other values of x for which (1) is convergent, then these values form an interval, called the **convergence interval**. If the convergence interval is finite then it is of the form $|x - x_0| < R$. The constant R is called the **radius of convergence** of (1).

The radius of convergence of the series $\sum_{m=0}^{\infty} a_m (x - x_0)^m$ can be found by using either of the following formulae :

(*i*) $R = \dfrac{1}{\lim\limits_{m \to \infty} \sqrt[m]{|a_m|}}$ (*ii*) $R = \dfrac{1}{\lim\limits_{m \to \infty} \left| \dfrac{a_{m+1}}{a_m} \right|}$.

In this case, the above limits are non-zero finite numbers.

In case, $\lim\limits_{m \to \infty} \sqrt[m]{|a_m|} \left(\text{or } \lim\limits_{m \to \infty} \left| \dfrac{a_{m+1}}{a_m} \right| \right)$ is zero, then the power series (1) converges for all x and its convergence interval is infinite and radius of convergence, $R = \infty$.

If the power series (1) converges only at its centre x_0, then its radius of convergence, R is defined to be zero.

Thus, we see that radius of convergence exists for each type of power series. If the radius of convergence R is finite and non-zero, then the power series is convergent inside the interval $|x - x_0| < R$ *i.e.*, $x_0 - R < x < x_0 + R$ and divergent outside this interval. A power series may or may not converge at the end points of its interval of convergence.

4. OPERATIONS ON POWER SERIES

(*i*) **Termwise differentiation.** Let $\sum_{m=0}^{\infty} a_0 (x - x_0)^m$ be a power series in $x - x_0$ with centre x_0 and real coefficients $a_0, a_1, a_2, \ldots\ldots$. Let R (> 0) be the radius of convergence of this power series.

∴ This power series converges in the interval of convergence $|x - x_0| < R$. Let its sum be deonoted by $f(x)$.

$$\therefore \quad f(x) = \sum_{m=0}^{\infty} a_0 (x - x_0)^m = a_0 + a_1 (x - x_0) + a_2 (x - x_0)^2 + \ldots \text{ for } |x - x_0| < R.$$

It can be proved that the power series on the right side can be differentiated term by term and we have

Sol. (*i*) Comparing $\sum_{m=0}^{\infty} \frac{(x-1)^m}{(m+1)!}$ with $\sum_{m=0}^{\infty} a_m (x-1)^m$, we get

$$a_m = \frac{1}{(m+1)!}.$$

$$\therefore \quad \frac{a_{m+1}}{a_m} = \frac{1}{(m+2)!} + \frac{1}{(m+1)!} = \frac{(m+1)!}{(m+2)!} = \frac{1}{m+2}$$

$$\therefore \quad \lim_{m \to \infty} \left| \frac{a_{m+1}}{a_m} \right| = \lim_{m \to \infty} \left| \frac{1}{m+2} \right| = \lim_{m \to \infty} \frac{1}{m+2} = 0.$$

$\therefore$ Radius of convergence, R = ∞.

(*ii*) Let $m + 1 = k$.

$$\therefore \quad \sum_{m=0}^{\infty} (m+2)(m+3)\, x^{m+1} = \sum_{k=1}^{\infty} (k+1)(k+2)\, x^k$$

Replacing k by m, the given series reduces to $\sum_{m=1}^{\infty} (m+1)(m+2)\, x^m$.

Comparing $\sum_{m=1}^{\infty} (m+1)(m+2)\, x^m$ by $\sum_{m=1}^{\infty} a_m x^m$, we get

$$a_m = (m+1)(m+2).$$

$$\therefore \quad \frac{a_{m+1}}{a_m} = \frac{(m+2)(m+3)}{(m+1)(m+2)} = \frac{m+3}{m+1}$$

$$\therefore \quad \lim_{m \to \infty} \left| \frac{a_{m+1}}{a_m} \right| = \lim_{m \to \infty} \left| \frac{m+3}{m+1} \right| = \lim_{m \to \infty} \frac{m+3}{m+1} = \lim_{m \to \infty} \frac{1+\frac{3}{m}}{1+\frac{1}{m}} = \frac{1+0}{1+0} = 1.$$

$\therefore$ Radius of convergence, $R = \frac{1}{1} = \mathbf{1}$.

(*iii*) Comparing $\sum_{m=0}^{\infty} \frac{x^m}{2^m}$ with $\sum_{m=0}^{\infty} a_m x^m$, we get $a_m = \frac{1}{2^m}$.

$$\therefore \quad \frac{a_{m+1}}{a_m} = \frac{2^m}{2^{m+1}} = \frac{1}{2}$$

$$\therefore \quad \lim_{m \to \infty} \left| \frac{a_{m+1}}{a_m} \right| = \lim_{m \to \infty} \left| \frac{1}{2} \right| = \frac{1}{2}$$

$\therefore$ Radius of convergence, $R = \frac{1}{1/2} = \mathbf{2}$.

(*iv*) Comparing $\sum_{m=2}^{\infty} m^m (x - x_0)^m$ with $\sum_{m=2}^{\infty} a_m (x - x_0)^m$, we get $a_m = m^m$.

$$\therefore \quad \sqrt[m]{|a_m|} = \sqrt[m]{|m^m|} = (m^m)^{1/m} = m$$

$$\therefore \quad \lim_{m \to \infty} \sqrt[m]{|a_m|} = \lim_{m \to \infty} m = \infty$$

$\therefore$ Radius of convergence, R = 0.

WORKING RULES FOR FINDING RADIUS OF CONVERGENCE

Step I. Express the given series in the form $\sum_{m=\lambda}^{\infty} a_m (x - x_0)^m$ where x_0 may or may not be zero and λ is a non-negative integer.

Step II. Find $\left|\frac{a_{m+1}}{a_m}\right|$ and simplify it.

Step III. Find $\lim_{m \to \infty} \left|\frac{a_{m+1}}{a_m}\right|$ and let it be l.

Step IV. (*i*) If $l = 0$, then R = ∞.
(*ii*) If $l > 0$ is finite, then R = $1/l$.
(*iii*) If $l = \infty$, then R = 0.

Note. In case a_m contains m as index, then we use $R = \dfrac{1}{\lim_{m \to \infty} \sqrt[m]{|a_m|}}$

EXERCISE 1

1. Express the following sums in terms of x^m and verify the result :

(*i*) $\sum_{m=1}^{\infty} m a_m x^{m-1}$ (*ii*) $\sum_{m=2}^{\infty} m(m-1) a_m x^{m-2}$ (*iii*) $\sum_{m=0}^{\infty} (m+2)^3 x^{m+2}$

(*iv*) $\sum_{m=0}^{\infty} \frac{(m+1)^2}{(m+2)!} x^{m+3}$ (*v*) $\sum_{m=0}^{\infty} \frac{(2m+3)!}{(2m-1)^2} x^{m+2}$ (*vi*) $\sum_{m=3}^{\infty} \frac{(m+1)^2}{(m-2)^3} x^{m-2}$

2. Find the radius of convergence of the following series :

(*i*) $\sum_{m=0}^{\infty} (m+1)!(x - x_0)^m$ (*ii*) $\sum_{m=0}^{\infty} (2m-1)!\, x^m$ (*iii*) $\sum_{m=0}^{\infty} \frac{1}{(m+2)!} (x-3)^m$

(*iv*) $\sum_{m=0}^{\infty} (m+1)^2 x^m$ (*v*) $\sum_{m=0}^{\infty} \frac{(-1)^m}{8^m} (x+2)^m$ (*vi*) $\sum_{m=0}^{\infty} \frac{(3m)!}{(m!)^3} x^m$

3. Find the radius of convergence of the following series :

(i) $\sum_{m=0}^{\infty} \frac{1}{3^m} x^{2m}$ (ii) $\sum_{m=0}^{\infty} (-1)^m (x-2)^{2m}$ (iii) $\sum_{m=0}^{\infty} \frac{(-1)^m}{5^m} (x+1)^{3m}$

(iv) $\sum_{m=0}^{\infty} \left(\frac{5}{4}\right)^m x^{4m}$ (v) $\sum_{m=0}^{\infty} m^m (x-5)^{2m}$ (vi) $\sum_{m=0}^{\infty} (m+2)^m (x-4)^{2m}$

Answers

1. (i) $\sum_{m=0}^{\infty} (m+1)\, a_{m+1}\, x^m$ (ii) $\sum_{m=0}^{\infty} (m+2)(m+1)\, a_{m+2}\, x^m$ (iii) $\sum_{m=2}^{\infty} m^3 x^m$

(iv) $\sum_{m=3}^{\infty} \frac{(m-2)^2}{(m-1)!} x^m$ (v) $\sum_{m=2}^{\infty} \frac{(2m-1)!}{(2m-5)^2} x^m$ (vi) $\sum_{m=1}^{\infty} \frac{(m+3)^2}{m^3} x^m$

2. (i) R = 0 (ii) R = 0 (iii) R = ∞ (iv) R = 1 (v) R = 8 (vi) R = 1/27

3. (i) R = $\sqrt{3}$ (ii) R = 1 (iii) R = $\sqrt[3]{5}$ (iv) R = $\sqrt[4]{4/5}$ (v) R = 0 (vi) R = 0.

Hints

3. (i) $\sum_{m=0}^{\infty} \frac{1}{3^m} x^{2m} = \sum_{m=0}^{\infty} \frac{1}{3^m} (x^2)^m = \sum_{m=0}^{\infty} \frac{1}{3^m} y^m$, where $y = x^2$.

Here $\frac{a_{m+1}}{a_m} = \frac{1}{3^{m+1}} \div \frac{1}{3^m} = \frac{1}{3}$

$\therefore \lim_{m \to \infty} \left| \frac{a_{m+1}}{a_m} \right| = \frac{1}{3}$

$\therefore$ R for $\sum_{m=0}^{\infty} \frac{1}{3^m} y^m$ is $\frac{1}{1/3} = 3$

$\therefore$ Given series converges for $|y| < 3$ *i.e.* $|x^2| < 3$ or $|x| < \sqrt{3}$.

$\therefore$ Radius of convergence for given series is $\sqrt{3}$.

6. ANALYTIC FUNCTION

A real function $f(x)$ is called **analytic** at a point x_0 if it can be represented by a power series $\sum_{m=0}^{\infty} a_m (x - x_0)^m$ in powers of $x - x_0$ with radius of convergence $R > 0$.

Thus, the series $\sum_{m=0}^{\infty} a_m (x - x_0)^m$ converges to $f(x)$ for all x in $|x - x_0| < R$.

The following results are used in judging the analyticity of real functions at given points in their domain :

1. The polynomial functions are analytic at all points.
2. e^x, $\sin x$, $\cos x$ are analytic at all points.

3. If $f(x)$ and $g(x)$ are analytic at $x = x_0$ then the functions $f(x) + g(x)$, $f(x) - g(x)$, $f(x)g(x)$ are also analytic at $x = x_0$. The quotient function $f(x)/g(x)$ is also analytic at $x = x_0$ provided $g(x_0) \neq 0$.

4. If $g(x)$ is analytic at $x = x_0$ and $f(x)$ is analytic at $x = g(x_0)$, then the function $(fog)(x)$ is analytic at $x = x_0$.

7. ORDINARY AND SINGULAR POINTS

Let
$$p_0(x)\frac{d^2y}{dx^2} + p_1(x)\frac{dy}{dx} + p_2(x)y = 0 \qquad ...(1)$$

be a second order differential equation with variable coefficients $p_0(x)$, $p_1(x)$ and $p_2(x)$.

Dividing (1) by $p_0(x)$, we get

$$\frac{d^2y}{dx^2} + \frac{p_1(x)}{p_0(x)}\frac{dy}{dx} + \frac{p_2(x)}{p_0(x)}y = 0$$

$$\Rightarrow \quad \frac{d^2y}{dx^2} + P(x)\frac{dy}{dx} + Q(x)y = 0 \qquad ...(2)$$

where
$$P(x) = \frac{p_1(x)}{p_0(x)} \quad \text{and} \quad Q(x) = \frac{p_2(x)}{p_0(x)}$$

(2) is called the *normalized form* of the equation (1). A point x_0 is called an **ordinary point** of the differential equation (1) if the functions $P(x)$ and $Q(x)$ are both analytic at x_0. If either (or both) of these functions is not analytic at x_0, then x_0 is called a **singular point** of the differential equation (1). Singular points are of two types.

If x_0 is a singular point of the differential equation (1) and the functions $(x - x_0)P(x)$ and $(x - x_0)^2 Q(x)$ are both analytic at x_0 then x_0 is called a **regular singular point** of the differential equation (1). If either (or both) of the functions $(x - x_0)P(x)$ and $(x - x_0)^2 Q(x)$ is not analytic at x_0, then x_0 is called an **irregular singular point** of the differential equation (1).

Illustrations : 1. Consider the differential equation :

$$\frac{d^2y}{dx^2} + (x+4)\frac{dy}{dx} + (x^3 + 2x + 7)y = 0.$$

Here $P(x) = x + 4$ and $Q(x) = x^3 + 2x + 7$. The functions $P(x)$ and $Q(x)$ are polynomial functions and so they are analytic everywhere. Every point is an ordinary point of this differential equation.

2. Consider the differential equation :

$$(x-1)\frac{d^2y}{dx^2} - (3x-2)\frac{dy}{dx} + 2xy = 0 \qquad ...(1)$$

Dividing (1) by $x - 1$, we get

$$\frac{d^2y}{dx^2} - \frac{3x-2}{x-1}\frac{dy}{dx} + \frac{2x}{x-1}y = 0 \qquad ...(2)$$

Here $P(x) = -\dfrac{3x-2}{x-1}$ and $Q(x) = \dfrac{2x}{x-1}$.

The functions $P(x)$ and $Q(x)$ are quotient of polynomial functions.

$\therefore$ $P(x)$ and $Q(x)$ are analytic everywhere except at $x = 1$.

$\therefore$ Every point except '1' is an ordinary point of the differential equation (1).

'1' is a singular point of the differential equation (1).

Also $(x-1)\,P(x) = -(3x-2)$ and $(x-1)^2\,Q(x) = 2x(x-1)$.

These functions are polynomial functions and so are analytic every where.

$\therefore$ The singular point '1' is a regular singular point of the given differential equation.

3. Consider the differential equation :

$$x^2(x-4)^2 \frac{d^2y}{dx^2} + 3(x-4)\frac{dy}{dx} + 8(x+7)\,y = 0 \qquad ...(1)$$

Dividing (1) by $x^2(x-4)^2$, we get

$$\frac{d^2y}{dx^2} + \frac{3}{x^2(x-4)}\frac{dy}{dx} + \frac{8(x+7)}{x^2(x-4)^2}\,y = 0 \qquad ...(2)$$

Here $P(x) = \dfrac{3}{x^2(x-4)}$ and $Q(x) = \dfrac{8(x+7)}{x^2(x-4)^2}$

$\therefore$ P(x) and Q(x) are analytic everywhere except at 0 and 4.

$\therefore$ Every point except 0 and 4 is an ordinary point of the differential equation (1). 0 and 4 are singular points of the differential equation (1).

Now $xP(x) = \dfrac{3}{x(x-4)}$ and $x^2Q(x) = \dfrac{8(x+7)}{(x-4)^2}$.

The function $xP(x)$ is not analytic at 0, whereas $x^2Q(x)$ is analytic at 0.

$\therefore$ The singular point 0 is an irregular singular point of the given differential equation.

Also $(x-4)P(x) = \dfrac{3}{x^2}$ and $(x-4)^2\,Q(x) = \dfrac{8(x+7)}{x^2}$

Here the functions $(x-4)P(x)$ and $(x-4)^2\,Q(x)$ are both analytic at the point 4.

$\therefore$ The singular point 4 is a regular singular point.

WORKING RULES FOR FINDING ORDINARY AND SINGULAR POINTS OF A DIFFERENTIAL EQUATION

Step I. Express the differential equation in the form $\dfrac{d^2y}{dx^2} + P(x)\dfrac{dy}{dx} + Q(x)\,y = 0$.

Step II. Points where both P(x) and Q(x) are analytic are ordinary points.

Step III. Points which are not ordinary points are singular points.

Step IV. The singular point x_0 is a regular singular point if the function $(x-x_0)\,P(x)$ and $(x-x_0)^2\,Q(x)$ are both analytic at x_0, otherwise the singular point x_0 is an irregular singular point.

Example 1. *Find the ordinary points, regular singular points and irregular singular points of the following differential equations :*

(i) $2x^2\dfrac{d^2y}{dx^2} - x\dfrac{dy}{dx} + (x+1)\,y = 0$ (ii) $(x-1)^2x^2\dfrac{d^2y}{dx^2} + 3(x-1)\dfrac{dy}{dx} + 7y = 0$.

Sol. (*i*) We have $2x^2 \dfrac{d^2y}{dx^2} - x \dfrac{dy}{dx} + (x+1)\,y = 0$ ...(1)

Dividing (1) by $2x^2$, we get

$$\frac{d^2y}{dx^2} - \frac{1}{2x}\frac{dy}{dx} + \frac{x+1}{2x^2}\,y = 0 \qquad \text{...(2)}$$

Here $P(x) = -\dfrac{1}{2x}$ and $Q(x) = \dfrac{x+1}{2x^2}$.

The functions $P(x)$ and $Q(x)$ are analytic everywhere except at the point 0.

$\therefore$ Every point except 0 is an ordinary point of the given differential equation.

0 is a singular point of (1).

Now, $xP(x) = -\dfrac{1}{2}$ and $x^2Q(x) = \dfrac{x+1}{2}$.

These functions are analytic at 0.

$\therefore$ 0 is a regular singular point of (1). There is no irregular singular point of the given differential equation.

(*ii*) We have $(x-1)^2x^2 \dfrac{d^2y}{dx^2} + 3(x-1)\dfrac{dy}{dx} + 7y = 0$ ...(1)

Dividing (1) by $(x-1)^2x^2$, we get

$$\frac{d^2y}{dx^2} + \frac{3}{(x-1)\,x^2}\frac{dy}{dx} + \frac{7}{(x-1)^2x^2}\,y = 0 \qquad \text{...(2)}$$

Here $P(x) = \dfrac{3}{(x-1)\,x^2}$ and $Q(x) = \dfrac{7}{(x-1)^2x^2}$.

The functions $P(x)$ and $Q(x)$ are analytic everywhere except at the points 0 and 1.

$\therefore$ Every point except 0 and 1 is an ordinary point of the given differential equation.

0 and 1 are singular points of (1).

Now, $xP(x) = \dfrac{3}{(x-1)\,x}$ and $x^2Q(x) = \dfrac{7}{(x-1)^2}$.

The function $xP(x)$ is not analytic at $x = 0$.

$\therefore$ 0 is an irregular singular point.

Also, $(x-1)\,P(x) = \dfrac{3}{x^2}$ and $(x-1)^2\,Q(x) = \dfrac{7}{x^2}$.

These functions are analytic at $x = 1$.

$\therefore$ 1 is a regular singular point.

EXERCISE 2

Find the ordinary points, regular singular points and irregular singular points of the following differential equations :

1. $\dfrac{d^2y}{dx^2} + 6x\dfrac{dy}{dx} + 11(x-1)\,y = 0$

2. $x\dfrac{d^2y}{dx^2} + 7x^2\dfrac{dy}{dx} + 4xy = 0$

3. $\frac{d^2y}{dx^2} + \frac{1}{x-2}\frac{dy}{dx} + 14y = 0$

4. $(x+1)\frac{d^2y}{dx^2} + 3\frac{dy}{dx} + 7y = 0$

5. $(x-1)(x+2)\frac{d^2y}{dx^2} + x^2\frac{dy}{dx} + xy = 0$

6. $x^3\frac{d^2y}{dx^2} + 4\frac{dy}{dx} + 6(x+1)y = 0$

7. $x(x+1)^2\frac{d^2y}{dx^2} + (x-1)\frac{dy}{dx} + 16x^3y = 0$

8. $(x-1)^4\frac{d^2y}{dx^2} + x\frac{dy}{dx} + y = 0.$

Answers

1. All points ; no point ; no point
2. All points ; no point ; no point
3. All points except 2 ; 2 ; no point
4. All points except − 1 ; − 1 ; no point
5. All points except − 2, 1 ; − 2, 1 ; no point
6. All points except 0 ; no point, 0
7. All points except − 1, 0 ; 0 ; − 1
8. All points except 1 ; no point ; 1.

---

8. SERIES SOLUTION OF DIFFERENTIAL EQUATIONS

In the present chapter, we shall confine ourselves to the series solution of second order differential equations with variable coefficients and expressible in the form

$$p_0(x)\frac{d^2y}{dx^2} + p_1(x)\frac{dy}{dx} + p_2(x)y = 0$$

where $p_0(x)$, $p_1(x)$ and $p_2(x)$ are functions of x. There are two methods of solving such differential equations, depending upon the nature of functions $p_0(x)$, $p_1(x)$ and $p_2(x)$. These methods are :

1. Power series method
2. Frobenius method.

9. POWER SERIES METHOD

If x_0 is an ordinary point of the differential equation

$$p_0(x)\frac{d^2y}{dx^2} + p_1(x)\frac{dy}{dx} + p_2(x)y = 0$$

then the **power series method** is used to find a power series (in powers of $x - x_0$) solution of this differential equation.

Theorem. If x_0 is an ordinary point of the differential equation $p_0(x)\frac{d^2y}{dx^2} + p_1(x)\frac{dy}{dx} + p_2(x)y = 0$, then every solution of this differential equation is analytic at $x = x_0$ and can thus be represented by a power series in powers of $x - x_0$ with radius of convergence $R > 0$.

Note. The proof of this theorem is beyond the scope of this book.

Method. Let x_0 be an ordinary point of the differential equation

$$p_0(x)\frac{d^2y}{dx^2} + p_1(x)\frac{dy}{dx} + p_2(x)y = 0 \qquad ...(1)$$

Let $$y = a_0 + a_1(x - x_0) + a_2(x - x_0)^2 + ... = \sum_{m=0}^{\infty} a_m(x - x_0)^m$$

be a solution of the differential equation (1).

Let the radius of convergence of this power series be R(> 0).

∴ The power series converges on the interval $| x - x_0 | < R$ about x_0.

∴ This power series can be differentiated term by term on this interval twice in succession.

$$\therefore \quad \frac{dy}{dx} = a_1 + 2a_2(x - x_0) + 3a_3(x - x_0)^2 + \ldots\ldots = \sum_{m=1}^{\infty} m a_m (x - x_0)^{m-1}$$

and
$$\frac{d^2y}{dx^2} = 2a_2 + 6a_3(x - x_0) + 12a_4(x - x_0)^2 + \ldots\ldots = \sum_{m=2}^{\infty} m(m-1)a_m (x - x_0)^{m-2}.$$

Substituting the values of $y, \dfrac{dy}{dx}$ and $\dfrac{d^2y}{dx^2}$ in (1), we get

$$p_0(x) \sum_{m=2}^{\infty} m(m-1)\, a_m\, (x - x_0)^{m-2} + p_1(x) \sum_{m=1}^{\infty} m a_m (x - x_0)^{m-1} + p_2(x) \sum_{m=0}^{\infty} a_m (x - x_0)^m = 0$$

On simplification, let this reduces to

$$A_0 + A_1(x - x_0) + A_2(x - x_0)^2 + \ldots\ldots = 0 \qquad \ldots(2)$$

The coefficients $A_0, A_1, A_2, \ldots\ldots$ are functions of $a_0, a_1, a_2, \ldots\ldots$.

(2) is true for all x in the interval $| x - x_0 | < R$.

∴ We have $A_0 = A_1 = A_2 = \ldots\ldots = 0$.

Solving these, we get the values of the coefficients $a_0, a_1, a_2, \ldots\ldots$.

Substituting the values of $a_0, a_1, a_2, \ldots\ldots$ in $y = \sum_{m=0}^{\infty} a_m (x - x_0)^m$, we get the required solution of the given differential equation.

WORKING RULES FOR SOLVING $\mathbf{p_0(x)\dfrac{d^2y}{dx^2} + p_1(x)\dfrac{dy}{dx} + p_2(x)y = 0}$ WHERE $\mathbf{x_0}$ IS AN ORDINARY POINT

Step I. Make sure that 'x_0' is an ordinary point of the given differential equation.

Step II. Assume the solution to be $y = \sum_{m=0}^{\infty} a_m (x - x_0)^m$.

Step III. Write $\dfrac{dy}{dx} = \sum_{m=1}^{\infty} m a_m (x - x_0)^{m-1}$ and $\dfrac{d^2y}{dx^2} = \sum_{m=2}^{\infty} m(m-1)\, a_m (x - x_0)^{m-2}$.

Step IV. Substitute the values of y, $\dfrac{dy}{dx}$ and $\dfrac{d^2y}{dx^2}$ in the given differential equation.

Step V. Shift the summation index so that each term is written in terms of $(x - x_0)^m$.

Step VI. Equate to constant term and coefficients of various powers of $x - x_0$ to zero.

Step VII. Solve these equations to find the values of $a_0, a_1, a_2, \ldots\ldots$ and substitute these values in $y = \sum_{m=0}^{\infty} a_m (x - x_0)^m$.

Type I. On finding series solution about '0'

Example 1. *Find the power series solution of the differential equation*

$$\frac{d^2y}{dx^2} + x\frac{dy}{dx} + x^2y = 0$$

about '0' i.e. in powers of x.

Sol. We have $$\frac{d^2y}{dx^2} + x\frac{dy}{dx} + x^2y = 0 \quad ...(1)$$

Comparing (1) with $\frac{d^2y}{dx^2} + P(x)\frac{dy}{dx} + Q(x)y = 0$, we get $P(x) = x$ and $Q(x) = x^2$.

The functions $P(x)$ and $Q(x)$ are both analytic at $x = 0$.

∴ '0' is an ordinary point of (1).

Let $$y = \sum_{m=0}^{\infty} a_m x^m \quad ...(2)$$

be the power series solution of (1) about '0'.

$$(2) \Rightarrow \quad \frac{dy}{dx} = \sum_{m=1}^{\infty} m a_m x^{m-1} \text{ and } \frac{d^2y}{dx^2} = \sum_{m=2}^{\infty} m(m-1)\, a_m x^{m-2}.$$

Putting the values of y, $\frac{dy}{dx}$ and $\frac{d^2y}{dx^2}$ in (1), we get

$$\sum_{m=2}^{\infty} m(m-1)\, a_m x^{m-2} + x\sum_{m=1}^{\infty} m a_m x^{m-1} + x^2 \sum_{m=0}^{\infty} a_m x^m = 0.$$

$$\Rightarrow \quad \sum_{m=2}^{\infty} m(m-1)\, a_m x^{m-2} + \sum_{m=1}^{\infty} m a_m x^m + \sum_{m=0}^{\infty} a_m x^{m+2} = 0 \quad ...(3)$$

Let $k = m - 2$. ∴ $m = k + 2$

$$\therefore \quad \sum_{m=2}^{\infty} m(m-1)\, a_m x^{m-2} = \sum_{k=0}^{\infty} (k+2)(k+1)\, a_{k+2} x^k = \sum_{m=0}^{\infty} (m+2)(m+1)\, a_{m+2} x^m$$

(By replacing k by m)

Let $k = m + 2$. ∴ $m = k - 2$.

$$\therefore \quad \sum_{m=0}^{\infty} a_m x^{m+2} = \sum_{k=2}^{\infty} a_{k-2} x^k = \sum_{m=2}^{\infty} a_{m-2} x^m$$

(By replacing k by m)

$$\therefore \ (3) \Rightarrow \quad \sum_{m=0}^{\infty} (m+2)(m+1)\, a_{m+2} x^m + \sum_{m=1}^{\infty} m\, a_m x^m + \sum_{m=2}^{\infty} a_{m-2} x^m = 0$$

$$\Rightarrow \left[2a_2 + 6a_3 x + \sum_{m=2}^{\infty} (m+2)(m+1)\, a_{m+2} x^m\right] + \left[a_1 x + \sum_{m=2}^{\infty} m\, a_m x^m\right] + \sum_{m=2}^{\infty} a_{m-2} x^m = 0$$

$$\Rightarrow \quad 2a_2 + (a_1 + 6a_3)x + \sum_{m=2}^{\infty}\left[(m+2)(m+1)a_{m+2} + m\,a_m + a_{m-2}\right]x^m = 0 \qquad ...(4)$$

(4) is an identity for all x in the interval of convergence of $y = \sum_{m=0}^{\infty} a_m x^m$

$$\therefore \quad 2a_2 = 0 \qquad ...(5)$$

$$a_1 + 6a_3 = 0 \qquad ...(6)$$

and
$$(m+2)(m+1)a_{m+2} + m\,a_m + a_{m-2} = 0 \quad \forall \quad m \geq 2 \qquad ...(7)$$

$$(5) \Rightarrow \quad a_2 = 0, \qquad (6) \Rightarrow \quad a_3 = -\frac{1}{6}a_1$$

$$(7) \Rightarrow \quad a_{m+2} = -\frac{m\,a_m + a_{m-2}}{(m+2)(m+1)} \quad \text{for } m \geq 2 \qquad ...(8)$$

$$m = 2 \text{ in } (8) \quad \Rightarrow \quad a_4 = -\frac{2a_2 + a_0}{4 \times 3} = -\frac{a_0}{12}$$

$$m = 3 \text{ in } (8) \quad \Rightarrow \quad a_5 = -\frac{3a_3 + a_1}{5 \times 4} = -\frac{3(-a_1/6) + a_1}{20} = -\frac{a_1}{40}$$

$$m = 4 \text{ in } (8) \quad \Rightarrow \quad a_6 = -\frac{4a_4 + a_2}{6 \times 5} = -\frac{4(-a_0/12) + 0}{30} = \frac{a_0}{90}$$

....

Putting these values in (2), we get

$$y = a_0 + a_1 x + 0.x^2 + \left(-\frac{a_1}{6}\right)x^3 + \left(-\frac{a_0}{12}\right)x^4 + \left(-\frac{a_1}{40}\right)x^5 + \left(\frac{a_0}{90}\right)x^6 + ...$$

$$\therefore \quad \mathbf{y = a_0\left(1 - \frac{x^4}{12} + \frac{x^6}{90} + ...\right) + a_1\left(x - \frac{x^3}{6} - \frac{x^5}{40} + ...\right)}.$$

This is the required power series solution of the given equation. Here a_0 and a_1 are arbitrary constants.

Remark. For the given differential equation, the power series $1 - \frac{x^4}{12} + \frac{x^6}{90} + ...$ and $x - \frac{x^3}{6} - \frac{x^5}{40} + ...$ are two linearly independent solutions.

Example 2. *Find the power series solution of the differential equation*

$$(x^3 - 1)\frac{d^2y}{dx^2} + x^2\frac{dy}{dx} + xy = 0 \quad \textit{about '0' i.e. in powers of } x.$$

Sol. We have
$$(x^3 - 1)\frac{d^2y}{dx^2} + x^2\frac{dy}{dx} + xy = 0. \qquad ...(1)$$

Dividing (1) by $x^3 - 1$, we get
$$\frac{d^2y}{dx^2} + \frac{x^2}{x^3 - 1}\frac{dy}{dx} + \frac{x}{x^3 - 1}y = 0 \qquad ...(2)$$

Comparing (2) with $\frac{d^2y}{dx^2} + P(x)\frac{dy}{dx} + Q(x)\,y = 0$, we get

$$P(x) = \frac{x^2}{x^3 - 1} \text{ and } Q(x) = \frac{x}{x^3 - 1}.$$

The functions P(x) and Q(x) are both analytic at $x = 0$.

∴ '0' is an ordinary point of (1).

Let $$y = \sum_{m=0}^{\infty} a_m x^m \qquad ...(3)$$

be the power series solution of (1) about '0'.

$$(3) \Rightarrow \quad \frac{dy}{dx} = \sum_{m=1}^{\infty} m\, a_m x^{m-1} \text{ and } \frac{d^2y}{dx^2} = \sum_{m=2}^{\infty} m(m-1)\, a_m x^{m-2}.$$

Putting the values of y, $\frac{dy}{dx}$ and $\frac{d^2y}{dx^2}$ in (1), we get

$$(x^3 - 1)\sum_{m=2}^{\infty} m(m-1)\,a_m x^{m-2} + x^2 \sum_{m=1}^{\infty} m\, a_m x^{m-1} + x\sum_{m=0}^{\infty} a_m x^m = 0$$

$$\Rightarrow \sum_{m=2}^{\infty} m(m-1)\,a_m x^{m+1} - \sum_{m=2}^{\infty} m(m-1)\,a_m x^{m-2} + \sum_{m=1}^{\infty} m\,a_m x^{m+1} + \sum_{m=0}^{\infty} a_m x^{m+1} = 0$$

$$\Rightarrow \sum_{m=3}^{\infty} (m-1)(m-2)\,a_{m-1} x^m - \sum_{m=0}^{\infty} (m+2)(m+1)\,a_{m+2} x^m$$

$$+ \sum_{m=2}^{\infty} (m-1)\,a_{m-1} x^m + \sum_{m=1}^{\infty} a_{m-1} x^m = 0$$

(By shifting of indices)

$$\Rightarrow \sum_{m=3}^{\infty} (m-1)(m-2)\,a_{m-1} x^m - \left[2a_2 + 6a_3 x + 12a_4 x^2 + \sum_{m=3}^{\infty} (m+2)(m+1)\,a_{m+2} x^m\right]$$

$$+ \left[a_1 x^2 + \sum_{m=3}^{\infty} (m-1)\,a_{m-1} x^m\right] + \left[a_0 x + a_1 x^2 + \sum_{m=3}^{\infty} a_{m-1} x^m\right] = 0$$

$$\Rightarrow -2a_2 + (a_0 - 6a_3)\,x + (2a_1 - 12a_4)\,x^2$$

$$+ \sum_{m=3}^{\infty} [(m-1)(m-2)\,a_{m-1} - (m+2)(m+1)\,a_{m+2} + (m-1)\,a_{m-1} + a_{m-1}]\,x^m = 0 \qquad ...(4)$$

(4) is an identity for all x in the interval of convergence of $y = \sum_{m=0}^{\infty} a_m x^m$.

∴

$$-2a_2 = 0 \qquad ...(5)$$

$$a_0 - 6a_3 = 0 \qquad ...(6)$$

$$2a_1 - 12a_4 = 0 \qquad ...(7)$$

$$(m-1)(m-2)a_{m-1}-(m+2)(m+1)a_{m+2}+(m-1)a_{m-1}+a_{m-1}=0 \ \forall \ m\geq 3$$

$$\Rightarrow \quad (m^2-2m+2)a_{m-1}-(m+2)(m+1)a_{m+2}=0 \ \forall \ m\geq 3 \qquad ...(8)$$

$$(5) \Rightarrow \quad a_2=0, \qquad (6) \Rightarrow a_3=\frac{1}{6}a_0. \qquad (7) \Rightarrow a_4=\frac{1}{6}a_1$$

$$(8) \Rightarrow \quad a_{m+2}=\frac{m^2-2m+2}{(m+2)(m+1)}a_{m-1} \ \forall \ m\geq 3 \qquad ...(9)$$

$$m=3 \text{ in } (9) \quad \Rightarrow \quad a_5=\frac{1}{4}a_2=\frac{1}{4}\times 0=0$$

$$m=4 \text{ in } (9) \quad \Rightarrow \quad a_6=\frac{1}{3}a_3=\frac{1}{18}a_0$$

$$m=5 \text{ in } (9) \quad \Rightarrow \quad a_7=\frac{17}{42}a_4=\frac{17}{252}a_1$$

....

Putting these values in (3), we get

$$y=a_0+a_1x+0.x^2+\frac{1}{6}a_0x^3+\frac{1}{6}a_1x^4+0.x^5-\frac{1}{18}a_0x^6+......$$

$$\therefore \quad \mathbf{y=a_0\left(1+\frac{1}{6}x^3+\frac{1}{18}x^6+......\right)+a_1\left(x+\frac{1}{6}x^4+\frac{17}{252}x^7+......\right)}$$

This is the required power series solution. Here a_0 and a_1 are arbitrary solutions.

Remark. For the given differential equation, the power series $1+\frac{x^3}{6}+\frac{x^6}{18}+......$ and $x+\frac{x^4}{6}+\frac{17x^7}{252}+......$ are two linearly independent solutions.

Type II. On finding series solution about a non-zero point.

Example 3. *Find the power series solution of the differential equation*

$$x\frac{d^2y}{dx^2}+\frac{dy}{dx}+2y=0 \text{ about '1' i.e. in powers of } x-1. \qquad \text{(KU 2005 S)}$$

Sol. We have
$$x\frac{d^2y}{dx^2}+\frac{dy}{dx}+2y=0. \qquad ...(1)$$

Dividing (1) by x, we get
$$\frac{d^2y}{dx^2}+\frac{1}{x}\frac{dy}{dx}+\frac{2}{x}y=0 \qquad ...(2)$$

Comparing (2) with $\frac{d^2y}{dx^2}+P(x)\frac{dy}{dx}+Q(x)y=0$, we get

$$P(x)=\frac{1}{x} \text{ and } Q(x)=\frac{2}{x}.$$

The functions P(x) and Q(x) are both analytic at $x=1$.

$\therefore$ '1' is an ordinary point of (1).

Let $$y = \sum_{m=0}^{\infty} a_m (x-1)^m \qquad ...(3)$$

be the power series solution of (1) about '1'.

(3) $\Rightarrow$ $$\frac{dy}{dx} = \sum_{m=1}^{\infty} m\, a_m (x-1)^{m-1} \text{ and } \frac{d^2y}{dx^2} = \sum_{m=2}^{\infty} m(m-1)\, a_m (x-1)^{m-2}.$$

Putting the values of y, $\frac{dy}{dx}$ and $\frac{d^2y}{dx^2}$ in (1), we get

$$x \sum_{m=2}^{\infty} m(m-1)\, a_m (x-1)^{m-2} + \sum_{m=1}^{\infty} m\, a_m (x-1)^{m-1} + 2\sum_{m=0}^{\infty} a_m (x-1)^m = 0$$

$$\Rightarrow \quad [(x-1)+1] \sum_{m=2}^{\infty} m(m-1)\, a_m (x-1)^{m-2} + \sum_{m=1}^{\infty} m\, a_m (x-1)^{m-1} + 2\sum_{m=0}^{\infty} a_m (x-1)^m = 0$$

$$\Rightarrow \quad \sum_{m=2}^{\infty} m(m-1)\, a_m (x-1)^{m-1} + \sum_{m=2}^{\infty} m(m-1)\, a_m (x-1)^{m-2}$$
$$+ \sum_{m=1}^{\infty} m\, a_m (x-1)^{m-1} + 2\sum_{m=0}^{\infty} a_m (x-1)^m = 0$$

$$\Rightarrow \quad \sum_{m=1}^{\infty} (m+1)\, m\, a_{m+1} (x-1)^m + \sum_{m=0}^{\infty} (m+2)(m+1)\, a_{m+2} (x-1)^m$$
$$+ \sum_{m=0}^{\infty} (m+1)\, a_{m+1} (x-1)^m + 2\sum_{m=0}^{\infty} a_m (x-1)^m = 0$$

(By shifting of indices)

$$\Rightarrow \quad \sum_{m=1}^{\infty} (m+1)\, m\, a_{m+1} (x-1)^m + \left[2a_2 + \sum_{m=1}^{\infty} (m+2)(m+1)\, a_{m+2} (x-1)^m\right]$$
$$+ \left[a_1 + \sum_{m=1}^{\infty} (m+1)\, a_{m+1} (x-1)^m\right] + \left[2a_0 + 2\sum_{m=1}^{\infty} a_m (x-1)^m\right] = 0$$

$$\Rightarrow \quad 2a_0 + a_1 + 2a_2 + \sum_{m=1}^{\infty} [(m+1)\, m\, a_{m+1} + (m+2)(m+1)\, a_{m+2}$$
$$+ (m+1)a_{m+1} + 2a_m] (x-1)^m = 0 \qquad ...(4)$$

(4) is an identity for all x in the interval of convergence of $y = \sum_{m=0}^{\infty} a_m (x-1)^m$.

$$\therefore \quad 2a_0 + a_1 + 2a_2 = 0 \qquad ...(5)$$

and $$(m+1)\, m\, a_{m+1} + (m+2)(m+1)\, a_{m+2} + (m+1)\, a_{m+1} + 2a_m = 0 \text{ for } m \geq 1$$

$$\therefore \quad a_{m+2} = -\frac{(m+1)^2\, a_{m+1} + 2a_m}{(m+1)(m+2)} \quad \text{for } m \geq 1 \qquad ...(6)$$

$$(5) \Rightarrow \qquad a_2 = -a_0 - \frac{1}{2}a_1$$

$$m = 1 \text{ in } (6) \Rightarrow \qquad a_3 = -\frac{4a_2 + 2a_1}{6} = -\frac{2}{3}\left(-a_0 - \frac{1}{2}a_1\right) - \frac{1}{3}a_1 = \frac{2}{3}a_0$$

$$m = 2 \text{ in } (6) \Rightarrow \qquad a_4 = -\frac{9a_3 + 2a_2}{12} = -\frac{3}{4}\left(\frac{2}{3}a_0\right) - \frac{1}{6}\left(-a_0 - \frac{1}{2}a_1\right) = -\frac{1}{3}a_0 + \frac{1}{12}a_1$$

....

Putting these values in (3), we get

$$y = a_0 + a_1(x-1) + \left(-a_0 - \frac{1}{2}a_1\right)(x-1)^2 + \left(\frac{2}{3}a_0\right)(x-1)^3 + \left(-\frac{1}{3}a_0 + \frac{1}{12}a_1\right)(x-1)^4 + \ldots\ldots$$

$$\therefore \qquad \mathbf{y = a_0\left(1 - (x-1)^2 + \frac{2}{3}(x-1)^3 - \frac{1}{3}(x-1)^4 + \ldots\ldots\right) + a_1\left((x-1) - \frac{1}{2}(x-1)^2 + \frac{1}{12}(x-1)^4 + \ldots\ldots\right)}.$$

This is the required power series solution. Here a_0 and a_1 are arbitrary constants.

Example 4. *Find the power series solution of the differential equation*

$$(x^2 - 4x + 5)\frac{d^2y}{dx^2} + (x-2)\frac{dy}{dx} - (x-2)\,y = 0$$

in powers of x – 2.

Sol. We have $\qquad (x^2 - 4x + 5)\dfrac{d^2y}{dx^2} + (x-2)\dfrac{dy}{dx} - (x-2)\,y = 0.$ ...(1)

Dividing (1) by $x^2 - 4x + 5$, we get

$$\frac{d^2y}{dx^2} + \frac{x-2}{x^2-4x+5}\frac{dy}{dx} - \frac{x-2}{x^2-4x+5}\,y = 0 \qquad \ldots(2)$$

Comparing (2) with $\dfrac{d^2y}{dx^2} + P(x)\dfrac{dy}{dx} + Q(x)\,y = 0$, we get

$$P(x) = \frac{x-2}{x^2-4x+5} \quad \text{and} \quad Q(x) = -\frac{x-2}{x^2-4x+5}.$$

The functions P(x) and Q(x) are both analytic at $x = 2$, because $4 - 8 + 5 = 1 \neq 0$.

∴ '2' is an ordinary point of (1).

Let $$y = \sum_{m=0}^{\infty} a_m (x-2)^m \qquad \ldots(3)$$

be the power series solution of (1) about '2'.

Let $t = x - 2$. $\qquad \therefore \quad x = t + 2$

$$\therefore \quad \frac{dy}{dx} = \frac{dy}{dt} . 1 = \frac{dy}{dt} \quad \text{and}$$

$$\frac{d^2y}{dx^2} = \frac{d}{dx}\left(\frac{dy}{dx}\right) = \frac{d}{dx}\left(\frac{dy}{dt}\right) = \frac{d^2y}{dt^2}\frac{dt}{dx} = \frac{d^2y}{dt^2} . 1 = \frac{d^2y}{dt^2} .$$

$$\therefore \ (1) \Rightarrow \ [(t+2)^2 - 4(t+2) + 5]\frac{d^2y}{dt^2} + (t+2-2)\frac{dy}{dt} - (t+2-2)\, y = 0$$

$$\Rightarrow \quad (t^2+1)\frac{d^2y}{dt^2} + t\frac{dy}{dt} - t\, y = 0 \cdot \qquad ...(4)$$

$$(3) \Rightarrow \quad y = \sum_{m=0}^{\infty} a_m t^m \qquad ...(5)$$

$$(5) \Rightarrow \quad \frac{dy}{dt} = \sum_{m=1}^{\infty} m\, a_m\, t^{m-1} \text{ and } \frac{d^2y}{dt^2} = \sum_{m=2}^{\infty} m(m-1)\, a_m\, t^{m-2}.$$

Putting the values of y, $\frac{dy}{dt}$ and $\frac{d^2y}{dt^2}$ in (4), we get

$$(t^2+1)\sum_{m=2}^{\infty} m(m-1)\, a_m\, t^{m-2} + t\sum_{m=1}^{\infty} m\, a_m\, t^{m-1} - t\sum_{m=0}^{\infty} a_m\, t^m = 0$$

$$\Rightarrow \quad \sum_{m=2}^{\infty} m(m-1)\, a_m\, t^m + \sum_{m=2}^{\infty} m(m-1)\, a_m\, t^{m-2} + \sum_{m=1}^{\infty} m\, a_m\, t^m - \sum_{m=0}^{\infty} a_m\, t^{m+1} = 0$$

$$\Rightarrow \quad \sum_{m=2}^{\infty} m(m-1)\, a_m\, t^m + \sum_{m=0}^{\infty} (m+2)(m+1)\, a_{m+2}\, t^m + \sum_{m=1}^{\infty} m\, a_m\, t^m - \sum_{m=1}^{\infty} a_{m-1}\, t^m = 0$$

(On shifting of indices)

$$\Rightarrow \quad \sum_{m=2}^{\infty} m(m-1)\, a_m\, t^m + \left[2a_2 + 6a_3 t + \sum_{m=2}^{\infty} (m+2)(m+1)\, a_{m+2}\, t^m\right] + \left[a_1 t + \sum_{m=2}^{\infty} m\, a_m\, t^m\right] - \left[a_0 t + \sum_{m=2}^{\infty} a_{m-1}\, t^m\right] = 0$$

$$\Rightarrow \quad 2a_2 + (6a_3 + a_1 - a_0)t + \sum_{m=2}^{\infty} [m(m-1)\, a_m + (m+2)(m+1)\, a_{m+2} + m\, a_m - a_{m-1}]\, t^m = 0 \qquad ...(6)$$

(6) is an identity for all t in the interval of convergence of $y = \sum_{m=0}^{\infty} a_m t^m$.

$$\therefore \quad 2a_2 = 0 \quad \ldots(7) \qquad 6a_3 + a_1 - a_0 = 0 \quad \ldots(8)$$

and $\quad m(m-1)a_m + (m+2)(m+1)a_{m+2} + m a_m - a_{m-1} = 0 \quad \forall\ m \geq 2$

$$\Rightarrow \quad m^2 a_m + (m+1)(m+2)a_{m+2} - a_{m-1} = 0$$

$$\therefore \quad a_{m+2} = \frac{a_{m-1} - m^2 a_m}{(m+1)(m+2)} \text{ for } m \geq 2 \quad \ldots(9)$$

$$(7) \Rightarrow \quad a_2 = 0, \quad (8) \Rightarrow \quad a_3 = \frac{1}{6}(a_0 - a_1)$$

$$m = 2 \text{ in } (9) \Rightarrow \quad a_4 = \frac{a_1 - 4a_2}{12} = \frac{1}{12}a_1$$

$$m = 3 \text{ in } (9) \Rightarrow \quad a_5 = \frac{a_2 - 9a_3}{20} = -\frac{9}{20}\left(\frac{1}{6}(a_0 - a_1)\right) = -\frac{3}{40}(a_0 - a_1)$$

....

Putting these values in (5), we get

$$y = a_0 + a_1 t + 0.t^2 + \frac{1}{6}(a_0 - a_1)t^3 + \frac{1}{12}a_1 t^4 - \frac{3}{40}(a_0 - a_1)t^5 + \ldots\ldots$$

$$\therefore \quad y = a_0\left(1 + \frac{1}{6}t^3 - \frac{3}{40}t^5 + \ldots\ldots\right) + a_1\left(t - \frac{1}{6}t^3 + \frac{1}{12}t^4 + \frac{3}{40}t^5 + \ldots\ldots\right)$$

Putting $t = x - 2$, we get

$$\mathbf{y = a_0\left(1 + \frac{1}{6}(x-2)^3 - \frac{3}{40}(x-2)^5 + \ldots\ldots\right)}$$

$$\mathbf{+ a_1\left(x - 2 - \frac{1}{6}(x-2)^3 + \frac{1}{12}(x-2)^4 + \frac{3}{40}(x-2)^5 + \ldots\ldots\right)}.$$

This is the required power series solution. Here a_0 and a_1 are arbitrary constants.

Remark. The given differential equation can also be solved without introducing the variable 't'.

Type III. On finding series solution when initial values are given.

Example 5. *Find the power series solution of the initial value problem*

$$(x^2 - 1)\frac{d^2y}{dx^2} + 3x\frac{dy}{dx} + xy = 0,\ y(2) = 4,\ y'(2) = 6.$$

Sol. We have $\quad (x^2 - 1)\dfrac{d^2y}{dx^2} + 3x\dfrac{dy}{dx} + xy = 0. \quad \ldots(1)$

Dividing (1) by $x^2 - 1$, we get

$$\frac{d^2y}{dx^2} + \frac{3x}{x^2 - 1}\frac{dy}{dx} + \frac{x}{x^2 - 1}y = 0 \quad \ldots(2)$$

Comparing (2) with $\frac{d^2y}{dx^2} + P(x)\frac{dy}{dx} + Q(x) = 0$, we get

$$P(x) = \frac{3x}{x^2 - 1} \text{ and } Q(x) = \frac{x}{x^2 - 1}.$$

Since the initial values of (1) are given at $x = 2$, we must have power series solution of (1) in powers of $x - 2$*.

Now, P(x) and Q(x) are both analytic at $x = 2$, because $(2)^2 - 1 = 3 \neq 0$.

$\therefore$ '2' is an ordinary point of (1).

Let $$y = \sum_{m=0}^{\infty} a_m (x-2)^m \qquad ...(3)$$

be the power series solution of (1) about '2'.

Let $t = x - 2$. $\therefore$ $x = t + 2$

$$\therefore \quad \frac{dy}{dx} = \frac{dy}{dt} \text{ and } \frac{d^2y}{dx^2} = \frac{d^2y}{dt^2}$$

$$\therefore \quad (1) \Rightarrow \quad ((t+2)^2 - 1)\frac{d^2y}{dt^2} + 3(t+2)\frac{dy}{dt} + (t+2)\,y = 0$$

$$\Rightarrow \quad (t^2 + 4t + 3)\frac{d^2y}{dt^2} + (3t+6)\frac{dy}{dt} + (t+2)\,y = 0 \qquad ...(4)$$

$$(3) \Rightarrow \quad y = \sum_{m=0}^{\infty} a_m t^m \qquad ...(5)$$

$$(5) \Rightarrow \quad \frac{dy}{dt} = \sum_{m=1}^{\infty} m\, a_m t^{m-1} \text{ and } \frac{d^2y}{dt^2} = \sum_{m=2}^{\infty} m(m-1)\, a_m t^{m-2}$$

Putting the values of y, $\frac{dy}{dt}$ and $\frac{d^2y}{dt^2}$ in (4), we get

$$(t^2 + 4t + 3)\sum_{m=2}^{\infty} m(m-1)\,a_m t^{m-2} + (3t+6)\sum_{m=1}^{\infty} m\,a_m t^{m-1} + (t+2)\sum_{m=0}^{\infty} a_m t^m = 0.$$

$$\Rightarrow \sum_{m=2}^{\infty} m(m-1)\,a_m t^m + \sum_{m=2}^{\infty} 4m(m-1)\,a_m t^{m-1} + \sum_{m=2}^{\infty} 3m(m-1)\,a_m t^{m-2}$$

$$+ \sum_{m=1}^{\infty} 3m\,a_m t^m + \sum_{m=1}^{\infty} 6m\,a_m t^{m-1} + \sum_{m=0}^{\infty} a_m t^{m+1} + \sum_{m=0}^{\infty} 2a_m t^m = 0$$

---

*If $y = \sum_{m=0}^{\infty} a_m (x-2)^m$, then $y_1 = \sum_{m=1}^{\infty} m\, a_m (x-2)^{m-1}$.

$\therefore$ At $x = 2$, y reduces to a_0 and y_1 reduces to a_1.

$$\Rightarrow \sum_{m=2}^{\infty} m(m-1)a_m t^m + \sum_{m=1}^{\infty} 4(m+1)m a_{m+1} t^m + \sum_{m=0}^{\infty} 3(m+2)(m+1)a_{m+2} t^m$$

$$+ \sum_{m=1}^{\infty} 3m a_m t^m + \sum_{m=0}^{\infty} 6(m+1)a_{m+1} t^m + \sum_{m=1}^{\infty} a_{m-1} t^m + \sum_{m=0}^{\infty} 2a_m t^m = 0$$

(On shifting of indices)

$$\Rightarrow \sum_{m=2}^{\infty} m(m-1)a_m t^m + \left[8a_2 t + \sum_{m=2}^{\infty} 4(m+1)m a_{m+1} t^m\right]$$

$$+\left[6a_2 + 18a_3 t + \sum_{m=2}^{\infty} 3(m+2)(m+1)a_{m+2} t^m\right]$$

$$+\left[3a_1 t + \sum_{m=2}^{\infty} 3m a_m t^m\right] + \left[6a_1 + 12a_2 t + \sum_{m=2}^{\infty} 6(m+1)a_{m+1} t^m\right]$$

$$+\left[a_0 t + \sum_{m=2}^{\infty} a_{m-1} t^m\right] + \left[2a_0 + 2a_1 t + \sum_{m=2}^{\infty} 2a_m t^m\right] = 0$$

$$\Rightarrow (6a_2 + 6a_1 + 2a_0) + (8a_2 + 18a_3 + 3a_1 + 12a_2 + a_0 + 2a_1]t$$

$$+ \sum_{m=2}^{\infty} [m(m-1)a_m + 4(m+1)ma_{m+1} + 3(m+2)(m+1)a_{m+2}$$

$$+ 3m a_m + 6(m+1)a_{m+1} + a_{m-1} + 2a_m]t^m = 0$$

$$\Rightarrow 2(a_0 + 3a_1 + 3a_2) + (a_0 + 5a_1 + 20a_2 + 18a_3)t$$

$$+ \sum_{m=2}^{\infty} [a_{m-1} + (m^2 + 2m + 2)a_m + 2(2m^2 + 5m + 3)a_{m+1}$$

$$+ 3(m+1)(m+2)a_{m+2}]t^m = 0 \qquad \text{...(6)}$$

(6) is an identity for all t in the interval of convergence of $y = \sum_{m=0}^{\infty} a_m t^m$.

$$\therefore \qquad a_0 + 3a_1 + 3a_2 = 0 \qquad \text{...(7)}$$

$$a_0 + 5a_1 + 20a_2 + 18a_3 = 0 \qquad \text{...(8)}$$

and

$$a_{m-1} + (m^2 + 2m + 2)a_m + 2(2m^2 + 5m + 3)a_{m+1}$$

$$+ 3(m+1)(m+2)a_{m+2} = 0 \quad \text{for } m \geq 2 \qquad \text{...(9)}$$

Now $y = \sum_{m=0}^{\infty} a_m (x-2)^m$ and $y(2) = 4$, $y'(2) = 6$.

$$\therefore \qquad \sum_{m=0}^{\infty} a_m (2-2)^m = 4 \text{ or } a_0 = 4.$$

Also $$\sum_{m=1}^{\infty} m\, a_m\,(2-2)^{m-1} = 6 \text{ or } a_1 = 6.$$

$$\therefore\ (7) \Rightarrow \quad 3a_2 = -22 \text{ or } a_2 = -\frac{22}{3}$$

$$(8) \Rightarrow \quad 18a_3 = -4-30-20\left(-\frac{22}{3}\right) = \frac{338}{3} \text{ or } a_3 = \frac{169}{27}$$

Putting $m = 2$ in (9), we get $a_1 + 10a_2 + 42a_3 + 36a_4 = 0$

$$\Rightarrow \quad 36a_4 = -6-10\left(-\frac{22}{3}\right)-42\left(\frac{169}{27}\right) = -\frac{5280}{27} \Rightarrow a_4 = -\frac{440}{27}.$$

Putting these values in (5), we get

$$\mathbf{y = 4 + 6\,(x-2) - \frac{22}{3}\,(x-2)^2 + \frac{169}{27}\,(x-2)^3 - \frac{440}{27}\,(x-2)^4 + \ldots\ldots}$$

This is the required solution of the given equation.

EXERCISE 3

Find the power series solution of the following differential equations about '0' i.e. in powers of x :

1. $\dfrac{d^2y}{dx^2} + x\dfrac{dy}{dx} + (2x^2+1)\,y = 0$
2. $\dfrac{d^2y}{dx^2} + x\dfrac{dy}{dx} + y = 0$
3. $(x^2+1)\dfrac{d^2y}{dx^2} + x\dfrac{dy}{dx} + xy = 0$
4. $\dfrac{d^2y}{dx^2} + x\dfrac{dy}{dx} + (3x+2)\,y = 0$
5. $\dfrac{d^2y}{dx^2} - x\dfrac{dy}{dx} - py = 0$
6. $(1-x^2)\dfrac{d^2y}{dx^2} - 2x\dfrac{dy}{dx} + 2y = 0$
7. $(x^2-1)\dfrac{d^2y}{dx^2} + 4x\dfrac{dy}{dx} + 2y = 0$
8. $(1-x^2)\dfrac{d^2y}{dx^2} + 2y = 0$
9. $\dfrac{d^2y}{dx^2} + x\dfrac{dy}{dx} + (x^2+2)\,y = 0$.

Find the power series solution of the following differential equations :

10. $\dfrac{d^2y}{dx^2} + (x-1)\dfrac{dy}{dx} + y = 0$ about $x = 1$
11. $\dfrac{d^2y}{dx^2} + (x-3)\dfrac{dy}{dx} + y = 0$ about $x = 2$
12. $(x^2+2x)\dfrac{d^2y}{dx^2} + (x+1)\dfrac{dy}{dx} - y = 0$ about $x = -1$.

Find the power series solution of the following initial value problems :

13. $\dfrac{d^2y}{dx^2} - x\dfrac{dy}{dx} - y = 0,\ y(0) = 1,\ y'(0) = 0$
14. $(x^2+1)\dfrac{d^2y}{dx^2} + x\dfrac{dy}{dx} + 2xy = 0,\ y(0) = 2,\ y'(0) = 3$
15. $(x^2-1)\dfrac{d^2y}{dx^2} + 3x\dfrac{dy}{dx} + xy = 0,\ y(0) = 4,\ y'(0) = 6$

16. $x\dfrac{d^2y}{dx^2}+\dfrac{dy}{dx}+2y=0,\ y(1)=1,\ y'(1)=2.$ *(DLU 2004)*

Answers

1. $y=a_0\left(1-\dfrac{x^2}{2}-\dfrac{x^4}{24}-\ldots\right)+a_1\left(x-\dfrac{x^3}{3}-\dfrac{x^5}{30}+\ldots\right)$

2. $y=a_0\left(1-\dfrac{x^2}{2}+\dfrac{x^4}{8}+\ldots\right)+a_1\left(x-\dfrac{x^3}{3}+\dfrac{x^5}{15}+\ldots\right)$

3. $y=a_0\left(1-\dfrac{x^3}{6}+\dfrac{3x^5}{40}+\ldots\right)+a_1\left(x-\dfrac{x^3}{6}-\dfrac{x^4}{12}+\dfrac{3x^5}{40}+\ldots\right)$

4. $y=a_0\left(1-x^2-\dfrac{x^3}{2}+\dfrac{x^4}{3}+\dfrac{11x^5}{40}+\ldots\right)+a_1\left(x-\dfrac{x^3}{2}-\dfrac{x^4}{4}+\dfrac{x^5}{8}+\ldots\right)$

5. $y=a_0\left(1+\dfrac{p}{2!}x^2+\dfrac{p(p+2)}{4!}x^4+\ldots\right)+a_1\left(x+\dfrac{p+1}{3!}x^3+\dfrac{(p+1)(p+3)}{5!}x^5+\ldots\right)$

6. $y=a_0\left(1-x^2-\dfrac{x^4}{3}-\dfrac{x^6}{5}-\dfrac{x^8}{7}+\ldots\right)+a_1x$

7. $y=a_0(1+x^2+x^4+\ldots)+a_1(x+x^3+x^5+\ldots)$

8. $y=a_0(1-x^2)+a_1\left(x-\dfrac{x^3}{3}-\dfrac{x^5}{15}-\dfrac{x^7}{35}+\ldots\right)$

9. $y=a_0\left(1-x^2+\dfrac{x^4}{4}+\ldots\right)+a_1\left(x-\dfrac{x^3}{2}+\dfrac{3x^5}{40}+\ldots\right)$

10. $y=a_0\left(1-\dfrac{(x-1)^2}{2}+\dfrac{(x-1)^4}{8}+\ldots\right)+a_1\left(x-1-\dfrac{(x-1)^3}{3}+\dfrac{(x-1)^5}{15}+\ldots\right)$

11. $y=a_0\left(1-\dfrac{(x-2)^2}{2}-\dfrac{(x-2)^3}{6}+\dfrac{(x-2)^4}{12}+\ldots\right)+a_1\left(x-2+\dfrac{(x-2)^2}{2}-\dfrac{(x-2)^3}{6}-\dfrac{(x-2)^4}{6}+\ldots\right)$

12. $y=a_0\left(1-\dfrac{(x+1)^2}{2}-\dfrac{(x+1)^4}{8}-\dfrac{(x+1)^6}{16}+\ldots\right)+a_1(x+1)$

13. $y=1+\dfrac{x^2}{2}+\dfrac{x^4}{8}+\dfrac{x^6}{48}+\ldots\ldots$ **14.** $y=2+3x-\dfrac{7x^3}{6}-\dfrac{x^4}{2}+\dfrac{21x^5}{40}+\ldots\ldots$

15. $y=4+6x+\dfrac{11x^3}{3}+\dfrac{x^4}{2}+\dfrac{11x^5}{4}+\ldots\ldots$

16. $y=1+2(x-1)-2(x-1)^2+\dfrac{2(x-1)^3}{3}-\dfrac{(x-1)^4}{6}+\ldots\ldots.$

10. FROBENIUS METHOD

If x_0 is a regular singular point of the differential equation

$$p_0(x)\frac{d^2y}{dx^2} + p_1(x)\frac{dy}{dx} + p_2(x)\,y = 0$$

then **Frobenius method** is used to find a series (in powers of $x - x_0$) solution of this differential equation. If $x_0 \neq 0$ then shift the origin to the point x_0 so that 0 is a regular singular point of the transformed equation. Therefore, it is sufficient to discuss this method for the regular singular point 0.

Theorem. If 0 is a regular singular point of the differential equation $p_0(x)\frac{d^2y}{dx^2} + p_1(x)\frac{dy}{dx} + p_2(x)\,y = 0$, then there exists at least one solution of this differential equation that can be represented in the form $x^r \sum_{m=0}^{\infty} a_m x^m$, $a_0 \neq 0$, where r is a constant and this solution is valid in the interval $0 < x < R$ for some positive R.

Note. The proof of this theorem is beyond the scope of this book.

Method. Let 0 be a regular singular point of the differential equation

$$p_0(x)\frac{d^2y}{dx^2} + p_1(x)\frac{dy}{dx} + p_2(x)\,y = 0. \qquad \text{...(1)}$$

Let $$y = x^r \sum_{m=0}^{\infty} a_m x^m = \sum_{m=0}^{\infty} a_m x^{m+r}, \; a_0 \neq 0$$

be a series solution of (1) about '0'.

$$\therefore \quad y = a_0 x^r + a_1 x^{r+1} + a_2 x^{r+2} + \ldots\ldots$$

Let this solution converges for $0 < x < R$.

$\therefore$ This series can be differentiated term by term twice in succession.

$$\therefore \quad \frac{dy}{dx} = r a_0 x^{r-1} + (r+1)\,a_1 x^r + (r+2)\,a_2 x^{r+1} + \ldots = \sum_{m=0}^{\infty} (m+r)\,a_m\, x^{m+r-1}$$

and
$$\frac{d^2y}{dx^2} = r(r-1)\,a_0 x^{r-2} + (r+1)\,r a_1 x^{r-1} + (r+2)(r+1)\,a_2 x^r + \ldots\ldots$$

$$= \sum_{m=0}^{\infty} (m+r)(m+r-1)\,a_m\, x^{m+r-2}$$

Substituting the values of y, $\frac{dy}{dx}$ and $\frac{d^2y}{dx^2}$ in (1), we get

$$p_0(x)\sum_{m=0}^{\infty} (m+r)(m+r-1)\,a_m\, x^{m+r-2} + p_1(x)\sum_{m=0}^{\infty} (m+r)\,a_m x^{m+r-1}$$

$$+\, p_2(x)\sum_{m=0}^{\infty} a_m\, x^{m+r} = 0$$

On simplification, let this equation reduces to

$$A_0x^{r+k} + A_1x^{r+k+1} + A_2x^{r+k+2} + \ldots\ldots = 0 \qquad \ldots(2)$$

where k is some integer. The coefficients $A_0, A_1, A_2, \ldots\ldots$ are functions of r and $a_0, a_1, a_2, \ldots\ldots$

(2) is true for all x in the interval $0 < x < R$.

$\therefore$ We have $A_0 = A_1 = A_2 = \ldots\ldots = 0$

$A_0 = 0$ gives a quadratic equation in r. This quadratic equation is called the **indicial equation** of the given differential equation (1). The roots of the indicial equation are called the **exponents** of the differential equation (1). Let the roots of the indicial equation be r_1 and r_2. The roots r_1 and r_2 may or may not be equal. Here we assume that the roots r_1 and r_2 are unequal and their difference is not an integer. We now equate to zero the remaining coefficients $A_1, A_2, \ldots\ldots$ to zero. We put $r = r_1$ and get the values of $a_0, a_1, a_2, \ldots\ldots$ We call the series $\sum a_m x^{m+r}$ as y_1. Similarly for $r = r_2$, we obtain another solution y_2. For arbitrary constants C_1 and C_2, $y = C_1y_1 + C_2y_2$ gives the general solution of the given differential equation.

Remark. If the roots r_1 and r_2 of the indicial equation are either equal or differing by an integer, then the solutions y_1 and y_2 may not be linearly independent and we cannot say that $y = C_1y_1 + C_2y_2$ is the general solution of the given differential equation.

WORKING RULES FOR SOLVING $p_0(x)\frac{d^2y}{dx^2} + p_1(x)\frac{dy}{dx} + p_2(x)\,y = 0$

WHERE '0' IS A REGULAR SINGULAR POINT

Step I. Make sure that '0' is a regular singular point of the given differential equation.

Step II. Assume the solution about '0' to be $y = x^r \sum_{m=0}^{\infty} a_m x^m$, $a_0 \neq 0$.

Step III. Write

$$\frac{dy}{dx} = \sum_{m=0}^{\infty} (m+r)a_m x^{m+r-1} \text{ and } \frac{d^2y}{dx^2} = \sum_{m=0}^{\infty} (m+r)(m+r-1)\,a_m x^{m+r-2}$$

Step IV. Substitute the values of y, $\frac{dy}{dx}$ and $\frac{d^2y}{dx^2}$ in the given differential equation.

Step V. Equation to zero, the coefficient of least power of x. This gives the indicial equation. Solve the indicial equation and make sure that the roots are distinct and not differing by an integer.

Step VI. Equate to zero, the coefficients of different powers of x.

Step VII. For each root of indicial equation, find the values of $a_0, a_1, a_2, \ldots\ldots$. Let y_1 and y_2 be the series corresponding to roots of the indicial equation.

Step VIII. Write the general solution $y = C_1y_1 + C_2y_2$ where C_1 and C_2 are arbitrary constants.

Example 1. *Find the series solution of the differential equation*

$$2x^2\frac{d^2y}{dx^2} - x\frac{dy}{dx} + (x-5)\,y = 0 \text{ about '0'}.$$

Sol. We have $$2x^2 \frac{d^2y}{dx^2} - x\frac{dy}{dx} + (x-5)\,y = 0. \qquad ...(1)$$

Dividing (1) by $2x^2$, we get

$$\frac{d^2y}{dx^2} - \frac{1}{2x}\frac{dy}{dx} + \frac{x-5}{2x^2}\,y = 0 \qquad ...(2)$$

Comparing (2) with $\frac{d^2y}{dx^2} + P(x)\frac{dy}{dx} + Q(x)\,y = 0$, we get

$$P(x) = -\frac{1}{2x} \text{ and } Q(x) = \frac{x-5}{2x^2}.$$

'0' is not an ordinary point of (1) because neither $P(x)$ nor $Q(x)$ is analytic at $x = 0$.

Here $$xP(x) = -\frac{1}{2} \text{ and } x^2Q(x) = \frac{x-5}{2}.$$

Both these functions are analytic at $x = 0$

$\therefore$ 0 is a regular singular point of (1).

Let $$y = x^r \sum_{m=0}^{\infty} a_m x^m = \sum_{m=0}^{\infty} a_m x^{m+r}, \; a_0 \neq 0 \qquad ...(3)$$

be a series solution of (1) about '0'

$$(3) \Rightarrow \quad \frac{dy}{dx} = \sum_{m=0}^{\infty} (m+r)\,a_m x^{m+r-1} \text{ and } \frac{d^2y}{dx^2} = \sum_{m=0}^{\infty} (m+r)(m+r-1)\,a_m x^{m+r-2}.$$

Putting the values of y, $\frac{dy}{dx}$ and $\frac{d^2y}{dx^2}$ in (1), we get

$$2x^2 \sum_{m=0}^{\infty} (m+r)(m+r-1)\,a_m x^{m+r-2} - x\sum_{m=0}^{\infty} (m+r)\,a_m x^{m+r-1} + (x-5)\sum_{m=0}^{\infty} a_m x^{m+r} = 0$$

$$\Rightarrow \quad 2\sum_{m=0}^{\infty} (m+r)(m+r-1)\,a_m x^{m+r} - \sum_{m=0}^{\infty} (m+r)\,a_m x^{m+r} + \sum_{m=0}^{\infty} a_m x^{m+r+1} - 5\sum_{m=0}^{\infty} a_m x^{m+r} = 0$$

$$\Rightarrow \quad \sum_{m=0}^{\infty} \left[2(m+r)(m+r-1) - (m+r) - 5\right] a_m x^{m+r} + \sum_{m=1}^{\infty} a_{m-1} x^{m+r} = 0$$

(By shifting of indices)

$$\Rightarrow \quad \sum_{m=0}^{\infty} \left[(m+r)(2m+2r-3) - 5\right] a_m x^{m+r} + \sum_{m=1}^{\infty} a_{m-1} x^{m+r} = 0$$

$$\Rightarrow \quad (r(2r-3)-5)\,a_0 x^r + \sum_{m=1}^{\infty} [(m+r)(2m+2r-3)-5+a_{m-1}]\,x^{m+r} = 0 \qquad ...(4)$$

Equating to zero the coefficient of lowest power of x, we get $(2r^2 - 3r - 5)\,a_0 = 0$

$$\Rightarrow \qquad 2r^2 - 3r - 5 = 0 \qquad (\because \; a_0 \neq 0)$$

This is the indicial equation and its roots are $r = -1, 5/2$.

Here the roots are distinct and their difference is not an integer.

(4) $\Rightarrow$ $((m+r)(2m+2r-3)-5)\,a_m + a_{m-1} = 0$ for $m \geq 1$

$$\Rightarrow \quad a_m = -\frac{a_{m-1}}{(m+r)(2m+2r-3)-5} \quad \text{for } m \geq 1 \qquad ...(5)$$

Case I. r = – 1

$$(5) \Rightarrow \quad a_m = -\frac{a_{m-1}}{(m-1)(2m-5)-5} = \frac{a_{m-1}}{m(7-2m)} \quad \text{for } m \geq 1 \qquad ...(6)$$

$m = 1$ in (6) $\Rightarrow$ $a_1 = \dfrac{a_0}{5}$

$m = 2$ in (6) $\Rightarrow$ $a_2 = \dfrac{a_1}{6} = \dfrac{a_0}{30}$

$m = 3$ in (6) $\Rightarrow$ $a_3 = \dfrac{a_2}{3} = \dfrac{a_0}{90}$

. . . .

$$\therefore \; (3) \Rightarrow \quad y_1 = x^{-1}\left(a_0 + \frac{a_0}{5}x + \frac{a_0}{30}x^2 + \frac{a_0}{90}x^3 + ...\right)$$

or
$$y_1 = x^{-1}\left(1 + \frac{x}{5} + \frac{x^2}{30} + \frac{x^3}{90} + ...\right) \qquad \text{(Letting } a_0 = 1)$$

Case II. r = 5/2

$$(5) \Rightarrow \quad a_m = -\frac{a_{m-1}}{\left(m+\frac{5}{2}\right)(2m+5-3)-5} = -\frac{a_{m-1}}{m(2m+7)}, \; m \geq 1 \qquad ...(7)$$

$m = 1$ in (7) $\Rightarrow$ $a_1 = -\dfrac{a_0}{9}$

$m = 2$ in (7) $\Rightarrow$ $a_2 = -\dfrac{a_1}{22} = \dfrac{a_0}{198}$

$m = 3$ in (7) $\Rightarrow$ $a_3 = -\dfrac{a_2}{39} = -\dfrac{a_0}{7722}$

. . . .

$$\therefore \; (3) \Rightarrow \quad y_2 = x^{5/2}\left(a_0 - \frac{a_0}{9}x + \frac{a_0}{198}x^2 - \frac{a_0}{7722}x^3 + ...\right)$$

or
$$y_2 = x^{5/2}\left(1 - \frac{x}{9} + \frac{x^2}{198} - \frac{x^3}{7722} + ...\right) \qquad \text{(Letting } a_0 = 1)$$

$\therefore$ The general solution of (1) is $y = C_1 y_1 + C_2 y_2$

or
$$\mathbf{y} = \mathbf{C}_1\mathbf{x}^{-1}\left(1+\frac{\mathbf{x}}{5}+\frac{\mathbf{x}^2}{30}+\frac{\mathbf{x}^3}{90}+\ldots\right)+\mathbf{C}_2\mathbf{x}^{5/2}\left(1-\frac{\mathbf{x}}{9}+\frac{\mathbf{x}^2}{198}-\frac{\mathbf{x}^3}{7722}+\ldots\right),$$

where C_1 and C_2 are arbitrary constants.

Example 2. *Find the series solution of the differential equation*

$$2x^2\frac{d^2y}{dx^2}-x\frac{dy}{dx}+(1-x^2)\,y=0 \ \text{about '0'}.$$

Sol. We have
$$2x^2\frac{d^2y}{dx^2}-x\frac{dy}{dx}+(1-x^2)\,y=0. \qquad \ldots(1)$$

Dividing (1) by $2x^2$, we get

$$\frac{d^2y}{dx^2}-\frac{1}{2x}\frac{dy}{dx}+\frac{1-x^2}{2x^2}y=0 \qquad \ldots(2)$$

Comparing (2) with $\frac{d^2y}{dx^2}+P(x)\frac{dy}{dx}+Q(x)\,y=0$, we get

$$P(x)=-\frac{1}{2x} \text{ and } Q(x)=\frac{1-x^2}{2x^2}.$$

'0' is not an ordinary point of (1) because neither $P(x)$ nor $Q(x)$ is analytic at $x = 0$.

Here $xP(x)=-\frac{1}{2}$ and $x^2Q(x)=\frac{1-x^2}{2}$.

Both these functions are analytic at $x = 0$.

$\therefore$ '0' is a regular singular point of (1).

Let
$$y=x^r\sum_{m=0}^{\infty}a_m x^m=\sum_{m=0}^{\infty}a_m x^{m+r},\ a_0\neq 0 \qquad \ldots(3)$$

be a series solution of (1) about '0'.

$$(3) \Rightarrow \frac{dy}{dx}=\sum_{m=0}^{\infty}(m+r)\,a_m x^{m+r-1} \text{ and } \frac{d^2y}{dx^2}=\sum_{m=0}^{\infty}(m+r)(m+r-1)\,a_m x^{m+r-2}$$

Putting the values of y, $\frac{dy}{dx}$ and $\frac{d^2y}{dx^2}$ in (1), we get

$$2x^2\sum_{m=0}^{\infty}(m+r)(m+r-1)\,a_m x^{m+r-2}-x\sum_{m=0}^{\infty}(m+r)\,a_m x^{m+r-1}+(1-x^2)\sum_{m=0}^{\infty}a_m x^{m+r}=0$$

$$\Rightarrow \quad 2\sum_{m=0}^{\infty}(m+r)(m+r-1)\,a_m x^{m+r}-\sum_{m=0}^{\infty}(m+r)\,a_m x^{m+r}$$
$$+\sum_{m=0}^{\infty}a_m x^{m+r}-\sum_{m=0}^{\infty}a_m x^{m+r+2}=0$$

$$\Rightarrow \quad \sum_{m=0}^{\infty} [2(m+r)(m+r-1)-(m+r)+1]\, a_m x^{m+r} - \sum_{m=2}^{\infty} a_{m-2} x^{m+r} = 0$$

$$\Rightarrow \quad \sum_{m=0}^{\infty} (2m+2r-1)(m+r-1)\, a_m x^{m+r} - \sum_{m=2}^{\infty} a_{m-2} x^{m+r} = 0$$

$$(2r-1)(r-1)\, a_0 x^r + (2r+1) r a_1 x^{r+1} + \sum_{m=2}^{\infty} [(2m+2r-1)(m+r-1)\, a_m - a_{m-2}]\, x^{m+r} = 0 \quad \text{...(4)}$$

Equating to zero the coefficient of lowest power of x, we get $(2r-1)(r-1)a_0 = 0$.

$$\Rightarrow \quad (2r-1)(r-1) = 0 \qquad (\because\ a_0 \neq 0)$$

This is the indicial equation and its roots are $r = 1/2, 1$.

Here the roots are distinct and their difference is not an integer.

$$(4) \Rightarrow \quad (2r+1) r a_1 = 0 \quad \text{...(5)}$$

$$\text{and} \quad (2m+2r-1)(m+r-1)\, a_m - a_{m-2} = 0, \quad m \geq 2 \quad \text{...(6)}$$

$$(6) \Rightarrow \quad a_m = \frac{a_{m-2}}{(2m+2r-1)(m+r-1)}, \; m \geq 2 \quad \text{...(7)}$$

Case I. r = 1/2

$$(5) \Rightarrow \quad a_1 = 0$$

$$(7) \Rightarrow \quad a_m = \frac{a_{m-2}}{2m\left(m - \frac{1}{2}\right)} = \frac{a_{m-2}}{m(2m-1)}, \; m \geq 2 \quad \text{...(8)}$$

$$m = 2 \text{ in } (8) \Rightarrow \quad a_2 = \frac{a_0}{2.3}$$

$$m = 3 \text{ in } (8) \Rightarrow \quad a_3 = \frac{a_1}{6\left(3 - \frac{1}{2}\right)} = 0$$

$$m = 4 \text{ in } (8) \Rightarrow \quad a_4 = \frac{a_2}{4.7} = \frac{a_0}{2.3.4.7}$$

. . . .

$$\therefore \; (3) \Rightarrow \quad y_1 = x^{1/2}\left(a_0 + 0.x + \frac{a_0}{2.3} x^2 + 0.x^3 + \frac{a_0}{2.3.4.7} x^4 + \ldots\right)$$

or

$$y_1 = x^{1/2}\left(1 + \frac{x^2}{2.3} + \frac{x^4}{2.3.4.7} + \ldots\right). \qquad (\text{Letting } a_0 = 1)$$

Case II. r = 1

$$(5) \Rightarrow \quad a_1 = 0$$

$$(7) \Rightarrow \quad a_m = \frac{a_{m-2}}{(2m+1)\, m}, \; m \geq 2 \quad \text{...(9)}$$

$m = 2$ in (9) $\Rightarrow$ $a_2 = \dfrac{a_0}{5.2}$

$m = 3$ in (9) $\Rightarrow$ $a_3 = \dfrac{a_1}{7.3} = 0$

$m = 4$ in (9) $\Rightarrow$ $a_4 = \dfrac{a_2}{9.4} = \dfrac{a_0}{9.4.5.2}$

....

$$\therefore \quad (3) \Rightarrow \quad y_2 = x^1\left(a_0 + 0.x + \frac{a_0}{2.5}x^2 + 0.x^3 + \frac{a_0}{2.4.5.9}x^4 + \ldots\right)$$

or
$$y_2 = x\left(1 + \frac{x^2}{2.5} + \frac{x^4}{2.4.5.9} + \ldots\right). \qquad \text{(Letting } a_0 = 1\text{)}$$

$\therefore$ The general solution of (1) is $y = C_1y_1 + C_2y_2$

or
$$\mathbf{y = C_1x^{1/2}\left(1 + \frac{x^2}{2.3} + \frac{x^4}{2.3.4.7} + \ldots\right) + C_2x\left(1 + \frac{x^2}{2.5} + \frac{x^4}{2.4.5.9} + \ldots\right)},$$

where C_1 and C_2 are arbitrary constants.

Example 3. *Find the series solution of the differential equation*

$$9x\,(1 - x)\frac{d^2y}{dx^2} - 12\frac{dy}{dx} + 4y = 0 \text{ about '0'.}$$

Sol. We have $\quad 9x\,(1 - x)\dfrac{d^2y}{dx^2} - 12\dfrac{dy}{dx} + 4y = 0$. ...(1)

Dividing (1) by $9x(1 - x)$, we get

$$\frac{d^2y}{dx^2} - \frac{4}{3x\,(1 - x)}\frac{dy}{dx} + \frac{4}{9x\,(1 - x)}y = 0 \qquad \text{...(2)}$$

Comparing (2) with $\dfrac{d^2y}{dx^2} + P(x)\dfrac{dy}{dx} + Q(x)\,y = 0$, we get

$$P(x) = -\frac{4}{3x\,(1 - x)} \text{ and } Q(x) = \frac{4}{9x\,(1 - x)}.$$

'0' is not an ordinary point of (1) because neither $P(x)$ nor $Q(x)$ is analytic at $x = 0$.

Here $\quad xP(x) = -\dfrac{4}{3\,(1 - x)}$ and $x^2Q(x) = \dfrac{4x}{9\,(1 - x)}$.

Both these functions are analytic at $x = 0$.

$\therefore$ '0' is a regular singular point of (1).

Let $\quad y = x^r\displaystyle\sum_{m=0}^{\infty} a_m\,x^m = \sum_{m=0}^{\infty} a_m\,x^{m+r}, a_0 \neq 0$ ...(3)

be a series solution of (1) about '0'.

$$(3) \Rightarrow \quad \frac{dy}{dx} = \sum_{m=0}^{\infty}(m + r)\,a_m\,x^{m+r-1}$$

and $$\frac{d^2y}{dx^2} = \sum_{m=0}^{\infty} (m+r)(m+r-1)\, a_m\, x^{m+r-2}$$

Putting the values of y, $\frac{dy}{dx}$ and $\frac{d^2y}{dx^2}$ in (1), we get

$$9x(1-x)\sum_{m=0}^{\infty}(m+r)(m+r-1)\,a_m\,x^{m+r-2} - 12\sum_{m=0}^{\infty}(m+r)\,a_m\,x^{m+r-1} + 4\sum_{m=0}^{\infty}a_m\,x^{m+r} = 0$$

$$\Rightarrow \quad 9\sum_{m=0}^{\infty}(m+r)(m+r-1)a_m x^{m+r-1} - 9\sum_{m=0}^{\infty}(m+r)(m+r-1)a_m x^{m+r} - 12\sum_{m=0}^{\infty}(m+r)a_m x^{m+r-1} + 4\sum_{m=0}^{\infty}a_m x^{m+r} = 0$$

$$\Rightarrow \quad \sum_{m=0}^{\infty}(m+r)(9m+9r-21)\,a_m\,x^{m+r-1} - \sum_{m=0}^{\infty}[9(m+r)(m+r-1)-4]\,a_m\,x^{m+r} = 0$$

$$\Rightarrow \quad \sum_{m=-1}^{\infty}(m+r+1)(9m+9r-12)a_{m+1}x^{m+r} - \sum_{m=0}^{\infty}[9(m+r)(m+r-1)-4]a_m x^{m+r} = 0$$

$$\Rightarrow \quad r(9r-21)\,a_0\,x^{r-1} + \sum_{m=0}^{\infty}[(m+r+1)(9m+9r-12)a_{m+1} - [9(m+r)(m+r-1)-4]\,a_m\,]\,x^{m+r} = 0 \quad \text{...(4)}$$

Equating to zero the coefficient of lowest power of x, we get $r(9r-21)\,a_0 = 0$

$\Rightarrow \quad r(3r-7) = 0 \qquad (\because a_0 \neq 0)$

This is the *indicial equation* and its roots are $r = 0, 7/3$.

Here the roots are distinct and their difference is not an integer.

(4) $\Rightarrow \quad 3(m+r+1)(3m+3r-4)\,a_{m+1} - [9(m+r)(m+r-1)-4]\,a_m = 0 \quad$ for $m \geq 0$

$$\therefore \quad a_{m+1} = \frac{9(m+r)(m+r-1)-4}{3(m+r+1)(3m+3r-4)}\,a_m \quad \text{for } m \geq 0 \qquad \text{...(5)}$$

Case I. r = 0

$$(5) \Rightarrow \quad a_{m+1} = \frac{9m(m-1)-4}{3(m+1)(3m-4)}\,a_m = \frac{(3m+1)(3m-4)}{3(m+1)(3m-4)}\,a_m$$

$$\therefore \quad a_{m+1} = \frac{3m+1}{3(m+1)}\,a_m, \quad m \geq 0 \qquad \text{...(6)}$$

$m = 0$ in (6) $\Rightarrow$ $a_1 = \frac{1}{3} a_0$

$m = 1$ in (6) $\Rightarrow$ $a_2 = \frac{4}{6} a_1 = \frac{2}{9} a_0$

$m = 2$ in (6) $\Rightarrow$ $a_3 = \frac{7}{9} a_2 = \frac{14}{81} a_0$

....

$\therefore$ (3) $\Rightarrow$ $y_1 = x^0 \left(a_0 + \frac{1}{3} a_0 x + \frac{2}{9} a_0 x^2 + \frac{14}{81} a_0 x^3 + \ldots \right)$

or $y_1 = 1 + \frac{x}{3} + \frac{2x^2}{9} + \frac{14x^3}{81} + \ldots$ (Letting $a_0 = 1$)

Case II. r = 7/3

(5) $\Rightarrow$
$$a_{m+1} = \frac{9\left(m + \frac{7}{3}\right)\left(m + \frac{7}{3} - 1\right) - 4}{3\left(m + \frac{7}{3} + 1\right)(3m + 7 - 4)} a_m$$

$\therefore$
$$a_{m+1} = \frac{3m + 8}{3m + 10} a_m, \; m \geq 0 \qquad \ldots(7)$$

$m = 0$ in (7) $\Rightarrow$ $a_1 = \frac{8}{10} a_0 = \frac{4}{5} a_0$

$m = 1$ in (7) $\Rightarrow$ $a_2 = \frac{11}{13} a_1 = \frac{44}{65} a_0$

$m = 2$ in (7) $\Rightarrow$ $a_3 = \frac{14}{16} a_1 = \frac{7}{8} \cdot \frac{44}{65} a_0 = \frac{77}{130} a_0$

$\therefore$ (3) $\Rightarrow$ $y_2 = x^{7/3} \left(a_0 + \frac{4}{5} a_0 x + \frac{44}{65} a_0 x^2 + \frac{77}{130} a_0 x^3 + \ldots\ldots \right)$

or $y_2 = x^{7/3} \left(1 + \frac{4}{5} x + \frac{44}{65} x^2 + \frac{77}{130} x^3 + \ldots\ldots \right)$. (Letting $a_0 = 1$)

$\therefore$ The general solution of (1) is $y = C_1 y_1 + C_2 y_2$

or
$$\mathbf{y = C_1 \left(1 + \frac{x}{3} + \frac{2x^2}{9} + \frac{14x^3}{81} + \ldots \right) + C_2 x^{7/3} \left(1 + \frac{4}{5} x + \frac{44}{65} x^2 + \frac{77}{130} x^3 + \ldots\ldots \right)},$$

where C_1 and C_2 are arbitrary constants.

EXERCISE 4

Find the series solution of the following differential equation about '0' :

1. $2x^2 \frac{d^2 y}{dx^2} + x \frac{dy}{dx} + (x^2 - 3) y = 0$

2. $3x \frac{d^2 y}{dx^2} - (x - 2) \frac{dy}{dx} - 2y = 0$

3. $2x^2 \frac{d^2y}{dx^2} + x\frac{dy}{dx} + (x^2 - 1)\,y = 0$ (MDU 2004)

4. $x^2 \frac{d^2y}{dx^2} - x\frac{dy}{dx} + \left(x^2 + \frac{8}{9}\right) y = 0$

5. $2x \frac{d^2y}{dx^2} + (x+1)\frac{dy}{dx} + 3y = 0$

6. $(2x + x^3)\frac{d^2y}{dx^2} - \frac{dy}{dx} - 6xy = 0$

7. $2x(1-x)\frac{d^2y}{dx^2} + (1-x)\frac{dy}{dx} + 3y = 0$

8. $2x^2 \frac{d^2y}{dx^2} - x\frac{dy}{dx} + (x^2+1)y = 0.$

Answers

1. $y = C_1 x^{-1}\left(1 + \frac{x^2}{2} - \frac{x^4}{24} + \ldots\right) + C_2 x^{3/2}\left(1 - \frac{x^2}{18} + \frac{x^4}{936} + \ldots\right)$

2. $y = C_1\left(1 + x + \frac{3x^2}{10} + \ldots\right) + C_2 x^{1/3}\left(1 + \frac{7x}{12} + \frac{5x^2}{36} + \ldots\right)$

3. $y = C_1 x\left(1 - \frac{x^2}{14} + \frac{x^4}{616} + \ldots\right) + C_2 x^{-1/2}\left(1 - \frac{x^2}{2} + \frac{x^4}{40} + \ldots\right)$

4. $y = C_1 x^{4/3}\left(1 - \frac{3x^2}{16} + \frac{9x^4}{896} + \ldots\right) + C_2 x^{2/3}\left(1 - \frac{3x^2}{8} + \frac{9x^4}{320} + \ldots\right)$

5. $y = C_1\left(1 - 3x + 2x^2 - \frac{2x^3}{3} + \ldots\right) + C_2\sqrt{x}\left(1 - \frac{7x}{6} + \frac{21x^2}{40} - \frac{11x^3}{80} + \ldots\right)$

6. $y = C_1\left(1 + 3x^2 + \frac{3x^4}{5} + \ldots\right) + C_2 x^{3/2}\left(1 + \frac{3x^2}{8} - \frac{3x^4}{128} + \ldots\right)$

7. $y = C_1\left(1 - 3x + x^2 + \frac{x^3}{5} + \frac{3x^4}{35} + \ldots\right) + C_2\sqrt{x}\,(1-x)$

8. $y = C_1 x\left(1 - x^2 + \frac{x^4}{360} + \ldots\right) + C_2\sqrt{x}\left(1 - \frac{x^2}{6} + \frac{x^4}{168} + \ldots\right).$

---

11. FROBENIUS METHOD (Continued)

Let '0' be a regular singularity of the differential equation $p_0(x)\frac{d^2y}{dx^2} + p_1(x)\frac{dy}{dx} + p_2(x)y = 0$.

In the Frobenius method, we assume that $y = x^r \sum_{m=0}^{\infty} a_m x^m$, $a_0 \neq 0$, is a series solution of the given equation about '0'. The indicial equation of the differential equation is a quadratic equation in r. There are three possibilities ;

Case I. Roots are distinct and not differing by an integer.

In this case, the series solutions are obtained corresponding to both values of r. Let the solutions be $y = y_1$ and $y = y_2$. In this case, the solutions y_1 and y_2 are linearly independent and so we can write the general solution as $y = C_1y_1 + C_2y_2$, where C_1 and C_2 are arbitrary constants. We have already discussed this case in detail.

Case II. Roots are equal.

In this case, the series solutions corresponding to both values of r are same and are thus not linearly independent.

Let the roots of the indicial equation be r_1, r_1. Let $y = \bar{y}$ be the series obtained from $x^r \sum_{m=0}^{\infty} a_m x^m$ in terms of a_0 and the variable r. The general solution of the given differential equation is given by

$$y = C_1 \left(\bar{y} \Big|_{r=r_1} \right) + C_2 \left(\frac{\partial \bar{y}}{\partial r} \Big|_{r=r_1} \right).$$

Case III. Roots are distinct and differ by an integer

Let the roots of the indicial equation be r_1 and r_2 with $r_1 < r_2$. In this case, the solutions corresponding to the values r_1 and r_2 may or may not be linearly independent. There are two methods of finding the general solution of the given differential equation.

Method 1. By using the smaller root r_1 of the indicial equation, let $y = y_1$ be a series solution of the given differential equation. It is sometime possible that the solution $y = y_1$ may contain two arbitrary constants. In that case, this solution would become the general solution of the given differential equation. In such a case, we need not find solution corresponding to the larger root r_2.

Method 2. Let $y = \bar{y}$ be the series obtained from $x^r \sum_{m=0}^{\infty} a_m x^m$ in terms of a_0 and the variable r. The general solution of the given differential equation is given by

$$y = C_1 \left(\bar{y} \Big|_{r=r_1} \right) + C_2 \left(\frac{\partial \bar{y}}{\partial r} \Big|_{r=r_1} \right).$$

If some coefficients of $\bar{y}$ become infinite on putting $r = r_1$, then we modify the form of $\bar{y}$ by replacing a_0 by $b_0 (r - r_1)$.

Type I. Roots of indicial equation are equal.

Example 1. *Find the series solution of the differential equation*

$$x \frac{d^2y}{dx^2} + \frac{dy}{dx} + xy = 0 \text{ about '0'}.$$

Sol. We have
$$x \frac{d^2y}{dx^2} + \frac{dy}{dx} + xy = 0. \quad \text{...(1)}$$

Dividing (1) by x, we get

$$\frac{d^2y}{dx^2} + \frac{1}{x}\frac{dy}{dx} + y = 0 \quad \text{...(2)}$$

Comparing (2) with $\frac{d^2y}{dx^2} + P(x)\frac{dy}{dx} + Q(x) = 0$, we get $P(x) = \frac{1}{x}$ and $Q(x) = 1$.

'0' is not an ordinary point of (1) because $P(x)$ is not analytic at 0. Here $xP(x) = 1$ and $x^2Q(x) = x^2$. Both these functions are analytic at $x = 0$

$\therefore$ '0' is a regular singular point of (1).

Let $$y = x^r \sum_{m=0}^{\infty} a_m x^m = \sum_{m=0}^{\infty} a_m x^{m+r},\ a_0 \neq 0 \qquad \text{...(3)}$$

be a series solution of (1) about '0'.

$$(3) \Rightarrow \frac{dy}{dx} = \sum_{m=0}^{\infty} (m+r) a_m x^{m+r-1} \text{ and } \frac{d^2y}{dx^2} = \sum_{m=0}^{\infty} (m+r)(m+r-1) a_m x^{m+r-2}$$

Putting the values of y, $\frac{dy}{dx}$ and $\frac{d^2y}{dx^2}$ in (1), we get

$$x \sum_{m=0}^{\infty} (m+r)(m+r-1) a_m x^{m+r-2} + \sum_{m=0}^{\infty} (m+r) a_m x^{m+r-1} + x \sum_{m=0}^{\infty} a_m x^{m+r} = 0$$

$$\Rightarrow \sum_{m=0}^{\infty} (m+r)(m+r-1) a_m x^{m+r-1} + \sum_{m=0}^{\infty} (m+r) a_m x^{m+r-1} + \sum_{m=0}^{\infty} a_m x^{m+r+1} = 0$$

$$\Rightarrow \sum_{m=0}^{\infty} (m+r)(m+r) a_m x^{m+r-1} + \sum_{m=2}^{\infty} a_{m-2} x^{m+r-1} = 0$$

$$\Rightarrow r^2 a_0 x^{r-1} + (1+r)^2 a_1 x^r + \sum_{m=2}^{\infty} [(m+r)^2 a_m + a_{m-2}] x^{m+r-1} = 0 \qquad \text{...(4)}$$

Equating to zero, the coefficients of lowest power of x, we get $r^2 = 0$. $(\because a_0 \neq 0)$
This is the indicial equation and its roots are $r = 0, 0$. Here the roots are equal.

$(4) \Rightarrow (1+r)^2 a_1 = 0 \Rightarrow a_1 = 0$ $(\because r \neq -1)$

Also $(m+r)^2 a_m + a_{m-2} = 0 \ \forall \ m \geq 2$

$$\Rightarrow a_m = -\frac{a_{m-2}}{(m+r)^2},\ m \geq 2 \qquad \text{...(5)}$$

$m = 2$ in (5) $\Rightarrow a_2 = -\dfrac{a_0}{(r+2)^2}$

$m = 3$ in (5) $\Rightarrow a_3 = -\dfrac{a_1}{(r+3)^2} = 0$

$m = 4$ in (5) $\Rightarrow a_4 = -\dfrac{a_2}{(r+4)^2} = \dfrac{a_0}{(r+2)^2 (r+4)^2}$

....

We note that $a_5, a_7, \ldots\ldots$ are all zero. Using (3), let

$$\bar{y} = x^r \left(a_0 + 0 \,.\, x - \frac{a_0}{(r+2)^2} x^2 + 0 \,.\, x^3 + \frac{a_0}{(r+2)^2 (r+4)^2} x^4 + \ldots \right)$$

(Note that the value of r is not yet used.)

$$\therefore \quad \bar{y} = x^r \left(1 - \frac{x^2}{(r+2)^2} + \frac{x^4}{(r+2)^2 (r+4)^2} + \ldots \right) \qquad (\text{Taking } a_0 = 1)$$

Let $\quad y_1 = \bar{y}\Big|_{r=0} \quad \therefore \; y_1 = 1 - \dfrac{x^2}{2^2} + \dfrac{x^4}{2^2 \,.\, 4^2} + \ldots\ldots$

Differentiating $\bar{y}$ partially w.r.t. r, we get

$$\frac{\partial \bar{y}}{\partial r} = \left(1 - \frac{x^2}{(r+2)^2} + \frac{x^4}{(r+2)^2\,(r+4)^2} + \ldots\right) x^r \log x$$

$$+ x^r \,.\left(0 - x^2(-2)(r+2)^{-3} + x^4\left(\frac{1}{(r+2)^2}\cdot\frac{-2}{(r+4)^3} + \frac{1}{(r+4)^2}\cdot\frac{-2}{(r+2)^3}\right) + \ldots\right)$$

$$= \bar{y}\log x + x^r\left(\frac{2x^2}{(r+2)^3} - \frac{2x^4}{(r+2)^2\,(r+4)^2}\left(\frac{1}{r+2} + \frac{1}{r+4}\right) + \ldots\right)$$

Let $\quad y_2 = \dfrac{\partial \bar{y}}{\partial r}\Big|_{r=0} \quad \therefore \; y_2 = y_1 \log x + \dfrac{x^2}{2^2} - \dfrac{2x^4}{2^2\,.\,4^2}\left(\dfrac{1}{2} + \dfrac{1}{4}\right) + \ldots\ldots$

$$= y_1 \log x + \frac{x^2}{2^2} - \frac{1}{2^2\,.\,4^2}\left(1 + \frac{1}{2}\right)x^4 + \ldots\ldots$$

$\therefore$ The general solution of (1) is $y = C_1 y_1 + C_2 y_2$

or $\quad y = C_1 y_1 + C_2\left(y_1 \log x + \dfrac{x^2}{2^2} - \dfrac{1}{2^2\,.\,4^2}\left(1 + \dfrac{1}{2}\right)x^4 + \ldots\right)$

or $\quad \mathbf{y = (C_1 + C_2 \log x)\left(1 - \dfrac{x^2}{2^2} + \dfrac{x^4}{2^2\,.\,4^2} + \ldots\right) + C_2\left(\dfrac{x^2}{2^2} - \dfrac{1}{2^2\,.\,4^2}\left(1 + \dfrac{1}{2}\right)x^4 + \ldots\right)}$,

where C_1 and C_2 are arbitrary constants.

Example 2. *Find the series solution of the differential equation*

$$x\frac{d^2y}{dx^2} + \frac{dy}{dx} + x^2 y = 0 \textit{ about `0'.}$$

Sol. We have $\quad x\dfrac{d^2y}{dx^2} + \dfrac{dy}{dx} + x^2 y = 0\,. \qquad \ldots(1)$

Dividing (1) by x, we get

$$\frac{d^2y}{dx^2} + \frac{1}{x}\frac{dy}{dx} + xy = 0 \qquad \ldots(2)$$

Comparing (2) with $\dfrac{d^2y}{dx^2} + P(x)\dfrac{dy}{dx} + Q(x)\,y = 0$, we get $P(x) = \dfrac{1}{x}$ and $Q(x) = x$.

'0' is not an ordinary point of (1) because P(x) is not analytic at 0. Here $xP(x) = 1$ and $x^2Q(x) = x^3$. Both these functions are analytic at $x = 0$.

$\therefore$ '0' is a regular singular point of (1).

Let $\quad y = x^r \displaystyle\sum_{m=0}^{\infty} a_m x^m = \sum_{m=0}^{\infty} a_m x^{m+r}, \; a_0 \neq 0 \qquad \ldots(3)$

be a series solution of (1) about '0'.

$$(3) \Rightarrow \frac{dy}{dx} = \sum_{m=0}^{\infty} (m+r) a_m x^{m+r-1} \text{ and } \frac{d^2y}{dx^2} = \sum_{m=0}^{\infty} (m+r)(m+r-1) a_m x^{m+r-2}.$$

Putting the values of y, $\frac{dy}{dx}$ and $\frac{d^2y}{dx^2}$ in (1), we get

$$x \sum_{m=0}^{\infty} (m+r)(m+r-1) a_m x^{m+r-2} + \sum_{m=0}^{\infty} (m+r) a_m x^{m+r-1} + x^2 \sum_{m=0}^{\infty} a_m x^{m+r} = 0$$

$$\Rightarrow \sum_{m=0}^{\infty} (m+r)(m+r-1) a_m x^{m+r-1} + \sum_{m=0}^{\infty} (m+r) a_m x^{m+r-1} + \sum_{m=0}^{\infty} a_m x^{m+r+2} = 0$$

$$\Rightarrow \sum_{m=0}^{\infty} (m+r)^2 a_m x^{m+r-1} + \sum_{m=3}^{\infty} a_{m-3} x^{m+r-1} = 0$$

$$\Rightarrow r^2 a_0 x^{r-1} + (r+1)^2 a_1 x^r + (r+2)^2 a_2 x^{r+1}$$

$$+ \sum_{m=3}^{\infty} [(m+r)^2 a_m + a_{m-3}] x^{m+r-1} = 0 \qquad \text{...(4)}$$

Equating to zero, the coefficients of lowest power of x, we get $r^2 a_0 = 0$.

$\Rightarrow$ $r^2 = 0$. This is the indicial equation and its roots are $r = 0, 0$. Here the roots are equal.

(4) $\Rightarrow$ $(r+1)^2 a_1 = 0$ or $a_1 = 0$, $(r+2)^2 a_2 = 0$ or $a_2 = 0$ $\quad (\because \; r \neq -1, -2)$

Also $(m+r)^2 a_m + a_{m-3} = 0, \; m \geq 3$

$$\Rightarrow \qquad a_m = -\frac{a_{m-3}}{(m+r)^2}, m \geq 3 \qquad \text{...(5)}$$

$m = 3$ in (5) $\Rightarrow$ $a_3 = -\dfrac{a_0}{(r+3)^2}$

$m = 4$ in (5) $\Rightarrow$ $a_4 = -\dfrac{a_1}{(r+4)^2} = 0$

Similarly, $a_5 = 0$, $\quad a_6 = \dfrac{a_0}{(r+3)^2 (r+6)^2}$, $a_7 = 0$, $a_8 = 0$

$$a_9 = -\frac{a_0}{(r+3)^2 (r+6)^2 (r+9)^2}, \ldots\ldots$$

Using (3), let

$$\bar{y} = x^r \left(a_0 - \frac{a_0}{(r+3)^2} x^3 + \frac{a_0}{(r+3)^2 (r+6)^2} x^6 - \frac{a_0}{(r+3)^2 (r+6)^2 (r+9)^2} x^9 + \ldots \right)$$

(Note that the value of r is not yet used.)

$$\therefore \qquad \bar{y} = x^r \left(1 - \frac{x^3}{(r+3)^2} + \frac{x^6}{(r+3)^2 (r+6)^2} - \frac{x^9}{(r+3)^2 (r+6)^2 (r+9)^2} + \ldots \right)$$

(Taking $a_0 = 1$)

Let $\quad y_1 = \bar{y}\Big|_{r=0} \quad \therefore \quad y_1 = 1 - \dfrac{x^3}{3^2} + \dfrac{x^6}{3^2 . 6^2} - \dfrac{x^9}{3^2 . 6^2 . 9^2} + \ldots\ldots$

Differentiating $\bar{y}$ partially w.r.t. r, we get

$$\frac{\partial \bar{y}}{\partial r} = x^r \log x \cdot \left(1 - \frac{x^3}{(r+3)^2} + \frac{x^6}{(r+3)^2 (r+6)^2} - \frac{x^9}{(r+3)^2 (r+6)^2 (r+9)^2} + \ldots\right)$$

$$+ x^r \cdot \left[0 + \frac{2x^3}{(r+3)^3} - x^6 \left(\frac{2}{(r+3)^2 (r+6)^3} + \frac{2}{(r+3)^3 (r+6)^2}\right)\right.$$

$$\left. + x^9 \left(\frac{2}{(r+3)^3 (r+6)^2 (r+9)^2} + \frac{2}{(r+3)^2 (r+6)^3 (r+9)^2} + \frac{2}{(r+3)^2 (r+6)^2 (r+9)^3}\right) + \ldots\right]$$

Let $y_2 = \left.\frac{\partial \bar{y}}{\partial r}\right|_{r=0}$ $\therefore y_2 = y_1 \log x$

$$+ 2\left(\frac{x^3}{3^3} + \frac{1}{3^5 (2!)^2}\left(1 + \frac{1}{2}\right) x^6 + \frac{1}{3^7 (3!)^2}\left(1 + \frac{1}{2} + \frac{1}{3}\right) x^9 + \ldots\ldots\right)$$

$\therefore$ The general solution is $y = C_1 y_1 + C_3 y_2$ where C_1 and C_2 are arbitrary constants.

Type II. Roots of indicial equation are distinct and differing by an integer

Example 3. *Find the series solution of the differential equation*

$$x^2 \frac{d^2y}{dx^2} - x \frac{dy}{dx} - \left(x^2 + \frac{5}{4}\right) y = 0 \text{ about '0'.} \qquad (KU\ 2004)$$

Sol. We have $$x^2 \frac{d^2y}{dx^2} - x \frac{dy}{dx} - \left(x^2 + \frac{5}{4}\right) y = 0. \qquad \ldots(1)$$

Dividing (1) by x^2, we get

$$\frac{d^2y}{dx^2} - \frac{1}{x}\frac{dy}{dx} - \left(1 + \frac{5}{4x^2}\right) y = 0 \qquad \ldots(2)$$

Comparing (2) with $\frac{d^2y}{dx^2} + P(x)\frac{dy}{dx} + Q(x)\, y = 0$, we get

$$P(x) = -\frac{1}{x} \text{ and } Q(x) = -\left(1 + \frac{5}{4x^2}\right).$$

'0' is not an ordinary point of (1) because neither $P(x)$ nor $Q(x)$ is analytic at $x = 0$.

Here $$xP(x) = -1 \text{ and } x^2Q(x) = -\left(x^2 + \frac{5}{4}\right).$$

Both these functions are analytic at $x = 0$

$\therefore$ 0 is a regular singular point of (1).

Let $$y = x^r \sum_{m=0}^{\infty} a_m x^m = \sum_{m=0}^{\infty} a_m x^{m+r}, a_0 \neq 0 \qquad \ldots(3)$$

be a series solution of (1) about '0'.

(3) $\Rightarrow$ $\dfrac{dy}{dx} = \sum_{m=0}^{\infty} (m+r) a_m x^{m+r-1}$ and $\dfrac{d^2y}{dx^2} = \sum_{m=0}^{\infty} (m+r)(m+r-1) a_m x^{m+r-2}$.

Putting the values of y, $\dfrac{dy}{dx}$ and $\dfrac{d^2y}{dx^2}$ in (1), we get

$$x^2 \sum_{m=0}^{\infty} (m+r)(m+r-1) a_m x^{m+r-2} - x \sum_{m=0}^{\infty} (m+r) a_m x^{m+r-1} - \left(x^2 + \frac{5}{4}\right) \sum_{m=0}^{\infty} a_m x^{m+r} = 0$$

$$\Rightarrow \sum_{m=0}^{\infty} (m+r)(m+r-1) a_m x^{m+r} - \sum_{m=0}^{\infty} (m+r) a_m x^{m+r} - \sum_{m=0}^{\infty} a_m x^{m+r+2} - \frac{5}{4} \sum_{m=0}^{\infty} a_m x^{m+r} = 0$$

$$\Rightarrow \sum_{m=0}^{\infty} \left[(m+r)(m+r-1) - (m+r) - \frac{5}{4}\right] a_m x^{m+r} - \sum_{m=0}^{\infty} a_m x^{m+r+2} = 0$$

$$\Rightarrow \sum_{m=0}^{\infty} \left[(m+r)(m+r-2) - \frac{5}{4}\right] a_m x^{m+r} - \sum_{m=2}^{\infty} a_{m-2} x^{m+r} = 0$$

$$\Rightarrow \left(r(r-2) - \frac{5}{4}\right) a_0 x^r + \left((r+1)(r-1) - \frac{5}{4}\right) a_1 x^{r+1} + \sum_{m=2}^{\infty} \left[\left((m+r)(m+r-2) - \frac{5}{4}\right) a_m - a_{m-2}\right] x^{m+r} = 0 \quad \text{...(4)}$$

Equating to zero, the coefficients of lowest power of x, we get $\left(r(r-2) - \dfrac{5}{4}\right) a_0 = 0$.

$\Rightarrow$ $r^2 - 2r - \dfrac{5}{4} = 0$. This is the indicial equation and its roots are $r = \dfrac{5}{2}, -\dfrac{1}{2}$.

Here the roots are distinct and differ by an integer. Let $r_1 = \dfrac{5}{2}, r_2 = -\dfrac{1}{2}$.

We find the solution for the smaller root $r = -1/2$.

(4) $\Rightarrow$ $\left(r^2 - 1 - \dfrac{5}{4}\right) a_1 = 0 \Rightarrow \left(r^2 - \dfrac{9}{4}\right) a_1 = 0 \Rightarrow a_1 = 0$ $\left(\because r^2 \neq \dfrac{9}{4}\right)$

Also $\left[(m+r)(m+r-2) - \dfrac{5}{4}\right] a_m - a_{m-2} = 0$, for $m \geq 2$ ...(5)

The smaller root of the indicial equation is $-1/2$. For $r = -1/2$ and $m = 3$,

(5) $\Rightarrow$ $\left[\left(3 - \dfrac{1}{2}\right)\left(3 - \dfrac{1}{2} - 2\right) - \dfrac{5}{4}\right] a_3 - a_1 = 0$

$\Rightarrow \quad 0 \,.\, a_3 - 0 = 0 \quad \Rightarrow \quad 0 \,.\, a_3 = 0 \qquad (\because \; a_1 = 0)$

$\therefore$ a_3 may be any constant.

$\therefore$ We find the series solution of (1) for the smaller root $-1/2$.

Putting $r = -1/2$ in (5), we have

$$\left[\left(m-\frac{1}{2}\right)\left(m-\frac{5}{2}\right)-\frac{5}{4}\right]a_m - a_{m-2} = 0,\ m \geq 2 \qquad \text{...(6)}$$

$$\Rightarrow \quad a_m = \frac{1}{\left(m-\frac{1}{2}\right)\left(m-\frac{5}{2}\right)-\frac{5}{4}}\,a_{m-2}$$

$$\Rightarrow \quad a_m = \frac{1}{m(m-3)}\,a_{m-2},\ m \geq 2,\ m \neq 3 \qquad \text{...(7)}$$

$m = 2$ in (7) $\Rightarrow$ $a_2 = -\dfrac{1}{2}\,a_0$

$m = 3$ in (6) $\Rightarrow$ $\left[\left(3-\frac{1}{2}\right)\left(3-\frac{5}{2}\right)-\frac{5}{4}\right]a_3 - a_1 = 0 \;\Rightarrow\; 0\,.\,a_3 = 0$

$\therefore$ a_3 may be any constant.

$m = 4$ in (7) $\Rightarrow$ $a_4 = \dfrac{1}{4}\,a_2 = \dfrac{1}{4}\left(-\dfrac{1}{2}\,a_0\right) = -\dfrac{1}{8}\,a_0$

Similarly, $\quad a_5 = \dfrac{a_3}{10},\ a_6 = \dfrac{a_4}{18} = -\dfrac{a_0}{144},\ a_7 = \dfrac{a_5}{28} = \dfrac{a_3}{280},\ a_8 = \dfrac{a_6}{40} = -\dfrac{a_0}{5760},\ \ldots\ldots$

$$\therefore \quad (3) \Rightarrow y = x^{-1/2}\left(a_0 + 0\,.\,x - \frac{a_0}{2}\,x^2 + a_3\,x^3 - \frac{a_0}{8}\,x^4 + \frac{a_3}{10}\,x^5 - \frac{a_0}{144}\,x^6 + \frac{a_3}{280}\,x^7 - \frac{a_0}{5760}\,x^8 + \ldots\right)$$

$$\therefore \quad y = a_0\,x^{-1/2}\left(1 - \frac{x^2}{2} - \frac{x^4}{8} - \frac{x^6}{144} - \frac{x^8}{5760} + \ldots\right) + a_3\,x^{-1/2}\left(x^3 + \frac{x^5}{10} + \frac{x^7}{280} + \ldots\right)$$

or

$$\mathbf{y = a_0\,x^{-1/2}\left(1 - \frac{x^2}{2} - \frac{x^4}{8} - \frac{x^6}{144} - \frac{x^8}{5760} + \ldots\right) + a_3\,x^{5/2}\left(1 + \frac{x^2}{10} + \frac{x^4}{280} + \ldots\right)} \qquad \text{...(7)}$$

This represents the general solution because a_0 and a_3 are arbitrary constants and $a_0 \neq 0$.

By taking $r = 5/2$, we can show that the solution is $y = x^{5/2}\left(1 + \dfrac{x^2}{10} + \dfrac{x^4}{280} + \ldots\right)$.

$\therefore$ (7) is a solution even if $a_0 = 0$.

Example 4. *Find the series solution of the differential equation*

$$x\frac{d^2y}{dx^2}-3\frac{dy}{dx}+xy=0 \text{ about '0'}. \quad \text{(KU 2004 S)}$$

Sol. We have
$$x\frac{d^2y}{dx^2}-3\frac{dy}{dx}+xy=0. \quad ...(1)$$

Dividing (1) by x, we get

$$\frac{d^2y}{dx^2}-\frac{3}{x}\frac{dy}{dx}+y=0 \quad ...(2)$$

Comparing (2) with $\frac{d^2y}{dx^2}+P(x)\frac{dy}{dx}+Q(x)y=0$, we get $P(x)=-\frac{3}{x}$ and $Q(x)=1$.

'0' is not an ordinary point of (1) because $P(x)$ is not analytic at 0.

Here $xP(x)=-3$ and $x^2P(x)=x^2$. Both these functions are analytic at $x=0$.

$\therefore$ '0' is a regular singular point of (1).

Let
$$y=x^r\sum_{m=0}^{\infty}a_m x^m=\sum_{m=0}^{\infty}a_m x^{m+r}, a_0\neq 0 \quad ...(3)$$

be a series solution of (1) about '0'.

$$(3) \Rightarrow \quad \frac{dy}{dx}=\sum_{m=0}^{\infty}(m+r)a_m x^{m+r-1}$$

and
$$\frac{d^2y}{dx^2}=\sum_{m=0}^{\infty}(m+r)(m+r-1)a_m x^{m+r-2}.$$

Putting the values of $\frac{dy}{dx}$ and $\frac{d^2y}{dx^2}$ in (1), we get

$$x\sum_{m=0}^{\infty}(m+r)(m+r-1)a_m x^{m+r-2}-3\sum_{m=0}^{\infty}(m+r)a_m x^{m+r-1}+x\sum_{m=0}^{\infty}a_m x^{m+r}=0$$

$$\Rightarrow \sum_{m=0}^{\infty}(m+r)(m+r-1)a_m x^{m+r-1}-3\sum_{m=0}^{\infty}(m+r)a_m x^{m+r-1}+\sum_{m=0}^{\infty}a_m x^{m+r+1}=0$$

$$\Rightarrow \sum_{m=0}^{\infty}(m+r)(m+r-4)a_m x^{m+r-1}+\sum_{m=2}^{\infty}a_{m-2}x^{m+r-1}=0$$

$$\Rightarrow r(r-4)a_0x^{r-1}+(r+1)(r-3)a_1x^r$$
$$+\sum_{m=2}^{\infty}[(m+r)(m+r-4)a_m+a_{m-2}]x^{m+r-1}=0 \quad ...(4)$$

Equating to zero, the coefficients of lowest power of x, we get $r(r-4)a_0=0$.

$\Rightarrow$ $r(r-4)=0$. This is the indicial equation and its roots are $r = 0, 4$. Here the roots are distinct and differ by an integer.

(4) $\Rightarrow$ $(r+1)(r-3)a_1 = 0 \;\Rightarrow\; a_1 = 0$ $(\because r \neq -1, 3)$

Also $(m+r)(m+r-4)a_m + a_{m-2} = 0,\ m \geq 2$

$$\Rightarrow \quad a_m = -\frac{a_{m-2}}{(m+r)(m+r-4)},\ m \geq 2 \quad ...(5)$$

$m = 2$ in (5) $\Rightarrow a_2 = -\dfrac{a_0}{(r+2)(r-2)}$

$m = 3$ in (5) $\Rightarrow a_3 = -\dfrac{a_1}{(r+3)(r-1)} = 0$

$m = 4$ in (5) $\Rightarrow a_4 = -\dfrac{a_2}{(r+4)r} = \dfrac{a_0}{(r-2)r(r+2)(r+4)}$

$m = 5$ in (5) $\Rightarrow a_5 = -\dfrac{a_3}{(r+5)(r+1)} = 0$

$m = 6$ in (5) $\Rightarrow a_6 = -\dfrac{a_4}{(r+6)(r+2)} = -\dfrac{a_0}{(r-2)(r+2)^2 r(r+4)(r+6)}$

....

Using (3), let

$$\bar{y} = x^r\left(a_0 + 0.x - \frac{a_0}{(r+2)(r-2)}x^2 + 0.x^3 + \frac{a_0}{(r-2)r(r+2)(r+4)}x^4 + 0.x^5 - \frac{a_0}{(r-2)r(r+2)^2(r+4)(r+6)}x^6 + \ldots\right)$$

or
$$\bar{y} = a_0 x^r\left(1 - \frac{x^2}{(r+2)(r-2)} + \frac{x^4}{(r-2)r(r+2)(r+4)} - \frac{x^6}{(r-2)r(r+2)^2(r+4)(r+6)} + \ldots\right)$$

The smaller root of the indicial equation is 0. We shall use this root. For $r = 0$, the coefficients of x^4, x^6, ... tend to infinity.

$\therefore$ We replace a_0 by $b_0(r-0)$ *i.e.* by $b_0 r$.

$$\therefore \quad \bar{y} = b_0 x^r\left[r - \frac{rx^2}{(r+2)(r-2)} + \frac{x^4}{(r-2)(r+2)(r+4)} - \frac{x^6}{(r-2)(r+2)^2(r+4)(r+6)} + \ldots\right]$$

$$\therefore \quad \bar{y} = x^r\left(r - \frac{rx^2}{(r+2)(r-2)} + \frac{x^4}{(r-2)(r+2)(r+4)} - \frac{x^6}{(r-2)(r+2)^2(r+4)(r+6)} + \ldots\right)$$

(Taking $b_0 = 1$)

Let
$$y_1 = \bar{y}\Big|_{r=0} \qquad \therefore\ y_1 = x^0\left(0 - 0 + \frac{x^4}{(-2).2.4} - \frac{x^6}{(-2).(2)^2.4.6} + \ldots\right)$$

or
$$y_1 = -\frac{x^4}{2^3.2!} + \frac{x^6}{2^5.3!} + \ldots\ldots$$

Differentiating $\bar{y}$ partially w.r.t. r, we get

$$\frac{\partial \bar{y}}{\partial r} = x^r \log x \cdot \left[r - \frac{rx^2}{(r+2)(r-2)} + \frac{x^4}{(r-2)(r+2)(r+4)} - \frac{x^6}{(r-2)(r+2)^2(r+4)(r+6)} + \ldots \right]$$

$$+ x^r \left[1 + \frac{(r^2+4)x^2}{(r+2)^2(r-2)^2} - \frac{1}{(r-2)(r+2)(r+4)} \left(\frac{1}{r-2} + \frac{1}{r+2} + \frac{1}{r+4} \right) x^4 \right.$$

$$\left. + \frac{1}{(r-2)(r+2)^2(r+4)(r+6)} \left(\frac{1}{r-2} + \frac{2}{r+2} + \frac{1}{r+4} + \frac{1}{r+6} \right) x^6 + \ldots \right]$$

Let $y_2 = \left. \frac{\partial \bar{y}}{\partial r} \right|_{r=0}$ $\therefore$ $y_2 = y_1 \log x + 1 + \frac{4x^2}{2^2 \cdot 2^2} + \frac{1}{2.2.4} \left(\frac{1}{-2} + \frac{1}{2} + \frac{1}{4} \right) x^4$

$$- \frac{1}{2.2^2.4.6} \left(\frac{1}{-2} + \frac{2}{2} + \frac{1}{4} + \frac{1}{6} \right) x^6 + \ldots$$

$$= y_1 \log x + 1 + \frac{1}{2^2} x^2 + \frac{1}{2^5 \cdot 2!} x^4 - \frac{1}{2^6 \cdot 3!} \left(1 + \frac{1}{2} + \frac{1}{3} \right) x^6 + \ldots$$

$\therefore$ The general solution is $y = C_1 y_1 + C_2 y_2$ where C_1 and C_2 are arbitrary constants.

EXERCISE 5

Find the series solution of the following differential equations about '0' :

1. $x \frac{d^2y}{dx^2} + \frac{dy}{dx} - y = 0$ *(MDU 2005)*
2. $x^2 \frac{d^2y}{dx^2} - x \frac{dy}{dx} + (x^2 + 1) y = 0$
3. $x \frac{d^2y}{dx^2} + \frac{dy}{dx} + 2y = 0$
4. $(x - x^2) \frac{d^2y}{dx^2} + (1 - 5x) \frac{dy}{dx} - 4y = 0$
5. $x \frac{d^2y}{dx^2} + (x - 1) \frac{dy}{dx} - y = 0$
6. $x \frac{d^2y}{dx^2} + 2 \frac{dy}{dx} + xy = 0$
7. $x \frac{d^2y}{dx^2} - 2 \frac{dy}{dx} + y = 0$
8. $x(1 - x) \frac{d^2y}{dx^2} - 3x \frac{dy}{dx} - y = 0.$

Answers

1. $y = (C_1 + C_2 \log x) \left(1 + x + \frac{1}{(2!)^2} x^2 + \frac{1}{(3!)^2} x^3 + \ldots \right)$

$$- 2C_2 \left(x + \frac{1}{(2!)^2} \left(1 + \frac{1}{2} \right) x^2 + \frac{1}{(3!)^2} \left(1 + \frac{1}{2} + \frac{1}{3} \right) x^3 + \ldots \right)$$

2. $y = (C_1 + C_2 \log x)\, x \left(1 - \frac{x^2}{2^2} + \frac{x^4}{2^4 (2!)^2} - \frac{x^6}{2^6 (3!)^2} + \ldots \right)$

$$+ C_2 x \left(\frac{x^2}{2^2} - \frac{x^4}{2^4 (2!)^2} \left(1 + \frac{1}{2} \right) + \frac{x^6}{2^6 (3!)^2} \left(1 + \frac{1}{2} + \frac{1}{3} \right) + \ldots \right)$$

3. $y = (C_1 + C_2 \log x)\left(1 - \frac{2x}{(1!)^2} + \frac{2^2x^2}{(2!)^2} - \frac{2^3x^3}{(3!)^2} + \ldots\right) + C_2\left(4x - 3x^2 + \frac{22x^3}{7} + \ldots\right)$

4. $y = (C_1 + C_2 \log x)(1 + 2^2x + 3^2x^2 + 4^2x^3 + \ldots) - 2C_2(1.2x + 2.3x^2 + 3.4x^3 + \ldots)$

5. $y = C_1(1 - x) + C_2e^{-x}$

6. $y = C_1x^{-1}\left(1 - \frac{x^2}{2!} + \frac{x^4}{4!} + \ldots\right) + C_2\left(1 - \frac{x^2}{3!} + \frac{x^4}{5!} + \ldots\right)$

7. $y = (C_1 + C_2 \log x)\left(-\frac{x^3}{12} + \frac{x^4}{48} - \frac{x^5}{480} + \ldots\right) + C_2\left(1 + \frac{x}{2} + \frac{x^2}{4} + \frac{x^3}{36} - \frac{19x^4}{576} + \frac{137x^5}{28800} + \ldots\right)$

8. $y = (C_1 + C_2 \log x)(x + 2x^2 + 3x^3 + 4x^4 + \ldots) + C_2(1 + x + x^2 + x^3 + x^4 + \ldots)$.

2

Legendre Equation

1. INTRODUCTION

With the knowledge of series method of solving second order differential equations, we are ready to solve three very important differential equations of Physics. The present chapter and the next two chapters would be devoted to these differential equations. In this chapter, we shall consider the differential equation known as Legendre equation*. This differential equation occurs particularly in boundary value problems for spheres.

2. LEGENDRE EQUATION AND ITS SOLUTION

The Legendre equation is $(1-x^2)\frac{d^2y}{dx^2} - 2x\frac{dy}{dx} + n(n+1)\,y = 0$. ...(1)

The parameter n is a real number.

Dividing (1) by $1 - x^2$, we get

$$\frac{d^2y}{dx^2} - \frac{2x}{1-x^2}\frac{dy}{dx} + \frac{k}{1-x^2}y = 0 \qquad ...(2)$$

[Putting $k = n(n+1)$]

Comparing (2) with $\frac{d^2y}{dx^2} + P(x)\frac{dy}{dx} + Q(x).\,y = 0$, we get

$$P(x) = -\frac{2x}{1-x^2} \text{ and } Q(x) = \frac{k}{1-x^2}.$$

The functions P(x) and Q(x) are analytic at 0.

$\therefore$ '0' is an ordinary point of (1).

We use *power series* method to find the solution of (1) about '0'.

Let $$y = \sum_{m=0}^{\infty} a_m x^m \qquad ...(3)$$

be the power series solution of (1) about '0'.

(3) $\Rightarrow$ $$\frac{dy}{dx} = \sum_{m=1}^{\infty} m a_m x^{m-1} \text{ and } \frac{d^2y}{dx^2} = \sum_{m=2}^{\infty} m(m-1)a_m x^{m-2}.$$

Putting the values of y, $\frac{dy}{dx}$ and $\frac{d^2y}{dx^2}$ in (1), we get

$$(1-x^2)\sum_{m=2}^{\infty} m\,(m-1)\,a_m x^{m-2} - 2x\sum_{m=1}^{\infty} m a_m x^{m-1} + k\sum_{m=0}^{\infty} a_m x^m = 0$$

***Adrien Marie Legendre** (1752—1833). French mathematician, who become a professor in Paris in 1775 and made important contribution to special functions and calculus of variations.

$$\Rightarrow \sum_{m=2}^{\infty} m(m-1)a_m x^{m-2} - \sum_{m=2}^{\infty} m(m-1)a_m x^m - 2\sum_{m=1}^{\infty} m\,a_m x^m + k\sum_{m=0}^{\infty} a_m x^m = 0$$

$$\Rightarrow \sum_{m=0}^{\infty} (m+2)(m+1)a_{m+2}x^m - \sum_{m=2}^{\infty} m(m-1)a_m x^m$$

$$-2\sum_{m=1}^{\infty} m\,a_m x^m + k\sum_{m=0}^{\infty} a_m x^m = 0$$

(By shifting of indices)

$$\Rightarrow \left(2a_2 + 6a_3x + \sum_{m=2}^{\infty} (m+2)(m+1)a_{m+2}x^m\right) - \sum_{m=2}^{\infty} m(m-1)a_m x^m$$

$$-2\left(a_1x + \sum_{m=2}^{\infty} m\,a_m x^m\right) + k\left(a_0 + a_1x + \sum_{m=2}^{\infty} a_m x^m\right) = 0$$

$$\Rightarrow (2a_2 + ka_0) + (6a_3 - 2a_1 + ka_1)x$$

$$+ \sum_{m=2}^{\infty} [(m+2)(m+1)a_{m+2} - m(m-1)a_m - 2m\,a_m + ka_m]\,x^m = 0$$

$$\Rightarrow (2a_2 + ka_0) + (6a_3 - 2a_1 + ka_1)x$$

$$+ \sum_{m=2}^{\infty} [(m+2)(m+1)a_{m+2} + (n-m)(n+m+1)a_m]\,x^m = 0 \quad ...(4)$$

$$(\because -m^2 + m - 2m + k = -m^2 - m + n^2 + n = n^2 - m^2 + (n-m) = (n-m)(n+m+1))$$

(4) is an identity for all values of x in the interval of convergence of the series (3).

$\therefore \quad 2a_2 + ka_0 = 0$ ...(5)

$6a_3 - 2a_1 + ka_1 = 0$ ...(6)

and $(m+2)(m+1)a_{m+2} + (n-m)(n+m+1)a_m = 0,\ m \geq 2$ ...(7)

$$(5) \Rightarrow a_2 = -\frac{n(n+1)}{2!}a_0, \quad (6) \Rightarrow a_3 = \frac{2 - n(n+1)}{6}a_1 = -\frac{(n-1)(n+2)}{3!}a_1$$

$(\because\ k = n(n+1))$

$$(7) \Rightarrow a_{m+2} = -\frac{(n-m)(n+m+1)a_m}{(m+2)(m+1)},\ m \geq 2 \quad ...(8)$$

Putting $m = 0$ and $m = 1$ in (8), we get the values of a_2 and a_3 respectively.

$\therefore$ (8) is also true for $m = 0, 1$.

$$\therefore \quad a_{m+2} = -\frac{(n-m)(n+m+1)a_m}{(m+2)(m+1)},\ m \geq 0$$

This is called **recurrence relation** of the Legendre equation.

$$m = 2 \text{ in } (8) \Rightarrow a_4 = -\frac{(n-2)(n+3)}{4\,.\,3}a_2 = \frac{(n-2)n(n+1)(n+3)}{4!}a_0$$

$$m = 3 \text{ in } (8) \quad \Rightarrow \quad a_5 = -\frac{(n-3)(n+4)a_3}{5.4} = \frac{(n-3)(n-1)(n+2)(n+4)}{5!}a_1$$

....

Putting these values in (3), we get

$$y = a_0 + a_1 x - \frac{n(n+1)}{2!}a_0 x^2 - \frac{(n-1)(n+2)}{3!}a_1 x^3$$

$$+ \frac{(n-2)n(n+1)(n+3)}{4!}a_0 x^4 + \frac{(n-3)(n-1)(n+2)(n+4)}{5!}a_1 x^5 + \ldots$$

$$= a_0\left(1 - \frac{n(n+1)}{2!}x^2 + \frac{(n-2)n(n+1)(n+3)}{4!}x^4 + \ldots\right)$$

$$+ a_1\left(x - \frac{(n-1)(n+2)}{3!}x^3 + \frac{(n-3)(n-1)(n+2)(n+4)}{5!}x^5 + \ldots\right)$$

Let $\quad y_1(x) = 1 - \frac{n(n+1)}{2!}x^2 + \frac{(n-2)n(n+1)(n+3)}{4!}x^4 + \ldots$

and $\quad y_2(x) = x - \frac{(n-1)(n+2)}{3!}x^3 + \frac{(n-3)(n-1)(n+2)(n+4)}{5!}x^5 + \ldots$

$\therefore \quad y = a_0 y_1(x) + a_1 y_2(x).$

Taking $a_0 = 1$ and $a_1 = 0$, we see that $y_1(x)$ is a solution of (1). Similarly $y_2(x)$ is a solution of (1). Also, $y_1(x)/y_2(x)$ is not a constant, so $y_1(x)$ and $y_2(x)$ are linearly independent solutions of (1).

$\therefore \quad y = a_0 y_1(x) + a_1 y_2(x)$ represents the general solution of Legendre equation.

In the above solution, $y_1(x)$ contains only even powers of x and $y_2(x)$ contains only odd powers of x.

If n is a positive even integer then $y_1(x)$ terminates at the term containing x^n and all succeeding terms vanish. Thus, $y_1(x)$ reduces to a polynomial of degree n. In this case, $y_2(x)$ remains an infinite series.

If n is a positive odd integer, then $y_2(x)$ terminates at the term containing x^n and all succeeding terms vanish. Thus, $y_2(x)$ reduces to a polynomial of degree n. In this case, $y_1(x)$ remains an infinite series.

Radius of convergence. Let n be not an integer.

For $y_1(x)$, $\quad \lim_{k\to\infty}\left|\frac{a_{2k+2}}{a_{2k}}\right| = \lim_{k\to\infty}\left|-\frac{(n-2k)(n+2k+1)}{(2k+2)(2k+1)}\right|$

$$= \lim_{k\to\infty}\left|\frac{\left(1-\frac{n}{2k}\right)\left(1+\frac{n+1}{2k}\right)}{\left(1+\frac{1}{k}\right)\left(1+\frac{1}{2k}\right)}\right| = \lim_{k\to\infty}\frac{\left(1-\frac{n}{2k}\right)\left(1+\frac{n+1}{2k}\right)}{\left(1+\frac{1}{k}\right)\left(1+\frac{1}{2k}\right)}$$

$$= \frac{(1-0)(1+0)}{(1+0)(1+1)} = 1$$

$\therefore$ Radius of convergence $= \frac{1}{1} = 1$.

For $y_2(x)$, $$\lim_{k \to \infty} \left| \frac{a_{2k+3}}{a_{2k+1}} \right| = \lim_{k \to \infty} \left| -\frac{(n-(2k+1))(n+2k+1+1)}{(2k+1+2)(2k+1+1)} \right|$$

$$= \lim_{k \to \infty} \left| -\frac{(n-2k-1)(n+2k+2)}{(2k+3)(2k+2)} \right| = \lim_{k \to \infty} \left| \frac{\left(1-\frac{n-1}{2k}\right)\left(1+\frac{n+2}{2k}\right)}{\left(1+\frac{3}{2k}\right)\left(1+\frac{1}{k}\right)} \right|$$

$$= \lim_{k \to \infty} \frac{\left(1-\frac{n-1}{2k}\right)\left(1+\frac{n+2}{2k}\right)}{\left(1+\frac{3}{2k}\right)\left(1+\frac{1}{k}\right)} = \frac{(1-0)(1+0)}{(1+0)(1+0)} = 1.$$

$\therefore$ Radius of convergence $= \frac{1}{1} = 1$.

$\therefore$ The general solution is convergent in $|x| < 1$ *i.e.* in $-1 < x < 1$.

3. LEGENDRE POLYNOMIALS

We know that '0' is an ordinary point of the Legendre equation

$$(1-x^2)\frac{d^2y}{dx^2} - 2x\frac{dy}{dx} + n(n+1)\,y = 0\,,\; n \in \mathbf{R}. \qquad \ldots(1)$$

If the power series solution about '0' is $y = \sum_{m=0}^{n} a_m x^m$, the recurrence relation is

$$a_{m+2} = -\frac{(n-m)(n+m+1)}{(m+2)(m+1)} a_m\,,\; m \geq 0 \qquad \ldots(2)$$

and the power series solution is $y = a_0 y_1(x) + a_1 y_2(x)$ where

$$y_1(x) = 1 - \frac{n(n+1)}{2!}x^2 + \frac{(n-2)\,n\,(n+1)\,(n+3)}{4!}x^4 + \ldots$$

and $$y_2(x) = x - \frac{(n-1)(n+2)}{3!}x^3 + \frac{(n-3)(n-1)(n+2)(n+4)}{5!}x^5 + \ldots$$

Also, this power series solution about '0' is convergent for $|x| < 1$.

Let n be a non-negative integer.

$\therefore$ If n is even, then $y_1(x)$ is a polynomial of degree n and if n is odd then $y_2(x)$ is a polynomial of degree n.

The polynomials $y_1(x)$ and $y_2(x)$ multiplied by some definite constants are called *Legendre polynomials*.

If n is even (resp. odd), then the constant multiple of $y_1(x)$ (resp. $y_2(x)$) with coefficient of x^n as $\frac{(2n)!}{2^n (n!)^2}$ is called the **Legendre polynomial** of degree n and is denoted by $P_n(x)$.

$$\therefore \qquad P_n(x) = \begin{cases} a_0 + a_2x^2 + \dots\dots + a_nx^n & \text{if } n \text{ is even} \\ a_1x + a_3x^3 + \dots\dots + a_nx^n & \text{if } n \text{ is odd,} \end{cases}$$

where $a_n = \dfrac{(2n)!}{2^n (n!)^2}$.

In descending powers of x, we have

$$P_n(x) = \begin{cases} a_nx^n + a_{n-2}x^{n-2} + \dots\dots + a_0 & \text{if } n \text{ is even} \\ a_nx^n + a_{n-2}x^{n-2} + \dots\dots + a_1x & \text{if } n \text{ is odd,} \end{cases}$$

where $a_n = \dfrac{(2n)!}{2^n (n!)^2}$

Equivalently, $P_n(x) = \sum\limits_{m=0}^{M} a_{n-2m} x^{n-2m}$

where $a_n = \dfrac{(2n)!}{2^n (n!)^2}$ and $M = \begin{cases} n/2 & \text{if } n \text{ is even or zero} \\ (n-1)/2 & \text{if } n \text{ is odd.} \end{cases}$

Now we shall find the values of $a_{n-2}, a_{n-4}, \dots\dots, a_0(\text{or } a_1)$.

Since, n is a non-negative integer, we have

$$a_{n+2} = 0, a_{n+4} = 0, \dots\dots \text{ and}$$

$$a_{m+2} = -\frac{(n-m)(n+m+1)}{(m+2)(m+1)} a_m, \quad 0 \le m \le n-2.$$

$$\therefore \qquad a_m = -\frac{(m+2)(m+1)}{(n-m)(n+m+1)} a_{m+2}, \quad 0 \le m \le n-2 \qquad \dots(1)$$

$$m = n-2 \text{ in } (1) \Rightarrow a_{n-2} = -\frac{n(n-1)}{2(2n-1)} a_n = -\frac{n(n-1)}{2(2n-1)} \cdot \frac{(2n)!}{2^n (n!)^2}$$

$$= -\frac{n(n-1)}{2(2n-1)} \cdot \frac{2n(2n-1).(2n-2)!}{2^n n.(n-1)!\, n(n-1).(n-2)!} = -\frac{(2n-2)!}{2^n (n-1)!\,(n-2)!}$$

Similarly, $a_{n-4} = -\dfrac{(n-2)(n-3)}{4(2n-3)} a_{n-2} = -\dfrac{(n-2)(n-3)}{4(2n-3)} \cdot -\dfrac{(2n-2)!}{2^n (n-1)!\,(n-2)!}$

$$= \frac{(-1)^2 (n-2)(n-3)}{4(2n-3)} \cdot \frac{(2n-2)(2n-3).(2n-4)!}{2^n (n-1)(n-2)!\,(n-2)(n-3).(n-4)!}$$

$$= \frac{(-1)^2 (2n-4)!}{2^n .2!\,(n-2)!\,(n-4)!}$$

In general, $a_{n-2m} = \dfrac{(-1)^m (2n-2m)!}{2^n m!\,(n-m)!\,(n-2m)!}, \; n-2m \ge 0$

$$\therefore \qquad \mathbf{P_n(x)} = \sum_{m=0}^{M} \frac{(-1)^m (2n-2m)!}{2^n m!\,(n-m)!\,(n-2m)!} x^{n-2m},$$

where $M = \begin{cases} n/2 & \textbf{if n is even or zero} \\ (n-1)/2 & \textbf{if n is odd.} \end{cases}$

Particular cases.

$$n = 0 \quad \Rightarrow \quad P_0(x) = \frac{(-1)^0\,(0-0)!}{2^0\,(0!)\,0!\,0!}\,x^0 = 1$$

$$n = 1 \quad \Rightarrow \quad P_1(x) = \sum_{m=0}^{0} \frac{(-1)^m\,(2-2m)!}{2.m!(1-m)!(1-2m)!}\,x^{1-2m} = \frac{1(2!)}{2.0!1!1!}\,x^1 = x$$

$$n = 2 \quad \Rightarrow \quad P_2(x) = \sum_{m=0}^{1} \frac{(-1)^m\,(4-2m)!}{2^2.m!(2-m)!(2-2m)!}\,x^{2-2m}$$

$$= \frac{1(4!)}{(4).0!2!2!}\,x^2 + \frac{(-1)2!}{(4)1!1!0!}\,x^0 = \frac{3}{2}x^2 - \frac{1}{2} = \frac{1}{2}(3x^2 - 1)$$

$$n = 3 \quad \Rightarrow \quad P_3(x) = \sum_{m=0}^{1} \frac{(-1)^m\,(6-2m)!}{2^3.m!(3-m)!(3-2m)!}\,x^{3-2m}$$

$$= \frac{1.6!}{8.(0!)3!3!}\,x^3 + \frac{(-1)4!}{(8)(1!)(2!)(1!)}\,x = \frac{5}{2}x^3 - \frac{3}{2}x = \frac{1}{2}(5x^3 - 3x)$$

$$n = 4 \quad \Rightarrow \quad P_4(x) = \sum_{m=0}^{2} \frac{(-1)^m\,(8-2m)!}{2^4\,m!(4-m)!(4-2m)!}\,x^{4-2m}$$

$$= \frac{1.(8!)}{16(0!)4!4!}\,x^4 + \frac{(-1)6!}{16(1!)3!2!}\,x^2 + \frac{1(4!)}{16(2!)2!0!}\,x^0$$

$$= \frac{35}{8}x^4 - \frac{15}{4}x^2 + \frac{3}{8} = \frac{1}{8}(35x^4 - 30x^2 + 3)$$

....

$\therefore$

$$\mathbf{P_0(x) = 1}$$

$$\mathbf{P_1(x) = x}$$

$$\mathbf{P_2(x) = \frac{1}{2}(3x^2 - 1)}$$

$$\mathbf{P_3(x) = \frac{1}{2}(5x^3 - 3x)}$$

$$\mathbf{P_4(x) = \frac{1}{8}(35x^4 - 30x^2 + 3)}$$

....

Remark. It is worth while to note that $y = P_n(x)$ is a particular solution of the Legendre equation

$$(1 - x^2)\frac{d^2y}{dx^2} - 2x\frac{dy}{dx} + n(n+1)\,y = 0,$$

where n is a non-negative integer.

4. ALTERNATIVE FORM OF LEGENDRE POLYNOMIAL

We know that if $y = \sum_{m=0}^{\infty} a_m x^m$ be a power series solution about '0' of the Legendre equation

$$(1-x^2)\frac{d^2y}{dx^2} - 2x\frac{dy}{dx} + n(n+1)y = 0,\ n \in \mathbf{R},$$ then we have

$$a_{m+2} = -\frac{(n-m)(n+m+1)}{(m+2)(m+1)} a_m,\ m \geq 0.$$

In particular, let n be a non-negative integer.

In this case, $a_{n+2} = 0, a_{n+4} = 0, \ldots\ldots$ and

$$a_{m+2} = -\frac{(n-m)(n+m+1)}{(m+2)(m+1)} a_m,\ 0 \leq m \leq n-2$$

$$\therefore \quad a_m = -\frac{(m+2)(m+1)}{(n-m)(n+m+1)} a_{m+2},\ 0 \leq m \leq n-2 \qquad \ldots(1)$$

$m = n-2$ in (1) $\Rightarrow$ $a_{n-2} = -\frac{n(n-1)}{2(2n-1)} a_n$

$m = n-4$ in (1) $\Rightarrow$ $a_{n-4} = -\frac{(n-2)(n-3)}{4(2n-3)} a_{n-2}$

$$= -\frac{(n-2)(n-3)}{4(2n-3)} \cdot -\frac{n(n-1)}{2(2n-1)} a_n = \frac{n(n-1)(n-3)(n-4)}{2.4(2n-1)(2n-3)} a_n$$

....

Let $P_n(x)$ be the Legendre polynomial.

$$\therefore \quad P_n(x) = \begin{cases} a_n x^n + a_{n-2}x^{n-2} + \ldots\ldots + a_0 & \text{if } n \text{ is even or zero} \\ a_n x^n + a_{n-2}x^{n-2} + \ldots\ldots + a_1 x & \text{if } n \text{ is odd,} \end{cases}$$

where $a_n = \frac{(2n)!}{2^n (n!)^2}$.

$$\therefore \quad P_n(x) = a_n x^n + a_{n-2}x^{n-2} + a_{n-4}x^{n-4} + \ldots\ldots$$

The last term on the right side depend upon the nature of n.

$$\therefore \quad P_n(x) = a_n x^n - \frac{n(n-1)}{2(2n-1)} a_n x^{n-2} + \frac{n(n-1)(n-2)(n-3)}{2.4(2n-1)(2n-3)} a_n x^{n-4} + \ldots\ldots$$

or

$$P_n(x) = a^n \left[x^n - \frac{n(n-1)}{2(2n-1)} x^{n-2} + \frac{n(n-1)(n-2)(n-3)}{2.4(2n-1)(2n-3} x^{n-4} + \ldots\ldots \right] \qquad \ldots(2)$$

Now $\quad a_n = \dfrac{(2n)!}{2^n (n!)^2} = \dfrac{1.2.3.4.5.6.......(2n-1)2n}{2^n (n!)^2}$

$$= \frac{1.3.5.......(2n-1)\,2.4.6.......2n}{n! \times 2^n . n!} = \frac{1.3.5......(2n-1)}{n!}.$$

$$\therefore \quad (2) \Rightarrow \mathbf{P_n(x)} = \frac{\mathbf{1.3.5......(2n-1)}}{\mathbf{n!}}\left[\mathbf{x^n} - \frac{\mathbf{n(n-1)}}{\mathbf{2(2n-1)}}\mathbf{x^{n-2}} + \frac{\mathbf{n(n-1)(n-2)(n-3)}}{\mathbf{2.4(2n-1)(2n-3)}}\mathbf{x^{n-4}} + ...\right]$$

Particular Cases :

$n = 0 \Rightarrow \quad P_0(x) = 1 . x^0 = 1$

$n = 1 \Rightarrow \quad P_1(x) = \dfrac{1}{1!} . x^1 = x$

$n = 2 \Rightarrow \quad P_2(x) = \dfrac{1.3}{2!}\left(x^2 - \dfrac{2.1}{2.3}x^0\right) = \dfrac{1}{2}(3x^2 - 1)$

$n = 3 \Rightarrow \quad P_3(x) = \dfrac{1.3.5}{3!}\left(x^3 - \dfrac{3.2}{2.5}x^1\right) = \dfrac{1}{2}(5x^3 - 3x)$

$n = 4 \Rightarrow \quad P_4(x) = \dfrac{1.3.5.7}{4!}\left(x^4 - \dfrac{4.3}{2.7}x^2 + \dfrac{4.3.2.1}{2.4.7.5}x^0\right)$

$$= \frac{35}{8}\left(x^4 - \frac{6}{7}x^2 + \frac{3}{35}\right) = \frac{1}{8}(35x^4 - 30x^2 + 3).$$

WORKING RULES FOR SOLVING PROBLEMS

Rule I. Legendre equation is $(1 - x^2)\dfrac{d^2y}{dx^2} - 2x\dfrac{dy}{dx} + n(n+1)\,y = 0$.

The parameter n is a real number.

Rule II. General solution of Legendre equation is $y = C_1 y_1(x) + C_2 y_2(x)$,

where $\quad y_1(x) = 1 - \dfrac{n(n+1)}{2!}x^2 + \dfrac{(n-2)n(n+1)(n+3)}{4!}x^4 + ...$

and $\quad y_2(x) = x - \dfrac{(n-1)(n+2)}{3!}x^3 + \dfrac{(n-3)(n-1)(n+2)(n+4)}{5!}x^5 + ...$

Rule III. General solution of Legendre equation is convergent in $|x| < 1$.

Rule IV. $P_n(x) = \displaystyle\sum_{m=0}^{M} \frac{(-1)^m (2n-2m)!}{2^n\, m!(n-m)!(n-2m)!} x^{n-2m}$,

where $\quad M = \begin{cases} \dfrac{n}{2} & \text{if } n \text{ is even or zero} \\ \dfrac{n-1}{2} & \text{if } n \text{ is odd.} \end{cases}$

Rule V. $P_n(x) = \frac{1.3.5....(2n-1)}{n!}\left[x^n - \frac{n(n-1)}{2(2n-1)}x^{n-2} + \frac{n(n-1)(n-2)(n-3)}{2.4(2n-1)(2n-3)}x^{n-4} + ...\right]$.

Rule VI. $P_0(x) = 1$, $P_1(x) = x$, $P_2(x) = \frac{1}{2}(3x^2 - 1)$,

$P_3(x) = \frac{1}{2}(5x^3 - 3x)$, $P_4(x) = \frac{1}{8}(35x^4 - 30x^2 + 3)$.

Example 1. *Verify that the Legendre polynomial*

$$P_4(x) = \frac{1}{8}(35x^4 - 30x^2 + 3)$$

satisfies the Legendre equation when the parameter n is equal to 4.

Sol. The Legendre equation is $(1-x^2)\frac{d^2y}{dx^2} - 2x\frac{dy}{dx} + n(n+1)y = 0$. ...(1)

We have $n = 4$.

$\therefore$ (1) $\Rightarrow$ $$(1-x^2)\frac{d^2y}{dx^2} - 2x\frac{dy}{dx} + 20y = 0 \quad ...(2)$$

Let $$y = P_4(x) = \frac{1}{8}(35x^4 - 30x^2 + 3)$$

$$\therefore \quad \frac{dy}{dx} = \frac{35}{2}x^3 - \frac{15}{2}x \quad \text{and} \quad \frac{d^2y}{dx^2} = \frac{105}{2}x^2 - \frac{15}{2}.$$

$y = P_4(x)$ is a solution of (2)

if $$(1-x^2)\left(\frac{105}{2}x^5 - \frac{15}{2}\right) - 2x\left(\frac{35}{2}x^3 - \frac{15}{2}x\right) + 20\left(\frac{35}{8}x^4 - \frac{15}{4}x^2 + \frac{3}{8}\right) = 0$$

if $$\left(-\frac{105}{2} - 35 + \frac{175}{2}\right)x^4 + \left(\frac{105}{2} + \frac{15}{2} + 15 - 75\right)x^2 + \left(-\frac{15}{2} + \frac{15}{2}\right) = 0$$

if $0 = 0$, which is true.

$\therefore$ $P_4(x)$ is a solution of (2).

Example 2. *Express $f(x) = x^4 + 3x^3 - x^2 + 5x - 2$ in terms of Legendre polynomials.*

Sol. We have

$$P_0(x) = 1, \quad P_1(x) = x,$$

$$P_2(x) = \frac{1}{2}(3x^2 - 1), \quad P_3(x) = \frac{1}{2}(5x^3 - 3x),$$

$$P_4(x) = \frac{1}{8}(35x^4 - 30x^2 + 3).$$

$$\therefore \quad x^2 = \frac{1}{3}(2P_2(x) + 1) = \frac{2}{3}P_2(x) + \frac{1}{3}$$

$$x^3 = \frac{1}{5}(2P_3(x) + 3x) = \frac{2}{5}P_3(x) + \frac{3}{5}P_1(x)$$

$$x^4 = \frac{1}{35}(8P_4(x) + 30x^2 - 3) = \frac{8}{35}P_4(x) + \frac{6}{7}\left(\frac{2}{3}P_2(x) + \frac{1}{3}\right) - \frac{3}{35}$$

$$= \frac{8}{35}P_4(x) + \frac{4}{7}P_2(x) + \frac{1}{5}.$$

$\therefore$
$$f(x) = x^4 + 3x^3 - x^2 + 5x - 2$$

$$= \left[\frac{8}{35}P_4(x) + \frac{4}{7}P_2(x) + \frac{1}{5}\right] + 3\left[\frac{2}{5}P_3(x) + \frac{3}{5}P_1(x)\right] - \left[\frac{2}{3}P_2(x) + \frac{1}{3}\right] + 5P_1(x) - 2$$

$$= \frac{8}{35}P_4(x) + \frac{6}{5}P_3(x) + \left(\frac{4}{7} - \frac{2}{3}\right)P_2(x) + \left(\frac{9}{5} + 5\right)P_1(x) + \left(\frac{1}{5} - \frac{1}{3} - 2\right)$$

$$= \mathbf{\frac{8}{35}P_4(x) + \frac{6}{5}P_3(x) - \frac{2}{21}P_2(x) - \frac{32}{15}P_1(x).}$$

EXERCISE 1

1. Solve the Legendre equation when the parameter n is equal to 0 and show that its solution is

$$y = C_1 + C_2 \log \frac{1+x}{1-x},$$ where C_1 and C_2 are arbitrary constants.

2. Solve the Legendre equation when the parameter n is equal to 0 by using the substitution $z = \frac{dy}{dx}$.

3. Solve the Legendre equation when the parameter n is equal to 1 and show that its solution is

$$y = C_1\left(1 - \frac{x}{2}\log\frac{1+x}{1-x}\right) + C_2 x.$$

4. (*i*) Verify that the Legendre polynomial $P_2(x) = \frac{1}{2}(3x^2 - 1)$ satisfies the Legendre equation when the parameter n is equal to 2.

   (*ii*) Verify that the Legendre polynomial $P_3(x) = \frac{1}{2}(5x^3 - 3x)$ satisfies the Legendre equation when the parameter n is equal to 3.

5. Verify that $P_2(1) = 1$, $P_3(1) = 1$, $P_4(1) = 1$.

6. Show that :

   (*i*) $P_5(x) = \frac{1}{8}(63x^5 - 70x^3 + 15x)$ (*ii*) $P_6(x) = \frac{1}{16}[231x^6 - 315x^4 + 105x^2 - 5]$.

7. Show that :

   (*i*) $\frac{1}{3}[P_0(x) + 2P_2(x)] = x^2$ (*ii*) $\frac{1}{5}[3P_1(x) + 2P_3(x)] = x^3$.

8. Express the following polynomials in terms of Legendre polynomials :

   (*i*) $4x^2 - 3x + 2$ (*ii*) $x^3 + 2x^2 - x - 3$ (*KU 2004*)

   (*iii*) $4x^3 - 2x^2 - 3x + 8$ (*KU 2005*) (*iv*) $x^4 + 3x^3 - x^2 + 5x - 2$.

Answers

2. $y = C_1 + C_2 \log \frac{1+x}{1-x}$

8. (i) $\frac{8}{3} P_2(x) - 3P_1(x) + \frac{10}{3} P_0(x)$

(ii) $\frac{2}{5} P_3(x) + \frac{4}{3} P_2(x) - \frac{2}{5} P_1(x) - \frac{7}{3} P_0(x)$ (iii) $\frac{8}{5} P_3(x) - \frac{4}{3} P_2(x) - \frac{3}{5} P_1(x) + \frac{22}{3} P_0(x)$

(iv) $\frac{8}{35} P_4(x) + \frac{6}{5} P_3(x) - \frac{2}{21} P_2(x) + \frac{34}{5} P_1(x) - \frac{32}{15} P_0(x).$

---

5. GENERATING FUNCTION OF A SEQUENCE

Let $\{f_n(x)\}$ be a sequence of functions. A function $G(t, x)$ is called a **generating function** of the sequence $\{f_n(x)\}$ if the function $G(t, x)$ can be expressed as $\sum_{n=0}^{\infty} f_n(x)\, t^n$.

6. GENERATING FUNCTION OF THE SEQUENCE OF LEGENDRE POLYNOMIALS

(MDU 2006)

We shall prove that the function $(1 - 2xt + t^2)^{-1/2}$ is a generating function of the Legendre polynomials, where $|x| < 1$, $|t| < 1/3$.

For $|z| < 1$, by binomial theorem,

$$(1-z)^{-1/2} = 1 + \frac{1}{2} z + \frac{\left(-\frac{1}{2}\right)\left(-\frac{3}{2}\right)}{2!}(-z)^2 + \ldots + \frac{\left(-\frac{1}{2}\right)\left(-\frac{3}{2}\right)\ldots\left(-\frac{1}{2}-(n-1)\right)}{n!}(-z)^n + \ldots$$

$$= 1 + \frac{1}{2} z + \frac{1.3}{2^2 . 2!} z^2 + \ldots + \frac{1.3 \ldots (2n-1)}{2^n . n!} z^n + \ldots$$

$$\therefore \quad (1-z)^{-1/2} = 1 + \frac{1}{2} z + \frac{1.3}{2^2 . 2!} z^2 + \ldots + \frac{1.3 \ldots (2n-5)}{2^{n-2} . (n-2)!} z^{n-2} + \ldots$$

$$+ \frac{1.3 \ldots (2n-3)}{2^{n-1} . (n-1)!} z^{n-1} + \frac{1.3 \ldots (2n-1)}{2^n . n!} z^n + \ldots \qquad \ldots(1)$$

Let $z = 2xt - t^2$. $\therefore$ $|z| = |2xt - t^2| = |t(2x - t)| = |t| . |2x - t|$

$$\le |t| (|2x| + |t|) \le |t| (2|x| + |t|) < \frac{1}{3}\left(2(1) + \frac{1}{3}\right) = \frac{7}{9} < 1.$$

$$\therefore \quad (1) \Rightarrow (1 - (2xt - t^2))^{-1/2} = (1 - 2xt + t^2)^{-1/2} = 1 + \frac{1}{2}(2xt - t^2) + \frac{1.3}{2^2 . 2!}(2xt - t^2)^2 + \ldots$$

$$+ \frac{1.3 \ldots (2n-5)}{2^{n-2} . (n-2)!}(2xt - t^2)^{n-2} + \frac{1.3 \ldots (2n-3)}{2^{n-1} . (n-1)!}(2xt - t^2)^{n-1}$$

$$+ \frac{1.3 \ldots (2n-1)}{2^n . n!}(2xt - t^2)^n + \ldots \qquad \ldots(2)$$

Now $(2xt - t^2)^n = (2x)^n t^n + \ldots$

$$(2xt - t^2)^{n-1} = (2x)^{n-1} t^{n-1} - (n-1)(2x)^{n-2} t^n + \ldots$$

$$(2xt - t^2)^{n-2} = (2x)^{n-2} t^{n-2} - (n-2)(2x)^{n-3} t^{n-1} + \frac{(n-2)(n-3)}{1.2}(2x)^{n-4} t^n + \ldots$$

....

Substituting these values in (2), we get

$$(1 - 2xt + t^2)^{-1/2} = 1 + xt + \left(-\frac{1}{2} + \frac{3}{8}.4x^2\right)t^2 + \ldots$$

$$+\left[\frac{1.3\ldots.(2n-1)}{2^n.n!}(2x)^n - \frac{1.3\ldots.(2n-3)}{2^{n-1}(n-1)!}(n-1)(2x)^{n-2}\right.$$

$$\left. + \frac{1.3\ldots.(2n-5)}{2^{n-2}.(n-2)!}\frac{(n-2)(n-3)}{1.2}(2x)^{n-4} + \ldots\right]t^n + \ldots$$

$$= 1 + xt + \frac{1}{2}(3x^2 - 1)t^2 + \ldots\ldots + \frac{1.3\ldots.(2n-1)}{n!}\left[x^n - \frac{n(n-1)}{2(2n-1)}x^{n-2}\right.$$

$$\left. + \frac{n(n-1)(n-2)(n-3)}{2.4(2n-1)(2n-3)}x^{n-4} + \ldots\right]t^n + \ldots$$

$$= P_0(x) + P_1(x)t + P_2(x)t^2 + \ldots\ldots + P_n(x)t^n + \ldots\ldots$$

∴ $\mathbf{(1 - 2xt + t^2)^{-1/2} = P_0(x) + P_1(x)\,t + P_2(x)\,t^2 + \ldots\ldots + P_n(x)\,t^n + \ldots\ldots}$

∴ $(1 - 2xt + t^2)^{-1/2}$ is a generating function of Legendre polynomials.

Example 1. *Using generating function of Legendre polynomials, show that*

$$P_n(0) = \begin{cases} \dfrac{(-1)^{n/2}\,1.3.5\ldots.(n-1)}{2.4.6\ldots.n} & \text{if } n \text{ is even} \\ 0 & \text{if } n \text{ is odd.} \end{cases}$$

Sol. Generating function of Legendre polynomials is $(1 - 2xt + t^2)^{-1/2}$.

∴ $P_n(x)$ = coefficient of t_n in $(1 - 2xt + t^2)^{-1/2}$

∴ $P_n(0)$ = coefficient of t^n in $(1 - 2(0)t + t^2)^{-1/2}$ *i.e.* in $(1 + t^2)^{-1/2}$ ...(1)

Case I. n is even.

Let $n = 2m.$

(1) ⇒ $P_n(0)$ = coefficient of t^{2m} *i.e.,* $(t^2)^m$ in $(1 + t^2)^{-1/2}$

$$= \frac{\left(-\frac{1}{2}\right)\left(-\frac{3}{2}\right)\ldots\left(-\frac{1}{2}-(m-1)\right)}{1.2\ldots.m}$$

$$= \frac{(-1)^m\,1.3\ldots.(2m-1)}{2.4\ldots.(2m)} = \frac{(-1)^{n/2}\,\mathbf{1.3\ldots.(n-1)}}{\mathbf{2.4\ldots.n}}.$$

Case II. n is odd.

Let $n = 2m + 1.$

(1) ⇒ $P_n(0)$ = coefficient of t^{2m+1} in $(1 + t^2)^{-1/2}$

$= \mathbf{0}$, because each term in $(1 + t^2)^{-1/2}$ contains even power of t.

Example 2. *Show that*

$$P_n\left(-\frac{1}{2}\right) = P_0\left(-\frac{1}{2}\right)P_{2n}\left(\frac{1}{2}\right) + P_1\left(-\frac{1}{2}\right)P_{2n-1}\left(\frac{1}{2}\right) + \ldots + P_{2n}\left(-\frac{1}{2}\right)P_0\left(\frac{1}{2}\right).$$

Sol. We have $(1-2xt+t^2)^{-1/2} = \sum_{n=0}^{\infty} P_n(x)\,t^n$ ...(1)

Putting $x = 1/2$ and $-1/2$ successively in (1), we get

$$(1-t+t^2)^{-1/2} = \sum_{n=0}^{\infty} P_n\left(\frac{1}{2}\right)t^n \qquad \ldots(2)$$

and

$$(1+t+t^2)^{-1/2} = \sum_{n=0}^{\infty} P_n\left(-\frac{1}{2}\right)t^n \qquad \ldots(3)$$

Replacing t by t^2 in (3), we get

$$(1+t^2+t^4)^{-1/2} = \sum_{n=0}^{\infty} P_n\left(-\frac{1}{2}\right)t^{2n} \qquad \ldots(4)$$

Now $1+t^2+t^4 = (1+2t^2+t^4) - t^2 = (1+t^2)^2 - t^2 = (1+t+t^2)(1-t+t^2)$

$$\therefore \quad (1+t^2+t^4)^{-1/2} = (1+t+t^2)^{-1/2}(1-t+t^2)^{-1/2}$$

$$\therefore \quad \sum_{n=0}^{\infty} P_n\left(-\frac{1}{2}\right)t^{2n} = \left(\sum_{n=0}^{\infty} P_n\left(-\frac{1}{2}\right)t^n\right)\left(\sum_{n=0}^{\infty} P_n\left(\frac{1}{2}\right)t^n\right) \quad \text{(By using (2), (3), (4))}$$

$$= \left[P_0\left(-\frac{1}{2}\right) + P_1\left(-\frac{1}{2}\right)t + \ldots + P_{2n-1}\left(-\frac{1}{2}\right)t^{2n-1} + P_{2n}\left(-\frac{1}{2}\right)t^{2n} + \ldots\right]$$

$$\times\left[P_0\left(\frac{1}{2}\right) + P_1\left(\frac{1}{2}\right)t + \ldots + P_{2n-1}\left(\frac{1}{2}\right)t^{2n-1} + P_{2n}\left(\frac{1}{2}\right)t^{2n} + \ldots\right].$$

Comparing the coefficients of t^{2n}, we get

$$\mathbf{P_n\left(-\frac{1}{2}\right) = P_0\left(-\frac{1}{2}\right)P_{2n}\left(\frac{1}{2}\right) + P_1\left(-\frac{1}{2}\right)P_{2n-1}\left(\frac{1}{2}\right) + \ldots + P_{2n}\left(-\frac{1}{2}\right)P_0\left(\frac{1}{2}\right)}.$$

Example 3. *Show that*

$$1 + \frac{1}{2}P_1(\cos\theta) + \frac{1}{3}P_2(\cos\theta) + \ldots = \log\frac{1+\sin\frac{1}{2}\theta}{\sin\frac{1}{2}\theta}.$$

Sol. We have $\sum_{n=0}^{\infty} P_n(x)\,t^n = (1-2xt+t^2)^{-1/2}$. ...(1)

Integrating (1) w.r.t. t from 0 to 1, we get

$$\int_0^1 \sum_{n=0}^{\infty} P_n(x)\,t^n\,dt = \int_0^1 \frac{dt}{\sqrt{1-2xt+t^2}}$$

$$\Rightarrow \quad \sum_{n=0}^{\infty}\left[P_n(x)\int_0^1 t^n\,dt\right]=\int_0^1 \frac{dt}{\sqrt{1-2xt+t^2}}$$

$$\Rightarrow \quad \sum_{n=0}^{\infty}\frac{P_n(x)}{n+1}=\int_0^1 \frac{dt}{\sqrt{1-2xt+t^2}}=\int_0^1 \frac{dt}{\sqrt{(t-x)^2+(1-x^2)}}$$

$$=\log\left((t-x)+\sqrt{(t-x)^2+(1-x^2)}\right)\Bigg|_0^1$$

$$=\log\left(1-x+\sqrt{2(1-x)}\right)-\log\left(-x+\sqrt{1}\right)$$

$$=\log\frac{1-x+\sqrt{2}\,\sqrt{1-x}}{1-x}=\log\frac{\sqrt{1-x}+\sqrt{2}}{\sqrt{1-x}}.$$

Putting $x=\cos\theta$, we get $\displaystyle\sum_{n=0}^{\infty}\frac{P_n(\cos\theta)}{n+1}=\log\frac{\sqrt{1-\cos\theta}+\sqrt{2}}{\sqrt{1-\cos\theta}}$

$$\Rightarrow \quad P_0(\cos\theta)+\frac{1}{2}P_1(\cos\theta)+\frac{1}{3}P_2(\cos\theta)+\ldots=\log\frac{\sqrt{2}\sin\frac{1}{2}\theta+\sqrt{2}}{\sqrt{2}\sin\frac{1}{2}\theta}$$

$$\Rightarrow \quad \mathbf{1+\frac{1}{2}P_1(\cos\theta)+\frac{1}{3}P_2(\cos\theta)+\ldots=\log\frac{\sin\frac{1}{2}\theta+1}{\sin\frac{1}{2}\theta}}. \qquad (\text{Using } P_0(x)=1)$$

Example 4. *Show that* $\displaystyle\frac{1+t}{t\sqrt{1-2xt+t^2}}-\frac{1}{t}=\sum_{n=0}^{\infty}(P_n+P_{n+1})t^n.$

Sol. L.H.S. $\displaystyle=\frac{1+t}{t\sqrt{1-2xt+t^2}}-\frac{1}{t}=\frac{1}{t}(1-2xt+t^2)^{-1/2}+(1-2xt+t^2)^{-1/2}-\frac{1}{t}$

$$\therefore \quad \text{L.H.S.}=\frac{1}{t}\sum_{n=0}^{\infty}P_n t^n+\sum_{n=0}^{\infty}P_n t^n-\frac{1}{t} \qquad \ldots(1)$$

Now $\displaystyle\sum_{n=0}^{\infty}P_n t^n=P_0+P_1t+P_2t^2+P_3t^3+\ldots\ldots$

$$=1+t(P_1+P_2t+P_3t^2+\ldots\ldots)=1+t\sum_{n=0}^{\infty}P_{n+1}t^n.$$

$$\therefore \quad (1) \Rightarrow \text{L.H.S.}=\frac{1}{t}\left[1+t\sum_{n=0}^{\infty}P_{n+1}t^n\right]+\sum_{n=0}^{\infty}P_n t^n-\frac{1}{t}$$

$$=\sum_{n=0}^{\infty}P_{n+1}t^n+\sum_{n=0}^{\infty}P_n t^n=\sum_{n=0}^{\infty}(P_n+P_{n+1})t^n.$$

7. RECURRENCE RELATIONS

In this section, we shall prove some recurrence relations. For the sake of simplicity, we shall write $P_n(x)$ as P_n.

(*i*) $n\,P_n = (2n-1)\,x\,P_{n-1} - (n-1)\,P_{n-2},\ n \ge 2$

(*ii*) $n\,P_n = x\,P_n{}' - P'_{n-1}$ (*KU 2005 S*) (*iii*) $(2n+1)\,P_n = P'_{n+1} - P'_{n-1}$

(*iv*) $(n+1)\,P_n = P'_{n+1} - x\,P_n{}'$ (*v*) $(1-x^2)\,P_n{}' = n\,(P_{n-1} - x\,P_n)$

(*vi*) $(1-x^2)\,P_n{}' = (n+1)\,(x\,P_n - P_{n+1})$.

Proof. (*i*) We have $$(1-2xt+t^2)^{-1/2} = \sum_{n=0}^{\infty} P_n\,t^n$$

Differentiating w.r.t. t, we get

$$-\frac{1}{2}(1-2xt+t^2)^{-3/2}(-2x+2t) = 0 + \sum_{n=1}^{\infty} nP_n t^{n-1} = \sum_{n=0}^{\infty} n\,P_n\,t^{n-1}$$

$$\Rightarrow \quad (x-t)(1-2xt+t^2)^{-3/2} = \sum_{n=0}^{\infty} n\,P_n\,t^{n-1}$$

$$\Rightarrow \quad (x-t)(1-2xt+t^2)^{-1/2} = (1-2xt+t^2)\sum_{n=0}^{\infty} n\,P_n\,t^{n-1}$$

$$\Rightarrow \quad (x-t)\sum_{n=0}^{\infty} P_n\,t^n = \sum_{n=0}^{\infty} n\,P_n\,t^{n-1} - 2x\sum_{n=0}^{\infty} n\,P_n\,t^n + \sum_{n=0}^{\infty} n\,P_n\,t^{n+1}$$

Equating the coefficients of t^n, we get

$$x\,P_n - P_{n-1} = (n+1)\,P_{n+1} - 2xn\,P_n + (n-1)\,P_{n-1}$$

$$\therefore \quad (n+1)\,P_{n+1} = (2n+1)\,x\,P_n - n\,P_{n-1}$$

Replacing n by $n-1$, we get

$$\mathbf{n\,P_n = (2n-1)\,x\,P_{n-1} - (n-1)\,P_{n-2},\ n \ge 2.}$$

Remark. In (*i*), if we raplace n by $n+1$, we get

$$(n+1)\,P_{n+1} = (2n+1)\,xP_n - nP_{n-1},\ n \ge 1. \qquad (KU\ 2006)$$

(*ii*) We have $$(1-2xt+t^2)^{-1/2} = \sum_{n=0}^{\infty} P_n\,t^n. \qquad ...(1)$$

Differentiating (1) w.r.t. t, we get

$$-\frac{1}{2}(1-2xt+t^2)^{-3/2}(-2x+2t) = 0 + \sum_{n=1}^{\infty} nP_n t^{n-1} = \sum_{n=0}^{\infty} n\,P_n\,t^{n-1}$$

$$\Rightarrow \quad (x-t)(1-2xt+t^2)^{-3/2} = \sum_{n=0}^{\infty} n\,P_n\,t^{n-1} \qquad ...(2)$$

Differentiating (1) w.r.t. x, we get

$$-\frac{1}{2}(1-2xt+t^2)^{-3/2}(-2t) = \sum_{n=0}^{\infty} P_n' t^n$$

$$\Rightarrow \quad t(1-2xt+t^2)^{-3/2} = \sum_{n=0}^{\infty} P_n' t^n$$

$$\Rightarrow \quad t(x-t)(1-2xt+t^2)^{-3/2} = (x-t)\sum_{n=0}^{\infty} P_n' t^n$$

$$\Rightarrow \quad t\sum_{n=0}^{\infty} n P_n t^{n-1} = (x-t)\sum_{n=0}^{\infty} P_n' t^n \qquad \text{(Using (2))}$$

Comparing the coefficients of t^n, we get

$$\mathbf{nP_n = xP_n' - P'_{n-1}.}$$

(*iii*) We have $\quad (1-2xt+t^2)^{-1/2} = \sum_{n=0}^{\infty} P_n t^n. \qquad ...(1)$

Differentiating (1) w.r.t. t, we get

$$\Rightarrow \quad (x-t)(1-2xt+t^2)^{-3/2} = 0 + \sum_{n=1}^{\infty} nP_n t^{n-1}$$

$$= \sum_{n=0}^{\infty} nP_n t^{n-1} \qquad ...(2)$$

Differentiating (1) w.r.t. x, we get

$$t(1-2xt+t^2)^{-3/2} = \sum_{n=0}^{\infty} P_n' t^n$$

$$\Rightarrow \quad (1-2xt+t^2)^{-3/2} = \sum_{n=0}^{\infty} P_n' t^{n-1} \qquad ...(3)$$

Multiplying (2) by $2t$ and (3) by $1-t^2$ and subtracting, we get

$$(2xt-2t^2-1+t^2)(1-2xt+t^2)^{-3/2} = 2\sum_{n=0}^{\infty} n P_n t^n - (1-t^2)\sum_{n=0}^{\infty} P_n' t^{n-1}$$

$$\Rightarrow \quad -(1-2xt+t^2)^{-1/2} = 2\sum_{n=0}^{\infty} n P_n t^n - \sum_{n=0}^{\infty} P_n' t^{n-1} + \sum_{n=0}^{\infty} P_n' t^{n+1}$$

$$\Rightarrow \quad \sum_{n=0}^{\infty} P_n t^n = -2\sum_{n=0}^{\infty} nP_n t^n + \sum_{n=0}^{\infty} P_n' t^{n-1} - \sum_{n=0}^{\infty} P_n' t^{n+1}$$

Comparing the coefficients of t^n, we get

$$P_n = -2n P_n + P'_{n+1} - P'_{n-1}$$

$$\therefore \quad \mathbf{(2n+1)\, P_n = P'_{n+1} - P'_{n-1}.}$$

(*iv*) From part (*iii*), $(2n+1) P_n = P'_{n+1} - P'_{n-1}$

From part (*ii*), $n P_n = x P'_n - P'_{n-1}$

Subtracting, we get $\mathbf{(n+1) P_n = P'_{n+1} - x P'_n}$.

(*v*) From part (*ii*), $n P_n = x P_n' - P'_{n-1}$

$\Rightarrow$ $$nx P_n = x^2 P_n' - x P'_{n-1} \qquad ...(1)$$

From part (*iv*), $(n+1) P_n = P'_{n+1} - x P'_n$.

Replacing n by $n-1$, we get

$$n P_{n-1} = P'_n - x P'_{n-1} \qquad ...(2)$$

$(2) - (1) \Rightarrow$ $n P_{n-1} - nx P_n = (1-x^2) P_n'$

$\Rightarrow$ $$\mathbf{(1 - x^2) P_n' = n (P_{n-1} - x P_n)}.$$

(*vi*) From part (*iv*), $(n+1) P_n = P'_{n+1} - x P'_n$.

Replacing n by $n-1$, we get

$$n P_{n-1} = P_n' - x P'_{n-1}.$$

$\Rightarrow$ $$nx P_{n-1} = x P_n' - x^2 P'_{n-1} \qquad ...(1)$$

From part (*ii*), $$n P_n = x P_n' - P'_{n-1} \qquad ...(2)$$

$(1) - (2) \Rightarrow$ $n [x P_{n-1} - P_n] = (1 - x^2) P'_{n-1}$

Replacing n by $n+1$, we get

$$\mathbf{(1 - x^2) P_n' = (n+1) (x P_n - P_{n+1})}.$$

Example 5. *Prove the Christoffel's expansion :*

$$P_n' = (2n-1)P_{n-1} + (2n-5) P_{n-3} + (2n-9) P_{n-5} + \text{......} .$$

with last term $3P_1$ if n is even and P_0 if n is odd.

Sol. We know that

$$(2n+1)P_n = P'_{n+1} - P'_{n-1}$$

$\Rightarrow$ $$P'_{n+1} - P'_{n-1} = (2n+1)P_n \qquad ...(1)$$

Case I. n is even

Replacing n in (1) by $n-1, n-3, n-5, \text{......} 1$, we get

$$P_n' - P'_{n-2} = (2n-1) P_{n-1}$$
$$P'_{n-2} - P'_{n-4} = (2n-5) P_{n-3}$$
$$P'_{n-4} - P'_{n-6} = (2n-9) P_{n-5}$$
$$\text{..}$$
$$P_2' - P_0' = 3P_1$$

Adding vertically, we get

$$P_n' - P_0' = (2n-1) P_{n-1} + (2n-5) P_{n-3} + (2n-9) P_{n-5} + \text{......} + 3P_1$$

$\Rightarrow$ $$\mathbf{P_n' = (2n-1)P_{n-1} + (2n-5)P_{n-3} + (2n-9) P_{n-5} + ... + 3P_1}. \qquad (\because P_0' = 0)$$

Case II. n is odd

Replacing n by $n-1, n-3, n-5, \ldots\ldots, 2$, we get

$$P_n' - P'_{n-2} = (2n-1)\,P_{n-1}$$
$$P'_{n-2} - P'_{n-4} = (2n-5)\,P_{n-3}$$
$$P'_{n-4} - P'_{n-6} = (2n-9)\,P_{n-5}$$
$$\ldots\ldots\ldots\ldots\ldots\ldots\ldots\ldots\ldots\ldots\ldots\ldots$$
$$P_3' - P_1' = 5P_2$$

Adding vertically, we get

$$P_n' - P_1' = (2n-1)\,P_{n-1} + (2n-5)\,P_{n-3} + (2n-9)\,P_{n-5} + \ldots\ldots + 5P_2$$

$$\Rightarrow \quad P_n' = (2n-1)\,P_{n-1} + (2n-5)\,P_{n-5} + (2n-9)\,P_{n-5} + \ldots\ldots + 5P_2 + 1$$

$$(\because \; P_1 = x \;\Rightarrow\; P_1' = 1)$$

$$\Rightarrow \quad \mathbf{P_n' = (2n-1)\,P_{n-1} + (2n-5)\,P_{n-5} + (2n-9)\,P_{n-5} + \ldots\ldots + 5P_2 + P_0}.$$

$$(\because \; P_0 = 1)$$

8. RODRIGUE'S FORMULA

The Rodrigue's formula is

$$\mathbf{P_n(x) = \frac{1}{2^n\, n!}\frac{d^n}{dx^n}(x^2-1)^n}. \qquad \text{(KU 2004 S, 2005 ; MDU 2005)}$$

Proof. By binomial theorem,

$$(x^2-1)^n = \sum_{r=0}^{n} {}^nC_r\,(x^2)^{n-r}(-1)^r = \sum_{r=0}^{n} (-1)^r\, {}^nC_r\, x^{2n-2r}$$

$$\therefore \quad \frac{d^n}{dx^n}(x^2-1)^n = \frac{d^n}{dx^n}\sum_{r=0}^{n}(-1)^r\,{}^nC_r\,x^{2n-2r} = \sum_{r=0}^{n}(-1)^r\,{}^nC_r\,\frac{d^n}{dx^n}x^{2n-2r} \ldots \qquad \ldots(1)$$

Now $\dfrac{d^n}{dx^n}x^m = \dfrac{m!}{(m-n)!}x^{m-n}$ if $n \le m$ and $\dfrac{d^n}{dx^n}x^m = 0$ if $n > m$.

$$\therefore \quad \frac{d^n}{dx^n}x^{2n-2r} = 0 \quad \text{if } n > 2n-2r \;\; i.e. \;\; r > \frac{n}{2}.$$

Case I. n is even. Let $M = n/2$

$$\therefore \quad \frac{d^n}{dx^n}x^{2n-2r} = 0 \quad \text{if } r > M$$

Case II. n is odd. Let $M = (n-1)/2$

$$\therefore \quad \frac{d^n}{dx^n}x^{2n-2r} = 0 \quad \text{if } r > M.$$

($\because$ r is an integer greater than $n/2$ implies $r > (n-1)/2$)

$$\therefore \; (1) \;\Rightarrow\; \frac{d^n}{dx^n}(x^2-1)^n = \sum_{r=0}^{M}(-1)^r\,{}^nC_r\,\frac{d^n}{dx^n}x^{2n-2r}$$

$$= \sum_{r=0}^{M}(-1)^r\,{}^nC_r\,\frac{(2n-2r)!}{(2n-2r-n)!}x^{2n-2r-n}$$

$$= \sum_{r=0}^{M} (-1)^r \frac{n!}{r!(n-r)!} \cdot \frac{(2n-2r)!}{(n-2r)!} x^{n-2r}$$

$$\therefore \quad \frac{1}{2^n \, n!} \frac{d^n}{dx^n} (x^2-1)^n = \sum_{r=0}^{M} \frac{(-1)^r}{2^n \, n!} \cdot \frac{n!}{r!(n-r)!} \frac{(2n-2r)!}{(n-2r)!} x^{n-2r}$$

$$= \sum_{r=0}^{M} (-1)^r \frac{(2n-2r)!}{2^n \, r!(n-r)!(n-2r)!} x^{n-2r}$$

$$\text{where} \quad M = \begin{cases} n/2 & \text{if } n \text{ is even} \\ (n-1)/2 & \text{if } n \text{ is odd.} \end{cases}$$

$$= P_n(x).$$

$$\therefore \quad \mathbf{P_n(x) = \frac{1}{2^n \, n!} \frac{d^n}{dx^n} (x^2-1)^n}.$$

Example 6. *Using Rodrigue's formula, find the value of $P_4(x)$.*

Sol. The Rodrigue's formula is

$$P_n(x) = \frac{1}{2^n \, n!} \frac{d^n}{dx^n} (x^2-1)^n .$$

$$\therefore \quad P_4(x) = \frac{1}{2^4 . 4!} \frac{d^4}{dx^4} (x^2-1)^4 = \frac{1}{384} \frac{d^4}{dx^4} (x^8 - 4x^6 + 6x^4 - 4x^2 + 1)$$

$$= \frac{1}{384} \frac{d^3}{dx^3} (8x^7 - 24x^5 + 24x^3 - 8x + 0)$$

$$= \frac{1}{384} \frac{d^2}{dx^2} (56x^6 - 120x^4 + 72x^2 - 8)$$

$$= \frac{1}{384} \frac{d}{dx} (336x^5 - 480x^3 + 144x - 0)$$

$$= \frac{1}{384} (1680x^4 - 1440x^2 + 144)$$

$$= \mathbf{\frac{1}{8} (35x^4 - 30x^2 + 3)}.$$

Example 7. *Show that*

$$\int_{-1}^{1} P_n(x) \, dx = \begin{cases} 2 & \text{if } n = 0 \\ 0 & \text{if } n \geq 1. \end{cases}$$

Sol. Let $n = 0$.

$$\therefore \quad \int_{-1}^{1} P_n(x) \, dx = \int_{-1}^{1} P_0(x) \, dx = \int_{-1}^{1} 1 \, dx = x \Big|_{-1}^{1} = 1 - (-1) = \mathbf{2}.$$

Let $n \geq 1$.

$$\int_{-1}^{1} P_n(x) \, dx = \int_{-1}^{1} \frac{1}{2^n \, n!} \frac{d^n}{dx^n} (x^2-1)^n \, dx \qquad \text{(By using Rodrigue's formula)}$$

$$= \frac{1}{2^n n!} \int_{-1}^{1} \frac{d^n}{dx^n} (x^2 - 1)^n \, dx = \frac{1}{2^n \, n!} \left[\frac{d^{n-1}}{dx^{n-1}} (x^2 - 1)^n \right]_{-1}^{1}$$

$$(x^2 - 1)^n = (x - 1)^n (x + 1)^n = uv \quad \text{(say)}$$

$$\therefore \quad \frac{d^{n-1}}{dx^{n-1}} (x^2 - 1)^n = (uv)_{n-1} = {}^{n-1}C_0 \, u_{n-1} v + {}^{n-1}C_1 \, u_{n-2} v_1 + {}^{n-1}C_2 \, u_{n-3} \, v_2$$

$$+ \ldots\ldots + {}^{n-1}C_{n-1} \, u v_{n-1}$$

$$= {}^{n-1}C_0 \frac{n!}{1!} (x-1)^1 \, . \, (x+1)^n + {}^{n-1}C_1 \frac{n!}{2!} (x-1)^2 \, . \, \frac{n!}{(n-1)!} (x+1)^{n-1}$$

$$+ {}^{n-1}C_2 \frac{n!}{3!} (x-1)^3 \, . \, \frac{n!}{(n-2)!} (x+1)^{n-2} + \ldots\ldots$$

$$+ {}^{n-1}C_{n-1} (x-1)^n \, . \, \frac{n!}{1!} (x+1)^1$$

$$\left(\text{Using } \frac{d^k}{dx^k} (ax+b)^m = \frac{m!}{(m-k)!} a^k (ax+b)^{m-k}, \text{ where } \; k \le m \right)$$

The values of R.H.S. at $x = 1$ and $x = -1$ are zero each.

$$\therefore \quad \frac{d^{n-1}}{dx^{n-1}} (x^2 - 1)^n = 0 - 0 = 0.$$

$$\therefore \quad \int_{-1}^{1} P_n(x) = \frac{1}{2^n n!} \times 0 = \mathbf{0}.$$

9. ORTHOGONALITY OF FUNCTIONS

Let $y_1(x), y_2(x), \ldots\ldots$ be functions defined on some interval $[a, b]$. These functions are called **orthogonal with respect to a weight function** $p(x) > 0$ on $[a, b]$

if $$\int_a^b p(x) \, y_m(x) \, y_n(x) \, dx = 0 \quad \text{for } m \neq n.$$

If the weight function $p(x)$ is the constant function '1', then we simply say that the functions are orthogonal.

Thus, the functions $y_1(x), y_2(x), \ldots\ldots$ defined on $[a, b]$ are called **orthogonal** on $[a, b]$

if $$\int_a^b y_m(x) \, y_n(x) \, dx = 0 \qquad \text{for } m \neq n.$$

Illustration : Consider the functions $y_n(x) = \sin nx$, $n = 1, 2, 3, \ldots\ldots$

For $m \neq n$, we have

$$\int_0^\pi y_m(x) \, y_n(x) \, dx = \int_0^\pi \sin mx \sin nx \, dx$$

$$= \frac{1}{2} \int_0^\pi [\cos (m-n) x - \cos (m+n) x] \, dx$$

$$= \frac{1}{2} \left[\frac{\sin (m-n) x}{m-n} - \frac{\sin (m+n) x}{m+n} \right]_0^\pi$$

$$= 0.$$

$\therefore \quad \int_0^{\pi} y_m(x)\, y_n(x)\, dx = 0 \quad$ for $m \neq n$.

$\therefore$ The functions $y_n(x) = \sin nx,\ n = 1, 2, 3, \ldots\ldots$ are orthogonal on the interval $[0, \pi]$.

Example 8. *Show that the functions 1, cos 4nx, sin 4nx, n = 1, 2, 3, ... are orthogonal on [0, π/2].*

Sol. The functions are 1, cos 4x, sin 4x, cos 8x, sin 8x, ...

We shall show that the integration of the product of any two distinct functions from 0 to π/2 is zero.

Case I. Let $I = \int_0^{\pi/2} 1 . \cos 4nx\, dx. \qquad \therefore \quad I = \left.\frac{\sin 4nx}{4n}\right|_0^{\pi/2} = 0.$

Case II. Let $I = \int_0^{\pi/2} 1 . \sin 4nx\, dx.$

$$\therefore \quad I = -\left.\frac{\cos 4nx}{4n}\right|_0^{\pi/2} = -\frac{1}{4n}[\cos 2n\pi - \cos 0] = -\frac{1}{4n}[1 - 1] = 0.$$

Case III. Let $I = \int_0^{\pi/2} \cos 4mx \cos 4nx\, dx,\ m \neq n.$

$$\therefore \quad I = \frac{1}{2}\int_0^{\pi/2} [\cos 4(m+n)x + \cos 4(m-n)x]\, dx$$

$$= \frac{1}{2}\left[\frac{\sin 4(m+n)x}{4(m+n)} + \frac{\sin 4(m-n)x}{4(m-n)}\right]_0^{\pi/2} = 0.$$

Case IV. Let $I = \int_0^{\pi/2} \sin 4mx \sin 4nx\, dx,\ m \neq n.$

$$\therefore \quad I = \frac{1}{2}\int_0^{\pi/2} [\cos 4(m-n)x - \cos 4(m+n)x]\, dx$$

$$= \frac{1}{2}\left[\frac{\sin 4(m-n)x}{4(m-n)} - \frac{\sin 4(m+n)x}{4(m+n)}\right]_0^{\pi/2} = 0.$$

Case V. Let $I = \int_0^{\pi/2} \sin 4nx \cos 4nx\, dx.$

$$\therefore \quad I = \frac{1}{2}\int_0^{\pi/2} \sin 8nx\, dx = \frac{1}{2}\left.\left(-\frac{\cos 8nx}{8n}\right)\right|_0^{\pi/2} = -\frac{1}{16n}[\cos 4n\pi - \cos 0] = 0.$$

Case VI. Let $I = \int_0^{\pi/2} \sin 4mx \cos 4nx\, dx,\ m \neq n.$

$$\therefore \quad I = \frac{1}{2}\int_0^{\pi/2} [\sin 4(m+n)x + \sin 4(m-n)x]\, dx$$

$$= \frac{1}{2}\left[-\frac{\cos 4(m+n)x}{4(m+n)} - \frac{\cos 4(m-n)x}{4(m-n)}\right]_0^{\pi/2}$$

$$= -\frac{1}{8}\left[\left(\frac{\cos 2(m+n)\pi}{m+n} + \frac{\cos 2(m-n)\pi}{m-n}\right) - \left(\frac{\cos 0}{m+n} + \frac{\cos 0}{m-n}\right)\right] = 0.$$

$\therefore$ The functions 1, cos 4nx, sin 4nx, where $n = 1, 2, 3, \ldots\ldots$ are orthogonal on $[0, \pi/2]$.

10. ORTHOGONALITY OF LEGENDRE POLYNOMIALS

Theorem. Prove that Legendre polynomials are orthogonal on the interval [– 1, 1].

Proof. Let P_m and P_n be Legendre polynomials, where $m \neq n$.

$\therefore$ P_m satisfies the Legendre equation

$$(1-x^2)\frac{d^2y}{dx^2} - 2x\frac{dy}{dx} + m(m+1)y = 0.$$

$$\therefore \quad (1-x^2)P_m'' - 2xP_m' + m(m+1)P_m = 0 \qquad ...(1)$$

Similarly, $(1-x^2)P_n'' - 2xP_n' + n(n+1)P_n = 0$ ...(2)

Multiplying (1) by P_n and (2) by P_m and subtracting, we get

$$(1-x^2)(P_n P_m'' - P_m P_n'') - 2x(P_n P_m' - P_m P_n') + (m(m+1) - n(n+1))P_m P_n = 0$$

$$\Rightarrow \quad (1-x^2)\frac{d}{dx}(P_n P_m' - P_m P_n') - 2x(P_n P_m' - P_m P_n') = (n^2 - m^2 + n - m)P_m P_n$$

$$\Rightarrow \quad \frac{d}{dx}[(1-x^2)(P_n P_m' - P_m P_n')] = (n-m)(n+m+1)P_m P_n$$

Integrating w.r.t. x from – 1 to 1, we get

$$(1-x^2)(P_n P_m' - P_m P_n')\Big|_{-1}^{1} = (n-m)(n+m+1)\int_{-1}^{1} P_m P_n \, dx$$

$$\Rightarrow \quad (n-m)(n+m+1)\int_{-1}^{1} P_m P_n \, dx = 0$$

$$\Rightarrow \quad \int_{-1}^{1} P_m P_n \, dx = 0 \qquad (\because \; n-m \neq 0, n+m+1 \neq 0)$$

$$\therefore \quad \int_{-1}^{1} P_m P_n \, dx = 0 \quad \text{for } m \neq n.$$

$\therefore$ **Legendre polynomials are orthogonal on the interval [– 1, 1].**

Example 9. *Show that*

$$\int_{-1}^{1} (P_n(x))^2 \, dx = \frac{2}{2n+1}.$$

Sol. We have

$$(1 - 2xt + t^2)^{-1/2} = \sum_{m=0}^{\infty} P_m(x)t^m \qquad ...(1)$$

Also $$(1 - 2xt + t^2)^{-1/2} = \sum_{n=0}^{\infty} P_n(x)t^n \qquad ...(2)$$

Multiplying (1) and (2), we get

$$(1 - 2xt + t^2)^{-1} = \sum_{m=0}^{\infty}\sum_{n=0}^{\infty} P_m(x)P_n(x)t^{m+n}$$

$$\Rightarrow \quad \int_{-1}^{1}(1-2xt+t^2)^{-1}\,dx = \sum_{m=0}^{\infty}\sum_{n=0}^{\infty}\int_{-1}^{1} P_m(x)\,P_n(x)\,t^{m+n}\,dx$$

$$\Rightarrow \quad \int_{-1}^{1}\frac{dx}{1+t^2-2xt} = \sum_{n=0}^{\infty}\int_{-1}^{1}(P_n(x))^2\,t^{2n}\,dx \qquad \left(\because \int_{-1}^{1} P_m(x)\,P_n(x)\,dx = 0 \text{ for } m \neq n\right)$$

$$\therefore \quad \sum_{n=0}^{\infty}\int_{-1}^{1}(P_n(x))^2\,t^{2n}\,dx = \left.\frac{\log(1+t^2-2xt)}{-2t}\right|_{-1}^{1}$$

$$\Rightarrow \quad \sum_{n=0}^{\infty}\left(\int_{-1}^{1}(P_n(x))^2\,dx\right)t^{2n} = -\frac{1}{2t}\,[\log(1+t^2-2t)-\log(1+t^2+2t)] = -\frac{1}{2t}\log\frac{(1-t)^2}{(1+t)^2}$$

$$= \frac{1}{t}\log\frac{1+t}{1-t} = \frac{1}{t}\,.\,2\left(t+\frac{t^3}{3}+\frac{t^5}{5}+\ldots\right) = 2\left(1+\frac{t^2}{3}+\frac{t^4}{5}+\ldots\right)$$

$$\therefore \quad \sum_{n=0}^{\infty}\left(\int_{-1}^{1}(P_n(x))^2\,dx\right)t^{2n} = 2\left(1+\frac{t^2}{3}+\frac{t^4}{5}+\ldots+\frac{t^{2n}}{2n+1}+\ldots\right).$$

Comparing the coefficients of t^{2n}, we get

$$\int_{-1}^{1}(\mathbf{P_n(x)})^2\,\mathbf{dx} = \frac{\mathbf{2}}{\mathbf{2n+1}}.$$

Example 10. *Show that*

$$\int_{-1}^{1} xP_n(x)\,P'_n(x)\,dx = \frac{2n}{n+1}.$$

Sol. Let $\qquad I = \int_{-1}^{1} xP_n(x)\,.\,P'_n(x)\,dx$

Integrating by parts, we have

$$I = xP_n(x)\,.\,P_n(x)\Big|_{-1}^{1} - \int_{-1}^{1}(xP'_n(x)+1\,.\,P_n(x))\,P_n(x)\,dx$$

$$= 1\,.\,(P_n(1))^2-(-1)(P_n(-1))^2-\int_{-1}^{1} x\,P_n'(x)\,P(x)\,dx-\int_{-1}^{1}(P_n(x))^2\,dx$$

$$\therefore \quad I = (1)^2+(-1)^2-I-\int_{-1}^{1}(P_n(x))^2\,dx$$

$$\therefore \quad 2I = 2-\int_{-1}^{1}(P_n(x))^2\,dx = 2-\frac{2}{2n+1} = \frac{4n}{2n+1}$$

$$\left(\text{Using } \int_{-1}^{1}(P_n(x))^2\,dx = \frac{2}{2n+1}\right)$$

$$\therefore \quad I = \frac{\mathbf{2n}}{\mathbf{2n+1}}.$$

WORKING RULES FOR SOLVING PROBLEMS

Rule I. $(1-2xt+t^2)^{-1/2} = P_0(x) + P_1(x)\,t + P_2(x)\,t^2 + \ldots\ldots$

Rule II. (*i*) $n\,P_n = (2n-1)\,x\,P_{n-1} - (n-1)\,P_{n-2},\ n \geq 2$

(*ii*) $n\,P_n = x\,P_n' - P'_{n-1}$ (*iii*) $(2n+1)\,P_n = P'_{n+1} - P'_{n-1}$

(*iv*) $(n+1)\,P_n = P'_{n+1} - x\,P_n'$ (*v*) $(1-x^2)\,P_n' = n\,(P_{n-1} - x\,P_n)$

(*vi*) $(1-x^2)\,P_n' = (n+1)\,(x\,P_n - P_{n+1})$

Rule III. $P_n(x) = \dfrac{1}{2^n \,.\, n!}\dfrac{d^n}{dx^n}(x^2-1)^n$.

Rule IV. Legendre polynomials are orthogonal on the interval $[-1, 1]$.

EXERCISE 2

1. Using generating function of Legendre polynomials, show that :
(*i*) $P_n(1) = 1$ (*ii*) $P_n(-1) = (-1)^n$.
2. If m is any non-negative integer, show that :
(*i*) $P_{2m+1}(0) = 0$ (*ii*) $P_{2m}(0) = \dfrac{(-1)^m\,(2m)!}{2^{2m}\,(m!)^2}$.
3. Show that :
(*i*) $P_n'(1) = \dfrac{n(n+1)}{2}$ (*ii*) $P_n'(-1) = \dfrac{(-1)^{n-1}\,n(n+1)}{2}$.
4. Show that $P_n(-x) = (-1)^n\,P_n(x)$. Also deduce that $P_n(-1) = (-1)^n$.
5. Show that :
(*i*) $P_n(x)$ is an odd function if n is odd. (*ii*) $P_n(x)$ is an even function if n is even.
6. Show that $\displaystyle\sum_{n=0}^{\infty}(2n+1)\,P_n(x)\,t^n = \frac{1-t^2}{(1-2xt+t^2)^{3/2}}$.
7. Using the recurrence relation $nP_n(x) = (2n-1)x\,P_{n-1}(x) - (n-1)\,P_{n-2}(x)$ and $P_0(x) = 1$, $P_1(x) = x$, find the values of $P_2(x)$, $P_3(x)$, $P_4(x)$, $P_5(x)$ and $P_6(x)$.
8. If $P_n(x)$ is a Legendre polynomial of degree n and α is such that $P_n(\alpha) = 0$. Show that $P_{n-1}(\alpha)$ and $P_{n+1}(\alpha)$ are of opposite signs.
9. Find the values of $P_1(x)$, $P_2(x)$, and $P_3(x)$ by using Rodrigue's formula. *(MDU 2004)*
10. Find the value of $P_5(x)$ and $P_6(x)$ by using Rodrigue's formula.
11. Show that the functions $\sin nx$, $n = 1, 2, 3, \ldots\ldots$ are orthogonal on the interval $[-\pi, \pi]$.
12. Verify that the Legendre polynomials $P_0(x)$, $P_1(x)$, $P_2(x)$, $P_3(x)$ are orthogonal on the interval $[-1, 1]$.
13. Show that : $\displaystyle\int_{-1}^{1} P_n(x)(1-2xt+t^2)^{-1/2}\,dx = \frac{2t^2}{2n+1}$.
14. Show that : $\displaystyle\int_{-1}^{1}(1-x^2)\,P_m'(x)\,P_n'(x)\,dx = \begin{cases} 0 & \text{if } m \neq n \\ \dfrac{2n(n+1)}{2n+1} & \text{if } m = n. \end{cases}$
15. Using Rodrigue's formula, show that $P_n(x)$ satisfies the differential equation

$$\frac{d}{dx}\left[(1-x^2)\frac{d}{dx}P_n(x)\right] + n(n+1)P_n(x) = 0.$$ *(CDLU 2004)*

Answers

7. $P_2(x) = \frac{1}{2}(3x^2 - 1), P_3(x) = \frac{1}{2}(5x^3 - 3x), P_4(x) = \frac{1}{8}(35x^4 - 30x^2 + 3),$

$P_5(x) = \frac{1}{8}(63x^5 - 70x^3 + 15x), P_6(x) = \frac{1}{16}(231x^6 - 315x^4 + 105x^2 - 5)$

9. $P_1(x) = x, P_2(x) = \frac{1}{2}(3x^2 - 1), P_3(x) = \frac{1}{2}(5x^3 - 3x)$

10. $P_5(x) = \frac{1}{8}(63x^5 - 70x^3 + 15x), P_6(x) = \frac{1}{16}(231x^6 - 315x^4 + 105x^2 - 5).$

Hints

1. (*i*) $P_n(1)$ is the coefficient of t^n in the expansion of $(1 - 2(1)t + t^2)^{-1/2}$.

3. (*i*) $P_n(x)$ is a solution of $(1 - x^2)\frac{d^2y}{dx^2} - 2x\frac{dy}{dx} + n(n+1)y = 0$.

Now put $x = 1$ and use $P_n(1) = 1$.

4. Replace x by $-x$ and t by $-t$ in succession in $(1 - 2xt + t^2)^{-1/2}$.

6. We have $(1 - 2xt + t^2)^{-1/2} = \sum_{n=0}^{\infty} P_n(x)t^n$ ...(1)

$\Rightarrow \quad (x - t)(1 - 2xt + t^2)^{-3/2} = \sum_{n=1}^{\infty} nP_n(x)t^{n-1}$ ...(2)

Multiplying (2) by $2t$ and add (1) to it.

8. Use the recurrence relation : $(2n+1)xP_n(x) = (n+1)P_{n+1}(x) + nP_{n-1}(x)$.

15. Let $y = (x^2 - 1)^n$. $\Rightarrow$ $y_1 = 2nx(x^2 - 1)^{n-1}$

$\Rightarrow$ $(x^2 - 1)y_1 = 2nxy$ $\Rightarrow$ $(x^2 - 1)y_2 + 2xy_1 = 2n(xy_1 + y)$

$\Rightarrow$ $(x^2 - 1)y_2 + 2(1 - n)xy_1 - 2xy = 0$. By *Leibnitz's theorem*, we have

$$\left(y_{n+2}(x^2 - 1) + ny_{n+1}\,2x + \frac{n(n-1)}{2}y_n\,2\right) + 2(1-n)(y_{n+1}x + ny_n) - 2xy_n = 0$$

$\Rightarrow$ $(1 - x^2)y_{n+2} - 2xy_{n+1} + n(n+1)y_n = 0$ $\Rightarrow$ $((1 - x^2)y_{n+1})' + n(n+1)y_n = 0$

$$\Rightarrow \quad \frac{d}{dx}\left[(1 - x^2)\frac{d}{dx}\left(\frac{d^n}{dx^n}(x^2 - 1)^n\right)\right] + n(n+1)\frac{d^n}{dx^n}(x^2 - 1)^n = 0$$

Dividing by $n!2^n$, we get $\frac{d}{dx}\left[(1 - x^2)\frac{d}{dx}(P_n(x))\right] + n(n+1)P_n(x) = 0.$

3

Bessel Equation

1. INTRODUCTION

In this chapter, we shall study a very important differential equation called Bessel equation*. This differential equation appears in problems relating to electric fields, viberations, heat conduction, etc.

2. BESSEL EQUATION AND ITS SOLUTION

The Bessel equation is $x^2 \dfrac{d^2y}{dx^2} + x\dfrac{dy}{dx} + (x^2 - n^2)y = 0$. ...(1)

The parameter n is a non-negative real number and is also called the *order of* the Bessel equation (1).

Dividing (1) by x^2, we get

$$\frac{d^2y}{dx^2} + \frac{1}{x}\frac{dy}{dx} + \left(1 - \frac{n^2}{x^2}\right)y = 0 \qquad ...(2)$$

Comparing (2) with $\dfrac{d^2y}{dx^2} + P(x)\dfrac{dy}{dx} + Q(x)y = 0$, we get

$$P(x) = \frac{1}{x} \quad \text{and} \quad Q(x) = 1 - \frac{n^2}{x^2}.$$

'0' is not an ordinary point of (1), because neither P(x) nor Q(x) is analytic at 0.

Here $\quad xP(x) = 1 \quad$ and $\quad x^2 Q(x) = x^2 - n^2$.

Both these functions are analytic at 0.

∴ '0' is a regular singular point of (1). We use *Frobenius method* to find the solution of (1) about '0'.

Let
$$y = x^r \sum_{m=0}^{\infty} a_m x^m = \sum_{m=0}^{\infty} a_m x^{m+r}, a_0 \neq 0 \qquad ...(3)$$

be a series solution of (1) about '0'.

$$(3) \Rightarrow \quad \frac{dy}{dx} = \sum_{m=0}^{\infty} (m+r)a_m x^{m+r-1}$$

and
$$\frac{d^2y}{dx^2} = \sum_{m=0}^{\infty} (m+r)(m+r-1)a_m x^{m+r-2}.$$

***Friedrich Wilhelm Bessel** (1784—1846), German astronomer and mathematician, who worked as the director of the new Königsberg observatory. His paper on Bessel functions appeared in 1826.

Putting the values of y, $\frac{dy}{dx}$ and $\frac{d^2y}{dx^2}$ in (1), we get

$$x^2 \sum_{m=0}^{\infty} (m+r)(m+r-1) a_m x^{m+r-2} + x \sum_{m=0}^{\infty} (m+r) a_m x^{m+r-1}$$

$$+ (x^2 - n^2) \sum_{m=0}^{\infty} a_m x^{m+r} = 0$$

$$\Rightarrow \sum_{m=0}^{\infty} (m+r)(m+r-1) a_m x^{m+r} + \sum_{m=0}^{\infty} (m+r) a_m x^{m+r} + \sum_{m=0}^{\infty} a_m x^{m+r+2}$$

$$- n^2 \sum_{m=0}^{\infty} a_m x^{m+r} = 0$$

$$\Rightarrow \sum_{m=0}^{\infty} ((m+r)(m+r-1+1) - n^2) a_m x^{m+r} + \sum_{m=2}^{\infty} a_{m-2} x^{m+r} = 0$$

(By shifting of indices)

$$\Rightarrow \sum_{m=0}^{\infty} ((m+r)^2 - n^2) a_m x^{m+r} + \sum_{m=2}^{\infty} a_{m-2} x^{m+r} = 0$$

$$\Rightarrow (r^2 - n^2) a_0 x^r + ((r+1)^2 - n^2) a_1 x^{r+1} + \sum_{m=2}^{\infty} [((m+r)^2 - n^2) a_m + a_{m-2}] x^{m+r} = 0$$

...(4)

Equating to zero the coefficient of lowest power of x, we get

$$(r^2 - n^2) a_0 = 0 \quad \Rightarrow \quad r^2 - n^2 = 0. \qquad (\because \; a_0 \neq 0)$$

This is the indicial equation and its roots are $r = n, -n$. We assume that n is not an integer.

(4) $\Rightarrow$ $((r+1)^2 - n^2) a_1 = 0 \;\Rightarrow\; a_1 = 0$ $\qquad (\because \; r = \pm n)$

(4) $\Rightarrow$ $((m+r)^2 - n^2) a_m + a_{m-2} = 0, \quad m \geq 2$

$$\Rightarrow \qquad a_m = -\frac{a_{m-2}}{(m+r)^2 - n^2}, \quad m \geq 2 \qquad \text{...(5)}$$

Case I. r = n

(5) $\Rightarrow$ $a_m = -\dfrac{a_{m-2}}{m^2 + 2mn} = -\dfrac{a_{m-2}}{m(m+2n)}, \quad m \geq 2$ ...(6)

(6) $\Rightarrow$ $a_3 = 0, a_5 = 0, a_7 = 0, \ldots\ldots$

Also, $m = 2$ $\Rightarrow$ $a_2 = -\dfrac{a_0}{2^2 (n+1)}$

$m = 4$ $\Rightarrow$ $a_4 = -\dfrac{a_2}{2^2 . 2(n+2)} = \dfrac{a_0}{2^4 \, 2!(n+1)(n+2)}$

$$n = 6 \quad \Rightarrow \quad a_6 = -\frac{a_4}{2^2 . 3(n+3)} = \frac{(-1)^3 a_0}{2^6\, 3!(n+1)(n+2)(n+3)}$$

....

$\therefore$ In general, $$a_{2m} = \frac{(-1)^m a_0}{2^{2m}\, m!(n+1)(n+2)......(n+m)}, \qquad m \geq 1 \qquad ...(7)$$

Let y_1 be the series solution when, $r = n$.

$$\therefore \ (3) \Rightarrow \quad y_1 = x^n \left(a_0 + 0.x - \frac{a_0}{2^2(n+1)} x^2 + 0.x^3 + \frac{a_0}{2^4\, 2!(n+1)(n+2)} x^4 + ... + \frac{(-1)^m a_0}{2^{2m}\, m!(n+1)(n+2)...(n+m)} x^{2m} + ... \right)$$

or $$y_1 = x^n \left(1 - \frac{x^2}{2^2(n+1)} + \frac{x^4}{2^4\, 2!(n+1)(n+2)} + ... + \frac{(-1)^m x^{2m}}{2^{2m}\, m!(n+1)(n+2)...(n+m)} + ... \right).$$

(Letting $a_0 = 1$)

Case II. r = – n

Let y_2 be the series solution when $r = -n$.

Replacing n by $-n$ in y_1, we get

$$y_2 = x^{-n} \left(1 - \frac{x^2}{2^2(1-n)} + \frac{x^4}{2^4\, 2!(1-n)(2-n)} + ... + \frac{(-1)^m x^{2m}}{2^{2m}\, m!(1-n)(2-n)...(m-n)} + ... \right)$$

Since n is not an integer, the solutions y_1 and y_2 are linearly independent.

$\therefore$ The general solution is $y = C_1 y_1 + C_2 y_2$, where C_1 and C_2 are arbitrary constants.

Now we assume that n is an integer. Let n be equal to zero.

$\therefore$ Roots of indicial equation are 0, 0.

$$(4) \Rightarrow \quad r^2 a_0 x^r + (r+1)^2 a_1 x^{r+1} + \sum_{m=2}^{\infty} [(m+r)^2 a_m + a_{m-2}] x^{m+r} = 0$$

$$\Rightarrow \quad a_1 = 0, \qquad a_m = -\frac{a_{m-2}}{(m+r)^2}, \quad m \geq 2 \qquad ...(8)$$

$$(8) \Rightarrow \quad a_3 = 0, a_5 = 0, a_7 = 0, ...$$

Also, $$m = 2 \quad \Rightarrow \quad a_2 = -\frac{a_0}{(r+2)^2}$$

$$m = 4 \quad \Rightarrow \quad a_4 = -\frac{a_2}{(r+4)^2} = \frac{(-1)^2 a_0}{(r+2)^2 (r+4)^2}$$

....

Let $$\bar{y} = x^r \left(a_0 + 0.x - \frac{a_0}{(r+2)^2} x^2 + 0.x^3 + \frac{(-1)^2 a_0}{(r+2)^2 (r+4)^2} x^4 + ... \right)$$

$$\therefore \quad \bar{y} = x^r \left(1 - \frac{x^2}{(r+2)^2} + \frac{x^4}{(r+2)^2 (r+4)^2} + ... \right) \qquad \text{(Taking } a_0 = 1)$$

Let $\quad y_1 = \bar{y}\Big|_{r=0}$. $\quad \therefore \quad y_1 = 1 - \dfrac{x^2}{2^2} + \dfrac{x^4}{2^2\,4^2} + \ldots$

Differentiating $\bar{y}$ partially w.r.t. r, we get

$$\frac{\partial \bar{y}}{\partial r} = \left(1 - \frac{x^2}{(r+2)^2} + \frac{x^4}{(r+2)^2\,(r+4)^2} + \ldots\right) x^r \log x$$

$$+ x^r \left(0 + \frac{x^2 \,.\, 2}{(r+2)^3} - \frac{2x^4}{(r+2)^2\,(r+4)^2}\left(\frac{1}{r+2} + \frac{1}{r+4}\right) + \ldots\right)$$

$$= \bar{y} \log x + x^r \left(\frac{2x^2}{(r+2)^3} - \frac{2x^4}{(r+2)^2\,(r+4)^2}\left(\frac{1}{r+2} + \frac{1}{r+4}\right) + \ldots\right)$$

Let $\quad y_2 = \dfrac{\partial \bar{y}}{\partial r}\Big|_{r=0}$. $\quad \therefore \quad y_2 = y_1 \log x + \dfrac{x^2}{2^2} - \dfrac{2x^4}{2^2 \,.\, 4^2}\left(\dfrac{1}{2} + \dfrac{1}{4}\right) + \ldots$

$$= y_1 \log x + \frac{x^2}{2^2} - \frac{x^4}{2^2 \,.\, 4^2}\left(1 + \frac{1}{2}\right) + \ldots$$

$\therefore$ The general solution is $y = C_1 y_1 + C_2 y_2$, where C_1 and C_2 are arbitrary constants.

Now we consider the last possibility for the value of n. Let n be a positive integer. In this case, the difference of roots (n and $-n$) of the indicial equation is an integer.

We have already seen that

$$y_1 = x^n \left(1 - \frac{x^2}{2^2\,(n+1)} + \frac{x^4}{4^2\; 2!\,(n+1)(n+2)} + \ldots + \frac{(-1)^m\, x^{2m}}{2^{2m}\; m!\,(n+1)(n+2)\ldots(n+m)} + \ldots\right)$$

is a solution of (1).

We find another solution of (1) and linearly independent of y_1, by the method of 'reduction of order'.

Let $\; y = uy_1$ be a solution of (1).

$$\therefore \qquad x^2 \frac{d^2}{dx^2}(uy_1) + x\frac{d}{dx}(uy_1) + (x^2 - n^2)(uy_1) = 0$$

$$\Rightarrow \quad x^2\,(u''y_1 + 2u'y_1' + uy_1'') + x\,(u'y_1 + uy_1') + (x^2 - n^2)\,uy_1 = 0$$

$$\Rightarrow \quad u\,(x^2 y_1'' + xy_1' + (x^2 - n^2)\,y_1) + x^2u''y_1 + 2x^2u'y_1' + xu'y_1 = 0$$

$$\Rightarrow \qquad x^2 y_1 u'' + (2x^2 y_1' + xy_1)\,u' = 0$$

($\because$ y_1 is a solution of Bessel equation)

$$\Rightarrow \qquad \frac{u''}{u'} + \frac{2x^2 y_1' + xy_1}{x^2 y_1} = 0 \quad \Rightarrow \quad \frac{u''}{u'} + 2\frac{y_1'}{y_1} + \frac{1}{x} = 0$$

$$\Rightarrow \quad \frac{d}{dx}(\log u') + 2\frac{d}{dx}(\log y_1) + \frac{d}{dx}(\log x) = 0 \quad \Rightarrow \quad \frac{d}{dx}(\log(u'y_1^2\, x)) = 0$$

Let $\log(u'y_1^2\, x) = \log A$. $\quad \therefore \quad u'y_1^2\, x = A$ or $u' = \dfrac{A}{xy_1^2}$

$$\Rightarrow \quad u = A\int \frac{dx}{xy_1^2} + B. \quad \therefore \quad y = uy_1 \quad \Rightarrow \quad y = Ay_1\int \frac{dx}{xy_1^2} + By_1.$$

Let $y_2 = y\Big|_{B=0}$. $\therefore \; y_2 = Ay_1\int \frac{dx}{xy_1^2}$. This is a solution of the Bessel equation.

$\therefore$ The general solution is $\quad y = C_1y_1 + C_2'y_2$

or $$y = C_1y_1 + C_2'\left(Ay_1\int \frac{dx}{xy_1^2}\right) = C_1y_1 + C_2\, y_1\int \frac{dx}{xy_1^2}, \qquad (C_2 = AC_2')$$

where C_1 and C_2 are arbitrary constants.

3. BESSEL FUNCTIONS

We know that '0' is a regular singular point of the Bessel equation

$$x^2 \frac{d^2y}{dx^2} + x\frac{dy}{dx} + (x^2 - n^2)\,y = 0 \qquad \text{...(1)}$$

of order n, where n is a non-negative real number.

If the series solution of (1) about '0' is $y = x^r \sum_{m=0}^{\infty} a_m x^m$, then $y_1(x) = x^n \sum_{m=0}^{\infty} a_m x^m$ is a solution, where $a_0 = 1, a_1 = 0, a_3 = 0, a_5 = 0, \ldots\ldots$

and $$a_{2m} = \frac{(-1)^m}{2^{2m}\, m!\,(n+1)(n+2)\ldots\ldots(n+m)}, \; m \geq 1.$$

$$\therefore \quad y_1(x) = x^n \left(1 - \frac{x^2}{2^2(n+1)} + \frac{x^4}{2^4\, 2!\,(n+1)(n+2)} + \ldots\ldots \right.$$
$$\left. + \frac{(-1)^m x^{2m}}{2^{2m}\, m!\,(n+1)(n+2)\ldots\ldots(n+m)} + \ldots\ldots\right)$$

or $$y_1(x) = x^n \sum_{m=0}^{\infty} \frac{(-1)^m x^{2m}}{2^{2m}\, m!\,(n+1)(n+2)\ldots\ldots(n+m)}. \qquad \text{...(2)}$$

The function obtained by multiplying $y_1(x)$ by $\frac{1}{2^n\,\Gamma(n+1)}$* is called the **Bessel function of the first kind** of order n and is denoted by $J_n(x)$.

***Gamma function, Γ(n).** If n is a positive real number, then the improper integral $\int_0^{\infty} e^{-t}\, t^{n-1}\, dt$ is called the **gamma function** and is denoted by $\Gamma(n)$.

1. If $n > 0$, then $\Gamma(n+1) = n\,\Gamma(n)$.
2. If n is a positive integer, then $\Gamma(n+1) = n\,!$, because

$$\Gamma(1) = \int_0^{\infty} e^{-t}\, dt = -e^{-t}\Big|_0^{\infty} = -\left[\lim_{t\to\infty} \frac{1}{e^t} - e^0\right] = 1.$$

3. If n is a negative non-integral real number, then $\Gamma(n)$ is defined as $\Gamma(n) = \frac{\Gamma(n+k+1)}{n(n+1)\ldots\ldots(n+k)}$, where k is the smallest integer such that $n + k + 1 > 0$.
4. If n is zero or negative integer, then $\Gamma(n)$ is taken as infinite.

$$\therefore \quad J_n(x) = \frac{1}{2^n \Gamma(n+1)} x^n \sum_{m=0}^{\infty} \frac{(-1)^m x^{2m}}{2^{2m} m!(n+1)(n+2)\ldots\ldots(n+m)}$$

We know that $\Gamma(n+1) = n\,\Gamma(n)$ for any non-negative real number n.

$$\therefore \quad J_n(x) = x^n \sum_{m=0}^{\infty} \frac{(-1)^m x^{2m}}{2^{2m+n} m!\,\Gamma(n+m+1)},$$

because $\Gamma(n+1)(n+1)(n+2)\ldots\ldots(n+m+1)$

$= \Gamma(n+2)(n+2)\ldots\ldots(n+m+1)$

$= \Gamma(n+3)\ldots\ldots(n+m+1)$

....

$= \Gamma(n+m+1)$.

Since $J_n(x)$ is a constant multiple of $y_1(x)$, it is also a particular solution of the Bessel equation of order n.

Radius of convergence

Let $u_{2k} = \dfrac{(-1)^k}{2^{2k}\,k!(n+1)(n+2)\ldots\ldots(n+k)}, k \geq 1$

$$\therefore \quad \lim_{k\to\infty}\left|\frac{u_{2k+2}}{u_{2k}}\right|$$

$$= \lim_{k\to\infty}\left|\frac{(-1)^{k+1}}{2^{2k+2}(k+1)!(n+1)\ldots\ldots(n+k+1)}\cdot\frac{2^{2k}k!(k+1)\ldots\ldots(n+k)}{(-1)^k}\right|$$

$$= \lim_{k\to\infty}\frac{1}{4(k+1)(n+k+1)} = 0.$$

$\therefore$ Radius of convergence $= \infty$

$\therefore$ $y_1(x)$ is convergent for all real values of x.

$\therefore$ $J_n(x)$, being a constant multiple of $y_1(x)$, is also convergent for all real values of x.

Now replacing n by $-n$ in $J_n(x)$, we get

$$J_{-n}(x) = \frac{1}{2^{-n}\Gamma(1-n)} x^{-n} \sum_{m=0}^{\infty} \frac{(-1)^m x^{2m}}{2^{2m} m!(1-n)(2-n)\ldots\ldots(m-n)} \quad \ldots(3)$$

and equivalently

$$J_{-n}(x) = x^{-n} \sum_{m=0}^{\infty} \frac{(-1)^m x^{2m}}{2^{2m-n} m!\,\Gamma(-n+m+1)}.$$

(3) $\Rightarrow$ $J_{-n}(x) = \dfrac{1}{2^{-n}\Gamma(1-n)} y_2(x)$, where $y_2(x)$ is obtained from (2) by replacing n by $-n$. Since, $(-n)^2$ is also n^2, (1) shows that $y_2(x)$ is also a solution of (1).

$\therefore$ $J_{-n}(x)$, being a constant multiple of $y_2(x)$, is also a particular solution of the Bessel equation of order n.

If n is non-integral positive real number, then the solutions $y_1(x)$ and $y_2(x)$ are linearly independent particular solutions of the Bessel equation.

$\therefore$ $J_n(x)$ and $J_{-n}(x)$ are linearly independent particular solutions.

$\therefore\ y = C_1 J_n(x) + C_2 J_{-n}(x)$ is the general solution of the Bessel equation of order n, where C_1 and C_2 are arbitrary constants.

Remarks :

1. The above general solution holds only when $x \neq 0$, because $J_{-n}(x)$ contains the factor x^{-n} with $n > 0$.

2. If n is a positive integer, then $y = C_1J_n(x) + C_2J_{-n}(x)$ does not represent the general solution, because $J_n(x)$ and $J_{-n}(x)$ are not linearly independent. This is proved in the next theorem.

Theorem. *If n is a non-negative integer then prove that $J_{-n}(x) = (-1)^n J_n(x)$.*

(MDU 2004)

Proof. We have $$J_n(x) = x^n \sum_{m=0}^{\infty} \frac{(-1)^m x^{2m}}{2^{2m+n}\, m!\,\Gamma(m+n+1)}$$

and $$J_{-n}(x) = x^{-n} \sum_{m=0}^{\infty} \frac{(-1)^m x^{2m}}{2^{2m-n}\, m!\,\Gamma(m-n+1)}\,.$$

Proof. The result is trivially true for $n = 0$. So, let n be a positive integer. Here $m - n + 1$ may or may not be positive.

Since n is a positive integer, $\dfrac{1}{\Gamma(m-n+1)}$ is zero if $m - n + 1 \le 0$ or if $m \le n - 1$.

$\therefore$ The first term in $J_{-n}(x)$ starts with $m = n$.

$$\therefore \quad J_{-n}(x) = x^{-n} \sum_{m=n}^{\infty} \frac{(-1)^m x^{2m}}{2^{2m-n}\, m!\,\Gamma(m-n+1)} = x^{-n} \sum_{m=n}^{\infty} \frac{(-1)^m x^{2m}}{2^{2m-n}\, m!\,(m-n)!}$$

Let $m = n + \lambda$.

$$\therefore \quad J_{-n}(x) = x^{-n} \sum_{\lambda=0}^{\infty} \frac{(-1)^{n+\lambda} x^{2n+2\lambda}}{2^{2\lambda+n}\,(n+\lambda)!\,\lambda!} = (-1)^n x^n \sum_{\lambda=0}^{\infty} \frac{(-1)^{\lambda} x^{2\lambda}}{2^{2\lambda+n}\,\lambda!\,(n+\lambda)!}$$

$$= (-1)^n x^n \sum_{m=0}^{\infty} \frac{(-1)^m x^{2m}}{2^{2m+n}\, m!\,\Gamma(m+n+1)} \qquad \text{(By replacing } \lambda \text{ by } m\text{)}$$

$$= (-1)^n J_n(x).$$

$\therefore$ If n is a non-negative integer, then $\mathbf{J_{-n}(x) = (-1)^n J_n(x)}$.

4. GENERAL SOLUTION OF BESSEL EQUATION IN TERMS OF BESSEL FUNCTIONS

The Bessel equation is

$$x^2 \frac{d^2y}{dx^2} + x\frac{dy}{dx} + (x^2 - n^2)\,y = 0 \qquad \text{...(1)}$$

where the parameter n is a non-negative real number.

Case I. $\mathbf{n \neq 0, 1, 2, 3, \ldots}$

In this case, $J_n(x)$ and $J_{-n}(x)$ are linearly independent solutions of (1).

$\therefore$ The general solution of (1) is $y = C_1 J_n(x) + C_2 J_{-n}(x)$, where C_1 and C_2 are arbitrary constants.

Case II. n = 0.

In this case, we have seen that $y_1(x) = 1 - \frac{x^2}{2^2} + \frac{x^4}{2^2 . 4^2} + \ldots$ and

$y_1(x) \log x + \frac{x^2}{2^2} - \frac{x^4}{2^2 . 4^2}\left(1+\frac{1}{2}\right) + \ldots\ldots$ are linearly independent solutions of (1).

By definition

$$J_0(x) = \frac{1}{2^0\ \Gamma(0+1)}\ y_1(x) = y_1(x).$$

$\therefore$ $J_0(x)$ and $J_0(x) \log x + \frac{x^2}{2^2} - \frac{x^4}{2^2 . 4^2}\left(1+\frac{1}{2}\right) + \ldots\ldots$ are linearly independent solutions of (1).

The solution $J_0(x) \log x + \frac{x^2}{2^2} - \frac{x^4}{2^2 . 4^2}\left(1+\frac{1}{2}\right) + \ldots\ldots$ is denoted by $Y_0(x)$ and is called the **Bessel function of second kind of order zero.**

$\therefore$ The general solution of (1) is $y = C_1 J_0(x) + C_2 Y_0(x)$, where C_1 and C_2 are arbitrary constants.

Case III. n = 1, 2, 3, ...

In this case, we have seen that $J_n(x)$ and $J_{-n}(x)$ are solutions of (1). Also, $J_{-n}(x)$ and $J_n(x)$ are not linearly independent, because $J_{-n}(x) = (-1)^n J_n(x)$. By using the method of 'reduction of order', we can show that $J_n(x) \int \frac{dx}{x(J_n(x))^2}$ is also a solution of (1) and is also linearly independent of the solution $J_n(x)$.

The solution $J_n(x) \int \frac{dx}{x(J_n(x))^2}$ is denoted by $Y_n(x)$ and is called **Bessel function of second kind of order n.**

$\therefore$ The general solution of (1) is $y = C_1 J_n(x) + C_2 Y_n(x)$, where C_1 and C_2 are arbitrary constants.

Thus, the general solution of the Bessel equation $x^2 \frac{d^2y}{dx^2} + x\frac{dy}{dx} + (x^2 - n^2)\, y = 0, n \geq 0$ is

$$y = \begin{cases} C_1 J_n(x) + C_2 J_{-n}(x) \text{ if } n \text{ is non-integral} \\ C_1 J_n(x) + C_2 Y_n(x) \text{ if } n \text{ is integral,} \end{cases}$$

where C_1 and C_2 are arbitrary constants.

Example 1. *Write the general solution of the given differential equations :*

(i) $x^2\frac{d^2y}{dx^2} + x\frac{dy}{dx} + \left(x^2 - \frac{9}{16}\right) y = 0$ (ii) $\frac{d^2y}{dx^2} + \frac{1}{x}\frac{dy}{dx} + \left(1 - \frac{1}{6.25\, x^2}\right) y = 0$

(iii) $t\frac{d^2y}{dt^2} + \frac{dy}{dt} + ty = 0$ (iv) $x^2\frac{d^2z}{dx^2} + x\frac{dz}{dx} + (x^2 - 64)\, z = 0.$

Sol. (*i*) We have

$$x^2\frac{d^2y}{dx^2}+x\frac{dy}{dx}+\left(x^2-\left(\frac{3}{4}\right)^2\right)y=0.$$

This is a Bessel equation of order 3/4, which is not an integer.

$\therefore$ Its general solution is $\mathbf{y = C_1\, J_{3/4}(x) + C_2\, J_{-3/4}(x)}$, where C_1 and C_2 are arbitrary constants.

(*ii*) We have

$$\frac{d^2y}{dx^2}+\frac{1}{x}\frac{dy}{dx}+\left(1-\frac{1}{6.25\,x^2}\right)y=0.$$

Multiplying by x^2, we get

$$x^2\frac{d^2y}{dx^2}+x\frac{dy}{dx}+\left(x^2-\frac{1}{6.25}\right)y=0$$

$$\Rightarrow \qquad x^2\frac{d^2y}{dx^2}+x\frac{dy}{dx}+\left(x^2-\left(\frac{2}{5}\right)^2\right)y=0$$

This is a Bessel equation of order 2/5, which is not an integer.

$\therefore$ Its general solution is $\mathbf{y = C_1\, J_{2/5}(x) + C_2\, J_{-2/5}(x)}$, where C_1 and C_2 are arbitrary constants.

(*iii*) We have $t\dfrac{d^2y}{dt^2}+\dfrac{dy}{dt}+ty=0.$

$$\Rightarrow \quad t^2\frac{d^2y}{dt^2}+t\frac{dy}{dt}+t^2y=0 \quad \Rightarrow \quad t^2\frac{d^2y}{dt^2}+t\frac{dy}{dt}+(t^2-(0)^2)\,y=0.$$

This is a Bessel equation of order 0.

$\therefore$ Its general solution is $\mathbf{y = C_1\, J_0(t) + C_2\, Y_0(t)}$, where C_1 and C_2 are arbitrary constants.

(*iv*) We have $x^2\dfrac{d^2z}{dx^2}+x\dfrac{dz}{dx}+(x^2-(8)^2)\,z=0.$

This is a Bessel equation of order 8, which is an integer.

$\therefore$ Its general solution is $\mathbf{z = C_1\, J_8(x) + C_2\, Y_8(x)}$, where C_1 and C_2 are arbitrary constants.

Example 2. *Solve the differential equation*

$$x^2\frac{d^2y}{dx^2}+x\frac{dy}{dx}+\left(4x^4-\frac{1}{4}\right)y=0.$$

Sol. We have

$$x^2\frac{d^2y}{dx^2}+x\frac{dy}{dx}+\left(4x^4-\frac{1}{4}\right)y=0. \qquad \text{...(1)}$$

Let $\quad z=x^2. \quad \therefore \quad \dfrac{dy}{dx}=\dfrac{dy}{dz}\,.\,2x$

and

$$\frac{d^2y}{dx^2}=\frac{d}{dx}\left(2x\frac{dy}{dz}\right)=2\frac{dy}{dz}+2x\frac{d^2y}{dz^2}\,.\,2x=4x^2\frac{d^2y}{dz^2}+2\frac{dy}{dz}.$$

$$\therefore \quad (1) \quad \Rightarrow \quad x^2\left(4x^2\frac{d^2y}{dz^2}+2\frac{dy}{dz}\right)+x\frac{dy}{dz}2x+\left(4x^4-\frac{1}{4}\right)y=0$$

$$\Rightarrow \quad 4z^2\frac{d^2y}{dz^2}+2z\frac{dy}{dz}+2z\frac{dy}{dz}+\left(4z^2-\frac{1}{4}\right)y=0$$

$$\Rightarrow \quad z^2\frac{d^2y}{dz^2}+z\frac{dy}{dz}+\left(z^2-\frac{1}{16}\right)y=0. \quad ...(2)$$

(2) is a Bessel equation of order 1/4. Since 1/4 is a positive non-integral real number, the general solution of (1) is $y = C_1J_{1/4}(z) + C_2J_{-1/4}(z)$ *i.e.*, $y = C_1J_{1/4}(x^2) + C_2J_{-1/4}(x^2)$, where C_1 and C_2 are arbitrary constants.

Example 3. *Solve the differential equation* $x\frac{d^2y}{dx^2}+\frac{dy}{dx}+\frac{1}{4}y=0$ *by using the substitution* $z=\sqrt{x}$.

Sol. We have

$$x\frac{d^2y}{dx^2}+\frac{dy}{dx}+\frac{1}{4}y=0 \quad ...(1)$$

Also, $z=\sqrt{x}$.

$$\therefore \quad \frac{dy}{dx}=\frac{dy}{dz}\cdot\frac{1}{2\sqrt{x}}$$

and

$$\frac{d^2y}{dx^2}=\frac{dy}{dz}\cdot\frac{1}{2}\left(-\frac{1}{2}x^{-3/2}\right)+\frac{1}{2\sqrt{x}}\left(\frac{d^2y}{dz^2}\cdot\frac{1}{2\sqrt{x}}\right)$$

$$=\frac{1}{4x}\frac{d^2y}{dz^2}-\frac{1}{4x^{3/2}}\frac{dy}{dz}=\frac{1}{4z^2}\frac{d^2y}{dz^2}-\frac{1}{4z^3}\frac{dy}{dz}.$$

$$\therefore \quad (1) \quad \Rightarrow \quad z^2\left(\frac{1}{4z^2}\frac{d^2y}{dz^2}-\frac{1}{4z^3}\frac{dy}{dz}\right)+\frac{1}{2z}\frac{dy}{dz}+\frac{1}{4}y=0$$

$$\Rightarrow \quad \frac{d^2y}{dz^2}-\frac{1}{z}\frac{dy}{dz}+\frac{2}{z}\frac{dy}{dz}+y=0 \quad \Rightarrow \quad \frac{d^2y}{dz^2}+\frac{1}{z}\frac{dy}{dz}+y=0$$

$$\Rightarrow \quad z\frac{d^2y}{dz^2}+\frac{dy}{dz}+zy=0 \quad \Rightarrow \quad z^2\frac{d^2y}{dz^2}+z\frac{dy}{dz}+(z^2-(0)^2)\,y=0.$$

This is a Bessel equation of order 0.

$\therefore$ Its general solution is $y = C_1J_0(z) + C_2Y_0(z)$ or $\mathbf{y = C_1J_0(\sqrt{x}) + C_2Y_0(\sqrt{x})}$, where C_1 and C_2 are arbitrary constants.

Example 4. *Solve the differential equation* $x\frac{d^2z}{dx^2}-2\frac{dz}{dx}+xz=0$ *by using the substitution* $y=\frac{z}{x^{3/2}}$.

Sol. We have

$$x\frac{d^2z}{dx^2}-2\frac{dz}{dx}+xz=0. \quad ...(1)$$

$$y=\frac{z}{x^{3/2}} \quad \Rightarrow \quad z=yx^{3/2}$$

$$\therefore \quad \frac{dz}{dx} = y \cdot \frac{3}{2} x^{1/2} + x^{3/2} \frac{dy}{dx}$$

and
$$\frac{d^2z}{dx^2} = \frac{3}{2}\left(y \cdot \frac{1}{2} x^{-1/2} + x^{1/2} \frac{dy}{dx}\right) + \left(\frac{3}{2} x^{1/2} \frac{dy}{dx} + x^{3/2} \frac{d^2y}{dx^2}\right)$$

$$= x^{3/2} \frac{d^2y}{dx^2} + 3\sqrt{x} \frac{dy}{dx} + \frac{3}{4\sqrt{x}} y.$$

$$\therefore \quad (1) \Rightarrow \quad x\left(x^{3/2} \frac{d^2y}{dx^2} + 3\sqrt{x} \frac{dy}{dx} + \frac{3}{4\sqrt{x}} y\right) - 2\left(x^{3/2} \frac{dy}{dx} + \frac{3}{2} \sqrt{x}\, y\right) + x \cdot y\, x^{3/2} = 0$$

$$\Rightarrow \quad x^{5/2} \frac{d^2y}{dx^2} + x^{3/2} \frac{dy}{dx} - \frac{9}{4} \sqrt{x}\, y + x^{5/2} y = 0$$

Dividing by $\sqrt{x}$, we get

$$x^2 \frac{d^2y}{dx^2} + x \frac{dy}{dx} - \frac{9}{4} y + x^2 y = 0.$$

$$\Rightarrow \quad x^2 \frac{d^2y}{dx^2} + x \frac{dy}{dx} + \left(x^2 - \left(\frac{3}{2}\right)^2\right) y = 0$$

This is a Bessel equation of order 3/2, which is not an integer.

$\therefore$ Its general solution is $y = C_1 J_{3/2}(x) + C_2 J_{-3/2}(x)$

or $\mathbf{z = C_1 x^{3/2} J_{3/2}(x) + C_2\, x^{3/2}\, J_{-3/2}(x)}$, where C_1 and C_2 are arbitrary constants.

Example 5. *Solve the equation*

$$x \frac{d^2y}{dx^2} + 2 \frac{dy}{dx} + \frac{1}{2} xy = 0$$

in terms of Bessel's functions. (KU 2005)

Sol. We have $x \dfrac{d^2y}{dx^2} + 2 \dfrac{dy}{dx} + \dfrac{1}{2} xy = 0.$ ...(1)

Let $z = \sqrt{x} y. \quad \therefore \quad y = \dfrac{z}{\sqrt{x}}$

$$\therefore \quad \frac{dy}{dx} = \frac{1}{\sqrt{x}} \frac{dz}{dx} + \left(-\frac{1}{2x^{3/2}}\right) z$$

and
$$\frac{d^2y}{dx^2} = \left[\frac{1}{\sqrt{x}} \frac{d^2z}{dx^2} + \left(-\frac{1}{2x^{3/2}}\right) \frac{dz}{dx}\right] + \left[-\frac{1}{2x^{3/2}} \frac{dz}{dx} + \frac{3}{4x^{5/2}} z\right]$$

$$= \frac{1}{\sqrt{x}} \frac{d^2z}{dx^2} - \frac{1}{x^{3/2}} \frac{dz}{dx} + \frac{3}{4x^{5/2}} z$$

Putting the values of y, $\dfrac{dy}{dx}$ and $\dfrac{d^2y}{dx^2}$ in (1), we get

$$x\left(\frac{1}{\sqrt{x}} \frac{d^2z}{dx^2} - \frac{1}{x^{3/2}} \frac{dz}{dx} + \frac{3}{4x^{5/2}} z\right) + 2\left(\frac{1}{\sqrt{x}} \frac{dz}{dx} - \frac{1}{2x^{3/2}} z\right) + \frac{1}{2} x \cdot \frac{z}{\sqrt{x}} = 0$$

$$\Rightarrow \qquad \sqrt{x}\,\frac{d^2z}{dx^2} + \frac{1}{\sqrt{x}}\frac{dz}{dx} - \frac{1}{4x^{3/2}}\,z + \frac{1}{2}\sqrt{x}z = 0$$

Multiplying by $x\sqrt{x}$, we get

$$x^2\frac{d^2z}{dx^2} + x\frac{dz}{dx} - \frac{1}{4}z + \frac{1}{2}x^2z = 0$$

$$\Rightarrow \qquad x^2\frac{d^2z}{dx^2} + x\frac{dz}{dx} + \left(\frac{1}{2}x^2 - \frac{1}{4}\right)z = 0 \qquad \text{...(2)}$$

Let $$t = \frac{1}{\sqrt{2}}x$$

$$\therefore \qquad \frac{dz}{dx} = \frac{dz}{dt}\cdot\frac{1}{\sqrt{2}} = \frac{1}{\sqrt{2}}\frac{dz}{dt}$$

and $$\frac{d^2z}{dx^2} = \frac{1}{\sqrt{2}}\cdot\frac{d^2z}{dt^2}\cdot\frac{1}{\sqrt{2}} = \frac{1}{2}\frac{d^2z}{dt^2}$$

$$\therefore \quad (2) \Rightarrow \quad 2t^2\cdot\frac{1}{2}\frac{d^2z}{dt^2} + \sqrt{2}\,t\cdot\frac{1}{\sqrt{2}}\frac{dz}{dt} + \left(\frac{1}{2}\cdot 2t^2 - \frac{1}{4}\right)z = 0$$

$$\Rightarrow \qquad t^2\frac{d^2z}{dt^2} + t\frac{dz}{dt} + \left(t^2 - \left(\frac{1}{2}\right)^2\right)z = 0 \qquad \text{...(3)}$$

(3) is a Bessel equation of order 1/2. Since 1/2 is a positive non-integral real number, the general solution of (3) is

$$z = C_1J_{1/2}(t) + C_2J_{-1/2}(t).$$

$\therefore$ The general solution of (1) is $\sqrt{x}\,y = \mathbf{C_1J_{1/2}\left(\frac{1}{\sqrt{2}}x\right) + C_2J_{-1/2}\left(\frac{1}{\sqrt{2}}x\right)}$,

where $\mathbf{C_1}$ and $\mathbf{C_2}$ are arbitrary constants.

Example 6. *If n is a positive integer, then show that $J_n(x)$ is an even or odd function of x according as n is even or odd respectively.*

Sol. We have $$J_n(x) = x^n\sum_{m=0}^{\infty}\frac{(-1)^m x^{2m}}{2^{2m+n}\,m!\,\Gamma(n+m+1)}.$$

Case I. n is even.

$$J_n(-x) = (-x)^n\sum_{m=0}^{\infty}\frac{(-1)^m(-x)^{2m}}{2^{2m+n}\,m!\,\Gamma(n+m+1)}$$

$$= (-1)^n x^n\sum_{m=0}^{\infty}\frac{(-1)^m(-1)^{2m}x^{2m}}{2^{2m+n}\,m!\,\Gamma(n+m+1)}$$

$$= x^n\sum_{m=0}^{\infty}\frac{(-1)^m x^{2m}}{2^{2m+n}\,m!\,\Gamma(n+m+1)} \qquad (\because\ (-1)^n = 1)$$

$= J_n(x)$. $\quad\therefore\quad J_n(x)$ is even.

Case II. n is odd.

$$J_n(-x) = (-x)^n \sum_{m=0}^{\infty} \frac{(-1)^m (-x)^{2m}}{2^{2m+n}\, m!\,\Gamma(n+m+1)}$$

$$= (-1)^n x^n \sum_{m=0}^{\infty} \frac{(-1)^m (-1)^{2m} x^{2m}}{2^{2m+n}\, m!\,\Gamma(n+m+1)}$$

$$= -x^n \sum_{m=0}^{\infty} \frac{(-1)^m x^{2m}}{2^{2m+n}\, m!\,\Gamma(n+m+1)} \qquad (\because \ (-1)^n = -1)$$

$= -J_n(x)$. $\quad \therefore \ J_n(x)$ is odd.

5. PARTICULAR FORMS OF BESSEL FUNCTIONS

If n is a non-negative real number, then the Bessel equation

$$x^2 \frac{d^2y}{dx^2} + x\frac{dy}{dx} + (x^2 - n^2)\, y = 0$$

has $y = J_n(x)$ as a particular solution,

where $$J_n(x) = x^n \sum_{m=0}^{\infty} \frac{(-1)^m x^{2m}}{2^{2m+n}\, m!\,\Gamma(n+m+1)}.$$

Particular cases.

n = 0. $$J_0(x) = x^0 \sum_{m=0}^{\infty} \frac{(-1)^m x^{2m}}{2^{2m}\, m!\,\Gamma(m+1)} = \sum_{m=0}^{\infty} \frac{(-1)^m x^{2m}}{2^{2m}\, m!\, m!}$$

$$\therefore \qquad \mathbf{J_0(x) = 1 - \frac{x^2}{2^2 (1!)^2} + \frac{x^4}{2^4 (2!)^2} - \frac{x^6}{2^6 (3!)^2} + \ldots\ldots}$$

n = 1. $$J_1(x) = x \sum_{m=0}^{\infty} \frac{(-1)^m x^{2m}}{2^{2m+1}\, m!\,\Gamma(m+2)} = \sum_{m=0}^{\infty} \frac{(-1)^m x^{2m+1}}{2^{2m+1}\, m!\,(m+1)!}$$

$$\therefore \qquad \mathbf{J_1(x) = \frac{x}{2} - \frac{x^3}{2^3\, 1!\,2!} + \frac{x^5}{2^5\, 2!\,3!} - \frac{x^7}{2^7\, 3!\,4!} + \ldots\ldots}$$

6. ELEMENTARY BESSEL FUNCTIONS

Bessel functions $J_n(x)$ of first kind of order $n = \pm\frac{1}{2}, \pm\frac{3}{2}, \pm\frac{5}{2}, \ldots\ldots$ are called **elementary Bessel functions**. We will see that elementary Bessel functions can be expressed by finitely many sines and cosines and powers of x.

We have $$J_n(x) = x^n \sum_{m=0}^{\infty} \frac{(-1)^m x^{2m}}{2^{2m+n}\, m!\,\Gamma(n+m+1)}.$$

Let $\qquad n = 1/2.$

$\therefore$ $$\mathbf{J_{1/2}(x)} = \sqrt{x} \sum_{m=0}^{\infty} \frac{(-1)^m x^{2m}}{2^{2m+\frac{1}{2}} m!\,\Gamma\left(m+\frac{3}{2}\right)}$$

$$= \sqrt{\frac{2}{x}} \sum_{m=0}^{\infty} \frac{(-1)^m x^{2m+1}}{2^{2m+1} m!\,\Gamma\left(m+\frac{3}{2}\right)}$$

$$= \sqrt{\frac{2}{x}} \left[\frac{x}{2\,\Gamma\left(\frac{3}{2}\right)} - \frac{x^3}{2^3\,\Gamma\left(\frac{5}{2}\right)} + \frac{x^5}{2^5 . 2!\,\Gamma\left(\frac{7}{2}\right)} + \ldots \right]$$

$$= \sqrt{\frac{2}{x}} \left[\frac{x}{2 . \frac{1}{2} . \sqrt{\pi}} - \frac{x^3}{2^3 . \frac{3}{2} . \frac{1}{2} . \sqrt{\pi}} + \frac{x^5}{2^5 . 2! . \frac{5}{2} . \frac{3}{2} . \frac{1}{2} . \sqrt{\pi}} + \ldots \right]$$

$$\left(\because \Gamma\left(\frac{1}{2}\right) = \sqrt{\pi} \right)$$

$$= \sqrt{\frac{2}{\pi x}} \left[\frac{x}{1!} - \frac{x^3}{3!} + \frac{x^5}{5!} + \ldots \right] = \sqrt{\frac{2}{\pi x}} \sin x.$$

$\therefore$ $$\mathbf{J_{1/2}(x) = \sqrt{\frac{2}{\pi x}} \sin x.}$$

Also $$J_{-n}(x) = x^{-n} \sum_{m=0}^{\infty} \frac{(-1)^m x^{2m}}{2^{2m-n} m!\,\Gamma(m-n+1)}.$$

Let $n = 1/2.$

$\therefore$ $$\mathbf{J_{-1/2}(x)} = x^{-1/2} \sum_{m=0}^{\infty} \frac{(-1)^m x^{2m}}{2^{2m-\frac{1}{2}} m!\,\Gamma\left(m+\frac{1}{2}\right)}$$

$$= \sqrt{\frac{2}{x}} \sum_{m=0}^{\infty} \frac{(-1)^m x^{2m}}{2^{2m} m!\,\Gamma\left(m+\frac{1}{2}\right)}$$

$$= \sqrt{\frac{2}{x}} \left[\frac{1}{\Gamma\left(\frac{1}{2}\right)} - \frac{x^2}{2^3\,\Gamma\left(\frac{3}{2}\right)} + \frac{x^4}{2^4 . 2!\,\Gamma\left(\frac{5}{2}\right)} + \ldots \right]$$

$$= \sqrt{\frac{2}{x}} \left[\frac{1}{\sqrt{\pi}} - \frac{x^2}{2^2 . \frac{1}{2} . \sqrt{\pi}} + \frac{x^4}{2^4 . 2! \frac{3}{2} . \frac{1}{2} . \sqrt{\pi}} + \ldots \right]$$

$$= \sqrt{\frac{2}{\pi x}} \left[1 - \frac{x^2}{2!} + \frac{x^4}{4!} + \ldots \right] = \sqrt{\frac{2}{\pi x}} \cos x.$$

$\therefore$ $$\mathbf{J_{-1/2}(x) = \sqrt{\frac{2}{\pi x}} \cos x.}$$

Example 7. *Verify that the Bessel function* $J_{1/2}(x) = \sqrt{\dfrac{2}{\pi x}} \sin x$ *satisfies the Bessel equation of order 1/2.* (MDU 2006)

Sol. Bessel equation is $$x^2 \frac{d^2y}{dx^2} + x\frac{dy}{dx} + (x^2 - n^2)y = 0. \quad \ldots(1)$$

We have $n = \dfrac{1}{2}$.

$\therefore$ (1) $\Rightarrow$ $$x^2 \frac{d^2y}{dx^2} + x\frac{dy}{dx} + \left(x^2 - \frac{1}{4}\right)y = 0 \quad \ldots(2)$$

Let $$y = J_{1/2}(x) = \sqrt{\frac{2}{\pi x}} \sin x. \quad \therefore y = \sqrt{\frac{2}{\pi}} \cdot \frac{\sin x}{\sqrt{x}}.$$

$$\therefore \quad \frac{dy}{dx} = \sqrt{\frac{2}{\pi}}\left[\frac{\sqrt{x}\cos x - \sin x \cdot \left(\frac{1}{2}x^{-1/2}\right)}{x}\right] = \sqrt{\frac{2}{\pi}}\left[\frac{2x\cos x - \sin x}{2x^{3/2}}\right]$$

and $$\frac{d^2y}{dx^2} = \sqrt{\frac{2}{\pi}}\left[\frac{2x^{3/2}(2\cos x - 2x\sin x - \cos x) - (2x\cos x - \sin x)\,3x^{1/2}}{4x^3}\right]$$

$$= \sqrt{\frac{2}{\pi}}\left[\frac{-4x^{3/2}\cos x - 4x^{5/2}\sin x + 3x^{1/2}\sin x}{4x^3}\right]$$

$y = J_{1/2}(x)$ is a solution of (2) if

$$x^2\sqrt{\frac{2}{\pi}}\left[\frac{-4x^{3/2}\cos x - 4x^{5/2}\sin x + 3x^{1/2}\sin x}{4x^3}\right] + x\sqrt{\frac{2}{\pi}}\left[\frac{2x\cos x - \sin x}{2x^{3/2}}\right] + \left(x^2 - \frac{1}{4}\right)\sqrt{\frac{2}{\pi}}\,\frac{\sin x}{\sqrt{x}} = 0$$

or if $$\sqrt{\frac{2}{\pi}}\left[-\sqrt{x}\cos x - x^{3/2}\sin x + \frac{3\sin x}{4\sqrt{x}} + \sqrt{x}\cos x - \frac{\sin x}{2\sqrt{x}} + x^{3/2}\sin x - \frac{\sin x}{4\sqrt{x}}\right] = 0$$

or if $0 = 0$, which is true. $\therefore$ The result holds.

Example 8. *Show that* $J_{-3/2}(x) = \sqrt{\dfrac{2}{\pi x}}\left(-\dfrac{1}{x}\cos x - \sin x\right)$.

Sol. We have $J_{-n}(x) = x^{-n} \displaystyle\sum_{m=0}^{\infty} \frac{(-1)^m x^{2m}}{2^{2m-n}\, m!\,\Gamma(m-n+1)}$ for $n \ge 0$.

Let $n = 3/2$.

$$\therefore \quad J_{-3/2}(x) = x^{-3/2} \sum_{m=0}^{\infty} \frac{(-1)^m x^{2m}}{2^{2m-\frac{3}{2}}\, m!\,\Gamma\left(m - \frac{1}{2}\right)}$$

$$= x^{-3/2}\left[\frac{1}{2^{-3/2}\,\Gamma\left(-\frac{1}{2}\right)} - \frac{x^2}{2^{1/2}\,\Gamma\left(\frac{1}{2}\right)} + \frac{x^4}{2^{5/2}\,2!\,\Gamma\left(\frac{3}{2}\right)} + \ldots\right]$$

$$= \sqrt{\frac{2}{x}} \cdot \frac{1}{x} \left[\frac{1}{2^{-1} \frac{\Gamma\left(\frac{1}{2}\right)}{-1/2}} - \frac{x^2}{2\Gamma\left(\frac{1}{2}\right)} + \frac{x^4}{2^3 \, 2! \frac{1}{2} \Gamma\left(\frac{1}{2}\right)} + \ldots \right]$$

$$= - \sqrt{\frac{2}{\pi x}} \cdot \frac{1}{x} \left[1 + \frac{x^2}{2} - \frac{x^4}{8} + \ldots \right]$$

$$= - \sqrt{\frac{2}{\pi x}} \cdot \frac{1}{x} \left[1 + \left(1 - \frac{1}{2}\right) x^2 - \left(\frac{1}{6} - \frac{1}{24}\right) x^4 + \ldots \right]$$

$$= - \sqrt{\frac{2}{\pi x}} \cdot \frac{1}{x} \left[\left(1 - \frac{x^2}{2} + \frac{x^4}{24} + \ldots \right) + \left(x^2 - \frac{x^4}{6} + \ldots \right) \right]$$

$$= \sqrt{\frac{2}{\pi x}} \left[-\frac{1}{x} \left(1 - \frac{x^2}{2!} + \frac{x^4}{4!} + \ldots \right) - \left(x - \frac{x^3}{3!} + \ldots \right) \right]$$

$$= \sqrt{\frac{2}{\pi \mathbf{x}}} \left[-\frac{1}{\mathbf{x}} \cos \mathbf{x} - \sin \mathbf{x} \right].$$

WORKING RULES FOR SOLVING PROBLEMS

Rule I. Bessel equation is $x^2 \frac{d^2 y}{dx^2} + x \frac{dy}{dx} + (x^2 - n^2) y = 0$.

The parameter n is a non-negative real number and is also called the order of the Bessel equation.

Rule II. $y = x^n \sum_{m=0}^{\infty} \frac{(-1)^m x^{2m}}{2^{2m} \, m!(n+1)(n+2) \ldots\ldots (n+m)}$

is a particular solution of the Bessel equation of order n. The other solution, linearly independent of y, depends upon n.

Rule III. The above solution of Bessel equation is convergent for all values of x.

Rule IV. $J_n(x) = x^n \sum_{m=0}^{\infty} \frac{(-1)^m x^{2m}}{2^{2m+n} \, m! \, \Gamma(n+m+1)}, \quad n \geq 0$

$J_n(x)$ is called Bessel function of first kind of order n.

Rule V. $Y_0(x) = J_0(x) \log x + \frac{x^2}{2^2} - \frac{x^4}{2^2 \cdot 4^2} \left(1 + \frac{1}{2}\right) + \ldots\ldots$

and $Y_n(x) = J_n(x) \int \frac{dx}{x (J_n(x))^2}, \; n = 1, 2, 3, \ldots\ldots$

The function $Y_n(x)$, $n = 0, 1, 2, 3, \ldots\ldots$ is called Bessel function of second kind of order n.

Rule VI. The general solution of Bessel equation

$$x^2 \frac{d^2y}{dx^2} + x\frac{dy}{dx} + (x^2 - n^2)\,y = 0,\ n \geq 0 \text{ of order } n \text{ is}$$

(*i*) $y = C_1 J_n(x) + C_2 J_{-n}(x)$ if n is non-integral

(*ii*) $y = C_1 J_n(x) + C_2 Y_n(x)$ if n is integral.

Rule VII. $J_{1/2}(x) = \sqrt{\frac{2}{\pi x}} \sin x$, $\quad J_{-1/2}(x) = \sqrt{\frac{2}{\pi x}} \cos x$,

$J_{-3/2}(x) = \sqrt{\frac{2}{\pi x}}\left(-\frac{\cos x}{x} - \sin x\right)$, $\quad J_{3/2}(x) = \sqrt{\frac{2}{\pi x}}\left(\frac{\sin x}{x} - \cos x\right)$.

EXERCISE 1

1. Write the general solution of the following differential equations :

   (*i*) $x^2 \frac{d^2y}{dx^2} + x\frac{dy}{dx} + \left(x^2 - \frac{1}{9}\right)y = 0$

   (*ii*) $z\frac{d^2y}{dz^2} + \frac{dy}{dz} + zy = 0$

   (*iii*) $x^2 \frac{d^2y}{dx^2} + x\frac{dy}{dx} + (x^2 - 25)\,y = 0.$ (*MDU 2006*)

2. Solve the differential equation

$$x^2 \frac{d^2y}{dx^2} + x\frac{dy}{dx} + (\lambda^2 x^2 - n^2)y = 0,\ \lambda \neq 0,\ n \geq 0.$$

3. Solve the differential equation

$$\frac{d^2y}{dx^2} + \frac{1}{x}\frac{dy}{dx} + 4\left(x^2 - \frac{n^2}{x^2}\right)y = 0,\ n \geq 0,$$

   by using the substitution $z = x^2$.

4. Solve the differential equation

$$9x^2 \frac{d^2y}{dx^2} + 9x\frac{dy}{dx} + (36x^4 - 16)\,y = 0 \text{ by using}$$

   the substitution $z = x^2$.

5. Verify that the Bessel function $J_{-1/2}(x) = \sqrt{\frac{2}{\pi x}} \cos x$ satisfies the Bessel equation of order $\frac{1}{2}$.

6. Show that :

   (*i*) $J_{-1/2}(x) = J_{1/2}(x) \cot x$.

   (*ii*) $(J_{1/2}(x))^2 + (J_{-1/2}(x))^2 = \frac{2}{\pi x}$

7. Show that $\frac{d}{dx}(J_0(x)) = -J_1(x)$.

8. Show that $J_{3/2}(x) = \sqrt{\frac{2}{\pi x}}\left(\frac{\sin x}{x} - \cos x\right)$. (*KU 2004 S*)

Answers

1. (i) $y = C_1J_{1/3}(x) + C_2J_{-1/3}(x)$
   (ii) $y = C_1J_0(z) + C_2Y_0(z)$
   (iii) $y = C_1J_5(x) + C_2Y_5(x)$
2. $y = C_1J_n(\lambda x) + C_2J_{-n}(\lambda x)$ if n is non-integral
   $y = C_1J_n(\lambda x) + C_2Y_n(\lambda x)$ if n is integral
3. $y = C_1J_n(x^2) + C_2J_{-n}(x^2)$ if n is non-integral
   $y = C_1J_n(x^2) + C_2Y_n(x^2)$ if n is integral
4. $y = C_1J_{2/3}(x^2) + C_2J_{-2/3}(x^2)$.

---

7. GENERATING FUNCTION OF THE BESSEL FUNCTIONS

Let n be a non-negative integer, then

$$J_n(x) = x^n \sum_{m=0}^{\infty} \frac{(-1)^m x^{2m}}{2^{2m+n}\, m!\,(n+m)!} = \left(\frac{x}{2}\right)^n \sum_{m=0}^{\infty} \frac{(-1)^m}{m!(n+m)!}\left(\frac{x}{2}\right)^{2m}$$

$$= \left(\frac{x}{2}\right)^n \left[\frac{1}{n!} - \frac{1}{1!(n+1)!}\left(\frac{x}{2}\right)^2 + \frac{1}{2!(n+2)!}\left(\frac{x}{2}\right)^4 - \frac{1}{3!(n+2)!}\left(\frac{x}{2}\right)^6 + \ldots\right].$$

Also $J_{-n}(x) = (-1)^n J_n(x)$. ($\because$ n is non-negative integer)

We shall prove that $e^{\frac{x}{2}\left(t - \frac{1}{t}\right)}$ is a generating function of the Bessel functions.

$$e^{\frac{x}{2}\left(t-\frac{1}{t}\right)} = e^{\frac{xt}{2} - \frac{x}{2t}} = e^{\frac{xt}{2}} \cdot e^{-\frac{x}{2t}}$$

$$= \left[1 + \frac{xt}{2} + \frac{1}{2!}\left(\frac{xt}{2}\right)^2 + \frac{1}{3!}\left(\frac{xt}{2}\right)^3 + \ldots\ldots + \frac{1}{n!}\left(\frac{xt}{2}\right)^n + \ldots\ldots\right]$$

$$\times\left[1 - \frac{x}{2t} + \frac{1}{2!}\left(\frac{x}{2t}\right)^2 - \frac{1}{3!}\left(\frac{x}{2t}\right)^3 + \ldots\ldots + \frac{(-1)^n}{n!}\left(\frac{x}{2t}\right)^n + \ldots\ldots\right]$$

$$= \left[1 + \frac{xt}{2} + \frac{x^2t^2}{2!2^2} + \frac{x^3t^3}{3!2^3} + \ldots\ldots + \frac{x^nt^n}{n!2^n} + \ldots\ldots\right]$$

$$\times\left[1 - \frac{x}{2t} + \frac{x^2}{2!2^2t^2} - \frac{x^3}{3!2^3t^3} + \ldots\ldots + \frac{(-1)^n x^n}{n!2^nt^n} + \ldots\ldots\right]$$

In this product, the coefficient of t^0 is

$$1 - \frac{x^2}{2^2} + \frac{x^4}{(2!)^2\, 2^4} - \frac{x^6}{(3!)^2\, 2^6} + \ldots\ldots + \frac{(-1)^n x^{2n}}{(n!)^2\, 2^{2n}} + \ldots\ldots$$

$$= 1 - \frac{1}{1!}\left(\frac{x}{2}\right)^2 + \frac{1}{(2!)^2}\left(\frac{x}{2}\right)^4 - \frac{1}{(n!)^2}\left(\frac{x}{2}\right)^6 + \ldots\ldots$$

$$= J_0(x).$$

In this product, the coefficient of t^n is

$$\frac{x^n}{n!2^n}.1+\frac{x^{n+1}}{(n+1)!2^{n+1}}.\left(-\frac{x}{2}\right)+\frac{x^{n+2}}{(n+2)!2^{n+2}}.\left(\frac{x^2}{2!2^2}\right)+\frac{x^{n+3}}{(n+3)!2^{n+2}}.\left(-\frac{x^3}{3!2^3}\right)+\ldots\ldots$$

$$=\frac{1}{n!}\left(\frac{x}{2}\right)^n-\frac{1}{1!(n+1)!}\left(\frac{x}{2}\right)^{n+2}+\frac{1}{2!(n+2)!}\left(\frac{x}{2}\right)^{n+4}-\frac{1}{3!(n+3)!}\left(\frac{x}{2}\right)^{n+6}+\ldots\ldots$$

$$=\left(\frac{x}{2}\right)^n\left[\frac{1}{n!}-\frac{1}{1!(n+1)!}\left(\frac{x}{2}\right)^2+\frac{1}{2!(n+2)!}\left(\frac{x}{2}\right)^4-\frac{1}{3!(n+3)!}\left(\frac{x}{2}\right)^6+\ldots\ldots\right]$$

$$= J_n(x).$$

In the above product, the coefficient of t^{-n} is

$$1.\frac{(-1)^n x^n}{n!2^n}+\frac{x}{2}.\frac{(-1)^{n+1}x^{n+1}}{(n+1)!2^{n+1}}+\frac{x^2}{2!2^2}.\frac{(-1)^{n+2}x^{n+2}}{(n+2)!2^{n+2}}+\frac{x^3}{3!2^3}.\frac{(-1)^{n+3}x^{n+3}}{(n+3)!2^{n+3}}+\ldots\ldots$$

$$=(-1)^n\left[\frac{1}{n!}\left(\frac{x}{2}\right)^n-\frac{1}{1!(n+1)!}\left(\frac{x}{2}\right)^{n+2}+\frac{1}{2!(n+2)!}\left(\frac{x}{2}\right)^{n+4}-\frac{1}{3!(n+3)!}\left(\frac{x}{2}\right)^{n+6}+\ldots\ldots\right]$$

$$=(-1)^n\left(\frac{x}{2}\right)^n\left[\frac{1}{n!}-\frac{1}{1!(n+1)!}\left(\frac{x}{2}\right)^2+\frac{1}{2!(n+2)!}\left(\frac{x}{2}\right)^4-\frac{1}{3!(n+3)!}\left(\frac{x}{2}\right)^6+\ldots\ldots\right]$$

$$= (-1)^n J_n(x) = J_{-n}(x).$$

$$\therefore \quad \mathbf{e^{\frac{x}{2}\left(t-\frac{1}{t}\right)} = \sum_{n=-\infty}^{\infty} J_n(x)\, t^n}.$$

$\therefore$ $e^{\frac{x}{2}\left(t-\frac{1}{t}\right)}$ is a generating function of Bessel functions.

Remark 1. For the sake of simplicity, we may write $J_n(x)$ as J_n.

Remark 2. $\displaystyle\sum_{n=-\infty}^{\infty} J_n t^n = J_0 + \sum_{n=1}^{\infty} (J_n t^n + J_{-n} t^{-n})$

$$= J_0 + \sum_{n=1}^{\infty} (J_n t^n + (-1)^n J_n t^{-n})$$

$$= J_0 + \sum_{n=1}^{\infty} (t^n + (-1)^n t^{-n}) J_n$$

$$\therefore \quad \mathbf{e^{\frac{x}{2}\left(t-\frac{1}{t}\right)} = J_0 + (t-t^{-1})J_1 + (t^2+t^{-2})J_2 + (t^3-t^{-3})J_3 + \ldots\ldots}$$

Example 1. *Show that $J_n(-x) = (-1)^n J_n(x)$, where n is a non-negative integer.*

Sol. We have $e^{\frac{x}{2}\left(t-\frac{1}{t}\right)} = \displaystyle\sum_{n=-\infty}^{\infty} J_n(x)\, t^n$. ...(1)

Replacing x by $-x$ in (1), we get

$$\sum_{n=-\infty}^{\infty} J_n(-x)\, t^n = e^{-\frac{x}{2}\left(t-\frac{1}{t}\right)} = e^{\frac{x}{2}\left(-t-\frac{1}{-t}\right)}$$

$$= \sum_{n=-\infty}^{\infty} J_n(x)\,(-t)^n = (-1)^n \sum_{n=-\infty}^{\infty} J_n(x)\, t^n .$$

Comparing the coefficients of t^n, we get

$$\mathbf{J_n(-x) = (-1)^n J_n(x).}$$

Example 2. *Show that :*

(*i*) $\cos(x \sin\phi) = J_0 + 2J_2 \cos 2\phi + 2J_4 \cos 4\phi + \ldots\ldots$ (KU 2005 S)

(*ii*) $\sin(x \sin\phi) = 2J_1 \sin\phi + 2J_3 \sin 3\phi + 2J_5 \sin 5\phi + \ldots\ldots$ (KU 2006)

(*iii*) $\cos(x \cos\phi) = J_0 - 2J_2 \cos 2\phi + 2J_4 \cos 4\phi + \ldots\ldots$

(*iv*) $\sin(x \cos\phi) = 2J_1 \cos\phi - 2J_3 \cos 3\phi + 2J_5 \cos 5\phi + \ldots\ldots$

Sol. We know that

$$e^{\frac{x}{2}\left(t-\frac{1}{t}\right)} = J_0 + (t - t^{-1}) J_1 + (t^2 + t^{-2}) J_2 + (t^3 - t^{-3}) J_3 + \ldots\ldots \quad \ldots(1)$$

Let $t = e^{i\phi}$. $\therefore$ $t^n = e^{in\phi}$ and $t^{-n} = e^{-in\phi}$.

$$\therefore \quad (1) \Rightarrow \quad e^{\frac{x}{2}(e^{i\phi} - e^{-i\phi})} = J_0 + (e^{i\phi} - e^{-i\phi}) J_1 + (e^{2i\phi} + e^{-2i\phi}) J_2 + (e^{3i\phi} - e^{-3i\phi}) J_3 + \ldots\ldots \quad \ldots(2)$$

Now $\cos n\phi = \dfrac{1}{2}(e^{in\phi} + e^{-in\phi})$ and $\sin n\phi = \dfrac{1}{2i}(e^{in\phi} - e^{-in\phi})$

$$\therefore \quad (2) \Rightarrow \quad e^{xi \sin\phi} = J_0 + (2i \sin\phi) J_1 + (2\cos 2\phi) J_2 + (2i \sin 3\phi) J_3 + \ldots\ldots$$

$$\Rightarrow \cos(x \sin\phi) + i \sin(x \sin\phi) = [J_0 + 2J_2 \cos 2\phi + 2J_4 \cos 4\phi + \ldots\ldots] + 2i\,[J_1 \sin\phi + J_3 \sin 3\phi + J_5 \sin 5\phi + \ldots\ldots] \quad \ldots(3)$$

(*i*) Equating real parts in (3), we get

$$\mathbf{\cos(x \sin\phi) = J_0 + 2J_2 \cos 2\phi + 2J_4 \cos 4\phi + \ldots\ldots} \quad \ldots(4)$$

(*ii*) Equating imaginary parts in (3), we get

$$\mathbf{\sin(x \sin\phi) = 2J_1 \sin\phi + 2J_3 \sin 3\phi + 2J_5 \sin 5\phi + \ldots\ldots} \quad \ldots(5)$$

(*iii*) Replacing ϕ by $\dfrac{\pi}{2} - \phi$ in (4), we get

$$\mathbf{\cos(x \cos\phi) = J_0 - 2J_2 \cos 2\phi + 2J_4 \cos 4\phi + \ldots\ldots}$$

(*iv*) Replacing ϕ by $\dfrac{\pi}{2} - \phi$ in (5), we get

$$\mathbf{\sin(x \cos\phi) = 2J_1 \cos\phi - 2J_3 \cos 3\phi + 2J_5 \cos 5\phi + \ldots\ldots}$$

Note. The series given in (*i*) and (*ii*) are called **Jacobi series.**

Example 3. *Using* $\cos(x \sin\phi) = J_0 + 2J_2 \cos 2\phi + 2J_4 \cos 4\phi + \ldots\ldots$, *show that*

$$x \sin x = 2\,(2^2 J_2 - 4^2 J_4 + 6^2 J_6 + \ldots\ldots).$$

Sol. We have $\cos(x \sin\phi) = J_0 + 2J_2 \cos 2\phi + 2J_4 \cos 4\phi + \ldots\ldots \quad \ldots(1)$

Differentiating (1) w.r.t. ϕ, we get

$$-\sin(x\sin\phi)\,.\,x\cos\phi = 0 - 4J_2\sin 2\phi - 8J_4\sin 4\phi + \ldots\ldots$$

Differentiating again w.r.t. ϕ, we get

$$-\cos(x\sin\phi)\,.\,x^2\cos^2\phi + \sin(x\sin\phi)\,.\,x\sin\phi$$
$$= -8\,J_2\cos 2\phi - 32\,J_4\cos 4\phi + \ldots\ldots$$

Putting $\phi = \pi/2$, we get

$$x\sin x = 8\,J_2 - 32\,J_4 + \ldots\ldots$$

or
$$\mathbf{x\sin x = 2\,(2^2\,J_2 - 4^2\,J_4 + \ldots\ldots).}$$

Example 4. *Show that*

$$J_n(x) = \frac{1}{\pi}\int_0^\pi \cos(n\phi - x\sin\phi)\,d\phi \text{ where } n \text{ is any integer.} \qquad \text{(KU 2004)}$$

Sol. The Jacobi series are $\cos(x\sin\phi) = J_0 + 2J_2\cos 2\phi + 2J_4\cos 4\phi + \ldots\ldots$ ...(1)

and
$$\sin(x\sin\phi) = 2J_1\sin\phi + 2J_3\sin 3\phi + 2J_5\sin 5\phi + \ldots\ldots \qquad \text{...(2)}$$

Also
$$\int_0^\pi \cos p\theta\cos q\theta\,d\theta = \int_0^\pi \sin p\theta\sin q\theta\,d\theta = \begin{cases}\pi/2 & \text{if } p = q\\ 0 & \text{if } p \ne q.\end{cases}$$

We first assume that n is a positive integer.

Multiplying (1) by $\cos n\phi$ and integrating w.r.t. ϕ between 0 and π, we get

$$\int_0^\pi \cos(x\sin\phi)\cos n\phi\,d\phi = J_0\int_0^\pi \cos n\phi\,d\,\phi + 2J_2\int_0^\pi \cos 2\phi\cos n\phi\,d\phi$$
$$+ 2J_4\int_0^\pi \cos 4\phi\cos n\phi\,d\phi + \ldots\ldots \qquad \text{...(3)}$$

Case I. n is odd

$$(3) \Rightarrow \int_0^\pi \cos(x\sin\phi)\cos n\phi\,d\phi = J_0\,.\,0 + 2J_2\,.\,0 + 2J_4\,.\,0 + \ldots = 0$$

Case II. n is even

$$(3) \Rightarrow \int_0^\pi \cos(x\sin\phi)\cos n\phi\,d\phi = J_0\,.\,0 + 2J_2\,.\,0 + \ldots\ldots + 2J_n\,.\,(\pi/2) + 2J_{n+2}\,.\,0 + \ldots\ldots$$
$$= \pi\,J_n.$$

$$\therefore \quad \int_0^\pi \cos(x\sin\phi)\cos n\phi\,d\phi = \begin{cases}0 & \text{if } n \text{ is odd}\\ \pi J_n & \text{if } n \text{ is even.}\end{cases}$$

Similarly by multiplying (2) by $\sin n\phi$ and integrating w.r.t. ϕ between 0 and π, we get

$$\int_0^\pi \sin(x\sin\phi)\sin n\phi\,d\phi = \begin{cases}\pi J_n & \text{if } n \text{ is odd}\\ 0 & \text{if } n \text{ is even.}\end{cases}$$

If n is odd, then by adding, we get

$$\int_0^\pi (\cos(x\sin\phi)\cos n\phi + \sin(x\sin\phi)\sin n\phi)\,d\phi = 0 + \pi J_n = \pi J_n$$

$$\Rightarrow \qquad \int_0^\pi \cos(n\phi - x\sin\phi)\,d\phi = \pi J_n\,.$$

If n is even, then by adding, we get

$$\int_0^{\pi} (\cos (x \sin \phi) \cos n\phi + \sin (x \sin \phi) \sin n\phi)\, d\phi = \pi J_n + 0 = \pi J_n .$$

$$\Rightarrow \qquad \int_0^{\pi} \cos (n\phi - x \sin \phi)\, d\phi = \pi J_n .$$

$$\therefore \qquad J_n(x) = \frac{1}{\pi} \int_0^{\pi} \cos (n\phi - x \sin \phi)\, d\phi \text{ for any positive integer, } n.$$

Now let n be a negative integer.

Let $\quad n = -m. \quad \therefore \quad m > 0.$

Let $$I = \int_0^{\pi} \cos (n\phi - x \sin \phi)\, d\phi.$$

$$\therefore \qquad I = \int_0^{\pi} \cos (-m\phi - x \sin \phi)\, d\phi.$$

Let $\quad \theta = \pi - \phi$

$$\therefore \qquad I = -\int_{\pi}^{0} \cos (-m(\pi - \theta) - x \sin (\pi - \theta))\, d\theta$$

$$= \int_0^{\pi} \cos (-m\pi + m\theta - x \sin \theta)\, d\theta = \int_0^{\pi} \cos [(m\theta - x \sin \theta) - m\pi]\, d\theta$$

$$= \int_0^{\pi} [\cos (m\theta - x \sin \theta) \cos m\pi + \sin (m\theta - x \sin \theta) \sin m\pi]\, d\theta$$

$$= (-1)^m \int_0^{\pi} \cos (m\theta - x \sin \theta)\, d\theta \qquad (\because \quad \cos m\pi = (-1)^m, \sin m\pi = 0)$$

$$= (-1)^m \pi . \frac{1}{\pi} \int_0^{\pi} \cos (m\phi - x \sin \phi)\, d\phi \qquad \text{(Replacing } \theta \text{ by } \phi)$$

$$= (-1)^m \pi J_m (x) = \pi J_{-m} (x) = \pi J_n (x).$$

$$\therefore \qquad J_n (x) = \frac{1}{\pi} \int_0^{\pi} \cos (n\phi - x \sin \phi)\, d\phi \text{ for any negative integer, } n.$$

Let $\quad n = 0.$

$$\therefore \qquad \frac{1}{\pi} \int_0^{\pi} \cos(n\phi - x \sin \phi)\, d\phi = \frac{1}{\pi} \int_0^{\pi} \cos(0 - x \sin \phi)\, d\phi$$

$$= \frac{1}{\pi} \int_0^{\pi} \cos(x \sin \phi)\, d\phi = \frac{1}{\pi} \int_0^{\pi} (J_0 + 2J_2 \cos 2\phi + 4J_4 \cos 4\phi + \ldots\ldots)\, d\phi$$

$$= \frac{1}{\pi} \left[J_0 \int_0^{\pi} d\phi + 2J_2 \int_0^{\pi} \cos 2\phi\, d\phi + 4J_4 \int_0^{\pi} \cos 4\phi\, d\phi + \ldots\ldots \right]$$

$$= \frac{1}{\pi} [J_0 . \pi + 2J_2 . 0 + 4J_4 . 0 + \ldots\ldots]$$

$$= J_0 .$$

$\therefore$ The result is also true for $n = 0$.

Combining, we get

$$J_n (x) = \frac{1}{\pi} \int_0^{\pi} \cos (n\phi - x \sin \phi)\, d\phi \text{ , where } n \text{ is any integer.}$$

8. RECURRENCE RELATIONS

In this section, we shall prove some recurrence relations. For the sake of simplicity, we shall write $J_n(x)$ as J_n. Let n be a non-negative integer.

(*i*) $\dfrac{d}{dx}(x^n J_n) = x^n J_{n-1}$

(*ii*) $\dfrac{d}{dx}(x^{-n} J_n) = -x^{-n} J_{n+1}$

(*iii*) $J_n' + \dfrac{n}{x} J_n = J_{n-1}$ (*KU 2005*)

(*iv*) $J_n' - \dfrac{n}{x} J_n = -J_{n+1}$

(*v*) $J_n = \dfrac{x}{2n}[J_{n-1} + J_{n+1}]$

(*vi*) $J_n' = \dfrac{1}{2}[J_{n-1} - J_{n+1}]$.

Proof. (*i*) We have $J_n = x^n \displaystyle\sum_{m=0}^{\infty} \frac{(-1)^m x^{2m}}{2^{2m+n}\, m!\,\Gamma(n+m+1)}$. ...(1)

$$\therefore \quad x^n J_n = \sum_{m=0}^{\infty} \frac{(-1)^m x^{2m+2n}}{2^{2m+n}\, m!\,\Gamma(n+m+1)}$$

$$\therefore \quad \frac{d}{dx}(x^n J_n) = \sum_{m=0}^{\infty} \frac{(-1)^m (2m+2n) x^{2m+2n-1}}{2^{2m+n}\, m!\,\Gamma(n+m+1)}$$

$$= x^n \sum_{m=0}^{\infty} \frac{(-1)^m\, 2(m+n) x^{2m+(n-1)}}{2^{2m+n}\, m!\,\Gamma(n+m+1)}$$

$$= x^n \sum_{m=0}^{\infty} \frac{(-1)^m (m+n) x^{2m+n-1}}{2^{2m+n-1}\, m!\,(n+m)\,\Gamma(n+m)}$$

$$= x^n \sum_{m=0}^{\infty} \frac{(-1)^m x^{2m+(n-1)}}{2^{2m+(n-1)}\, m!\,\Gamma(n-1+m+1)} = x^n J_{n-1}.$$

$$\therefore \quad \mathbf{\frac{d}{dx}(x^n J_n) = x^n J_{n-1}}.$$

(*ii*)
$$J_n = x^n \sum_{m=0}^{\infty} \frac{(-1)^m x^{2m}}{2^{2m+n}\, m!\,\Gamma(n+m+1)}$$

$$\therefore \quad x^{-n} J_n = \sum_{m=0}^{\infty} \frac{(-1)^m x^{2m}}{2^{2m+n}\, m!\,\Gamma(n+m+1)}$$

$$\therefore \quad \frac{d}{dx}(x^{-n} J_n) = \sum_{m=0}^{\infty} \frac{(-1)^m\, 2m\, x^{2m-1}}{2^{2m+n}\, m!\,\Gamma(n+m+1)}$$

$$= 0 + x^{-n} \sum_{m=1}^{\infty} \frac{(-1)^m\, 2m\, x^{2m+n-1}}{2^{2m+n}\, m!\,\Gamma(n+m+1)}$$

$$= x^{-n} \sum_{m=0}^{\infty} \frac{(-1)^{m+1}\, 2(m+1)\, x^{2(m+1)+n-1}}{2^{2(m+1)+n}\, (m+1)!\,\Gamma(n+m+1+1)} \quad \text{(By shifting of index)}$$

$$= -x^{-n} \sum_{m=0}^{\infty} \frac{(-1)^m x^{2m+n+1}}{2^{2m+n+1} m! \Gamma(n+1+m+1)} = -x^{-n} J_{n+1}.$$

$$\therefore \quad \mathbf{\frac{d}{dx}(x^{-n} J_n) = -x^{-n} J_{n+1}}.$$

(*iii*) From part (*i*),

$$\frac{d}{dx}(x^n J_n) = x^n J_{n-1}.$$

$$\Rightarrow \quad x^n J_n' + nx^{n-1} J_n = x^n J_{n-1}$$

Dividing by x^n, we get

$$\mathbf{J_n' + \frac{n}{x} J_n = J_{n-1}}.$$

(*iv*) From part (*ii*),

$$\frac{d}{dx}(x^{-n} J_n) = -x^{-n} J_{n+1}.$$

$$\Rightarrow \quad x^{-n} J_n' - nx^{-n-1} J_n = -x^{-n} J_{n+1}$$

Dividing by x^{-n}, we get

$$\mathbf{J_n' - \frac{n}{x} J_n = -J_{n+1}}.$$

(*v*) From part (*i*), $\frac{d}{dx}(x^n J_n) = x^n J_{n-1}$.

$$\Rightarrow \quad x^n J_n' + nx^{n-1} J_n = x^n J_{n-1}$$

Dividing by x^n, we get $J_n' + \frac{n}{x} J_n = J_{n-1}$ ...(1)

From part (*ii*), $\frac{d}{dx}(x^{-n} J_n) = -x^{-n} J_{n+1}$

$$\Rightarrow \quad x^{-n} J_n' - nx^{-n-1} J_n = -x^{-n} J_{n+1}$$

$$\Rightarrow \quad J_n' - \frac{n}{x} J_n = -J_{n+1} \qquad ...(2)$$

Subtracting (2) from (1), we get

$$\frac{2n}{x} J_n = J_{n-1} + J_{n+1}$$

or

$$J_n = \mathbf{\frac{x}{2n}[J_{n-1} + J_{n+1}]}.$$

(*vi*) Adding (1) and (2), we get $2J_n' = J_{n-1} - J_{n+1}$

or

$$\mathbf{J_n' = \frac{1}{2}[J_{n-1} - J_{n+1}]}.$$

Example 5. *Express $J_5(x)$ in terms of $J_0(x)$ and $J_1(x)$.*

Sol. We have $J_n(x) = \frac{x}{2n}[J_{n-1}(x) + J_{n+1}(x)]$

$$\Rightarrow \qquad J_{n+1}(x) = \frac{2n}{x} J_n(x) - J_{n-1}(x) \qquad \text{...(1)}$$

$$n = 1 \text{ in (1)} \quad \Rightarrow \quad J_2(x) = \frac{2}{x} J_1(x) - J_0(x) \qquad \text{...(2)}$$

$$n = 2 \text{ in (1)} \quad \Rightarrow \quad J_3(x) = \frac{4}{x} J_2(x) - J_1(x) \qquad \text{...(3)}$$

$$n = 3 \text{ in (1)} \quad \Rightarrow \quad J_4(x) = \frac{6}{x} J_3(x) - J_2(x) \qquad \text{...(4)}$$

$$n = 4 \text{ in (1)} \quad \Rightarrow \quad J_5(x) = \frac{8}{x} J_4(x) - J_3(x)$$

$$\therefore \qquad J_5(x) = \frac{8}{x}\left(\frac{6}{x} J_3(x) - J_2(x)\right) - J_3(x) \qquad \text{(Using (4))}$$

$$= \left(\frac{48}{x^2} - 1\right) J_3(x) - \frac{8}{x} J_2(x)$$

$$= \left(\frac{48}{x^2} - 1\right)\left[\frac{4}{x} J_2(x) - J_1(x)\right] - \frac{8}{x} J_2(x) \qquad \text{(Using (3))}$$

$$= \left(\frac{192}{x^3} - \frac{4}{x} - \frac{8}{x}\right) J_2(x) - \left(\frac{48}{x^2} - 1\right) J_1(x)$$

$$= \left(\frac{192}{x^3} - \frac{12}{x}\right)\left(\frac{2}{x} J_1(x) - J_0(x)\right) - \left(\frac{48}{x^2} - 1\right) J_1(x) \qquad \text{(Using (2))}$$

$$= \left(\frac{384}{x^4} - \frac{24}{x^2} - \frac{48}{x^2} + 1\right) J_1(x) - \left(\frac{192}{x^3} - \frac{12}{x}\right) J_0(x)$$

$$\therefore \qquad \mathbf{J_5(x) = \left(\frac{384}{x^4} - \frac{72}{x^2} + 1\right) J_1(x) + \left(-\frac{192}{x^3} + \frac{12}{x}\right) J_0(x)}.$$

Example 6. *Using* $J_{1/2}(x) = \sqrt{\frac{2}{\pi x}} \sin x$ *and* $J_{-1/2}(x) = \sqrt{\frac{2}{\pi x}} \cos x$, *show that :*

(*i*) $J_{-3/2}(x) = -\sqrt{\frac{2}{\pi x}}\left(\frac{\cos x}{x} + \sin x\right)$ (*ii*) $J_{-5/2}(x) = \sqrt{\frac{2}{\pi x}}\left(\frac{3 - x^2}{x^2} \cos x + \frac{3}{x} \sin x\right)$

Sol. We know that

$$J_n(x) = \frac{x}{2n}\,[J_{n-1}(x) + J_{n+1}(x)] \quad \Rightarrow \quad J_{n-1}(x) = \frac{2n}{x} J_n(x) - J_{n+1}(x) \qquad \text{...(1)}$$

$$(i)\ n = -\frac{1}{2} \text{ in (1)} \quad \Rightarrow \quad J_{-3/2}(x) = \frac{2\left(-\frac{1}{2}\right)}{x} J_{-1/2}(x) - J_{1/2}(x)$$

$$\therefore \qquad J_{-3/2}(x) = -\frac{1}{x} J_{-1/2}(x) - J_{1/2}(x) = -\frac{1}{x}\cdot\sqrt{\frac{2}{\pi x}} \cos x - \sqrt{\frac{2}{\pi x}} \sin x$$

$$\therefore \qquad \mathbf{J_{-3/2}(x) = -\sqrt{\frac{2}{\pi x}}\left(\frac{\cos x}{x} + \sin x\right)}.$$

(ii) $n = -\frac{3}{2}$ in (1) $\Rightarrow$ $J_{-5/2}(x) = \frac{2(-3/2)}{x} J_{-3/2}(x) - J_{-1/2}(x)$

$$\therefore \quad J_{-5/2}(x) = -\frac{3}{x} J_{-3/2}(x) - J_{-1/2}(x)$$

$$= -\frac{3}{x}\left[-\sqrt{\frac{2}{\pi x}}\left(\frac{\cos x}{x} + \sin x\right)\right] - \sqrt{\frac{2}{\pi x}} \cos x$$

$$= \sqrt{\frac{2}{\pi x}}\left[\frac{3}{x^2}\cos x - \frac{3}{x}\sin x - \cos x\right]$$

$$\therefore \quad \mathbf{J_{-5/2}(x) = \sqrt{\frac{2}{\pi x}}\left(\frac{3 - x^2}{x^2}\cos x - \frac{3}{x}\sin x\right).}$$

Example 7. *Show that* $\int J_3(x)\,dx = -J_2(x) - \frac{2}{x} J_0(x) + C$. (KU 2005 S)

Sol. We have $\frac{d}{dx}(x^{-n} J_n(x)) = -x^{-n} J_{n+1}(x)$.

$$\Rightarrow \quad x^{-n} J_n(x) = -\int x^{-n} J_{n+1}(x)\,dx$$

$$\Rightarrow \quad \int x^{-n} J_{n+1}(x)\,dx = -x^{-n} J_n(x) \qquad \text{...(1)}$$

Now $\int J_3(x)\,dx = \int x^2 (x^{-2} J_3(x))\,dx$

$$= x^2 \int x^{-2} J_3(x)\,dx - \int \left(2x \int x^{-2} J_3(x)\,dx\right) dx$$

$$= x^2(-x^{-2} J_2(x)) - \int 2x(-x^{-2} J_2(x))\,dx \qquad \text{(Using (1) with } n = 2)$$

$$= -J_2(x) + 2\int x^{-1} J_2(x)\,dx$$

$$= -J_2(x) + 2[-x^{-1} J_1(x)] \qquad \text{(Using (1) with } n = 1)$$

$$= -J_2(x) - \frac{2}{x} J_1(x) + C.$$

9. ORTHOGONALITY OF BESSEL FUNCTIONS

Theorem. Let n be any fixed non-negative integer. Let R be any fixed positive real number. Let $\lambda_1, \lambda_2, \ldots\ldots$ be the roots of the equation $J_n(\lambda R) = 0$. Prove that the Bessel functions $J_n(\lambda_1 x), J_n(\lambda_2 x), \ldots\ldots$ are orthogonal with respect to the weight function 'x' on the interval [0, R].

Proof. Let $J_n(\lambda_i x)$ and $J_n(\lambda_j x)$ be Bessel functions, where $\lambda_i \neq \lambda_j$.

$J_n(z)$ satisfies the Bessel equation

$$z^2 \frac{d^2y}{dz^2} + z\frac{dy}{dz} + (z^2 - n^2)y = 0. \qquad \text{...(1)}$$

Let $z = \lambda_i x$.

$$\therefore \qquad \frac{dy}{dz} = \frac{dy}{dx} \cdot \frac{dx}{dz} = \frac{1}{\lambda_i} \frac{dy}{dx}$$

and
$$\frac{d^2y}{dz^2} = \frac{d}{dz}\left(\frac{1}{\lambda_i}\frac{dy}{dx}\right) = \frac{1}{\lambda_i}\frac{d^2y}{dx^2} \cdot \frac{1}{\lambda_i} = \frac{1}{\lambda_i^2}\frac{d^2y}{dx^2}.$$

$$\therefore \quad (1) \Rightarrow \lambda_i^2 x^2 \left(\frac{1}{\lambda_i^2}\frac{d^2y}{dx^2}\right) + \lambda_i x \left(\frac{1}{\lambda_i}\frac{dy}{dx}\right) + (\lambda_i^2 x^2 - n^2)\, y = 0$$

$$\Rightarrow \qquad x^2 \frac{d^2y}{dx^2} + x\frac{dy}{dx} + (\lambda_i^2 x^2 - n^2)\, y = 0 \qquad ...(2)$$

$\therefore$ $J_n(\lambda_i x)$ is a solution of (2). $(\because \; z = \lambda_i x)$

Let $u_i = J_n(\lambda_i x)$.

$\therefore$ We have $x^2 u_i'' + x u_i' + (\lambda_i^2 x^2 - n^2)\, u_i = 0$ ...(3)

Similarly, $x^2 u_j'' + x u_j' + (\lambda_j^2 x^2 - n^2)\, u_j = 0$ ...(4)

where $u_j = J_n(\lambda_j x)$.

Multiplying (3) by u_j and (4) by u_i and subtracting, we get

$$x^2 (u_j u_i'' - u_i u_j'') + x(u_j u_i' - u_i u_j') + x^2 u_i u_j (\lambda_i^2 - \lambda_j^2) = 0$$

$$\Rightarrow \quad x(u_j u_i'' - u_i u_j'') + u_j u_i' - u_i u_j' = x(\lambda_j^2 - \lambda_i^2)\, u_i u_j$$

$$\Rightarrow \quad x\frac{d}{dx}(u_j u_i' - u_i u_j') + (u_j u_i' - u_i u_j') = x(\lambda_j^2 - \lambda_i^2)\, u_i u_j$$

$$\Rightarrow \qquad \frac{d}{dx}[x(u_j u_i' - u_i u_j')] = x(\lambda_j^2 - \lambda_i^2)\, u_i u_j$$

Integrating w.r.t. x from 0 to R, we get

$$x(u_j u_i' - u_i u_j')\Big|_0^R = (\lambda_j^2 - \lambda_i^2)\int_0^R x\, u_i u_j \, dx$$

$$\Rightarrow \quad R\,(J_n(\lambda_j R)\, J_n'(\lambda_i R) - J_n(\lambda_i R)\, J_n'(\lambda_j R)) - 0 = (\lambda_j^2 - \lambda_i^2)\int_0^R x\, u_i u_j\, dx$$

$$\Rightarrow \qquad (\lambda_j^2 - \lambda_i^2)\int_0^R x\, u_i u_j\, dx = 0 \qquad (\because \; J_n(\lambda_i R) = 0,\; J_n(\lambda_j R) = 0)$$

$$\Rightarrow \qquad \int_0^R x\, J_n(\lambda_i x)\, J_n(\lambda_j x)\, dx = 0 \qquad (\because \; \lambda_i \neq \lambda_j)$$

$$\therefore \qquad \int_0^R x\, J_n(\lambda_i x)\, J_n(\lambda_j x)\, dx = 0 \quad \text{for } \lambda_i \neq \lambda_j$$

$\therefore$ **Bessel functions $J_n(\lambda_1 x)$, $J_n(\lambda_2 x)$, ... are orthogonal w.r.t. weight function 'x' on the interval [0, R].**

WORKING RULES FOR SOLVING PROBLEMS

Rule I. $e^{\frac{x}{2}\left(t-\frac{1}{t}\right)} = \sum_{n=-\infty}^{\infty} J_n(x)\, t^n$.

Rule II. (*i*) $\cos(x \sin \phi) = J_0 + 2J_2 \cos 2\phi + 2J_4 \cos 4\phi + \ldots\ldots$

(*ii*) $\sin(x \sin \phi) = 2J_1 \sin \phi + 2J_3 \sin 3\phi + 2J_5 \sin 5\phi + \ldots\ldots$

Rule III. $J_n(x) = \dfrac{1}{\pi}\displaystyle\int_0^{\pi} \cos(n\phi - x \sin \phi)\, d\phi$, where n is any integer.

Rule IV. (*i*) $\dfrac{d}{dx}(x^n J_n) = x^n J_{n-1}$ (*ii*) $\dfrac{d}{dx}(x^{-n} J_n) = -x^{-n} J_{n+1}$

(*iii*) $J_n = \dfrac{x}{2n}[J_{n-1} + J_{n+1}]$ (*iv*) $J_n' = \dfrac{1}{2}[J_{n-1} - J_{n+1}]$.

Rule V. Let n be any fixed non-negative integer and $R \in (0, \infty)$. If $\lambda_1, \lambda_2, \ldots\ldots$ are the roots of $J_n(\lambda R) = 0$, then the Bessel functions $J_n(\lambda_1 x), J_n(\lambda_2 x), \ldots\ldots$ are orthogonal w.r.t. weight function 'x' on $[0, R]$.

EXERCISE 2

1. Show that :

(*i*) $\cos x = J_0 - 2J_1 + 2J_4 + \ldots\ldots = J_0 + 2\displaystyle\sum_{n=1}^{\infty} (-1)^n J_{2n}$

(*ii*) $\sin x = 2J_1 - 2J_3 + 2J_5 + \ldots\ldots = 2\displaystyle\sum_{n=0}^{\infty} (-1)^n J_{2n+1}$.

2. Using $\sin(x \sin \phi) = 2J_1 \sin \phi + 2J_2 \sin 3\phi + 2J_5 \sin 5\phi + \ldots\ldots$, show that

$$x \cos x = 2(1^2 J_1 - 3^2 J_3 + 5^2 J_5 + \ldots\ldots).$$

3. Show that $J_0(x) = \dfrac{1}{\pi}\displaystyle\int_0^{\pi} \cos(x \sin \phi)\, d\phi = \dfrac{1}{\pi}\int_0^{\pi} \cos(x \cos \phi)\, d\phi$.

4. Express $J_4(x)$ in terms of $J_0(x)$ and $J_1(x)$.

5. Using $J_{1/2}(x) = \sqrt{\dfrac{2}{\pi x}} \sin x$ and $J_{-1/2}(x) = \sqrt{\dfrac{2}{\pi x}} \cos x$, show that :

(*i*) $J_{3/2}(x) = \sqrt{\dfrac{2}{\pi x}}\left(\dfrac{\sin x}{x} - \cos x\right)$ (*ii*) $J_{5/2}(x) = \sqrt{\dfrac{2}{\pi x}}\left(\dfrac{3-x^2}{x^2}\sin x - \dfrac{3}{x}\cos x\right)$.

(*KU 2006*)

6. Show that

$$J_0^2 + 2J_1^2 + 2J_2^2 + 2J_3^2 + \ldots\ldots = 1.$$

7. Show that

$$\int \frac{J_4(x)}{x}\, dx = -\left[\frac{1}{x} J_3(x) + \frac{2}{x^2} J_2(x)\right] + C$$

8. Show that $\int x J_0^2(x)\,dx = \dfrac{x^2}{2}[J_0^2(x) + J_1^2(x)] + C.$

9. (*i*) Show that $x^n J_n$ is a solution of $x\dfrac{d^2y}{dx^2} + (1-2n)\dfrac{dy}{dx} + xy = 0.$ (*CDLU 2004*)

(*ii*) Show that $x^{-n}J_n(x)$ is a solution of $x\dfrac{d^2y}{dx^2} + (1+2n)\dfrac{dy}{dx} + xy = 0.$ (*MDU 2005*)

Answers

4. $\left(\dfrac{48}{x^3} - \dfrac{8}{x}\right) J_1(x) + \left(-\dfrac{24}{x^2} + 1\right) J_0(x).$

Hints

1. Put $\phi = \dfrac{\pi}{2}$ in expressions for $\cos(x \sin \phi)$ and $\sin(x \sin \phi)$.

3. Integrate $\cos(x \sin \phi) = J_0 + 2J_2 \cos 2\phi - 2J_4 \cos 4\phi + \ldots\ldots$ w.r.t. ϕ between 0 and π.

Put $\theta = \dfrac{\pi}{2} - \phi$ to get the second equality.

8. $$\int J_0^2(x)\, x\, dx = \frac{1}{2}x^2 J_0^2(x) - \int x^2 J_0(x) J_0'(x)\,dx$$

Now $\dfrac{d}{dx}(x^{-n} J_n(x)) = -x^{-n} J_{n+1}$ implies $\dfrac{d}{dx}(J_0(x)) = -J_1(x).$

Also $\dfrac{d}{dx}(x^n J_n(x)) = x^n J_{n-1}$ implies $\dfrac{d}{dx}(x J_1(x)) = x J_0(x).$

$$\therefore \int x^2 J_0(x) J_0'(x)\,dx = -\int x^2 J_0(x) J_1(x)\,dx = -\int \left[x J_1(x) \frac{d}{dx}(x J_1(x))\right] dx.$$

9. (*i*) $y = x^n J_n \Rightarrow y' = (x^n J_n)' = x^n J_{n-1} \Rightarrow y'' = x^n J'_{n-1} + n x^{n-1} J_{n-1}.$

$$\therefore xy'' + (1-2n)y' + xy = x(x^n J'_{n-1} + n x^{n-1} J_{n-1}) + (1-2n)x^n J_{n-1} + x \,.\, x^n J_n$$

$$= x^{n+1} J'_{n-1} - (n-1)x^n J_{n-1} + x^{n+1} J_n = x^{n+1}\left[J'_{n-1} - \frac{n-1}{x} J_{n-1}\right] + x^{n+1} J_n$$

$$= x^{n+1}(-J_n) + x^{n+1} J_n = 0. \qquad \left(\text{By using } J'_n - \frac{n}{x} J_n = x^n J_n\right)$$

4

Hypergeometric Equation

1. INTRODUCTION

In this chapter, we shall study the third very important differential equation used very widely in applied mathematics. This differential equation is called Gauss hypergeometric equation* or simply hypergeometric equation.

2. HYPERGEOMETRIC EQUATION AND ITS SOLUTION

The hypergeometric equation is

$$x(1-x)\frac{d^2y}{dx^2}+[c-(a+b+1)\,x]\frac{dy}{dx}-aby=0, \quad \text{...(1)}$$

where a, b and c are constants.

Dividing (1) by $x(1-x)$, we get

$$\frac{d^2y}{dx^2}+\frac{c-(a+b+1)\,x}{x(1-x)}\frac{dy}{dx}-\frac{ab}{x(1-x)}\,y=0 \quad \text{...(2)}$$

Comparing (2) with $\dfrac{d^2y}{dx^2}+\text{P}(x)\dfrac{dy}{dx}+\text{Q}(x)=0$, we get

$$\text{P}(x)=\frac{c-(a+b+1)\,x}{x\,(1-x)} \quad \text{and} \quad \text{Q}(x)=-\frac{ab}{x\,(1-x)}\,.$$

'0' is not an ordinary point of (1) because neither P(x) nor Q(x) is analytic at 0.

Here $$x\,\text{P}(x)=\frac{c-(a+b+1)\,x}{1-x} \quad \text{and} \quad x^2\,\text{Q}(x)=-\frac{abx}{1-x}\,.$$

Both these functions are analytic at 0.

$\therefore$ '0' is a regular singular point of (1). We use *Frobenius method* to find the solution of (1) about '0'.

Let $$y=x^r\sum_{m=0}^{\infty}a_m\,x^m=\sum_{m=0}^{\infty}a_m\,x^{m+r},\quad a_0\neq 0 \quad \text{...(3)}$$

be a solution of (1), about '0'.

***Carl Friedrich Gauss** (1777—1855), German mathematician, who became the director of the observatory at Göttingen. His work was of basic importance in algebra, number theory, differential equations, astronomy and theoretical mechanics.

(3) $\Rightarrow$ $$\frac{dy}{dx} = \sum_{m=0}^{\infty} (m+r) a_m \, x^{m+r-1} \text{ and } \frac{d^2y}{dx^2} = \sum_{m=0}^{\infty} (m+r)(m+r-1) a_m \, x^{m+r-2}$$

Putting the values of y, $\frac{dy}{dx}$ and $\frac{d^2y}{dx^2}$ in (1), we get

$$x(1-x) \sum_{m=0}^{\infty} (m+r)(m+r-1) a_m \, x^{m+r-2}$$

$$+ [c-(a+b+1)x] \sum_{m=0}^{\infty} (m+r) a_m \, x^{m+r-1} - ab \sum_{m=0}^{\infty} a_m \, x^{m+r} = 0$$

$$\Rightarrow \quad \sum_{m=0}^{\infty} (m+r)(m+r-1) a_m \, x^{m+r-1} - \sum_{m=0}^{\infty} (m+r)(m+r-1) a_m \, x^{m+r}$$

$$+ c \sum_{m=0}^{\infty} (m+r) a_m \, x^{m+r-1} - (a+b+1) \sum_{m=0}^{\infty} (m+r) a_m \, x^{m+r} - ab \sum_{m=0}^{\infty} a_m \, x^{m+r} = 0$$

$$\Rightarrow \quad \sum_{m=0}^{\infty} (m+r)(m+r-1+c) a_m \, x^{m+r-1}$$

$$- \sum_{m=0}^{\infty} [(m+r)(m+r-1) + (a+b+1)(m+r) + ab] a_m \, x^{m+r} = 0$$

$$\Rightarrow \quad \sum_{m=-1}^{\infty} (m+r+1)(m+r+c) a_{m+1} \, x^{m+r} - \sum_{m=0}^{\infty} (m+r+a)(m+r+b) a_m \, x^{m+r} = 0$$

(By shifting of indices)

$$\Rightarrow \quad r(r+c-1) \, a_0 \, x^{r-1}$$

$$+ \sum_{m=0}^{\infty} [(m+r+1)(m+r+c) a_{m+1} - (m+r+a)(m+r+b) a_m] x^{m+r} = 0 \qquad \text{...(4)}$$

Equating to zero the coefficient of lowest power of x, we get $r(r+c-1) \, a_0 = 0$

$$\Rightarrow \quad r(r+c-1) = 0. \qquad (\because \; a_0 \neq 0)$$

This is the indicial equation and its roots are $r = 0, 1 - c$. We assume that c is not an integer.

$\therefore$ The roots are distinct and their difference is not an integer.

(4) $\Rightarrow$ $(m+r+1)(m+r+c) \, a_{m+1} - (m+r+a)(m+r+b) \, a_m = 0, \quad m \geq 0$

$$\Rightarrow \quad a_{m+1} = \frac{(m+r+a)(m+r+b) a_m}{(m+r+1)(m+r+c)}, m \geq 0 \qquad \text{...(5)}$$

Case I. r = 0

(5) $\Rightarrow$ $$a_{m+1} = \frac{(a+m)(b+m)}{(1+m)(c+m)} a_m, \; m \geq 0 \qquad \text{...(6)}$$

$m = 0$ in (6) $\Rightarrow$ $a_1 = \dfrac{ab}{c} a_0$

$m = 1$ in (6) $\Rightarrow$ $a_2 = \dfrac{(a+1)(b+1)}{2(c+1)} a_1 = \dfrac{a(a+1)b(b+1)}{2!c(c+1)} a_0$

$m = 2$ in (6) $\Rightarrow$ $a_3 = \dfrac{(a+2)(b+2)}{3(c+2)} a_2 = \dfrac{a(a+1)(a+2)b(b+1)(b+2)}{3!c(c+1)(c+2)} a_0$

....

Let y_1 be the series solution when $r = 0$.

$$\therefore \quad (3) \Rightarrow \quad y_1 = x^0 \left[a_0 + \frac{ab}{1!c} a_0 x + \frac{a(a+1)b(b+1)}{2!c(c+1)} a_0 x^2 + \frac{a(a+1)(a+2)b(b+1)(b+2)}{3!c(c+1)(c+2)} a_0 x^3 + \ldots\ldots \right]$$

$$\Rightarrow \quad y_1 = 1 + \frac{ab}{1!c} x + \frac{a(a+1)b(b+1)}{2!c(c+1)} x^2 + \frac{a(a+1)(a+2)b(b+1)(b+2)}{3!c(c+1)(c+2)} x^3 + \ldots\ldots$$

(Letting $a_0 = 1$)

Case II. r = 1 – c

$$(5) \Rightarrow \quad a_{m+1} = \frac{(m+1-c+a)(m+1-c+b)}{(m+1-c+1)(m+1-c+c)} a_m$$

$$\Rightarrow \quad a_{m+1} = \frac{(a'+m)(b'+m)}{(1+m)(c'+m)} a_m, \quad m \geq 0 \qquad \ldots(7)$$

where $\qquad a' = a + 1 - c,\ b' = b + 1 - c,\ c' = 2 - c.$

Let y_2 be the series solution when $r = 1 - c$.

Proceeding as in **Case I**, we get

$$y_2 = x^{1-c} \left[1 + \frac{a'b'}{1!c'} x + \frac{a'(a'+1)b'(b'+1)}{2!c'(c'+1)} x^2 + \frac{a'(a'+1)(a'+2)b'(b'+1)(b'+2)}{3!c'(c'+1)(c'+2)} x^3 + \ldots\ldots \right]$$

$\therefore$ The general solution is $y = C_1 y_1 + C_2 y_2$, where y_1 and y_2 are arbitrary constants.

Radius of convergence. For y_1, we have

$$\lim_{m \to \infty} \left| \frac{a_{m+1}}{a_m} \right| = \lim_{m \to \infty} \left| \frac{(a+m)(b+m)}{(1+m)(c+m)} \right| = \lim_{m \to \infty} \frac{\left| \frac{a}{m} + 1 \right| \left| \frac{b}{m} + 1 \right|}{\left| \frac{1}{m} + 1 \right| \left| \frac{c}{m} + 1 \right|} = 1.$$

$\therefore$ Radius of convergence $= \dfrac{1}{1} = 1$

$\therefore$ The solution y_1 is convergent in $|x| < 1$ *i.e.* in $-1 < x < 1$.

Similarly, the solution y_2 is convergent in $|x| < 1$.

Remark. If c is allowed to take positive integral values, then the power series y_1 and y_2 are solutions of (1) but the solutions y_1 and y_2 may not be linearly independent.

3. HYPERGEOMETRIC FUNCTIONS

We know that '0' is a regular singular point of the hypergeometric equation

$$x(1-x)\frac{d^2y}{dx^2}+[c-(a+b+1)x]\frac{dy}{dx}-aby=0, \quad ...(1)$$

where a, b and c are constants. Let $c \neq 0, -1, -2, ...$

$$\therefore \quad y_1 = 1+\frac{ab}{1!c}x+\frac{a(a+1)b(b+1)}{2!c(c+1)}x^2+\frac{a(a+1)(a+2)b(b+1)(b+2)}{3!c(c+1)(c+2)}x^3+......$$

is defined and we have already seen that it is a solution of the differential equation (1). The sum of this series is denoted by $F(a, b, c ; x)$ and is called the **hypergeometric function**.

If c is not an integer, then the other solution of (1) and linearly independent of the solution y_1 is $x^{1-c}F(a', b', c' ; x)$, where $a' = a+1-c$, $b' = b+1-c$ and $c' = 2-c$.

Thus if c is not an integer, then the general solution of the hypergeometric equation

$$x(1-x)\frac{d^2y}{dx^2}+[c-(a+b+1)x]\frac{dy}{dx}-aby=0 \text{ is}$$

$$y = C_1F(a, b, c ; x)+C_2x^{1-c}F(a+1-c, b+1-c, 2-c ; x),$$

where C_1 and C_2 are arbitrary constants.

Remarks 1. The hypergeometric function $F(a, b, c ; x)$ is defined only if (*i*) a, b are any real numbers (*ii*) c is any real number such that $c \neq 0, -1, -2, ...$ (*iii*) the variable x satisfies $|x| < 1$.

2. If either a or b is a negative integer, then $F(a, b, c ; x)$ reduces to a polynomial, because after some terms, the coefficient of each term will be zero. For example,

$$F(-2, b, c ; x) = 1+\frac{(-2)b}{c}x+\frac{(-2)(-1)b(b+1)}{2!c(c+1)}x^2+0+......$$

4. FACTORIAL FUNCTION

Let x be a variable taking real number values and $n \in \mathbf{N}$. The **factorial function** of x is denoted by $(x)_n$ and given by $x(x+1)(x+2)......(x+n-1)$. By definition, $(x)_0 = 1$.

Illustrations : (*i*) $(1)_n = 1(1+1)(1+2)......(1+n-1) = n!$

(*ii*) $(1/2)_4 = (1/2)(3/2)(5/2)(7/2) = 105/16$.

Remarks. $(x)_{n+1} = x(x+1)(x+2)......(x+n)$

$= [x(x+1)(x+2)......(x+n-1)](x+n) = (x)_n(x+n).$

Also, $(x)_{n+1} = x(x+1)(x+2)......(x+n)$

$= x[(x+1)(x+1+1)......(x+1+n-1)] = x.(x+1)_n.$

$\therefore$ $\mathbf{(x)_{n+1} = (x)_n(x+n)}$ **and** $\mathbf{(x)_{n+1} = x.(x+1)_n}$.

5. ALTERNATIVE FORM OF HYPERGEOMETRIC FUNCTION

If $F(a, b, c ; x)$ is denoted by $\sum_{m=0}^{\infty} a_m x^m$, then $a_0 = 1$ and for $m \geq 1$

$$a_m = \frac{a(a+1)...(a+m-1)b(b+1)...(b+m-1)}{m!c(c+1)...(c+m-1)}.$$

$$\therefore \quad a_m = \frac{(a)_m(b)_m}{m!(c)_m} \text{ for } m \geq 0$$

$$\therefore \quad \mathbf{F(a, b, c ; x)} = \sum_{m=0}^{\infty}\frac{(a)_m(b)_m}{(c)_m}\cdot\frac{x^m}{m!}.$$

6. PARTICULAR SOLUTION OF HYPERGEOMETRIC EQUATION

If a, b and c are real numbers such that $c \neq 0, -1, -2, \ldots\ldots$ then the hypergeometric equation

$$x(1-x)\frac{d^2y}{dx^2} + [c - (a+b+1)\,x]\frac{dy}{dx} - aby = 0$$

has a particular solution $y = F(a, b, c\,; x)$, where

$$F(a, b, c\,; x) = \sum_{m=0}^{\infty} \frac{(a)_m\,(b)_m}{(c)_m} \cdot \frac{x^m}{m!}.$$

Example 1. *Show that :*

(*i*) $F(1, b, b\,; x) = \dfrac{1}{1-x}$ (*ii*) $F(-n, b, b\,; -x) = (1+x)^n, \quad n \in \mathbf{N}$

(*iii*) $F\left(\dfrac{1}{2}, 1, \dfrac{3}{2}\,; x^2\right) = \dfrac{1}{2x}\log\dfrac{1+x}{1-x}$.

Sol. (*i*) Using $F(a, b, c\,; x) = 1 + \dfrac{ab}{1!\,c}x + \dfrac{a(a+1)\,b\,(b+1)}{2!\,c(c+1)}x^2 + \ldots\ldots$, we have

$$F(1, b, b\,; x) = 1 + \frac{1.\,b}{1!\,b}x + \frac{1.\,2.\,b(b+1)}{2!\,b\,(b+1)}x^2 + \ldots\ldots$$

$$= 1 + x + x^2 + \ldots\ldots = \mathbf{\frac{1}{1-x}}. \qquad (\because \quad |x| < 1)$$

(*ii*) Using $F(a, b, c\,; x) = 1 + \dfrac{ab}{1!\,c}x + \dfrac{a(a+1)\,b\,(b+1)}{2!\,c\,(c+1)}x^2 + \ldots\ldots$, we have

$$F(-n, b, b\,; -x) = 1 + \frac{(-n)\,b}{b}(-x) + \frac{(-n)(-n+1)\,b\,(b+1)}{2!\,b\,(b+1)}(-x)^2 + \ldots\ldots$$

$$= 1 + nx + \frac{(-n)(-n+1)}{2!}x^2 + \ldots\ldots + \frac{(-n)(-n+1)\ldots\ldots(-2)(-1)}{n!}(-x)^n + 0 + \ldots\ldots$$

$$= 1 + nx + \frac{n(n-1)}{2!}x^2 + \ldots\ldots + \frac{n(n-1)\ldots 2.\,1}{n!}x^n = \mathbf{(1+x)^n}.$$

(*iii*) Using $F(a, b, c, x) = 1 + \dfrac{ab}{1!\,c}x + \dfrac{a(a+1)\,b(b+1)}{2!\,c(c+1)}x^2 + \ldots\ldots$, we have

$$F\left(\frac{1}{2}, 1, \frac{3}{2}\,; x^2\right) = 1 + \frac{\frac{1}{2}.\,1}{\frac{3}{2}}x^2 + \frac{\frac{1}{2}.\frac{3}{2}.\,1.\,2}{2!.\frac{3}{2}.\frac{5}{2}}x^4 + \frac{\frac{1}{2}.\frac{3}{2}.\frac{5}{2}.\,1.\,2.\,3}{3!.\frac{3}{2}.\frac{5}{2}.\frac{7}{2}}x^6 + \ldots\ldots$$

$$= 1 + \frac{x^2}{3} + \frac{x^4}{5} + \frac{x^6}{7} + \ldots\ldots = \frac{1}{x}\left[x + \frac{x^3}{3} + \frac{x^5}{5} + \frac{x^7}{7} + \ldots\ldots\right]$$

$$= \frac{1}{x}.\frac{1}{2}\log\frac{1+x}{1-x} = \mathbf{\frac{1}{2x}\log\frac{1+x}{1-x}}.$$

Example 2. *Find the solution of the differential equation*

$$8x(1-x)\frac{d^2y}{dx^2}+(4-14x)\frac{dy}{dx}-y=0 \text{ about '0'.}$$

Sol. We have $$8x(1-x)\frac{d^2y}{dx^2}+(4-14x)\frac{dy}{dx}-y=0. \quad ...(1)$$

$$\Rightarrow \quad x(1-x)\frac{d^2y}{dx^2}+\left(\frac{1}{2}-\frac{7}{4}x\right)\frac{dy}{dx}-\frac{1}{8}y=0 \quad ...(2)$$

Comparing (2) with $x(1-x)\frac{d^2y}{dx^2}+[c-(a+b+1)x]\frac{dy}{dx}-aby=0$,

we get $$c=\frac{1}{2},\quad a+b+1=\frac{7}{4},\quad ab=\frac{1}{8}.$$

Solving, we get $$a=\frac{1}{2},\quad b=\frac{1}{4},\quad c=\frac{1}{2}.$$

Here c is not an integer.

∴ The general solution of (1) is $y = C_1y_1 + C_2y_2$, where

$y_1 = F(a, b, c ; x)$ and $y_2 = x^{1-c} F(a+1-c, b+1-c, 2-c ; x)$.

$$\therefore \quad y_1=F\left(\frac{1}{2},\frac{1}{4},\frac{1}{2};x\right)=1+\frac{\frac{1}{2}\cdot\frac{1}{4}}{1!\frac{1}{2}}x+\frac{\frac{1}{4}\cdot\frac{5}{4}}{2!}x^2+\frac{\frac{1}{4}\cdot\frac{5}{4}\cdot\frac{9}{4}}{3!}x^3+\ldots\ldots$$

$$=1+\left(-\frac{1}{4}\right)(-x)+\frac{\left(-\frac{1}{4}\right)\left(-\frac{1}{4}-1\right)}{2!}(-x)^2+\frac{\left(-\frac{1}{4}\right)\left(-\frac{5}{4}\right)\left(-\frac{9}{4}\right)}{3!}(-x)^3+\ldots\ldots$$

$$=(1-x)^{-1/4}.$$

$$y_2=x^{1-\frac{1}{2}}F\left(\frac{1}{2}+1-\frac{1}{2},\frac{1}{4}+1-\frac{1}{2},2-\frac{1}{2};x\right)=\sqrt{x}\,F\left(1,\frac{3}{4},\frac{3}{2};x\right).$$

∴ The general solution of (1) is $\mathbf{y = C_1(1-x)^{-1/4} + C_2\sqrt{x}\,F(1, 3/4, 3/2 ; x)}$, **where C_1 and C_2 are arbitrary constants.**

Example 3. *Solve the Legendre equation* $(1-x^2)\frac{d^2y}{dx^2}-2x\frac{dy}{dx}+n(n+1)y=0$ *by changing it to a hypergeometric equation.* (MDU 2004)

Sol. We have $$(1-x^2)\frac{d^2y}{dx^2}-2x\frac{dy}{dx}+n(n+1)y=0. \quad ...(1)$$

Let $z = x^2$.

$$\therefore \quad \frac{dy}{dx}=\frac{dy}{dz}\cdot 2x=2x\frac{dy}{dz}$$

and $$\frac{d^2y}{dx^2}=\frac{d}{dx}\left(2x\frac{dy}{dz}\right)=2x\frac{d^2y}{dz^2}\cdot 2x+2\frac{dy}{dz}=4z\frac{d^2y}{dz^2}+2\frac{dy}{dz}.$$

$$\therefore \quad (1) \Rightarrow \quad (1-z)\left(4z\frac{d^2y}{dz^2}+2\frac{dy}{dz}\right)-4z\frac{dy}{dz}+n(n+1)\,y=0$$

$$\Rightarrow \quad z(1-z)\frac{d^2y}{dz^2}+\left(\frac{1}{2}-\frac{3}{2}z\right)\frac{dy}{dz}+\frac{n\,(n+1)}{4}\,y=0 \qquad \text{...(2)}$$

Comparing (2) with $z(1-z)\dfrac{d^2y}{dz^2}+[c-(a+b+1)\,z]\dfrac{dy}{dz}-aby=0$, we get

$$c=\frac{1}{2},\quad a+b+1=\frac{3}{2},\quad ab=-\frac{n(n+1)}{4}.$$

Solving, we get $a=\dfrac{n+1}{2}, b=-\dfrac{n}{2}, c=\dfrac{1}{2}$.

Here c is not an integer.

$\therefore$ The general solution of (2) is

$$y=C_1\,F(a,b,c\,;z)+C_2\,z^{1-c}\,F(a+1-c,b+1-c,2-c\,;z).$$

$$\Rightarrow \quad y=C_1\,F\left(\frac{n+1}{2},-\frac{n}{2},\frac{1}{2};z\right)+C_2\,z^{1/2}\,F\left(\frac{n+1}{2}+1-\frac{1}{2},-\frac{n}{2}+1-\frac{1}{2},2-\frac{1}{2};z\right)$$

or

$$\mathbf{y=C_1\,F\left(\frac{n+1}{2},-\frac{n}{2},\frac{1}{2};x^2\right)+C_2\,x\,F\left(\frac{n+2}{2},-\frac{n-1}{2},\frac{3}{2};x^2\right)}.$$

This represents the general solution of the given Legendre equation.

WORKING RULES FOR SOLVING PROBLEMS

Rule I. Hypergeometric equation is $x(1-x)\dfrac{d^2y}{dx^2}+[c-(a+b+1)\,x]\dfrac{dy}{dx}-aby=0$,

where a, b, c are constants.

Rule II. If $c \neq 0, -1, -2, \ldots\ldots$, then $y=F(a,b,c\,;x)=\displaystyle\sum_{m=0}^{\infty}\frac{(a)_m\,(b)_m}{(c)_m}\cdot\frac{x^m}{m!}$ is a particular solution of the hypergeometric equation. If c is not an integer then another solution, linearly independent of the solution $y=F(a,b,c\,;x)$ is given by

$$y=x^{1-c}\,F(a+1-c,b+1-c,2-c\,;x).$$

Rule III. The solution of hypergeometric equation is convergent for $|x|<1$.

Rule IV. $F(a,b,c\,;x)$ is called a hypergeometric function, where a, b, c are constants and $c \neq 0, -1, -2, \ldots\ldots$ and $|x|<1$.

EXERCISE 1

1. Show that $F(1,1,1\,;x)=F(a,1,a\,;x)=\dfrac{1}{1-x}$.
2. Show that $1-nx\,F(1-n,1,2\,;x)=(1-x)^n$, $n \in \mathbf{N}$.

3. Show that $xF(1, 1, 2\,; -x) = \log(1 + x)$.
4. Show that $-xF(1, 1, 2\,; x) = \log(1 - x)$.
5. Show that $\lim\limits_{a \to \infty} F\left(1, a, 1\,; \dfrac{x}{a}\right) = e^x$.
6. Show that $\lim\limits_{a, b \to \infty} F\left(a, b, \dfrac{1}{2}\,; \dfrac{x^2}{4ab}\right) = \cosh x$.
7. Find the solution of the following differential equations :

(*i*) $4x(1-x)\dfrac{d^2y}{dx^2} + \dfrac{dy}{dx} + 8y = 0$ about '0'.

(*ii*) $x(1-x)\dfrac{d^2y}{dx^2} + \left(\dfrac{3}{2} - 2x\right)\dfrac{dy}{dx} + 2y = 0$ about '0'. (*KU 2004 S*)

(*iii*) $(x - x^2)\dfrac{d^2y}{dx^2} + \left(\dfrac{3}{2} - 2x\right)\dfrac{dy}{dx} - \dfrac{1}{4}y = 0$ about '0'. (*KU 2004*)

Answers

7. (*i*) $y = C_1\left(1 - 8x + \dfrac{32}{5}x^2\right) + C_2\, x^{3/4}\, F\left(\dfrac{7}{4}, -\dfrac{5}{4}, \dfrac{7}{4}\,; x\right)$

(*ii*) $y = C_1\left(1 - \dfrac{4}{3}x\right) + C_2\, x^{-1/2}\, F\left(\dfrac{3}{2}, -\dfrac{3}{2}, \dfrac{1}{2}\,; x\right)$

(*iii*) $y = C_1\, F\left(\dfrac{1}{2}, \dfrac{1}{2}, \dfrac{3}{2}\,; x\right) + \dfrac{C_2}{\sqrt{x}}$.

Hints

7. (*i*) We have $c = \dfrac{1}{4}, a + b + 1 = 0, ab = -2$.

7. PROPERTIES OF HYPERGEOMETRIC FUNCTIONS

(*i*) **F(a, b, c ; x) = F(b, a, c ; x).**

Proof.
$$F(a, b, c\,; x) = \sum_{m=0}^{\infty} \frac{(a)_m\,(b)_m}{(c)_m}\cdot\frac{x^m}{m!} = \sum_{m=0}^{\infty} \frac{(b)_m\,(a)_m}{(c)_m}\cdot\frac{x^m}{m!}$$
$$= F(b, a, c\,; x).$$

$\therefore$ **F(a, b, c ; x) = F(b, a, c ; x).**

(*ii*) $\dfrac{\mathbf{d}}{\mathbf{dx}}\,\mathbf{F(a, b, c\,; x)} = \dfrac{\mathbf{ab}}{\mathbf{c}}\,\mathbf{F(a+1, b+1, c+1\,; x)}$. (*KU 2006*)

Proof.
$$\frac{d}{dx}F(a, b, c\,; x) = \frac{d}{dx}\sum_{m=0}^{\infty} \frac{(a)_m\,(b)_m}{(c)_m}\cdot\frac{x^m}{m!}$$
$$= 0 + \sum_{m=1}^{\infty} \frac{(a)_m\,(b)_m}{(c)_m}\cdot\frac{mx^{m-1}}{m!} = \sum_{m=1}^{\infty} \frac{(a)_m\,(b)_m}{(c)_m}\cdot\frac{x^{m-1}}{(m-1)!}$$
$$= \sum_{m=0}^{\infty} \frac{(a)_{m+1}\,(b)_{m+1}}{(c)_{m+1}}\cdot\frac{x^m}{m!} \qquad \text{(By shifting of index } m\text{)}$$

$$= \sum_{m=0}^{\infty} \frac{a(a+1)_m\, b(b+1)_m}{c(c+1)_m} \cdot \frac{x^m}{m!} = \frac{ab}{c} \sum_{m=0}^{\infty} \frac{(a+1)_m (b+1)_m}{(c+1)_m} \cdot \frac{x^m}{m!}$$

$$= \frac{ab}{c} \mathrm{F}(a+1, b+1, c+1\,; x).$$

$$\therefore \quad \frac{\mathbf{d}}{\mathbf{dx}} \mathbf{F(a, b, c\,; x)} = \frac{\mathbf{ab}}{\mathbf{c}} \mathbf{F(a+1, b+1, c+1; x)}.$$

(*iii*) $$\frac{\mathbf{d^n}}{\mathbf{dx^n}} \mathbf{F(a, b, c\,; x)} = \frac{\mathbf{(a)_n (b)_n}}{\mathbf{(c)_n}} \mathbf{F(a+n, b+n, c+n\,; x)}.$$

Proof. We shall prove this result by using P.M.I. on n.

By property (*ii*), the result is true for $n = 1$.

Let the result be true for $n = k$.

$$\therefore \quad \frac{d^k}{dx^k} \mathrm{F}(a, b, c\,; x) = \frac{(a)_k (b)_k}{(c)_k} \mathrm{F}(a+k, b+k, c+k\,; x) \quad \ldots(1)$$

Let $n = k + 1$.

$$\frac{d^{k+1}}{dx^{k+1}} \mathrm{F}(a, b, c\,; x) = \frac{d}{dx}\left[\frac{d^k}{dx^k} \mathrm{F}(a, b, c\,; x)\right]$$

$$= \frac{d}{dx}\left[\frac{(a)_k (b)_k}{(c)_k} \mathrm{F}(a+k, b+k, c+k\,; x)\right] \quad \text{(By using (1))}$$

$$= \frac{(a)_k (b)_k}{(c)_k} \frac{d}{dx} \mathrm{F}(a+k, b+k, c+k\,; x)$$

$$= \frac{(a)_k (b)_k}{(c)_k} \cdot \frac{(a+k)(b+k)}{c+k} \mathrm{F}(a+k+1, b+k+1, c+k+1\,; x)$$

(By using property (*ii*))

$$= \frac{(a)_{k+1} (b)_{k+1}}{(c)_{k+1}} \mathrm{F}(a+k+1, b+k+1, c+k+1\,; x).$$

∴ The result is true for $n = k + 1$.

∴ By P.M.I., the result is true for $n = 1, 2, 3, \ldots\ldots$

$$\therefore \quad \frac{\mathbf{d^n}}{\mathbf{dx^n}} \mathbf{F(a, b, c\,; x)} = \frac{\mathbf{(a)_n (b)_n}}{\mathbf{(c)_n}} \mathbf{F(a+n, b+n, c+n\,; x)}.$$

Remark. $$\left.\frac{d^n}{dx^n} \mathrm{F}(a, b, c\,; x)\right|_{x=0} = \frac{(a)_n (b)_n}{(c)_n} \mathrm{F}(a+n, b+n, c+n\,; 0)$$

$$= \frac{(a)_n (b)_n}{(c)_n}\left[1 + \frac{(a+n)(b+n)}{1!(c+n)}(0) + \frac{(a+n)(a+n+1)(b+n)(b+n+1)}{2!(c+n)(c+n+1)}(0)^2 + \ldots\ldots\right] = \frac{(a)_n (b_n)}{c_n}.$$

$$\therefore \quad \left.\frac{\mathbf{d^n}}{\mathbf{dx^n}} \mathbf{F(a, b, c\,; x)}\right|_{\mathbf{x=0}} = \frac{\mathbf{(a)_n (b)_n}}{\mathbf{(c)_n}}.$$

(*iv*) $$\mathbf{F(a, b, c\,; x)} = \frac{1}{\mathbf{B(b, c-b)}} \int_0^1 \mathbf{t^{b-1}\,(1-t)^{c-b-1}\,(1-xt)^{-a}\,dt}.$$

Proof. For $m \in \mathbf{N}$, $$(\alpha)_m = \alpha\,(\alpha+1)\,......\,(\alpha+m-1)$$

$$= \frac{\Gamma(\alpha)\,\alpha\,(\alpha+1)......(\alpha+m-1)}{\Gamma(\alpha)} = \frac{\Gamma(\alpha+m)}{\Gamma(\alpha)}.$$

$\therefore$ $$(\alpha)_m = \frac{\Gamma(\alpha+m)}{\Gamma(\alpha)} \text{ for } m \in \mathbf{N}.$$

Now $$F(a, b, c\,; x) = \sum_{m=0}^{\infty} \frac{(a)_m\,(b)_m}{(c)_m} \cdot \frac{x^m}{m!} = \sum_{m=0}^{\infty} (a)_m \cdot \frac{\Gamma(b+m)}{\Gamma(b)} \cdot \frac{\Gamma(c)}{\Gamma(c+m)} \cdot \frac{x^m}{m!}$$

$$= \frac{\Gamma(c)}{\Gamma(b)} \sum_{m=0}^{\infty} (a)_m \cdot \frac{\Gamma(b+m)}{\Gamma(c+m)} \cdot \frac{x^m}{m!}$$

$$= \frac{\Gamma(c)}{\Gamma(b)\,\Gamma(c-b)} \sum_{m=0}^{\infty} (a)_m \cdot \frac{\Gamma(b+m)\,\Gamma(c-b)}{\Gamma(b+m+c-b)} \cdot \frac{x^m}{m!}$$

$$= \frac{\Gamma(b+c-b)}{\Gamma(b)\,\Gamma(c-b)} \sum_{m=0}^{\infty} (a)_m \,.\, B(b+m, c-b)\,.\,\frac{x^m}{m!}$$

(Assuming $b + m > 0$, $c - b > 0$)

$$= \frac{1}{B(b, c-b)} \sum_{m=0}^{\infty} (a)_m \cdot \left[\int_0^1 t^{b+m-1}\,(1-t)^{c-b-1}\,dt\right] \frac{x^m}{m!}$$

$$= \frac{1}{B(b, c-b)} \int_0^1 \left(t^{b-1}\,(1-t)^{c-b-1} \sum_{m=0}^{\infty} \frac{(a)_m\,(xt)^m}{m!}\right) dt$$

$$= \frac{1}{B(b, c-b)} \int_0^1 t^{b-1}\,(1-t)^{c-b-1}\,(1-xt)^{-a}\,dt.$$

(By using Binomial theorem)

$$\therefore\ \mathbf{F(a, b, c\,; x)} = \frac{1}{\mathbf{B(b, c-b)}} \int_0^1 \mathbf{t^{b-1}\,(1-t)^{c-b-1}\,(1-xt)^{-a}\,dt}.$$

Note. Beta function, B(m, n). If m and n are positive real numbers, then the integral $\int_0^1 t^{m-1}\,(1-t)^{n-1}\,dt$ is called a **Beta function** and is denoted by $B(m, n)$. In terms of Gamma functions :

$$B\,(m, n) = \frac{\Gamma(m)\,\Gamma(n)}{\Gamma(m+n)}. \text{ Also, } \quad B(m, n) = B\,(n, m).$$

Example 1. *Find the third derivative of the hypergeometric function F (2, 3, 1 ; x), w.r.t. x.*

Sol. We have $$\frac{d^3}{dx^3} F(2, 3, 1\,; x) = \frac{(2)_3\,(3)_3}{(1)_3} F(2+3, 3+3, 1+3\,; x) \qquad \text{(By property (}iii\text{))}$$

$$= \frac{2\,.\,3\,.\,4\,.\,3\,.\,4\,.\,5}{1\,.\,2\,.\,3} F(5, 6, 4\,; x) = \mathbf{240\ F(5, 6, 4\,; x)}.$$

8. GAUSS THEOREM

Prove that $\mathbf{F(a, b, c\,;1) = \dfrac{\Gamma(c)\,\Gamma(c-a-b)}{\Gamma(c-a)\,\Gamma(c-b)}}$ **where** $\mathbf{c > a, c > b, c > a+b, b > 0, c > 0.}$

Proof. We have $F(a, b, c\,; x) = \dfrac{1}{B(b, c-b)} \displaystyle\int_0^1 t^{b-1}(1-t)^{c-b-1}(1-xt)^{-a}\, dt.$

(By property (*iv*))

$$\therefore \quad F(a, b, c\,; 1) = \frac{\Gamma(b+c-b)}{\Gamma(b)\,\Gamma(c-b)} \int_0^1 t^{b-1}(1-t)^{c-b-1}(1-t)^{-a}\, dt$$

$$= \frac{\Gamma(c)}{\Gamma(b)\,\Gamma(c-b)} \int_0^1 t^{b-1}(1-t)^{c-a-b-1}\, dt$$

$$= \frac{\Gamma(c)}{\Gamma(b)\,\Gamma(c-b)} . B(b, c-a-b) = \frac{\Gamma(c)}{\Gamma(b)\,\Gamma(c-b)} . \frac{\Gamma(b)\,\Gamma(c-a-b)}{\Gamma(b+c-a-b)}$$

$$\therefore \quad \mathbf{F(a, b, c\,; 1) = \frac{\Gamma(c)\,\Gamma(c-a-b)}{\Gamma(c-a)\,\Gamma(c-b)}}.$$

9. VANDERMONDE THEOREM

Prove that $\mathbf{F(-n, b, c\,; 1) = \dfrac{(c-b)_n}{(c)_n}}$**, where** $\mathbf{n \in N, c > -n, c > b, c > b-n,}$ $\mathbf{b > 0, c > 0.}$

Proof. By *Gauss theorem*, we have $F(-n, b, c\,; 1) = \dfrac{\Gamma(c)\,\Gamma(c+n-b)}{\Gamma(c+n)\,\Gamma(c-b)}.$

$$= \frac{\Gamma(c)}{\Gamma(c-b)} . \frac{(c-b+n-1)(c-b+n-2)......(c-b)\,\Gamma(c-b)}{(c+n-1)(c+n-2)......c\,\Gamma(c)}$$

$$= \frac{(c-b+n-1)(c-b+n-2)......(c-b)}{(c+n-1)(c+n-2)......c}$$

$$= \frac{(c-b)(c-b+1)......(c-b+n-2)(c-b+n-1)}{c(c+1)......(c+n-2)(c+n-1)} = \frac{(c-b)_n}{(c)_n}.$$

$$\therefore \quad \mathbf{F(-n, b, c\,; 1) = \frac{(c-b)_n}{(c)_n}}.$$

Example 2. *Prove that* $F\left(-n, n+1, 1; \dfrac{1-x}{2}\right) = P_n(x)$, *where* $P_n(x)$ *is the Legendre function of the order n.*

Sol. By *Rodrigue's formula*, we have $P_n(x) = \dfrac{1}{n!\,2^n} \dfrac{d^n}{dx^n}(x^2-1)^n.$

$$\therefore \quad P_n(x) = \frac{(-1)^n}{n!\,2^n} \frac{d^n}{dx^n}(1-x^2)^n$$

$$= \frac{(-1)^n}{n!} \frac{d^n}{dx^n}\left[(1-x)^n \left(\frac{1+x}{2}\right)^n\right] = \frac{(-1)^n}{n!} \frac{d^n}{dx^n}\left[(1-x)^n \left(1 - \frac{1-x}{2}\right)^n\right]$$

$$= \frac{(-1)^n}{n!} \frac{d^n}{dx^n}\left[(1-x)^n \left\{1 - n\left(\frac{1-x}{2}\right) + \frac{n(n-1)}{2!}\left(\frac{1-x}{2}\right)^2 + \ldots\ldots + (-1)^n \left(\frac{1-x}{2}\right)^n\right\}\right]$$

$$= \frac{(-1)^n}{n!} \frac{d^n}{dx^n}\left[(1-x)^n - \frac{n}{2}(1-x)^{n+1} + \frac{n(n-1)}{2!\,2^2}(1-x)^{n+2} + \ldots\ldots + \frac{(-1)^n}{2^n}(1-x)^{2n}\right]$$

$$= \frac{(-1)^n}{n!}\left[(-1)^n\, n! - (-1)^n \cdot \frac{n}{2} \cdot \frac{(n+1)!}{1!}(1-x) + (-1)^n \cdot \frac{n(n-1)}{2!\,2^2} \cdot \frac{(n+2)!}{2!}(1-x)^2 \right.$$

$$\left. + \ldots\ldots + \frac{(-1)^n}{2^n} \cdot (-1)^n \cdot \frac{(2n)!}{n!}(1-x)^n\right]$$

$$= \frac{(-1)^{2n}}{n!}\left[n! - \frac{n(n+1)}{2} n!(1-x) + \frac{n(n-1)(n+2)(n+1) \cdot n!}{2!\,2!\,2^2}(1-x)^2 \right.$$

$$\left. + \ldots\ldots + \frac{(-1)^n}{2^n} \cdot \frac{2n \cdot (2n-1) \ldots\ldots (n+1) \cdot n!}{n!}(1-x)^n\right]$$

$$= 1 - n(n+1)\left(\frac{1-x}{2}\right) + \frac{n(n-1)(n+2)(n+1)}{2!\,2!}\left(\frac{1-x}{2}\right)^2$$

$$+ \ldots\ldots + \frac{(-1)^n\, 2n(2n-1) \ldots\ldots (n+1)}{n!}\left(\frac{1-x}{2}\right)^n$$

$$= 1 + \frac{(-n)(n+1)}{1!(1)}\left(\frac{1-x}{2}\right) + \frac{(-n)(-n+1)(n+1)(n+2)}{(2!)1 \cdot 2}\left(\frac{1-x}{2}\right)^2$$

$$+ \ldots\ldots + \frac{(-n)(-n+1) \ldots\ldots (-n+n-1)(n+1)(n+2) \ldots\ldots 2n}{(n!)1 \cdot 2 \ldots\ldots n}\left(\frac{1-x}{2}\right)^n$$

$$= \mathrm{F}\left(-n, n+1, 1; \frac{1-x}{2}\right).$$

$$\therefore \quad \mathbf{P_n(x) = F\left(-n, n+1, 1; \frac{1-x}{2}\right).}$$

WORKING RULES FOR SOLVING PROBLEMS

Rule I. $\mathrm{F}(a, b, c; x) = \mathrm{F}(b, a, c; x)$.

Rule II. $\dfrac{d}{dx}\mathrm{F}(a, b, c; x) = \dfrac{ab}{c}\mathrm{F}(a+1, b+1, c+1; x)$.

Rule III. $\dfrac{d^n}{dx^n}\mathrm{F}(a, b, c; x) = \dfrac{(a)_n\,(b)_n}{(c)_n}\mathrm{F}(a+n, b+n, c+n; x)$.

Rule IV. $\mathrm{F}(a, b, c; x) = \dfrac{1}{\mathrm{B}(b, c-b)}\displaystyle\int_0^1 t^{b-1}(1-t)^{c-b-1}(1-xt)^{-a}\,dt$.

Rule V. **Gauss Theorem.** $F(a, b, c\,;1) = \dfrac{\Gamma(c)\,\Gamma(c-a-b)}{\Gamma(c-a)\,\Gamma(c-b)}$, where $c > a, c > b, c > a + b,$ $b > 0, c > 0.$

Rule VI. **Vandermonde Theorem.** $F(-n, b, c\,;1) = \dfrac{(c-b)_n}{(c)_n}$, where $n \in \mathbf{N}, c > -n, c > b,$ $c > b - n, b > 0, c > 0.$

EXERCISE 2

1. Show that $\left[\dfrac{d}{dx} F(a,b,c\,;x)\right]_{x=0} = \dfrac{ab}{c}$.
2. Find the second derivative of the following hypergeometric functions w.r.t. x :
   (*i*) $F(2, 1, 1\,; x)$ (*ii*) $F(2, 5, 3\,; x)$.
3. Find the fourth derivative of the following hypergeometric functions w.r.t. x :
   (*i*) $F(2, 1, 4\,; x)$ (*ii*) $F(2, -2, 5\,; x)$.
4. Show that $\dfrac{2}{\pi}\displaystyle\int_0^{\pi/2} \frac{d\theta}{\sqrt{1-x^2\sin^2\theta}} = F\left(\frac{1}{2}, \frac{1}{2}, 1\,; x^2\right), |x| < 1$.
5. Show that $\dfrac{2}{\pi}\displaystyle\int_0^{\pi/2} \sqrt{1-x^2\sin^2\theta}\,d\theta = F\left(-\frac{1}{2}, \frac{1}{2}, 1\,; x^2\right), |x| < 1$.

Answers

2. (*i*) $6\,F(4, 3, 3\,; x)$ (*ii*) $15\,F(4, 7, 5\,; x)$ 3. (*i*) $\dfrac{24}{7}\,F(6, 5, 8\,; x)$ (*ii*) 0.

Hints

5. Try $t = \sin^2\theta$.

5

Sturm-Liouville Problems

1. INTRODUCTION

In the present chapter, we shall study the solution of a special type of second order differential equations with given conditions. This type of differential equations with given conditions are called Sturm-Liouville problems.* These problems will introduce us to the concepts of 'eigen value' and 'eigen function'.

2. STURM-LIOUVILLE PROBLEM

A second order differential equation of the form

$$\frac{d}{dx}\left[p(x)\frac{dy}{dx}\right]+[q(x)+\lambda r(x)]\,y=0 \qquad \text{...(1)}$$

where $p(x)$, $q(x)$, $r(x)$ are real functions and $p(x)$, $p'(x)$, $q(x)$, $r(x)$ are continuous functions and $p(x)>0$, $r(x)>0$ on an interval $[a, b]$ and λ is a parameter independent of x and two conditions

$$\left.\begin{aligned} A_1y(a)+A_2y'(a)=0 \\ B_1y(b)+B_2y'(b)=0 \end{aligned}\right] \qquad \text{...(2)}$$

where A_1, A_2, B_1, B_2 are real constants such that A_1 and A_2 are not both zero and B_1 and B_2 are not both zero is called a **Sturm-Liouville problem.**

The equation (1) is called a **Sturm-Liouville equation.** The conditions (2) are called **boundary conditions** at the end points a and b of the interval $[a, b]$. A problem containing a given differential equation with given boundary conditions is called a **boundary value problem.**

Remarks 1. If A_2 and B_2 are zero then the boundary conditions take the form $y(a)=0$, $y(b)=0$.

2. If A_1 and B_1 are zero, then the boundary conditions take the form $y'(a)=0$, $y'(b)=0$.

Illustration : Consider the equation $\quad \dfrac{d^2y}{dx^2}+\lambda y=0 \qquad$ ...(1)

with the conditions $y(0)=0$, $y(\pi)=0$.

(1) can be written as $\quad \dfrac{d}{dx}\left[1.\dfrac{dy}{dx}\right]+[0+\lambda.1]\,y=0$

$\therefore$ (1) is a Sturm-Liouville equation with $\quad p(x)=1, q(x)=0, r(x)=1.$

---

*__Jacques Charles Francois Sturm__ (1803—1855), was born in Switzerland and became the successor of Poisson in the chair of mechanics at the Sorbonne.

Joseph Liouville (1809—1882), professor of mathematics in Paris and is known for his work in special functions, complex analysis and number theory.

Also, the given conditions can be written as

$$A_1 y(a) + A_2 y'(a) = 0$$

and

$$B_1 y(b) + B_2 y'(b) = 0$$

with

$$A_1 = 1, A_2 = 0, B_1 = 1, B_2 = 0, a = 0, b = \pi.$$

$\therefore$ The given boundary value problem is a Sturm-Liouville problem.

3. EIGENVALUE AND EIGENFUNCTION

For a Sturm-Liouville problem, a non-zero solution, if it exists, is called an **eigen function** of the Sturm-Liouville problem and the value of the parameter λ, for which an eigen function exists, is called an **eigenvalue** of the problem.

Remarks 1. For a Sturm-Liouville problem, $y = 0$, is always a solution. This solution is called the trivial solution of the problem.

2. The eigenfunction and eigenvalue of a Sturm-Liouville problem are also called **characteristic function** and **characteristic value** respectively.

4. REALITY OF EIGENVALUES

Theorem 1. The eigenvalues of a Sturm-Liouville problem are always real.

Theorem 2. For the Sturm-Liouville problem given above, there exists an infinite number of eigenvalues λ_n. These eigenvalues λ_n can be arranged in an increasing sequence

$$\lambda_1 < \lambda_2 < \lambda_3 < \ldots\ldots$$

such that $\lambda_n \to \infty$ as $n \to \infty$. Also, corresponding to each eigenvalue λ_n there exists a one-parameter family of eigenfunctions. Each of these eigenfunctions is defined on $a \le x \le b$, and any two eigenfunctions corresponding to the same eigenvalue are non-zero constant multiple of each other.

Note. The proofs of the above theorems are beyond the scope of this book.

Example 1. *Solve the Sturm-Liouville problem :*

$$\frac{d^2y}{dx^2} + \lambda y = 0 \text{ with } y(0) = 0, y(\pi) = 0.$$

Sol. We have

$$\frac{d^2y}{dx^2} + \lambda y = 0. \qquad \ldots(1)$$

The boundary conditions are $y(0) = 0, y(\pi) = 0$.

The parameter λ is either zero or negative or positive.

Case I. $\lambda = 0$.

In this case, (1) $\Rightarrow$ $\dfrac{d^2y}{dx^2} = 0.$

$\Rightarrow$ $y = C_1 x + C_2$, where C_1 and C_2 are arbitrary constants.

$$y(0) = 0 \Rightarrow C_1(0) + C_2 = 0 \Rightarrow C_2 = 0$$

$$y(\pi) = 0 \Rightarrow C_1\pi + C_2 = 0 \Rightarrow C_1 = 0. \qquad (\because C_2 = 0 \text{ and } \pi \neq 0)$$

$\therefore$ $\mathbf{y = 0.}$

$\therefore$ Given problem has only the trivial solution.

Case II. $\lambda < 0$. The A.E. of (1) is $D^2 + \lambda = 0$.

Its roots are $\pm\sqrt{-\lambda}$ and these are real and distinct.

$\therefore$ Solution of (1) is $y = C_1 e^{\sqrt{-\lambda}\,x} + C_2 e^{-\sqrt{-\lambda}\,x}$.

$$y(0) = 0 \Rightarrow C_1 + C_2 = 0$$

and $$y(\pi) = 0 \Rightarrow C_1 e^{\sqrt{-\lambda}\,\pi} + C_2 e^{-\sqrt{-\lambda}\,\pi} = 0$$

Solving these equations, we get $C_1 = 0$, $C_2 = 0$.

$\therefore$ $\mathbf{y = 0.}$

$\therefore$ Given problem has only the trivial solution.

Case III. $\boldsymbol{\lambda > 0}$. In this case, the roots of the A.E. are $\pm\sqrt{\lambda}\, i$ and these are imaginary numbers.

$\therefore$ Solution of (1) is $y = C_1 \cos \sqrt{\lambda}\, x + C_2 \sin \sqrt{\lambda}\, x$

$$y(0) = 0 \Rightarrow C_1 \cos 0 + C_2 \sin 0 = 0 \Rightarrow C_1 = 0$$

$$y(\pi) = 0 \Rightarrow C_1 \cos \sqrt{\lambda}\, \pi + C_2 \sin \sqrt{\lambda}\, \pi = 0$$

$$\Rightarrow C_2 \sin \sqrt{\lambda}\, \pi = 0. \qquad (\because C_1 = 0)$$

$\therefore$ In order to get non-trivial solution, we should have $\sin \sqrt{\lambda}\, \pi = 0$ for otherwise C_2 and hence y would become '0'.

Now $\sin \sqrt{\lambda}\, \pi = 0 \Rightarrow \sqrt{\lambda} = 1, 2, 3, \ldots\ldots \qquad (\because \lambda > 0)$

$$\Rightarrow \lambda = 1, 4, 9, \ldots\ldots \text{ i.e., } \lambda = n^2, n \in \mathbf{N}$$

$\therefore$ If $\lambda = n^2, n \in \mathbf{N}$, then the given problem has non-trivial solution given by $y = C_2 \sin \sqrt{\lambda}\, x$, where $C_2 \neq 0$.

Thus the given problem has non-trivial solution only when $\lambda = n^2$, $n \in \mathbf{N}$ and for $\lambda = n^2, n \in \mathbf{N}$, the solution is $\mathbf{y = k_n \sin nx}$, where $\mathbf{k_n}$ is an arbitrary non-zero constant.

Remark. The eigenvalues of the above problem are 1, 4, 9, ... and the corresponding eigenfunctions are $k_1 \sin x$, $k_2 \sin 2x$, $k_3 \sin 3x$, ...

Example 2. *Show that Legendre equation and Bessel equation can be expressed as Sturm-Liouville equations.*

Sol. (*i*) The Legendre equation is

$$(1 - x^2)\frac{d^2y}{dx^2} - 2x\frac{dy}{dx} + n(n+1)\, y = 0. \qquad \ldots(1)$$

$$\Rightarrow \frac{d}{dx}\left[(1 - x^2)\frac{dy}{dx}\right] + n(n+1)\, y = 0$$

This equation can be written as Sturm-Liouville equation

$$\frac{d}{dx}\left[p(x)\frac{dy}{dx}\right] + [q(x) + \lambda r(x)]\, y = 0,$$

where $p(x) = 1 - x^2$, $q(x) = 0$, $r(x) = 1$ and the parameter is $\lambda = n(n + 1)$.

(*ii*) The Bessel equation of order n is

$$x^2\frac{d^2y}{dx^2} + x\frac{dy}{dx} + (x^2 - n^2)y = 0. \qquad \ldots(2)$$

Let $x = kz$.

$$\therefore \quad \frac{dy}{dx} = \frac{dy}{dz} \cdot \frac{1}{k} \quad \text{and} \quad \frac{d^2y}{dx^2} = \frac{d^2y}{dz^2} \cdot \frac{1}{k^2}.$$

$$\therefore \quad (2) \Rightarrow \quad \frac{x^2}{k^2}\frac{d^2y}{dz^2} + \frac{x}{k}\frac{dy}{dz} + (x^2 - n^2)y = 0$$

$$\Rightarrow \quad z^2\frac{d^2y}{dz^2} + z\frac{dy}{dz} + (k^2z^2 - n^2)y = 0$$

$$\Rightarrow \quad z\frac{d^2y}{dz^2} + \frac{dy}{dz} + \left(k^2z - \frac{n^2}{z}\right)y = 0$$

$$\Rightarrow \quad \frac{d}{dz}\left[z\frac{dy}{dz}\right] + \left[-\frac{n^2}{z} + k^2z\right]y = 0$$

This equation can be written as Sturm-Liouville equation

$$\frac{d}{dz}\left[p(z)\frac{dy}{dz}\right] + [q(z) + \lambda r(z)]y = 0,$$

where $p(z) = z$, $q(z) = -\dfrac{n^2}{z}$, $r(z) = z$ and the parameter is $\lambda = k^2$.

Example 3. *Find the eigenvalues and eigenfunctions of the Sturm-Liouville problem :*

$$\frac{d^2y}{dx^2} + \lambda y = 0 \ \text{ with } \ y(0) = 0, \ \ y\left(\frac{\pi}{2}\right) = 0.$$

Sol. We have
$$\frac{d^2y}{dx^2} + \lambda y = 0. \qquad \text{...(1)}$$

The boundary conditions are $y(0) = 0$, $y\left(\frac{\pi}{2}\right) = 0$.

The parameter λ is either 0 or negative or positive.

Case I. $\lambda = 0$. In this case, (1) $\Rightarrow \dfrac{d^2y}{dx^2} = 0 \Rightarrow y = C_1x + C_2$.

$$y(0) = 0 \Rightarrow C_1(0) + C_2 = 0 \Rightarrow C_2 = 0$$

$$y\left(\frac{\pi}{2}\right) = 0 \Rightarrow C_1\frac{\pi}{2} + C_2 = 0 \Rightarrow C_1\frac{\pi}{2} = 0 \Rightarrow C_1 = 0 \qquad (\because \ C_2 = 0)$$

$\therefore$ $y = 0$. This is not a non-trivial solution.

$\therefore$ $\lambda = 0$ is not an eigenvalue.

Case II. $\lambda < 0$. The A.E. of (1) is $D^2 + \lambda = 0$.

Its roots are $\pm\sqrt{-\lambda}$ and these are real and distinct.

$\therefore$ Solution of (1) is $y = C_1 e^{\sqrt{-\lambda}\,x} + C_2 e^{-\sqrt{-\lambda}\,x}$.

$$y(0) = 0 \Rightarrow C_1 + C_2 = 0$$

$$y\left(\frac{\pi}{2}\right) = 0 \Rightarrow C_1 e^{\alpha\pi/2} + C_2 e^{-\alpha\pi/2} = 0 \qquad \text{(Putting } \alpha = \sqrt{-\lambda}\text{)}$$

$$\Rightarrow C_1 (e^{\alpha\pi/2} - e^{-\alpha\pi/2}) = 0 \Rightarrow C_1 = 0 \text{ and } C_2 = 0 \qquad (\because C_2 = -C_1)$$

$\therefore$ $y = 0$. This is not a non-trivial solution.

No negative number is an eigenvalue.

Case III. $\lambda > 0$. In this case, the roots of the A.E. are $\pm\sqrt{\lambda}\,i$ and these are imaginary numbers.

$\therefore$ Solution of (1) is $y = C_1 \cos\sqrt{\lambda}\,x + C_2 \sin\sqrt{\lambda}\,x$.

$$y(0) = 0 \Rightarrow C_1 \cos 0 + C_2 \sin 0 = 0 \Rightarrow C_1 = 0$$

$$y\left(\frac{\pi}{2}\right) = 0 \Rightarrow C_1 \cos\sqrt{\lambda}\,\frac{\pi}{2} + C_2 \sin\sqrt{\lambda}\,\frac{\pi}{2} = 0$$

$$\Rightarrow C_2 \sin\sqrt{\lambda}\,\frac{\pi}{2} = 0 \qquad (\because C_1 = 0)$$

In order to have non-trivial solution, we should have $\sin\sqrt{\lambda}\,\frac{\pi}{2} = 0$ for otherwise C_2 and hence y would become '0'.

Now $\sin\sqrt{\lambda}\,\frac{\pi}{2} = 0 \Rightarrow \frac{\sqrt{\lambda}}{2} = 1, 2, 3, \ldots\ldots \qquad (\because \lambda > 0)$

$$\Rightarrow \lambda = 4n^2, n \in \mathbf{N}.$$

$\therefore$ If $\lambda = 4n^2, n \in \mathbf{N}$, then the given problem has non-trivial solution and is given by $y = C_2 \sin\sqrt{\lambda}\,x$, where $C_2 \neq 0$.

Thus the given problem has non-trivial solution only when $\lambda = 4n^2, n \in \mathbf{N}$ and for $\lambda = 4n^2, n \in \mathbf{N}$, the solution is $\mathbf{y = k_n \sin 2nx}$, where $\mathbf{k_n} \neq 0$.

$\therefore$ Eigenvalues are $\mathbf{4n^2}$, **n =1, 2, ...** and the corresponding eigenfunctions are

$$\mathbf{y = k_n \sin 2nx, n = 1, 2, 3, \ldots\ldots}$$

Example 4. *Find the eigenvalues and eigenfunctions of the sturm-Liouville problem*

$$\frac{d^2y}{dx^2} + \lambda y = 0 \text{ with } y(0) = 0, y'(l) = 0.$$

Sol. We have $$\frac{d^2y}{dx^2} + \lambda y = 0 \qquad \ldots(1)$$

The boundary conditions are $y(0) = 0, y'(l) = 0$.

The parameter λ is either 0 or negative or positive.

Case I. $\lambda = 0$. In this case, (1) $\Rightarrow \frac{d^2y}{dx^2} = 0 \Rightarrow y = C_1x + C_2$

$$y(0) = 0 \Rightarrow C_1(0) + C_2 = 0 \Rightarrow C_2 = 0$$

$\therefore$ $y = C_1x + 0$ or $y = C_1x$

$\therefore$ $y' = C_1$. $\quad\therefore\ y'(l) = 0 \Rightarrow C_1 = 0$

$\therefore$ $y = 0$. This is not a non-trivial solution.

$\therefore$ $\lambda = 0$ is not an eigenvalue.

Case II. $\lambda < 0$. The A.E. of (1) is $D^2 + \lambda = 0$.

Its roots are $\pm\sqrt{-\lambda}$ and these are real and distinct

$\therefore$ The solution of (1) is $y = C_1 e^{\sqrt{-\lambda}x} + C_2 e^{-\sqrt{-\lambda}x}$

$$y(0) = 0 \Rightarrow C_1 + C_2 = 0 \Rightarrow C_2 = -C_1$$

$$\therefore \quad y = C_1 (e^{\sqrt{-\lambda}x} - e^{-\sqrt{-\lambda}x})$$

$$\Rightarrow \quad \frac{dy}{dx} = C_1(\sqrt{-\lambda}\, e^{\sqrt{-\lambda}x} + \sqrt{-\lambda}\, e^{-\sqrt{-\lambda}x}) = C_1 \sqrt{-\lambda}\,(e^{\sqrt{-\lambda}x} + e^{-\sqrt{-\lambda}x})$$

$$\therefore \quad y'(l) = 0 \Rightarrow C_1\sqrt{-\lambda}\,(e^{\sqrt{-\lambda}l} + e^{-\sqrt{-\lambda}l}) = 0 \Rightarrow C_1 = 0$$

$\therefore$ $y = 0$. This is not a non-trivial solution.

$\therefore$ No negative number is an eigenvalue.

Case III. $\lambda > 0$. In this case, the roots are $\pm\sqrt{\lambda}i$ and these are imaginary numbers.

$\therefore$ Solution of (1) is

$$y = C_1 \cos\sqrt{\lambda}x + C_2 \sin\sqrt{\lambda}x.$$

$$y(0) = 0 \Rightarrow C_1 \cos 0 + C_2 \sin 0 = 0 \Rightarrow C_1 = 0$$

$$\therefore \quad y = C_2 \sin\sqrt{\lambda}x$$

$$\therefore \quad y' = C_2\sqrt{\lambda}\cos\sqrt{\lambda}x$$

$$y'(l) = 0 \Rightarrow C_2\sqrt{\lambda}\cos\sqrt{\lambda}l = 0 \Rightarrow C_2\cos\sqrt{\lambda}l = 0 \qquad (\because \lambda \neq 0)$$

In order to have non-trivial solution, we should have $\cos\sqrt{\lambda}l = 0$ for otherwise C_2 and hence y would become '0'.

Now $\cos\sqrt{\lambda}l = 0 \Rightarrow \sqrt{\lambda}l = (2n+1)\frac{\pi}{2}$, $n = 0, 1, 2, \ldots\ldots$

$$\Rightarrow \lambda = \left((2n+1)\frac{\pi}{2l}\right)^2, n = 0, 1, 2, \ldots\ldots$$

If $\lambda = \left((2n+1)\frac{\pi}{2l}\right)^2$, $n = 0, 1, 2, \ldots\ldots$ then the given problem has non-trivial solution and is given by $y = C_2 \sin\sqrt{\lambda}x$, where $C_2 \neq 0$.

Thus the given problem has non-trivial solution only when $\lambda = \left((2n+1)\frac{\pi}{2l}\right)^2$, $n = 0, 1, 2, \ldots\ldots$ and for $\lambda = \left((2n+1)\frac{\pi}{2l}\right)^2$, $n = 0, 1, 2, \ldots\ldots$ the solution is $y = k_n \sin\frac{(2n+1)\pi x}{2l}$, where $k_n \neq 0$.

$\therefore$ Eigenvalues are $\left((2n+1)\frac{\pi}{2l}\right)^2$, **n = 0, 1, 2, ...** and the corresponding eigen functions are

$$y = k_n \sin\frac{(2n+1)\pi x}{2l}, n = 0, 1, 2, \ldots\ldots.$$

Example 5. *Find the eigenvalues and eigenfunctions of the Sturm-Liouville problem :*

$$\frac{d}{dx}\left[x\frac{dy}{dx}\right]+\frac{\lambda}{x}y=0 \quad with \quad y(1)=0,\ y(e^{\pi})=0.$$

Sol. We have $\qquad \dfrac{d}{dx}\left[x\dfrac{dy}{dx}\right]+\dfrac{\lambda}{x}y=0.$ ...(1)

The boundary conditions are $\quad y(1)=0, \quad y(e^{\pi})=0.$

The parameter λ is either 0 or negative or positive.

Case I. $\lambda = 0$. In this case, (1) $\Rightarrow \quad \dfrac{d}{dx}\left(x\dfrac{dy}{dx}\right)=0.$

$$\Rightarrow \quad x\frac{dy}{dx}=C_1 \Rightarrow \frac{dy}{dx}=\frac{C_1}{x}$$

$$\Rightarrow \quad y=C_1\log|x|+C_2.$$

$$y(1)=0 \Rightarrow C_1\log|1|+C_2=0 \Rightarrow C_2=0$$

and $\quad y(e^{\pi})=0 \Rightarrow C_1\log|e^{\pi}|+C_2=0 \Rightarrow C_1\pi=0 \Rightarrow C_1=0 \quad (\because \ C_2=0)$

$\therefore \quad y=0$. This is not a non-trivial solution.

$\therefore \quad \lambda=0$ is not an eigenvalue.

Case II. $\lambda < 0$.

$$(1) \Rightarrow \quad x\frac{d^2y}{dx^2}+\frac{dy}{dx}+\frac{\lambda}{x}y=0$$

$$\Rightarrow \quad x^2\frac{d^2y}{dx^2}+x\frac{dy}{dx}+\lambda y=0 \qquad ...(2)$$

Let $\quad x>0$ and $z=\log x. \quad \therefore \quad x=e^z$

$$\therefore \quad \frac{dy}{dx}=\frac{dy}{dz}\cdot\frac{1}{x}=\frac{1}{x}\frac{dy}{dz}$$

and $$\frac{d^2y}{dx^2}=-\frac{1}{x^2}\frac{dy}{dz}+\frac{1}{x}\frac{d^2y}{dz^2}\cdot\frac{1}{x}=\frac{1}{x^2}\left(\frac{d^2y}{dz^2}-\frac{dy}{dz}\right).$$

$$\therefore \quad (2) \Rightarrow \quad \frac{d^2y}{dz^2}-\frac{dy}{dz}+\frac{dy}{dz}+\lambda y=0$$

$$\Rightarrow \quad \frac{d^2y}{dz^2}+\lambda y=0 \qquad ...(3)$$

The A.E. of (3) is $D^2+\lambda=0$.

Its roots are $\pm\sqrt{-\lambda}$ and these are real and distinct.

$\therefore \quad$ Solution is $\quad y=C_1e^{\sqrt{-\lambda}\,z}+C_2e^{-\sqrt{-\lambda}\,z}$

$$\Rightarrow \quad y=C_1x^{\sqrt{-\lambda}}+C_2x^{-\sqrt{-\lambda}}$$

$$y(1)=0 \Rightarrow C_1+C_2=0 \Rightarrow C_2=-C_1$$

$$y(e^{\pi})=0 \Rightarrow C_1e^{\sqrt{-\lambda}\pi}+C_2e^{-\sqrt{-\lambda}\pi}=0 \Rightarrow C_1(e^{\sqrt{-\lambda}\pi}-e^{-\sqrt{-\lambda}\pi})=0$$

$$\Rightarrow \quad C_1=0 \Rightarrow C_1, C_2=0$$

∴ $y = 0$. This is not a non-trivial solution.

∴ No negative number is an eigenvalue.

Case III. $\lambda > 0$. In this, the roots of A.E. are $\pm\sqrt{\lambda}i$ and these are imaginary numbers.

∴ Solution is $y = C_1 \cos\sqrt{\lambda}z + C_2 \sin\sqrt{\lambda}z$

$$\Rightarrow \quad y = C_1 \cos(\sqrt{\lambda}\log x) + C_2 \sin(\sqrt{\lambda}\log x)$$

$$y(1) = 0 \Rightarrow C_1 \cos 0 + C_2 \sin 0 = 0 \Rightarrow C_1 = 0$$

$$y(e^{\pi}) = 0 \Rightarrow C_1 \cos(\sqrt{\lambda}\,\pi) + C_2 \sin(\sqrt{\lambda}\,\pi) = 0 \Rightarrow C_2 \sin(\sqrt{\lambda}\,\pi) = 0$$

$$(\because \; C_1 = 0)$$

In order to have non-trivial solution, we should have $\sin\sqrt{\lambda}\,\pi = 0$ for otherwise C_2 and hence y would become '0'.

Now $\quad \sin\sqrt{\lambda}\,\pi = 0 \Rightarrow \sqrt{\lambda} = 1, 2, 3, \ldots\ldots \quad (\because \; \lambda > 0)$

$$\Rightarrow \quad \lambda = n^2, n = 1, 2, 3, \ldots\ldots$$

∴ If $\lambda = n^2$, $n \in \mathbf{N}$, then the given problem has non-trivial solution given by $y = C_2 \sin(\sqrt{\lambda}\log x)$, where $C_2 \neq 0$.

Thus, the given problem has non-trivial solution only when $\lambda = n^2$, $n \in \mathbf{N}$ and for $\lambda = n^2$, $n \in \mathbf{N}$, the solution is $y = k_n \sin(n \log x)$ where $k_n \neq 0$.

∴ Eigenvalues are $\mathbf{n^2}$, $\mathbf{n \in N}$ and the corresponding eigenfunctions are

$$\mathbf{y = k_n \sin(n \log x), n \in N.}$$

5. ORTHOGONALITY OF EIGENFUNCTIONS OF A STURM-LIOUVILLE PROBLEM

Theorem. Let $\frac{d}{dx}\left[p(x)\frac{dy}{dx}\right] + [q(x) + \lambda r(x)]\,y = 0 \quad \ldots(1)$

where p(x), q(x), r(x) are real functions and p(x), p′(x), q(x), r(x) are continuous functions and p(x) > 0, r(x) > 0, on an interval [a, b] and λ is a parameter independent of x and two conditions

$$\left.\begin{aligned} A_1 y(a) + A_2 y'(a) = 0 \\ B_1 y(b) + B_2 y'(b) = 0 \end{aligned}\right] \quad \ldots(2)$$

where A_1, A_2, B_1, B_2 are real constants such that A_1 and A_2 are not both zero and B_1 and B_2 are not both zero.

Let λ_m and λ_n be any two distinct eigenvalues of this problem. Let ϕ_m and ϕ_n be eigenfunctions corresponding to λ_m and λ_n respectively.

Prove that the eigenfunctions ϕ_m and ϕ_n are orthogonal with respect to the weight function r(x) on [a, b].

Proof. Since ϕ_m is an eigenfunction of (1) corresponding to λ_m, we have

$$\frac{d}{dx}(p\phi_m') + (q + \lambda_m r)\,\phi_m = 0 \quad \ldots(3)$$

Similarly, $\quad \frac{d}{dx}(p\phi_n') + (q + \lambda_n r)\,\phi_n = 0 \quad \ldots(4)$

Multiplying (3) by ϕ_n and (4) by ϕ_m and subtracting, we get

$$\phi_n \frac{d}{dx}(p\phi_m') - \phi_m \frac{d}{dx}(p\phi_n') + (\lambda_m - \lambda_n)\,r\phi_m\phi_n = 0$$

$$\Rightarrow \qquad (\lambda_m - \lambda_n) r\phi_m\phi_n = \phi_m \frac{d}{dx}(p\phi_n') - \phi_n \frac{d}{dx}(p\phi_m')$$

Integrating w.r.t. x from a to b, we get

$$(\lambda_m - \lambda_n) \int_a^b r\phi_m\phi_n \, dx = \left(\phi_m \, p\phi_n' \Big|_a^b - \int_a^b \phi_m' \, p\phi_n' \, dx\right) - \left(\phi_n \, p\phi_m' \Big|_a^b - \int_a^b \phi_n' \, p\phi_m' \, dx\right).$$

$$\Rightarrow \quad (\lambda_m - \lambda_n) \int_a^b r\phi_m\phi_n \, dx = p(\phi_m \phi_n' - \phi_m' \phi_n) \Big|_a^b$$

$$= p(b)\left[\phi_m(b)\phi_n'(b) - \phi_m'(b)\phi_n(b)\right] - p(a)\left[\phi_m(a)\phi_n'(a) - \phi_m'(a)\phi_n(a)\right] \qquad ...(5)$$

Case I. $A_2 = 0$, $B_2 = 0$. In this case, $y(a) = 0$, $y(b) = 0$.

$\therefore \quad \phi_m(a) = 0, \phi_n(a) = 0, \phi_n(b), \phi_n(b) = 0.$

$\therefore \quad$ R.H.S. of (5) is zero.

$$\therefore \quad (5) \Rightarrow (\lambda_m - \lambda_n) \int_a^b r\,\phi_m\phi_n \, dx = 0$$

$$\Rightarrow \qquad \int_a^b r\,\phi_m\phi_n \, dx = 0. \qquad (\because \lambda_m \neq \lambda_n)$$

Case II. $A_2 = 0$, $B_2 \neq 0$. In this case,

$y(a) = 0$ and $\beta y(b) + y'(b) = 0$, where $\beta = B_1/B_2$.

$\therefore \quad \phi_m(a) = 0, \phi_n(a) = 0, \beta\phi_m(b) + \phi_m'(b) = 0$ and $\beta\phi_n(b) + \phi_n'(b) = 0.$

Now $\phi_m(b)\,\phi_n'(b) - \phi_m'(b)\,\phi_n(b) = \phi_m(b) \,.\, -\beta\phi_n(b) + \beta\phi_m(b)\,\phi_n(b) = 0$

Also $\phi_m(a)\,\phi_n'(a) - \phi_m'(a)\,\phi_n(a) = 0 \,.\, \phi_n'(a) - \phi_m'(a) \,.\, 0 = 0$

$\therefore \quad$ R.H.S. of (5) is zero.

$$\therefore \quad (\lambda_m - \lambda_n) \int_a^b r\,\phi_m\phi_n \, dx = 0$$

$$\Rightarrow \qquad \int_a^b r\,\phi_m\phi_n \, dx = 0 \qquad (\because \lambda_m \neq \lambda_n)$$

Similarly in other cases, we have $\int_a^b r\,\phi_m\phi_n \, dx = 0$.

$\therefore$ **The eigenfunctions $\phi_m(x)$ and $\phi_n(x)$ are orthogonal w.r.t. the weight function $r(x)$ on the interval $[a, b]$.**

WORKING RULES FOR SOLVING PROBLEMS

Rule I. An equation of the form $\frac{d}{dx}\left[p(x)\frac{dy}{dx}\right] + [q(x) + \lambda r(x)]\,y = 0$

where $p(x)$, $q(x)$, $r(x)$ are real functions and $p(x)$, $p'(x)$, $q(x)$, $r(x)$ are continuous and $p(x) > 0$, $r(x) > 0$ on $[a, b]$ and λ is a parameter independent of x and two boundary conditions

$$A_1 y(a) + A_2 y'(a) = 0, \; B_1 y(b) + B_2 y'(b) = 0$$

where A_1, A_2, B_1, B_2 are real constants such that A_1 and A_2 are not both zero and B_1 and B_2 are not both zero is called a Sturm-Liouville problem.

Rule II. A non-zero solution of a Sturm-Liouville problem is called an eigenfunction of the problem and the corresponding value of λ, an eigenvalue of the problem.

Rule III. The eigenvalues of a Sturm-Liouville problem are always real.

Rule IV. Every Sturm-Liouville problem has infinitely many eigenvalues and these can be arranged in an increasing sequence.

Rule V. Distinct eigenfunctions of a Sturm-Liouville problem are orthogonal with respect to the weight function $r(x)$ on $[a, b]$.

EXERCISE 1

Find the eigenvalues and eigenfunctions of the following Sturm-Liouville problems :

1. $\dfrac{d^2y}{dx^2} + \lambda y = 0, \quad y(0) = 0, \quad y(a) = 0$

2. $\dfrac{d^2y}{dx^2} + \lambda y = 0, \quad y(0) = 0, \quad y'(1) = 0$

3. $\dfrac{d^2y}{dx^2} + \lambda y = 0, \quad y(0) = 0, \quad y'(\pi) = 0$

4. $\dfrac{d^2y}{dx^2} + \lambda y = 0, \quad y'(0) = 0, \quad y'(\pi) = 0$

(CDLU 2004 ; MDU 2005)

5. $\dfrac{d}{dx}\left[x\dfrac{dy}{dx}\right] + \dfrac{\lambda}{x}y = 0, \; y'(1) = 0, \; y'(e^{2\pi}) = 0$, **where the parameter λ is non-negative.**

6. $\dfrac{d}{dx}\left[(x^2+1)\dfrac{dy}{dx}\right] + \dfrac{\lambda}{x^2+1}y = 0, \; y(0) = 0, \; y(1) = 0$.

Answers

1. $\lambda = \left(\dfrac{n\pi}{a}\right)^2, n = 1, 2, 3, \ldots\ldots$

$y = k_n \sin\left(\dfrac{n\pi}{a}x\right), n = 1, 2, 3, \ldots\ldots$ **where $k_1, k_2, k_3, \ldots\ldots$ are non-zero arbitrary constants.**

2. $\lambda = \left[(2n+1)\dfrac{\pi}{2}\right]^2, n = 1, 2, 3, \ldots\ldots$

$y = k_n \sin\left((2n+1)\dfrac{\pi x}{2}\right), n = 0, 1, 2, 3, \ldots\ldots$ **where $k_0, k_1, k_2, k_3, \ldots\ldots$ are non-zero arbitrary constants.**

3. $\lambda = \left(\dfrac{2n+1}{2}\right)^2, n = 1, 2, 3, \ldots\ldots$

$y = k_n \sin\left(\dfrac{2n+1}{2}x\right), n = 0, 1, 2, 3, \ldots\ldots$ **where $k_0, k_1, k_2, k_3, \ldots\ldots$ are non-zero arbitrary constants.**

4. $\lambda = n^2, n = 0, 1, 2, 3, \ldots\ldots$

$y = k_n \cos nx, n = 0, 1, 2, 3, \ldots\ldots$ **where $k_0, k_1, k_2, k_3, \ldots\ldots$ are non-zero arbitrary constants.**

5. $\lambda = \dfrac{n^2}{4}, n = 0, 1, 2, 3, \ldots\ldots$

$y = k_n \cos\dfrac{n \log x}{2}, n = 0, 1, 2, 3, \ldots\ldots$ **where $k_0, k_1, k_2, k_3, \ldots\ldots$ are non-zero arbitrary constants.**

6. $\lambda = 16n^2, n = 1, 2, 3, \ldots\ldots, y = k_n \sin(4n \tan^{-1} x), n = 1, 2, 3, \ldots\ldots$ where $k_1, k_2, k_3, \ldots\ldots$ are non-zero constants.

Hints

6. Let $z = \tan^{-1} x$.

$$\therefore \quad \frac{dy}{dx} = \frac{dy}{dz} \cdot \frac{1}{x^2+1}.$$

$$\therefore \quad \text{Given equation becomes } \frac{d}{dx}\left(\frac{dy}{dz}\right) + \frac{\lambda}{x^2+1} y = 0$$

$$\Rightarrow \quad \frac{d^2y}{dz^2} \cdot \frac{1}{x^2+1} + \frac{\lambda}{x^2+1} y = 0 \text{ or } \frac{d^2y}{dz^2} + \lambda y = 0.$$

SECTION II

LAPLACE TRANSFORMATIONS

6

Laplace Transforms

1. INTRODUCTION

The Laplace transform* of a suitably defined function f of a real variable t is a related function F of a real variable s. The use of Laplace transforms provide a powerful method of solving differential and integral equations. The Laplace transform method also has the advantage that it solves initial value problems directly without first finding a general solution. The ready tables of Laplace transforms has reduced the problem of solving differential equations to merely algebraic manipulation.

2. LAPLACE TRANSFORM OF A FUNCTION

Let f be a real valued function of the real variable t, defined for $t \geq 0$. Let s be a real variable and consider the function F of s defined by

$$F(s) = \int_0^\infty e^{-st} f(t)\, dt$$

for all values of s for which this integral exists (*i.e.* has some finite value). The function F(s) defined by the integral $\int_0^\infty e^{-st} f(t)\, dt$ is called the **Laplace transform** of the function f and is denoted by L(f).

$$\therefore \qquad \mathbf{L(f) = F(s) = \int_0^\infty e^{-st}\, f(t)\, dt.}$$

Remarks 1. The original function f depends on t and its Laplace transform (F) depends on s.

2. Original functions are denoted by *lower case letters* and their Laplace transforms by the same letters in *capitals*.

WORKING RULES TO FIND LAPLACE TRANSFORMS OF f(t), t ≥ 0.
Step I. Write $L(f) = \int_0^\infty e^{-st} f(t)\, dt$.
Step II. Write this improper integral as $\lim_{T \to \infty} \int_0^T e^{-st} f(t)\, dt$ and simplify $e^{-st} f(t)$.
Step III. Evaluate $\int_0^T e^{-st} f(t)\, dt$.
Step IV. Find limit of $\int_0^T e^{-st} f(t)\, dt$ as $T \to \infty$. This gives the value of L(f).

*__Pierre Simon Marquis De Laplace__ (1749—1827) French mathematician, made contributions to special functions, probability theory, potential theory and astronomy.

3. LAPLACE TRANSFORMS OF ELEMENTARY FUNCTIONS

In this section, we shall find the Laplace transforms of some elementary functions.

Theorem. Prove that for $t \geq 0$,

1. $L(1) = \frac{1}{s}, s > 0$
2. $L(t^a) = \frac{\Gamma(a+1)}{s^{a+1}}, a > -1, s > 0$
3. $L(t^n) = \frac{n!}{s^{n+1}}, n = 0, 1, 2, \ldots\ldots; s > 0$
4. $L(e^{at}) = \frac{1}{s-a}, s > a$
5. $L(\sinh at) = \frac{a}{s^2 - a^2}, s > |a|$
6. $L(\cosh at) = \frac{s}{s^2 - a^2}, s > |a|$
7. $L(\sin at) = \frac{a}{s^2 + a^2}, s > 0$
8. $L(\cos at) = \frac{s}{s^2 + a^2}, s > 0.$

Proof. By definition, the improper integeral $\int_k^\infty g(t)\,dt$ is equal to $\lim_{T \to \infty} \int_k^T g(t)\,dt$.

1. By definition, $L(1) = \int_0^\infty e^{-st}.1\,dt$

$$\therefore \quad L(1) = \lim_{T \to \infty} \int_0^T e^{-st}\,dt = \lim_{T \to \infty} \left[\frac{e^{-st}}{-s}\right]_0^T$$

$$= -\frac{1}{s} \lim_{T \to \infty} \left[\frac{1}{e^{st}}\right]_0^T = -\frac{1}{s} \lim_{T \to \infty} \left[\frac{1}{e^{sT}} - 1\right]$$

$$= -\frac{1}{s}[0 - 1] = \frac{1}{s} \text{ for } s > 0.$$

$$\therefore \quad \mathbf{L(1) = \frac{1}{s}, s > 0.}$$

2. By definition, $L(t^a) = \int_0^\infty e^{-st} t^a\,dt$.

Let $st = u$. $\therefore$ $s\,dt = du$.

$$\therefore \quad L(t^a) = \int_0^\infty e^{-u} \left(\frac{u}{s}\right)^a \frac{du}{s} = \frac{1}{s^{a+1}} \int_0^\infty e^{-u} u^a\,du$$

$$= \frac{\Gamma(a+1)}{s^{a+1}}, \text{ provided } a > -1$$

$$\therefore \quad \mathbf{L(t^a) = \frac{\Gamma(a+1)}{s^{a+1}}, a > -1, s > 0.} \qquad (\because t \geq 0, u \geq 0, u = st \Rightarrow s \geq 0)$$

3. By definition, $L(t^n) = \int_0^\infty e^{-st} t^n\,dt$.

Let $st = u$. $\therefore$ $s\,dt = du$

$\therefore \quad L(t^n) = \int_0^\infty e^{-u} \left(\frac{u}{s}\right)^n \frac{du}{s} = \frac{1}{s^{n+1}} \int_0^\infty e^{-u} u^n \, du$

$= \frac{\Gamma(n+1)}{s^{n+1}}$, provided $n + 1 > 0$.

Let $\quad n = 0, 1, 2, \ldots\ldots \quad \therefore \quad \Gamma(n+1) = n\,!$

$\therefore \quad \mathbf{L(t^n) = \frac{n\,!}{s^{n+1}}, n = 0, 1, 2, \ldots\ldots; s > 0.} \qquad (\because \ t \ge 0, u \ge 0, u = st \Rightarrow s \ge 0)$

4. By definition, $L(e^{at}) = \int_0^\infty e^{-st} e^{at} \, dt$

$= \lim_{T \to \infty} \int_0^T e^{(a-s)t} \, dt = \lim_{T \to \infty} \left[\frac{e^{(a-s)t}}{a-s}\right]_0^T$

$= \frac{1}{a-s} \lim_{T \to \infty} \left[\frac{1}{e^{(s-a)T}} - 1\right] = \frac{1}{a-s} [0 - 1]$ for $s > a$ $= \frac{1}{s-a}$

$\therefore \quad \mathbf{L(e^{at}) = \frac{1}{s-a}, \ s > a.}$

5. $L(\sinh at) = L\left(\frac{e^{at} - e^{-at}}{2}\right) = \int_0^\infty e^{-st} \left(\frac{e^{at} - e^{-at}}{2}\right) dt$

$= \frac{1}{2} \int_0^\infty \left(e^{-(s-a)t} - e^{-(s+a)t}\right) dt = \frac{1}{2} \lim_{T \to \infty} \int_0^T \left(e^{-(s-a)t} - e^{-(s+a)t}\right) dt$

$= \frac{1}{2} \lim_{T \to \infty} \left[\frac{e^{-(s-a)t}}{a-s} + \frac{e^{-(s+a)t}}{s+a}\right]_0^T$

$= \frac{1}{2} \lim_{T \to \infty} \left[\frac{1}{a-s}\left(\frac{1}{e^{(s-a)T}} - 1\right) + \frac{1}{s+a}\left(\frac{1}{e^{(s+a)T}} - 1\right)\right]$

$= \frac{1}{2}\left[\frac{1}{a-s}(0-1) + \frac{1}{s+a}(0-1)\right]$ provided $s > a, s > -a$

$= \frac{1}{2}\left[\frac{2a}{s^2 - a^2}\right] = \frac{a}{s^2 - a^2}, \ s > |\,a\,|.$

$\therefore \quad \mathbf{L(\sinh at) = \frac{a}{s^2 - a^2}, \ s > |\,a\,|.}$

7. $L(\sin at) = \int_0^\infty e^{-st} \sin at \, dt$

$\therefore \quad L(\sin at) = \lim_{T \to \infty} \int_0^T e^{-st} \sin at \, dt$

Let $\quad I = \int e^{-st} \sin at \, dt$

$\therefore \quad I = e^{-st} \cdot \frac{-\cos at}{a} - \int -se^{-st} \cdot \frac{-\cos at}{a} \, dt$

$$= -\frac{e^{-st}\cos at}{a} - \frac{s}{a}\int e^{-st}\cos at\,dt$$

$$= -\frac{e^{-st}\cos at}{a} - \frac{s}{a}\left[e^{-st}\frac{\sin at}{a} - \int -se^{-st}.\frac{\sin at}{a}dt\right]$$

$$\therefore \quad I = -\frac{e^{-st}}{a^2}[a\cos at + s\sin at] - \frac{s^2}{a^2}I$$

$$\therefore \quad I = -\frac{e^{-st}}{s^2+a^2}[a\cos at + s\sin at]$$

$$\therefore \ L(\sin at) = \lim_{T\to\infty}\frac{-e^{-st}}{s^2+a^2}\Big[a\cos at + s\sin at\Big]_0^T$$

$$= \frac{-1}{s^2+a^2}\lim_{T\to\infty}\left[\frac{a\cos aT + s\sin aT}{e^{sT}} - \frac{a+0}{1}\right]$$

$$= \frac{-1}{s^2+a^2}[0-a] \text{ , provided } s > 0$$

$$= \frac{a}{s^2+a^2}, s > 0.$$

$$\therefore \quad \mathbf{L(\sin at) = \frac{a}{s^2+a^2}, s > 0.}$$

Remark. The proofs of the parts 6 and 8 are left for readers as exercises.

Example 1. *Find the Laplace transform of the following function :*

$$f(t) = \begin{cases} t+1 & 0 \le t \le 2 \\ 3 & t > 2. \end{cases}$$

Sol. $L(f) = \int_0^\infty e^{-st} f(t)\,dt$

$$= \int_0^2 e^{-st} f(t)\,dt + \int_2^\infty e^{-st} f(t)\,dt$$

$$= \int_0^2 e^{-st}(t+1)\,dt + \int_2^\infty e^{-st}.3\,dt$$

$$= \left[(t+1).\frac{e^{-st}}{-s}\Bigg|_0^2 - \int_0^2 1.\frac{e^{-st}}{-s}dt\right] + 3.\frac{e^{-st}}{-s}\Bigg|_2^\infty$$

$$= -\frac{3}{s}e^{-2s} + \frac{1}{s} - \frac{e^{-st}}{s^2}\Bigg|_0^2 - \frac{3}{s}\left[\lim_{T\to\infty} e^{-sT} - e^{-2s}\right]$$

$$= -\frac{3e^{-2s}}{s} + \frac{1}{s} - \frac{e^{-2s}}{s^2} + \frac{1}{s^2} - \frac{3}{s}(0 - e^{-2s})$$

$$= -\frac{3e^{-2s}}{s} + \frac{1}{s} - \frac{e^{-2s}}{s^2} + \frac{1}{s^2} + \frac{3e^{-2s}}{s} = \frac{1}{\mathbf{s^2}}[\mathbf{s - e^{-2s} + 1}] \text{ .}$$

Example 2. *Find the Laplace transform of the following function :*

$$f(t) = \begin{cases} 0, & 0 \le t < 1 \\ t, & 1 < t < 2 \\ 1, & t > 2. \end{cases}$$

Sol. $L(f) = \int_0^{\infty} e^{-st} f(t)\,dt$

$$= \int_0^1 e^{-st} f(t)\,dt + \int_1^2 e^{-st} f(t)\,dt + \int_2^{\infty} e^{-st} f(t)\,dt$$

$$= \int_0^1 e^{-st} .0\,dt + \int_1^2 e^{-st}\, t\,dt + \int_2^{\infty} e^{-st} .1\,dt$$

$$= \int_0^1 0\,dt + \left[t.\frac{e^{-st}}{-s}\Bigg|_1^2 - \int_1^2 1.\frac{e^{-st}}{-s}\,dt \right] + \lim_{T\to\infty} \left[\frac{e^{-st}}{-s} \right]_2^T$$

$$= 0 - \frac{2}{se^{2s}} + \frac{1}{se^{s}} + \frac{e^{-st}}{-s^2}\Bigg|_1^2 - \frac{1}{s} \lim_{T\to\infty} \left[\frac{1}{e^{sT}} - \frac{1}{e^{2s}} \right]$$

$$= -\frac{2}{se^{2s}} + \frac{1}{se^{s}} - \frac{1}{s^2}\left[\frac{1}{e^{2s}} - \frac{1}{e^{s}} \right] - \frac{1}{s}\left[0 - \frac{1}{e^{2s}} \right], \quad s > 0$$

$$= -\frac{2}{se^{2s}} + \frac{1}{se^{s}} - \frac{1}{s^2e^{2s}} + \frac{1}{s^2e^{s}} + \frac{1}{se^{2s}}, \quad s > 0$$

$$= \frac{1}{s^2}\left[-se^{-2s} + se^{-s} - e^{-2s} + e^{-s} \right], \quad s > 0$$

$$= \frac{\mathbf{1}}{\mathbf{s^2}} (\mathbf{e^{-s} - e^{-2s}})\,(\mathbf{s+1}), \quad \mathbf{s > 0.}$$

Example 3. *Find the Laplace transform of the function shown in the graph.*

Sol. From the graph, we have

$$f(t) = \begin{cases} t \tan 135° + 1 & 0 \le t \le 1 \\ 0 & t \ge 1 \end{cases}$$

or

$$f(t) = \begin{cases} -t + 1 & 0 \le t \le 1 \\ 0 & t \ge 1 \end{cases}$$

$\therefore \quad L(f) = \int_0^{\infty} e^{-st} f(t)\,dt$

$$= \int_0^1 e^{-st} f(t)\,dt + \int_1^{\infty} e^{-st} f(t)\,dt = \int_0^1 e^{-st}(-t+1)\,dt + \int_1^{\infty} e^{-st} .0\,dt$$

$$= \int_0^1 (1-t)\,e^{-st}\,dt + \int_1^{\infty} 0\,dt = (1-t).\frac{e^{-st}}{-s}\Bigg|_0^1 - \int_0^1 -1.\frac{e^{-st}}{-s}\,dt + 0$$

$$= 0 + \frac{e^0}{s} - \frac{e^{-st}}{-s^2}\Bigg|_0^1 = \frac{1}{s} + \frac{1}{s^2}\left[\frac{1}{e^{s}} - \frac{1}{e^0} \right] = \frac{\mathbf{1}}{\mathbf{s}} + \frac{\mathbf{1}}{\mathbf{s^2}}\left[\frac{\mathbf{1}}{\mathbf{e^{s}}} - \mathbf{1} \right], \quad \mathbf{s \ne 0.}$$

Example 4. *Show that*

$$\int_0^{\infty} \cos x^2 \, dx = \frac{1}{2}\sqrt{\frac{\pi}{2}}. \qquad \text{(MDU 2005)}$$

Sol. Let $\quad I = \int_0^{\infty} \cos x^2 \, dx.$

$$t = x^2 \Rightarrow dt = 2x\,dx \Rightarrow dx = \frac{dt}{2\sqrt{t}}$$

$x \to \infty \Rightarrow t \to \infty,\ x = 0 \Rightarrow t = (0)^2 = 0$

$$\therefore \quad I = \int_0^{\infty} \frac{\cos t\,dt}{2\sqrt{t}} = \frac{1}{2}\int_0^{\infty} \frac{e^{it} + e^{-it}}{2\sqrt{t}}\,dt$$

$$= \frac{1}{4}\left[\int_0^{\infty} e^{it}\,.\,t^{-1/2}\,dt + \int_0^{\infty} e^{-it}\,.\,t^{-1/2}\,dt\right]$$

$$= \frac{1}{4}\,[L(t^{-1/2})\,|_{s=-i} + L(t^{-1/2})\,|_{s=i}]$$

$$= \frac{1}{4}\left[\frac{\Gamma(1/2)}{s^{1/2}}\bigg|_{s=-i} + \frac{\Gamma(1/2)}{s^{1/2}}\bigg|_{s=i}\right]$$

$$= \frac{1}{4}\left[\frac{\sqrt{\pi}}{\sqrt{-i}} + \frac{\sqrt{\pi}}{\sqrt{i}}\right] = \frac{\sqrt{\pi}}{4}\left[\frac{1}{\frac{1}{\sqrt{2}} - \frac{1}{\sqrt{2}}i} + \frac{1}{\frac{1}{\sqrt{2}} + \frac{1}{\sqrt{2}}i}\right] \qquad \text{(Note this step)}$$

$$= \frac{\sqrt{2\pi}}{4}\left[\frac{1}{1-i} + \frac{1}{1+i}\right] = \frac{\sqrt{2\pi}}{4}\left[\frac{2}{2}\right] = \frac{1}{2}\sqrt{\frac{\pi}{2}}.$$

EXERCISE 1

1. By using standard formulae, write the Laplace transform of the following functions :
   (*i*) $t^{3/2}$ (*ii*) $t^{5/3}$ (*iii*) t^7
   (*iv*) e^{3t} (*v*) e^{-10t} (*vi*) sinh $5t$
   (*vii*) cosh $7t$ (*viii*) sin $4t$ (*ix*) cos $6t$.
2. Find the Laplace transform of the function $f(t) = t,\ t \geq 0$.
3. Find the Laplace transform of the function $f(t) = 4t + 3,\ t \geq 0$.
4. Find the Laplace transform of the function $f(t) = \cosh at,\ t \geq 0$.
5. Find the Laplace transform of the function $f(t) = \cos at,\ t \geq 0$.
6. Find the Laplace transform of the following functions :

   (*i*) $f(t) = \begin{cases} 4, & 0 \leq t < 3 \\ 2, & t > 3 \end{cases}$ (*ii*) $f(t) = \begin{cases} t, & 0 \leq t < 2 \\ 3, & t > 2 \end{cases}$.
7. Find the Laplace transform of the following function :

$$f(t) = \begin{cases} t & 0 \leq t \leq 1/2 \\ t - 1 & 1/2 < t \leq 1 \\ 0 & t > 1 \end{cases}.$$

8. Find the Laplace transform of the functions whose graphs are given :

(i) 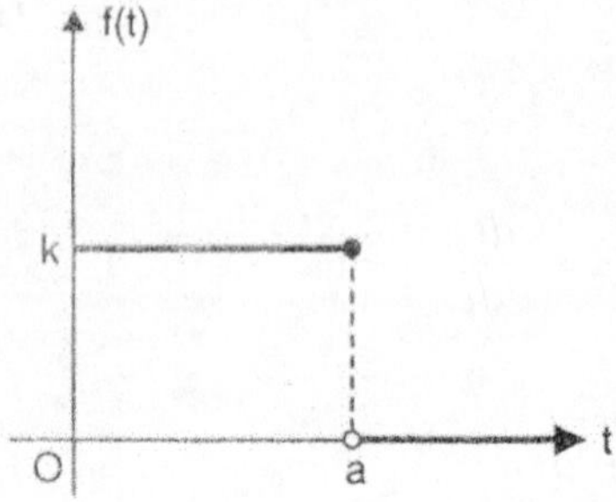

(ii) 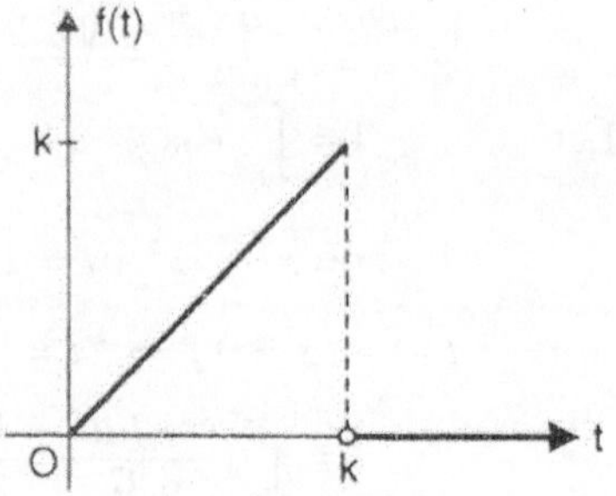

9. Show that :

(i) $\int_0^{\infty} e^{-x^2}\, dx = \frac{\sqrt{\pi}}{2}$ (ii) $\int_0^{\infty} \sin x^2\, dx = \frac{1}{2}\sqrt{\frac{\pi}{2}}$.

Answers

1. (i) $\frac{3\sqrt{\pi}}{4s^{5/2}}, s > 0$ (ii) $\frac{10\,\Gamma(2/3)}{9s^{8/3}}, s > 0$ (iii) $\frac{5040}{s^8}, s > 0$

(iv) $\frac{1}{s-3}, s > 3$ (v) $\frac{1}{s+10}, s > -10$ (vi) $\frac{s}{s^2-25}, s > 5$

(vii) $\frac{s}{s^2-49}, s > 7$ (viii) $\frac{4}{s^2+16}, s > 0$ (ix) $\frac{s}{s^2+36}, s > 0$

2. $\frac{1}{s^2}, \quad s > 0$ 3. $\frac{3s+4}{s^2}, \quad s > 0$ 4. $\frac{s}{s^2-a^2}, \quad s > |a|$

5. $\frac{s}{s^2+a^2}, \quad s > 0$ 6. (i) $\frac{2}{s}(2 - e^{-3s}), \quad s > 0$ (ii) $\frac{1}{s^2} + \frac{e^{-2s}}{s} - \frac{e^{-2s}}{s^2}, \quad s > 0$

7. $\frac{1}{s^2}\left[1 - se^{-s/2} - e^{-s}\right], \quad s > 0$ 8. (i) $\frac{k}{s}(1 - e^{-as}), \quad s > 0$

(ii) $\frac{1}{s^2}(1 - e^{-ks}) - \frac{k}{s}e^{-ks}, \quad s > 0$.

4. LINEARITY OF THE LAPLACE TRANSFORM

Theorem. If f(t) and g(t) be any functions of t for t ≥ 0 whose Laplace transforms exists and a and b be any constants, then

$$\mathbf{L\{af(t) + bg(t)\} = aL\{f(t)\} + bL\{g(t)\}}.$$

Proof. We have $L\{f(t)\} = \int_0^{\infty} e^{-st} f(t)\, dt$ and $L\{g(t)\} = \int_0^{\infty} e^{-st} g(t)\, dt$.

Now
$$L\{af(t) + bg(t)\} = \int_0^{\infty} e^{-st}\, [af(t) + bg(t)]\, dt$$

$$= a\int_a^{\infty} e^{-st} f(t)\, dt + b\int_0^{\infty} e^{-st} g(t)\, dt$$

$$= aL\{f(t)\} + bL\{g(t)\}$$

∴ $$\mathbf{L\{af(t) + bg(t)\} = aL\{f(t)\} + bL\{g(t)\}}.$$

Example 1. *Find Laplace transform of the function cosh at, $t \geq 0$ using linearity property.*

Sol. We have $L(\cosh at) = L\left(\frac{e^{at} + e^{-at}}{2}\right)$

$$= L\left(\frac{1}{2}e^{at} + \frac{1}{2}e^{-at}\right) = \frac{1}{2}L(e^{at}) + \frac{1}{2}L(e^{-at})$$

$$= \frac{1}{2} \cdot \frac{1}{s-a} + \frac{1}{2} \cdot \frac{1}{s-(-a)}, s > a, s > -a$$

$$= \frac{s}{s^2 - a^2}, s > |a| \qquad \left(\because L(e^{at}) = \frac{1}{s-a}, s > a\right)$$

$$\therefore \qquad \mathbf{L(\cosh at) = \frac{s}{s^2 - a^2}, s > |a|.}$$

Example 2. *Find the Laplace transform of the following functions of t, $t \geq 0$:*

(*i*) $6t + 9$ (*ii*) $2t^2 - t + 5$ (*iii*) $\sin^2 t$

(*iv*) $\sin 2t \sin 3t$ (CDLU 2004) (*v*) $\cos^3 t$ (*vi*) $e^{4t} + e^{2t} + t^3 + \sin^2 t$.

Sol. (*i*) $L(6t + 9) = 6L(t) + L(1)$ (By linearity)

$$= 6\left(\frac{1!}{s^{1+1}}\right) + \frac{1}{s}, s > 0 = \mathbf{\frac{6 + s}{s^2}, s > 0}$$

(*ii*) $L(2t^2 - t + 5) = 2L(t^2) - L(t) + L(5)$

$$= 2.\left(\frac{2!}{s^3}\right) - \frac{1!}{s^2} + \frac{5}{s}, s > 0 = \mathbf{\frac{4 - s + 5s^2}{s^3}, s > 0.}$$

(*iii*) $L(\sin^2 t) = L\left(\frac{1 - \cos 2t}{2}\right) = L\left(\frac{1}{2} - \frac{1}{2}\cos 2t\right)$

$$= \frac{1}{2}L(1) - \frac{1}{2}L(\cos 2t) = \frac{1}{2}\left(\frac{1}{s}\right) - \frac{1}{2}\left(\frac{s}{s^2 + 4}\right), s > 0 = \mathbf{\frac{2}{s(s^2 + 4)}, s > 0.}$$

(*iv*) $L(\sin 2t \sin 3t) = L\left(\frac{1}{2}(2 \sin 2t \sin 3t)\right)$

$$= L\left(\frac{1}{2}\cos t - \frac{1}{2}\cos 5t\right) = \frac{1}{2}L(\cos t) - \frac{1}{2}L(\cos 5t)$$

$$= \frac{1}{2} \cdot \left(\frac{s}{s^2 + 1^2}\right) - \frac{1}{2} \cdot \left(\frac{s}{s^2 + 5^2}\right) s > |1|, s > |5|$$

$$= \mathbf{\frac{12s}{(s^2 + 1)(s^2 + 25)}, s > 5.}$$

(*v*) We have $\cos 3\theta = 4\cos^3\theta - 3\cos\theta$.

$$\Rightarrow \qquad \cos^3\theta = \frac{1}{4}\cos 3\theta + \frac{3}{4}\cos\theta$$

$\therefore \quad \cos^3 t = \frac{1}{4} \cos 3t + \frac{3}{4} \cos t.$

$\therefore \quad L(\cos^3 t) = \frac{1}{4} L(\cos 3t) + \frac{3}{4} L(\cos t)$ (By linearity)

$$= \frac{1}{4}\left(\frac{s}{s^2+3^2}\right) + \frac{3}{4}\left(\frac{s}{s^2+1^2}\right), s > 0$$

$$= \frac{s}{4}\left[\frac{1}{s^2+9} + \frac{3}{s^2+1}\right], s > 0 = \mathbf{\frac{(s^2+7)\,s}{(s^2+9)\,(s^2+1)}}, \mathbf{s > 0.}$$

(*vi*) $L(e^{4t} + e^{2t} + t^3 + \sin^2 t)$

$$= L(e^{4t}) + L(e^{2t}) + L(t^3) + L\left(\frac{1-\cos 2t}{2}\right)$$ (By linearity)

$$= L(e^{4t}) + L(e^{2t}) + L(t^3) + \frac{1}{2} L(1) - \frac{1}{2} L(\cos 2t)$$

$$= \frac{1}{s-4} + \frac{1}{s-2} + \frac{3!}{s^{3+1}} + \frac{1}{2}\left(\frac{1}{s}\right) - \frac{1}{2}\left(\frac{s}{s^2+2^2}\right), s > 4, s > 2, s > 0$$

$$= \mathbf{\frac{1}{s-4} + \frac{1}{s-2} + \frac{6}{s^4} + \frac{1}{2s} - \frac{s}{2(s^2+4)}, s > 4.}$$

Example 3. *Find the Laplace transform of the function sin (ωt + δ), t ≥ 0.*

Sol. $L(\sin(\omega t + \delta)) = L(\sin \omega t \cos \delta + \cos \omega t \sin \delta)$

$$= \cos \delta\, L(\sin \omega t) + \sin \delta\, L(\cos \omega t)$$ (By linearity)

$$= \cos \delta \left(\frac{\omega}{s^2+\omega^2}\right) + \sin \delta \left(\frac{s}{s^2+\omega^2}\right), s > 0$$

$$= \mathbf{\frac{1}{s^2+\omega^2}[\omega \cos \delta + s \sin \delta], s > 0.}$$

WORKING RULES FOR SOLVING PROBLEMS

Step I. Simplify the given functions and write it as a linear combination of functions with known Laplace transforms.

Step II. Apply linearity theorem.

Step III. Simplify the terms as far as possible.

EXERCISE 2

1. Find the Laplace transform of the following functions of t, $t \geq 0$:

(*i*) $5t + 9$ (*ii*) $t^2 + 8t - 15$

(*iii*) $t^3 + 4$ (*iv*) $t^{10} + t^4 + 2$.

2. Find the Laplace transform of the following functions of t, $t \geq 0$:
(*i*) $e^{5t} + t^2$ (*ii*) $e^{-4t} + e^{2t}$
(*iii*) $e^{3t} + t^3$ (*iv*) $e^{-5t} + t^2 + 6t$.

3. Find the Laplace transform of the following functions of t, $t \geq 0$:
(*i*) $\sinh 4t + \cosh 4t$ (*ii*) $t - \sinh 2t$ *(CDLU 2004)*
(*iii*) $\sin \pi t + e^{6t}$ (*iv*) $\cos (at + b)$.

4. Find the Laplace transform of the following functions of t, $t \geq 0$:
(*i*) $\sin^2 2t$ *(KU 2005 S)* (*ii*) $\sin^2 3t$
(*iii*) $\cos^2 4t$ (*iv*) $7 \cos^2 t$.

5. Find the Laplace transform of the following functions of t, $t \geq 0$:
(*i*) $\sin^3 t$ (*ii*) $\sin^3 2t$ *(CDLU 2004)*
(*iii*) $\cos^3 2t + t^2$ (*iv*) $\cos^3 4t + t$.

6. Find the Laplace transform of the following functions of t, $t \geq 0$:
(*i*) $\sin 3t \cos 2t$ *(KU 2005 S)* (*ii*) $\cos 5t \sin 2t$
(*iii*) $\cos 4t \cos t$ (*iv*) $\sin 3t \sin 7t$.

7. Find the Laplace transform of the following functions of t:
(*i*) $(\sin t - \cos t)^2$, $t \geq 0$ (*ii*) $1 + \sqrt{t} + \dfrac{3}{\sqrt{t}}$, $t > 0$
(*iii*) $\sin at \sin bt$, $t \geq 0$ (*iv*) $\cosh at - \cos at$, $t \geq 0$.

Answers

1. (*i*) $\dfrac{5}{s^2} + \dfrac{9}{s}$, $s > 0$ (*ii*) $\dfrac{2}{s^3} + \dfrac{8}{s^2} - \dfrac{15}{s}$, $s > 0$
(*iii*) $\dfrac{6}{s^4} + \dfrac{4}{s}$, $s > 0$ (*iv*) $\dfrac{10!}{s^{11}} + \dfrac{24}{s^5} + \dfrac{2}{s}$, $s > 0$

2. (*i*) $\dfrac{1}{s-5} + \dfrac{2}{s^3}$, $s > 5$ (*ii*) $\dfrac{2(s+1)}{(s+4)(s-2)}$, $s > 2$
(*iii*) $\dfrac{1}{s-3} + \dfrac{6}{s^4}$, $s > 3$ (*iv*) $\dfrac{1}{s+5} + \dfrac{2}{s^3} + \dfrac{6}{s^2}$, $s > 0$

3. (*i*) $\dfrac{1}{s-4}$, $s > 4$ (*ii*) $\dfrac{4+s^2}{s^2(4-s^2)}$, $s > 2$
(*iii*) $\dfrac{\pi}{s^2+\pi^2} + \dfrac{1}{s-6}$, $s > 6$ (*iv*) $\dfrac{s \cos b - a \sin b}{s^2 + a^2}$, $s > 0$

4. (*i*) $\dfrac{8}{s(s^2+16)}$, $s > 0$ (*ii*) $\dfrac{18}{s(s^2+36)}$, $s > 0$
(*iii*) $\dfrac{s^2+32}{s(s^2+64)}$, $s > 0$ (*iv*) $\dfrac{7(s^2+2)}{s(s^2+4)}$, $s > 0$

5. (*i*) $\dfrac{6}{(s^2+1)(s^2+9)}$, $s > 0$ (*ii*) $\dfrac{48}{(s^2+4)(s^2+36)}$, $s > 0$
(*iii*) $\dfrac{s(s^2+28)}{(s^2+4)(s^2+36)} + \dfrac{2}{s^3}$, $s > 0$ (*iv*) $\dfrac{s(s^2+112)}{(s^2+16)(s^2+144)} + \dfrac{1}{s^2}$, $s > 0$

6. (i) $\dfrac{3s^2+15}{(s^2+1)(s^2+25)}, s>0$ (ii) $\dfrac{2s^2-42}{(s^2+9)(s^2+49)}, s>0$

(iii) $\dfrac{s(s^2+17)}{(s^2+9)(s^2+25)}, s>0$ (iv) $\dfrac{42s}{(s^2+16)(s^2+100)}, s>0$

7. (i) $\dfrac{s^2-2s+4}{s(s^2+4)}, s>0$ (ii) $\dfrac{1}{s}+\dfrac{\sqrt{\pi}}{2s^{3/2}}+\dfrac{3\sqrt{\pi}}{s^{1/2}}, s>0$

(iii) $\dfrac{2abs}{(s^2+(a-b)^2)(s^2+(a+b)^2)}, s>0$ (iv) $\dfrac{2a^2s}{s^4-a^4}, s>|a|$.

5. SHIFTING THEOREMS

There are two shifting theorems. In the first theorem the variable s of the function $L(f(t))$ is replaced by $s-a$ and in the second theorem the variable t of the function $f(t)$ is replaced by $t-a$.

6. FIRST SHIFTING THEOREM

If f(t) be a function of t for t ≥ 0 whose Laplace transform F(s) exists for s > k then for any constant 'a' the function e^{at} f(t) has the Laplace transform F(s – a) for s > k + a.

Proof. We have $F(s) = L(f) = \int_0^\infty e^{-st} f(t)\,dt, s>k$.

Replacing s by $s-a$, we get $F(s-a) = \int_0^\infty e^{-(s-a)t} f(t)\,dt, s-a>k$.

$\Rightarrow \quad F(s-a) = \int_0^\infty e^{-st}(e^{at} f(t))\,dt, s>k+a$

$\therefore$ Laplace transform of the function $e^{at} f(t)$ is $F(s-a)$ for $s>k+a$.

Remark. The result of above theorem can be easily remembered as follows :

If $L(f(t)) = F(s), s>k$ then for any a, $L(e^{at} f(t)) = F(s-a), s>k+a$.

Theorem. Using first shifting theorem. Show that for t ≥ 0 :

1. $L(e^{at}) = \dfrac{1}{s-a}, \quad s>a$

2. $L(e^{at} t^b) = \dfrac{\Gamma(b+1)}{(s-a)^{b+1}}, b>-1, \; s>a$

3. $L(e^{at} t^n) = \dfrac{n!}{(s-a)^{n+1}}, n = 0, 1, 2, \ldots\ldots, s>a$

4. $L(e^{at} \sinh bt) = \dfrac{b}{(s-a)^2-b^2}, \; s>|b|+a$

5. $L(e^{at} \cosh bt) = \dfrac{s-a}{(s-a)^2-b^2}, \; s>|b|+a$

6. $L(e^{at} \sin bt) = \dfrac{b}{(s-a)^2+b^2}, \; s>a$

7. $\mathbf{L(e^{at}\cos bt) = \dfrac{s-a}{(s-a)^2+b^2}}$, $\mathbf{s > a}$.

Proof. 1. We have $L(1) = \dfrac{1}{s}$, $s > 0$.

$\therefore$ By **first shifting theorem,**

$$L(e^{at}.1) = \frac{1}{s-a}, \ s > a$$

$\therefore$
$$\mathbf{L(e^{at}) = \frac{1}{s-a}, \ s > a.}$$

2. We have $L(t^b) = \dfrac{\Gamma(b+1)}{s^{b+1}}$, $b > -1$, $s > 0$.

$\therefore$ By **first shifting theorem,**

$$\mathbf{L(e^{at}\,t^b) = \frac{\Gamma(b+1)}{(s-a)^{b+1}}, \ b > -1, \ s > a.}$$

3. We have $L(t^n) = \dfrac{n!}{s^{n+1}}$, $n = 0, 1, 2, \ldots\ldots; s > 0$.

$\therefore$ By **first shifting theorem,**

$$\mathbf{L(e^{at}\,t^n) = \frac{n!}{(s-a)^{n+1}}, \ n = 0, 1, 2, \ldots\ldots; s > a.}$$

4. We have $L(\sinh bt) = \dfrac{b}{s^2-b^2}$, $s > |b|$.

$\therefore$ By **first shifting theorem,**

$$\mathbf{L(e^{at}\sinh bt) = \frac{b}{(s-a)^2-b^2}, \ s > |b| + a.}$$

5. We have $L(\cosh bt) = \dfrac{s}{s^2-b^2}$, $s > |b|$.

$\therefore$ By **first shifting theorem,**

$$\mathbf{L(e^{at}\cosh bt) = \frac{s-a}{(s-a)^2-b^2}, \ s > |b| + a.}$$

6. We have $L(\sin bt) = \dfrac{b}{s^2+b^2}$, $s > 0$.

$\therefore$ By **first shifting theorem,**

$$\mathbf{L(e^{at}\sin bt) = \frac{b}{(s-a)^2+b^2}, \ s > a.}$$

7. We have $L(\cos bt) = \dfrac{s}{s^2+b^2}$, $s > 0$.

$\therefore$ By **first shifting theorem,**

$$\mathbf{L(e^{at}\cos bt) = \frac{s-a}{(s-a)^2+b^2}, \ s > a.}$$

Example 1. *Find the Laplace transform of the following functions :*

(i) $t^3 e^{-3t}, t \geq 0$ (ii) $e^{-3t} (2 \cos 5t - 3 \sin 5t), t \geq 0$

(iii) $e^{4t} \sin 2t \cos t, t \geq 0$ (iv) $\sinh t \cos t, t \geq 0$

(v) $e^{-t} (3 \sinh 2t - 5 \cosh 2t)$.

Sol. (i) We have $L(t^3) = \dfrac{3!}{s^{3+1}} = \dfrac{6}{s^4}, \ s > 0$.

∴ By **first shifting theorem,**

$$L(t^3 e^{-3t}) = \frac{6}{(s-(-3))^4}, s > 0 + (-3) = \mathbf{\frac{6}{(s+3)^4}, \ s > -3.}$$

(ii) We have L(2 cos 5*t* – 3 sin 5*t*)

$$= 2L(\cos 5t) - 3L(\sin 5t) \qquad \text{(By linearity)}$$

$$= 2\left(\frac{s}{s^2+5^2}\right) - 3\left(\frac{5}{s^2+5^2}\right), \ s > 0 = \frac{2s-15}{s^2+25}, \ s > 0.$$

∴ By **first shifting theorem,**

L(e^{-3t} (2 cos 5*t* – 3 sin 5*t*))

$$= \frac{2(s-(-3))-15}{(s-(-3))^2+25}, \ s > 0 + (-3) = \mathbf{\frac{2s-9}{s^2+6s+34}, \ s > -3.}$$

(iii) $$L(\sin 2t \cos t) = L\left(\frac{1}{2}(\sin 3t + \sin t)\right)$$

$$= \frac{1}{2} L(\sin 3t) + \frac{1}{2} L(\sin t) = \frac{1}{2}\left(\frac{3}{s^2+3^2}\right) + \frac{1}{2}\left(\frac{1}{s^2+1^2}\right), s > 0$$

$$= \frac{1}{2}\left[\frac{3}{s^2+9} + \frac{1}{s^2+1}\right], s > 0.$$

∴ By **first shifting theorem,**

$$L(e^{4t} \sin 2t \cos t) = \frac{1}{2}\left[\frac{3}{(s-4)^2+9} + \frac{1}{(s-4)^2+1}\right], s > 0 + 4$$

$$= \mathbf{\frac{1}{2}\left[\frac{3}{s^2-8s+25} + \frac{1}{s^2-8s+17}\right], s > 4.}$$

(iv) $$\sinh t \cos t = \frac{e^t - e^{-t}}{2} \cos t = e^t\left(\frac{\cos t}{2}\right) - e^{-t}\left(\frac{\cos t}{2}\right).$$

Now $$L\left(\frac{\cos t}{2}\right) = \frac{1}{2} L(\cos t) = \frac{1}{2}\left(\frac{s}{s^2+1^2}\right) = \frac{s}{2(s^2+1)}, \ s > 0.$$

∴ $$L(\sinh t \cos t) = L\left(e^t \cdot \frac{\cos t}{2} - e^{-t} \cdot \frac{\cos t}{2}\right)$$

$$= L\left(e^t \cdot \frac{\cos t}{2}\right) - L\left(e^{-t} \cdot \frac{\cos t}{2}\right) \qquad \text{(By linearity)}$$

$$= \frac{s-1}{2((s-1)^2+1)} - \frac{s-(-1)}{2((s-(-1))^2+1)}, \ s > 0 + 1, s > 0 + (-1)$$

$$= \frac{s-1}{2(s^2-2s+2)} - \frac{s+1}{2(s^2+2s+2)}, \ s > 1 = \frac{\mathbf{s^2-2}}{\mathbf{s^4+4}}, \ \mathbf{s > 1.}$$

(v) We have L(3 sinh $2t$ – 5 cosh $2t$)

$$= 3\text{L}(\sinh 2t) - 5\text{L}(\cosh 2t) = 3 \cdot \frac{2}{s^2-4} - 5 \cdot \frac{s}{s^2-4}, \ s > |2|$$

$$= \frac{6-5s}{s^2-4}, \ s > 2.$$

By **first shifting theorem,**

$$\text{L}(e^{-t}(3\sinh 2t - 5\cosh 2t)) = \frac{6-5(s+1)}{(s+1)^2-4}, \ s > 2+(-1) \ = \frac{\mathbf{1-5s}}{\mathbf{s^2+2s-3}}, \ \mathbf{s > 1.}$$

Example 2. *If the Laplace transform of the function f(t) of t for t ≥ 0 is F(s), then show that*

$$L[(\sinh at)\, f(t)] = \frac{1}{2}[F(s-a) - F(s+a)].$$

Hence evaluate L(sinh 2t sin 3t).

Sol. $\text{L}[(\sinh at)\, f(t)] = \text{L}\left[\frac{e^{at}-e^{-at}}{2} f(t)\right]$ $\left(\because \sinh at = \frac{e^{at}-e^{-at}}{2}\right)$

$$= \text{L}\left[\frac{1}{2}e^{at} f(t) - \frac{1}{2}e^{-at} f(t)\right]$$

$$= \frac{1}{2}\text{L}(e^{at} f(t)) - \frac{1}{2}\text{L}(e^{-at} f(t)) \qquad \text{(By linearity)}$$

$$= \frac{1}{2}\text{F}(s-a) - \frac{1}{2}\text{F}(s-(-a)) \qquad \text{(By first shifting theorem)}$$

$$= \frac{\mathbf{1}}{\mathbf{2}}[\mathbf{F(s-a) - F(s+a)}].$$

Also, $\quad \text{L}(\sin 3t) = \frac{3}{s^2+3^2} = \frac{3}{s^2+9}, \ s > 0.$

$$\therefore \ \text{L}(\sinh 2t \sin 3t) = \frac{1}{2}\left[\frac{3}{(s-2)^2+9} - \frac{3}{(s+2)^2+9}\right], \ s > 0+2, \ s > 0+(-2)$$

$$= \frac{3}{2}\left[\frac{1}{s^2-4s+13} - \frac{1}{s^2+4s+13}\right], \ s > 2$$

$$= \frac{\mathbf{12s}}{\mathbf{s^4+10s^2+169}}, \ \mathbf{s > 2}.$$

7. UNIT STEP FUNCTION

Let $a \geq 0$. The function of t taking value 0 if $t < a$ and 1 if $t > a$, is called a **unit step function** and is denoted by $u_a(t)$.

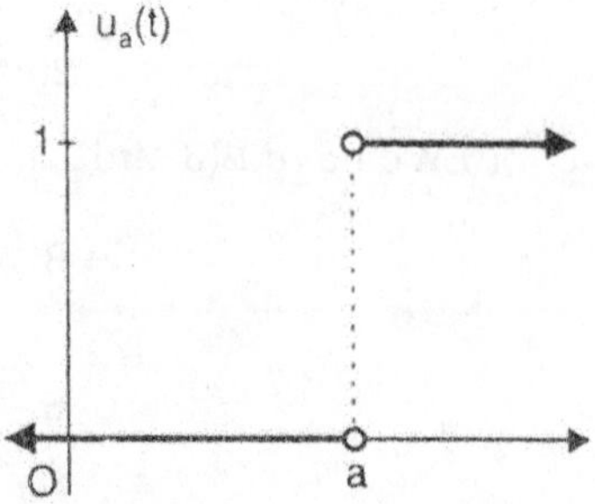

$$\therefore \qquad u_a(t) = \begin{cases} 0 & \text{if } t < a \\ 1 & \text{if } t > a. \end{cases}$$

8. SECOND SHIFTING THEOREM

If f(t) be a function of t for t ≥ 0 whose Laplace transform F(s) exists then for any constant a (≥ 0), the function f(t – a) u_a(t) has the Laplace transform e^{-as} F(s).

Proof. $t < a \Rightarrow f(t-a)\, u_a(t) = f(t-a)\,.\,0 = 0$

and $t > a \Rightarrow f(t-a)\, u_a(t) = f(t-a)\,.\,1 = f(t-a)$

$$\therefore \qquad f(t-a)\, u_a(t) = \begin{cases} 0 & \text{if } t < a \\ f(t-a) & \text{if } t > a \end{cases}$$

Also, $$F(s) = L(f(t)) = \int_0^\infty e^{-st} f(t)\, dt \qquad \text{...(1)}$$

Now $$L(f(t-a)\, u_a(t)) = \int_0^\infty e^{-st} f(t-a)\, u_a(t)\, dt$$

$$= \int_0^a e^{-st} f(t-a) u_a(t) dt + \int_a^\infty e^{-st} f(t-a) u_a(t) dt$$

$$= \int_0^a e^{-st}\,.\,0\, dt + \int_a^\infty e^{-st} f(t-a)\, dt$$

$$= 0 + \int_0^\infty e^{-s(a+u)} f(u)\, du, \text{ where } u = t - a$$

$$= e^{-sa} \int_0^\infty e^{-su} f(u)\, du = e^{-sa} \int_0^\infty e^{-st} f(t)\, dt \qquad \text{(By replacing } u \text{ by } t)$$

$$= e^{-as}\, F(s) \qquad \text{(By using (1))}$$

$\therefore$ **L(f(t – a) u_a(t)) = e^{-as} F(s), where F(s) = L(f(t)).**

Remark. The result of above theorem can be easily remembered as follows :

If **L(f(t)) = F(s), then for any a ≥ 0, L(f(t – a) u_a(t)) = e^{-as} F(s).**

Example 3. *Find the Laplace transform of the function* $t^2 u_1(t)$.

Sol. Let $g(t) = t^2 u_1(t)$.

$\therefore$ $g(t) = ((t-1)+1)^2 u_1(t) = f(t-1)\, u_1(t)$, where $f(t) = (t+1)^2$.

Now $L(f(t)) = L((t+1)^2) = L(t^2 + 2t + 1)$

$$= L(t^2) + 2L(t) + L(1) = \frac{2!}{s^3} + 2\left(\frac{1!}{s^2}\right) + \frac{1}{s},\ s > 0 = \frac{2 + 2s + s^2}{s^3},\ s > 0.$$

∴ By **second shifting theorem,**

$$L(g(t)) = L(f(t-1))\,u_1(t)) = e^{-1.s}\,L(f(t))$$

$$= e^{-s} \cdot \frac{2+2s+s^2}{s^3},\quad s>0.$$

Example 4. *Find the Laplace transform of the following function of t :*

$$g(t) = \begin{cases} 0, & 0<t<\pi/2 \\ \sin t, & t>\pi/2. \end{cases}$$

Sol. Given function $g(t)$ can be written as

$$g(t) = \begin{cases} 0, & 0<t<\pi/2 \\ \cos\left(t-\frac{\pi}{2}\right), & t>\frac{\pi}{2}. \end{cases}$$

$$\therefore \quad g(t) = \cos\left(t-\frac{\pi}{2}\right) u_{\pi/2}(t)$$

$$\therefore \quad g(t) = f\left(t-\frac{\pi}{2}\right) u_{\pi/2}(t), \text{ where } f(t) = \cos t$$

Now $$L(f(t)) = L(\cos t) = \frac{s}{s^2+1^2} = \frac{s}{s^2+1},\; s>0$$

∴ By **second shifting theorem,**

$$L(g(t)) = L\left(f\left(t-\frac{\pi}{2}\right) u_{\pi/2}(t)\right)$$

$$= e^{-(\pi/2)s}\,L(f(t)) = \frac{e^{-\pi s/2}\,s}{s^2+1},\; s>0.$$

Example 5. *Find the Laplace transform of the function* $g(t) = \begin{cases} 0, & 0<t<2 \\ t & t>2 \end{cases}$ *by using (i) definition (ii) second shifting theorem. Verify that the results are same :*

Sol. We have $g(t) = \begin{cases} 0, & 0<t<2 \\ t, & t>2. \end{cases}$

(i) $$L(g) = \int_0^\infty e^{-st}\,g(t)\,dt$$

$$= \int_0^2 e^{-st}\,g(t)\,dt + \int_2^\infty e^{-st}\,g(t)\,dt = \int_0^2 e^{-st}.0\,dt + \int_2^\infty e^{-st}\,t\,dt$$

$$= 0 + t \cdot \left.\frac{e^{-st}}{-s}\right|_2^\infty - \int_2^\infty 1 \cdot \frac{e^{-st}}{-s}\,dt = -\frac{1}{s}\left[\lim_{T\to\infty} \frac{T}{e^{sT}} - \frac{2}{e^{2s}}\right] + \left.\frac{e^{-st}}{-s^2}\right|_2^\infty$$

$$= -\frac{1}{s}\left[\lim_{T\to\infty} \frac{1}{se^{sT}} - \frac{2}{e^{2s}}\right] - \frac{1}{s^2}\left[\lim_{T\to\infty} \frac{1}{e^{sT}} - \frac{1}{e^{2s}}\right]$$

(Using L'Hospital's Rule)

$$= -\frac{1}{s}\left[0 - \frac{2}{e^{2s}}\right] - \frac{1}{s^2}\left[0 - \frac{1}{e^{2s}}\right] = \frac{2}{se^{2s}} + \frac{1}{s^2e^{2s}} = \frac{2s+1}{s^2\,e^{2s}},\; s>0.$$

(*ii*) $$g(t) = \begin{cases} 0, & 0 < t < 2 \\ (t-2)+2, & t > 2 \end{cases}.$$

$\therefore$ $g(t) = f(t-2)\, u_2(t)$, where $f(t) = t + 2$

Now $L(f(t)) = L(t+2) = L(t) + 2L(1)$

$$= \frac{1!}{s^{1+1}} + 2\left(\frac{1}{s}\right), s > 0 = \frac{1+2s}{s^2}, s > 0$$

By **second shifting theorem,**

$$L(g(t)) = L(f(t-2)\, u_2(t)) = e^{-2s}\, L(f(t))$$

$$= e^{-2s} \cdot \frac{1+2s}{s^2}, s > 0 = \frac{\mathbf{2s+1}}{\mathbf{s^2\, e^{2s}}}, \mathbf{s > 0.}$$

9. CHANGE OF SCALE PROPERTY

Theorem. If f(t) be a function of t for t ≥ 0 whose Laplace transform F(s) exists, then for any positive constant 'a', the function f(at) has the Laplace transform $\frac{1}{a} F\left(\frac{s}{a}\right)$.

Proof. We have $F(s) = L(f(t)) = \int_0^\infty e^{-st} f(t)\, dt$.

Now $$L(f(at)) = \int_0^\infty e^{-st} f(at)\, dt = \int_0^\infty e^{-sz/a} f(z) \frac{dz}{a}, \text{ where } z = at$$

$$= \frac{1}{a}\int_0^\infty e^{-(s/a)z} f(z)\, dz = \frac{1}{a}\int_0^\infty e^{-(s/a)t} f(t)\, dt$$

(By replacing variable z by t)

$$= \frac{1}{a} F\left(\frac{s}{a}\right).$$

$\therefore$ $$\mathbf{L(f(at)) = \frac{1}{a} F\left(\frac{s}{a}\right).}$$

Remark. The above theorem can be easily remembered as follows :

If $\mathbf{L(f(t)) = F(s)}$**, then for any a (> 0),** $\mathbf{L(f(at)) = \frac{1}{a} F\left(\frac{s}{a}\right)}$.

Example 6. *Find $L(f(\lambda t))$ where λ is any positive constant and $f(t)$ is a function of t for $t \geq 0$:*

(*i*) $f(t) = t^n$, $n \in \mathbf{N}$ (*ii*) $f(t) = e^t$ (*iii*) $f(t) = \sinh t$

(*iv*) $f(t) = \cosh t$ (*v*) $f(t) = \sin t$ (*vi*) $f(t) = \cos t$.

Sol. (*i*) $f(t) = t^n$, $n \in \mathbf{N}$

$\therefore$ $L(f(t)) = L(t^n) = \frac{n!}{s^{n+1}}, s > 0$

By **change of scale property,** $L(f(\lambda t)) = \frac{1}{\lambda} \cdot \frac{n!}{(s/\lambda)^{n+1}}, \frac{s}{\lambda} > 0$

$$= \frac{\mathbf{\lambda^n\, n!}}{\mathbf{s^{n+1}}}, \mathbf{s > 0.} \qquad (\because \lambda > 0)$$

(*ii*) $f(t) = e^t$

$$\therefore \quad L(f(t)) = L(e^t) = \frac{1}{s-1}, \quad s > 1$$

By **change of scale property,** $L(f(\lambda t)) = \frac{1}{\lambda} \cdot \frac{1}{(s/\lambda) - 1}, \quad \frac{s}{\lambda} > 1$

$$= \frac{1}{s - \lambda}, s > \lambda.$$

(*iii*) $f(t) = \sinh t$

$$\therefore \quad L(f(t)) = L(\sinh t) = \frac{1}{s^2 - (1)^2}, s > |1| = \frac{1}{s^2 - 1}, s > 1$$

By **change of scale property,** $L(f(\lambda t)) = \frac{1}{\lambda} \cdot \frac{1}{(s/\lambda)^2 - 1}, \quad \frac{s}{\lambda} > 1$

$$= \frac{\lambda}{s^2 - \lambda^2}, s > \lambda.$$

(*iv*) $f(t) = \cosh t$

$$\therefore \quad L(f(t)) = L(\cosh t) = \frac{s}{s^2 - 1}, s > 1$$

By **change of scale property,** $L(f(\lambda t)) = \frac{1}{\lambda} \cdot \frac{s/\lambda}{(s/\lambda)^2 - 1}, \quad \frac{s}{\lambda} > 1$

$$= \frac{s}{s^2 - \lambda^2}, s > \lambda.$$

(*v*) $f(t) = \sin t$

$$\therefore \quad L(f(t)) = L(\sin t) = \frac{1}{s^2 + 1}, s > 0$$

By **change of scalar property,** $L(f(\lambda t)) = \frac{1}{\lambda} \cdot \frac{1}{(s/\lambda)^2 + 1}, \quad \frac{s}{\lambda} > 0$

$$= \frac{\lambda}{s^2 + \lambda^2}, s > 0.$$

(*vi*) $f(t) = \cos t$

$$\therefore \quad L(f(t)) = L(\cos t) = \frac{s}{s^2 + 1}, s > 0$$

By **change of scalar property,** $L(f(\lambda t)) = \frac{1}{\lambda} \cdot \frac{s/\lambda}{(s/\lambda)^2 + 1}, \quad \frac{s}{\lambda} > 0$

$$= \frac{s}{s^2 + \lambda^2}, s > 0.$$

WORKING RULES FOR SOLVING PROBLEMS

Rule I. If $L(f(t)) = F(s)$, $s > k$ then for any a, $L(e^{at} f(t)) = F(s-a)$, $s > k + a$.

Rule II. For $a \geq 0$, the unit step function $u(t-a)$ is defined as $u(t-a) = \begin{cases} 0 & \text{if } t < a \\ 1 & \text{if } t > a. \end{cases}$

Rule III. If $L(f(t)) = F(s)$ then for any $a \geq 0$, $L(f(t-a)\,u(t-a)) = e^{-as} L(f(t))$.

Rule IV. If $L(f(t)) = F(s)$ then for any $a (> 0)$, $L(f(at)) = \frac{1}{a} F\left(\frac{s}{a}\right)$.

EXERCISE 3

1. Find the Laplace transform of the following functions of t for $t \geq 0$:

   (i) $e^t t^k$, $k > -1$ (ii) $e^{2t} t^4$ (iii) $e^t \sinh t$

   (iv) $e^{3t} \cosh 3t$ (v) $e^{2t} \sin t$ (vi) $e^{2t} \cos 2t$.

2. Find the Laplace transform of the following functions of t for $t \geq 0$:

   (i) $e^{-4t} t^{3/2}$ (ii) $e^{-6t} t^7$ (iii) $e^{-2t} \sinh 6t$

   (iv) $e^{-5t} \cosh 3t$ (v) $e^{-5t} \sin 8t$ (vi) $e^{-3t} \cos 4t$.

3. Find the Laplace transform of the following functions of t for $t \geq 0$:

   (i) $e^{3t} \sin^2 t$ (ii) $(t+2)^2 e^t$

   (iii) $\sinh 3t \cos^2 t$ *(KU 2004)* (iv) $\cosh at \sin at$.

4. Find the Laplace transform of the following functions of t for $t \geq 0$:

   (i) $e^{-t} \sin^2 t$ (ii) $5e^{2t} \sinh 2t$

   (iii) $e^{-at} \sinh bt$ (iv) $\cosh 4t \sin 6t$.

5. If the Laplace transform of the function $f(t)$ of t for $t \geq 0$ is $F(s)$, then show that

   $$L[(\cosh at)\, f(t)] = \frac{1}{2}[F(s-a) + F(s+a)].$$

   Hence evaluate $L(\cosh 3t \cos 2t)$. *(MDU 2004)*

6. Show that $L\{(1 + te^{-t})^3\} = \frac{1}{s} + \frac{3}{(s+1)^2} + \frac{6}{(s+2)^3} + \frac{6}{(s+3)^4}$, $s > 0$.

7. Find the Laplace transform of the following functions :

   (i) $(t-1)\, u_1(t)$ (ii) $(5 \cos t)\, u_\pi(t)$.

8. Find the Laplace transform of the function : $g(t) = \begin{cases} 0, & 0 < t < \pi/2 \\ \cos t, & t > \pi/2. \end{cases}$

9. Find the Laplace transform of the function : $g(t) = \begin{cases} \cos(t - 2\pi/3), & t > 2\pi/3 \\ 0, & 0 < t < 2\pi/3. \end{cases}$

10. Find the Laplace transform of the function $g(t) = \begin{cases} 0, & 0 < t < 5 \\ t, & t > 5 \end{cases}$ by using (*i*) definition (*ii*) second shifting theorem. Verify that the results are same.

Answers

1. (i) $\dfrac{\Gamma(k+1)}{(s-1)^{k+1}}$, $s>1$ (ii) $\dfrac{24}{(s-2)^5}$, $s>2$ (iii) $\dfrac{1}{s^2-2s}$, $s>2$

(iv) $\dfrac{s}{s^2-6s}$, $s>6$ (v) $\dfrac{1}{s^2-4s+5}$, $s>2$ (vi) $\dfrac{s-2}{s^2-4s+8}$, $s>2$

2. (i) $\dfrac{3\sqrt{\pi}}{4(s+4)^{5/2}}$, $s>-4$ (ii) $\dfrac{5040}{(s+6)^8}$, $s>-6$ (iii) $\dfrac{6}{s^2+4s-32}$, $s>4$

(iv) $\dfrac{s+5}{s^2+10s+16}$, $s>-2$ (v) $\dfrac{8}{s^2+10s+89}$, $s>-5$ (vi) $\dfrac{s+3}{s^2+6s+25}$, $s>-3$

3. (i) $\dfrac{2}{(s-3)(s^2-6s+13)}$, $s>3$ (ii) $\dfrac{2}{(s-1)^3}[(2s^2-2s+1)]$, $s>1$

(iii) $\dfrac{1}{2}\left[\dfrac{s^2-6s+11}{(s-3)(s^2-6s+13)}+\dfrac{s^2+6s+11}{(s+3)(s^2+6s+13)}\right]$, $s>3$ (iv) $\dfrac{a(s^2+2a^2)}{s^4+4a^4}$, $s>|a|$

4. (i) $\dfrac{2}{(s+1)(s^2+2s+5)}$, $s>-1$ (ii) $\dfrac{10}{s^2-4s}$, $s>4$

(iii) $\dfrac{b}{s^2+2as+a^2-b^2}$, $s>|b|-a$ (iv) $\dfrac{6(s^2+52)}{s^4+40s^2+2704}$, $s>4$

5. $\dfrac{s^3-5s}{s^4-10s^2+169}$, $s>3$ **7.** (i) $\dfrac{e^{-s}}{s^2}$, $s>0$ (ii) $\dfrac{-5se^{-\pi s}}{s^2+1}$, $s>0$

8. $-\dfrac{e^{-\pi s/2}}{s^2+1}$, $s>0$ **9.** $\dfrac{e^{-2\pi s/3}s}{s^2+1}$, $s>0$ **10.** $\dfrac{(5s+1)e^{-5s}}{s^2}$, $s>0$

Hints

8. Use $\cos t = -\sin\left(t-\dfrac{\pi}{2}\right)$

10. PIECE WISE CONTINUOUS FUNCTION

A function $f(t)$ is called **piece wise continuous (or sectionally continuous)** on a finite interval $[a, b]$ if this interval can be divided into a finite number of sub-intervals such that (i) $f(t)$ is continuous in the interior of each of these sub-intervals and (ii) $f(t)$ approaches a finite limit as t approaches either endpoint of each of the sub-interval from its interior.

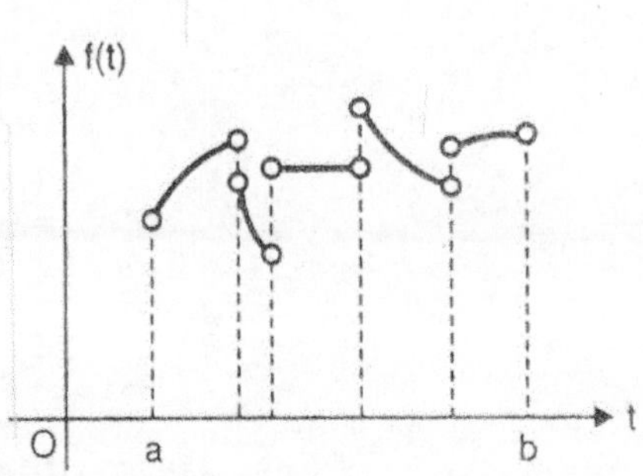

Thus a piece wise continuous function has finitely many jumps as discontinuities. Clearly every continuous function is a piece wise continuous function. Also, if $f(t)$ is a piece wise continuous function on $[a, b]$, then $f(x)$ is integrable on $[a, b]$.

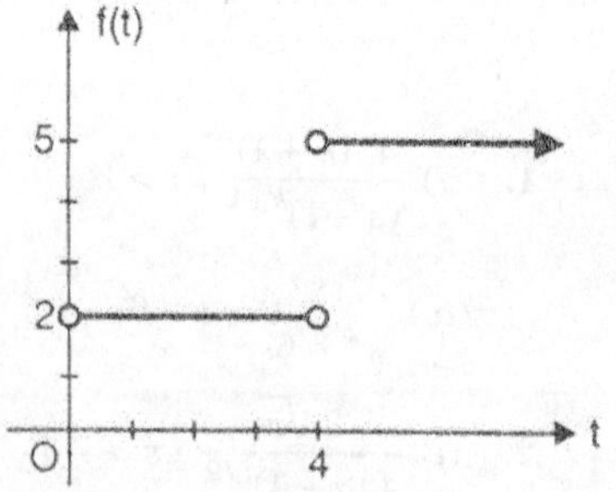

For example, let $f(t) = \begin{cases} 2 & 0 < t < 4 \\ 5 & t > 4. \end{cases}$

The function $f(x)$ is piece wise continuous on every finite interval $[0, b]$, where b is a positive real number.

11. EXISTENCE THEOREM FOR LAPLACE TRANSFORMS

The Laplace transform of any arbitrary function may not exist. For the existence of the Laplace transform of a function, the function is expected to fulfil certain conditions. In the ensuing theorem, we shall establish the criterion for the existence of Laplace transform of a function.

Theorem. Let f(t) be a real function such that

(*i*) f(t) is piece wise continuous on every finite interval in the range $t \geq 0$ and

(*ii*) there exists constants k and M such that $|f(t)| \leq Me^{kt}$ for $t \geq 0$, then prove that the Laplace transform of f(t) exists for all $s > k$. (KU 2004 S)

Proof. Since $f(t)$ is piece wise continuous on every finite interval in the range $t \geq 0$, $f(t)$ is piece wise continuous on the finite interval $[0, T]$ for $T > 0$.

Also e^{-st} is continuous on the finite interval $[0, T]$ for $T > 0$

$\therefore$ $e^{-st} f(t)$ is piece wise continuous on $[0, T]$ for $T > 0$.

$\therefore$ $e^{-st} f(t)$ is integrable on $[0, T]$ for $T > 0$.

$\therefore$ $\int_0^T e^{-st} f(t)\,dt$ exists for all $T > 0$.

Now
$$\int_0^\infty e^{-st} f(t)\,dt = \lim_{T\to\infty} \int_0^T e^{-st} f(t)\,dt$$

and
$$\left| \int_0^\infty e^{-st} f(t)\,dt \right| \leq \int_0^\infty \left| e^{-st} f(t) \right| dt = \int_0^\infty e^{-st} |f(t)|\,dt$$

$$\leq \int_0^\infty e^{-st} \cdot Me^{kt}\,dt = M\int_0^\infty e^{(k-s)t}\,dt = M \lim_{T\to\infty} \left[\frac{e^{(k-s)t}}{k-s} \right]_0^T$$

$$= \frac{M}{k-s} \lim_{T\to\infty} \left[\frac{1}{e^{(s-k)T}} - 1 \right] = \frac{M}{k-s}[0-1] \quad \text{for } s > k$$

$$= \frac{M}{s-k} \quad \text{for } s > k.$$

$$\therefore \quad \int_0^\infty e^{-st} f(t)\,dt \leq \frac{M}{s-k} \quad \text{for } s > k$$

$$\therefore \quad L(f) = \int_0^\infty e^{-st} f(t)\,dt \text{ exists for } s > k.$$

12. LAPLACE TRANSFORMS OF DERIVATIVES

Theorem 1. (Laplace transform of the first derivative). Let f(t) be a real function such that

(*i*) f(t) is continuous for all $t \geq 0$

(*ii*) there exists constants k and M such that $|f(t)| \leq Me^{kt}$ for $t \geq 0$

(*iii*) f′(t) is piece wise continuous on every finite interval in the range $t \geq 0$,

then the Laplace transform of the derivative f ′(t) exists and

$$L(f') = sL(f) - f(0) \quad \text{for } s > k.$$

Proof. By definition

$L(f') = \lim_{T \to \infty} \int_0^T e^{-st} f'(t)\, dt$, provided this limit has some finite value.

Let T be any positive number.

Using (*iii*), $f'(t)$ is piece wise continuous on [0, T].

$\therefore$ $f'(t)$ has at most a finite number of discontinuities, say $t_1, t_2, \ldots\ldots, t_n$, where

$$0 < t_1 < t_2 < \ldots\ldots < t_n \leq T$$

$$\therefore \quad \int_0^T e^{-st} f'(t)\, dt = \int_0^{t_1} e^{-st} f'(t)\, dt + \ldots\ldots + \int_{t_n}^T e^{-st} f'(t)\, dt$$

The integrand of each of the integrals on the right is continuous.

$\therefore$ By using integration by parts, we have

$$\int_0^T e^{-st} f'(t)\, dt = \left[e^{-st} f(t)\right]_0^{t_1} + s\int_0^{t_1} e^{-st} f(t)\, dt + \ldots\ldots$$

$$+ \left[e^{-st} f(t)\right]_{t_n}^T + s\int_{t_n}^T e^{-st} f(t)\, dt$$

$$= \left[e^{-st_1} f(t_1) - f(0)\right] + s\int_0^{t_1} e^{-st} f(t)\, dt + \ldots\ldots$$

$$+ \left[e^{-sT} f(T) - e^{-st_n} f(t_n)\right] + s\int_{t_n}^T e^{-st} f(t)\, dt$$

$$= e^{-sT} f(T) - f(0) + s\left[\int_0^{t_1} e^{-st} f(t)\, dt + \ldots\ldots + \int_{t_n}^T e^{-st} f(t)\, dt\right]$$

$$\therefore \quad \int_0^T e^{-st} f'(t)\, dt = e^{-sT} f(T) - f(0) + s\int_0^T e^{-st} f(t)\, dt$$

($\because$ f is continuous for $t \geq 0$)

$$\therefore \quad \lim_{T \to \infty} \int_0^T e^{-st} f'(t)\, dt = \lim_{T \to \infty} e^{-sT} f(T) - f(0) + \lim_{T \to \infty} s\int_0^T e^{-st} f(t)\, dt \quad \ldots(1)$$

Now using (*ii*), $e^{-sT} f(T) \leq e^{-sT} |f(T)| \leq e^{-sT} . Me^{kT} = \frac{M}{e^{(s-k)T}}$

$$\therefore \quad \lim_{T \to \infty} e^{-sT} f(T) = 0 \text{ for } s > k$$

Also $\quad \lim_{T \to \infty} s\int_0^T e^{-st} f(t)\, dt = sL(f)$

$\therefore$ (1) $\Rightarrow$ $\lim_{T \to \infty} \int_0^T e^{-st} f'(t)\,dt = 0 - f(0) + sL(f).$

$\therefore$ **L(f′) = sL(f) − f(0) for s > k.**

Example 1. *Using* $L(t^n) = \frac{n!}{s^{n+1}}$ *, find the value of* $L(t^{n+1})$*.*

Sol. Let $f(t) = t^{n+1}$.

$\therefore$ $f'(t) = (n+1)\,t^n$.

We have $L(f') = sL(f) - f(0)$.

$\therefore$ $L((n+1)\,t^n) = sL(t^{n+1}) - (0)^{n+1} \Rightarrow (n+1)\,L(t^n) = sL(t^{n+1})$

$\therefore$ $L(t^{n+1}) = \frac{n+1}{s}\,L(t^n) = \frac{n+1}{s}\cdot\frac{n!}{s^{n+1}} = \mathbf{\frac{(n+1)!}{s^{n+2}}}$.

Example 2. *Find the Laplace transform of the function* $\sin^2 at \cos at$*,* $t \geq 0$*.*

Sol. Let $f(t) = \sin^3 at$.

$\therefore$ $f'(t) = 3\sin^2 at \,.\, a\cos at = 3a\cos at \sin^2 at$

We have $L(f') = sL(f) - f(0)$.

$\therefore$ $L(3a\cos at \sin^2 at) = sL(\sin^3 at) - \sin^3 0$

$\Rightarrow$ $3a\,L(\cos at \sin^2 at) = sL(\sin^3 at)$ ...(1)

Now, $\sin 3x = 3\sin x - 4\sin^3 x \Rightarrow \sin^3 x = \frac{3}{4}\sin x - \frac{1}{4}\sin 3x$

$\therefore$ $\sin^3 at = \frac{3}{4}\sin at - \frac{1}{4}\sin 3at$

$\therefore$ $L(\sin^3 at) = \frac{3}{4}L(\sin at) - \frac{1}{4}L(\sin 3at)$

$$= \frac{3}{4}\left(\frac{a}{s^2+a^2}\right) - \frac{1}{4}\left(\frac{3a}{s^2+(3a)^2}\right)$$

$$= \frac{3a}{4}\left(\frac{1}{s^2+a^2} - \frac{1}{s^2+9a^2}\right) = \frac{6a^3}{(s^2+a^2)(s^2+9a^2)}$$

$\therefore$ (1) $\Rightarrow$ $3a\,L(\cos at \sin^2 at) = s\,.\,\frac{6a^3}{(s^2+a^2)(s^2+9a^2)} - 0$

$\therefore$ $L(\cos at \sin^2 at) = \frac{1}{3a}\cdot\frac{6a^3 s}{(s^2+a^2)(s^2+9a^2)} = \mathbf{\frac{2a^2 s}{(s^2+a^2)(s^2+9a^2)}}$.

Alternative method

$$\sin^2 at \cos at = \frac{1}{2}.\sin at\,.\,2\sin at \cos at$$

$$= \frac{1}{2}\sin at \sin 2at = \frac{1}{4}.\,2\sin 2at \sin at$$

$$= \frac{1}{4}(\cos at - \cos 3at).$$

$\therefore \quad L(\sin^2 at \cos at) = L\left(\frac{1}{4}(\cos at - \cos 3at)\right)$

$$= \frac{1}{4}[L(\cos at) - L(\cos 3at)] = \frac{1}{4}\left[\frac{s}{s^2+a^2} - \frac{s}{s^2+9a^2}\right]$$

$$= \frac{s}{4}\left[\frac{8a^2}{(s^2+a^2)(s^2+9a^2)}\right] = \frac{\mathbf{2a^2 s}}{\mathbf{(s^2+a^2)(s^2+9a^2)}}.$$

Theorem 2. (Laplace transform of the derivative of any order n). Let f(t) be a real function such that

(*i*) **$f(t), f'(t), f''(t), \ldots\ldots, f^{(n-1)}(t)$ are continuous for all $t \geq 0$**

(*ii*) **there exists constants k and M such that**

$$| f(t) | \leq Me^{kt} \text{ for } t \geq 0 \text{ and } \quad | f^{(i)}(t) | \leq Me^{kt} \text{ for } t \geq 0 \text{ and } i = 1, 2, \ldots\ldots, n-1$$

(*iii*) **$f^{(n)}(t)$ is piece wise continuous on every finite interval in the range $t \geq 0$ then the Laplace transform of $f^{(n)}(t)$ exists and**

$$L(f^{(n)}) = s^n L(f) - s^{n-1} f(0) - s^{n-2} f'(0) - \ldots\ldots - f^{(n-1)}(0) \quad \text{for } s > k.$$

Proof. Using (*i*), $f'(t)$ is piece wise continuous on every finite interval in the range $t \geq 0$.

$\therefore$ By **theorem 1,** $L(f') = s\,L(f) - f(0)$, $s > k$

By applying **theorem 1** to the function $f'(t)$, we get

$$L(f'') = s\,L(f') - f'(0).$$

$$\therefore \quad L(f'') = s\,[s\,L(f) - f(0)] - f'(0)$$

or $$L(f'') = s^2 L(f) - s f(0) - f'(0)$$

Let the result be true for $f^{(m)}(t)$, the mth derivative of $f(t)$.

$$\therefore \quad L(f^{(m)}) = s^m L(f) - s^{m-1} f(0) - \ldots\ldots f^{(m-1)}(0) \qquad \ldots(1)$$

Now (*i*) $f^{(m)}(t)$ is continuous for all $t \geq 0$.

(*ii*) $| f^{(m)}(t) | \leq M e^{kt}$ for $t \geq 0$.

(*iii*) By given condition (*i*), $f^{(m+1)}(t)$ is piece wise continuous on every finite interval in the range $t \geq 0$.

$\therefore$ By **theorem 1**, the Laplace transform of the derivative $f^{(m+1)}(t)$ exists and

$$L(f^{(m+1)}) = s\,L(f^{(m)}) - f^{(m)}(0). \qquad \ldots(2)$$

Using (1), we get

$$L(f^{(m+1)}) = s\,[s^m L(f) - s^{m-1} f(0) - \ldots\ldots - f^{(m-1)}(0)] - f^{(m)}(0)$$

or $$L(f^{(m+1)}) = s^{m+1} L(f) - s^m f(0) - s^{m-1} f(0) - \ldots\ldots - f^m(0)$$

$\therefore$ By P.M.I., we have

$$L(f^{(n)}) = s^n L(f) - s^{n-1} f(0) - s^{n-2} f'(0) - \ldots\ldots - f^{(n-1)}(0) \quad \text{for } s > k.$$

In particular

$n = 1 \Rightarrow$ $\mathbf{L(f') = sL(f) - f(0)}$

$n = 2 \Rightarrow$ $\mathbf{L(f'') = s^2L(f) - sf(0) - f'(0)}$

$n = 3 \Rightarrow$ $\mathbf{L(f''') = s^3L(f) - s^2f(0) - sf'(0) - f''(0).}$

Example 3. *Given* $L(t^3) = \frac{6}{s^4}$, *find the value of* $L(t^6)$.

Sol. Let $f(t) = t^6$.

$\therefore$ $f'(t) = 6t^5, f''(t) = 30t^4$ and $f'''(t) = 120t^3$.

We have $L(f''') = s^3L(f) - s^2 f(0) - sf'(0) - f''(0)$.

$\therefore$ $L(120t^3) = s^3L(t^6) - s^2 . (0)^6 - s . 6(0)^5 - 30(0)^4$

$\Rightarrow$ $120L(t^3) = s^3L(t^6) - 0 - 0 - 0$

$\Rightarrow$ $120\left(\frac{6}{s^4}\right) = s^3L(t^6)$ (Given)

$\Rightarrow$ $L(t^6) = \frac{1}{s^3}\left(\frac{720}{s^4}\right) = \mathbf{\frac{720}{s^7}}$.

Example 4. *Find the Laplace transform of the function cos at,* $t \geq 0$.

Sol. Let $f(t) = \cos at, t \geq 0$.

$\therefore$ $f'(t) = -a \sin at$ and $f''(t) = -a^2 \cos at$.

We have $L(f'') = s^2 L(f) - sf(0) - f'(0)$.

$\therefore$ $L(-a^2 \cos at) = s^2 L(\cos at) - s \cos 0 - (-a \sin 0)$

$\Rightarrow$ $-a^2 L(\cos at) = s^2 L(\cos at) - s - 0$

$\Rightarrow$ $(s^2 + a^2) L(\cos at) = s$

$\therefore$ $L(\cos at) = \mathbf{\frac{s}{s^2 + a^2}}$.

Example 5. *Find the Laplace transform of the function t sin bt.*

Sol. Let $f(t) = t \sin bt$.

$\therefore$ $f'(t) = t(b \cos bt) + 1 . \sin bt = bt \cos bt + \sin bt$

and $f''(t) = b[t(-b \sin bt) + 1 . \cos bt] + b \cos bt = -b^2t \sin bt + 2b \cos bt$

We have $L(f'') = s^2L(f) - sf(0) - f'(0)$.

$\therefore$ $L(-b^2t \sin bt + 2b \cos bt) = s^2L(t \sin bt) - s(0 . \sin 0) - (b . 0 . \cos 0 + \sin 0)$

$\Rightarrow$ $-b^2L(t \sin bt) + 2bL(\cos bt) = s^2L(t \sin bt) - 0 - (0 + 0)$

$\Rightarrow$ $(s^2 + b^2) L(t \sin bt) = 2bL(\cos bt) = 2b\left(\frac{s}{s^2 + b^2}\right)$

$\Rightarrow$ $L(t \sin bt) = \frac{1}{s^2 + b^2}\left(\frac{2bs}{s^2 + b^2}\right) = \mathbf{\frac{2bs}{(s^2 + b^2)^2}}$.

WORKING RULES FOR SOLVING PROBLEMS

Rule I. $L(f') = sL(f) - f(0)$.

Rule II. $L(f^{(n)}) = s^n L(f) - s^{n-1} f(0) - s^{n-2} f'(0) - \ldots\ldots - f^{(n-1)}(0)$.

Rule III. (*i*) $L(f'') = s^2L(f) - sf(0) - f'(0)$

(*ii*) $L(f''') = s^3L(f) - s^2f(0) - sf'(0) - f''(0)$.

EXERCISE 4

1. Using $L(1) = \frac{1}{s}$, find $L(t)$.

2. (*i*) Using $L(\sinh at) = \frac{a}{s^2 - a^2}$, find $L(\cosh at)$.

   (*ii*) Using $L(\cosh at) = \frac{s}{s^2 - a^2}$, find $L(\sinh at)$.

3. (*i*) Using $L(\sin bt) = \frac{b}{s^2 + b^2}$, find $L(\cos bt)$.

   (*ii*) Using $L(\cos bt) = \frac{s}{s^2 + b^2}$, find $L(\sin bt)$.

4. Find the Laplace transform of the function $\sin bt \cos^2 bt$, $t \geq 0$.

5. Using $L(1) = \frac{1}{s}$, find $L(t^2)$.

6. Given $L(t^2) = \frac{2}{s^3}$, find the value of $L(t^5)$.

7. Find the Laplace transform of the following functions by using the result of Laplace transform of second derivative of a function :

   (*i*) e^{at} (*ii*) $\sinh at$ (*iii*) $\cosh at$ (*iv*) $\sin at$.

8. Find the Laplace transform of the function $t \cos at$.

Answers

1. $\frac{1}{s^2}$ 2. (*i*) $\frac{s}{s^2 - a^2}$ (*ii*) $\frac{a}{s^2 - a^2}$ 3. (*i*) $\frac{s}{s^2 + b^2}$ (*ii*) $\frac{b}{s^2 + b^2}$

4. $\frac{b(s^2 + 3b^2)}{(s^2 + b^2)(s^2 + 9b^2)}$ 5. $\frac{2}{s^3}$ 6. $\frac{120}{s^6}$ 7. (*i*) $\frac{1}{s - a}$

(*ii*) $\frac{a}{s^2 - a^2}$ (*iii*) $\frac{s}{s^2 - a^2}$ (*iv*) $\frac{a}{s^2 + a^2}$ 8. $\frac{s^2 - a^2}{(s^2 + a^2)^2}$.

Hints

8. Let $f(t) = t \cos at$.

   Use $L(f'') = s^2 L(f) - sf(0) - f'(0)$.

13. LAPLACE TRANSFORMS OF INTEGRALS

Theorem. Let f(t) be a real function such that

(*i*) f(t) is piece wise continuous on every finite interval in the range $t \geq 0$

(*ii*) there exists constants k and M such that $|f(t)| \leq Me^{kt}$ for $t \geq 0$, then the Laplace transform of the integral $\int_0^t f(T)\,dT$ exists and

$$L\left(\int_0^t f(T)\,dT\right) = \frac{1}{s} L(f(t)) \text{ for } s > k.$$

Proof. If k in (*ii*) is negative, then $-k > 0$ and

$$(ii) \Rightarrow |f(t)| \le Me^{kt} = \frac{M}{e^{-kt}} \le Me^{-kt}. \qquad (\because \ e^{-kt} > 1)$$

$\therefore$ We can assume that k is positive.

Let $$g(t) = \int_0^t f(T)\, dT, \quad t \ge 0$$

$\therefore$ $g(t)$ is continuous for all $t \ge 0$.

Now $$|g(t)| = \left| \int_0^t f(T)\,dT \right| \le \int_0^t |f(T)|\,dT \le \int_0^t |Me^{kT}|\,dT = M\int_0^t e^{kT}\, dT$$

$$= \frac{M}{k}(e^{kt} - 1) \le \frac{M}{k} e^{kt}. \qquad (\because \ k > 0 \Rightarrow e^{kt} > 1)$$

$$\therefore \quad |g(t)| \le \frac{M}{k} e^{kt} \quad \text{for } t \ge 0$$

Also $g'(t) = f(t)$ except for points at which $f(t)$ is discontinuous.

$\therefore$ $g'(t)$ is piece wise continuous on every finite interval in the range $t \ge 0$.

$\therefore$ The Laplace transform of $g'(t)$ exists and

$$L(g') = sL(g) - g(0) \quad \text{for } s > k$$

$$\Rightarrow \quad L(g') = sL(g) \quad \text{for } s > k \qquad \left(\because \ g(0) = \int_0^0 f(T)\, dT = 0\right)$$

$$\Rightarrow \quad L(g) = \frac{1}{s} L(g')$$

$$\Rightarrow \quad \mathbf{L}\left(\int_0^t \mathbf{f(T)\, dT} \right) = \frac{\mathbf{1}}{\mathbf{s}} \mathbf{L(f(t))} \quad \textbf{for } \mathbf{s > k.}$$

WORKING RULE FOR SOLVING PROBLEMS

Rule I. $L\left(\int_0^t f(T)\, dT\right) = \frac{1}{s} L(f(t)).$

Example 1. *Using* $L(1) = \frac{1}{s}$, *find* $L(t^2)$.

Sol. Let $f(t) = 1$. $\quad \therefore \quad L(f) = L(1) = \frac{1}{s}$ (Given)

We have $$L\left(\int_0^t f(T)\, dT\right) = \frac{1}{s} L(f).$$

$$\therefore \quad L\left(\int_0^t 1\, dT\right) = \frac{1}{s}\left(\frac{1}{s}\right)$$

$$\Rightarrow \quad L\left(T \Big|_0^t\right) = \frac{1}{s^2} \Rightarrow L(t) = \frac{1}{s^2}.$$

Let $g(t) = t$. $\therefore$ $L(g) = L(t) = \dfrac{1}{s^2}$

We have $L\left(\int_0^t g(T)\,dT\right) = \dfrac{1}{s}L(g)$

$$\therefore \quad L\left(\int_0^t T\,dT\right) = \frac{1}{s}\cdot\frac{1}{s^2}$$

$$\Rightarrow \quad L\left(\frac{T^2}{2}\Bigg|_0^t\right) = \frac{1}{s^3} \Rightarrow L\left(\frac{t^2}{2}\right) = \frac{1}{s^3}$$

$$\Rightarrow \quad \frac{1}{2}L(t^2) = \frac{1}{s^3} \Rightarrow L(t^2) = \frac{2}{s^3}.$$

Example 2. *Using* $L(\sin bt) = \dfrac{b}{s^2 + b^2}$, *find* $L(\cos bt)$. (KU 2005 S)

Sol. Let $f(t) = \sin bt$. $\therefore$ $L(f) = L(\sin bt) = \dfrac{b}{s^2 + b^2}$. (Given)

We have $L\left(\int_0^t f(T)\,dT\right) = \dfrac{1}{s}L(f)$.

$$\therefore \quad L\left(\int_0^t \sin bT\,dT\right) = \frac{1}{s}\cdot\frac{b}{s^2 + b^2} \Rightarrow L\left(-\frac{\cos bT}{b}\Bigg|_0^t\right) = \frac{b}{s(s^2 + b^2)}$$

$$\Rightarrow \quad L\left(\frac{1}{b} - \frac{\cos bT}{b}\right) = \frac{b}{s(s^2 + b^2)} \Rightarrow \frac{1}{b}L(1) - \frac{1}{b}L(\cos bt) = \frac{b}{s(s^2 + b^2)}$$

$$\Rightarrow \quad \frac{1}{b}L(\cos bt) = \frac{1}{b}\cdot\frac{1}{s} - \frac{b}{s(s^2 + b^2)} = \frac{s}{b(s^2 + b^2)}$$

$$\therefore \quad L(\cos bt) = \frac{s}{s^2 + b^2}.$$

Example 3. *Using* $L(1) = \dfrac{1}{s}$, *find the Laplace transform of the function* $\cos bt$.

Sol. Let $f(t) = \cos bt$.

We have $L\left(\int_0^t f(T)\,dT\right) = \dfrac{1}{s}L(f)$.

$$\Rightarrow \quad L\left(\int_0^t \cos bT\,dT\right) = \frac{1}{s}L(\cos bt) \Rightarrow L\left(\frac{\sin bT}{b}\Bigg|_0^t\right) = \frac{1}{s}L(\cos bt)$$

$$\Rightarrow \quad L\left(\frac{\sin bt}{b} - 0\right) = \frac{1}{s}L(\cos bt) \Rightarrow L(\sin bt) = \frac{b}{s}L(\cos bt) \quad \ldots(1)$$

Let $g(t) = \sin bt$.

We have $L\left(\int_0^t g(T)\,dT\right) = \dfrac{1}{s}L(g)$.

$$\Rightarrow \quad L\left(\int_0^t \sin bT\, dT\right) = \frac{1}{s}L(\sin bt) = \frac{1}{s}\cdot\left(\frac{b}{s}L(\cos bt)\right) \qquad \text{(By using (1))}$$

$$\Rightarrow \quad L\left(-\frac{\cos bT}{b}\Big|_0^t\right) = \frac{b}{s^2}L(\cos bt) \quad \Rightarrow \quad L\left(-\frac{\cos bt}{b} + \frac{1}{b}\right) = \frac{b}{s^2}L(\cos bt)$$

$$\Rightarrow \quad -\frac{1}{b}L(\cos bt) + \frac{1}{b}L(1) = \frac{b}{s^2}L(\cos bt) \quad \Rightarrow \quad \frac{1}{b}\cdot\frac{1}{s} = \left(\frac{b}{s^2} + \frac{1}{b}\right)L(\cos bt)$$

$$\Rightarrow \quad \frac{1}{bs} = \frac{b^2 + s^2}{bs^2}L(\cos bt) \quad \Rightarrow \quad L(\cos bt) = \frac{\mathbf{s}}{\mathbf{s^2 + b^2}}.$$

EXERCISE 5

1. Using $L(t) = \frac{1}{s^2}$, find the values of $L(t^2)$ and $L(t^3)$.

2. Using $L(\cos at) = \frac{s}{s^2 + a^2}$, find $L(3 \sin 8t)$.

3. Using $L(1) = \frac{1}{s}$ and $L(\sinh at) = \frac{a}{s^2 - a^2}$, find $L(4 \cosh 6t)$.

4. Using $L(\cosh at) = \frac{s}{s^2 - a^2}$, find $L(2 \sinh pt)$.

5. Using $L(1) = \frac{1}{s}$, find the Laplace transform of the function $\frac{1}{5}\sin \pi t$.

6. Using $L(1) = \frac{1}{s}$, find the Laplace transform of the function $b \cosh pt$.

7. Using $L(1) = \frac{1}{s}$, find the Laplace transform of the function $b \sinh at$.

8. Evaluate $L\left(\int_0^t e^{-x} \cos x\, dx\right)$.

Answers

1. $\frac{2}{s^3}, \frac{6}{s^4}$ 2. $\frac{24}{s^2 + 64}$ 3. $\frac{4s}{s^2 - 36}$ 4. $\frac{2p}{s^2 - p^2}$

5. $\frac{\pi}{5(s^2 + \pi^2)}$ 6. $\frac{bs}{s^2 - p^2}$ 7. $\frac{ab}{s^2 - a^2}$ 8. $\frac{s+1}{s(s^2 + 2s + 2)}$.

14. DIFFERENTIATION OF LAPLACE TRANSFORMS

Theorem. Let f(t) be a real function such that

(*i*) f(t) is piece wise continuous on every finite interval in the range $t \geq 0$

(*ii*) there exists constants k and M such that $|f(t)| \leq Me^{kt}$ for $t \geq 0$, then

$$F'(s) = -L(t\, f(t)), \text{ where } F(s) = L(f(t)).$$

Note. The proof of this theorem is beyond the scope of this book.

Remark. The result of the above theorem can be easily remembered as follows :

If $L(f(t)) = F(s)$, then $L(t\, f(t)) = -F'(s)$.

Corollary. We have $L(t\, f(t)) = -F'(s)$.

Applying this result successively, we get

$$L(t^2 f(t)) = (-1)^2 F''(s)$$
$$L(t^3 f(t)) = (-1)^3 F'''(s)$$
$$\dots\dots\dots\dots$$
$$\therefore \quad \mathbf{L(t^n f(t)) = (-1)^n F^{(n)}(s).}$$

Example 1. *Find the Laplace transform of the following functions of t for $t \geq 0$:*

(i) $t\, e^{at}$ *(ii)* $t^2 \cosh \pi t$ *(iii)* $t^2 \sin 3t$.

Sol. *(i)* We have $L(e^{at}) = \dfrac{1}{s-a}$

$\therefore$ By **differentiability of Laplace transform,**

$$L(t\,.\,e^{at}) = -\frac{d}{ds}\left(\frac{1}{s-a}\right) = -(-(s-a)^{-2}) = \frac{1}{\mathbf{(s-a)^2}}.$$

(ii) We have $L(\cosh \pi t) = \dfrac{s}{s^2 - \pi^2}$

$\therefore$ By **differentiability of Laplace transform,**

$$L(t\,.\cosh \pi t) = -\frac{d}{ds}\left(\frac{s}{s^2-\pi^2}\right) = -\left[\frac{(s^2-\pi^2)\,.\,1 - s\,.\,2s}{(s^2-\pi^2)^2}\right] = \frac{s^2+\pi^2}{(s^2-\pi^2)^2}$$

Again by using the same formula,

$$L(t\,.\,t\cosh \pi t) = -\frac{d}{ds}\left(\frac{s^2+\pi^2}{(s^2-\pi^2)^2}\right)$$
$$= -\left[\frac{(s^2-\pi^2)^2\,.\,2s - (s^2+\pi^2)\,.\,2(s^2-\pi^2)\,.\,2s}{(s^2-\pi^2)^4}\right] = \frac{2s(s^2+3\pi^2)}{(s^2-\pi^2)^3}.$$

$$\therefore \quad L(t^2 \cosh \pi t) = \frac{\mathbf{2s(s^2+3\pi^2)}}{\mathbf{(s^2-\pi^2)^3}}.$$

Alternative method

$$L(t^2 \cosh \pi t) = L\left(t^2\,.\,\frac{e^{\pi t}+e^{-\pi t}}{2}\right) = \frac{1}{2}L(e^{\pi t}t^2 + e^{-\pi t}t^2)$$
$$= \frac{1}{2}[L(e^{\pi t}t^2) + L(e^{-\pi t}t^2)] = \frac{1}{2}\left[\frac{2!}{(s-\pi)^3} + \frac{2!}{(s-(-\pi))^3}\right]$$

(Using $L(t^2) = \dfrac{2!}{s^3}$ and first shifting theorem)

$$= \frac{1}{(s-\pi)^3} + \frac{1}{(s+\pi)^3} = \frac{(s+\pi)^3 + (s-\pi)^3}{(s^2-\pi^2)^3}$$

$$= \frac{2s^3 + 6s\pi^2}{(s^2-\pi^2)^3} = \frac{2s(s^2+3\pi^2)}{(s^2-\pi^2)^3}.$$

(*iii*) We have $L(\sin 3t) = \frac{3}{s^2+(3)^2} = \frac{3}{s^2+9}$

By **differentiability of Laplace transform,**

$$L(t \,.\, \sin 3t) = -\frac{d}{ds}\left(\frac{3}{s^2+9}\right) = -3(-(s^2+9)^{-2} \,.\, 2s) = \frac{6s}{(s^2+9)^2}$$

Again by using the same formula,

$$L(t \,.\, t \sin 3t) = -\frac{d}{ds}\left(\frac{6s}{(s^2+9)^2}\right)$$

$$= -6\left[\frac{(s^2+9)^2 \,.\, 1 - s \,.\, 2(s^2+9) \,.\, 2s}{(s^2+9)^4}\right] = \frac{18(s^2-3)}{(s^2+9)^3}$$

$\therefore$ $L(t^2 \sin 3t) = \mathbf{\frac{18(s^2-3)}{(s^2+9)^3}}$.

Example 2. *Find the Laplace transform of the function $3te^{5t} \sin 7t$ for $t \geq 0$.*

Sol. We have $L(\sin 7t) = \frac{7}{s^2+49}$.

By **first shifting theorem,**

$$L(e^{5t} \sin 7t) = \frac{7}{(s-5)^2+49} = \frac{7}{s^2-10s+74}.$$

By **differentiability of Laplace transform,**

$$L(te^{5t} \sin 7t) = -\frac{d}{ds}\left(\frac{7}{s^2-10s+74}\right) = \frac{7 \,.\, (2s-10)}{(s^2-10s+74)^2} = \frac{14\,(s-5)}{(s^2-10s+74)^2}$$

By **linearity of Laplace transform,**

$$L(3te^{5t} \sin 7t) = 3L(te^{5t} \sin 7t) = \mathbf{\frac{42\,(s-5)}{(s^2-10s+74)^2}}.$$

Example 3. *Prove that* $L\left[\frac{1}{2a^3}(\sin at - at \cos at)\right] = \frac{1}{(s^2+a^2)^2}$. *(KU 2004)*

Sol. We have $L(\sin at) = \frac{a}{s^2+a^2}$. ...(1)

Also $L(\cos at) = \frac{s}{s^2+a^2}$

By **differentiability of Laplace transform,**

$$L(t \cos at) = -\frac{d}{ds}\left(\frac{s}{s^2+a^2}\right).$$

$$= -\left[\frac{(s^2+a^2).1 - s.2s}{(s^2+a^2)^2}\right] = \frac{s^2-a^2}{(s^2+a^2)^2}$$

Now $\quad L\left[\frac{1}{2a^3}(\sin at - at\cos at)\right]$

$$= \frac{1}{2a^3}\,[L(\sin at) - aL(t\cos at)]$$

$$= \frac{1}{2a^3}\left[\frac{a}{s^2+a^2} - a\left(\frac{s^2-a^2}{(s^2+a^2)^2}\right)\right]$$

$$= \frac{1}{2a^3}\left[\frac{as^2+a^3-as^2+a^3}{(s^2+a^2)^2}\right] = \frac{1}{(\mathbf{s^2+a^2})^2}.$$

Example 4. *Evaluate* $\int_0^\infty te^{-2t}\sin t\, dt$. (KU 2005)

Sol. We have $\quad L(\sin t) = \frac{1}{s^2+1^2} = \frac{1}{s^2+1}.$

$$\therefore \quad L(t\sin t) = -\frac{d}{ds}\left(\frac{1}{s^2+1}\right) = -(-(s^2+1)^2 . 2s) = \frac{2s}{(s^2+1)^2}$$

$$\therefore \quad \int_0^\infty e^{-st}.\, t\sin t\, dt = \frac{2s}{(s^2+1)^2}$$

$$\therefore \quad \int_0^\infty e^{-2t}\, t\sin t\, dt = \left.\frac{2s}{(s^2+1)^2}\right|_{s=2} = \frac{2(2)}{((2)^2+1)^2} = \frac{\mathbf{4}}{\mathbf{25}}.$$

WORKING RULES FOR SOLVING PROBLEMS

Rule I. If $L(f(t)) = F(s)$, then $L(t\,f(t)) = -F'(s)$.

Rule II. If $L(f(t)) = F(s)$, then

$L(t^2 f(t)) = (-1)^2 F''(s)$

$L(t^3 f(t)) = (-1)^3 F'''(s)$

....

$L(t^n f(t)) = (-1)^n F^{(n)}(s)$.

EXERCISE 6

1. Find the Laplace transform of the following functions of t for $t \ge 0$:
   (i) $t\,e^{5t}$ (ii) $4t\cos 3t$ (iii) $6t\sin 5t$
   (iv) $2t\sinh 2t$ (v) $3t\cosh 4t$.
2. Using $L(t^2) = \frac{2}{s^3}$, find the Laplace transform of t^3 and t^4.
3. Find the Laplace transform of the following functions of t for $t \ge 0$:
   (i) $2t^2 e^{3t}$ (ii) $t^2\cos 4t$ (iii) $t^2\sin at$ (MDU 2005)
   (iv) $6t^2\sinh 3t$ (v) $5t^2\cosh 7t$.

4. Find the Laplace transform of the following functions of t for $t \geq 0$:

(i) $t^3 e^{2t}$ (ii) $3t^3 \cos \pi t$ (iii) $4t^3 \sin 4t$

(iv) $5t^3 \sinh 4t$ (v) $6t^3 \cosh (t/2)$.

5. Find the Laplace transform of the following functions of t for $t \geq 0$: (KU 2005)

(i) $t e^{2t} \cos 4t$ (ii) $t e^{-t} \sin 3t$

(iii) $t e^{3t} \sinh 3t$ (iv) $3t e^{2t} \cosh 7t$.

6. Prove that $L\left(\frac{1}{2a}(\sin at + at \cos at)\right) = \frac{s^2}{(s^2+a^2)^2}$.

7. Evaluate $\int_0^\infty t^3 e^{-t} \sin t \, dt$.

Answers

1. (i) $\frac{1}{(s-5)^2}$ (ii) $\frac{4(s^2-9)}{(s^2+9)^2}$ (iii) $\frac{60s}{(s^2+25)^2}$

(iv) $\frac{8s}{(s^2-4)^2}$ (v) $\frac{3(s^2+16)}{(s^2-16)^2}$ 2. $\frac{6}{s^4}, \frac{24}{s^5}$

3. (i) $\frac{4}{(s-3)^3}$ (ii) $\frac{2s(s^2-48)}{(s^2+16)^3}$ (iii) $\frac{2a(3s^2-a^2)}{(s^2+a^2)^3}$

(iv) $\frac{108(s^2+3)}{(s^2-9)^3}$ (v) $\frac{10s(s^2+147)}{(s^2-49)^3}$ 4. (i) $\frac{6}{(s-2)^4}$

(ii) $\frac{18(\pi^4-6\pi^2 s^2-s^4)}{(s^2+\pi^2)^4}$ (iii) $\frac{384s(s^2-16)}{(s^2+16)^4}$ (iv) $\frac{480s(s^2+16)}{(s^2-16)^4}$

(v) $\frac{576(16s^4+24s^2+1)}{(4s^2-1)^4}$ 5. (i) $\frac{s^2-4s-12}{(s^2-4s+20)^2}$ (ii) $\frac{6(s+1)}{(s^2+2s+10)^2}$

(iii) $\frac{6(s-3)}{(s^2-6s)^2}$ (iv) $\frac{3(s^2-4s+53)}{(s^2-4s-45)^2}$ 7. 0.

---

15. INTEGRATION OF LAPLACE TRANSFORMS

Theorem. Let f(t) be a real function such that

(i) f(t) is piece wise continuous on every finite interval in the range $t \geq 0$

(ii) there exists constants k and M such that $|f(t)| \leq Me^{kt}$ for $t \geq 0$

(iii) $\lim_{t \to 0^+} \frac{f(t)}{t}$ exists finitely, then

$$\int_s^\infty F(S)\, dS = L\left(\frac{f(t)}{t}\right), \; s > k \text{ where } F(s) = L(f(t)).$$

Note. The proof of this theorem is beyond the scope of this book.

Remark. The result of the above theorem can be easily remembered as follows :

If $L(f(t)) = F(s)$, then $L\left(\frac{f(t)}{t}\right) = \int_s^\infty F(S)\, dS$.

Example 1. *Find the Laplace transform of the function* $\frac{2}{t}(1-\cos at)$, *for* $t \geq 0$.

Sol. We have $L(2(1-\cos at)) = 2L(1-\cos at) = 2[L(1) - L(\cos at)]$

$$= 2\left[\frac{1}{s} - \frac{s}{s^2+a^2}\right] = \left(\frac{2}{s} - \frac{2s}{s^2+a^2}\right)^*.$$

By **integration of Laplace transform,**

$$L\left(\frac{2(1-\cos at)}{t}\right) = \int_s^\infty \left[\frac{2}{S} - \frac{2S}{S^2+a^2}\right] dS$$

$$= \left[2\log S - \log(S^2+a^2)\right]_s^\infty = \log \frac{S^2}{S^2+a^2}\Bigg|_s^\infty$$

$$= \lim_{S\to\infty}\left(\log\frac{S^2}{S^2+a^2}\right) - \log\frac{s^2}{s^2+a^2}$$

$$= \log\left(\lim_{S\to\infty}\frac{1}{1+\frac{a^2}{S^2}}\right) - \log\frac{s^2}{s^2+a^2}$$

$$= \log\left(\frac{1}{1+0}\right) - \log\frac{s^2}{s^2+a^2} = 0 + \log\frac{s^2}{s^2+a^2} = \log\frac{s^2+a^2}{s^2}.$$

$$\therefore \quad L\left(\frac{2}{t}(1-\cos at)\right) = \mathbf{\log\frac{s^2+a^2}{s^2}}.$$

Example 2. *Find the Laplace transformation of the function* $\frac{2(e^t - \cos t)}{t}$.

Sol. We have $L(2(e^t - \cos t)) = 2L(e^t - \cos t)$

$$= 2\left[\frac{1}{s-1} - \frac{s}{s^2+1}\right] = \frac{2}{s-1} - \frac{2s}{s^2+1}.$$

By **integration of Laplace transform,**

$$L\left(\frac{2(e^t-\cos t)}{t}\right) = \int_s^\infty \left(\frac{2}{S-1} - \frac{2S}{S^2+1}\right) dS$$

$$= \left[2\log(S-1) - \log(S^2+1)\right]_s^\infty = \log\frac{(S-1)^2}{S^2+1}\Bigg|_s^\infty$$

$$= \lim_{S\to\infty}\log\frac{(S-1)^2}{S^2+1} - \log\frac{(s-1)^2}{s^2+1}$$

---

*__Why this step.__ We have not simplified $\frac{2}{s} - \frac{2s}{s^2+a^2}$ because we shall be integrating it in the next

$$= \log \lim_{S\to\infty} \frac{(1-1/S)^2}{1+1/S^2} - \log \frac{(s-1)^2}{s^2+1}$$

$$= \log \frac{(1-0)^2}{1+0} - \log \frac{(s-1)^2}{s^2+1} = 0 + \log \frac{s^2+1}{(s-1)^2}$$

$$\therefore \quad L\left(\frac{2(e^t - \cos t)}{t}\right) = \log \frac{s^2+1}{(s-1)^2}.$$

Example 3. *Find the Laplace transform of the function* $\dfrac{\sin at}{t}$.

Sol. We have $L(\sin at) = \dfrac{a}{s^2+a^2} = F(s)$ (say)

By **integration of Laplace transform,**

$$L\left(\frac{\sin at}{t}\right) = \int_s^\infty F(S)\, dS.$$

$$\therefore \quad L\left(\frac{\sin at}{t}\right) = \int_s^\infty \frac{a}{S^2+a^2}\, dS = a \cdot \frac{1}{a} \tan^{-1} \frac{S}{a}\Big|_s^\infty$$

$$= \frac{\pi}{2} - \tan^{-1}\frac{s}{a} = \cot^{-1}\frac{s}{a}.$$

$$\therefore \quad L\left(\frac{\sin at}{t}\right) = \cot^{-1}\frac{s}{a}.$$

Example 4. *Show that :*

$$\int_0^\infty \frac{e^{-t} - e^{-3t}}{t}\, dt = \log 3.$$

Sol. $L(e^{-t} - e^{-3t}) = L(e^{-t}) - L(e^{-3t}) = \dfrac{1}{s+1} - \dfrac{1}{s+3}$

$\therefore$ *By integration of Laplace transform,*

$$L\left(\frac{e^{-t} - e^{-3t}}{t}\right) = \int_s^\infty \left(\frac{1}{S+1} - \frac{1}{S+3}\right) dS$$

$$= \Big[\log(S+1) - \log(S+3)\Big]_s^\infty = \log \frac{S+1}{S+3}\Big|_s^\infty$$

$$= \lim_{S\to\infty}\left(\log\frac{S+1}{S+3}\right) - \log\frac{s+1}{s+3} = \log\left(\lim_{S\to\infty}\frac{1+\frac{1}{S}}{1+\frac{3}{S}}\right) - \log\frac{s+1}{s+3}$$

$$= \log\left(\frac{1+0}{1+0}\right) + \log\frac{s+3}{s+1} = \log\frac{s+3}{s+1}$$

$$\therefore \quad L\left(\frac{e^{-t} - e^{-3t}}{t}\right) = \log\frac{s+3}{s+1}$$

$$\therefore \int_0^{\infty} e^{-st} \cdot \frac{e^{-t} - e^{-3t}}{t} dt = \log \frac{s+3}{s+1}$$

In particular, let $s = 0$,

$$\therefore \quad \int_0^{\infty} e^{0} \cdot \frac{e^{-t} - e^{-3t}}{t} dt = \log \frac{0+3}{0+1}$$

$$\Rightarrow \quad \int_0^{\infty} \frac{e^{-t} - e^{-3t}}{t} dt = \log 3.$$

WORKING RULE FOR SOLVING PROBLEMS

Rule I. If $L(f(t)) = F(s)$, then $L\left(\frac{f(t)}{t}\right) = \int_s^{\infty} F(S)\, dS$.

EXERCISE 7

1. Find the Laplace transform of the following functions of t for $t > 0$:

   (i) $\frac{\sin t}{t}$ (ii) $\frac{1 - \cos 2t}{t}$.

2. Find the Laplace transform of the following functions of t for $t > 0$:

   (i) $\frac{1 - e^{t}}{t}$ (ii) $\frac{e^{-at} - e^{-bt}}{t}$.

3. Find the Laplace transform of the following functions of t for $t > 0$:

   (i) $\frac{e^{at} - \cos bt}{t}$ (ii) $\frac{\cos 2t - \cos 3t}{t}$.

4. Find the Laplace transform of the following functions of t for $t > 0$:

   (i) $\frac{\cos \alpha t - \cos \beta t}{t}$ (ii) $\frac{e^{-t} \sin t}{t}$.

5. Show that the Laplace transform of the function $\frac{\cos at}{t}$ does not exist.

6. Show that :

   (i) $\int_0^{\infty} \frac{\sin t}{t} dt = \frac{\pi}{2}$ (ii) $\int_0^{\infty} \frac{e^{-t} \sin t}{t} dt = \frac{\pi}{4}$. *(KU 2004 S)*

   (iii) $\int_0^{\infty} \frac{\cos 6t - \cos 4t}{t} dt = \log \frac{2}{3}$.

7. Show that :

   (i) $L\left(\int_0^t \frac{\sin x}{x} dx\right) = \frac{1}{s} \cot^{-1} s$ (ii) $L\left(\int_0^t \frac{1 - e^{-2x}}{x} dx\right) = \frac{1}{s} \log\left(1 + \frac{2}{s}\right)$.

   (KU 2006)

   (iii) $L\left(\int_0^t \frac{e^{x} \sin x}{x} dx\right) = \frac{\cot^{-1}(s-1)}{s}$.

Answers

1. (*i*) $\cot^{-1} s$ (*ii*) $\frac{1}{2}\log\frac{s^2+4}{s^2}$ 2. (*i*) $\log\frac{s-1}{s}$ (*ii*) $\log\frac{s+b}{s+a}$

3. (*i*) $\frac{1}{2}\log\frac{s^2+b^2}{(s-a)^2}$ (*ii*) $\frac{1}{2}\log\frac{s^2+9}{s^2+4}$ 4. (*i*) $\frac{1}{2}\log\frac{s^2+\beta^2}{s^2+\alpha^2}$ (*ii*) $\cot^{-1}(s+1)$

Hints

6. We have $L\left(\frac{\sin t}{t}\right)=\cot^{-1} s$

$$\therefore \quad \int_0^{\infty}\frac{e^{-st}\sin t}{t}\,dt=\cot^{-1} s$$

For part (*i*), take $s = 0$.
For part (*ii*), take $s = 1$.

7. (*i*) $L(\sin t)=\frac{1}{s^2+1} \Rightarrow L\left(\frac{\sin t}{t}\right)=\cot^{-1} s.$

Now using Laplace transform of integral of $\frac{\sin t}{t}$, we have

$$L\left(\int_0^t \frac{\sin T}{T}\,dT\right)=\frac{1}{s}\,.\,\cot^{-1} s.$$

7

Inverse Laplace Transforms

1. INTRODUCTION

We have already noted that the main purpose of studying Laplace transforms is for solving various types of differential equations. During the process of solving a differential equation, we shall also require to find a function when its Laplace transform is known. This is the reverse process of finding the Laplace transform of a function. In the present chapter, we shall learn to find the function whose Laplace transform is known.

2. INVERSE LAPLACE TRANSFORM OF A FUNCTION

Let f be a real valued function of the real variable t, defined for $t \geq 0$. Let the Laplace transform F(s) of $f(t)$ exists. Therefore the infinite integral $\int_0^\infty e^{-st} f(t)\,dt$ exists and equals F(s). The function $f(t)$ is called the **inverse Laplace transform** of the function F(s) and we write $L^{-1}(F(s)) = f(t)$.

In other words, $L^{-1}(F(s))$ is that function whose Laplace transform is the function F(s).

For example,

(*i*) $L^{-1}\left(\dfrac{1}{s-a}\right) = e^{at}$, because $L(e^{at}) = \dfrac{1}{s-a}$

(*ii*) $L^{-1}\left(\dfrac{s}{s^2+9}\right) = \cos 3t$, because $L(\cos 3t) = \dfrac{s}{s^2+9}$

3. EXISTENCE AND UNIQUENESS OF INVERSE LAPLACE TRANSFORM

A given function F(s) of s may or may not have its inverse Laplace transform. So far as the uniqueness of inverse Laplace transforms, we have the following result :

If $f_1(t)$ and $f_2(t)$ be two continuous functions for $t \geq 0$ having the same Laplace transform F(s) i.e. $L^{-1}(F(s)) = f_1(t)$ and $L^{-1}(F(s)) = f_2(t)$, then $f_1(t) = f_2(t) \quad \forall\ t \geq 0$.

We accept this result without proof.

Illustration : The functions $f_1(t) = 1$

and
$$f_2(t) = \begin{cases} 1, & 1 \leq t < 4 \\ 5, & t = 4 \\ 1, & t > 4 \end{cases}$$

have the same Laplace transform $\dfrac{1}{s}$. Here the above result is not applicable because the function $f_1(t)$ is continuous for $t \geq 0$ but the function $f_2(t)$ is not continuous for $t \geq 0$.

4. ELEMENTARY INVERSE LAPLACE TRANSFORM FORMULAE

In this section, we shall find some elementary inverse Laplace transform formulae.

1. We have $L(1) = \frac{1}{s}, \; s > 0$

$\therefore$ By definition, $\mathbf{L^{-1}\left(\frac{1}{s}\right) = 1, \; s > 0}$.

2. We have $L(t^a) = \frac{\Gamma(a+1)}{s^{a+1}}, \; a > -1, \; s > 0$.

$\therefore$ By definition, $\mathbf{L^{-1}\left(\frac{\Gamma(a+1)}{s^{a+1}}\right) = t^a, a > -1, \; s > 0}$.

3. We have $L(t^n) = \frac{n!}{s^{n+1}}, \; n = 0, 1, 2, \ldots\ldots; s > 0$

$\therefore$ By definition, $\mathbf{L^{-1}\left(\frac{n!}{s^{n+1}}\right) = t^n, \; n = 0, 1, 2, \ldots\ldots; s > 0}$.

4. We have $L(e^{at}) = \frac{1}{s-a}, \; s > a$.

$\therefore$ By definition, $\mathbf{L^{-1}\left(\frac{1}{s-a}\right) = e^{at}, \; s > a}$.

5. We have $L(\sinh at) = \frac{a}{s^2 - a^2}, \; s > |a|$

$\therefore$ By definition, $\mathbf{L^{-1}\left(\frac{a}{s^2 - a^2}\right) = \sinh at, \; s > |a|}$.

6. We have $L(\cosh at) = \frac{s}{s^2 - a^2}, \; s > |a|$

$\therefore$ By definition, $\mathbf{L^{-1}\left(\frac{s}{s^2 - a^2}\right) = L(\cosh at), \; s > |a|}$.

7. We have $L(\sin at) = \frac{a}{s^2 + a^2}, \; s > 0$

$\therefore$ By definition, $\mathbf{L^{-1}\left(\frac{a}{s^2 + a^2}\right) = \sin at, \; s > 0}$.

8. We have $L(\cos at) = \frac{s}{s^2 + a^2}, \; s > 0$.

$\therefore$ By definition, $\mathbf{L^{-1}\left(\frac{s}{s^2 + a^2}\right) = \cos at, \; s > 0}$.

Remarks 1. $L^{-1}\left(\frac{\Gamma(a+1)}{s^{a+1}}\right) = t^a \Rightarrow L^{-1}\left(\frac{1}{s^{a+1}}\right) = \frac{t^a}{\Gamma(a+1)}$; $a > -1,\ s > 0$.

$\therefore$ $$L^{-1}\left(\frac{1}{s^a}\right) = \frac{t^{a-1}}{\Gamma(a)},\ a > 0,\ s > 0.$$

2. $L^{-1}\left(\frac{n!}{s^{n+1}}\right) = t^n \Rightarrow L^{-1}\left(\frac{1}{s^{n+1}}\right) = \frac{t^n}{n!}$, $n = 0, 1, 2, \ldots\ldots; s > 0$

$\therefore$ $$L^{-1}\left(\frac{1}{s^n}\right) = \frac{t^{n-1}}{(n-1)!},\quad n \in N, s > 0.$$

WORKING RULES FOR SOLVING PROBLEMS

Rule I. If $L(f(t)) = F(s)$, then $L^{-1}(F(s)) = f(t)$.

Rule II. (*i*) $L^{-1}\left(\frac{1}{s}\right) = 1$ (*ii*) $L^{-1}\left(\frac{\Gamma(a+1)}{s^{a+1}}\right) = t^a$, $a > -1$

(*iii*) $L^{-1}\left(\frac{n!}{s^{n+1}}\right) = t^n$ (*iv*) $L^{-1}\left(\frac{1}{s-a}\right) = e^{at}$

(*v*) $L^{-1}\left(\frac{a}{s^2 - a^2}\right) = \sinh at$ (*vi*) $L^{-1}\left(\frac{s}{s^2 - a^2}\right) = \cosh at$

(*vii*) $L^{-1}\left(\frac{a}{s^2 + a^2}\right) = \sin at$ (*viii*) $L^{-1}\left(\frac{s}{s^2 + a^2}\right) = \cos at$.

Example 1. *Find the values of :*

(*i*) $L^{-1}\left(\frac{\Gamma(5/2)}{s^{5/2}}\right)$ (*ii*) $L^{-1}\left(\frac{5040}{s^8}\right)$

(*iii*) $L^{-1}\left(\frac{1}{s+5}\right)$ (*iv*) $L^{-1}\left(\frac{3}{s^2-9}\right)$

(*v*) $L^{-1}\left(\frac{s}{s^2+16}\right)$ (*vi*) $L^{-1}\left(\frac{6}{s^2+36}\right)$.

Sol. (*i*) We have $L^{-1}\left(\frac{\Gamma(a+1)}{s^{a+1}}\right) = t^a$.

$\therefore$ $$L^{-1}\left(\frac{\Gamma(5/2)}{s^{5/2}}\right) = t^{\frac{5}{2}-1} = t^{3/2}$$

(*ii*) We have $$L^{-1}\left(\frac{n!}{s^{n+1}}\right) = t^n.$$

$\therefore$ $$L^{-1}\left(\frac{5040}{s^8}\right) = L^{-1}\left(\frac{7!}{s^{7+1}}\right) = t^7.$$

(*iii*) We have $L^{-1}\left(\dfrac{1}{s-a}\right)=e^{at}$.

$\therefore \quad L^{-1}\left(\dfrac{1}{s+5}\right)=L^{-1}\left(\dfrac{1}{s-(-5)}\right)=\mathbf{e^{-5t}}.$

(*iv*) We have $L^{-1}\left(\dfrac{a}{s^2-a^2}\right)=\sinh at.$

$\therefore \quad L^{-1}\left(\dfrac{3}{s^2-9}\right)=L^{-1}\left(\dfrac{3}{s^2-3^2}\right)=\mathbf{\sinh 3t}.$

(*v*) We have $L^{-1}\left(\dfrac{s}{s^2+a^2}\right)=\cos at$

$\therefore \quad L^{-1}\left(\dfrac{s}{s^2+16}\right)=L^{-1}\left(\dfrac{s}{s^2+4^2}\right)=\mathbf{\cos 4t}.$

(*vi*) We have $L^{-1}\left(\dfrac{a}{s^2+a^2}\right)=\sin at$

$\therefore \quad L^{-1}\left(\dfrac{6}{s^2+36}\right)=L^{-1}\left(\dfrac{6}{s^2+6^2}\right)=\mathbf{\sin 6t}.$

5. LINEARITY OF THE INVERSE LAPLACE TRANSFORM

Theorem. If f(t) and g(t) be any functions of t for t ≥ 0 such that L(f(t)) = F(s) and L(g(t)) = G(s) and a and b be any constants, then

$$\mathbf{L^{-1}(aF(s)+bG(s))=aL^{-1}(F(s))+bL^{-1}(G(s)).}$$

Proof. We have $L(f(t)) = F(s)$ and $L(g(t)) = G(s)$.

$\therefore \quad aF(s)+bG(s)=aL(f(t))+bL(g(t))$

$\qquad = L(af(t)+bg(t))$

$\therefore \quad L^{-1}(aF(s)+bG(s))=af(t)+bg(t)$

or $\quad \mathbf{L^{-1}(aF(s)+bG(s))=aL^{-1}(F(s))+bL^{-1}(G(s)).}$

Example 2. *Find the value of* $L^{-1}\left(\dfrac{1}{s+3}+\dfrac{2}{s+5}+\dfrac{6}{s^4}\right)$.

Sol. $L^{-1}\left(\dfrac{1}{s+3}+\dfrac{2}{s+5}+\dfrac{6}{s^4}\right)$

$=L^{-1}\left(\dfrac{1}{s+3}\right)+2L^{-1}\left(\dfrac{1}{s+5}\right)+L^{-1}\left(\dfrac{6}{s^4}\right)$ (Using linearity)

$=L^{-1}\left(\dfrac{1}{s-(-3)}\right)+2L^{-1}\left(\dfrac{1}{s-(-5)}\right)+L^{-1}\left(\dfrac{3!}{s^{3+1}}\right)$

$=\mathbf{e^{-3t}+2e^{-5t}+t^3}.$

Example 3. *Find the value of* $L^{-1}\left(\frac{s}{4s^2-16}+\frac{9}{s^2+25}+\frac{4s}{9s^2+4}+\frac{1}{4s-1}\right)$

Sol. $L^{-1}\left(\frac{s}{4s^2-16}+\frac{9}{s^2+25}+\frac{4s}{9s^2+4}+\frac{1}{4s-1}\right)$

$$= L^{-1}\left(\frac{s}{4s^2-16}\right)+L^{-1}\left(\frac{9}{s^2+25}\right)+L^{-1}\left(\frac{4s}{9s^2+4}\right)+L^{-1}\left(\frac{1}{4s-1}\right)$$

$$= \frac{1}{4}L^{-1}\left(\frac{s}{s^2-2^2}\right)+\frac{9}{5}L^{-1}\left(\frac{5}{s^2+5^2}\right)+\frac{4}{9}L^{-1}\left(\frac{s}{s^2+\left(\frac{2}{3}\right)^2}\right)+\frac{1}{4}L^{-1}\left(\frac{1}{s-\frac{1}{4}}\right)$$

$$= \mathbf{\frac{1}{4}\cosh 2t+\frac{9}{5}\sin 5t+\frac{4}{9}\cos\frac{2}{3}t+\frac{1}{4}e^{\frac{1}{4}t}}.$$

Example 4. *Find the inverse Laplace transform of the following functions :*

(*i*) $\frac{4s-8}{9-s^2}$ (*ii*) $\frac{2s-5}{4s^2+25}$

Sol. (*i*) $$\frac{4s-8}{9-s^2}=-4\left(\frac{s-2}{s^2-9}\right)=-4\cdot\frac{s}{s^2-9}+\frac{8}{3}\cdot\frac{3}{s^2-9}$$

$$\therefore \quad L^{-1}\left(\frac{4s-8}{9-s^2}\right)=L^{-1}\left(-4\cdot\frac{s}{s^2-9}+\frac{8}{3}\cdot\frac{3}{s^2-9}\right)$$

$$=-4L^{-1}\left(\frac{s}{s^2-3^2}\right)+\frac{8}{3}L^{-1}\left(\frac{3}{s^2-3^2}\right)=\mathbf{-4\cosh 3t+\frac{8}{3}\sinh 3t}.$$

(*ii*) $$\frac{2s-5}{4s^2+25}=\frac{2}{4}\left(\frac{s-\frac{5}{2}}{s^2+\frac{25}{4}}\right)=\frac{1}{2}\cdot\frac{s}{s^2+\frac{25}{4}}-\frac{5}{4}\cdot\frac{1}{s^2+\frac{25}{4}}$$

$$\therefore \quad L^{-1}\left(\frac{2s-5}{4s^2+25}\right)=L^{-1}\left(\frac{1}{2}\cdot\frac{s}{s^2+(5/2)^2}-\frac{1}{2}\cdot\frac{5/2}{s^2+(5/2)^2}\right)$$

$$=\frac{1}{2}L^{-1}\left(\frac{s}{s^2+(5/2)^2}\right)-\frac{1}{2}L^{-1}\left(\frac{5/2}{s^2+(5/2)^2}\right)$$

$$=\mathbf{\frac{1}{2}\cos\frac{5}{2}t-\frac{1}{2}\sin\frac{5}{2}t}.$$

EXERCISE 1

Find the inverse Laplace transform of the following functions :

1. (*i*) $\dfrac{720}{s^7}$ (*ii*) $\dfrac{40320}{s^9}$ (*iii*) $\dfrac{\Gamma(3/2)}{s^{3/2}}$ (*iv*) $\dfrac{1}{s-7}$

2. (*i*) $\dfrac{s}{s^2+25}$ (*ii*) $\dfrac{s}{s^2-49}$ (*iii*) $\dfrac{8}{s^2-64}$ (*iv*) $\dfrac{4}{s^2+16}$

3. (*i*) $\dfrac{60+6s^2+s^4}{s^7}$ (*ii*) $\dfrac{s-4}{s^2-16}$ (*iii*) $\dfrac{0.1s+0.9}{s^2+3.24}$ (*iv*) $\dfrac{s}{a^2s^2+b^2c^2}$

4. (*i*) $\dfrac{6}{s-4}+\dfrac{3}{s+5}+\dfrac{9}{s-7}$ (*ii*) $\dfrac{2}{2s+1}-\dfrac{4}{5s+7}+\dfrac{11}{1+5s}$

5. (*i*) $\dfrac{4}{s^2+1}-\dfrac{9s}{s^2+5}+\dfrac{6}{4s^2+1}+\dfrac{8s}{s^2+25}$ (*ii*) $\dfrac{2}{(s-1)(s+1)}+\dfrac{6s}{s^2-25}-\dfrac{4s}{s^2-9}+\dfrac{1}{6s^2-1}$

6. (*i*) $\dfrac{3}{s^2-1}-\dfrac{4}{s^2+9}+\dfrac{s}{s^2+16}-\dfrac{5}{s^2-16}$ (*ii*) $\dfrac{5}{3s^2+27}+\dfrac{6}{5s^2-9}-\dfrac{5}{36s^2+1}+\dfrac{9}{5+s^2}$.

Answers

1. (*i*) t^6 (*ii*) t^8 (*iii*) $\sqrt{t}$ (*iv*) e^{7t}

2. (*i*) $\cos 5t$ (*ii*) $\cosh 7t$ (*iii*) $\sinh 8t$ (*iv*) $\sin 4t$

3. (*i*) $\dfrac{1}{12}t^6+\dfrac{1}{4}t^4+\dfrac{1}{2}t^2$ (*ii*) e^{-4t}

(*iii*) $\dfrac{1}{10}\cos 1.8\,t+\dfrac{1}{2}\sin 1.8\,t$ (*iv*) $\dfrac{1}{a^2}\cos\dfrac{bc}{a}t$

4. (*i*) $6e^{4t}+3e^{-5t}+9e^{7t}$ (*ii*) $e^{-\frac{1}{2}t}-\dfrac{4}{5}e^{-\frac{7}{5}t}+\dfrac{11}{5}e^{-\frac{1}{5}t}$

5. (*i*) $4\sin t-9\cos\sqrt{5}\,t+3\sin\dfrac{t}{2}+8\cos 5t$ (*ii*) $2\sinh t+6\cosh 5t-4\cosh 3t+\dfrac{1}{\sqrt{6}}\sinh\dfrac{t}{\sqrt{6}}$

6. (*i*) $3\sinh t-\dfrac{4}{3}\sin 3t+\cos 4t-\dfrac{5}{4}\sinh 4t$ (*ii*) $\dfrac{5}{9}\sin 3t+\dfrac{2}{\sqrt{5}}\sinh\dfrac{3}{\sqrt{5}}t-\dfrac{5}{6}\sin\dfrac{t}{6}+\dfrac{9}{\sqrt{5}}\sin\sqrt{5}t.$

6. VALUE OF $L^{-1}(F(s-a))$ IN TERMS OF $L^{-1}(F(s))$

By the **first shifting theorem** of Laplace transforms,

if $$L(f(t)) = F(s), \text{ then } L(e^{at}f(t)) = F(s-a).$$

$\therefore$ **If $L^{-1}(F(s)) = f(t)$ then $L^{-1}(F(s-a)) = e^{at} f(t)$.**

Equivalently, $L^{-1}(F(s-a)) = e^{at} L^{-1}(F(s))$.

Remark. In the formula, $L^{-1}(F(s-a)) = e^{at}L^{-1}(F(s))$, if we replace a by $-a$, the formula takes the form,

$$\mathbf{L^{-1}(F(s+a)) = e^{-at} L^{-1}(F(s))}.$$

For example, $$L^{-1}\left(\frac{s-2}{(s-2)^2+5^2}\right) = e^{2t}L^{-1}\left(\frac{s}{s^2+5^2}\right) = e^{2t}\cos 5t.$$

Theorem. Using the formula $L^{-1}(F(s-a)) = e^{at} L^{-1}(F(s))$ prove that :

1. $L^{-1}\left(\frac{1}{s-a}\right) = e^{at}$

2. $L^{-1}\left(\frac{\Gamma(b+1)}{(s-a)^{b+1}}\right) = e^{at} t^b, b > -1$

3. $L^{-1}\left(\frac{n!}{(s-a)^{n+1}}\right) = e^{at} t^n, n = 0, 1, 2, \ldots\ldots$

4. $L^{-1}\left(\frac{b}{(s-a)^2 - b^2}\right) = e^{at} \sinh bt$

5. $L^{-1}\left(\frac{s-a}{(s-a)^2 - b^2}\right) = e^{at} \cosh bt$

6. $L^{-1}\left(\frac{b}{(s-a)^2 + b^2}\right) = e^{at} \sin bt$

7. $L^{-1}\left(\frac{s-a}{(s-a)^2 + b^2}\right) = e^{at} \cos bt.$

Proof. 1. We have $L^{-1}\left(\frac{1}{s}\right) = 1.$

$$\therefore \quad L^{-1}\left(\frac{1}{s-a}\right) = e^{at} . L^{-1}\left(\frac{1}{s}\right) = e^{at} .1$$

$$\therefore \quad L^{-1}\left(\frac{1}{s-a}\right) = e^{at}.$$

2. We have $L^{-1}\left(\frac{\Gamma(b+1)}{s^{b+1}}\right) = t^b, b > -1.$

$$\therefore \quad L^{-1}\left(\frac{\Gamma(b+1)}{(s-a)^{b+1}}\right) = e^{at} L^{-1}\left(\frac{\Gamma(b+1)}{s^{b+1}}\right) = e^{at} t^b$$

$$\therefore \quad L^{-1}\left(\frac{\Gamma(b+1)}{(s-a)^{b+1}}\right) = e^{at} t^b, b > -1.$$

3. We have $L^{-1}\left(\frac{n!}{s^{n+1}}\right) = t^n, n = 0, 1, 2, \ldots\ldots$

$$\therefore \quad L^{-1}\left(\frac{n!}{(s-a)^{n+1}}\right) = e^{at} L^{-1}\left(\frac{n!}{s^{n+1}}\right) = e^{at} t^n$$

$$\therefore \quad L^{-1}\left(\frac{n!}{(s-a)^{n+1}}\right) = e^{at} t^n, n = 0, 1, 2, \ldots\ldots$$

4. We have $L^{-1}\left(\frac{b}{s^2-b^2}\right)=\sinh bt$.

$$\therefore \quad L^{-1}\left(\frac{b}{(s-a)^2-b^2}\right)=e^{at}\,L^{-1}\left(\frac{b}{s^2-b^2}\right)=e^{at}\sinh bt$$

$$\therefore \quad \mathbf{L^{-1}\left(\frac{b}{(s-a)^2-b^2}\right)=e^{at}\sinh bt.}$$

5. We have $L^{-1}\left(\frac{s}{s^2-b^2}\right)=\cosh bt$.

$$\therefore \quad L^{-1}\left(\frac{s-a}{(s-a)^2-b^2}\right)=e^{at}\,L^{-1}\left(\frac{s}{s^2-b^2}\right)=e^{at}\cosh bt$$

$$\therefore \quad \mathbf{L^{-1}\left(\frac{s-a}{(s-a)^2-b^2}\right)=e^{at}\cosh bt.}$$

6. We have $L^{-1}\left(\frac{b}{s^2+b^2}\right)=\sin bt$.

$$\therefore \quad L^{-1}\left(\frac{b}{(s-a)^2+b^2}\right)=e^{at}\,L^{-1}\left(\frac{b}{s^2+b^2}\right)=e^{at}\sin bt$$

$$\therefore \quad \mathbf{L^{-1}\left(\frac{b}{(s-a)^2+b^2}\right)=e^{at}\sin bt.}$$

7. We have $L^{-1}\left(\frac{s}{s^2+b^2}\right)=\cos bt$.

$$\therefore \quad L^{-1}\left(\frac{s-a}{(s-a)^2+b^2}\right)=e^{at}\,L^{-1}\left(\frac{s}{s^2+b^2}\right)=e^{at}\cos bt$$

$$\therefore \quad \mathbf{L^{-1}\left(\frac{s-a}{(s-a)^2+b^2}\right)=e^{at}\cos bt.}$$

Example 1. *Find the inverse Laplace transform of the function* $\frac{12}{(s-4)^3}$.

Sol. $L^{-1}\left(\frac{12}{(s-4)^3}\right)=6L^{-1}\left(\frac{2}{(s-4)^3}\right)$

$$=6e^{4t}\,L^{-1}\left(\frac{2}{s^3}\right)=6e^{4t}\,L^{-1}\left(\frac{2!}{s^{2+1}}\right) \qquad (\because L^{-1}(F(s-a))=e^{at}L^{-1}(F(s)))$$

$$= \mathbf{6e^{4t}.t^2}.$$

Example 2. *Find the inverse Laplace transform of the following functions :*

(*i*) $\dfrac{3s+1}{(s+1)^4}$ (*ii*) $\displaystyle\sum_{k=1}^{5} \frac{\lambda_k}{s+k^2}$.

Sol. (*i*) $L^{-1}\left(\dfrac{3s+1}{(s+1)^4}\right) = L^{-1}\left(\dfrac{3(s+1)-2}{(s+1)^4}\right)$

$$= e^{-t} L^{-1}\left(\frac{3s-2}{s^4}\right) = e^{-t} L^{-1}\left(\frac{3}{s^3} - \frac{2}{s^4}\right)$$

$(\because L^{-1}(F(s-a)) = e^{at} L^{-1}(F(s)))$

$$= e^{-t}\left[\frac{3}{2} L^{-1}\left(\frac{2!}{s^3}\right) - \frac{2}{6} L^{-1}\left(\frac{3!}{s^4}\right)\right] = \mathbf{e^{-t}\left[\frac{3}{2}t^2 - \frac{1}{3}t^3\right]}.$$

(*ii*) $$L^{-1}\left(\sum_{k=1}^{5} \frac{\lambda_k}{s+k^2}\right) = \sum_{k=1}^{5} \lambda_k L^{-1}\left(\frac{1}{s+k^2}\right) = \sum_{k=1}^{5} \lambda_k e^{-k^2 t}.$$

Example 3. *Find the inverse Laplace transform of the following functions :*

(*i*) $\dfrac{s+3}{(s+3)^2+4}$ (*ii*) $\dfrac{3s}{s^2+2s-8}$.

Sol. (*i*) $L\left(\dfrac{s+3}{(s+3)^2+4}\right) = e^{-3t} L^{-1}\left(\dfrac{s}{s^2+2^2}\right) = \mathbf{e^{-3t}\cos 2t}$.

$(\because L^{-1}(F(s-a)) = e^{at} L^{-1}(F(s)))$

(*ii*) $$\frac{3s}{s^2+2s-8} = \frac{3s}{(s+1)^2-9} = \frac{3s+3-3}{(s+1)^2-9} = \frac{3(s+1)}{(s+1)^2-9} - \frac{3}{(s+1)^2-9}$$

$$\therefore \quad L^{-1}\left(\frac{3s}{s^2+2s-8}\right) = L^{-1}\left(\frac{3(s+1)}{(s+1)^2-9} - \frac{3}{(s+1)^2-9}\right)$$

$$= 3L^{-1}\left(\frac{s+1}{(s+1)^2-9}\right) - L^{-1}\left(\frac{3}{(s+1)^2-9}\right)$$

$$= 3e^{-1.t} L^{-1}\left(\frac{s}{s^2-3^2}\right) - e^{-1.t} L^{-1}\left(\frac{3}{s^2-3^2}\right)$$

$$= 3e^{-t}\cosh 3t - e^{-t}\sinh 3t$$

$$= \mathbf{e^{-t}(3\cosh 3t - \sinh 3t)}.$$

Example 4. *Find the inverse Laplace transform of the function*

$$\frac{1}{s^2+4s+13} - \frac{s+4}{s^2+8s+97} + \frac{s+2}{s^2-4s+29}.$$ *(KU 2004)*

Sol. $$\frac{1}{s^2+4s+13} - \frac{s+4}{s^2+8s+97} + \frac{s+2}{s^2-4s+29}$$

$$= \frac{1}{(s+2)^2+9} - \frac{s+4}{(s+4)^2+81} + \frac{s+2}{(s-2)^2+25}$$

$$= \frac{1}{(s+2)^2+9} - \frac{s+4}{(s+4)^2+81} + \frac{s-2}{(s-2)^2+25} + \frac{4}{(s-2)^2+25}$$

$$\therefore \quad L^{-1}\left(\frac{1}{s^2+4s+13} - \frac{s+4}{s^2+8s+97} + \frac{s+2}{s^2-4s+29}\right)$$

$$= L^{-1}\left(\frac{1}{(s+2)^2+9}\right) - L^{-1}\left(\frac{s+4}{(s+4)^2+81}\right) + L^{-1}\left(\frac{s-2}{(s-2)^2+25}\right) + L^{-1}\left(\frac{4}{(s-2)^2+25}\right)$$

$$= e^{-2t} L^{-1}\left(\frac{1}{s^2+9}\right) - e^{-4t} L^{-1}\left(\frac{s}{s^2+81}\right) + e^{2t} L^{-1}\left(\frac{s}{s^2+25}\right) + e^{2t} L^{-1}\left(\frac{4}{s^2+25}\right)$$

$$= \frac{1}{3} e^{-2t} L^{-1}\left(\frac{3}{s^2+3^2}\right) - e^{-4t} L^{-1}\left(\frac{s}{s^2+9^2}\right) + e^{2t} L^{-1}\left(\frac{s}{s^2+5^2}\right) + \frac{4}{5} e^{2t} L^{-1}\left(\frac{5}{s^2+5^2}\right)$$

$$= \frac{1}{3} e^{-2t} \sin 3t - e^{-4t} \cos 9t + e^{2t} \cos 5t + \frac{4}{5} e^{2t} \sin 5t.$$

7. VALUE OF $L^{-1}(e^{-as} F(s))$ IN TERMS OF $L^{-1}(F(s))$

By the **second shifting theorem** of Laplace transforms,

if $L(f(t)) = F(s)$ then for any $a \geq 0$, $L(f(t-a)\, u_a(t)) = e^{-as} F(s)$.

$\therefore$ **If $L^{-1}(F(s)) = f(t)$ then $L^{-1}(e^{-as} F(s)) = f(t-a)\, u_a(t)$ for any $a \geq 0$.**

Remark. It may be recalled that for $a \geq 0$, $u_a(t)$ is the *unit step function* defined as :

$$u_a(t) = \begin{cases} 0 & \text{if } t < a \\ 1 & \text{if } t > a. \end{cases}$$

$\therefore$ The function $f(t-a)\, u_a(t)$ can also be written as

$$f(t-a)\, u_a(t) = \begin{cases} 0 & \text{if } t < a \\ f(t-a) & \text{if } t > a. \end{cases}$$

Example 5. *Find the inverse Laplace transform of the function* $\frac{2s+1}{s^2 e^{2s}}$.

Sol. $\frac{2s+1}{s^2 e^{2s}} = e^{-2s} \cdot \frac{2s+1}{s^2} = e^{-2s} F(s)$, where $F(s) = \frac{2s+1}{s^2}$.

$$L^{-1}(F(s)) = L^{-1}\left(\frac{2s+1}{s^2}\right) = L^{-1}\left(\frac{2}{s} + \frac{1}{s^2}\right) = 2L^{-1}\left(\frac{1}{s}\right) + L^{-1}\left(\frac{1}{s^2}\right)$$

$$= 2(1) + t = t + 2 = f(t), \text{ say.}$$

$$\therefore \quad L^{-1}\left(\frac{2s+1}{s^2 e^{2s}}\right) = L^{-1}(e^{-2s} F(s))$$

$$= f(t-2)\, u_2(t) = ((t-2)+2)\, u_2(t) = t \cdot u_2(t) = \begin{cases} 0 & \text{if } t < 2 \\ t & \text{if } t > 2 \end{cases}.$$

$$\therefore \quad L^{-1}\left(\frac{2s+1}{s^2 e^{2s}}\right) = g(t), \text{ where } g(t) = \begin{cases} 0 & \text{if } t < 2 \\ t & \text{if } t > 2 \end{cases}.$$

Example 6. *Find the inverse Laplace transform of the function* $\dfrac{e^{-\pi s/2}\, s}{s^2+1}$.

Sol. $$\frac{e^{-\pi s/2} s}{s^2+1} = e^{-(\pi/2)s} \cdot \frac{s}{s^2+1} = e^{-(\pi/2)s}\, F(s), \text{ where } F(s) = \frac{s}{s^2+1}.$$

$$L^{-1}(F(s)) = L^{-1}\left(\frac{s}{s^2+1}\right) = \cos t = f(t), \text{ say.}$$

$$\therefore \quad L^{-1}\left(\frac{e^{-\pi s/2}\, s}{s^2+1}\right) = L^{-1}\left(e^{-(\pi/2)s}\, F(s)\right)$$

$$= f\left(t-\frac{\pi}{2}\right) u_{\pi/2}(t) = \cos\left(t-\frac{\pi}{2}\right) u_{\pi/2}(t)$$

$$= \sin t \,.\, u_{\pi/2}(t) = \begin{cases} 0 & \text{if } t < \pi/2 \\ \sin t & \text{if } t > \pi/2 \end{cases}.$$

Example 7. *Find the inverse Laplace transform of the function* $\dfrac{3(1-e^{-\pi s})}{s^2+9}$.

(KU 2004 S)

Sol. $$L^{-1}\left(\frac{3(1-e^{-\pi s})}{s^2+9}\right) = L^{-1}\left(\frac{3}{s^2+9} - \frac{3e^{-\pi s}}{s^2+9}\right) = L^{-1}\left(\frac{3}{s^2+9}\right) - L^{-1}\left(\frac{3e^{-\pi s}}{s^2+9}\right)$$

$$\therefore \quad L^{-1}\left(\frac{3(1-e^{-\pi s})}{s^2+9}\right) = \sin 3t - L^{-1}\left(\frac{3e^{-\pi s}}{s^2+9}\right) \qquad \ldots(1)$$

$$\frac{3e^{-\pi s}}{s^2+9} = e^{-\pi s} \cdot \frac{3}{s^2+9} = e^{-\pi s}\, F(s), \text{ where } F(s) = \frac{3}{s^2+9}.$$

$$L^{-1}(F(s)) = L^{-1}\left(\frac{3}{s^2+9}\right) = \sin 3t = f(t), \text{ say.}$$

$$\therefore \quad L^{-1}\left(\frac{3e^{-\pi s}}{s^2+9}\right) = L^{-1}(e^{-\pi s}\, F(s)) = f(t-\pi)\, u_\pi(t) = \sin 3(t-\pi)\, u_\pi(t)$$

$$= -\sin(3\pi - 3t)\, u_\pi(t) = -\sin 3t \,.\, u_\pi(t).$$

$$\therefore \quad (1) \Rightarrow \quad L^{-1}\left(\frac{3(1-e^{-\pi s})}{s^2+9}\right) = \sin 3t - (-\sin 3t \,.\, u_\pi(t))$$

$$= \mathbf{(1 + u_\pi(t)) \sin 3t.}$$

8. VALUE OF L^{-1} F(s/a)) IN TERMS OF L^{-1} (F(s))

By the **change of scale property,**

if $\quad L(f(t)) = F(s)$ then for any $a > 0$, $L(f(at)) = \dfrac{1}{a} F\left(\dfrac{s}{a}\right)$ *i.e.* $L(af(at)) = F\left(\dfrac{s}{a}\right)$.

$\therefore$ **If $L^{-1}(F(s)) = f(t)$ then $L^{-1}\left(F\left(\dfrac{s}{a}\right)\right) = a\, f(at)$ for any $a > 0$.**

Example 8. *Find the inverse Laplace transform of the following functions :*

(*i*) $\dfrac{a}{\left(\dfrac{s}{\lambda}\right)^2 + a^2}$ (*ii*) $\dfrac{s}{\left(\dfrac{s}{7}\right)^2 + 9}$

Sol. (*i*) Let $F(s) = \dfrac{a}{s^2 + a^2}$.

$\therefore$ $L^{-1}(F(s)) = \sin at = f(t)$, say

$$\therefore \quad L^{-1}\left(\frac{a}{\left(\frac{s}{\lambda}\right)^2 + a^2}\right) = L^{-1}\left(F\left(\frac{s}{\lambda}\right)\right) = \lambda f(\lambda t) = \lambda \sin \lambda at.$$

Alternative method

$$L^{-1}\left(\frac{a}{\left(\frac{s}{\lambda}\right)^2 + a^2}\right) = L^{-1}\left(\frac{\lambda^2 a}{s^2 + a^2\lambda^2}\right) = \lambda L^{-1}\left(\frac{\lambda a}{s^2 + (\lambda a)^2}\right) = \lambda \sin \lambda at.$$

(*ii*) Let $F(s) = \dfrac{s}{s^2 + 9}$.

$\therefore$ $L^{-1}(F(s)) = \cos 3t = f(t)$, say

$$\therefore \quad L^{-1}\left(\frac{s}{\left(\frac{s}{7}\right)^2 + 9}\right) = 7L^{-1}\left(\frac{s/7}{(s/7)^2 + 9}\right) = 7(7 f(7t)) = 49 \cos (3(7t)) = 49 \cos 21t.$$

WORKING RULES FOR SOLVING PROBLEMS

Rule I. If $L^{-1}(F(s)) = f(t)$, then $L^{-1}(F(s - a)) = e^{at} f(t)$.

Rule II. If $L^{-1}(F(s)) = f(t)$, then

$L^{-1}(e^{-as} F(s)) = f(t - a)\, u_a(t), a \geq 0$.

Rule III. If $L^{-1}(F(s)) = f(t)$, then

$L^{-1}\left(F\left(\dfrac{s}{a}\right)\right) = a f(at), a > 0.$

EXERCISE 2

Find the inverse Laplace transform of the following functions :

1. (*i*) $\dfrac{1}{(s-4)^5}$ (*ii*) $\dfrac{4}{(s+2)^7}$

2. (i) $\dfrac{1}{s^2+6s+13}$ (ii) $\dfrac{s+3}{s^2-4s+13}$

3. (i) $\dfrac{s}{\left(s+\frac{1}{2}\right)^2+1}$ (ii) $\dfrac{4}{s^2+6s+18}$

4. (i) $\dfrac{5}{s^2-4s-3}$ (ii) $\dfrac{9}{s^2+s+\frac{1}{2}}$

5. (i) $\dfrac{s+2}{s^2+4s+7}$ (ii) $\dfrac{s+10}{s^2+8s+20}$

6. (i) $\dfrac{1}{(s-4)^5}+\dfrac{5}{s^2-4s+29}$ (ii) $\dfrac{1}{(s-3)^4}+\dfrac{s+3}{s^2+6s+45}$

7. (i) $\dfrac{1}{2s-5}+\dfrac{5s-2}{3s^2+s+8}+\dfrac{s+1}{s^2+2s+2}$

(ii) $\dfrac{1}{s^2-6s+10}+\dfrac{1}{s^2+8s+16}+\dfrac{3s-2}{s^2-4s+20}+\dfrac{3s+7}{s^2-2s-3}$

8. (i) $\dfrac{e^{-s}}{s^2}$ (ii) $\dfrac{e^{-3s}}{s^3}$

9. (i) $\dfrac{(5s+1)\,e^{-5s}}{s^2}$ (ii) $\dfrac{2+2s+s^2}{s^3\,e^s}$

10. (i) $-\dfrac{e^{-\pi s/2}}{s^2+1}$ (ii) $-\dfrac{5se^{-\pi s}}{s^2+1}$

11. (i) $\dfrac{se^{-2s}}{s^2+\pi^2}$ (ii) $\dfrac{e^{-2\pi s/3}}{s^2}$

12. (i) $\dfrac{e^{4-3s}}{(s+4)^{5/2}}$ (ii) $\dfrac{(s+1)\,e^{-\pi s}}{s^2+s+1}$.

Answers

1. (i) $\dfrac{1}{24}t^4 e^{4t}$ (ii) $\dfrac{1}{180}t^6 e^{-2t}$

2. (i) $\dfrac{1}{2}e^{-3t}\sin 2t$ (ii) $e^{2t}\left(\cos 3t+\dfrac{5}{3}\sin 3t\right)$

3. (i) $e^{-t/2}\left(\cos t-\dfrac{1}{2}\sin t\right)$ (ii) $\dfrac{4}{3}e^{-3t}\sin 3t$

4. (i) $\dfrac{5}{\sqrt{7}}e^{2t}\sinh\sqrt{7}t$ (ii) $18e^{-t/2}\sin\dfrac{t}{2}$

5. (i) $e^{-2t}\cos\sqrt{3}t$ (ii) $e^{-4t}\,[\cos 2t+3\sin 2t]$

6. (i) $\dfrac{1}{24}e^{4t}t^4+e^{2t}\sin 5t$ (ii) $\dfrac{1}{6}e^{3t}t^3+e^{-3t}\cos 6t$

7. (i) $\dfrac{1}{2}e^{5t/2}+e^{-\frac{t}{6}}\left[\dfrac{5}{3}\cos\dfrac{\sqrt{95}}{6}t-\dfrac{25}{3\sqrt{95}}\sin\dfrac{\sqrt{95}}{6}t\right]+e^{-t}\cos t$

(ii) $e^{3t}\sin t+te^{-4t}+3e^{2t}\cos 4t+e^{2t}\sin 4t+3e^{t}\cosh 2t+5e^{t}\sinh 2t$

8. (*i*) $(t-1)\,u_1(t)$ (*ii*) $\frac{1}{2}(t-3)^2\,u_3(t)$

9. (*i*) $t\,.\,u_5(t)$ (*ii*) $t^2u_1(t)$

10. (*i*) $\cos t\,.\,u_{\pi/2}(t)$ (*ii*) $5\cos t\,.\,u_\pi(t)$

11. (*i*) $\cos \pi t\,.\,u_2(t)$ (*ii*) $-\cos\left(\frac{\pi}{6}-t\right).u_{2\pi/3}(t)$

12. (*i*) $\frac{4}{3\sqrt{\pi}}e^{16-4t}(t-3)^{3/2}\,u_3(t)$

(*ii*) $e^{-\frac{1}{2}(t-\pi)}\left[\cos\frac{\sqrt{3}}{2}(t-\pi)+\frac{1}{\sqrt{3}}\sin\frac{\sqrt{3}}{2}(t-\pi)\right]u_\pi(t).$

---

9. VALUE OF L^{-1} (F(s)/s) IN TERMS OF L^{-1} (F(s))

By the property of **Laplace transforms of integrals,**

if $$L(f(t)) = F(s), \text{ then } L\left(\int_0^t f(T)\,dT\right) = \frac{1}{s}F(s).$$

$\therefore$ **If** $\mathbf{L^{-1}(F(s)) = f(t), \text{ then } L^{-1}\left(\frac{1}{s}F(s)\right) = \int_0^t f(T)\,dT.}$

Example 1. *Find the inverse Laplace transform of the function* $\frac{1}{s(s^2+a^2)}$.

Sol. $$\frac{1}{s(s^2+a^2)} = \frac{1}{s}\left(\frac{1}{s^2+a^2}\right) = \frac{1}{s}F(s), \text{ where } F(s) = \frac{1}{s^2+a^2}.$$

$$L^{-1}(F(s)) = L^{-1}\left(\frac{1}{s^2+a^2}\right) = \frac{1}{a}L^{-1}\left(\frac{a}{s^2+a^2}\right) = \frac{1}{a}\sin at = f(t), \text{ say.}$$

$\therefore$ By the **property of Laplace transform of integrals,**

$$L^{-1}\left(\frac{1}{s}F(s)\right) = \int_0^t f(T)\,dT = \int_0^t \frac{1}{a}\sin aT\,dT = \frac{1}{a}\left(-\frac{\cos aT}{a}\right)\Big|_0^t$$

$$= -\frac{1}{a^2}(\cos at - \cos 0) = \frac{1-\cos at}{a^2}$$

$\therefore$ $$L^{-1}\left(\frac{1}{s(s^2+a^2)}\right) = \mathbf{\frac{1-\cos at}{a^2}}.$$

Example 2. *Find the inverse Laplace transform of the function* $\frac{1}{s^5+s^3}$.

Sol. $$\frac{1}{s^5+s^3} = \frac{1}{s^3(s^2+1)} = \frac{1}{s^3}\left(\frac{1}{s^2+1}\right) = \frac{1}{s^3}F(s), \text{ where } F(s) = \frac{1}{s^2+1}.$$

$$L^{-1}(F(s)) = L^{-1}\left(\frac{1}{s^2+1}\right) = \sin t = f(t), \text{ say}$$

$\therefore$ By the **property of Laplace transform of integrals,**

$$L^{-1}\left(\frac{1}{s}F(s)\right)=\int_0^t F(T)\,dT=\int_0^t \sin T\,dT=-\cos T\Big|_0^t=-\cos t+\cos 0=1-\cos t.$$

Again by using the same formula,

$$L^{-1}\left(\frac{1}{s}\cdot\frac{1}{s}F(s)\right)=\int_0^t (1-\cos T)\,dT=(T-\sin T)\Big|_0^t=t-\sin t.$$

$$\therefore \quad L^{-1}\left(\frac{1}{s^2}F(s)\right)=t-\sin t.$$

Again by using the same formula,

$$L^{-1}\left(\frac{1}{s}\cdot\frac{1}{s^2}F(s)\right)=\int_0^t (T-\sin T)\,dT=\left(\frac{T^2}{2}+\cos T\right)\Bigg|_0^t=\frac{t^2}{2}+\cos t-1$$

$$\therefore \quad L^{-1}\left(\frac{1}{s^3}F(s)\right)=\frac{t^2}{2}+\cos t-1$$

or $$L^{-1}\left(\frac{1}{s^5+s^3}\right)=\frac{\mathbf{t^2}}{\mathbf{2}}+\mathbf{\cos t-1.}$$

Remark. The above problem can also be solved by the "method of partial fractions".

10. VALUE OF L^{-1} (F′(s)) IN TERMS OF L^{-1}(F(s))

By the property of **differentiation of Laplace transforms**

if $\quad L(f(t))=F(s)$, then $L(t\,f(t))=-F'(s)$.

$\therefore$ If $L^{-1}(F(s))=f(t)$, then $F'(s)=L(-t\,f(t))$.

$\therefore$ **If L^{-1} (F(s)) = f(t), then L^{-1} (F′(s)) = – t f(t).**

Example 3. *Find the inverse Laplace transform of the function* $\dfrac{s}{(s^2+4)^2}$

Sol. $$\int \frac{s}{(s^2+4)^2}\,ds=\frac{1}{2}\int\frac{2s}{(s^2+4)^2}\,ds=\frac{1}{2}\cdot\frac{(s^2+4)^{-1}}{-1}=-\frac{1}{2(s^2+4)}=F(s),\ \text{say.}$$

$$\therefore \quad F'(s)=\frac{s}{(s^2+4)^2}$$

Also $$L^{-1}(F(s))=L^{-1}\left(-\frac{1}{2(s^2+4)}\right)=-\frac{1}{4}L^{-1}\left(\frac{2}{s^2+2^2}\right)=-\frac{1}{4}\sin 2t=f(t),\ \text{say.}$$

$\therefore$ By the **property of differentiation of Laplace transforms,** we have

$$L^{-1}(F'(s))=-t\,f(t).$$

$$\therefore \quad L^{-1}\left(\frac{s}{(s^2+4)^2}\right)=-t\left(-\frac{1}{4}\sin 2t\right)=\frac{1}{4}t\sin 2t$$

$$\therefore \quad L^{-1}\left(\frac{s}{(s^2+4)^2}\right)=\frac{\mathbf{1}}{\mathbf{4}}\,\mathbf{t\sin 2t.}$$

Example 4. *Find the inverse Laplace transform of the function* $\dfrac{2s+6}{(s^2+6s+10)^2}$.

Sol. $L^{-1}\left[\dfrac{2s+6}{(s^2+6s+10)^2}\right] = L^{-1}\left[\dfrac{2(s+3)}{((s+3)^2+1)^2}\right] = e^{-3t}\, L^{-1}\left[\dfrac{2s}{(s^2+1)^2}\right]$ ...(1)

Now, we require the value of $L^{-1}\left[\dfrac{2s}{(s^2+1)^2}\right]$.

$$\int \frac{2s}{(s^2+1)^2}\, ds = \frac{(s^2+1)^{-1}}{-1} = -\frac{1}{s^2+1} = F(s), \text{ say.}$$

$\therefore$
$$F'(s) = \frac{2s}{(s^2+1)^2}$$

Also
$$L^{-1}(F(s)) = L^{-1}\left(-\frac{1}{s^2+1}\right) = -\sin t = f(t), \text{ say.}$$

$\therefore$ By the **property of differentiation of Laplace transforms,** we have

$$L^{-1}(F'(s)) = -t\, f(t).$$

$$\Rightarrow \quad L^{-1}\left(\frac{2s}{(s^2+1)^2}\right) = -t(-\sin t) \quad \Rightarrow \quad L^{-1}\left(\frac{2s}{(s^2+1)^2}\right) = t \sin t.$$

$$\therefore \ (1) \quad \Rightarrow \quad L^{-1}\left(\frac{2s+6}{(s^2+6s+10)^2}\right) = e^{-3t}\, t \sin t.$$

Example 5. *Find the inverse Laplace transform of the function* $\dfrac{1}{(s^2+a^2)^2}$.

Sol. Let $F(s) = \dfrac{1}{s^2+a^2}$.

$$\therefore \quad L^{-1}(F(s)) = L^{-1}\left(\frac{1}{s^2+a^2}\right) = \frac{1}{a} L^{-1}\left(\frac{a}{s^2+a^2}\right) = \frac{1}{a}\sin at = f(t), \text{ say.}$$

Using, $L^{-1}(F'(s)) = -t\, f(t)$, we get

$$L^{-1}\left(\left(\frac{1}{s^2+a^2}\right)'\right) = -t \cdot \frac{1}{a}\sin at.$$

$$\Rightarrow \quad L^{-1}\left(\frac{-2s}{(s^2+a^2)^2}\right) = -\frac{1}{a}\, t \sin at$$

$$\Rightarrow \quad L^{-1}\left(\frac{s}{(s^2+a^2)^2}\right) = \frac{1}{2a}\, t \sin at = g(t), \text{ say.}$$

Using formula for **Laplace transform of integrals,** we get

$$L^{-1}\left(\frac{1}{s} \cdot \frac{s}{(s^2+a^2)^2}\right) = \int_0^t g(T)\, dT.$$

$$\Rightarrow \quad L^{-1}\left(\frac{1}{(s^2+a^2)^2}\right) = \int_0^t \frac{1}{2a} T \sin aT\, dT = \frac{1}{2a}\left[-\frac{T\cos aT}{a} + \frac{\sin aT}{a^2}\right]_0^t$$

$$= \frac{1}{2a^3}[-at\cos at + \sin at]$$

$$\therefore \quad L^{-1}\left(\frac{1}{(s^2+a^2)^2}\right) = \frac{1}{2a^3}[\sin at - at\cos at].$$

11. VALUE OF $L^{-1}\left(\int_s^\infty F(s)\, ds\right)$ IN TERMS OF $L^{-1}(F(s))$

By the property of **integration of Laplace transforms**

if $\quad L(f(t)) = F(s)$, then $L\left(\frac{f(t)}{t}\right) = \int_s^\infty F(S)\, dS.$

$\therefore$ **If $L^{-1}(F(s)) = f(t)$, then $L^{-1}\left(\int_s^\infty F(S)\, dS\right) = \frac{f(t)}{t}$.**

Example 6. *Find the inverse Laplace transform of the function* $\log\left(1+\frac{a^2}{s^2}\right)$.

Sol. $\frac{d}{ds}\left(\log\left(1+\frac{a^2}{s^2}\right)\right) = \frac{d}{ds}\left(\log(s^2+a^2) - 2\log s\right) = \frac{2s}{s^2+a^2} - \frac{2}{s} = F(s)$, say.

$$\therefore \quad \int F(s)\, ds = \log\left(1+\frac{a^2}{s^2}\right)$$

Also, $\quad L^{-1}(F(s)) = L^{-1}\left(\frac{2s}{s^2+a^2} - \frac{2}{s}\right) = 2L^{-1}\left(\frac{s}{s^2+a^2}\right) - 2L^{-1}\left(\frac{1}{s}\right)$

$$= 2\cos at - 2(1) = 2\cos at - 2 = f(t), \text{ say.}$$

$\therefore$ By the **property of integration of Laplace transforms**, we have

$$L^{-1}\left(\int_s^\infty F(S)\, dS\right) = \frac{f(t)}{t}.$$

$$\therefore \quad L^{-1}\left(\log\left(1+\frac{a^2}{S^2}\right)\Bigg|_s^\infty\right) = \frac{2\cos at - 2}{t}$$

$$\therefore \quad L^{-1}\left(0 - \log\left(1+\frac{a^2}{s^2}\right)\right) = \frac{2\cos at - 2}{t}$$

$$\therefore \quad L^{-1}\left(\log\left(1+\frac{a^2}{s^2}\right)\right) = \frac{2 - 2\cos at}{t}.$$

Example 7. *Find the inverse Laplace transform of the function log* $\frac{s^2+1}{(s-1)^2}$.

Sol. $\frac{d}{ds}\left(\log\frac{s^2+1}{(s-1)^2}\right) = \frac{d}{ds}(\log(s^2+1) - 2\log(s-1)) = \frac{2s}{s^2+1} - \frac{2}{s-1} = F(s)$, say.

$\therefore \qquad \int F(s)\, ds = \log\frac{s^2+1}{(s-1)^2}$

Also $\qquad L^{-1}(F(s)) = L^{-1}\left(\frac{2s}{s^2+1} - \frac{2}{s-1}\right) = 2L^{-1}\left(\frac{s}{s^2+1}\right) - 2L^{-1}\left(\frac{1}{s-1}\right)$

$= 2\cos t - 2e^t = f(t)$, say.

By the **property of integration of Laplace transforms,** we have

$$L^{-1}\left(\int_s^\infty F(S)\, dS\right) = \frac{f(t)}{t}.$$

$$\therefore \qquad L^{-1}\left(\left(\log\frac{S^2+1}{(S-1)^2}\right)\Bigg|_s^\infty\right) = \frac{2\cos t - 2e^t}{t}$$

$$\therefore \qquad L^{-1}\left(0 - \log\frac{s^2+1}{(s-1)^2}\right) = -\frac{2e^t - 2\cos t}{t}$$

$$\therefore \qquad L^{-1}\left(\log\frac{s^2+1}{(s-1)^2}\right) = \frac{\mathbf{2e^t - 2\cos t}}{\mathbf{t}}.$$

Example 8. *Find the inverse Laplace transform of the function* $\cot^{-1}(s+1)$.

Sol. $\frac{d}{ds}(\cot^{-1}(s+1)) = \frac{-1}{(s+1)^2+1}\cdot 1 = -\frac{1}{(s+1)^2+1} = F(s)$, say.

$\therefore \qquad \int F(s)\, ds = \cot^{-1}(s+1)$

Also, $\qquad L^{-1}(F(s)) = L^{-1}\left(-\frac{1}{(s+1)^2+1}\right) = -L^{-1}\left(\frac{1}{(s+1)^2+1}\right)$

$= -e^{-t} L^{-1}\frac{1}{s^2+1} = -e^{-t}\sin t = f(t)$, say.

$\therefore$ By the **property of integration of Laplace transforms,** we have

$$L^{-1}\left(\int_s^\infty F(S)\, dS\right) = \frac{f(t)}{t}.$$

$$\therefore \qquad L^{-1}\left(\cot^{-1}(S+1)\Big|_s^\infty\right) = -\frac{e^{-t}\sin t}{t}$$

$$\Rightarrow \qquad L^{-1}(0 - \cot^{-1}(s+1)) = -\frac{e^{-t}\sin t}{t}$$

$$\therefore \qquad L^{-1}(\cot^{-1}(s+1)) = \frac{\mathbf{e^{-t}\sin t}}{\mathbf{t}}.$$

WORKING RULES FOR SOLVING PROBLEMS

Rule I. If $L^{-1}(F(s)) = f(t)$, then $L^{-1}\left(\frac{1}{s}F(s)\right) = \int_0^t f(T)\, dT$.

Rule II. If $L^{-1}(F(s)) = f(t)$, then $L^{-1}(F'(s)) = -t\, f(t)$.

Rule III. If $L^{-1}(F(s)) = f(t)$, then $L^{-1}\left(\int_s^{\infty} F(S)dS\right) = \frac{f(t)}{t}$.

EXERCISE 3

Find the inverse Laplace transform of the following functions :

1. (i) $\frac{1}{s^2+4s}$ (ii) $\frac{1}{s(s^2+16)}$ **2.** (i) $\frac{1}{s^3-s}$ (ii) $\frac{4}{s^3-2s^2}$

3. (i) $\frac{1}{s(s+a)^3}$ (ii) $\frac{1}{s(s^2+2s+2)}$ **4.** (i) $\frac{7}{s^4-s^2}$ (ii) $\frac{\pi^5}{s^4(s^2+\pi^2)}$

5. (i) $\frac{s}{(s^2+a^2)^2}$ (ii) $\frac{s}{(s^2-9)^2}$ **6.** (i) $\frac{s^2-\pi^2}{(s^2+\pi^2)^2}$ (ii) $\frac{s+1}{(s^2+2s+2)^2}$

7. (i) $\log\frac{s+a}{s+b}$ (ii) $\log\frac{s+1}{s-1}$ **8.** (i) $\log\left(1-\frac{a^2}{s^2}\right)$ (ii) $\log\frac{1+s}{s}$

9. (i) $\frac{1}{2}\log\frac{s^2+b^2}{s^2+a^2}$ (ii) $\log\frac{s^2+1}{s(s+1)}$ **10.** (i) $\log\frac{(s+1)^2}{(s+2)(s+3)}$ (ii) $\log\frac{s^2+1}{(s-1)^2}$

(MDU 2005)

11. (i) $\cot^{-1}\frac{s}{\pi}$ (ii) $\tan^{-1}\frac{2}{s}$.

Answers

1. (i) $\frac{1}{4}-\frac{e^{-4t}}{4}$ (ii) $\frac{1}{16}-\frac{\cos 4t}{16}$ **2.** (i) $\cosh t - 1$ (ii) $e^{2t}-2t-1$

3. (i) $\frac{1}{a^3}-\frac{e^{-at}}{a^3}\left(\frac{a^2}{2}t^2+at+1\right)$ (ii) $\frac{1}{2}\left[1-(\sin t+\cos t)\,e^{-t}\right]$

4. (i) $7(\sinh t - t)$ (ii) $\sin \pi t + \frac{\pi^3}{6}t^3 - \pi t$

5. (i) $\frac{1}{2a}t\sin at$ (ii) $\frac{1}{6}t\sinh 3t$ **6.** (i) $t\cos \pi t$ (ii) $\frac{1}{2}e^{-t}\, t\sin t$

7. (i) $\frac{e^{-bt}-e^{-at}}{t}$ (ii) $\frac{e^{t}-e^{-t}}{t}$ **8.** (i) $\frac{2(1-\cos at)}{t}$ (ii) $\frac{1-e^{-t}}{t}$

9. (*i*) $\dfrac{\cos at - \cos bt}{t}$ (*ii*) $\dfrac{1 + e^{-t} - 2\cos t}{t}$

10. (*i*) $\dfrac{e^{-2t} + e^{-3t} - 2e^{-t}}{t}$ (*ii*) $\dfrac{2(e^t - \cos t)}{t}$

11. (*i*) $\dfrac{\sin \pi t}{t}$ (*ii*) $\dfrac{\sin 2t}{t}$

Hints

6. (*i*) Use $\left(\dfrac{s}{s^2 + \pi^2}\right)' = -\dfrac{s^2 - \pi^2}{(s^2 + \pi^2)^2}$.

12. CONVOLUTION THEOREM

The convolution theorem is used to find the inverse Laplace transform of the product of two functions with known inverse Laplace transforms of the factors of the product. Let F(*s*) and G(*s*) be two functions with known inverse Laplace transforms *f*(*t*) and *g*(*t*) respectively. The convolution theorem would help us to find the inverse Laplace transform of the product F(*s*) G(*s*). In this theorem, we shall prove that the inverse Laplace transformation of the product F(*s*) G(*s*) is given by the function $\int_0^t f(T)\, g(t - T)\, dT$ of *t*. This integral is called the **convolution** of the functions *f* and *g* and it is denoted by $f * g$.

$$\therefore \quad (f * g)(t) = \int_0^t f(T)\, g(t - T)\, dT.$$

Let $z = t - T$. $\therefore$ $dz = -dT$

$$\therefore \quad (f * g)(t) = \int_t^0 f(t - z)\, g(z) \,.\, -dz = -\int_t^0 g(z)\, f(t - z)\, dz$$

$$= \int_0^t g(z)\, f(t - z)\, dz = \int_0^t g(T)\, f(t - T)\, dT \qquad \text{(Replacing } z \text{ by T)}$$

$$= (g * f)(t)$$

$$\therefore \quad \mathbf{f * g = g * f}$$

Statement. Let f(t) and g(t) be functions such that their Laplace transforms exist. Prove that

$$\mathbf{L(f * g) = L(f)\, L(g).} \qquad \textit{(CDLU 2004)}$$

Proof. It can be proved mathematically that the Laplace transform of the convolution of *f* and *g* *i.e.*, $f * g$ exists.

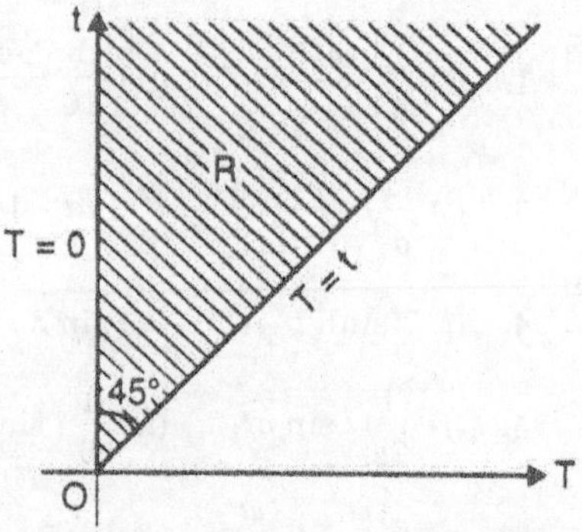

By definition, $L(f * g) = \int_0^\infty e^{-st}\, (f * g)(t)\, dt$

$$\therefore \quad L(f * g) = \int_0^\infty e^{-st} \left[\int_0^t f(T)\, g(t - T)\, dT\right] dt$$

$$= \int_0^\infty \int_0^t e^{-st} f(T)\, g(t - T)\, dT\, dt$$

$$= \iint_R e^{-st} f(T)\, g(t - T)\, dT\, dt,$$

where R is the 45° wedge bounded by the lines T = 0 and T = *t* in the T*t*-plane.

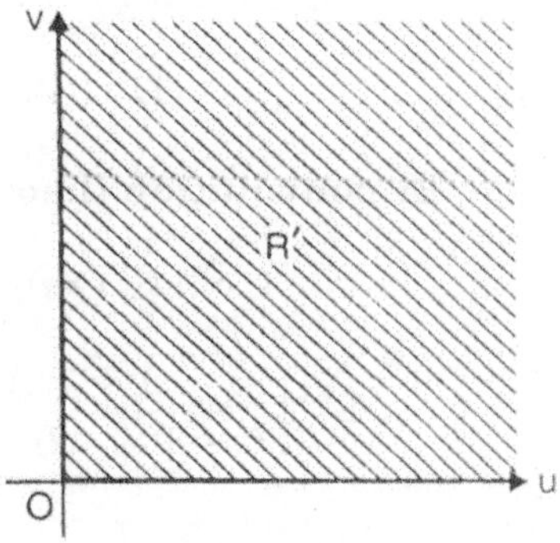

Let $u = T$ and $v = t - T$.

$\therefore$ $T = u$ and $t = u + v$

$$\therefore \quad J = \begin{vmatrix} \frac{\partial T}{\partial u} & \frac{\partial T}{\partial v} \\ \frac{\partial t}{\partial u} & \frac{\partial t}{\partial v} \end{vmatrix} = \begin{vmatrix} 1 & 0 \\ 1 & 1 \end{vmatrix} = 1$$

New variables transform the region R into the region R′ in the uv-plane defined by $u \geq 0$, $v \geq 0$.

$$\therefore \quad L(f * g) = \iint_{R'} e^{-s(u+v)} f(u)\, g(v)\, |J|\, du\, dv$$

$$= \int_0^\infty \int_0^\infty e^{-su} e^{-sv} f(u)\, g(v)\, du\, dv \qquad (\because |J| = |1| = 1)$$

$$= \left(\int_0^\infty e^{-su} f(u)\, du \right) \left(\int_0^\infty e^{-sv} g(v)\, dv \right)$$

$$= L(f)\, L(g).$$

$\therefore$ **L(f * g) = L(f) L(g).**

Corollary 1. Let $L(f) = F(s)$ and $L(g) = G(s)$.

$\therefore$ The result of the convolution theorem can be written as

$$L(f * g) = F(s)\, G(s).$$

$$\Rightarrow \quad L^{-1}(F(s)\, G(s)) = f * g$$

or

$$L^{-1}(F(s)\, G(s)) = \int_0^t f(T)\, g(t - T)\, dT.$$

$\therefore$ **If** $\mathbf{L^{-1}(F(s)) = f(t)}$ **and** $\mathbf{L^{-1}(G(s)) = g(t)}$,

then $$\mathbf{L^{-1}(F(s)\, G(s)) = \int_0^t f(T)\, g(t - T)\, dT.}$$

This formula is used to find the inverse Laplace transform of the product of two functions.

Corollary 2. Since $f * g = g * f$, we can also write $L^{-1}(F(s)\, G(s)) = \int_0^t g(T)\, f(t - T)\, dT.$

Example 1. *Find the inverse Laplace transform of the function* $\dfrac{1}{(s+3)(s-2)}$.

(KU 2005 S)

Sol. $$\frac{1}{(s+3)(s-2)} = \left(\frac{1}{s+3}\right)\left(\frac{1}{s-2}\right) = F(s)\, G(s),$$

where $$F(s) = \frac{1}{s+3} \text{ and } G(s) = \frac{1}{s-2}$$

$$L^{-1}(F(s)) = L^{-1}\left(\frac{1}{s+3}\right) = e^{-3t} = f(t), \text{ say}$$

and $$L^{-1}(G(s)) = L^{-1}\left(\frac{1}{s-2}\right) = e^{2t} = g(t), \text{ say}.$$

By **convolution theorem**, we have

$$L^{-1}(F(s)\,G(s)) = f * g = \int_0^t f(T)\,g(t-T)\,dT.$$

$$\therefore \quad L^{-1}\left(\frac{1}{(s+3)(s-2)}\right) = \int_0^t e^{-3T}\,e^{2(t-T)}\,dT$$

$$= \int_0^t e^{2t-5T}\,dT = \left.\frac{e^{2t-5T}}{-5}\right|_0^t = -\frac{1}{5}[e^{-3t} - e^{2t}] = \frac{e^{2t}}{5} - \frac{e^{-3t}}{5}.$$

Example 2. *Use convolution theorem to evaluate* $L^{-1}\left(\frac{1}{s^2(s^2+a^2)}\right)$. (MDU 2005)

Sol. $$\frac{1}{s^2(s^2+a^2)} = \left(\frac{1}{s^2}\right)\left(\frac{1}{s^2+a^2}\right) = F(s)\,G(s), \text{ where}$$

$$F(s) = \frac{1}{s^2} \quad \text{and} \quad G(s) = \frac{1}{s^2+a^2}.$$

$$L^{-1}(F(s)) = L^{-1}\left(\frac{1}{s^2}\right) = t = f(t), \text{ say}$$

and $$L^{-1}(G(s)) = L^{-1}\left(\frac{1}{s^2+a^2}\right) = \frac{1}{a}L^{-1}\left(\frac{a}{s^2+a^2}\right) = \frac{1}{a}\sin at = g(t), \text{ say}$$

By **convolution theorem,** we have

$$L^{-1}(F(s)\,G(s)) = f * g = g * f = \int_0^t g(T)\,f(t-T)\,dT$$

$$\therefore \quad L^{-1}\left(\frac{1}{s^2(s^2+a^2)}\right) = \int_0^t \left(\frac{1}{a}\sin aT\right)(t-T)\,dT$$

$$= \frac{t}{a}\int_0^t \sin aT\,dT - \frac{1}{a}\int_0^t T\sin aT\,dT$$

$$= \frac{t}{a}\left.\left(-\frac{\cos aT}{a}\right)\right|_0^t - \frac{1}{a}\left[\left.T\left(-\frac{\cos aT}{a}\right)\right|_0^t - \int_0^t 1.\left(-\frac{\cos aT}{a}\right)dT\right]$$

$$= -\frac{t}{a^2}(\cos at - 1) - \frac{1}{a}\left[-\frac{t\cos at}{a} + 0 + \frac{1}{a}.\left.\frac{\sin aT}{a}\right|_0^t\right]$$

$$= \frac{t}{a^2}(1-\cos at) + \frac{t}{a^2}\cos at - \frac{1}{a^3}\sin at - 0$$

$$= \frac{t}{a^2} - \frac{1}{a^3}\sin at = \frac{1}{a^3}\,(\mathbf{at - \sin at}).$$

Example 3. *Find the inverse Laplace transform of the function* $\frac{s}{(s^2+\pi^2)^2}$.

Sol. $$\frac{s}{(s^2+\pi^2)^2} = \left(\frac{s}{s^2+\pi^2}\right)\left(\frac{1}{s^2+\pi^2}\right) = F(s)\,G(s),$$

where $$F(s) = \frac{s}{s^2+\pi^2} \quad \text{and} \quad G(s) = \frac{1}{s^2+\pi^2}.$$

$$L^{-1}(F(s)) = L^{-1}\left(\frac{s}{s^2+\pi^2}\right) = \cos \pi t = f(t), \quad \text{say}$$

and $$L^{-1}(G(s)) = L^{-1}\left(\frac{1}{s^2+\pi^2}\right) = \frac{1}{\pi} L^{-1}\left(\frac{\pi}{s^2+\pi^2}\right) = \frac{1}{\pi}\sin \pi t = g(t), \quad \text{say.}$$

By **convolution theorem,** we have

$$L^{-1}(F(s)\,G(s)) = f * g = \int_0^t f(T)\,g(t-T)\,dT.$$

$$\therefore \quad L^{-1}\left(\frac{s}{(s^2+\pi^2)^2}\right) = \int_0^t \cos \pi T \,.\, \frac{1}{\pi}\sin \pi(t-T)\,dT$$

$$= \frac{1}{2\pi}\int_0^t [2\sin \pi(t-T)\cos \pi T\,dT$$

$$= \frac{1}{2\pi}\int_0^t [\sin \pi t + \sin \pi(t-2T)]\,dT = \frac{1}{2\pi}\left[T\sin \pi t - \frac{\cos \pi(t-2T)}{-2\pi}\right]_0^t$$

$$= \frac{1}{2\pi}\left[t\sin \pi t + \frac{1}{2\pi}\cos \pi t - 0 - \frac{1}{2\pi}\cos \pi t\right] = \frac{1}{2\pi}\, \mathbf{t \sin \pi t.}$$

Example 4. *Find the inverse Laplace transform of the function* $\dfrac{s+3}{(s^2+6s+13)^2}$.

Sol. $$\frac{s+3}{(s^2+6s+13)^2} = \left(\frac{s+3}{s^2+6s+13}\right)\left(\frac{1}{s^2+6s+13}\right) = F(s)\,G(s),$$

where $$F(s) = \frac{s+3}{s^2+6s+13} \quad \text{and} \quad G(s) = \frac{1}{s^2+6s+13}.$$

$$L^{-1}(F(s)) = L^{-1}\left(\frac{s+3}{s^2+6s+13}\right) = L^{-1}\left(\frac{s+3}{(s+3)^2+4}\right) = e^{-3t}L^{-1}\left(\frac{s}{s^2+4}\right)$$

$$= e^{-3t}\cos 2t = f(t), \text{ say}$$

and $$L^{-1}(G(s)) = L^{-1}\left(\frac{1}{s^2+6s+13}\right) = L^{-1}\left(\frac{1}{(s+3)^2+4}\right) = e^{-3t}L^{-1}\left(\frac{1}{s^2+4}\right)$$

$$= e^{-3t}\frac{\sin 2t}{2} = g(t), \text{ say.}$$

By **convolution theorem,** we have

$$L^{-1}(F(s)\,G(s)) = f * g = \int_0^t f(T)\,g(t-T)\,dt.$$

$$\therefore \quad L^{-1}\left(\frac{s+3}{(s^2+6s+13)^2}\right) = \int_0^t e^{-3T}\cos 2T \cdot \frac{1}{2}e^{-3(t-T)}\sin 2(t-T)\,dT.$$

$$= \frac{1}{2}\int_0^t e^{-3t}\cos 2T\sin 2(t-T)\,dT = \frac{e^{-3t}}{4}\int_0^t 2\sin 2(t-T)\cos 2T\,dT$$

$$= \frac{e^{-3t}}{4}\int_0^t (\sin 2t + \sin(2t-4T))\,dT$$

$$= \frac{e^{-3t}}{4}\left[(\sin 2t)\,T - \frac{\cos(2t-4T)}{-4}\right]\Bigg|_0^t$$

$$= \frac{e^{-3t}}{4}\left[t\sin 2t + \frac{1}{4}\cos 2t - 0 - \frac{1}{4}\cos 2t\right] = \frac{1}{4}\,\mathbf{te^{-3t}\sin 2t}.$$

Example 5. *Find the inverse Laplace transform of the function* $\dfrac{s}{(s^2+a^2)^3}$.

(MDU 2004)

Sol.
$$\frac{s}{(s^2+a^2)^3} = \left(\frac{1}{s^2+a^2}\right)\left(\frac{1}{s^2+a^2}\right)\left(\frac{s}{s^2+a^2}\right) = F(s)\,F(s)\,G(s),$$

where $F(s) = \dfrac{1}{s^2+a^2}$ and $G(s) = \dfrac{s}{s^2+a^2}$.

$$L^{-1}(F(s)) = L^{-1}\left(\frac{1}{s^2+a^2}\right) = \frac{1}{a}L^{-1}\left(\frac{a}{s^2+a^2}\right) = \frac{1}{a}\sin at = f(t), \text{ say}$$

and
$$L^{-1}(G(s)) = L^{-1}\left(\frac{s}{s^2+a^2}\right) = \cos at = g(t), \text{ say}.$$

By **convolution theorem,** we have

$$L^{-1}(F(s)\,F(s)) = f * f = \int_0^t f(T)\,f(t-T)\,dT.$$

$$\therefore \quad L^{-1}(F(s)\,F(s)) = \int_0^t \frac{1}{a}\sin aT \cdot \frac{1}{a}\sin a(t-T)\,dT$$

$$= \frac{1}{2a^2}\int_0^t 2\sin aT\sin(at-aT)\,dT$$

$$= \frac{1}{2a^2}\int_0^t [\cos(2aT-at) - \cos at]\,dT$$

$$= \frac{1}{2a^2}\left[\frac{\sin(2aT-at)}{2a} - T(\cos at)\right]\Bigg|_0^t$$

$$= \frac{1}{2a^2}\left[\frac{\sin at}{2a} - t\cos at - \frac{\sin(-at)}{2a} + 0\right]$$

$$= \frac{1}{2a^2}\left[\frac{\sin at}{a} - t\cos at\right] = \frac{1}{2a^3}[\sin at - at\cos at] = h(t), \text{ say}.$$

Again, by **convolution theorem,** we have

$$L^{-1}(F(s)\,F(s)\,.\,G(s)) = h * g = \int_0^t h(T)\,g(t-T)\,dT.$$

$$\therefore \quad L^{-1}\left(\frac{s}{(s^2+a^2)^3}\right) = \int_0^t \frac{1}{2a^3}(\sin a\mathrm{T} - a\mathrm{T}\cos a\mathrm{T})\cos a(t-\mathrm{T})\,d\mathrm{T}$$

$$= \frac{1}{2a^3}\int_0^t (\sin a\mathrm{T}\cos(at - a\mathrm{T}) - a\mathrm{T}\cos a\mathrm{T}\cos(at - a\mathrm{T}))\,d\mathrm{T}$$

$$= \frac{1}{4a^3}\int_0^t (2\sin a\mathrm{T}\cos(at - a\mathrm{T}) - a\mathrm{T}\,.\,2\cos a\mathrm{T}\cos(at - a\mathrm{T}))\,d\mathrm{T}$$

$$= \frac{1}{4a^3}\int_0^t (\sin at + \sin(2a\mathrm{T} - at) - a\mathrm{T}(\cos at + \cos(2a\mathrm{T} - at)))\,d\mathrm{T}$$

$$= \frac{1}{4a^3}\left[\sin at\int_0^t d\mathrm{T} + \int_0^t \sin(2a\mathrm{T} - at)\,d\mathrm{T} - a\cos at\int_0^t \mathrm{T}dt - a\int_0^t \mathrm{T}\cos(2a\mathrm{T} - at)\,d\mathrm{T}\right]$$

$$= \frac{1}{4a^3}\left[(\sin at)\mathrm{T}\Big|_0^t - \frac{\cos(2a\mathrm{T} - at)}{2a}\Big|_0^t - (a\cos at)\frac{\mathrm{T}^2}{2}\Big|_0^t - a\left(\mathrm{T}\,.\frac{\sin(2a\mathrm{T} - at)}{2a}\Big|_0^t - \int_0^t 1.\frac{\sin(2a\mathrm{T} - at)}{2a}\,d\mathrm{T}\right)\right]$$

$$= \frac{1}{4a^3}\left[t\sin at - 0 - \frac{1}{2a}(\cos at - \cos at) - \frac{at^2\cos at}{2} - \frac{1}{2}(t\sin at - 0) + \frac{1}{2}\left(\frac{-\cos(2a\mathrm{T} - at)}{2a}\right)\Big|_0^t\right]$$

$$= \frac{1}{4a^3}\left[t\sin at - \frac{1}{2}at^2\cos at - \frac{1}{2}t\sin at - \frac{1}{4a}(\cos at - \cos at)\right]$$

$$= \frac{1}{4a^3}\left[\frac{1}{2}t\sin at - \frac{1}{2}at^2\cos at\right].$$

$$= \frac{\mathbf{t}}{\mathbf{8a^3}}\,[\mathbf{\sin at - at\cos at}].$$

WORKING RULES FOR SOLVING PROBLEMS

Step I. Write the given function as the product of two functions say $F(s)$ and $G(s)$.

Step II. Find the inverse Laplace transforms of the functions $F(s)$ and $G(s)$ and call these functions as $f(t)$ and $g(t)$ respectively.

Step III. Write the result of convolution theorem as

$$L^{-1}(F(s)\,G(s)) = \int_0^t f(\mathrm{T})\,g(t - T)\,d\mathrm{T}.$$

Step IV. Substitute the values of $f(\mathrm{T})$ and $g(t - \mathrm{T})$ and simplify the integral on the right side.

EXERCISE 4

Find the inverse Laplace transform of the following functions by using convolution theorem :

1. (i) $\frac{1}{(s-2)(s+4)}$ (ii) $\frac{4}{(s-3)(s+7)}$
2. (i) $\frac{1}{s^2(s-1)}$ (ii) $\frac{1}{s(s^2+1)}$
3. (i) $\frac{1}{s^2(s+1)^2}$ (ii) $\frac{1}{s^3(s^2+1)}$
4. (i) $\frac{1}{(s+1)(s^2+1)}$ (ii) $\frac{1}{(s^2+1)^2}$
5. (i) $\frac{1}{s^2(s^2-a^2)}$ (ii) $\frac{a^2}{s(s+a)^2}$
6. (i) $\frac{1}{s(s+1)^3}$ (ii) $\frac{4}{s^3+s^2+s+1}$
7. (i) $\frac{s^2}{(s^2+4)^2}$ (ii) $\frac{s^2}{(s^2-9)^2}$
8. (i) $\frac{1}{s^3-a^3}$ (ii) $\frac{s+2}{(s^2+4s+5)^2}$.

Answers

1. (i) $\frac{1}{6}[e^{2t}-e^{-4t}]$ (ii) $\frac{2}{5}[e^{3t}-e^{-7t}]$
2. (i) e^t-t-1 (ii) $1-\cos t$
3. (i) $(t+2)e^{-t}+t-2$ (ii) $\cos t+\frac{t^2}{2}-1$
4. (i) $\frac{1}{2}[e^{-t}+\sin t-\cos t]$ (ii) $\frac{1}{2}(\sin t-t\cos t)$
5. (i) $\frac{1}{a^3}[\sinh at-at]$ (ii) $1-e^{-at}(1+at)$
6. (i) $-\frac{1}{e^t}\left[\frac{t^2}{2}+t+1\right]+1$ (ii) $2[e^{-t}+\sin t-\cos t]$
7. (i) $\frac{1}{2}\left[t\cos 2t+\frac{1}{2}\sin 2t\right]$ (ii) $\frac{1}{2}\left[t\cosh 3t+\frac{1}{3}\sinh 3t\right]$
8. (i) $\frac{1}{3a^2}\left[e^{at}-e^{-\frac{at}{2}}\left(\cos\frac{\sqrt{3}}{2}at+\sqrt{3}\sin\frac{\sqrt{3}}{2}at\right)\right]$ (ii) $\frac{1}{2}te^{-2t}\sin t$.

13. INVERSE LAPLACE TRANSFORMS BY THE METHOD OF PARTIAL FRACTIONS

Let $\dfrac{a_0s^m + a_1s^{m-1} + \ldots\ldots + a_m}{b_0s^n + b_1s^{n-1} + \ldots\ldots + b_n}$ be a proper rational algebraic function of s with $m < n$. The denominator of this quotient can be factorised into linear and quadratic factors. The given rational function can be expressed as the sum of partial fractions as per the rules given below :

(*i*) If $as + b$ is any linear non-repeated factor in the denominator, then there corresponds a partial fraction of the form $\dfrac{A}{as+b}$.

(*ii*) If $as + b$ is any linear factor repeated r ($\in$ **N**) times in the denominator, then there corresponds partial fractions of the form $\dfrac{A}{as+b}, \dfrac{B}{(as+b)^2}, \dfrac{C}{(as+b)^3}, \ldots\ldots r$ terms.

(*iii*) If $as^2 + bs + c$ is any irreducible quadratic factor in the denominator, then there corresponds partial fraction of the form $\dfrac{As+B}{as^2+bs+c}$.

(*iv*) If $as^2 + bs + c$ is any irreducible factor repeated r ($\in$ **N**) times in the denominator, then there corresponds partial fractions of the form $\dfrac{As+B}{as^2+bs+c}, \dfrac{Cs+D}{(as^2+bs+c)^2}, \ldots\ldots r$ terms.

The quantities A, B, C, D, ... are all constants independent of s.

The constants A, B, C, D, ... occurring in the numerators of the partial fractions are determined by simplifying the sum of partial fractions and then giving various values to s, to obtain equations involving unknown constants or by comparing the coefficients of like powers of s.

∴ The given proper fraction can be expressed as the sum of its partial fractions. Thus, by using linearity of inverse Laplace transform and elementary inverse Laplace transform formulae, the inverse Laplace transform of the given proper fraction is found.

If the given fraction is not proper, then division of numerator by denominator is carried first.

Example 1. *Find the inverse Laplace transform of the following functions :*

(*i*) $\dfrac{s^2+s-2}{s(s+3)(s-2)}$ (*ii*) $\dfrac{s^2-10s+13}{(s-7)(s^2-5s+6)}$.

Sol. (*i*) $\dfrac{s^2+s-2}{s(s+3)(s-2)}$ is a proper fraction.

Let $$\frac{s^2+s-2}{s(s+3)(s-2)} = \frac{A}{s} + \frac{B}{s+3} + \frac{C}{s-2}$$

Multiplying both sides by $s(s + 3)(s - 2)$, we get

$$s^2 + s - 2 = A(s + 3)(s - 2) + Bs(s - 2) + Cs(s + 3) \quad \ldots(1)$$

$s = 0$ in (1) $\Rightarrow$ $-2 = A(3)(-2) + 0 + 0$ $\Rightarrow$ $A = 2/-6 - 1/3$

$s = -3$ in (1) $\Rightarrow$ $9 - 3 - 2 = 0 + B(-3)(-5) + 0$ $\Rightarrow$ $B = 4/15$

$s = 2$ in (1) $\Rightarrow$ $4 + 2 - 2 = 0 + 0 + C(2)(5)$ $\Rightarrow$ $C = 4/10 = 2/5$

$$\therefore \quad \frac{s^2 + s - 2}{s(s+3)(s-2)} = \frac{1/3}{s} + \frac{4/15}{s+3} + \frac{2/5}{s-2} = \frac{1}{3}\left(\frac{1}{s}\right) + \frac{4}{15}\left(\frac{1}{s+3}\right) + \frac{2}{5}\left(\frac{1}{s-2}\right)$$

$$\therefore \quad L^{-1}\left(\frac{s^2 + s - 2}{s(s+3)(s-2)}\right) = \frac{1}{3}L^{-1}\left(\frac{1}{s}\right) + \frac{4}{15}L^{-1}\left(\frac{1}{s+3}\right) + \frac{2}{5}L^{-1}\left(\frac{1}{s-2}\right)$$

$$= \frac{1}{3}(1) + \frac{4}{15}e^{-3t} + \frac{2}{5}e^{2t} = \mathbf{\frac{1}{3} + \frac{4}{15}e^{-3t} + \frac{2}{5}e^{2t}}.$$

Note. Since the factors in the denominator are linear and non-repeated, the short-cut method can also be used.

(*ii*) $\dfrac{s^2 - 10s + 13}{(s-7)(s^2 - 5s + 6)} = \dfrac{s^2 - 10s + 13}{(s-7)(s-2)(s-3)}$ is a proper fraction.

The factors in the denominator are linear and non-repeated.

$\therefore$ By short-cut method,

$$\frac{s^2 - 10s + 13}{(s-7)(s^2 - 5s + 6)} = \frac{7^2 + 10(7) + 13}{(s-7)(5)(4)} + \frac{2^2 - 10(2) + 13}{(-5)(s-2)(-1)} + \frac{3^2 - 10(3) + 13}{(-4)(1)(s-3)}$$

$$= \frac{-8}{20(s-7)} + \frac{-3}{5(s-2)} + \frac{-8}{-4(s-3)}$$

$$= -\frac{2}{5(s-7)} - \frac{3}{5(s-2)} + 2 . \frac{1}{s-3}$$

$$\therefore \quad L^{-1}\left(\frac{s^2 - 10s + 13}{(s-7)(s^2 - 5s + 6)}\right) = L^{-1}\left(-\frac{2}{5(s-7)} - \frac{3}{5(s-2)} + 2 . \frac{1}{s-3}\right)$$

$$= -\frac{2}{5}L^{-1}\left(\frac{1}{s-7}\right) - \frac{3}{5}L^{-1}\left(\frac{1}{s-2}\right) + 2L^{-1}\left(\frac{1}{s-3}\right)$$

$$= \mathbf{-\frac{2}{5}e^{7t} - \frac{3}{5}e^{2t} + 2e^{3t}}.$$

Example 2. *Find the inverse Laplace transform of the function* $\dfrac{s^2}{(s^2 + a^2)(s^2 + b^2)}$ *by using (i) method of partial fractions (ii) convolution theorem.*

Sol. (*i*) $\dfrac{s^2}{(s^2 + a^2)(s^2 + b^2)} = \dfrac{z}{(z + a^2)(z + b^2)}$, where $z = s^2$

$$= \frac{-a^2}{(z + a^2)(-a^2 + b^2)} + \frac{-b^2}{(-b^2 + a^2)(z + b^2)}$$

$$= \frac{a^2}{a^2 - b^2} \cdot \frac{1}{z + a^2} - \frac{b^2}{a^2 - b^2} \cdot \frac{1}{z + b^2}$$

$$= \frac{a}{a^2 - b^2} \cdot \frac{a}{s^2 + a^2} - \frac{b}{a^2 - b^2} \cdot \frac{b}{s^2 + b^2}.$$

$$\therefore \quad L^{-1}\left(\frac{s^2}{(s^2 + a^2)(s^2 + b^2)}\right) = \frac{a}{a^2 - b^2} L^{-1}\left(\frac{a}{s^2 + a^2}\right) - \frac{b}{a^2 - b^2} L^{-1}\left(\frac{b}{s^2 + b^2}\right)$$

$$= \frac{a}{a^2 - b^2} \sin at - \frac{b}{a^2 - b^2} \sin bt$$

$$= \frac{\mathbf{a \sin at - b \sin bt}}{\mathbf{a^2 - b^2}}.$$

(*ii*) $$\frac{s^2}{(s^2 + a^2)(s^2 + b^2)} = \left(\frac{s}{s^2 + a^2}\right)\left(\frac{s}{s^2 + b^2}\right) = F(s)\, G(s),$$

where $F(s) = \frac{s}{s^2 + a^2}$ and $G(s) = \frac{s}{s^2 + b^2}$.

Also $$L^{-1}(F(s)) = L^{-1}\left(\frac{s}{s^2 + a^2}\right) = \cos at = f(t), \text{ say}$$

and $$L^{-1}(G(s)) = L^{-1}\left(\frac{s}{s^2 + b^2}\right) = \cos bt = g(t), \text{ say}$$

By **convolution theorem,** we have

$$L^{-1}(F(s)\, G(s)) = f * g = \int_0^t f(T)\, g(t - T)\, dT.$$

$$\therefore \quad L^{-1}\left(\frac{s^2}{(s^2 + a^2)(s^2 + b^2)}\right) = \int_0^t \cos aT \cos b(t - T)\, dT$$

$$= \frac{1}{2} \int_0^t [\cos(aT + bt - bT) + \cos(aT - bt + bT)]\, dT$$

$$= \frac{1}{2}\left[\frac{\sin((a - b)T + bt)}{a - b} + \frac{\sin((a + b)T - bt)}{a + b}\right]_0^t$$

$$= \frac{1}{2}\left[\frac{\sin at}{a - b} + \frac{\sin at}{a + b} - \frac{\sin bt}{a - b} + \frac{\sin bt}{a + b}\right]$$

$$= \frac{1}{2}\left[\frac{2a}{a^2 - b^2} \sin at - \frac{2b}{a^2 - b^2} \sin bt\right]$$

$$= \frac{\mathbf{a \sin at - b \sin bt}}{\mathbf{a^2 - b^2}}.$$

Example 3. *Find the inverse Laplace transform of the function* $\dfrac{1}{(s-1)^5\,(s+2)}$ *by using (i) method of partial fractions (ii) convolution theorem.*

Sol. (*i*) $\dfrac{1}{(s-1)^5\,(s+2)} = \dfrac{1}{z^5\,(z+3)}$, where $z = s - 1$.

We divide 1 by $z + 3$ as follows :

$$\begin{array}{r|l}
 & \dfrac{1}{3} - \dfrac{z}{9} + \dfrac{z^2}{27} - \dfrac{z^3}{81} + \dfrac{z^4}{243} \\
\hline
3+z & 1 \\
 & 1 + \dfrac{z}{3} \\
\cline{2-2}
 & -\dfrac{z}{3} \\
 & -\dfrac{z}{3} - \dfrac{z^2}{9} \\
\cline{2-2}
 & \dfrac{z^2}{9} \\
 & \dfrac{z^2}{9} + \dfrac{z^3}{27} \\
\cline{2-2}
 & -\dfrac{z^3}{27} \\
 & -\dfrac{z^3}{27} - \dfrac{z^4}{81} \\
\cline{2-2}
 & \dfrac{z^4}{81} \\
 & \dfrac{z^4}{81} + \dfrac{z^5}{243} \\
\cline{2-2}
 & -\dfrac{z^5}{243} \\
\cline{2-2}
\end{array}$$

$$\therefore \quad \frac{1}{3+z} = \frac{1}{3} - \frac{z}{9} + \frac{z^2}{27} - \frac{z^3}{81} + \frac{z^4}{243} - \frac{z^5/243}{3+z}$$

$$\therefore \quad \frac{1}{z^5(z+3)} = \frac{1}{z^5}\left(\frac{1}{3+z}\right) = \frac{1}{3z^5} - \frac{1}{9z^4} + \frac{1}{27z^3} - \frac{1}{81z^2} + \frac{1}{243z} - \frac{1}{243(3+z)}$$

$$\therefore \quad \frac{1}{(s-1)^5\,(s+2)} = \frac{1}{3(s-1)^5} - \frac{1}{9(s-1)^4} + \frac{1}{27(s-1)^3}$$

$$- \frac{1}{81(s-1)^2} + \frac{1}{243(s-1)} - \frac{1}{243(s+2)}$$

$$\therefore \quad L^{-1}\left(\frac{1}{(s-1)^5(s+2)}\right) = \frac{1}{3}L^{-1}\left(\frac{1}{(s-1)^5}\right) - \frac{1}{9}L^{-1}\left(\frac{1}{(s-1)^4}\right)$$

$$+\frac{1}{27}L^{-1}\left(\frac{1}{(s-1)^3}\right) - \frac{1}{81}L^{-1}\left(\frac{1}{(s-1)^2}\right) + \frac{1}{243}L^{-1}\left(\frac{1}{s-1}\right) - \frac{1}{243}L^{-1}\left(\frac{1}{s+2}\right)$$

$$= \frac{1}{3}e^t L^{-1}\left(\frac{1}{s^5}\right) - \frac{1}{9}e^t L^{-1}\left(\frac{1}{s^4}\right) + \frac{1}{27}e^t L^{-1}\left(\frac{1}{s^3}\right)$$

$$-\frac{1}{81}e^t L^{-1}\left(\frac{1}{s^2}\right) + \frac{1}{243}e^t L^{-1}\left(\frac{1}{s}\right) - \frac{1}{243}e^{-2t} L^{-1}\left(\frac{1}{s}\right)$$

$$= \frac{e^t}{3}\cdot\frac{1}{24}L^{-1}\left(\frac{4!}{s^5}\right) - \frac{e^t}{9}\cdot\frac{1}{6}L^{-1}\left(\frac{3!}{s^4}\right) - \frac{e^t}{27}\cdot\frac{1}{2}L^{-1}\left(\frac{2!}{s^3}\right) - \frac{e^t}{81}\cdot t + \frac{e^t}{243}\cdot 1 - \frac{e^{-2t}}{243}\cdot 1$$

$$= \mathbf{\frac{e^t}{72}t^4 - \frac{e^t}{54}t^3 - \frac{e^t}{54}t^2 - \frac{e^t}{81}t + \frac{e^t}{243} - \frac{e^{-2t}}{243}}.$$

(*ii*) $$\frac{1}{(s-1)^5(s+2)} = \left(\frac{1}{(s-1)^5}\right)\left(\frac{1}{s+2}\right) = F(s)\,G(s),$$

where $$F(s) = \frac{1}{(s-1)^5} \quad \text{and} \quad G(s) = \frac{1}{s+2}.$$

Also $$L^{-1}(F(s)) = L^{-1}\left(\frac{1}{(s-1)^5}\right) = e^{1.t}L^{-1}\left(\frac{1}{s^5}\right)$$

$$= e^t\cdot\frac{1}{24}L^{-1}\left(\frac{4!}{s^5}\right) = \frac{e^t}{24}t^4 = f(t), \text{ say}$$

and $$L^{-1}(G(s)) = L^{-1}\left(\frac{1}{s+2}\right) = e^{-2t} = g(t), \text{ say}.$$

By **convolution theorem,** we have

$$L^{-1}(F(s)\,G(s)) = f * g = \int_0^t f(T)\,g(t-T)\,dT.$$

$$\therefore \quad L^{-1}\left(\frac{1}{(s-1)^5(s+2)}\right) = \int_0^t \frac{e^T T^4}{24}\cdot e^{-2(t-T)}\,dT = \frac{e^{-2t}}{24}\int_0^t T^4 e^{3T}\,dT.$$

Now $$\int_0^t T^4 e^{3T}\,dT = \left.\frac{T^4 e^{3T}}{3}\right|_0^t - \int_0^t 4T^3\cdot\frac{e^{3T}}{3}\,dT$$

$$= \frac{t^4 e^{3t}}{3} - \frac{4}{3}\left[\left.\frac{T^3 e^{3T}}{3}\right|_0^t - \int_0^t 3T^2\cdot\frac{e^{3T}}{3}\,dT\right]$$

$$= \frac{t^4e^{3t}}{3} - \frac{4}{9}t^3e^{3t} + \frac{4}{3}\left[\frac{T^2e^{3T}}{3}\Bigg|_0^t - \int_0^t 2T\,.\frac{e^{3T}}{3}\,dT\right]$$

$$= \frac{t^4e^{3t}}{3} - \frac{4}{9}t^3e^{3t} + \frac{4}{9}t^2e^{3t} - \frac{8}{9}\left[\frac{Te^{3T}}{3}\Bigg|_0^t - \int_0^t 1.\frac{e^{3T}}{3}\,dT\right]$$

$$= \frac{t^4e^{3t}}{3} - \frac{4}{9}t^3e^{3t} + \frac{4}{9}t^2e^{3t} - \frac{8}{27}te^{3t} + \frac{8}{81}(e^{3t} - 1)$$

$$\therefore \quad L^{-1}\left(\frac{1}{(s-1)^5(s+2)}\right) = \frac{e^{-2t}}{24}\left[\frac{t^4e^{3t}}{3} - \frac{4}{9}t^3e^{3t} + \frac{4}{9}t^2e^{3t} - \frac{8}{27}te^{3t} + \frac{8}{81}e^{3t} - \frac{8}{81}\right]$$

$$= \frac{\mathbf{t^4e^t}}{\mathbf{72}} - \frac{\mathbf{t^3e^t}}{\mathbf{54}} + \frac{\mathbf{t^2e^t}}{\mathbf{54}} - \frac{\mathbf{te^t}}{\mathbf{81}} + \frac{\mathbf{e^t}}{\mathbf{243}} - \frac{\mathbf{e^{-2t}}}{\mathbf{243}}.$$

Example 4. *Find the inverse Laplace transform of the following functions :*

(*i*) $\dfrac{4s+5}{(s-1)^2\,(s+2)}$ (*ii*) $\dfrac{1+2s}{(s+2)^2\,(s-1)^2}$.

Sol. (*i*) $\dfrac{4s+5}{(s-1)^2\,(s+2)}$ is a proper fraction.

Let $\dfrac{4s+5}{(s-1)^2\,(s+2)} = \dfrac{A}{s-1} + \dfrac{B}{(s-1)^2} + \dfrac{C}{s+2}$

Multiplying both sides by $(s-1)^2\,(s+2)$, we get

$$4s + 5 = A(s-1)(s+2) + B(s+2) + C(s-1)^2. \qquad ...(1)$$

$s = 1$ in (1) $\Rightarrow$ $9 = 0 + 3B + 0$ $\Rightarrow$ $B = 3$

$s = -2$ in (1) $\Rightarrow$ $-3 = 0 + 0 + 9C$ $\Rightarrow$ $C = -1/3$

Let $s = 0$. $\therefore$ $5 = -2A + 2B + C$

$\Rightarrow$ $2A = 2(3) - (1/3) - 5 = 2/3$ $\Rightarrow$ $A = 1/3$.

$$\therefore \quad \frac{4s+5}{(s-1)^2\,(s+2)} = \frac{1/3}{s-1} + \frac{3}{(s-1)^2} + \frac{-1/3}{s+2} = \frac{1}{3}\left(\frac{1}{s-1}\right) + 3\left(\frac{1}{(s-1)^2}\right) - \frac{1}{3}\left(\frac{1}{s+2}\right)$$

$$\therefore \quad L^{-1}\left(\frac{4s+5}{(s-1)^2\,(s+2)}\right) = \frac{1}{3}L^{-1}\left(\frac{1}{s-1}\right) + 3L^{-1}\left(\frac{1}{(s-1)^2}\right) - \frac{1}{3}L^{-1}\left(\frac{1}{s+2}\right)$$

$$= \frac{1}{3}e^{1.t} + 3e^{1.t}\,L^{-1}\left(\frac{1}{s^2}\right) - \frac{1}{3}e^{-2t}$$

$$= \frac{1}{3}e^t + 3e^t\,t^1 - \frac{1}{3}e^{-2t} = \frac{\mathbf{1}}{\mathbf{3}}(\mathbf{(9t+1)\,e^t - e^{-2t}}).$$

(*ii*) $\dfrac{1+2s}{(s+2)^2\,(s-1)^2}$ is a proper fraction.

Let $\dfrac{1+2s}{(s+2)^2\,(s-1)^2} = \dfrac{A}{s+2} + \dfrac{B}{(s+2)^2} + \dfrac{C}{s-1} + \dfrac{D}{(s-1)^2}$

Multiplying both sides by $(s + 2)^2 (s - 1)^2$, we get

$$1 + 2s = A(s + 2)(s - 1)^2 + B(s - 1)^2 + C(s + 2)^2 (s - 1) + D(s + 2)^2. \quad ...(1)$$

$$s = 1 \text{ in } (1) \quad \Rightarrow \quad 3 = 0 + 0 + 0 + 9D \quad \Rightarrow \quad D = 1/3$$

$$s = -2 \text{ in } (1) \quad \Rightarrow \quad -3 = 0 + 9B + 0 + 0 \quad \Rightarrow \quad B = -1/3$$

Comparing coefficients of s^3 and s^2 in (1), we get

$$0 = A + C \quad ...(2) \qquad \text{and} \qquad 0 = B + 3C + D \quad ...(3)$$

$$(3) \quad \Rightarrow \quad 3C = -B - D = \frac{1}{3} - \frac{1}{3} = 0 \quad \Rightarrow \quad C = 0$$

$\therefore$ (2) $\Rightarrow$ $A = -C = 0$.

$$\therefore \quad \frac{1+2s}{(s+2)^2\,(s-1)^2} = \frac{0}{s+2} + \frac{-1/3}{(s+2)^2} + \frac{0}{s-1} + \frac{1/3}{(s-1)^2} = -\frac{1}{3}\left(\frac{1}{(s+2)^2}\right) + \frac{1}{3}\left(\frac{1}{(s-1)^2}\right)$$

$$\therefore \quad L^{-1}\left(\frac{1+2s}{(s+2)^2\,(s-1)^2}\right) = -\frac{1}{3}L^{-1}\left(\frac{1}{(s+2)^2}\right) + \frac{1}{3}L^{-1}\left(\frac{1}{(s-1)^2}\right)$$

$$= -\frac{1}{3}e^{-2t}\,L^{-1}\left(\frac{1}{s^2}\right) + \frac{1}{3}e^{1t}\,L^{-1}\left(\frac{1}{s^2}\right)$$

$$= -\frac{1}{3}e^{-2t}\,.\,t + \frac{1}{3}e^{t}\,.\,t = \frac{\mathbf{t}}{\mathbf{3}}\,(\mathbf{e}^{\mathbf{t}} - \mathbf{e}^{-2\mathbf{t}}).$$

Example 5. *Find the inverse Laplace transform of the following functions :*

(*i*) $\dfrac{3s+1}{(s+1)\,(s^2+1)}$ (*ii*) $\dfrac{2s^3+2s^2+4s+1}{(s^2+1)\,(s^2+s+1)}$.

Sol. (*i*) $\dfrac{3s+1}{(s+1)(s^2+1)}$ is a proper fraction.

Let $\dfrac{3s+1}{(s+1)(s^2+1)} = \dfrac{A}{s+1} + \dfrac{Bs+C}{s^2+1}$.

Multiplying both sides by $(s + 1)(s^2 + 1)$, we get

$$3s + 1 = A(s^2 + 1) + (Bs + C)(s + 1). \quad ...(1)$$

$s = -1$ in (1) $\Rightarrow$ $-2 = 2A + 0$ $\Rightarrow$ $A = -1$

Comparing coefficients of s^2 and s in (1), we get

$$0 = A + B \quad ...(2) \qquad \text{and} \qquad 3 = B + C \quad ...(3)$$

(2) $\Rightarrow$ $B = -A = -(-1) = 1$

(3) $\Rightarrow$ $C = 3 - B = 3 - 1 = 2$.

$$\therefore \quad \frac{3s+1}{(s+1)(s^2+1)} = \frac{-1}{s+1} + \frac{1\,s+2}{s^2+1} = -\frac{1}{s+1} + \frac{s}{s^2+1} + \frac{2}{s^2+1}$$

$$\therefore \quad L^{-1}\left(\frac{3s+1}{(s+1)(s^2+1)}\right) = -L^{-1}\left(\frac{1}{s+1}\right) + L^{-1}\left(\frac{s}{s^2+1}\right) + 2L^{-1}\left(\frac{1}{s^2+1}\right)$$

$$= -\mathbf{e^{t} + \cos t + 2 \sin t.}$$

(*ii*) Let $\quad F(s) = \dfrac{2s^3+2s^2+4s+1}{(s^2+1)(s^2+s+1)}$.

$\therefore$ F(*s*) is a proper fraction.

Let $\quad \dfrac{2s^3+2s^2+4s+1}{(s^2+1)(s^2+s+1)} = \dfrac{As+B}{s^2+1} + \dfrac{Cs+D}{s^2+s+1}$.

Multiplying both sides by $(s^2+1)(s^2+s+1)$, we get

$$2s^3 + 2s^2 + 4s + 1 = (As + B)(s^2 + s + 1) + (Cs + D)(s^2 + 1).$$

Comparing coefficients of s^3, s^2, s and constant terms, we get

$$2 = A + C \quad \text{...(1)}$$

$$2 = A + B + D \quad \text{...(2)}$$

$$4 = A + B + C \quad \text{...(3)}$$

$$1 = B + D \quad \text{...(4)}$$

(2) – (4) $\Rightarrow$ A = 1

(1) $\Rightarrow$ C = 2 – A = 2 – 1 = 1

(3) $\Rightarrow$ B = 4 – A – C = 4 – 1 – 1 = 2

(4) $\Rightarrow$ D = 1 – B = 1 – 2 = – 1.

$$\therefore \quad F(s) = \frac{1.s+2}{s^2+1} + \frac{1.s-1}{s^2+s+1} = \frac{s}{s^2+1} + 2\left(\frac{1}{s^2+1}\right) + \frac{s-1}{s^2+s+1}$$

$$\therefore \quad L^{-1}(F(s)) = L^{-1}\left(\frac{s}{s^2+1}\right) + 2L^{-1}\left(\frac{1}{s^2+1}\right) + L^{-1}\left(\frac{s-1}{s^2+s+1}\right)$$

$$= \cos t + 2 \sin t + L^{-1}\left(\frac{\left(s+\frac{1}{2}\right) - \frac{3}{2}}{\left(s+\frac{1}{2}\right)^2 + \frac{3}{4}}\right)$$

$$= \cos t + 2 \sin t + e^{-\frac{1}{2}t} L^{-1}\left(\frac{s - \frac{3}{2}}{s^2 + \frac{3}{4}}\right)$$

$$= \cos t + 2 \sin t + e^{-\frac{1}{2}t} L^{-1}\left(\frac{s}{s^2+\frac{3}{4}} - \sqrt{3}\,\frac{\sqrt{3}/2}{s^2+\frac{3}{4}}\right)$$

$$= \mathbf{\cos t + 2 \sin t + e^{-\frac{1}{2}t}\left(\cos \frac{\sqrt{3}}{2} t - \sqrt{3} \sin \frac{\sqrt{3}}{2} t\right).}$$

Example 6. *Find the inverse Laplace transform of the function* $\frac{s}{s^4 + 4a^4}$.

Sol. $$\frac{s}{s^4 + 4a^4} = \frac{s}{(s^2 + 2a^2)^2 - 4a^2s^2} = \frac{s}{(s^2 + 2as + 2a^2)(s^2 - 2as + 2a^2)}$$

$\therefore$ Let $$\frac{s}{s^4 + 4a^4} = \frac{As + B}{s^2 + 2as + 2a^2} + \frac{Cs + D}{s^2 - 2as + 2a^2}.$$

Multiplying both sides by $s^4 + 4a^4$, we get

$$s = (As + B)(s^2 - 2as + 2a^2) + (Cs + D)(s^2 + 2as + 2a^2).$$

Comparing coefficients of s^3, s^2, s and constant terms, we get

$$0 = A + C \quad ...(1)$$

$$0 = -2aA + B + 2aC + D \quad ...(2)$$

$$1 = 2a^2A - 2aB + 2a^2C + 2aD \quad ...(3)$$

$$0 = 2a^2B + 2a^2D \quad ...(4)$$

$$(4) \Rightarrow B + D = 0 \quad ...(5)$$

$$(2) - (5) \Rightarrow -2a(A - C) = 0 \Rightarrow A = C \quad ...(6)$$

$$\therefore (1) \text{ and } (6) \Rightarrow A = 0, C = 0$$

$$(3) \Rightarrow 1 = -2a(B - D) \Rightarrow B - D = -1/2a \quad ...(7)$$

Solving (5) and (7), we get $B = -1/4a$, $D = 1/4a$.

$$\therefore \frac{s}{s^4 + 4a^4} = \frac{0.s - 1/4a}{s^2 + 2as + 2a^2} + \frac{0.s + 1/4a}{s^2 - 2as + 2a^2}$$

$$= -\frac{1}{4a}\left(\frac{1}{s^2 + 2as + a^2}\right) + \frac{1}{4a}\left(\frac{1}{s^2 - 2as + 2a^2}\right)$$

$$= -\frac{1}{4a}\left(\frac{1}{(s + a)^2 + a^2}\right) + \frac{1}{4a}\left(\frac{1}{(s - a)^2 + a^2}\right)$$

$$\therefore L^{-1}\left(\frac{s}{s^4 + 4a^4}\right) = -\frac{1}{4a}L^{-1}\left(\frac{1}{(s + a)^2 + a^2}\right) + \frac{1}{4a}L^{-1}\left(\frac{1}{(s - a)^2 + a^2}\right)$$

$$= -\frac{1}{4a}e^{-at}L^{-1}\left(\frac{1}{s^2 + a^2}\right) + \frac{1}{4a}e^{at}L^{-1}\left(\frac{1}{s^2 + a^2}\right)$$

$$= \frac{1}{4a}(e^{at} - e^{-at}).\frac{1}{a}L^{-1}\left(\frac{a}{s^2 + a^2}\right) = \frac{1}{2a^2}\left(\frac{e^{at} - e^{-at}}{2}\right).\sin at$$

$$= \mathbf{\frac{1}{2a^2} \sinh at \sin at.}$$

EXERCISE 5

Find the inverse Laplace transform of the following functions by the method of partial fractions (Q No 1–12) :

1. (*i*) $\dfrac{1}{(s-1)(s-2)}$ (*ii*) $\dfrac{1}{(s+a)(s+b)}$

2. (*i*) $\dfrac{3s+7}{s^2-2s-3}$ (*ii*) $\dfrac{3s-11}{s^2-7s+12}$

3. (*i*) $\dfrac{2s^2+5s-4}{s^3+s^2-2s}$ (*ii*) $\dfrac{s^2-6}{s^3+4s^2+3s}$

4. (*i*) $\dfrac{1}{s^2(s^2+1)}$ (*ii*) $\dfrac{1}{s^2(s^2+1)(s^2+9)}$

5. (*i*) $\dfrac{s^2-2s+3}{(s-1)^2(s+1)}$ (*ii*) $\dfrac{1}{(s+2)^2(s-2)}$

6. (*i*) $\dfrac{5s-2}{s^2(s+2)(s-1)}$ (*ii*) $\dfrac{1}{s^2(s-a)^2}$

7. (*i*) $\dfrac{5s^2-15s-11}{(s+1)(s-2)^3}$ (*ii*) $\dfrac{3s^3-3s^2-40s+36}{(s^2-4)^2}$

8. (*i*) $\dfrac{1}{(s+1)(s^2+1)}$ (*ii*) $\dfrac{5s+3}{(s-1)(s^2+2s+5)}$

9. (*i*) $\dfrac{3s+1}{(s-1)(s^2+1)}$ (*ii*) $\dfrac{1}{s^3(s^2+1)}$

10. (*i*) $\dfrac{s}{s^4+s^2+1}$ (*CDLU 2004*) (*ii*) $\dfrac{1}{s^3-a^3}$

11. (*i*) $\dfrac{s^2+s}{(s^2+1)(s^2+2s+2)}$ (*KU 2005*) (*ii*) $\dfrac{s^3}{s^4-a^4}$

12. (*i*) $\dfrac{s}{(s+1)^2(s^2+1)}$ (*ii*) $\dfrac{a(s^2-2a^2)}{s^4+4a^4}$.

Answers

1. (*i*) $e^{2t}-e^{t}$ (*ii*) $\dfrac{e^{-at}-e^{-bt}}{b-a}$

2. (*i*) $4e^{3t}-e^{-t}$ (*ii*) $e^{4t}+2e^{3t}$

3. (*i*) $2+e^{t}-e^{-2t}$ (*ii*) $-2+\dfrac{5}{2}e^{-t}+\dfrac{1}{2}e^{-3t}$

4. (*i*) $t-\sin t$ (*ii*) $\dfrac{1}{9}t-\dfrac{1}{8}\sin t+\dfrac{1}{216}\sin 3t$

5. (*i*) $\left(t-\dfrac{1}{2}\right)e^{t}+\dfrac{3}{2}e^{-t}$ (*ii*) $\dfrac{1}{16}(e^{2t}-(4t+1)e^{-2t})$

6. (*i*) $t + e^t + e^{-2t} - 2$ (*ii*) $\frac{1}{a^3}[(2 + at) - (2 - at)e^{at}]$

7. (*i*) $e^{2t}\left[\frac{1}{3} + 4t - \frac{7}{2}t^2\right] - \frac{1}{3}e^{-t}$ (*ii*) $-10t \sinh 2t + 3e^{-2t} + 3te^{2t}$

8. (*i*) $\frac{1}{2}[e^{-t} - \cos t + \sin t]$ (*ii*) $e^t - e^{-t}\left(\cos 2t - \frac{3}{2}\sin 2t\right)$

9. (*i*) $2e^t - 2\cos t + \sin t$ (*ii*) $\frac{1}{2}t^2 + \cos t - 1$

10. (*i*) $\frac{2}{\sqrt{3}} \sin \frac{t\sqrt{3}}{2} \sinh \frac{t}{2}$

(*ii*) $\frac{1}{3a^2}\left[e^{at} - e^{-at/2}\left(\cos\left(\frac{\sqrt{3}}{2}at\right) + \sqrt{3}\sin\left(\frac{\sqrt{3}}{2}at\right)\right)\right]$

11. (*i*) $\frac{1}{5}(1 + e^{-t})\sin t + \frac{3}{5}(1 - e^{-t})\cos t$ (*ii*) $\frac{1}{2}[\cos at + \cosh at]$

12. (*i*) $\frac{1}{2}[\sin t - te^{-t}]$ (*ii*) $\cos at \sinh at$.

Hints

4. (*i*) $\frac{1}{s^2(s^2+1)} = \frac{1}{z(z+1)}$, where $z = s^2$

$$= \frac{1}{z(1)} + \frac{1}{(-1)(z+1)} = \frac{1}{z} - \frac{1}{z+1} = \frac{1}{s^2} - \frac{1}{s^2+1}.$$

10. (*i*) $s^4 + s^2 + 1 = (s^4 + 2s^2 + 1) - s^2$.

14. SOLUTION OF DIFFERENTIAL EQUATIONS BY USING LAPLACE TRANSFORMATION

We know that a differential equation with initial conditions is solved by first finding the general solution of the given equation and then finding the values of the arbitrary constants by using the given initial conditions. By using Laplace transformations, we find the required solution without first finding the general solution of the given equation.

Example 1. *Solve the following equations :*

(*i*) $\frac{d^2y}{dt^2} + y = 6\cos 2t$, *where* $y'(0) = 1$, $y(0) = 3$. (KU 2005)

(*ii*) $\frac{d^2y}{dt^2} + 2\frac{dy}{dt} - 3y = \sin t$, *where* $y = \frac{dy}{dt} = 0$, *when* $t = 0$. (MDU 2005)

(*iii*) $(D^2 + m^2)y = a\cos nt$, *where* $y = 0 = \frac{dy}{dt}$ *when* $t = 0$.

(*iv*) $\frac{d^3y}{dt^3} + 2\frac{d^2y}{dt^2} - \frac{dy}{dt} - 2y = 0$, *where* $y = 1$, $\frac{dy}{dt} = 2$, $\frac{d^2y}{dt^2} = 2$ at $t = 0$.

Sol. (*i*) We have

$$\frac{d^2y}{dt^2} + y = 6 \cos 2t.$$

$$\Rightarrow \qquad y'' + y = 6 \cos 2t$$

Taking Laplace Transform, we have

$$L(y'') + L(y) = 6L(\cos 2t)$$

$$\Rightarrow \qquad [s^2L(y) - s \,.\, y(0) - y'(0)] + L(y) = 6 \frac{s}{s^2 + (2)^2}$$

$$\Rightarrow \qquad s^2 \bar{y} - s \,.\, 3 - 1 + \bar{y} = \frac{6s}{s^2 + 4} \qquad \text{(Putting } \bar{y} = L(y))$$

$$\Rightarrow \qquad (s^2 + 1)\, \bar{y} = \frac{6s}{s^2 + 4} + 3s + 1$$

$$\Rightarrow \qquad \bar{y} = \frac{6s}{(s^2 + 1)(s^2 + 4)} + \frac{3s}{s^2 + 1} + \frac{1}{s^2 + 1}$$

Taking inverse Laplace transform, we have

$$y = 6L^{-1}\left(\frac{s}{(s^2 + 1)(s^2 + 4)}\right) + 3L^{-1}\left(\frac{s}{s^2 + 1}\right) + L^{-1}\left(\frac{1}{s^2 + 1}\right) \qquad ...(1)$$

$$\frac{s}{(s^2 + 1)(s^2 + 4)} = \frac{s}{s^2 + 1} \cdot \frac{1}{s^2 + 4} = F(s)\, G(s),$$

where $\quad F(s) = \dfrac{s}{s^2 + 1} \quad$ and $\quad G(s) = \dfrac{1}{s^2 + 4}.$

$$L^{-1}(F(s)) = L^{-1}\left(\frac{s}{s^2 + 1}\right) = \cos t = f(t), \text{ say}$$

and $\quad L^{-1}(G(s)) = L^{-1}\left(\dfrac{1}{s^2 + 4}\right) = \dfrac{1}{2} \sin 2t = g(t)$, say

By **convolution theorem,**

$$L^{-1}(F(s)\, G(s)) = f * g = \int_0^t f(T)\, g(t - T)\, dT$$

$$= \int_0^t (\cos T)\left(\frac{1}{2} \sin 2(t - T)\right) dT = \frac{1}{4}\int_0^t 2 \sin (2t - 2T) \cos T \, dT$$

$$= \frac{1}{4}\int_0^t (\sin (2t - T) + \sin (2t - 3T))\, dT$$

$$= \frac{1}{4}\left[-\frac{\cos (2t - T)}{-1} - \frac{\cos (2t - 3T)}{-3}\right]_0^t$$

$$= \frac{1}{4}\left[\cos t - \cos 2t + \frac{\cos t}{3} - \frac{\cos 2t}{3}\right]$$

$$= \frac{1}{4}\left[\frac{4}{3} \cos t - \frac{4}{3} \cos 2t\right] = \frac{1}{3} [\cos t - \cos 2t]$$

Also, $L^{-1}\left(\frac{s}{s^2+1}\right) = \cos t$ and $L^{-1}\left(\frac{1}{s^2+1}\right) = \sin t$

$\therefore$ (1) $\Rightarrow$ $y = 6 \cdot \frac{1}{3}(\cos t - \cos 2t) + 3\cos t + \sin t$

or $y = \mathbf{5\cos t + \sin t - 2\cos 2t.}$

(*ii*) We have

$$\frac{d^2y}{dt^2} + 2\frac{dy}{dt} - 3y = \sin t.$$

$\Rightarrow$ $y'' + 2y' - 3y = \sin t$

Taking Laplace transform, we have

$$L(y'') + 2L(y') - 3L(y) = L(\sin t)$$

$\Rightarrow$ $[s^2L(y) - s \cdot y(0) - y'(0)] + 2[sL(y) - y(0)] - 3L(y) = \frac{1}{s^2+1}$

$\Rightarrow$ $s^2\bar{y} - s.0 - 0 + 2[s\bar{y} - 0] - 3\bar{y} = \frac{1}{s^2+1}$

$\Rightarrow$ $(s^2 + 2s - 3)\bar{y} = \frac{1}{s^2+1}$

$\Rightarrow$ $\bar{y} = \frac{1}{(s^2+1)(s^2+2s-3)} = \frac{1}{(s^2+1)(s+3)(s-1)}$

Taking inverse Laplace transform, we have

$$y = L^{-1}\left(\frac{1}{(s^2+1)(s+3)(s-1)}\right)$$

Let $\frac{1}{(s^2+1)(s+3)(s-1)} = \frac{As+B}{s^2+1} + \frac{C}{s+3} + \frac{D}{s-1}$

Multiplying by $(s^2 + 1)(s + 3)(s - 1)$, we get

$$1 = (As + B)(s + 3)(s - 1) + C(s^2 + 1)(s - 1) + D(s^2 + 1)(s + 3) \quad \text{...(1)}$$

$s = -3$ $\Rightarrow$ $1 = 0 + c(10)(-4) + 0$ $\Rightarrow$ $C = -\frac{1}{40}$

$s = 1$ $\Rightarrow$ $1 = 0 + 0 + D(2)(4)$ $\Rightarrow$ $D = \frac{1}{8}$

Comparing the coefficients of s^3 and constant terms in (1), we get

$$0 = A + C + D \quad \text{...(2)}$$

$$1 = -3B - C + 3D \quad \text{...(3)}$$

(2) $\Rightarrow$ $A = -C - D = \frac{1}{40} - \frac{1}{8} = -\frac{1}{10}$

(3) $\Rightarrow$ $3B = -1 - C + 3D = -1 + \frac{1}{40} + \frac{3}{8} = -\frac{3}{5}$ $\therefore$ $B = -\frac{1}{5}$

$$\frac{1}{(s^2+1)(s+3)(s-1)} = \frac{-\frac{1}{10}s - \frac{1}{5}}{s^2+1} + \frac{-\frac{1}{40}}{s+3} + \frac{\frac{1}{8}}{s-1}$$

$$= -\frac{1}{10}\cdot\frac{s}{s^2+1} - \frac{1}{5}\cdot\frac{1}{s^2+1} - \frac{1}{40}\cdot\frac{1}{s+3} + \frac{1}{8}\cdot\frac{1}{s-1}$$

$$\therefore \qquad y = -\frac{1}{10}L^{-1}\left(\frac{s}{s^2+1}\right) - \frac{1}{5}L^{-1}\left(\frac{1}{s^2+1}\right) - \frac{1}{40}L^{-1}\left(\frac{1}{s+3}\right) + \frac{1}{8}L^{-1}\left(\frac{1}{s-1}\right)$$

$$= -\frac{1}{10}\cos t - \frac{1}{5}\sin t - \frac{1}{40}e^{-3t} + \frac{1}{8}e^{t}.$$

(*iii*) We have $(D^2 + m^2)\, y = a \cos nt$.

$$\Rightarrow \qquad y'' + m^2 y = a \cos nt$$

Taking Laplace transform, we have

$$L(y'') + m^2 L(y) = a\, L(\cos nt)$$

$$\Rightarrow \qquad [s^2 L(y) - s\,.\,y(0) - y'(0)] + m^2 L(y) = a\,.\,\frac{s}{s^2+n^2}$$

$$\Rightarrow \qquad s^2\bar{y} - s.0 - 0 + m^2\bar{y} = \frac{as}{s^2+n^2}$$

$$\Rightarrow \qquad (s^2+m^2)\,\bar{y} = \frac{as}{s^2+n^2}$$

$$\Rightarrow \qquad \bar{y} = \frac{as}{(s^2+m^2)(s^2+n^2)}$$

$$\therefore \qquad y = aL^{-1}\left(\frac{s}{(s^2+m^2)(s^2+n^2)}\right) \qquad \ldots(1)$$

$$\frac{s}{(s^2+m^2)(s^2+n^2)} = \frac{s}{s^2+m^2}\cdot\frac{1}{s^2+n^2} = F(s)\,G(s), \quad \text{where } F(s) = \frac{s}{s^2+m^2}$$

and $$G(s) = \frac{1}{s^2+n^2}.$$

$$L^{-1}(F(s)) = L^{-1}\left(\frac{s}{s^2+m^2}\right) = \cos mt = f(t), \text{ say}$$

and $$L^{-1}(G(s)) = L^{-1}\left(\frac{1}{s^2+n^2}\right) = \frac{1}{n}\sin nt = g(t), \text{ say}$$

By convolution theorem,

$$L^{-1}(F(s)\,G(s)) = f * g = \int_0^t f(T)\, g(t-T)\, dT$$

$$= \int_0^t \cos mT\,.\,\frac{1}{n}\sin n(t-T)\, dT$$

$$= \frac{1}{2n}\int_0^t 2\sin(nt-nT)\cos mT\, dT$$

$$= \frac{1}{2n}\int_0^t [\sin(nt+(m-n)T) + \sin(nt-(m+n)T)]\, dT$$

$$= \frac{1}{2n}\left[-\frac{\cos(nt+(m-n)T)}{m-n} - \frac{\cos(nt-(m+n)T)}{-(m+n)}\right]_0^t$$

$$= \frac{1}{2n}\left[-\frac{\cos mt}{m-n} + \frac{\cos nt}{m-n} + \frac{\cos mt}{m+n} - \frac{\cos nt}{m+n}\right]$$

$$= \frac{1}{2n}\left[\left(\frac{1}{m+n} - \frac{1}{m-n}\right)\cos mt + \left(\frac{1}{m-n} - \frac{1}{m+n}\right)\cos nt\right]$$

$$= \frac{1}{2n}\left[-\frac{2n\cos mt}{m^2-n^2} + \frac{2n\cos nt}{m^2-n^2}\right] = \frac{1}{m^2-n^2}(\cos nt - \cos mt)$$

$\therefore$ (1) $\Rightarrow$ $\quad y = \dfrac{\mathbf{a}}{\mathbf{m^2 - n^2}}\,\mathbf{(\cos nt - \cos mt).}$

(*iv*) We have

$$\frac{d^3y}{dt^3} + 2\frac{d^2y}{dt^2} - \frac{dy}{dt} - 2y = 0.$$

$\Rightarrow$ $\quad y''' + 2y'' - y' - 2y = 0$

Taking Laplace transform, we have

$$L(y''') + 2L(y'') - L(y') - 2L(y) = 0$$

$\Rightarrow$ $\quad [s^3L(y) - s^2 . y(0) - s . y'(0) - y''(0)] + 2[s^2L(y) - s . y(0) - y'(0)]$
$\qquad - [sL(y) - y(0)] - 2L(y) = 0$

$\Rightarrow$ $\quad (s^3\bar{y} - s^2.1 - s.2 - 2) + 2(s^2\bar{y} - s.1 - 2) - (s\bar{y} - 1) - 2\bar{y} = 0$

$\Rightarrow$ $\quad s^3\bar{y} - s^2 - 2s - 2 + 2s^2\bar{y} - 2s - 4 - s\bar{y} + 1 - 2\bar{y} = 0$

$\Rightarrow$ $\quad (s^3 + 2s^2 - s - 2)\,\bar{y} = s^2 + 4s + 5$

$$\bar{y} = \frac{s^2+4s+5}{s^3+2s^2-s-2} = \frac{s^2+4s+5}{s^2(s+2)-(s+2)}$$

$\therefore$
$$\bar{y} = \frac{s^2+4s+5}{(s-1)(s+1)(s+2)}$$

$$= \frac{1+4+5}{(s-1)(2)(3)} + \frac{1-4+5}{(-2)(s+1)(1)} + \frac{4-8+5}{(-3)(-1)(s+2)}$$

$$= \frac{5}{3}\cdot\frac{1}{s-1} - \frac{1}{s+1} + \frac{1}{4}\cdot\frac{1}{s+2}$$

$\therefore$
$$y = \frac{5}{3}L^{-1}\left(\frac{1}{s-1}\right) - L^{-1}\left(\frac{1}{s+1}\right) + \frac{1}{3}L^{-1}\left(\frac{1}{s+2}\right)$$

$$= \mathbf{\frac{5}{3}e^{t} - e^{-t} + \frac{1}{3}e^{-2t}.}$$

EXERCISE 6

Solve the following differential equations :

1. $\dfrac{d^2y}{dt^2} + y = t$, where $y(0) = 1,\ y'(0) = -2$.

2. $\dfrac{d^2y}{dt^2} + 4\dfrac{dy}{dt} + 3y = e^{-t}$, where $y(0) = y'(0) = 1$.

3. $\dfrac{d^2x}{dt^2} + \dfrac{dx}{dt} = 2$, where $x(0) = 3$, $x'(0) = 1$.

4. $y'' - 3y' + 2y = 4t + e^{3t}$, where $y(0) = 1$, $y'(0) = -1$.

5. $\dfrac{d^3y}{dt^3} - 3\dfrac{d^2y}{dt^2} + 3\dfrac{dy}{dt} - y = t^2e^t$, where $y(0) = 1$, $y'(0) = 0$, $y''(0) = -2$.

6. $(D^4 + 2D^2 + 1)\, y = 0$, where $y(0) = 0$, $y'(0) = 1$, $y''(0) = 2$, $y'''(0) = -3$.

Answers

1. $y = t - 3 \sin t + \cos t$

2. $y = -\dfrac{3}{4}e^{-3t} + \dfrac{7}{4}e^{-t} + \dfrac{1}{2}te^{-t}$

3. $y = 2t + e^{-t} + 2$

4. $y = 2t + 3 + \dfrac{1}{2}e^{3t} - \dfrac{1}{2}e^{t} - 2e^{2t}$

5. $y = e^t \left[\dfrac{t^5}{60} - \dfrac{t^2}{2} - t + 1\right]$

6. $y = t(\sin t + \cos t)$.

8

Solution of Integral Equations Using Laplace Transformation

1. INTRODUCTION

Integral equations occur very frequently in the fields of mechanics and mathematical physics. The development of the theory of integral equations began with the works of Italian mathematician **V. Volterra** (1896) and the Swedish mathematician **I. Fredholm** (1900).

2. DEFINITION OF INTEGRAL EQUATION

An equation involving an unknown function under the integral and perhaps also outside it is called an **integral equation.**

For example the equation $y(t) = f(t) + \int_a^b y(u)\,k(t, u)\,du$, where $f(t)$, $k(t, u)$ are known functions and the function $y(t)$ is to be determined, is an integral equation.

If the integral involved in an integral equation is of the form $\int_0^t y(u)\,k(t-u)\,du$, then the integral equation is said to be an **integral equation of convolution type.**

3. METHOD OF SOLVING INTEGRAL EQUATION OF CONVOLUTION TYPE

Let
$$y(t) = f(t) + \int_0^t y(u)\,k(t-u)\,du \qquad \ldots(1)$$
be an integral equation of convolution type.

The integral on the right side is the convolution of the functions $y(t)$ and $k(t)$.

$\therefore$ (1) can be written as $y(t) = f(t) + (y(t) * k(t))$

Taking the Laplace transform on both sides, we get

$$\mathrm{L}(y(t)) = \mathrm{L}(f(t)) + \mathrm{L}(y(t) * k(t)).$$

$$\Rightarrow \quad \mathrm{L}(y(t)) = \mathrm{L}(f(t)) + \mathrm{L}(y(t)).\mathrm{L}(k(t)) \qquad \text{(By convolution theorem)}$$

$\Rightarrow$ $\mathrm{Y}(s) = \mathrm{F}(s) + \mathrm{Y}(s)\,\mathrm{K}(s)$, where $\mathrm{L}(y(t)) = \mathrm{Y}(s)$, $\mathrm{L}(f(t)) = \mathrm{F}(s)$ and $\mathrm{L}(k(t)) = \mathrm{K}(s)$.

$$\Rightarrow \quad (1 - \mathrm{K}(s))\,\mathrm{Y}(s) = \mathrm{F}(s) \quad \Rightarrow \quad \mathrm{Y}(s) = \frac{\mathrm{F}(s)}{1 - \mathrm{K}(s)}$$

$$\Rightarrow \quad \mathrm{L}^{-1}(\mathrm{Y}(s)) = \mathrm{L}^{-1}\left(\frac{\mathrm{F}(s)}{1 - \mathrm{K}(s)}\right) \quad \therefore \quad \mathbf{y(t) = L^{-1}\left(\frac{L(f(t))}{1 - L(k(t))}\right)}.$$

This gives the solution of the given integral equation.

Example 1. *Solve the following integral equation by using Laplace transforms :*

$$y(t) = 1 + \int_0^t y(u) \sin(t-u)\, du.$$

Sol. We have $\quad y(t) = 1 + \int_0^t y(u) \sin(t-u)\, du.$

$\Rightarrow \quad y(t) = 1 + (y(t) * \sin t)$

Taking the Laplace transform, we get

$$L(y(t)) = L(1) + L(y(t) * \sin t)$$

$\Rightarrow \quad L(y(t)) = \frac{1}{s} + L(y(t))\,.\,L(\sin t)$ (By convolution theorem)

$\Rightarrow \quad Y(s) = \frac{1}{s} + Y(s)\,.\,\frac{1}{s^2+1}$, where $Y(s) = L(y(t))$

$\Rightarrow \quad \left(1 - \frac{1}{s^2+1}\right) Y(s) = \frac{1}{s} \quad \Rightarrow \quad Y(s) = \frac{s^2+1}{s^3} = \frac{1}{s} + \frac{1}{s^3}$

$\therefore \quad y(t) = L^{-1}(Y(s)) = L^{-1}\left(\frac{1}{s}\right) + L^{-1}\left(\frac{1}{s^3}\right) = 1 + \frac{1}{2} L^{-1}\left(\frac{2!}{s^{2+1}}\right) = 1 + \frac{1}{2} t^2.$

Example 2. *Solve the following integral equation by using Laplace transforms :*

$$y(t) = te^t - 2e^t \int_0^t y(u)\, e^{-u}\, du.$$

Sol. We have $\quad y(t) = te^t - 2e^t \int_0^t y(u)\, e^{-u}\, du.$

$\Rightarrow \quad y(t) = te^t - 2\int_0^t y(u)\, e^{t-u}\, du$

$\Rightarrow \quad y(t) = te^t - 2\,(y(t) * e^t)$

Taking the Laplace transform, we get

$$L(y(t)) = L(te^t) - 2L(y(t) * e^t).$$

$\Rightarrow \quad L(y(t)) = L(te^t) - 2(L(y(t))\,.\,L(e^t))$ (By convolution theorem)

$\Rightarrow \quad Y(s) = -\frac{d}{ds}\left(\frac{1}{s-1}\right) - 2Y(s)\left(\frac{1}{s-1}\right) \quad \Rightarrow \quad Y(s) = \frac{1}{(s-1)^2} - 2Y(s)\left(\frac{1}{s-1}\right)$

$\Rightarrow \quad \left(1 + \frac{2}{s-1}\right) Y(s) = \frac{1}{(s-1)^2} \quad \Rightarrow \quad Y(s) = \frac{1}{(s-1)(s+1)} = \frac{1}{s^2-1}$

$\therefore \quad y(t) = L^{-1}(Y(s)) = L^{-1}\left(\frac{1}{s^2-1}\right) = \sinh t.$

Example 3. *Solve the following integral equation by using Laplace transforms :*

$$y(t) = e^{-t} - 2\int_0^t y(u) \cos(t-u)\, du.$$

Sol. We have $\quad y(t) = e^{-t} - 2\int_0^t y(u) \cos(t-u)\, du.$

$\Rightarrow \qquad y(t) = e^{-t} - 2\,(y(t) * \cos t)$

Taking the Laplace transform, we get $\quad L(y(t)) = L(e^{-t}) - 2L(y(t) * \cos t)$

$\Rightarrow \qquad L(y(t)) = L(e^{-t}) - 2(L(y(t))\,.\,L(\cos t))$ (By convolution theorem)

$$\Rightarrow \qquad Y(s) = \frac{1}{s+1} - 2Y(s)\,.\,\frac{s}{s^2+1^2} \quad \Rightarrow \quad \left(1 + \frac{2s}{s^2+1}\right)Y(s) = \frac{1}{s+1}$$

$$\Rightarrow \qquad Y(s) = \frac{s^2+1}{(s+1)^3}$$

$$\therefore \qquad y(t) = L^{-1}(Y(s)) = L^{-1}\left(\frac{s^2+1}{(s+1)^3}\right) = e^{-t}L^{-1}\left(\frac{(s-1)^2+1}{s^3}\right)$$

$$= e^{-t}L^{-1}\left(\frac{s^2-2s+2}{s^3}\right) = e^{-t}\left[L^{-1}\left(\frac{1}{s}\right) - 2L^{-1}\left(\frac{1}{s^2}\right) + L^{-1}\left(\frac{2\,!}{s^3}\right)\right]$$

$$= e^{-t}[1 - 2t + t^2] = \mathbf{e^{-t}\,(1-t)^2}.$$

Example 4. *Solve the following integral equation by using Laplace transforms :*

$$y(t) = 1 - \sinh t + \int_0^t (1+u)\, y(t-u)\, du.$$

Sol. We have $\quad y(t) = 1 - \sinh t + \int_0^t (1+u)\, y(t-u)\, du.$

$\Rightarrow \qquad y(t) = 1 - \sinh t + ((1+t) * y(t))$

Taking the Laplace transform, we get

$$L(y(t)) = L(1) - L(\sinh t) + L((1+t) * y(t)).$$

$\Rightarrow \qquad L(y(t)) = \dfrac{1}{s} - \dfrac{1}{s^2-1} + L(1+t)\,.\,L(y(t))$ (By convolution theorem)

$\Rightarrow \qquad Y(s) = \dfrac{1}{s} - \dfrac{1}{s^2-1} + \left(\dfrac{1}{s} + \dfrac{1}{s^2}\right)Y(s)$, where $Y(s) = L(y(t))$

$$\Rightarrow \qquad \left(1 - \frac{1}{s} - \frac{1}{s^2}\right)Y(s) = \frac{s^2-1-s}{s(s^2-1)}$$

$$\Rightarrow \qquad Y(s) = \frac{s^2(s^2-1-s)}{(s^2-s-1)\,s(s^2-1)} = \frac{s}{s^2-1}$$

$$\therefore \qquad y(t) = L^{-1}(Y(s)) = L^{-1}\left(\frac{s}{s^2-1}\right) = \mathbf{\cosh t}.$$

Example 5. *Solve the following integral equation using Laplace transforms :*

$$\int_0^t \frac{y(u)}{\sqrt{t-u}}\, du = 1 + 2t - t^2.$$ (MDU 2004 ; KU 2004 S)

Sol. We have $\int_0^t y(u)\,(t-u)^{-1/2}\, du = 1 + 2t - t^2.$

$$\Rightarrow \qquad y(t) * t^{-1/2} = 1 + 2t - t^2$$

Taking the Laplace transform, we get

$$L\,(y(t) * t^{-1/2}) = L\,(1 + 2t - t^2)$$

$$L(y(t))\,.\,L(t^{-1/2}) = L(1) + 2L(t) - L(t^2) \quad \text{(By convolution theorem)}$$

$$\Rightarrow \qquad Y(s)\,.\,\frac{\Gamma(1/2)}{\sqrt{s}} = \frac{1}{s} + \frac{2}{s^2} - \frac{2!}{s^3}, \text{ where } Y(s) = L(y(t))$$

$$\Rightarrow \qquad Y(s)\frac{\sqrt{\pi}}{\sqrt{s}} = \frac{s^2 + 2s - 2}{s^3} \quad \Rightarrow \quad Y(s) = \frac{1}{\sqrt{\pi}}\left[\frac{1}{s^{1/2}} + \frac{2}{s^{3/2}} - \frac{2}{s^{5/2}}\right]$$

$$\therefore \qquad y(t) = L^{-1}(Y(s)) = \frac{1}{\sqrt{\pi}}\left[L^{-1}\left(\frac{1}{s^{1/2}}\right) + 2L^{-1}\left(\frac{1}{s^{3/2}}\right) - 2L^{-1}\left(\frac{1}{s^{5/2}}\right)\right]$$

$$= \frac{1}{\sqrt{\pi}}\left[\frac{t^{-1/2}}{\Gamma(1/2)} + 2\,.\,\frac{t^{1/2}}{\Gamma(3/2)} - 2\,.\,\frac{t^{3/2}}{\Gamma(5/2)}\right]$$

$$= \frac{1}{\sqrt{\pi}}\left[\frac{t^{-1/2}}{\sqrt{\pi}} + \frac{2t^{1/2}}{\frac{1}{2}\,.\sqrt{\pi}} - 2\,.\,\frac{t^{3/2}}{\frac{3}{2}\,.\,\frac{1}{2}\,.\sqrt{\pi}}\right]$$

$$\therefore \qquad y(t) = \frac{1}{\pi}\left[t^{-1/2} + 4t^{1/2} - \frac{8}{3}\,t^{3/2}\right].$$

4. INTEGRO-DIFFERENTIAL EQUATION

An equation involving an unknown function under the integral and perhaps also outside it and the derivatives of the unknown function is called an **integro-differential equation**.

The method of solving an integro-differential equation is same as that of solving an integral equation.

Example 6. *Solve the following integro-differential equation using Laplace transforms :*

$$y'(t) = t + \int_0^t (\cos u)\, y(t-u)\, du,\ y(0) = 4. \qquad \text{(KU 2006)}$$

Sol. We have $\quad y'(t) = t + \int_0^t (\cos u)\, y(t-u)\, du,\ y(0) = 4.$

$$\Rightarrow \qquad y'(t) = t + (\cos t * y(t))$$

Taking the Laplace transform, we get

$$L(y'(t)) = L(t) + L(\cos t * y(t)).$$

$$sL(y(t)) - y(0)^{*} = \frac{1}{s^2} + L(\cos t)\,.\,L(y(t)) \qquad \text{(By convolution theorem)}$$

$$\Rightarrow \qquad sY(s) - 4 = \frac{1}{s^2} + \frac{s}{s^2+1}\,.\,Y(s), \text{ where } Y(s) = L(y(t))$$

---

*__Why this step.__ Using $L(f') = sL(f') - f(0)$.

$$\Rightarrow \quad \left(s - \frac{s}{s^2+1}\right) Y(s) = \frac{1}{s^2} + 4 \quad \Rightarrow \quad Y(s) = \frac{s^2+1}{s^3}\left(\frac{1}{s^2} + 4\right)$$

$$\Rightarrow \quad Y(s) = \frac{1}{s^3} + \frac{1}{s^5} + \frac{4}{s} + \frac{4}{s^3} = \frac{5}{s^3} + \frac{1}{s^5} + \frac{4}{s}$$

$$\therefore \quad y(t) = L^{-1}(Y(s)) = 5L^{-1}\left(\frac{1}{s^3}\right) + L^{-1}\left(\frac{1}{s^5}\right) + 4L^{-1}\left(\frac{1}{s}\right)$$

$$= 5\left(\frac{t^2}{2!}\right) + \frac{t^4}{4!} + 4(1) = \frac{5}{2} t^2 + \frac{1}{24} t^4 + 4.$$

Example 7. *Solve the following integro-differential equation by using Laplace transforms :*

$$y'(t) + 4y(t) + 5\int_0^t y(u)\, du = e^{-t}, \; y(0) = 0.$$

Sol. We have $\quad y'(t) + 4y(t) + 5\int_0^t y(u)\, du = e^{-t}, \; y(0) = 0.$

$$\Rightarrow \quad y'(t) + 4y(t) + 5(y(t) * 1) = e^{-t}$$

Taking the Laplace transform, we get

$$L(y'(t)) + 4L(y(t)) + 5L(y(t) * 1) = L(e^{-t}).$$

$$\Rightarrow \quad (sL(y(t)) - y(0)) + 4L(y(t)) + 5(L(y(t)) \,.\, L(1)) = \frac{1}{s-(-1)} \qquad \text{(By convolution theorem)}$$

$$\Rightarrow \quad sY(s) - 0 + 4Y(s) + 5Y(s)\,.\,\frac{1}{s} = \frac{1}{s+1}.$$

$$\Rightarrow \quad \left(s + 4 + \frac{5}{s}\right) Y(s) = \frac{1}{s+1} \quad \Rightarrow \quad Y(s) = \frac{s}{(s+1)(s^2+4s+5)}$$

Using partial fractions, we have

$$Y(s) = -\frac{1}{2(s+1)} + \frac{s+5}{2(s^2+4s+5)} = -\frac{1}{2(s+1)} + \frac{(s+2)+3}{2((s+2)^2+1)}$$

$$\therefore \quad y(t) = L^{-1}(Y(s)) = -\frac{1}{2} L^{-1}\left(\frac{1}{s+1}\right) + \frac{1}{2} L^{-1}\left(\frac{(s+2)+3}{(s+2)^2+1}\right)$$

$$= -\frac{1}{2} e^{-t} + \frac{1}{2} e^{-2t} L^{-1}\left(\frac{s+3}{s^2+1}\right)$$

$$= -\frac{1}{2} e^{-t} + \frac{1}{2} e^{-2t}\left(L^{-1}\left(\frac{s}{s^2+1}\right) + 3L^{-1}\left(\frac{1}{s^2+1}\right)\right)$$

$$\therefore \quad y(t) = -\frac{1}{2} e^{-t} + \frac{1}{2} e^{-2t} (\cos t + 3 \sin t).$$

WORKING RULES FOR SOLVING PROBLEMS

Step I. Take the Laplace transform of the given equation.

Step II. Substitute the values of Laplace transforms.

Step III. Simplify the equation to get the value of Laplace transform of the unknown function.

Step IV. Find the unknown functions by taking the inverse Laplace transform.

EXERCISE 1

Solve the following integral equations by using Laplace transforms :

1. $y(t) = t + \int_0^t y(u) \sin (t - u)\, du$ *(KU 2005 S)*

2. $y(t) = 1 - \int_0^t y(u)(t - u)\, du$

3. $y(t) = t + 2 \int_0^t y(u) \cos (t - u)\, du$

4. $y(t) = 1 + 2 \int_0^t y(u) \cos (t - u)\, du$

5. $y(t) = \sin t + 2 \int_0^t y(u) \cos (t - u)\, du$

6. $y(t) = 3t^2 + \int_0^t y(u) \sin (t - u)\, du$

7. $y(t) = t^2 + \int_0^t y(u) \sin (t - u)\, du$

8. $y(t) = t + \frac{1}{6} \int_0^t y(u)(t - u)^3\, du$

9. $\int_0^t \frac{y(u)}{\sqrt{t - u}}\, du = 1$

10. $\int_0^t \frac{y(u)}{\sqrt{t - u}}\, du = 1 + t + t^2$

11. $\int_0^t y(u)\, y(t - u)\, du = 2y(t) + t - 2$

12. $y'(t) = 3 \int_0^t y(u) \cos 2(t - u)\, du + 2,\ y(0) = 1$

13. $y'(t) + 3y(t) + 2 \int_0^t y(u)\, du = t,\ y(0) = 1$

14. $y'(t) = \int_0^t y(u) \cos (t - u)\, du,\ y(0) = 1$

15. $y'(t) = t + \int_0^t (\cos u)\, y(t - u)\, du,\ y(0) = 1.$

Answers

1. $y(t) = t + \frac{t^3}{6}$ **2.** $y = \cos t$ **3.** $y(t) = 2e^t (t - 1) + 2 + t$ **4.** $y(t) = 1 + 2te^t$

5. $y = te^t$ **6.** $y(t) = 3t^2 + \frac{t^4}{4}$ **7.** $y(t) = t^2 + \frac{t^4}{12}$ **8.** $y(t) = \frac{1}{2}(\sin t + \sinh t)$

9. $y(t) = \frac{1}{\pi \sqrt{t}}$ **10.** $y(t) = \frac{1}{\pi}\left[\frac{1}{\sqrt{t}} + 2\sqrt{t} + \frac{8}{3} t^{3/2}\right]$ **11.** $y(t) = 1$

12. $y(t) = 4 + 8t - 3 \cos t - 6 \sin t$ **13.** $y(t) = \frac{1}{2} - 2e^{-t} + \frac{5}{2} e^{-2t}$ **14.** $y(t) = 1 + \frac{t^2}{2}$

15. $y(t) = 1 + t^2 + \frac{t^4}{24}$

Hints

11. If $L(y(t)) = Y(s)$, then $(Y(s))^2 - 2Y(s) - \frac{1-2s}{s^2} = 0$.

$\therefore \quad Y(s) = 2 - \frac{1}{s}$ or $\frac{1}{s}$

Rejecting $Y(s) = 2 - \frac{1}{s}$, we have $Y(s) = \frac{1}{s}$.

9

Solution of Systems of Differential Equations Using the Laplace Transformation

1. INTRODUCTION

In the present chapter, we shall study the method of solving a system of differential equations using Laplace transformations of functions. Our knowledge of finding Laplace transforms and inverse Laplace transforms would help us to solve the systems of differential equations. In the method of Laplace transforms, we would be able to find the required particular solution of the given system of differential equations with known initial conditions, without the necessity of first finding the general solution and then evaluating the arbitrary constants by using the given conditions.

2. METHOD OF SOLVING SYSTEM OF DIFFERENTIAL EQUATIONS

Let t be the independent variable and x, y the dependent variables of a given system of differential equations. We shall denote the Laplace transforms of the functions $x(t)$ and $y(t)$ by $\bar{x}(s)$ and $\bar{y}(s)$ respectively. Thus,

$$L(x(t)) = \bar{x}(s) \quad \text{and} \quad L(y(t)) = \bar{y}(s).$$

We take the Laplace transform of each differential equation of the given system. These equations are simplified to get the values of the functions $\bar{x}(s)$ and $\bar{y}(s)$. The values of the functions $x(t)$ and $y(t)$ are found by taking the inverse Laplace transforms of the functions $\bar{x}(s)$ and $\bar{y}(s)$ respectively.

Example 1. *Solve the following system of differential equations by the method of Laplace transforms :*

$$x' + y = 2 \cos t,\ x + y' = 0,\ x(0) = 0,\ y(0) = 1.$$

Sol. Given system is $x' + y = 2 \cos t$ ...(1)

$$x + y' = 0. \qquad ...(2)$$

Taking the Laplace transform, we get

$$L(x') + L(y) = L(2 \cos t) \qquad ...(3)$$

and

$$L(x) + L(y') = L(0). \qquad ...(4)$$

$$(3) \Rightarrow \quad [sL(x) - x(0)] + \bar{y} = \frac{2s}{s^2 + 1}$$

$$\Rightarrow \quad s\bar{x} + \bar{y} = \frac{2s}{s^2 + 1} \qquad (\because x(0) = 0) \quad ...(5)$$

(4) $\Rightarrow$ $\bar{x} + [sL(y) - y(0)] = 0 \Rightarrow \bar{x} + s\bar{y} - 1 = 0$ $(\because\ y(0) = 1)$

$\Rightarrow$ $\bar{x} + s\bar{y} = 1$ ...(6)

(5) $- s \times$ (6) $\Rightarrow$ $\bar{y} - s^2\bar{y} = \dfrac{2s}{s^2+1} - s = \dfrac{s - s^3}{s^2+1}$

$\Rightarrow$ $\bar{y} = \dfrac{s}{s^2+1} \Rightarrow y(t) = L^{-1}\left(\dfrac{s}{s^2+1}\right) = \cos t$

(6) $\Rightarrow$ $\bar{x} = 1 - s\bar{y} = 1 - s\left(\dfrac{s}{s^2+1}\right) = \dfrac{1}{s^2+1}$

$\Rightarrow$ $x = L^{-1}\left(\dfrac{1}{s^2+1}\right) = \sin t.$

$\therefore$ $x = \sin t, y = \cos t.$

Example 2. *Solve the following system of differential equations by the method of Laplace transforms :*

$$x' + 5x - 2y = t,\ y' + 2x + y = 0\ ;\ x(0) = 0,\ y(0) = 0.$$

Sol. Given system is $x' + 5x - 2y = t$ ...(1)

$y' + 2x + y = 0.$ ...(2)

Taking the Laplace transform, we get

$L(x') + 5L(x) - 2L(y) = L(t)$ ...(3)

and $L(y') + 2L(x) + L(y) = L(0).$ ...(4)

(3) $\Rightarrow$ $[sL(x) - x(0)] + 5\bar{x} - 2\bar{y} = \dfrac{1}{s^2}$

$\Rightarrow$ $s\bar{x} - 0 + 5\bar{x} - 2\bar{y} = \dfrac{1}{s^2} \Rightarrow (s+5)\bar{x} - 2\bar{y} - \dfrac{1}{s^2} = 0$ ...(5)

(4) $\Rightarrow$ $[sL(y) - y(0)] + 2\bar{x} + \bar{y} = 0$

$\Rightarrow$ $s\bar{y} - 0 + 2\bar{x} + \bar{y} = 0 \Rightarrow 2\bar{x} + (s+1)\bar{y} + 0 = 0$ ...(6)

Solving (5) and (6), we get

$$\frac{\bar{x}}{0 + \dfrac{s+1}{s^2}} = \frac{\bar{y}}{-\dfrac{2}{s^2} - 0} = \frac{1}{(s+5)(s+1)+4}$$

$\therefore$ $\bar{x} = \dfrac{s+1}{s^2(s^2+6s+9)} = \dfrac{s+1}{s^2(s+3)^2}$

Also $\bar{y} = -\dfrac{2}{s^2(s^2+6s+9)} = -\dfrac{2}{s^2(s+3)^2}.$

Using partial fractions,

$$\bar{x} = \frac{1}{27s} + \frac{1}{9s^2} - \frac{1}{27(s+3)} - \frac{2}{9(s+3)^2}.$$

$$\therefore \qquad x = L^{-1}(\bar{x}) = \frac{1}{27}L^{-1}\left(\frac{1}{s}\right) + \frac{1}{9}L^{-1}\left(\frac{1}{s^2}\right) - \frac{1}{27}L^{-1}\left(\frac{1}{s+3}\right) - \frac{2}{9}L^{-1}\left(\frac{1}{(s+3)^2}\right)$$

$$= \frac{1}{27}(1) + \frac{1}{9}.(t) - \frac{1}{27}(e^{-3t}) - \frac{2}{9}e^{-3t}L^{-1}\left(\frac{1}{s^2}\right)$$

$$\therefore \qquad \mathbf{x = \frac{1}{27} + \frac{t}{9} - \frac{1}{27}e^{-3t} - \frac{2}{9}e^{-3t}\,t.}$$

Using partial fractions,

$$\bar{y} = \frac{4}{27s} - \frac{2}{9s^2} - \frac{4}{27(s+3)} - \frac{2}{9(s+3)^2}.$$

$$\therefore \qquad y = L^{-1}(\bar{y}) = -\frac{4}{27}L^{-1}\left(\frac{1}{s}\right) - \frac{2}{9}L^{-1}(s^{-2}) - \frac{4}{27}L^{-1}\left(\frac{1}{s+3}\right) - \frac{2}{9}L^{-1}\left(\frac{1}{(s+3)^2}\right)$$

$$= -\frac{4}{27}(1) - \frac{2}{9}(t) - \frac{4}{27}(e^{-3t}) - \frac{2}{9}e^{-3t}L^{-1}\left(\frac{1}{s^2}\right)$$

$$\therefore \qquad \mathbf{y = -\frac{4}{27} - \frac{2}{9}t - \frac{4}{27}e^{-3t} - \frac{2}{9}e^{-3t}\,t.}$$

Example 3. *Solve the following system of differential equations by the method of Laplace transforms :*

$$x' + y = 3e^{2t},\ y' + x = 0,$$
$$x(0) = 2,\ y(0) = 0.$$

Sol. Given system is $x' + y = 3e^{2t}$ ...(1)

$y' + x = 0.$ ...(2)

Taking the Laplace transform, we get

$L(x') + L(y) = 3L(e^{2t})$ ...(3)

and $L(y') + L(x) = 0.$ ...(4)

(3) $\Rightarrow$ $[sL(x) - x(0)] + \bar{y} = 3.\dfrac{1}{s-2}$ $\Rightarrow$ $s\bar{x} - 2 + \bar{y} = \dfrac{3}{s-2}$

$\Rightarrow$ $s\bar{x} + \bar{y} = 2 + \dfrac{3}{s-2}$ ...(5)

(4) $\Rightarrow$ $[sL(y) - y(0)] + \bar{x} = 0 \Rightarrow s\bar{y} - 0 + \bar{x} = 0$

$\Rightarrow$ $\bar{x} + s\bar{y} = 0$ ...(6)

(5) – (6) × s $\Rightarrow$ $\bar{y} - s^2\bar{y} = 2 + \dfrac{3}{s-2} = \dfrac{2s-1}{s-2}$ $\Rightarrow$ $\bar{y} = \dfrac{2s-1}{(s-2)(1-s)(1+s)}$

(6) $\Rightarrow$ $\bar{x} = -s\bar{y} = \dfrac{-s(2s-1)}{(s-2)(1-s)(1+s)} = \dfrac{-s(2s-1)}{(s-2)(1-s)(1+s)}$

Using partial fractions,

$$\bar{x} = \frac{(-2)(3)}{(s-2)(-1)(3)} + \frac{(-1)(1)}{(-1)(1-s)(2)} + \frac{(1)(-3)}{(-3)(2)(1+s)}$$

$$= \frac{2}{s-2} - \frac{1}{2(s-1)} + \frac{1}{2(s+1)}.$$

$$\therefore \quad x = L^{-1}(\bar{x}) = 2L^{-1}\left(\frac{1}{s-2}\right) - \frac{1}{2}L^{-1}\left(\frac{1}{s-1}\right) + \frac{1}{2}L^{-1}\left(\frac{1}{s+1}\right)$$

$$= 2e^{2t} - \frac{1}{2}e^{t} + \frac{1}{2}e^{-t}.$$

Using partial fractions,

$$\bar{y} = \frac{3}{(s-2)(-3)} + \frac{1}{(-1)(1-s)(2)} + \frac{-3}{(-3)(2)(1+s)}$$

$$= -\frac{1}{s-2} + \frac{1}{2(s-1)} + \frac{1}{2(s+1)}.$$

$$\therefore \quad y = L^{-1}(\bar{y}) = -L^{-1}\left(\frac{1}{s-2}\right) + \frac{1}{2}L^{-1}\left(\frac{1}{s-1}\right) + \frac{1}{2}L^{-1}\left(\frac{1}{s+1}\right)$$

$$= -e^{2t} + \frac{1}{2}e^{t} + \frac{1}{2}e^{-t}.$$

$$\therefore \quad \mathbf{x = 2e^{2t} - \frac{1}{2}e^{t} + \frac{1}{2}e^{-t} \quad \text{and} \quad y = -e^{2t} + \frac{1}{2}e^{t} + \frac{1}{2}e^{-t}.}$$

Example 4. *Solve the following system of differential equations by the method of Laplace transforms :*

$$(D-2)x - (D+1)y = 6e^{3t}$$
$$(2D-3)x + (D-3)y = 6e^{3t},$$
$$x(0) = 3,\ y(0) = 0.$$

Sol. Given system is $\quad Dx - Dy - 2x - y = 6e^{3t}$ ...(1)

$$2Dx + Dy - 3x - 3y = 6e^{3t}. \quad ...(2)$$

Taking the Laplace transform, we get

$$L(Dx) - L(Dy) - 2L(x) - L(y) = 6L(e^{3t}) \quad ...(3)$$

and $\quad 2L(Dx) + L(Dy) - 3L(x) - 3L(y) = 6L(e^{3t}).$ ...(4)

$$(3) \Rightarrow \quad [sL(x) - x(0)] - [sL(y) - y(0)] - 2\bar{x} - \bar{y} = \frac{6}{s-3}$$

$$\Rightarrow \quad s\bar{x} - 3 - s\bar{y} + 0 - 2\bar{x} - \bar{y} = \frac{6}{s-3} \quad \Rightarrow \quad (s-2)\bar{x} - (s+1)\bar{y} = 3 + \frac{6}{s-3} \quad ...(5)$$

$$(4) \Rightarrow \quad 2[sL(x) - x(0)] + [sL(y) - y(0)] - 3\bar{x} - 3\bar{y} = \frac{6}{s-3}$$

$$\Rightarrow \quad 2(s\bar{x} - 3) + s\bar{y} - 0 - 3\bar{x} - 3\bar{y} = \frac{6}{s-3} \quad \Rightarrow \quad (2s-3)\bar{x} + (s-3)\bar{y} = 6 + \frac{6}{s-3} \quad ...(6)$$

$(5) \times (s-3) + (6) \times (s+1)$

$$\Rightarrow \quad [(s-3)(s-2) + (2s-3)(s+1)]\,\bar{x} = 3(s-3) + 6 + 6(s+1) + \frac{6(s+1)}{s-3}$$

$$\Rightarrow \quad 3(s-1)^2\,\bar{x} = \frac{3(3s^2-6s-1)}{s-3} \quad \Rightarrow \quad \bar{x} = \frac{3s^2-6s-1}{(s-1)^2\,(s-3)}.$$

Using partial fractions,

$$\bar{x} = \frac{1}{s-1} + \frac{2}{(s-1)^2} + \frac{2}{s-3}.$$

$$\therefore \quad x = L^{-1}\left(\frac{1}{s-1}\right) + 2\left(L^{-1}\left(\frac{1}{(s-1)^2}\right)\right) + 2L^{-1}\left(\frac{1}{s-3}\right)$$

$$= e^t + 2e^t\,L^{-1}\left(\frac{1}{s^2}\right) + 2e^{3t} = e^t + 2e^t\,t + 2e^{3t}.$$

$(5) \times (2s-3) - (6) \times (s-2)$

$$\Rightarrow \quad [-(2s-3)(s+1)-(s-2)(s-3)]\,\bar{y} = 3(2s-3) + \frac{6(2s-3)}{s-3} - 6(s-2) - \frac{6(s-2)}{s-3}$$

$$\Rightarrow \quad -3(s-1)^2\bar{y} = 3 + \frac{6s-6}{s-3}$$

$$\Rightarrow \quad \bar{y} = -\frac{1}{(s-1)^2} - \frac{2}{(s-1)(s-3)}$$

$$= -\frac{1}{(s-1)^2} - 2\left[\frac{1}{(s-1)(-2)} + \frac{1}{2(s-3)}\right]$$

$$= -\frac{1}{(s-1)^2} + \frac{1}{s-1} - \frac{1}{s-3}.$$

$$\therefore \quad y = -L^{-1}\left(\frac{1}{(s-1)^2}\right) + L^{-1}\left(\frac{1}{s-1}\right) - L^{-1}\left(\frac{1}{s-3}\right)$$

$$= -e^tL^{-1}\left(\frac{1}{s^2}\right) + e^t - e^{3t} = -e^t t + e^t - e^{3t}.$$

$$\therefore \quad x = \mathbf{e^t + 2te^t + 2e^{3t}} \text{ and } y = \mathbf{-te^t + e^t - e^{3t}}.$$

Example 5. *Solve the following system of differential equations by the method of Laplace transforms :*

$$x'' = x + 3y,\; y'' = 4x - 4e^t,$$
$$x(0) = 2,\; x'(0) = 3,\; y(0) = 1,\; y'(0) = 2.$$

Sol. Given system is $x'' = x + 3y$ ...(1)

$y'' = 4x - 4e^t.$ ...(2)

Taking the Laplace transform, we get

$L(x'') = L(x) + 3L(y)$ ...(3)

and $L(y'') = 4L(x) - 4L(e^t).$ ...(4)

$$(3) \Rightarrow \quad [s^2L(x) - sx(0) - x'(0)] = \bar{x} + 3\bar{y}$$

$$\Rightarrow \quad s^2\bar{x} - s.2 - 3 = \bar{x} + 3\bar{y}$$

$\Rightarrow \quad (s^2-1)\bar{x} - 3\bar{y} = 2s+3$ ...(5)

(4) $\Rightarrow \quad [s^2 L(y) - sy(0) - y'(0)] = 4\bar{x} - 4 \cdot \dfrac{1}{s-1}$

$\Rightarrow \quad s^2\bar{y} - s \cdot 1 - 2 = 4\bar{x} - \dfrac{4}{s-1}$

$\Rightarrow \quad -4\bar{x} + s^2\bar{y} = s + 2 - \dfrac{4}{s-1}$ ...(6)

(5) × 4 + (6) × (s^2-1) $\Rightarrow \quad -12\bar{y} + s^2(s^2-1)\bar{y} = 8s + 12 + (s^2-1)(s+2) - 4(s+1)$

$\Rightarrow \quad (s^2-4)(s^3+3)\bar{y} = 4(s+2) + (s^2-1)(s+2)$

$\Rightarrow \quad \bar{y} = \dfrac{(s+2)(s^2+3)}{(s^2-4)(s^2+3)} = \dfrac{1}{s-2}.$

$\therefore \quad y = L^{-1}\left(\dfrac{1}{s-2}\right) = e^{2t}$

(5) $\Rightarrow \quad (s^2-1)\bar{x} = 3\left(\dfrac{1}{s-2}\right) + 2s + 3 = \dfrac{(s+1)(2s-3)}{s-2}$

$\therefore \quad \bar{x} = \dfrac{2s-3}{(s-1)(s-2)} = \dfrac{(-1)}{(s-1)(-1)} + \dfrac{1}{1.(s-2)} = \dfrac{1}{s-1} + \dfrac{1}{s-2}.$

$\therefore \quad x = L^{-1}\left(\dfrac{1}{s-1}\right) + L^{-1}\left(\dfrac{1}{s-2}\right) = e^t + e^{2t}.$

$\therefore \quad \mathbf{x = e^t + e^{2t}}$ and $\mathbf{y = e^{2t}}$.

Example 6. *Solve the following system of differential equations by the method of Laplace transforms :*

$$(D^2+2)x - Dy = 1, \quad Dx + (D^2+2)y = 0,$$
$$x(0) = 0, \; x'(0) = 0, \; y(0) = 0, \; y'(0) = 0.$$ (KU 2004)

Sol. Given system is $\quad D^2x + 2x - Dy = 1$ ...(1)

$Dx + D^2y + 2y = 0.$ ...(2)

Taking the Laplace transform, we get

$L(x'') + 2L(x) - L(y') = L(1)$ ...(3)

and $\quad L(x') + L(y'') + 2L(y) = L(0).$ ...(4)

(3) $\Rightarrow \quad [s^2L(x) - sx(0) - x'(0)] + 2\bar{x} - [sL(y) - y(0)] = L(1)$

$\Rightarrow \quad s^2\bar{x} - s \cdot 0 - 0 + 2\bar{x} - s\bar{y} + 0 = \dfrac{1}{s}$

$\Rightarrow \quad (s^2+2)\bar{x} - s\bar{y} - \dfrac{1}{s} = 0$ ...(5)

(4) $\Rightarrow \quad [sL(x) - x(0)] + [s^2L(y) - sy(0) - y'(0)] + 2\bar{y} = 0$

$$\Rightarrow \quad s\bar{x} - 0 + s^2\bar{y} - s.0 - 0 + 2\bar{y} = 0$$

$$\Rightarrow \quad s\bar{x} + (s^2+2)\bar{y} + 0 = 0 \qquad ...(6)$$

Solving (5) and (6), we get

$$\frac{\bar{x}}{0 + \frac{s^2+2}{s}} = \frac{\bar{y}}{-1-0} = \frac{1}{(s^2+2)^2 + s^2}$$

$$\therefore \quad \bar{x} = \frac{s^2+2}{s}\left(\frac{1}{s^4+5s^2+4}\right) = \frac{s^2+2}{s(s^2+1)(s^2+4)}$$

and $$\bar{y} = \frac{-1}{(s^2+1)(s^2+4)}.$$

Using partial fractions, we get

$$\bar{x} = \frac{1}{2s} - \frac{s}{3(s^2+1)} - \frac{s}{6(s^2+4)}$$

and $$\bar{y} = -\frac{1}{3(s^2+1)} + \frac{1}{3(s^2+4)}.$$

$$\therefore \quad x = \frac{1}{2}L^{-1}\left(\frac{1}{s}\right) - \frac{1}{3}L^{-1}\left(\frac{s}{s^2+1}\right) - \frac{1}{6}L^{-1}\left(\frac{s}{s^2+4}\right)$$

$$= \frac{1}{2}.1 - \frac{1}{3}.\cos t - \frac{1}{6}\cos 2t$$

and $$y = -\frac{1}{3}L^{-1}\left(\frac{1}{s^2+1}\right) + \frac{1}{3}L^{-1}\left(\frac{1}{s^2+4}\right) = -\frac{1}{3}\sin t + \frac{1}{3}.\frac{1}{2}\sin 2t.$$

$$\therefore \quad \mathbf{x = \frac{1}{2} - \frac{1}{3}\cos t - \frac{1}{6}\cos 2t \text{ and } y = -\frac{1}{3}\sin t + \frac{1}{6}\sin 2t.}$$

Example 7. *Solve the following system of differential equations by the method of Laplace transforms :*

$$\frac{dx}{dt} + \frac{dy}{dt} = t, \quad \frac{d^2x}{dt^2} - y = e^{-t} \text{ with } x(0) = 3,\ x'(0) = -2,\ y(0) = 0.$$

Sol. Given system is $$\frac{dx}{dt} + \frac{dy}{dt} = t \qquad ...(1)$$

$$\frac{d^2x}{dt^2} - y = e^{-t}. \qquad ...(2)$$

Taking the Laplace transform, we get

$$L\left(\frac{dx}{dt}\right) + L\left(\frac{dy}{dt}\right) = L(t) \qquad ...(3)$$

and $$L\left(\frac{d^2x}{dt^2}\right) - L(y) = L(e^{-t}). \qquad ...(4)$$

$$(3) \Rightarrow [sL(x) - x(0)] + [sL(y) - y(0)] = \frac{1}{s^2}$$

$$\Rightarrow [s\bar{x} - 3] + [s\bar{y} - 0] = \frac{1}{s^2}$$

$$\Rightarrow s\bar{x} + s\bar{y} = 3 + \frac{1}{s^2}$$

$$\Rightarrow \bar{x} + \bar{y} = \frac{3}{s} + \frac{1}{s^3} \quad ...(5)$$

$$(4) \Rightarrow [s^2L(x) - sx(0) - x'(0)] - \bar{y} = \frac{1}{s+1}$$

$$\Rightarrow [s^2\bar{x} - s(3) - (-2)] - \bar{y} = \frac{1}{s+1}$$

$$\Rightarrow s^2\bar{x} - \bar{y} = \frac{1}{s+1} + 3s - 2 \quad ...(6)$$

$$(5) + (6) \Rightarrow (1 + s^2)\bar{x} = \frac{3}{s} + \frac{1}{s^3} + \frac{1}{s+1} + 3s - 2$$

$$\therefore \bar{x} = \frac{3}{s(s^2+1)} + \frac{1}{s^3(s^2+1)} + \frac{1}{(s+1)(s^2+1)} + \frac{3s}{s^2+1} - \frac{2}{s^2+1}.$$

We have $L^{-1}\frac{1}{s^2+1} = \sin t.$

$$\therefore L^{-1}\left(\frac{1}{s}\cdot\frac{1}{s^2+1}\right) = \int_0^t \sin T\,dT = -\cos T\Big|_0^t = 1 - \cos t$$

$$L^{-1}\left(\frac{1}{s}\cdot\frac{1}{s(s^2+1)}\right) = \int_0^t (1 - \cos T)\,dT = (T - \sin T)\Big|_0^t = t - \sin t$$

$$L^{-1}\left(\frac{1}{s}\cdot\frac{1}{s^2(s^2+1)}\right) = \int_0^t (T - \sin T)\,dT = \left(\frac{T^2}{2} + \cos T\right)\Bigg|_0^t = \frac{t^2}{2} + \cos t - 1.$$

Using partial fractions,

$$\frac{1}{(s+1)(s^2+1)} = \frac{1}{2(s+1)} + \frac{1}{2}\left(\frac{1-s}{s^2+1}\right)$$

$$= \frac{1}{2(s+1)} + \frac{1}{2(s^2+1)} - \frac{s}{2(s^2+1)}$$

$$\therefore L^{-1}\left(\frac{1}{(s+1)(s^2+1)}\right) = \frac{1}{2}e^{-t} + \frac{1}{2}\sin t - \frac{1}{2}\cos t.$$

$$\therefore x = 3(1 - \cos t) + \left(\frac{t^2}{2} + \cos t - 1\right) + \frac{1}{2}(e^{-t} + \sin t - \cos t) + 3\cos t - 2\sin t$$

or $$x = 2 + \frac{1}{2}\cos t + \frac{1}{2}t^2 + \frac{1}{2}e^{-t} - \frac{3}{2}\sin t$$

(5) $\Rightarrow$ $$\bar{y} = \frac{3}{s} + \frac{1}{s^3} - \bar{x}$$

$\therefore$ $$y = 3L^{-1}\left(\frac{1}{s}\right) + L^{-1}\left(\frac{1}{s^3}\right) - L^{-1}(\bar{x})$$

$$= 3(1) + \frac{1}{2}t^2 - 2 - \frac{1}{2}\cos t - \frac{1}{2}t^2 - \frac{1}{2}e^{-t} + \frac{3}{2}\sin t$$

or $$y = 1 - \frac{1}{2}\cos t - \frac{1}{2}e^{-t} + \frac{3}{2}\sin t.$$

WORKING RULES FOR SOLVING PROBLEMS

Step I. Take the Laplace transform of the given equations.

Step II. Substitute the values of Laplace transforms.

Step III. Simplify the equations to get the values of $\bar{x}$ and $\bar{y}$.

Step IV. Find the inverse Laplace transforms of $\bar{x}$ and $\bar{y}$ to get the values of x and y.

EXERCISE 1

Solve the following systems of differential equations by the method of Laplace transforms :

1. $x' + x - 4y = 0,\ y' = 3x - 2y,$ $x(0) = 3,\ y(0) = 4.$
2. $x' + x - y = 0,\ y' + x + y = 0,$ $x(0) = 1,\ y(0) = 0.$
3. $3x' + y' + 2x = 1,\ x' + 4y' + 3y = 0,$ $x(0) = 0,\ y(0) = 0.$ *(MDU 2004)*
4. $(D - 2)x + 3y = 0,\ 2x + (D - 1)y = 0,$ $x(0) = 8,\ y(0) = 3.$
5. $x' = 6x + 9y,\ y' = x + 6y,$ $x(0) = 3,\ y(0) = 3.$
6. $x' = 5x + y,\ y' = x + 5y,$ $x(0) = -3,\ y(0) = 7.$
7. $x' = -y,\ y' = x,$ $x(0) = 1,\ y(0) = 0.$
8. $x' = 2x - 4y,\ y' = x - 3y,$ $x(0) = 3,\ y(0) = 0.$
9. $x' = 2x + 4y,\ y' = x + 2y,$ $x(0) = -4,\ y(0) = -4.$
10. $x' = -2x + 3y,\ y' = 4x - y,$ $x(0) = 4,\ y(0) = 3.$
11. $x' + 2x - 4y = 0;\ y' - 2x = t,$ $x(0) = 0,\ y(0) = 3.$
12. $2x' + y' - x - y = e^{-t},\ x' + y' + 2x + y = e^{t},$ $x(0) = 2,\ y(0) = 1.$
13. $x'' - 3x' + y' + 2x - y = 0,$ $x' + y' - 2x + y = 0,$ $x(0) = 0,\ y(0) = -1,\ x'(0) = 0.$
14. $x'' = -5x + 2y,\ y'' = 2x - 2y,$ $x(0) = 3,\ x'(0) = 0,\ y(0) = 1,\ y'(0) = 0.$
15. $x'' + 3x - 2y = 0,\ x'' + y'' - 3x + 5y = 0,$ $x(0) = 0,\ x'(0) = 3,\ y(0) = 0,\ y'(0) = 2.$
16. $x'' - x + 5y' = t,\ -2x' + y'' - 4y = -2$ $x(0) = 0,\ x'(0) = 0,\ y(0) = 0,\ y'(0) = 0.$

Answers

1. $x = 4e^{2t} - e^{-5t},\ y = 3e^{2t} + e^{-5t}$
2. $x = e^{-t}\cos t,\ y = -e^{-t}\sin t$

3. $x = \frac{1}{10}(5 - 2e^{-t} - 3e^{-6t/11}),\ y = \frac{1}{5}(e^{-t} - e^{-6t/11})$

4. $x = 5e^{-t} + 3e^{4t}, y = 5e^{-t} - 2e^{4t}$

5. $x = -3e^{3t} + 6e^{9t}, y = e^{3t} + 2e^{9t}$

6. $x = -5e^{4t} + 2e^{6t}, y = 5e^{4t} + 2e^{6t}$

7. $x = \cos t, y = \sin t$

8. $x = 4e^{t} - e^{-2t}, y = e^{t} - e^{-2t}$

9. $x = 2 - 6e^{4t}, y = -1 - 3e^{4t}$

10. $x = 3e^{2t} + e^{-5t}, y = 4e^{2t} - e^{-5t}$

11. $x = \frac{13}{6}e^{2t} - \frac{49}{24}e^{-4t} - \frac{1}{2}t - \frac{1}{8},\ y = \frac{13}{6}e^{2t} + \frac{49}{48}e^{-4t} - \frac{1}{4}t - \frac{3}{16}$

12. $x = 8\sin t + 2\cos t,$

$y = -13\sin t + \cos t + \frac{e^{t}}{2} - \frac{e^{-t}}{2}$

13. $x = 2e^{t} - e^{2t} - 1,$

$y = e^{t} - 2$

14. $x = \cos t + 2\cos\sqrt{6}\,t, y = 2\cos t - \cos\sqrt{6}\,t$

15. $x = \frac{11}{4}\sin t + \frac{1}{12}\sin 3t,\ y = \frac{11}{4}\sin t - \frac{1}{4}\sin 3t$

16. $x = -t + 5\sin t - 2\sin 2t, y = 1 - 2\cos t + \cos 2t.$

SECTION III

PARTIAL DIFFERENTIAL EQUATIONS

10

Partial Differential Equations

1. INTRODUCTION

Partial differential equations arise in applied mathematics and mathematical physics when the functions involved depend on two or more independent variables. The use of partial differential equation is enormous as compared to that of ordinary differential equations. In the present course, we shall learn the method of solving various types of partial differential equations.

2. DEFINITION OF A PARTIAL DIFFERENTIAL EQUATION

An equation containing one or more partial derivatives of an unknown function of two or more independent variables is called a **partial differential equation.**

The following are some of the examples of partial differential equations :

1. $\frac{\partial z}{\partial x} + 3\frac{\partial z}{\partial y} = 5z + \tan(y - 3x)$ **2.** $xz\frac{\partial z}{\partial x} + yz\frac{\partial z}{\partial y} = xy$

3. $(y^2 + z^2)\frac{\partial z}{\partial x} - xy\frac{\partial z}{\partial y} -$ [illegible] **4.** $x\frac{\partial z}{\partial x} + 3y\frac{\partial z}{\partial y} = 2\left(z - x^2\left(\frac{\partial z}{\partial y}\right)^2\right)$

5. $2\frac{\partial^2 z}{\partial x^2} - 3\frac{\partial^2 z}{\partial x \partial y} - 2\frac{\partial^2 z}{\partial y^2} = 0$ **6.** $x^2\frac{\partial^2 z}{\partial x^2} - y^2\frac{\partial^2 z}{\partial y^2} - y\frac{\partial z}{\partial y} + x\frac{\partial z}{\partial x} = 0.$

3. ORDER OF A PARTIAL DIFFERENTIAL EQUATION

The **order** of a partial differential equation is defined as the order of the highest partial derivative occurring in the partial differential equation. For the partial differential equations (1–6) given above, the order of the first four equations are one each and the order of the last two equations are two each.

4. LINEAR PARTIAL DIFFERENTIAL EQUATION

A partial differential equation is said to be **linear** if the dependent variable and its partial derivatives occur only in the first degree and are not multiplied together. A partial differential equation which is not linear is called **non-linear.** Out of partial differential equations (1–6) given above the first, fifth and sixth equations are linear and others are non-linear.

The partial differential equation $z\frac{\partial z}{\partial x} + 5y = 7$ is not a linear partial differential equation because the dependent variable z and its partial derivative $\frac{\partial z}{\partial x}$ are multiplied together.

5. NOTATION

If $z = f(x, y)$ be a function of two independent variables x and y then we shall use the following notation :

$$\frac{\partial z}{\partial x} = p, \quad \frac{\partial z}{\partial y} = q, \quad \frac{\partial^2 z}{\partial x^2} = r, \quad \frac{\partial^2 z}{\partial x \partial y} = s, \quad \frac{\partial^2 z}{\partial y^2} = t.$$

6. FORMATION OF A PARTIAL DIFFERENTIAL EQUATION

There are two ways of forming partial differential equations depending on the given relation between variables. A relation between variables may contain arbitrary constants and arbitrary functions. The elimination of arbitrary constants (or functions) give rise to a partial differential equation.

7. FORMATION OF A PARTIAL DIFFERENTIAL EQUATION BY ELIMINATION OF ARBITRARY CONSTANTS

Let z be a function of two independent variables x and y defined by

$$f(x, y, z, a, b) = 0, \qquad \text{...(1)}$$

where a and b are arbitrary constants.

Differentiating (1) partially w.r.t. x and y, we get

$$\frac{\partial f}{\partial x} + \frac{\partial f}{\partial z}\frac{\partial z}{\partial x} = 0 \text{ and } \frac{\partial f}{\partial y} + \frac{\partial f}{\partial z}\frac{\partial z}{\partial y} = 0$$

$$\Rightarrow \quad \frac{\partial f}{\partial x} + p\frac{\partial f}{\partial z} = 0 \quad \text{...(2)} \quad \text{and} \quad \frac{\partial f}{\partial y} + q\frac{\partial f}{\partial z} = 0 \qquad \text{...(3)}$$

In general, a and b may be eliminated from (1), (2), (3) and we get an equation of the form $g(x, y, z, p, q) = 0$.

This is the required partial differential equation. The order of this equation shall be one.

Remark 1. If the number of arbitrary constants is less than the number of independent variables, then the elimination of arbitrary constants shall usually give rise to more than one differential equation of order one. For example, if $z = \lambda x + y$, then we have differential equations $p = \dfrac{z-y}{x}$ and $q = 1$.

2. If the number of arbitrary constants is greater than the number of independent variables, then the elimination of arbitrary constants shall give rise to a partial differential equation of order usually greater than one.

Example 1. *Form partial differential equations by eliminating arbitrary constants from the following relations :*

(*i*) $z = (x + a)(y + b)$ (*ii*) $z = ax^2 + by^2 + ab$

(*iii*) $z = (x^2 + a)(y^2 + b)$ (*iv*) $z = ae^{bx} \sin by$.

Sol. (*i*) We have $z = (x + a)(y + b)$. ...(1)

$$\Rightarrow \quad z = xy + ay + bx + ab$$

Differentiating z partially w.r.t. x and y, we get

$$\frac{\partial z}{\partial x} = y(1) + 0 + b(1) + 0 \qquad \text{...(2)}$$

and

$$\frac{\partial z}{\partial y} = x(1) + a(1) + 0 + 0 \qquad \text{...(3)}$$

(2) $\Rightarrow$ $b = \dfrac{\partial z}{\partial x} - y$ (3) $\Rightarrow$ $a = \dfrac{\partial z}{\partial y} - x$

Putting the values of a and b in (1), we get

$$z = \left(x + \frac{\partial z}{\partial y} - x\right)\left(y + \frac{\partial z}{\partial x} - y\right) \quad \text{or} \quad \mathbf{z = \frac{\partial z}{\partial x} \cdot \frac{\partial z}{\partial y}}$$

(*ii*) We have $z = ax^2 + by^2 + ab.$ ...(1)

Differentiating (1) partially w.r.t. x and y, we get

$$\frac{\partial z}{\partial x} = 2ax + 0 + 0 \quad \text{...(2)} \quad \text{and} \quad \frac{\partial z}{\partial y} = 0 + 2by + 0 \quad \text{...(3)}$$

(2) $\Rightarrow$ $p = 2ax$ $\Rightarrow$ $a = \dfrac{p}{2x}$ (3) $\Rightarrow$ $q = 2by$ $\Rightarrow$ $b = \dfrac{q}{2y}$.

Putting the values of a and b in (1), we get

$$z = \left(\frac{p}{2x}\right)x^2 + \left(\frac{q}{2y}\right)y^2 + \left(\frac{p}{2x}\right)\left(\frac{q}{2y}\right) \quad \text{or} \quad z = \frac{px}{2} + \frac{qy}{2} + \frac{pq}{4xy}$$

or $\mathbf{4xyz = 2px^2y + 2qxy^2 + pq.}$

(*iii*) We have $z = (x^2 + a)(y^2 + b).$ ...(1)

Differentiating (1) partially w.r.t. x and y, we get

$$\frac{\partial z}{\partial x} = (y^2 + b)(2x + 0) \quad \text{...(2)} \quad \text{and} \quad \frac{\partial z}{\partial y} = (x^2 + a)(2y + 0) \quad \text{...(3)}$$

(2) $\Rightarrow$ $p = 2x(y^2 + b)$ $\Rightarrow$ $y^2 + b = \dfrac{p}{2x}$

(3) $\Rightarrow$ $q = 2y(x^2 + a)$ $\Rightarrow$ $x^2 + a = \dfrac{q}{2y}$

Putting the values of $y^2 + b$ and $x^2 + a$ in (1), we get

$$z = \frac{q}{2y} \cdot \frac{p}{2x} \quad \text{or} \quad \mathbf{pq = 4xyz.}$$

(*iv*) We have $z = ae^{bx} \sin by.$ ...(1)

Differentiating (1) partially w.r.t. x and y, we get

$$\frac{\partial z}{\partial x} = (a \sin by) \cdot be^{bx} \quad \text{...(2)}$$

and $$\frac{\partial z}{\partial y} = (ae^{bx}) \cdot b \cos by \quad \text{...(3)}$$

(2) $\Rightarrow$ $p = abe^{bx} \sin by$ ...(4)

(3) $\Rightarrow$ $q = abe^{bx} \cos by$ ...(5)

Dividing (4) by (5), we get $\dfrac{p}{q} = \tan by.$

Also, (4) $\Rightarrow$ $p = bz$ $\Rightarrow$ $b = \dfrac{p}{z}.$

$$\therefore \quad \frac{p}{q} = \tan\left(\frac{p}{z}\right)y \quad \text{or} \quad \mathbf{p = q \tan \frac{py}{z}}$$

Example 2. *Find a partial differential equation by eliminating a, b and c from*

$$\frac{x^2}{a^2}+\frac{y^2}{b^2}+\frac{z^2}{c^2}=1.$$

Sol. We have $\frac{x^2}{a^2}+\frac{y^2}{b^2}+\frac{z^2}{c^2}=1.$ ...(1)

Differentiating (1) partially w.r.t. x and y, we get

$$\frac{2x}{a^2}+0+\frac{2z}{c^2}\frac{\partial z}{\partial x}=0 \quad \text{or} \quad c^2x+a^2z\frac{\partial z}{\partial x}=0 \qquad ...(2)$$

and $$0+\frac{2y}{b^2}+\frac{2z}{c^2}\frac{\partial z}{\partial y}=0 \quad \text{or} \quad c^2y+b^2z\frac{\partial z}{\partial y}=0 \qquad ...(3)$$

Differentiating (2) partially w.r.t. y, we get

$$0+a^2\left(z\frac{\partial^2 z}{\partial y\partial x}+\frac{\partial z}{\partial y}\frac{\partial z}{\partial x}\right)=0 \Rightarrow \mathbf{z\frac{\partial^2 z}{\partial y\partial x}+\frac{\partial z}{\partial x}\frac{\partial z}{\partial y}=0.}$$

Example 3. *Find the partial differential equation of all planes which are at a constant distance 'a' from the origin.*

Sol. Let $lx+my+nz=a$ ...(1)

be the equation of a plane where l, m, n are d.c.'s of the normal to the plane.

Differentiating (1) partially w.r.t. x and y, we get

$$l(1)+0+n\frac{\partial z}{\partial x}=0 \quad ...(2) \quad \text{and} \quad 0+m(1)+n\frac{\partial z}{\partial y}=0 \quad ...(3)$$

(2) $\Rightarrow$ $l+np=0$ or $l=-np$

(3) $\Rightarrow$ $m+nq=0$ or $m=-nq$

Also $l^2+m^2+n^2=1$

$\therefore$ $(-np)^2+(-nq)^2+n^2=1$

or $(p^2+q^2+1)n^2=1$ or $n=\frac{1}{\sqrt{p^2+q^2+1}}$ (Assuming $n>0$)

$\therefore$ $$l=-np=-\frac{p}{\sqrt{p^2+q^2+1}},\quad m=-nq=-\frac{q}{\sqrt{p^2+q^2+1}}$$

Putting the values of l, m and n in (1), we get

$$-\frac{px}{\sqrt{p^2+q^2+1}}-\frac{qy}{\sqrt{p^2+q^2+1}}+\frac{z}{\sqrt{p^2+q^2+1}}=a$$

or $$\mathbf{z=px+qy+a\sqrt{p^2+q^2+1}}.$$

Example 4. *Find the differential equation of the family of spheres of radius 7 with centres on the plane $x-y=0$.*

Sol. Let (a, a, b) be any point on the plane $x-y=0$.

$\therefore$ With centre at (a, a, b), the equation of the sphere of radius 7 is

$$(x-a)^2+(y-a)^2+(z-b)^2=49 \qquad ...(1)$$

$\therefore$ (1) represents a family of spheres where a and b are arbitrary constants.

Differentiating (1) partially w.r.t. x and y, we get

$$2(x-a)+0+2(z-b)\,p=0 \quad \text{...(2)}$$

and
$$0+2(y-a)+2(z-b)\,q=0 \quad \text{...(3)}$$

$$(2) \Rightarrow \quad x-a=-(z-b)p \quad \text{and} \quad (3) \Rightarrow \quad y-a=-(z-b)q$$

$$\therefore \quad (1) \Rightarrow \quad (z-b)^2p^2+(z-b)^2q^2+(z-b)^2=49$$

$$\Rightarrow \quad (p^2+q^2+1)\,(z-b)^2=49 \quad \text{...(4)}$$

$$(2)-(3) \Rightarrow \quad 2(x-y)=-2(z-b)\,(p-q) \quad \Rightarrow \quad z-b=-\frac{x-y}{p-q}$$

$$\therefore \quad (4) \Rightarrow \quad (p^2+q^2+1)\left(\frac{x-y}{p-q}\right)^2=49$$

or
$$\mathbf{(p^2+q^2+1)(x-y)^2=49(p-q)^2.}$$

Example 5. *Show that the differential equation of all cones which have their vertex at the origin is $px+qy=z$.*

Sol. The equation of the family of cones is the homogeneous equation

$$ax^2+by^2+cz^2+2fyz+2gzx+2hxy=0 \quad \text{...(1)}$$

where a, b, c, f, g, h are arbitrary constants.

Differentiating (1) partially w.r.t. x and y, we get

$$2ax+0+2czp+2fyp+2g(z.1+xp)+2hy=0 \quad \text{...(2)}$$

and
$$0+2by+2czq+2f(yq+z.1)+2gxq+2hx=0 \quad \text{...(3)}$$

$$(2) \Rightarrow \quad ax+gz+hy+p(cz+fy+gx)=0 \quad \text{...(4)}$$

$$(3) \Rightarrow \quad by+fz+hx+q(cz+fy+gx)=0 \quad \text{...(5)}$$

Multiplying (4) by x and (5) by y and adding, we get

$$ax^2+gxz+hxy+by^2+fyz+hxy+(px+qy)\,(cz+fy+gx)=0$$

or
$$ax^2+by^2+fyz+gzx+2hxy+(px+qy)\,(cz+fy+gx)=0$$

Using (1), we get $-(cz^2+fyz+gzx)+(px+qy)\,(cz+fy+gx)=0$

$$\Rightarrow \quad (cz+fy+gx)\,(-z+px+qy)=0 \quad \Rightarrow \quad \mathbf{px+qy=z.}$$

WORKING RULES FOR SOLVING PROBLEMS

Rule I. For a given relation involving variables and arbitrary constants, the relation is differentiated partially w.r.t. independent variables and arbitrary constants are eliminated to get the corresponding partial differential equation.

Rule II. If the number of arbitrary constants is less than the number of independent variables, then the elimination of arbitrary constants shall usually give rise to more than one differential equation of order one.

Rule III. If the number of arbitrary constants is equal to the number of independent variables, then the elimination of arbitrary constants shall give rise to one differential equation of order one.

Rule IV. If the number of arbitrary constants is greater than the number of independent variables then the elimination of arbitrary constants shall give rise to a differential equation of order usually greater than one.

EXERCISE 1

Form partial differential equations by eliminating arbitrary constants from the following relations (Q. no. 1—10) :

1. $az + b = a^2x + y$
2. $z = ax + (1 - a)y + b$
3. $z = ax + by + ab$
4. $z = ax + a^2y^2 + b$
5. $2z = \dfrac{x^2}{a^2} + \dfrac{y^2}{b^2}$ (*MDU 2006*)
6. $z = axe^y + \dfrac{1}{2}a^2e^{2y} + b$
7. $z = xy + y\sqrt{x^2 - a^2} + b$
8. $ax^2 + by^2 + cz^2 = 1$
9. $z = ax^2 + bxy + cy^2$
10. $z = ax + by + cxy.$
11. Form a partial differential equation by eliminating a and b from the equation
$$(x - a)^2 + (y - b)^2 + z^2 = k^2.$$
12. Find the partial differential equation of planes having equal x and y intercepts.
13. Find the differential equation of all spheres of fixed radius and having their centres in the xy-plane. (*KU 2005 ; MDU 2005*)
14. Find the differential equation of all spheres whose centre lies on z-axis.

Answers

1. $\dfrac{\partial z}{\partial x} \cdot \dfrac{\partial z}{\partial y} = 1$
2. $\dfrac{\partial z}{\partial x} + \dfrac{\partial z}{\partial y} = 1$
3. $z = x\dfrac{\partial z}{\partial x} + y\dfrac{\partial z}{\partial y} + \dfrac{\partial z}{\partial x} \cdot \dfrac{\partial z}{\partial y}$
4. $\dfrac{\partial z}{\partial y} = 2y\left(\dfrac{\partial z}{\partial x}\right)^2$
5. $2z = x\dfrac{\partial z}{\partial x} + y\dfrac{\partial z}{\partial y}$
6. $\dfrac{\partial z}{\partial y} = x\dfrac{\partial z}{\partial x} + \left(\dfrac{\partial z}{\partial x}\right)^2$
7. $\dfrac{\partial z}{\partial x}\dfrac{\partial z}{\partial y} = x\dfrac{\partial z}{\partial x} + y\dfrac{\partial z}{\partial y}$
8. $\dfrac{\partial z}{\partial x}\dfrac{\partial z}{\partial y} + z\dfrac{\partial^2 z}{\partial x \partial y} = 0$
9. $x\dfrac{\partial z}{\partial x} + y\dfrac{\partial z}{\partial y} = 2z$
10. $\dfrac{\partial^2 z}{\partial x^2} = 0, \dfrac{\partial^2 z}{\partial y^2} = 0, z = x\dfrac{\partial z}{\partial x} + y\dfrac{\partial z}{\partial y} - xy\dfrac{\partial^2 z}{\partial x \partial y}$
11. $z^2\left(\left(\dfrac{\partial z}{\partial x}\right)^2 + \left(\dfrac{\partial z}{\partial y}\right)^2 + 1\right) = k^2$
12. $\dfrac{\partial z}{\partial x} - \dfrac{\partial z}{\partial y} = 0$
13. $z^2\left(\left(\dfrac{\partial z}{\partial x}\right)^2 + \left(\dfrac{\partial z}{\partial y}\right)^2 + 1\right) = k^2$
14. $x\dfrac{\partial z}{\partial y} - y\dfrac{\partial z}{\partial x} = 0.$

8. FORMATION OF A PARTIAL DIFFERENTIAL EQUATION BY ELIMINATION OF ARBITRARY FUNCTIONS

Let u and v be independent functions of three variables x, y, z and let

$$f(u, v) = 0 \quad ...(1)$$

be an arbitrary relation between u and v. Regarding z as a function of x, y and differentiating (1) partially w.r.t. x, we get

$$\frac{\partial f}{\partial u}\left(\frac{\partial u}{\partial x} + \frac{\partial u}{\partial z}\frac{\partial z}{\partial x}\right) + \frac{\partial f}{\partial v}\left(\frac{\partial v}{\partial x} + \frac{\partial v}{\partial z}\frac{\partial z}{\partial x}\right) = 0$$

$$\Rightarrow \quad \frac{\partial f}{\partial u}\left(\frac{\partial u}{\partial x} + p\frac{\partial u}{\partial z}\right) + \frac{\partial f}{\partial v}\left(\frac{\partial v}{\partial x} + p\frac{\partial v}{\partial z}\right) = 0$$

$$\Rightarrow \quad \frac{\partial f}{\partial u}\Big/\frac{\partial f}{\partial v} = -\left(\frac{\partial v}{\partial x} + p\frac{\partial v}{\partial z}\right)\Big/\left(\frac{\partial u}{\partial x} + p\frac{\partial u}{\partial z}\right) \quad ...(2)$$

Similarly, differentiating (1) partially w.r.t. y, we get

$$\frac{\partial f}{\partial u}\Big/\frac{\partial f}{\partial v} = -\left(\frac{\partial v}{\partial y} + q\frac{\partial v}{\partial z}\right)\Big/\left(\frac{\partial u}{\partial y} + q\frac{\partial u}{\partial z}\right) \quad ...(3)$$

Eliminating f using (2) and (3), we get

$$-\left(\frac{\partial v}{\partial x} + p\frac{\partial v}{\partial z}\right)\Big/\left(\frac{\partial u}{\partial x} + p\frac{\partial u}{\partial z}\right) = -\left(\frac{\partial v}{\partial y} + q\frac{\partial v}{\partial z}\right)\Big/\left(\frac{\partial u}{\partial y} + q\frac{\partial u}{\partial z}\right)$$

$$\Rightarrow \quad \left(\frac{\partial v}{\partial x} + p\frac{\partial v}{\partial z}\right)\left(\frac{\partial u}{\partial y} + q\frac{\partial u}{\partial z}\right) = \left(\frac{\partial v}{\partial y} + q\frac{\partial v}{\partial z}\right)\left(\frac{\partial u}{\partial x} + p\frac{\partial u}{\partial z}\right)$$

$$\Rightarrow \quad \left(\frac{\partial u}{\partial y}\frac{\partial v}{\partial z} - \frac{\partial u}{\partial z}\frac{\partial v}{\partial y}\right)p + \left(\frac{\partial u}{\partial z}\frac{\partial v}{\partial x} - \frac{\partial u}{\partial x}\frac{\partial v}{\partial z}\right)q = \frac{\partial u}{\partial x}\frac{\partial v}{\partial y} - \frac{\partial u}{\partial y}\frac{\partial v}{\partial x}$$

$$\Rightarrow \quad \mathrm{P}p + \mathrm{Q}q = \mathrm{R},$$

where $\mathrm{P} = \frac{\partial u}{\partial y}\frac{\partial v}{\partial z} - \frac{\partial u}{\partial z}\frac{\partial v}{\partial y}$, $\mathrm{Q} = \frac{\partial u}{\partial z}\frac{\partial v}{\partial x} - \frac{\partial u}{\partial x}\frac{\partial v}{\partial z}$ and $\mathrm{R} = \frac{\partial u}{\partial x}\frac{\partial v}{\partial y} - \frac{\partial u}{\partial y}\frac{\partial v}{\partial x}$.

This is the required partial differential equation. The order of this equation is one.

Remark. The functions u and v are said to be *independent* if u/v is not merely a constant.

Example 1. *Form partial differential equations by eliminating arbitrary function from the following relations :*

(*i*) $z = f(x^2 + 2y^2)$ (*ii*) $f(x^2 + y^2 + z^2) = ax + by + cz$

(*iii*) $f(x^2 + y^2, z - xy) = 0$ (*iv*) $f(x^2 + y^2 + z^2, z^2 - 2xy) = 0.$

Sol. (*i*) We have $z = f(x^2 + 2y^2)$.

Differentiating (1) partially w.r.t. x and y, we get

$$\frac{\partial z}{\partial x} = p = f'(x^2 + 2y^2)\frac{\partial}{\partial x}(x^2 + 2y^2) = 2x\, f'(x^2 + 2y^2)$$

and

$$\frac{\partial z}{\partial y} = q = f'(x^2 + 2y^2)\frac{\partial}{\partial y}(x^2 + 2y^2) = 4y\, f'(x^2 + 2y^2)$$

Dividing we get $\frac{p}{q} = \frac{x}{2y}$ or $\mathbf{2py - qx = 0.}$

(*ii*) We have $f(x^2 + y^2 + z^2) = ax + by + cz.$ ...(1)

Differentiating (1) partially w.r.t. x and y, we get

$$f'(x^2 + y^2 + z^2).\left(2x + 0 + 2z\frac{\partial z}{\partial x}\right) = a\,.1 + 0 + c\frac{\partial z}{\partial x} \quad ...(2)$$

and

$$f'(x^2 + y^2 + z^2).\left(0 + 2y + 2z\frac{\partial z}{\partial y}\right) = 0 + b\,.1 + c\frac{\partial z}{\partial y} \quad ...(3)$$

$$(2) \Rightarrow \quad 2f'(x^2 + y^2 + z^2).(x + pz) = a + cp \quad ...(4)$$

$$(3) \Rightarrow \quad 2f'(x^2 + y^2 + z^2).(y + qz) = b + cq \quad ...(5)$$

Dividing (4) by (5), we get

$$\frac{x + pz}{y + qz} = \frac{a + cp}{b + cq} \text{ or } (x + pz)(b + cq) = (y + qz)(a + cp)$$

or $$bx + cxq + bpz + czpq = ay + cyp + aqz + czpq$$

or $$\mathbf{(bz - cy)p + (cx - az)q = ay - bx.}$$

(*iii*) We have $f(x^2 + y^2, z - xy) = 0.$ ...(1)

Let $u = x^2 + y^2$ and $v = z - xy.$

$\therefore$ (1) $\Rightarrow$ $f(u, v) = 0$ ...(2)

Differentiating (2) partially w.r.t. x, we get

$$\frac{\partial f}{\partial u}\frac{\partial u}{\partial x} + \frac{\partial f}{\partial v}\left(\frac{\partial v}{\partial x} + \frac{\partial v}{\partial z}\frac{\partial z}{\partial x}\right) = 0$$

$$\Rightarrow \quad \frac{\partial f}{\partial u} . 2x + \frac{\partial f}{\partial v}(-y + 1 . p) = 0$$

$$\Rightarrow \quad 2x\frac{\partial f}{\partial u} + (p - y)\frac{\partial f}{\partial v} = 0 \quad ...(3)$$

Differentiating (2) partially w.r.t. y, we get

$$\frac{\partial f}{\partial u}\frac{\partial u}{\partial y} + \frac{\partial f}{\partial v}\left(\frac{\partial v}{\partial y} + \frac{\partial v}{\partial z}\frac{\partial z}{\partial y}\right) = 0$$

$$\Rightarrow \quad \frac{\partial f}{\partial u} . 2y + \frac{\partial f}{\partial v}(-x + 1 . q) = 0$$

$$\Rightarrow \quad 2y\frac{\partial f}{\partial u} + (q - x)\frac{\partial f}{\partial v} = 0 \quad ...(4)$$

Eliminating $\frac{\partial f}{\partial u}$ and $\frac{\partial f}{\partial v}$ from (3) and (4), we get $\begin{vmatrix} 2x & p - y \\ 2y & q - x \end{vmatrix}^{*} = 0$

$$\Rightarrow \quad 2x(q - x) - 2y(p - y) = 0 \quad \text{or} \quad \mathbf{xq - yp = x^2 - y^2.}$$

(*iv*) We have $f(x^2 + y^2 + z^2, z^2 - 2xy) = 0.$ ...(1)

Let $u = x^2 + y^2 + z^2$ and $v = z^2 - 2xy.$

$\therefore$ (1) $\Rightarrow$ $f(u, v) = 0$ ...(2)

Differentiating (1) partially w.r.t. x, we get

$$\frac{\partial f}{\partial u}\left(\frac{\partial u}{\partial x} + \frac{\partial u}{\partial z}p\right) + \frac{\partial f}{\partial v}\left(\frac{\partial v}{\partial x} + \frac{\partial v}{\partial z}p\right) = 0$$

$$\Rightarrow \quad \frac{\partial f}{\partial u}(2x + 2zp) + \frac{\partial f}{\partial v}(-2y + 2zp) = 0$$

$$\Rightarrow \quad (x + zp)\frac{\partial f}{\partial u} + (zp - y)\frac{\partial f}{\partial v} = 0 \quad ...(3)$$

***Why this step.** If $ax + by = 0$ and $cx + dy = 0$, then $\frac{x}{y} = -\frac{b}{a}$ and $\frac{x}{y} = -\frac{d}{c}$.

$\therefore$ Eliminating x, y, we get $-\frac{b}{a} = -\frac{d}{c}$ or $ad - bc = 0$ or $\begin{vmatrix} a & b \\ c & d \end{vmatrix} = 0.$

Differentiating (1) partially w.r.t. y, we get

$$\frac{\partial f}{\partial v}\left(\frac{\partial u}{\partial y}+\frac{\partial u}{\partial z}q\right)+\frac{\partial f}{\partial v}\left(\frac{\partial v}{\partial y}+\frac{\partial v}{\partial z}q\right)=0$$

$$\Rightarrow \quad \frac{\partial f}{\partial u}(2y+2zq)+\frac{\partial f}{\partial v}(-2x+2zq)=0$$

$$\Rightarrow \quad (y+zq)\frac{\partial f}{\partial u}+(zq-x)\frac{\partial f}{\partial v}=0 \qquad ...(4)$$

Eliminating $\frac{\partial f}{\partial u}$ and $\frac{\partial f}{\partial v}$ from (3) and (4), we get $\begin{vmatrix} x+zp & zp-y \\ y+zq & zq-x \end{vmatrix}=0.$

$\Rightarrow \quad (x+zp)(zq-x)-(y+zq)(zp-y)=0$

$\Rightarrow \quad xzq-x^2+z^2pq-xzp-yzp+y^2-z^2pq+yzq=0$

$\Rightarrow \quad (x+y)zp-(x+y)zq=y^2-x^2 \quad \Rightarrow \quad \mathbf{z(p-q)=y-x.}$

Example 2. *Form partial differential equations by eliminating arbitrary functions from the following relations :*

(*i*) $z=x\phi(y)+y\psi(x)$ (*ii*) $z=f(x^2-y)+g(x^2+y)$

(*iii*) $x=f(z)+g(y)$ (*iv*) $z=f(y+ax)+g(y+bx),\ a\neq b.$

Sol. (*i*) We have $z=x\phi(y)+y\psi(x)$. ...(1)

Differentiating (1) partially w.r.t. x and y, we get

$$\frac{\partial z}{\partial x}=\phi(y).1+y\psi'(x) \quad ...(2) \quad \text{and} \quad \frac{\partial z}{\partial y}=x\phi'(y)+\psi(x).1 \qquad ...(3)$$

Differentiating (2) w.r.t. y, we get

$$\frac{\partial^2 z}{\partial y\partial x}=\phi'(y)+\psi'(x).1 \qquad ...(4)$$

$$\Rightarrow \quad \frac{\partial^2 z}{\partial y\partial x}=\frac{1}{x}\left(\frac{\partial z}{\partial y}-\psi(x)\right)+\frac{1}{y}\left(\frac{\partial z}{\partial x}-\phi(y)\right) \qquad \text{(Using (2) and (3))}$$

$$\Rightarrow \quad xy\frac{\partial^2 z}{\partial y\partial x}=x\frac{\partial z}{\partial x}+y\frac{\partial z}{\partial y}-(x\phi(y)+y\psi(x))$$

$$\Rightarrow \quad \mathbf{xy\frac{\partial^2 z}{\partial y\partial x}=x\frac{\partial z}{\partial x}+y\frac{\partial z}{\partial y}-z.}$$

(*ii*) We have $z=f(x^2-y)+g(x^2+y)$. ...(1)

Differentiating partially w.r.t. x and y, we get

$$p=f'(x^2-y)\frac{\partial}{\partial x}(x^2-y)+g'(x^2+y)\frac{\partial}{\partial x}(x^2+y) \qquad ...(2)$$

and

$$q=f'(x^2-y)\frac{\partial}{\partial y}(x^2-y)+g'(x^2+y)\frac{\partial}{\partial y}(x^2+y) \qquad ...(3)$$

(2) $\Rightarrow \quad p=2x\,f'(x^2-y)+2x\,g'(x^2+y)$ ...(4)

(3) $\Rightarrow \quad q=-f'(x^2-y)+1\,.\,g'(x^2+y)$ ...(5)

Differentiating (4) w.r.t. x, we get

$$r=2x\,f''(x^2-y)\,.\,2x+2.1\,f'(x^2-y)+2x\,g''(x^2+y)\,.\,2x+2.1\,g'(x^2+y)$$

or $$r = 4x^2 (f''(x^2 - y) + g''(x^2 + y)) + 2 (f'(x^2 - y) + g'(x^2 + y)) \quad ...(6)$$

Differentiating (5) w.r.t. y, we get

$$t = - f''(x^2 - y) . (- 1) + g''(x^2 + y) . 1 \quad \text{or} \quad t = f''(x^2 - y) + g''(x^2 + y) \quad ...(7)$$

$\therefore$ (6) $\Rightarrow$ $$r = 4x^2 t + 2\left(\frac{p}{2x}\right) \quad \text{(using (4) and (7))}$$

$$\Rightarrow \quad \mathbf{x \frac{\partial^2 z}{\partial x^2} = 4x^3 \frac{\partial^2 z}{\partial y^2} + \frac{\partial z}{\partial x}}.$$

(*iii*) We have $x = f(z) + g(y)$. ...(1)

Differentiating (1) partially w.r.t. x and y, we get

$$1 = f'(z)\, p + 0 \quad ...(2) \qquad \text{and} \quad 0 = f'(z)\, q + g'(y) \quad ...(3)$$

Differentiating (2) and (3) w.r.t. x, we get

$$0 = f''(z)\, p . p + f'(z)\, r \quad ...(4) \qquad \text{and} \quad 0 = f''(z)\, p . q + f'(z)\, s + 0 \quad ...(5)$$

(4) $\Rightarrow$ $f''(z)\, p^2 = - f'(z)\, r$

(5) $\Rightarrow$ $f''(z)\, pq = - f'(z)\, s$

Dividing, we get $\frac{p}{q} = \frac{r}{s}$ or $\mathbf{ps - qr = 0.}$

(*iv*) We have $z = f(y + ax) + g(y + bx)$. ...(1)

Differentiating (1) partially w.r.t. x and y, we get

$$p = f'(y + ax) . a + g'(y + bx) . b \quad ...(2)$$

and $$q = f'(y + ax) . 1 + g'(y + bx) . 1 \quad ...(3)$$

Differentiating (2) partially w.r.t. x and y, we get

$$r = f''(y + ax)\, a^2 + g''(y + bx)\, b^2 \quad ...(4)$$

and $$s = f''(y + ax)\, a . 1 + g''(y + bx)\, b . 1 \quad ...(5)$$

Differentiating (3) w.r.t. y, we get

$$t = f''(y + ax) . 1 + g''(y + bx) . 1 \quad ...(6)$$

(4) $\Rightarrow$ $a^2 f''(y + ax) + b^2 g''(y + bx) - r = 0$

(5) $\Rightarrow$ $a f''(y + ax) + b\, g''(y + bx) - s = 0$

(6) $\Rightarrow$ $f''(y + ax) + g''(y + bx) - t = 0$

Eliminating $f''(y + ax)$ and $g''(y + bx)$ from these three equations, we get

$$\begin{vmatrix} a^2 & b^2 & r \\ a & b & s \\ 1 & 1 & t \end{vmatrix} = 0$$

$\Rightarrow$ $(a - b)\, r - (a^2 - b^2)\, s + (a^2 b - ab^2)\, t = 0$

$$\Rightarrow \quad \mathbf{r - (a + b)s + abt = 0.}$$

Example 3. *The equation of any cone with vertex at* $P(x_0, y_0, z_0)$ *is of the form*

$$f\left(\frac{x - x_0}{z - z_0}, \frac{y - y_0}{z - z_0}\right) = 0.$$

Find the differential equation.

Sol. We have $$f\left(\frac{x-x_0}{z-z_0}, \frac{y-y_0}{z-z_0}\right)=0. \quad ...(1)$$

Let $$u=\frac{x-x_0}{z-z_0} \text{ and } v=\frac{y-y_0}{z-z_0}.$$

$\therefore$ (1) $\Rightarrow$ $$f(u, v)=0 \quad ...(2)$$

Differentiating (2) partially w.r.t. x, we get

$$\frac{\partial f}{\partial u}\left(\frac{1-0}{z-z_0}-\frac{x-x_0}{(z-z_0)^2}\frac{\partial z}{\partial x}\right)+\frac{\partial f}{\partial v}\left(-\frac{y-y_0}{(z-z_0)^2}\frac{\partial z}{\partial x}\right)=0$$

$$\Rightarrow \quad \frac{\partial f}{\partial u}\left(\frac{1}{z-z_0}-p\frac{x-x_0}{(z-z_0)^2}\right)+\frac{\partial f}{\partial v}\left(-p\frac{y-y_0}{(z-z_0)^2}\right)=0 \quad ...(3)$$

Differentiating (2) partially w.r.t. y, we get

$$\frac{\partial f}{\partial u}\left(-\frac{x-x_0}{(z-z_0)^2}\frac{\partial z}{\partial y}\right)+\frac{\partial f}{\partial v}\left(\frac{1-0}{z-z_0}-\frac{y-y_0}{(z-z_0)^2}\frac{\partial z}{\partial y}\right)=0$$

$$\Rightarrow \quad \frac{\partial f}{\partial u}\left(-q\frac{x-x_0}{(z-z_0)^2}\right)+\frac{\partial f}{\partial v}\left(\frac{1}{z-z_0}-q\frac{y-y_0}{(z-z_0)^2}\right)=0 \quad ...(4)$$

Eliminating $\frac{\partial f}{\partial u}$ **and** $\frac{\partial f}{\partial v}$ **from (3), (4), we get**

$$\begin{vmatrix} \frac{1}{z-z_0}-p\frac{x-x_0}{(z-z_0)^2} & -p\frac{y-y_0}{(z-z_0)^2} \\ -q\frac{x-x_0}{(z-z_0)^2} & \frac{1}{z-z_0}-q\frac{y-y_0}{(z-z_0)^2} \end{vmatrix}=0$$

$$\Rightarrow \quad \begin{vmatrix} z-z_0-p(x-x_0) & -p(y-y_0) \\ -q(x-x_0) & z-z_0-q(y-y_0) \end{vmatrix}=0$$

$$\Rightarrow \quad [z-z_0-p(x-x_0)][z-z_0-q(y-y_0)]-pq(x-x_0)(y-y_0)=0$$

$$\Rightarrow \quad (z-z_0)^2-p(x-x_0)(z-z_0)-(z-z_0)q(y-y_0)=0$$

$$\Rightarrow \quad \mathbf{p(x-x_0)+q(y-y_0)=z-z_0.}$$

WORKING RULES FOR SOLVING PROBLEMS

Rule I. For a given relation involving variables and arbitrary functions, the relation is differentiated partially w.r.t. independent variables and arbitrary functions are eliminated to get the corresponding partial differential equation.

Rule II. If the number of arbitrary functions is less than the number of independent variables then the elimination of arbitrary functions shall give rise to a differential equation of order one.

Rule III. If the number of arbitrary functions is equal to the number of independent variables, then the elimination of arbitrary functions shall give rise to a differential equation of order usually greater than one.

EXERCISE 2

Find partial differential equation by eliminating arbitrary functions from the following relations :

1. $z = f(x + ky)$
2. $z = f(x^2 - y^2)$
3. $f(x^2 + y^2 + z^2) = x + y + z$
4. $z = x + y + f(xy)$
5. $z = xy + f(x^2 + y^2)$
6. $z = f(xy/z)$ *(KU 2004 S)*
7. $f(x + y + z) = xyz$
8. $z = (x + y) f(x^2 - y^2)$
9. $z = f(x) + e^y g(x)$
10. $z = f(xy) + g(x + y)$
11. $z = f(xy) + g(x/y)$
12. $f(x + y + z, x^2 + y^2 - z^2) = 0$ *(CDLU 2004)*
13. $z = f(x \cos \alpha + y \sin \alpha - at) + g(x \cos \alpha + y \sin \alpha + at)$. *(KU 2004)*

Answers

1. $q = kp$
2. $yp + xq = 0$
3. $(y - z) p + (z - x) q = x - y$
4. $px - qy = x - y$
5. $py - qx = y^2 - x^2$
6. $px - qy = 0$
7. $x(y - z)p + y(z - x)q = z(x - y)$
8. $yp + xq = z$
9. $t - q = 0$
10. $x(y - x) r - (y^2 - x^2) s + y(y - x)t + (p - q) (x + y) = 0$
11. $x^2r - y^2t + xp - yq = 0$
12. $p(y + z) - (x + z)q = x - y$
13. $\dfrac{\partial^2 z}{\partial x^2} + \dfrac{\partial^2 z}{\partial y^2} = \dfrac{1}{a^2} \dfrac{\partial^2 z}{\partial t^2}$.

Hints

12. $u = x + y + z,\ v = x^2 + y^2 - z^2 \quad \Rightarrow \quad f(u, v) = 0$

Diff. w.r.t. x, we get $\dfrac{\partial f}{\partial u}\left(\dfrac{\partial u}{\partial x} + \dfrac{\partial u}{\partial z}\dfrac{\partial z}{\partial x}\right) + \dfrac{\partial f}{\partial v}\left(\dfrac{\partial v}{\partial x} + \dfrac{\partial v}{\partial z}\dfrac{\partial z}{\partial x}\right) = 0$

$\Rightarrow \quad \dfrac{\partial f}{\partial u}(1 + 1 \,.\, p) + \dfrac{\partial f}{\partial v}(2x - 2zp) = 0$

Similarly, $\quad \dfrac{\partial f}{\partial u}(1 + 1 \,.\, q) + \dfrac{\partial f}{\partial v}(2y - 2zq) = 0$

Eliminating $\dfrac{\partial f}{\partial u}, \dfrac{\partial f}{\partial v}$, we get $\begin{vmatrix} 1 + p & 2x - 2zp \\ 1 + q & 2y - 2zq \end{vmatrix} = 0.$

11

Partial Differential Equations of the First Order

(Equations linear in p and q)

1. INTRODUCTION

In the last chapter, we studied the methods of forming partial differential equations. The next step is to solve partial differential equations. Solving a partial differential equation means to find a function which satisfies the given partial differential equation. A function satisfying a partial differential equation is called its solution (or integral). In the present chapter, we shall confine ourselves to the solution of partial differential equations of first order and at the same time linear in p and q.

2. SOLUTION OF A PARTIAL DIFFERENTIAL EQUATION

A **solution** of a partial differential equation is a relation between the variables by means of which and the partial derivatives derived there from the given partial differential equation is satisfied.

A solution of a partial differential equation is also called an **integral** of the equation.

In the context of partial differential equations of first order, there are four types of solutions. These are :

(*i*) Complete solution (*ii*) Particular solution

(*iii*) Singular solution (*iv*) General solution.

3. COMPLETE SOLUTION

Let z be a function of two independent variables x and y defined by

$$f(x, y, z, a, b) = 0 \qquad ...(1)$$

where a and b are arbitrary constants.

Differentiating (1) partially w.r.t. x and y, we get

$$\frac{\partial f}{\partial x} + p\frac{\partial f}{\partial z} = 0 \quad ...(2) \qquad \text{and} \qquad \frac{\partial f}{\partial y} + q\frac{\partial f}{\partial z} = 0 \qquad ...(3)$$

Eliminating a and b from (1), (2) and (3), we get an equation of the form $g(x, y, z, p, q) = 0$. This is a partial differential equation of first order.

In (1), the number of arbitrary constants is two which is equal to the number of independent variables in $g(x, y, z, p, q) = 0$.

The function $f(x, y, z, a, b) = 0$ is called the **complete solution** of the equation $g(x, y, z, p, q) = 0$.

For example $z = (x + a)(y + b)$ is a complete solution of the equation $pq = z$.

4. PARTICULAR SOLUTION

A solution obtained by giving some particular values to the arbitrary constants in the complete solution of a partial differential equation of first order is called a **particular solution** of the concerned equation.

For example $z = (x + 1)(y + 4)$ is a particular solution of the equation $pq = z$.

5. SINGULAR SOLUTION

Let $f(x, y, z, a, b) = 0$ be the complete solution of a partial differential equation $g(x, y, z, p, q) = 0$. The relation between x, y and z obtained by eliminating the arbitrary constants a and b between the equations $f(x, y, z, a, b) = 0, \frac{\partial f}{\partial a} = 0, \frac{\partial f}{\partial b} = 0$ is called the **singular solution** of the equation $g(x, y, z, p, q) = 0$, provided it satisfies this equation. This solution represents the envelope of the surfaces represented by the complete solution of the given partial differential equation. The singular solution may or may not be contained in the complete solution of the equation.

For example, $z = ax + by - (a^2 + b^2)$ is the complete solution of the partial differential equation $z = px + qy - (p^2 + q^2)$.

Let $f(x, y, z, a, b) = z - ax - by + a^2 + b^2$.

$$\therefore \quad \frac{\partial f}{\partial a} = -x + 2a, \quad \frac{\partial f}{\partial b} = -y + 2b$$

Eliminating a and b from the equations,

$$z - ax - by + a^2 + b^2 = 0, \quad -x + 2a = 0, \quad -y + 2b = 0, \text{ we get } z = \frac{x^2 + y^2}{4}.$$

This also satisfy the given equation.

$\therefore \quad z = \frac{x^2 + y^2}{4}$ is the singular solution of the equation $z = px + qy - (p^2 + q^2)$.

6. GENERAL SOLUTION

Let $f(x, y, z, a, b) = 0$ be the complete solution of a partial differential equation $g(x, y, z, p, q) = 0$. Let $b = \phi(a)$.

$\therefore \quad f(x, y, z, a, \phi(a)) = 0$ is a one-parameter family of the surfaces of $g(x, y, z, p, q) = 0$. The relation between x, y and z obtained by eliminating the arbitrary constant a between the equations $f(x, y, z, a, \phi(a)) = 0$ and $\frac{\partial f}{\partial a} = 0$ is called the **general solution** of the equation $g(x, y, z, p, q) = 0$, provided it satisfies this equation. This solution represents the envelope of the surfaces represented by the equation $f(x, y, z, a, \phi(a)) = 0$.

If $b = \phi(a)$, where ϕ is an arbitrary function, then the elimination of a between the equations $f(x, y, z, a, \phi(a)) = 0$, and $\frac{\partial f}{\partial a} = 0$ is not possible. Thus the general solution of the equation $g(x, y, z, p, q) = 0$ is written as the set of equations $f(x, y, z, a, \phi(a)) = 0, \frac{\partial f}{\partial a} = 0$ where ϕ is any arbitrary function.

We know that if u and v be independent functions of x, y, z and

$$f(u, v) = 0 \qquad \text{...(1)}$$

be an arbitrary function of u and v, then $\quad Pp + Qq = R \qquad$ ...(2)

where $$P = \frac{\partial u}{\partial y}\frac{\partial v}{\partial z} - \frac{\partial u}{\partial z}\frac{\partial v}{\partial y}, \quad Q = \frac{\partial u}{\partial z}\frac{\partial v}{\partial x} - \frac{\partial u}{\partial x}\frac{\partial v}{\partial z}, \quad R = \frac{\partial u}{\partial x}\frac{\partial v}{\partial y} - \frac{\partial u}{\partial y}\frac{\partial v}{\partial x}.$$

(2) is a partial differential equation of first order.

Thus $f(u, v) = 0$ is a solution of the equation $Pp + Qq = R$. Since $f(u, v) = 0$ contains an arbitrary function 'f', it is the general solution of the equation (2).

7. LAGRANGE LINEAR EQUATION

We know that a partial differential quation of first order involves only the first order partial derivatives of the dependent variable (z) w.r.t. the independent variables (x and y). Thus an equation of first order involves x, y, z, p, q and may also involve powers of partial derivatives p and q.

In particular, a partial differential equation of first order and at the same time linear in p and q is of the form $Pp + Qq = R$ where P, Q, R are functions of x, y, z. This type of a partial differential equation is called a **Lagrange linear equation.**

For example $4xp + 6y^2q = x^2 + y^2 + z^2$ is a Lagrange linear equation.

8. SOLUTION OF LAGRANGE LINEAR EQUATION

Let $$Pp + Qq = R \quad \text{...(1)}$$

be a Lagrange linear equation where P, Q, R are functions of the dependent variable z and independent variables x and y. The system of equations

$$\frac{dx}{P} = \frac{dy}{Q} = \frac{dz}{R} \quad \text{...(2)}$$

is called the **Lagrange system** of ordinary differential equations for the equation (1).

Let $u = C_1$ and $v = C_2$ be two independent solutions of the equations (2).

Let $f(u, v) = 0$ ...(3)

be an arbitrary function of u and v.

Differentiating (3) partially w.r.t. x and y, we get

$$\frac{\partial f}{\partial u}\left(\frac{\partial u}{\partial x} + \frac{\partial u}{\partial z}p\right) + \frac{\partial f}{\partial v}\left(\frac{\partial v}{\partial x} + \frac{\partial v}{\partial z}p\right) = 0$$

and $$\frac{\partial f}{\partial u}\left(\frac{\partial u}{\partial y} + \frac{\partial u}{\partial z}q\right) + \frac{\partial f}{\partial v}\left(\frac{\partial v}{\partial y} + \frac{\partial v}{\partial z}q\right) = 0$$

Eliminating $\frac{\partial f}{\partial u}$ and $\frac{\partial f}{\partial v}$, we get $$\begin{vmatrix} \frac{\partial u}{\partial x} + p\frac{\partial u}{\partial z} & \frac{\partial v}{\partial x} + p\frac{\partial v}{\partial z} \\ \frac{\partial u}{\partial y} + q\frac{\partial u}{\partial z} & \frac{\partial v}{\partial y} + q\frac{\partial v}{\partial z} \end{vmatrix} = 0$$

$$\Rightarrow \left(\frac{\partial u}{\partial x} + p\frac{\partial u}{\partial z}\right)\left(\frac{\partial v}{\partial y} + q\frac{\partial v}{\partial z}\right) - \left(\frac{\partial v}{\partial x} + p\frac{\partial v}{\partial z}\right)\left(\frac{\partial u}{\partial y} + q\frac{\partial u}{\partial z}\right) = 0$$

$$\Rightarrow \left(\frac{\partial u}{\partial z}\frac{\partial v}{\partial y} - \frac{\partial u}{\partial y}\frac{\partial v}{\partial z}\right)p + \left(\frac{\partial u}{\partial x}\frac{\partial v}{\partial z} - \frac{\partial u}{\partial z}\frac{\partial v}{\partial x}\right)q + \frac{\partial u}{\partial x}\frac{\partial v}{\partial y} - \frac{\partial u}{\partial y}\frac{\partial v}{\partial x} = 0$$

$$\Rightarrow \left(\frac{\partial u}{\partial y}\frac{\partial v}{\partial z} - \frac{\partial u}{\partial z}\frac{\partial v}{\partial y}\right)p + \left(\frac{\partial u}{\partial z}\frac{\partial v}{\partial x} - \frac{\partial u}{\partial x}\frac{\partial v}{\partial z}\right)q = \frac{\partial u}{\partial x}\frac{\partial v}{\partial y} - \frac{\partial u}{\partial y}\frac{\partial v}{\partial x} \quad \text{...(4)}$$

$\therefore$ (3) is a solution of the equation (4).

Taking differentials of $u = C_1$ and $v = C_2$, we get

$$\frac{\partial u}{\partial x}dx + \frac{\partial u}{\partial y}dy + \frac{\partial u}{\partial z}dz = 0 \qquad ...(5)$$

and
$$\frac{\partial v}{\partial x}dx + \frac{\partial v}{\partial y}dy + \frac{\partial v}{\partial z}dz = 0 \qquad ...(6)$$

Since u and v are independent functions, we have

$$\frac{dx}{\frac{\partial u}{\partial y}\frac{\partial v}{\partial z} - \frac{\partial u}{\partial z}\frac{\partial v}{\partial y}} = \frac{dy}{\frac{\partial u}{\partial z}\frac{\partial v}{\partial x} - \frac{\partial u}{\partial x}\frac{\partial v}{\partial z}} = \frac{dz}{\frac{\partial u}{\partial x}\frac{\partial v}{\partial y} - \frac{\partial u}{\partial y}\frac{\partial v}{\partial x}} \qquad ...(7)$$

Using (2) and (7), we have

$$\frac{\frac{\partial u}{\partial y}\frac{\partial v}{\partial z} - \frac{\partial u}{\partial z}\frac{\partial v}{\partial y}}{P} = \frac{\frac{\partial u}{\partial z}\frac{\partial v}{\partial x} - \frac{\partial u}{\partial x}\frac{\partial v}{\partial z}}{Q} = \frac{\frac{\partial u}{\partial x}\frac{\partial v}{\partial y} - \frac{\partial u}{\partial y}\frac{\partial v}{\partial x}}{R} = \lambda \text{ (say)}$$

$$\therefore \quad \frac{\partial u}{\partial y}\frac{\partial v}{\partial z} - \frac{\partial u}{\partial z}\frac{\partial v}{\partial y} = \lambda P, \quad \frac{\partial u}{\partial z}\frac{\partial v}{\partial x} - \frac{\partial u}{\partial x}\frac{\partial v}{\partial z} = \lambda Q, \quad \frac{\partial u}{\partial x}\frac{\partial v}{\partial y} - \frac{\partial u}{\partial y}\frac{\partial v}{\partial x} = \lambda R.$$

$\therefore$ Putting these values in (4), we get $\lambda Pp + \lambda Qq = \lambda R$ or $Pp + Qq = R$, which is the given partial differential equation.

$\therefore$ If $u = C_1$ and $v = C_2$ be two independent solutions of the system of differential equations $\frac{dx}{P} = \frac{dy}{Q} = \frac{dz}{R}$, then any arbitrary function $f(u, v)$ of u and v is a solution of the Lagrange linear equation $Pp + Qq = R$. The solution $f(u, v) = 0$ is the general solution of the equation $Pp + Qq = R$. In particular, for arbitrary constants a and b, the solution $u = av + b$ is a complete solution of the equation $Pp + Qq = R$.

Remark. The Lagrange system of ordinary differential equations $\frac{dx}{P} = \frac{dy}{Q} = \frac{dz}{R}$ for the partial differential equation $Pp + Qq = R$ is also known as the **auxiliary system of equations** or simply as the **auxiliary equations** of the equation $Pp + Qq = R$.

WORKING RULES FOR SOLVING $Pp + Qq = R$

Step I. Indentify the functions P, Q and R.

Step II. Form the system : $\frac{dx}{P} = \frac{dy}{Q} = \frac{dz}{R}$.

Step III. Find two independent solutions $u = C_1$ and $v = C_2$ of the system given in **step II.**

Step IV. Write $f(u, v) = 0$ and call it the general solution of the given equation.

Type I. In this type, we shall consider the solution of the equation $Pp + Qq = R$ for which the equality of two factors of the auxiliary equations $\frac{dx}{P} = \frac{dy}{Q} = \frac{dz}{R}$ gives an equation in the variables whose differentials are involved. Two independent solutions of the auxiliary equations are calculated in this manner.

Example 1. *Find the general solution of the following Lagrange linear equations :*

(*i*) $2p + 5q = 1$ (*ii*) $y^2p + x^2q = x^2y^2z^2$ (*iii*) $\frac{y^2z}{x}p + xzq = y^2$

(*iv*) $zp = x$ (*v*) $(x^2 + 2y^2)\,p - xyq = xz.$ (KU 2005 S)

Sol. (*i*) We have $2p + 5q = 1.$

Here $P = 2, Q = 5, R = 1$

$\therefore$ Auxiliary equations are $\frac{dx}{P} = \frac{dy}{Q} = \frac{dz}{R}.$

$$\therefore \quad \frac{dx}{2} = \frac{dy}{5} = \frac{dz}{1} \quad ...(1)$$

Taking the first two fractions of (1), we get $5dx - 2dy = 0$ ...(2)

Integrating (2), we get $5x - 2y = C_1$ ...(3)

Taking the last two fractions of (1), we get $dy - 5dz = 0$ ...(4)

Integrating (4), we have $y - 5z = C_2$ ...(5)

From (3) and (5), the general solution of given equation is $\mathbf{f(5x - 2y, y - 5z) = 0}$, where f is any arbitrary function.

(*ii*) We have $y^2p + x^2q = x^2y^2z^2.$

Here $P = y^2, Q = x^2, R = x^2y^2z^2.$

$\therefore$ Auxiliary equations are $\frac{dx}{P} = \frac{dy}{Q} = \frac{dz}{R}.$

$$\therefore \quad \frac{dx}{y^2} = \frac{dy}{x^2} = \frac{dz}{x^2y^2z^2} \quad ...(1)$$

Taking the first two fractions of (1), we get $3x^2dx - 3y^2dy = 0$ ...(2)

Integrating (2), we get $x^3 - y^3 = C_1$ ...(3)

Taking the last two fractions of (1), we get $3y^2dy - 3z^{-2}dz = 0$ ...(4)

Integrating (4), we get $y^3 + 3z^{-1} = C_2$ ...(5)

From (3) and (5), the general solution of the given equation is $\mathbf{f(x^3 - y^3, y^3 + 3z^{-1}) = 0}$, where f is any arbitrary function.

(*iii*) We have $\frac{y^2z}{x}p + xzq = y^2.$

Here $P = \frac{y^2z}{x}, Q = xz, R = y^2$

$\therefore$ Auxiliary equations are $\frac{dx}{P} = \frac{dy}{Q} = \frac{dz}{R}.$

$$\therefore \quad \frac{xdx}{y^2z} = \frac{dy}{xz} = \frac{dz}{y^2} \quad ...(1)$$

Taking the first two fractions of (1), we get

$$x^2dx = y^2dy \quad \text{or} \quad 3x^2dx - 3y^2dy = 0 \quad ...(2)$$

Integrating (2), we have $x^3 - y^3 = C_1$ ...(3)

Taking the first and last fractions of (1), we get

$$xdx = zdz \quad \text{or} \quad 2xdx - 2zdz = 0 \qquad \text{...(4)}$$

Integrating (4), we have $x^2 - z^2 = C_2$ ...(5)

From (3) and (5), the general solution of the given equation is $\mathbf{f(x^3 - y^3, x^2 - z^2) = 0}$, where f is any arbitrary function.

(*iv*) We have $zp = x$. $\therefore$ $zp + 0.q = x$

Here $P = z, Q = 0, R = x$.

$\therefore$ Auxiliary equations are $\frac{dx}{P} = \frac{dy}{Q} = \frac{dz}{R}$.

$$\therefore \quad \frac{dx}{z} = \frac{dy}{0} = \frac{dz}{x} \qquad \text{...(1)}$$

Second fraction of (1) implies $dy = 0$

$$\therefore \quad y = C_1 \qquad \text{...(2)}$$

Taking the first and third fractions of (1), we get $xdx = zdz$

or $$2xdx - 2zdz = 0 \qquad \text{...(3)}$$

Integrating (3), we have $x^2 - z^2 = C_2$ ...(4)

From (2) and (4), the general solution of the given equation is $\mathbf{f(y, x^2 - z^2) = 0}$, where f is any arbitrary function.

(*v*) We have $(x^2 + 2y^2)\,p - xyq = xz$.

Here $P = x^2 + 2y^2, Q = -xy, R = xz$.

$\therefore$ Auxiliary equations are $\frac{dx}{P} = \frac{dy}{Q} = \frac{dz}{R}$.

$$\therefore \quad \frac{dx}{x^2 + 2y^2} = \frac{dy}{-xy} = \frac{dz}{xz} \qquad \text{...(1)}$$

Taking the first two fractions of (1), we get $\frac{dx}{x^2 + 2y^2} = \frac{dy}{-xy}$.

$$\Rightarrow \quad \frac{dx}{dy} = \frac{x^2 + 2y^2}{-xy} \quad \Rightarrow \quad 2x\frac{dx}{dy} = -\frac{2x^2}{y} - 4y$$

$$\Rightarrow \quad 2x\frac{dx}{dy} + x^2\left(\frac{2}{y}\right) = -4y \qquad \text{...(2)}$$

Let $z = x^2$.

$$\therefore \quad (2) \quad \Rightarrow \quad \frac{dz}{dy} + z\left(\frac{2}{y}\right) = -4y$$

This is a linear differential equation of order one.

$$\text{I.F.} = e^{\int \frac{2}{y} dy} = e^{2\log y} = y^2$$

$$\therefore \quad zy^2 = \int (-4y)\,y^2\,dy + C_1 \quad \text{or} \quad x^2y^2 + y^4 = C_1 \qquad \text{...(3)}$$

Taking the last two fractions of (1), we get $\frac{dy}{y} + \frac{dz}{z} = 0$ ...(4)

Integrating (4), we get $\log y + \log z = \log C_2$ or $yz = C_2$ ...(5)

From (3) and (5), the general solution of the given equation is $\mathbf{f(x^2y^2 + y^4, yz) = 0}$, where f is any arbitrary function.

Type II. In this type, we shall consider the solution of the equation $Pp + Qq = R$ for which the equality of two factors of the auxiliary equations $\frac{dx}{P} = \frac{dy}{Q} = \frac{dz}{R}$ gives an equation in the variables whose differentials are involved. Another independent solution of the auxiliary equations is found by using the first solution.

Example 2. *Find the general solution of the following Lagrange linear equations :*

(i) $p + 2q = 5z + \tan(y - 2x)$ (ii) $yp + xq = xyz^2 (x^2 - y^2)$

(iii) $xz(z^2 + xy) p - yz(z^2 + xy) q = x^4$ (iv) $z(p - q) = z^2 + (x + y)^2$.

Sol. (i) We have $p + 2q = 5z + \tan(y - 2x)$.

$\therefore$ Auxiliary equations are $\frac{dx}{1} = \frac{dy}{2} = \frac{dz}{5z + \tan(y - 2x)}$. ...(1)

Taking the first two fractions of (1), we get

$$dy - 2dx = 0 \qquad ...(2)$$

Integrating (2), we have $y - 2x = C_1$ ...(3)

Taking the last two fractions of (1) and using (3), we have

$$\frac{dy}{2} - \frac{dz}{5z + \tan C_1} = 0 \qquad ...(4)$$

Integrating (4), we have $\frac{1}{2}y - \frac{1}{5}\log|5z + \tan C_1| = C_2$

or $$5y - 2\log|5z + \tan(y - 2x)| = 10C_2 \qquad ...(5)$$

From (3) and (5), the general solution of the given equation is

$$\mathbf{f(y - 2x, 5y - 2\log|5z + \tan(y - 2x)|) = 0,}$$

where f is any arbitrary function.

(ii) We have $yp + xq = xyz^2 (x^2 - y^2)$.

$\therefore$ Auxiliary equations are $\frac{dx}{y} = \frac{dy}{x} = \frac{dz}{xyz^2(x^2 - y^2)}$. ...(1)

Taking the first two fractions of (1), we get $2xdx - 2ydy = 0$ ...(2)

Integrating (2), we have $x^2 - y^2 = C_1$ ...(3)

Taking the last two fractions of (1) and using (3), we have $ydy - \frac{dz}{C_1 z^2} = 0$ ...(4)

Integrating (4), we have $\frac{y^2}{2} - \frac{1}{C_1}\left(\frac{z^{-1}}{-1}\right) = C_2$

$$\Rightarrow \quad \frac{y^2}{2} + \frac{1}{z(x^2 - y^2)} = C_2 \qquad ...(5)$$

From (3) and (5), the general solution of the given equation is

$$\mathbf{f}\left(\mathbf{x}^2-\mathbf{y}^2, \frac{\mathbf{y}^2}{2}+\frac{1}{\mathbf{z}(\mathbf{x}^2-\mathbf{y}^2)}\right)=\mathbf{0}, \text{ where } f \text{ is any arbitrary function.}$$

(*iii*) We have $xz(z^2+xy)\,p - yz(z^2+xy)\,q = x^4$.

$\therefore$ Auxiliary equations are $\dfrac{dx}{xz(z^2+xy)}=\dfrac{dy}{-yz(z^2+xy)}=\dfrac{dz}{x^4}$. ...(1)

Taking the first two fractions of (1), we get $\dfrac{dx}{x}+\dfrac{dy}{y}=0$ ...(2)

Integrating (2), we have $\log x+\log y=\log C_1$ or $xy=C_1$ ...(3)

Taking the first and third fractions of (1) and using (3), we get $\dfrac{dx}{z(z^2+C_1)}=\dfrac{dz}{x^3}$

or $x^3dx-(z^3+C_1z)\,dz=0$ ...(4)

Integrating (4), we have $\dfrac{x^4}{4}-\left(\dfrac{z^4}{4}+\dfrac{C_1z^2}{2}\right)=C_2$

or $x^4-z^4-2xyz^2=4C_2$ ...(5)

From (3) and (5), the general solution of the given equation is $\mathbf{f(xy,\, x^4-z^4-2xyz^2)=0}$, where f is any arbitrary function.

(*iv*) We have $z(p-q)=z^2+(x+y)^2$.

$\Rightarrow$ $zp-zq=z^2+(x+y)^2$.

$\therefore$ Auxiliary equations are $\dfrac{dx}{z}=\dfrac{dy}{-z}=\dfrac{dz}{z^2+(x+y)^2}$. ...(1)

Taking the first two fractions of (1), we have $dx+dy=0$ ...(2)

Integrating, we have $x+y=C_1$ ...(3)

Taking the last two fractions of (1) and using (3), we have $dy+\dfrac{zdz}{z^2+C_1^2}=0$ ...(4)

Integrating (4), we get $y+\dfrac{1}{2}\log|z^2+C_1^2|=C_2$ or $y+\dfrac{1}{2}\log(z^2+(x+y)^2)=C_2$ ...(5)

From (3) and (5), the general solution of the given equation is

$$\mathbf{f}\left(\mathbf{x+y},\ \mathbf{y}+\frac{1}{2}\log\left(\mathbf{z}^2+(\mathbf{x+y})^2\right)\right)=\mathbf{0},$$

where f is any arbitrary function.

Type III. In this type, we shall consider the solution of the equation $Pp+Qq=R$ by using the formula :

$$\frac{dx}{P}=\frac{dy}{Q}=\frac{dz}{R}=\frac{P_1dx+Q_1dy+R_1dz}{P_1P+Q_1Q+R_1R},$$

where P_1, Q_1, R_1 are some functions of x, y and z. If for some choice of P_1, Q_1, R_1, the sum $P_1P+Q_1Q+R_1R$ is zero, then we have $P_1dx+Q_1dy+P_1dz=0$. We integrate this equation to get one solution of the auxiliary equations. P_1, Q_1, R_1 are called **multipliers**. By using different set of multipliers or by using two fractions of the auxiliary equations, we find another independent solution of the auxiliary equations.

Example 3. *Find the general solution of the following Lagrange linear equations*

(*i*) $x(y^2 - z^2)p + y(z^2 - x^2)q = z(x^2 - y^2)$ (*ii*) $x(y^2 + z)\,p - y(x^2 + z)\,q = z(x^2 - y^2)$

(*iii*) $(y^2 + z^2)p - xyq + xz = 0$ (*iv*) $(4y - 3z)p + (4x - 2z)q = 2y - 3x.$

Sol. (*i*) We have $x(y^2 - z^2)\,p + y(z^2 - x^2)\,q = z(x^2 - y^2).$

$\therefore$ Auxiliary equations are $\dfrac{dx}{x(y^2 - z^2)} = \dfrac{dy}{y(z^2 - x^2)} = \dfrac{dz}{z(x^2 - y^2)}$ ...(1)

Taking $\dfrac{1}{x}, \dfrac{1}{y}, \dfrac{1}{z}$ as multipliers, each fraction of (1)

$$= \frac{\frac{1}{x}dx + \frac{1}{y}dy + \frac{1}{z}dz}{(y^2 - z^2) + (z^2 - x^2) + (x^2 - y^2)} = \frac{\frac{1}{x}dx + \frac{1}{y}dy + \frac{1}{z}dz}{0}$$

$$\therefore \quad \frac{1}{x}dx + \frac{1}{y}dy + \frac{1}{z}dz = 0$$

Integrating, we get $\log|x| + \log|y| + \log|z| = \log C_1$

or $|xyz| = C_1$ or $xyz = \pm C_1$ ...(2)

Taking x, y, z as multipliers, each fraction of (1)

$$= \frac{xdx + ydy + zdz}{x^2(y^2 - z^2) + y^2(z^2 - x^2) + z^2(x^2 - y^2)} = \frac{xdx + ydy + zdz}{0}$$

$$\therefore \quad xdx + ydy + zdz = 0 \quad \text{or} \quad 2xdx + 2ydy + 2zdz = 0$$

Integrating, we get $x^2 + y^2 + z^2 = C_2$ ...(3)

From (2) and (3), the general solution of the given equation is $\mathbf{f(xyz, x^2 + y^2 + z^2) = 0}$, where f is any arbitrary function.

(*ii*) We have $x(y^2 + z)\,p - y(x^2 + z)\,q = z(x^2 - y^2).$

$\therefore$ Auxiliary equations are $\dfrac{dx}{x(y^2 + z)} = \dfrac{dy}{-y(x^2 + z)} = \dfrac{dz}{z(x^2 - y^2)}$ ...(1)

Taking $x, y, -1$ as multipliers, each fraction of (1)

$$= \frac{xdx + ydy + (-1)\,dz}{x^2(y^2 + z) - y^2(x^2 + z) - z(x^2 - y^2)} = \frac{xdx + ydy - dz}{0}$$

$$\therefore \quad 2xdx + 2ydy - 2dz = 0$$

Integrating, we get $x^2 + y^2 - 2z = C_1$ ...(2)

Taking $\dfrac{1}{x}, \dfrac{1}{y}, \dfrac{1}{z}$ as multiplier, each fraction of (1)

$$= \frac{\frac{1}{x}dx + \frac{1}{y}dy + \frac{1}{z}dz}{y^2 + z - x^2 - z + x^2 - y^2} = \frac{\frac{1}{x}dx + \frac{1}{y}dy + \frac{1}{z}dz}{0}$$

$$\therefore \quad \frac{1}{x}dx + \frac{1}{y}dy + \frac{1}{z}dz = 0$$

Integrating, we get $\log |x| + \log |y| + \log |z| = \log C_2$

or $$|xyz| = C_2 \quad \text{or} \quad xyz = \pm C_2 \qquad ...(3)$$

From (2) and (3), the general solution of the given equation is $\mathbf{f(x^2 + y^2 - 2z, xyz) = 0}$, where f is any arbitrary function.

(*iii*) We have $$(y^2 + z^2)\,p - xyq = -xz.$$

$\therefore$ Auxiliary equations are $$\frac{dx}{y^2 + z^2} = \frac{dy}{-xy} = \frac{dz}{-xz} \qquad ...(1)$$

Taking the last two fractions of (1), we get $\dfrac{dy}{y} - \dfrac{dz}{z} = 0$

Integrating, we have $\log |y| - \log |z| = \log C_1$

or $$\left|\frac{y}{z}\right| = C_1 \quad \text{or} \quad \frac{y}{z} = \pm C_1 \qquad ...(2)$$

Taking x, y, z as multipliers, each fraction of (1)

$$= \frac{xdx + ydy + zdz}{xy^2 + xz^2 - xy^2 - xz^2} = \frac{xdx + ydy + zdz}{0}$$

$\therefore$ $2xdx + 2ydy + 2zdz = 0$

Integrating, we have $x^2 + y^2 + z^2 = C_2$ ...(3)

From (2) and (3), the general solution of the given equation is $\mathbf{f(y/z, x^2 + y^2 + z^2) = 0}$, where f is any arbitrary function.

(*iv*) We have $(4y - 3z)\,p + (4x - 2z)\,q = 2y - 3x$.

$\therefore$ Auxiliary equations are $$\frac{dx}{4y - 3z} = \frac{dy}{4x - 2z} = \frac{dz}{2y - 3x} \qquad ...(1)$$

Taking a, b, c as multipliers, each fraction of (1)

$$= \frac{adx + bdy + cdz}{a(4y - 3z) + b(4x - 2z) + c(2y - 3x)}$$

Let $$a(4y - 3z) + b(4x - 2z) + c(2y - 3x) = 0 \qquad ...(2)$$

(2) $\Rightarrow$ $(4b - 3c)\,x + (4a + 2c)\,y + (-3a - 2b)\,z = 0$

Let $$4b - 3c = 0,\ 4a + 2c = 0,\ -3a - 2b = 0$$

$\Rightarrow$ $b : c = 3 : 4,\quad a : c = 1 : -2,\quad a : b = -2 : 3$

$\Rightarrow$ $a : b : c = -2 : 3 : 4$

$\therefore$ (2) is true for $a = -2,\ b = 3,\ c = 4$

$\therefore$ Each fraction of (1)

$$= \frac{-2dx + 3dy + 4dz}{-2(4y - 3z) + 3(4x - 2z) + 4(2y - 3x)} = \frac{-2dx + 3dy + 4dz}{0}$$

$\therefore$ $-2dx + 3dy + 4dz = 0$

Integrating, we have $-2x + 3y + 4z = C_1$ ...(3)

Also, (2) $\Rightarrow$ $4(ay + bx) - 3(az + cx) + 2(cy - bz) = 0$

Let $ay + bx = 0,\ az + cx = 0,\ cy - bz = 0$

$\therefore$ $a : b = -x : y,\quad a : c = -x : z,\quad b : c = y : z$

$\therefore$ $a : b : c = -x : y : z$

$\therefore$ (2) is true for $a = -x$, $b = y$, $c = z$.

$\therefore$ Each fraction of (1)

$$= \frac{-xdx + ydy + zdz}{-x(4y-3z)+y(4x-2z)+z(2y-3x)} = \frac{-xdx+ydy+zdz}{0}$$

$\therefore$ $-2xdx + 2ydy + 2zdz = 0$

Integrating, we get $-x^2 + y^2 + z^2 = C_2$ ...(4)

From (3) and (4), the general solution of the given equation is

$$\mathbf{f(-2x + 3y + 4z, -x^2 + y^2 + z^2) = 0,}$$

where f is any arbitrary function.

Type IV. In this type, we shall consider the solution of the equation $Pp + Qq = R$ by using the formula :

$$\frac{dx}{P} = \frac{dy}{Q} = \frac{dz}{R} = \frac{P_1dx + Q_1dy + R_1dz}{P_1P + Q_1Q + R_1R},$$

where P_1, Q_1, R_1 are some functions of x, y and z. If for some choice of P_1, Q_1, R_1, the sum $P_1dx + Q_1dy + R_1dz$ is exact differential of a factor of $P_1P + Q_1Q + R_1R$, then the quotient $\dfrac{P_1dx + Q_1dy + R_1dz}{P_1P + Q_1Q + R_1R}$ is equated with a suitable fraction of auxiliary equations to get one solution of the auxiliary equations. By using different set of multipliers or by using two fractions of the auxiliary equations, we find another independent solution of the auxiliary equations.

Example 4. *Find the general solution of the following Lagrange linear equations :*

(*i*) $(x^2 - yz)p + (y^2 - zx)q = z^2 - xy$ (*ii*) $(y + z)p + (z + x)q = x + y$

(MDU 2005)

(*iii*) $p \cos(x + y) + q \sin(x + y) = z + \dfrac{1}{z}$ (*iv*) $(y^2 + yz + z^2)p + (z^2 + zx + x^2)q = x^2 + xy + y^2$.

Sol. (*i*) We have $(x^2 - yz)p + (y^2 - zx)q = z^2 - xy$.

$\therefore$ Auxiliary equations are $\dfrac{dx}{x^2 - yz} = \dfrac{dy}{y^2 - zx} = \dfrac{dz}{z^2 - xy}$ ...(1)

Taking 1, 1, 1 and x, y, z as multipliers, each fraction of (1)

$$= \frac{1.dx + 1.dy + 1.dz}{x^2 - yz + y^2 - zx + z^2 - xy} = \frac{xdx + ydy + zdz}{x^3 - xyz + y^3 - xyz + z^3 - xyz}$$

$$\Rightarrow \frac{dx + dy + dz}{x^2 + y^2 + z^2 - yz - zx - xy} = \frac{xdx + ydy + zdz}{(x + y + z)(x^2 + y^2 + z^2 - yz - zx - xy)}$$

$$\Rightarrow (x + y + z)\,d(x + y + z) = \frac{1}{2}(2xdx + 2ydy + 2zdz)$$

$$\Rightarrow (x + y + z)\,d(x + y + z) - \frac{1}{2}d(x^2 + y^2 + z^2) = 0$$

Integrating, we get $\dfrac{1}{2}(x + y + z)^2 - \dfrac{1}{2}(x^2 + y^2 + z^2) = C_1$

or $xy + yz + zx = C_1$ ...(2)

Taking 1, – 1, 0 and 0, 1, – 1 as multipliers, each fraction of (1)

$$= \frac{dx - dy + 0}{(x^2 - yz) - (y^2 - zx) + 0} = \frac{0 + dy - dz}{0 + (y^2 - zx) - (z^2 - xy)}$$

$$\Rightarrow \quad \frac{dx - dy}{x^2 - y^2 + z(x - y)} = \frac{dy - dz}{y^2 - z^2 + x(y - z)}$$

$$\Rightarrow \quad \frac{dx - dy}{(x - y)(x + y + z)} = \frac{dy - dz}{(y - z)(y + z + x)} \quad \Rightarrow \quad \frac{d(x - y)}{x - y} - \frac{d(y - z)}{y - z} = 0$$

Integrating, we get $\log | x - y | - \log | y - z | = \log C_2$

or $$\left| \frac{x - y}{y - z} \right| = C_2 \quad \text{or} \quad \frac{x - y}{y - z} = \pm C_2 \qquad ...(3)$$

From (2) and (3), the general solution of the given equation is $f\left(xy + yz + zx, \frac{x - y}{y - z}\right) = 0$,

where f is any arbitrary function.

(*ii*) We have $(y + z)\, p + (z + x)\, q = x + y.$

∴ Auxiliary equations are $$\frac{dx}{y + z} = \frac{dy}{z + x} = \frac{dz}{x + y} \qquad ...(1)$$

Taking 1, – 1, 0 and 0, 1, – 1 as multipliers, each fraction of (1)

$$= \frac{dx - dy + 0}{(y + z) - (z + x) + 0} = \frac{0 + dy - dz}{0 + (z + x) - (x + y)} \qquad ...(2)$$

$$\Rightarrow \quad \frac{dx - dy}{-(x - y)} = \frac{dy - dz}{-(y - z)} \quad \Rightarrow \quad \frac{d(x - y)}{x - y} - \frac{d(y - z)}{y - z} = 0$$

Integrating, we get $\log | x - y | - \log | y - z | = \log C_1$

$$\Rightarrow \quad \left| \frac{x - y}{y - z} \right| = C_1 \quad \text{or} \quad \frac{x - y}{y - z} = \pm C_1 \qquad ...(3)$$

Taking 1, – 1, 0 and 1, 1, 1 as multipliers, each fraction of (1) and (2)

$$\frac{dx - dy + 0}{(y + z) - (z + x) + 0} = \frac{dx + dy + dz}{(y + z) + (z + x) + (x + y)}$$

$$\therefore \quad \frac{d(x - y)}{-(x - y)} = \frac{d(x + y + z)}{2(x + y + z)} \quad \text{or} \quad 2\frac{d(x - y)}{x - y} + \frac{d(x + y + z)}{x + y + z} = 0$$

Integrating, we get $2 \log | x - y | + \log | x + y + z | = \log C_2$

$\Rightarrow \quad (x - y)^2 \, | x + y + z | = C_2 \quad \Rightarrow \quad (x - y)^2 (x + y + z) = \pm C_2$ ...(4)

From (3) and (4), the general solution of the given equation is

$$\mathbf{f}\left(\frac{\mathbf{x - y}}{\mathbf{y - z}}, (\mathbf{x - y})^2 (\mathbf{x + y + z})\right) = 0,$$

where f is any arbitrary function.

(*iii*) We have $p \cos (x + y) + q \sin (x + y) = z + \dfrac{1}{z}.$

$\therefore$ Auxiliary equations are $\dfrac{dx}{\cos(x+y)} = \dfrac{dy}{\sin(x+y)} = \dfrac{dz}{z+\dfrac{1}{z}}$ ...(1)

Taking 1, 1, 0 and 1, – 1, 0 as multipliers, each fraction of (1)

$$= \frac{dx + dy + 0}{\cos(x+y) + \sin(x+y) + 0} = \frac{dx - dy + 0}{\cos(x+y) - \sin(x+y) + 0} \qquad ...(2)$$

(1) and (2) $\Rightarrow \dfrac{zdz}{z^2+1} = \dfrac{d(x+y)}{\cos(x+y)+\sin(x+y)}$

$\Rightarrow \dfrac{1}{2} \cdot \dfrac{2zdz}{z^2+1} = \dfrac{dt}{\cos t + \sin t} = \dfrac{dt}{\sqrt{2}\sin(t+\pi/4)}$, where $t = x + y$.

$\Rightarrow \dfrac{1}{\sqrt{2}} \cdot \dfrac{2z}{z^2+1} dz - \operatorname{cosec}\left(t + \dfrac{\pi}{4}\right) dt = 0$

Integrating, we get $\dfrac{1}{\sqrt{2}} \log|z^2+1| - \log \tan \dfrac{1}{2}\left(t + \dfrac{\pi}{4}\right) = \log C_1$

$$\Rightarrow \frac{(z^2+1)^{1/\sqrt{2}}}{\tan\left(\dfrac{x+y}{2} + \dfrac{\pi}{8}\right)} = C_1 \qquad ...(3)$$

Also, (2) $\Rightarrow \dfrac{\cos(x+y) - \sin(x+y)}{\cos(x+y) + \sin(x+y)} d(x+y) = d(x-y)$

$\Rightarrow \dfrac{\cos t - \sin t}{\cos t + \sin t} dt - d(x-y) = 0$, where $t = x + y$.

Integrating, we get $\log|\cos t + \sin t| - (x - y) = \log C_2$

$\Rightarrow |\cos t + \sin t|\, e^{y-x} = C_2$

$$\Rightarrow (\cos(x+y) + \sin(x+y))\, e^{y-x} = \pm C_2 \qquad ...(4)$$

From (3) and (4), the general solution of the given equation is

$$\mathbf{f}\left(\frac{(\mathbf{z}^2+1)^{1/\sqrt{2}}}{\tan\left(\dfrac{\mathbf{x}+\mathbf{y}}{2} + \dfrac{\pi}{8}\right)}, (\cos(\mathbf{x}+\mathbf{y}) + \sin(\mathbf{x}+\mathbf{y}))\, \mathbf{e}^{\mathbf{y}-\mathbf{x}}\right) = 0,$$

where f is any arbitrary function.

(*iv*) We have $(y^2 + yz + z^2)p + (z^2 + zx + x^2)q = x^2 + xy + y^2$.

$\therefore$ Auxiliary equations are $\dfrac{dx}{y^2+yz+z^2} = \dfrac{dy}{z^2+zx+x^2} = \dfrac{dz}{x^2+xy+y^2}$ ...(1)

Taking 1, – 1, 0 and 0, 1, – 1 as multipliers, each fraction of (1)

$$= \frac{dx - dy + 0}{(y^2+yz+z^2) - (z^2+zx+x^2) + 0} = \frac{0 + dy - dz}{0 + (z^2+zx+x^2) - (x^2+xy+y^2)}$$

$$\Rightarrow \quad \frac{dx - dy}{y^2 - x^2 + yz - zx} = \frac{dy - dz}{z^2 - y^2 + zx - xy}$$

$$\Rightarrow \quad \frac{dx - dy}{(y - x)(y + x + z)} = \frac{dy - dz}{(z - y)(z + y + x)}$$

$$\Rightarrow \quad \frac{d(x - y)}{-(x - y)} = \frac{d(y - z)}{-(y - z)} \quad \Rightarrow \quad \frac{d(y - z)}{y - z} - \frac{d(x - y)}{x - y} = 0$$

Integrating, we get $\log |y - z| - \log |x - y| = \log C_1$

$$\Rightarrow \quad \left|\frac{y - z}{x - y}\right| = C_1 \quad \text{or} \quad \frac{y - z}{x - y} = \pm C_1 \qquad ...(2)$$

Taking 1, – 1, 0 and 1, 0, – 1 as multipliers, each fraction of (1)

$$= \frac{dx - dy}{(y^2 + yz + z^2) - (z^2 + zx + x^2)} = \frac{dx - dz}{(y^2 + yz + z^2) - (x^2 + xy + y^2)}$$

$$\Rightarrow \quad \frac{dx - dy}{y^2 - x^2 + yz - zx} = \frac{dx - dz}{z^2 - x^2 + yz - xy}$$

$$\Rightarrow \quad \frac{dx - dy}{(y - x)(y + x + z)} = \frac{dx - dz}{(z - x)(z + x + y)}$$

$$\Rightarrow \quad \frac{dx - dy}{-(x - y)} = \frac{dx - dz}{-(x - z)} \quad \Rightarrow \quad \frac{d(x - z)}{x - z} - \frac{d(x - y)}{x - y} = 0$$

Integrating, we get $\log |x - z| - \log |x - y| = \log C_2$.

$$\Rightarrow \quad \left|\frac{x - z}{x - y}\right| = C_2 \quad \text{or} \quad \frac{x - z}{x - y} = \pm C_2 \qquad ...(3)$$

From (2) and (3), the general solution of the given equation is $\mathbf{f\left(\frac{y - z}{x - y}, \frac{x - z}{x - y}\right) = 0}$, where f is any arbitrary function.

EXERCISE 1

Find the general solution of the following Lagrange linear equations :

1. (*i*) $p + q = \sin x$ (*ii*) $ap + bq = c$
   (*iii*) $p \tan x + q \tan y = \tan z$ (*iv*) $yzp + zxq = xy$ (*KU 2005*)
   (*v*) $xp + yq = z$ (*vi*) $x^2p + y^2q = z^2$
   (*vii*) $(x - a)p + (y - b)q = z - c$ (*viii*) $y^2p - xyq = x(z - 2y)$
2. (*i*) $p - 2q = 3x^2 \sin(y + 2x)$ (*ii*) $p + 3q = z + \cot(y - 3x)$ (*MDU 2006*)
   (*iii*) $zp - zq = x + y$ (*iv*) $y^3q - xy^2p = axz$
   (*v*) $xyp + y^2q + 2x^2 - xyz = 0$ (*vi*) $(p - q)(x + y) = z$
   (*vii*) $z(xy + z^2)(px - qy) = x^4$ (*viii*) $xzp + yzq = xy$
3. (*i*) $(z - y)p + (x - z)q = y - x$ (*ii*) $x(y - z)p + y(z - x)q = z(x - y)$
   (*iii*) $\left(\frac{1}{z} - \frac{1}{y}\right)p + \left(\frac{1}{x} - \frac{1}{z}\right)q = \frac{1}{y} - \frac{1}{x}$ (*iv*) $x^2(y - z)p + y^2(z - x)q = z^2(x - y)$

(v) $\left(\frac{b-c}{a}\right)yzp + \left(\frac{c-a}{b}\right)zxq = \left(\frac{a-b}{c}\right)xy$ (vi) $z(x+y)p + z(x-y)q = x^2 + y^2$

(vii) $x(y^2 - z^2)p - y(z^2 + x^2)q = z(x^2 + y^2)$ (viii) $(x - y)p + (x + y)q = 2xz$

4. (i) $(x^2 - y^2 - z^2)p + 2xyq = 2xz$ (ii) $(1 + y)p + (1 + x)q = z$

(iii) $(x^2 - y^2 - yz)p + (x^2 - y^2 - zx)q = z(x - y)$ (iv) $xzp + yzq = xy$

(v) $x(x + y)p - y(x + y)q + (x - y)(2x + 2y + z) = 0$

(vi) $\big(y(x+y)+az\big)p + \big(x(x+y)-az\big)q = z(x+y)$

(vii) $xp + zq + y = 0$ (MDU 2004) (viii) $(x^2 + y^2)p + 2xyq = (x + y)z$.

Answers

1. (i) $f(x - y, z + \cos x) = 0$ (ii) $f(bx - ay, cy - bz) = 0$

(iii) $f\left(\frac{\sin x}{\sin y}, \frac{\sin x}{\sin z}\right) = 0$ (iv) $f(x^2 - y^2, x^2 - z^2) = 0$

(v) $f\left(\frac{x}{y}, \frac{y}{z}\right) = 0$ (vi) $f\left(\frac{1}{y} - \frac{1}{x}, \frac{1}{z} - \frac{1}{y}\right) = 0$

(vii) $f\left(\frac{x-a}{y-b}, \frac{y-b}{z-c}\right) = 0$ (viii) $f(x^2 + y^2, yz - y^2) = 0$

2. (i) $f(2x + y, x^3 \sin(2x + y) - z) = 0$ (ii) $f\,(y - 3x, x - \log|z + \cot(y - 3x)|) = 0$

(iii) $f(x + y, 2(x + y)x - z^2) = 0$ (iv) $f\left(xy, \log|z| + \frac{ax}{3y^2}\right) = 0$

(v) $f\left(\frac{x}{y}, x - \log\left|z - \frac{2x}{y}\right|\right) = 0$ (vi) $f(x + y, x - (x + y)\log|z|) = 0$

(vii) $f(xy, x^4 - 2xyz^2 - z^4) = 0$ (viii) $f\left(xy - z^2, \frac{x}{y}\right) = 0$

3. (i) $f(x + y + z, x^2 + y^2 + z^2) = 0$ (ii) $f(x + y + z, xyz) = 0$

(iii) $f(x + y + z, xyz) = 0$ (iv) $f\left(xyz, \frac{1}{x} + \frac{1}{y} + \frac{1}{z}\right) = 0$

(v) $f(ax^2 + by^2 + cz^2, a^2x^2 + b^2y^2 + c^2z^2) = 0$ (vi) $f(2xy - z^2, x^2 - y^2 - z^2) = 0$

(vii) $f(x^2 + y^2 + z^2, x/yz) = 0$ (viii) $f\left(x + y - \log|z|, (x^2 + y^2)e^{-2\tan^{-1}(y/x)}\right) = 0$

4. (i) $f\left(\frac{y}{z}, \frac{x^2 + y^2 + z^2}{z}\right) = 0$ (ii) $f\left((1 + x)^2 - (1 + y)^2, \frac{x + y + 2}{z}\right) = 0$

(iii) $f\left(z - x + y, \frac{x^2 - y^2}{z^2}\right) = 0$ (iv) $f\left(\frac{x}{y}, xy - z^2\right) = 0$

(v) $f\,(xy, (x + y)(x + y + z)) = 0$ (vi) $f\left(\frac{x + y}{z}, x^2 - y^2 - 2az\right) = 0$

(vii) $f\left(y^2 + z^2, \frac{x}{e^{\tan^{-1}(y/z)}}\right) = 0$ (viii) $f\left(\frac{y}{x^2 - y^2}, \frac{x + y}{z}\right) = 0$.

Hints

3. (*vi*) Try $x, -y, -z$ and $y, x, -z$ as multipliers.

(*vii*) Try x, y, z and $1/x, -1/y, -1/z$ as multipliers.

4. (*i*) Try x, y, z as multipliers. (*ii*) Try 1, 1, 0 as multipliers.

(*iii*) Try 1, – 1, 0 and $x, -y, 0$ as multipliers. (*iv*) Try $1/x, 1/y, 0$ as multipliers.

(*v*) Try 1, 1, 0 and 1, 1, 1 as multipliers. (*vi*) Try 1, 1, 0 and $x, -y, 0$ as multipliers.

(*vii*) We have $\dfrac{dx}{x} = \dfrac{0 + z\,dy - y\,dz}{z^2 + y^2} = \dfrac{\dfrac{1}{z}\,dy + \left(-\dfrac{y}{z^2}\right)dz}{1 + \left(\dfrac{y}{z}\right)^2} = \dfrac{d(y/z)}{1 + (y/z)^2}$

$$\therefore \quad \log|x| - \tan^{-1}\frac{y}{z} = \log C.$$

(*viii*) Try 1, 1, 0 and 1, – 1, 0 as multipliers.

12

Partial Differential Equations of the First Order

(Equations Non-linear in p and q)

1. INTRODUCTION

By now we have learnt the method of solving first order partial differential equations which are linear in partial derivatives p and q. A partial differential equation of first order need not be linear in p and q. In the present chapter, we shall study the methods of solving such equations. In the first part, we shall study the method of solving some special types of equations which can be solved easily by methods other than the general method. In the second part, we shall take up **Charpit's general method** of solution.

2. SPECIAL TYPE I : EQUATIONS CONTAINING ONLY p AND q

Let $$g(p, q) = 0 \qquad \ldots(1)$$
be a partial differential equation of first order and containing only p and q.

Let $$z = ax + \phi(a)\, y + c \qquad \ldots(2)$$
be the complete solution of (1), where $\phi(a)$ is some function of a.

$$(2) \quad \Rightarrow \quad p = \frac{\partial z}{\partial x} = a \quad \text{and} \quad q = \frac{\partial z}{\partial y} = \phi(a)$$

$\therefore$ (1) $\Rightarrow$ $g(a, \phi(a)) = 0$.

$\therefore$ Complete solution of (1) is

$$\mathbf{z = ax + \phi(a)\, y + c,}$$

where $g(a, \phi(a)) = 0$ and a, c are arbitrary constants.

To find the singular solution, let

$$f(x, y, z, a, c) = z - ax - \phi(a)\, y - c$$

$\therefore$ Using $f(x, y, z, a, c) = 0$, $\dfrac{\partial f}{\partial a} = 0$, $\dfrac{\partial f}{\partial c} = 0$, the singular solution is given by eliminating a and c from the equations :

$$z - ax - \phi(a)\, y - c = 0, \quad -x - \phi'(a)\, y = 0, \quad -1 = 0$$

This is impossible, because $-1 \neq 0$.

$\therefore$ There is no singular solution.

To find the general solution, let $c = \psi(a)$, where ψ is any arbitrary function.

$\therefore$ Using $f(x, y, z, a, \psi(a)) = 0$, $\dfrac{\partial f}{\partial a} = 0$, the general solution is given by

$$\mathbf{z - ax - \phi(a)\, y - \psi(a) = 0, \; - x - \phi'(a)\, y - \psi'(a) = 0.}$$

Example 1. *Solve the following partial differential equations :*

(*i*) $p^2 + q^2 = \lambda^2$ (*ii*) $p^2 - q^2 = k^2$

(*iii*) $p = 2q^2 + 1$ (*iv*) $p^2 + 6p + 2q + 4 = 0$.

Sol. (*i*) We have $p^2 + q^2 = \lambda^2$. ...(1)

This equation is of the form $g(p, q) = 0$.

Let $z = ax + \phi(a)\, y + c$ ...(2)

be the complete solution of (1), where $\phi(a)$ is some function of a.

$$(2) \Rightarrow \quad p = \frac{\partial z}{\partial x} = a \text{ and } q = \frac{\partial z}{\partial y} = \phi(a)$$

$$\therefore \quad (1) \Rightarrow \quad a^2 + (\phi(a))^2 = \lambda^2 \text{ or } \phi(a) = \pm\sqrt{\lambda^2 - a^2}$$

Let $\phi(a) = \sqrt{\lambda^2 - a^2}$ and $-\lambda \le a \le \lambda$.

$\therefore$ The complete solution is $\mathbf{z = ax + \sqrt{\lambda^2 - a^2}\, y + c}$, where a and c are arbitrary constants and $-\lambda \le a \le \lambda$. There is no singular solution.

To find the general solution, let $f(x, y, z, a, c) = z - ax - \sqrt{\lambda^2 - a^2}\, y - c$ and $c = \psi(a)$.

$\therefore$ Using $f(x, y, z, a, \psi(a)) = 0$, $\dfrac{\partial f}{\partial a} = 0$, the general solution is given by the equations :

$$\mathbf{z - ax - \sqrt{\lambda^2 - a^2}\, y - \psi(a) = 0,\ -x + \frac{a}{\sqrt{\lambda^2 - a^2}}\, y - \psi'(a) = 0,}$$

where ψ is any arbitrary function.

(*ii*) We have $p^2 - q^2 = k^2$. ...(1)

This equation is of the form $g(p, q) = 0$.

Let $z = ax + \phi(a)\, y + c$ ...(2)

be the complete solution of (1), where $\phi(a)$ is some function of a.

$$(2) \Rightarrow \quad p = \frac{\partial z}{\partial x} = a \text{ and } q = \frac{\partial z}{\partial y} = \phi(a)$$

$$\therefore \quad (1) \Rightarrow \quad a^2 - (\phi(a))^2 = k^2 \text{ or } \phi(a) = \pm\sqrt{a^2 - k^2}$$

Let $\phi(a) = \sqrt{a^2 - k^2}$ and $a^2 \ge k^2$.

$\therefore$ The complete solution is $\mathbf{z = ax + \sqrt{a^2 - k^2}\, y + c}$, where a and c are arbitrary constants and $a^2 \ge k^2$.

There is no singular solution.

To find the general solution, let

$$f(x, y, z, a, c) = z - ax - \sqrt{a^2 - k^2}\, y - c \text{ and } c = \psi(a).$$

$\therefore$ Using $f(x, y, z, a, \psi(a)) = 0$, $\dfrac{\partial f}{\partial a} = 0$, the general solution is given by the equations :

$$z - ax - \sqrt{a^2 - k^2}\ y - \psi(a) = 0,\ -x - \frac{a}{\sqrt{a^2 - k^2}}\ y - \psi'(a) = 0,$$

where ψ is any arbitrary function.

(*iii*) We have $p = 2q^2 + 1.$ ...(1)

This equation is of the form $g(p, q) = 0.$

Let $z = ax + \phi(a)\, y + c$ ...(2)

be the complete solution of (1), where $\phi(a)$ is some function of a.

$$(2) \Rightarrow \quad p = \frac{\partial z}{\partial x} = a \text{ and } q = \frac{\partial z}{\partial y} = \phi(a)$$

$$\therefore \quad (1) \Rightarrow \quad a = 2(\phi(a))^2 + 1 \text{ or } \phi(a) = \pm\sqrt{\frac{a-1}{2}}.$$

Let $\phi(a) = \sqrt{\frac{a-1}{2}}$ and $a \geq 1.$

$\therefore$ The complete solution is $z = ax + \sqrt{\frac{a-1}{2}}\ y + c$, where a and c are arbitrary constants and $a \geq 1$.

There is no singular solution. To find the general solution, let

$$f(x, y, z, a, c) = z - ax - \sqrt{\frac{a-1}{2}}\ y - c \text{ and } c = \psi(a).$$

$\therefore$ Using $f(x, y, z, a, \psi(a)) = 0$, $\frac{\partial f}{\partial a} = 0$, the general solution is given by the equations :

$$z - ax - \sqrt{\frac{a-1}{2}}\ y - \psi(a) = 0,\ -x - \frac{1}{2\sqrt{2}\sqrt{a-1}}\ y - \psi'(a) = 0,$$

where ψ is any arbitrary function.

(*iv*) We have $p^2 + 6p + 2q + 4 = 0.$ ...(1)

This equation is of the form $g(p, q) = 0.$

Let $z = ax + \phi(a)\, y + c$ ...(2)

be the complete solution of (1) where $\phi(a)$ is some function of a

$$(2) \Rightarrow \quad p = \frac{\partial z}{\partial x} = a \text{ and } q = \frac{\partial z}{\partial y} = \phi(a)$$

$$\therefore \quad (1) \Rightarrow \quad a^2 + 6a + 2\phi(a) + 4 = 0 \text{ or } \phi(a) = -\left(\frac{a^2}{2} + 3a + 2\right)$$

$\therefore$ The complete solution is $z = ax - \left(\frac{a^2}{2} + 3a + 2\right) y + c$, where a and c are arbitrary constants.

There is no singular solution. To find the general solution, let

$$f(x, y, z, a, c) = z - ax + \left(\frac{a^2}{2} + 3a + 2\right) y - c \text{ and } c = \psi(a).$$

$\therefore$ Using $f(x, y, z, a, \psi(a)) = 0, \dfrac{\partial f}{\partial a} = 0$, the general solution is given by the equations :

$$z - ax + \left(\frac{a^2}{2} + 3a + 2\right)y - \psi(a) = 0, -x + (a+3)y - \psi'(a) = 0,$$

where ψ is any arbitrary function.

WORKING RULES FOR SOLVING g(p, q) = 0

Step I. Take complete solution as $z = ax + \phi(a)y + c$ where a and c are arbitrary constants.

Step II. Find $p = \dfrac{\partial z}{\partial x} = a, \quad q = \dfrac{\partial z}{\partial y} = \phi(a)$.

Step III. Substitute the values of p and q in $g(p, q) = 0$ and find the value of $\phi(a)$ in terms of a. Put the value of $\phi(a)$ in the complete solution $z = ax + \phi(a)y + c$.

Step IV. For general solution take $f(x, y, z, a, c) = z - ax - \phi(a)y - c$, and $c = \psi(a)$. Differentiate 'f' partially w.r.t. a and write the general solution as $f(x, y, z, a, \psi(a)) = 0, \dfrac{\partial f}{\partial a} = 0$, *i.e.* $z - ax - \phi(a)y - \psi(a) = 0, -x - \phi'(a)y - \psi'(a) = 0$, where ψ is any arbitrary function.

Step V. Equation of the form $g(p, q) = 0$ has no singular solution.

EXERCISE 1

Solving the following partial differential equations.

1. $p^2 + q^2 = 16$
2. $p = q^2$
3. $p^2 - q^2 = 1$
4. $p + q = pq$
5. $p^2 + p = q^2$
6. $p + q + pq = 0$
7. $p = e^q$
8. $p^2 + q^2 = npq$
9. $p^2q^3 = 1$
10. $pq = k$.

Answers

1. **C.S.** $z = ax - \sqrt{16 - a^2}\, y + c$, where a and c are arbitrary constant and $-4 \le a \le 4$.
   S.S. No singular solution.
   G.S. $z - ax - \sqrt{16 - a^2} - \psi(a) = 0, -x + \dfrac{a}{\sqrt{16 - a^2}} y - \psi'(a) = 0$, where ψ is any arbitrary function.

2. **C.S.** $z = ax + \sqrt{a}\, y + c$, where a and c are arbitrary constants and $a \ge 0$.
   S.S. No singular solution.
   G.S. $z - ax - \sqrt{a}\, y - \psi(a) = 0, -x - \dfrac{1}{2\sqrt{a}} y - \psi'(a) = 0$, where ψ is any arbitrary function.

3. **C.S.** $z = ax + \sqrt{a^2 - 1}\, y + c$, where a and c are arbitrary constants and $|a| \ge 1$
   S.S. No singular solution.

G.S. $z - ax - \sqrt{a^2 - 1}\, y - \psi(a) = 0, - x - \dfrac{a}{\sqrt{a^2 - 1}} y - \psi'(a) = 0$, where ψ is any arbitrary function.

4. **C.S.** $z = ax + \dfrac{a}{a-1} y + c$ where a and c are arbitrary constants and $a \neq 1$.

S.S. No singular solution.

G.S. $z - ax - \dfrac{a}{a-1} y - \psi(a) = 0, - x + \dfrac{1}{(a-1)^2} y - \psi'(a) = 0$, where ψ is any arbitrary function.

5. **C.S.** $z = ax + \sqrt{a^2 + a}\, y + c$, where a and c are arbitrary constants and $a \in \mathbf{R} - (-1, 0)$.
S.S. No singular solution.

G.S. $z - ax - \sqrt{a^2 + a}\, y - \psi(a) = 0, - x - \dfrac{2a + 1}{2\sqrt{a^2 + a}} y - \psi'(a) = 0$, where ψ is any arbitrary function.

6. **C.S.** $z = ax - \dfrac{a}{a+1} y + c$ where a and c are arbitrary constants and $a \neq -1$.

S.S. No singular solution.

G.S. $z - ax + \dfrac{a}{a+1} y - \psi(a) = 0, - x + \dfrac{1}{(a+1)^2} y - \psi'(a) = 0$, where ψ is any arbitrary function.

7. **C.S.** $z = ax + y \log a + c$ where a and c are arbitrary constants and $a > 0$.
S.S. No singular solution.

G.S. $z - ax - y \log a - \psi(a) = 0, - x - \dfrac{y}{a} - \psi'(a) = 0$, where ψ is any arbitrary function.

8. **C.S.** $z = ax + \dfrac{a}{2}\left(n + \sqrt{n^2 - 4}\right) y + c$, where a and c are arbitrary constants.

S.S. No singular solution.

G.S. $z - ax - \dfrac{a}{2}\left(n + \sqrt{n^2 - 4}\right) y - \psi(a) = 0, - x - \dfrac{1}{2}\left(n + \sqrt{n^2 - 4}\right) y - \psi'(a) = 0$, where ψ is any arbitrary function.

9. **C.S.** $z = ax + a^{-2/3} y + c$, where a and c are arbitrary constants and $a \neq 0$.
S.S. No singular solution.

G.S. $z - ax - a^{-2/3} y - \psi(a) = 0, - x + \dfrac{2}{3} a^{-5/3} y - \psi'(a) = 0$, where ψ is any arbitrary function.

10. **C.S.** $z = ax + \dfrac{k}{a} y + c$, where a and c are arbitrary constants and $a \neq 0$.

S.S. No singular solution.

G.S. $z - ax - \dfrac{k}{a} y - \psi(a) = 0, - x + \dfrac{k}{a^2} y - \psi'(a) = 0$, where ψ is any arbitrary function.

---

3. SPECIAL TYPE II : EQUATIONS OF THE FORM z = px + qy + g(p, q)

Consider the equation $z = px + qy + g(p, q)$. ...(1)

Let $z = ax + by + c$ ...(2)

be a solution of (1).

(2) $\Rightarrow$ $$p = \frac{\partial z}{\partial x} = a \quad \text{and} \quad q = \frac{\partial z}{\partial y} = b$$

$\therefore$ (1) $\Rightarrow$ $ax + by + c = ax + by + g(a, b)$

$\Rightarrow$ $c = g(a, b)$

$\therefore$ (2) $\Rightarrow$ $z = ax + by + g(a, b)$.

$\therefore$ Complete solution of (1) is

$\mathbf{z = ax + by + g(a, b)}$, where a and b are arbitrary constants.

To find the singular solution, let $f(x, y, z, a, b) = z - ax - by - g(a, b)$.

$\because$ Using $f(x, y, z, a, b) = 0$, $\frac{\partial f}{\partial a} = 0$, $\frac{\partial f}{\partial b} = 0$, the singular solution is given by eliminating a and b from the equations :

$\mathbf{z - ax - by - g(a, b) = 0}$, $\mathbf{-x - \frac{\partial g}{\partial a} = 0}$, $\mathbf{-y - \frac{\partial g}{\partial b} = 0}$, provided it satisfies the given equation.

To find the general solution, let $b = \psi(a)$, where ψ is any arbitrary function.

$\therefore$ Using $f(x, y, z, a, \psi(a)) = 0$, $\frac{\partial f}{\partial a} = 0$, the general solution is given by

$$\mathbf{z - ax - \psi(a)y - g(a, \psi(a)) = 0, \ -x - \psi'(a)\,y - g'(a, \psi(a)) = 0.}$$

Remark. The partial differential equation $z = px + qy + g(p, q)$ is analogous to the **Clairaut's equation** $z = px + f(p)$. The equation $z = px + qy + g(p, q)$ is known **as extended Clairaut's equation.**

Example 1. *Solve the following partial differential equations :*

(*i*) $z = px + qy + pq$ (*ii*) $z = px + qy + p^2q^2$

(*iii*) $z = px + qy + 4\sqrt{1 + p^2 + q^2}$ (*iv*) $z = px + qy + \log(pq)$. (KU 2006)

Sol. (*i*) We have $z = px + qy + pq$. ...(1)

This equation is of the form $z = px + qy + g(p, q)$.

$\therefore$ Complete solution of (1) is $\mathbf{z = ax + by + ab}$, where a and b are arbitrary constants.

To find the singular solution, let

$$f(x, y, z, a, b) = z - ax - by - ab$$

$\therefore$ $$\frac{\partial f}{\partial a} = -x - b \quad \text{and} \quad \frac{\partial f}{\partial b} = -y - a$$

$\therefore$ $f(x, y, z, a, b) = 0 \Rightarrow z - ax - by - ab = 0$ ...(2)

$\frac{\partial f}{\partial a} = 0 \Rightarrow -x - b = 0$ ...(3)

$\frac{\partial f}{\partial b} = 0 \Rightarrow -y - a = 0$ ...(4)

Putting the values of a and b from (3) and (4) in (2), we get

$z - (-y)x - (-x)y - (-y)(-x) = 0$ or $z + xy = 0$ and it also satisfies (1).

$\therefore$ Singular solution is $\mathbf{z + xy = 0}$.

To find the general solution, let $b = \psi(a)$.

$\therefore$ Using $f(x, y, z, a, \psi(a)) = 0$, $\frac{\partial f}{\partial a} = 0$, the general solution is given by the equations :

$\mathbf{z - ax - \psi(a)\, y - a\, \psi(a) = 0,\ - x - \psi'(a)\, y - \psi(a) - a\psi'(a) = 0}$, where ψ is any arbitrary function.

(*ii*) We have $$z = px + qy + p^2q^2. \qquad ...(1)$$

This equation is of the form $z = px + qy + g(p, q)$.

$\therefore$ Complete solution of (1) is $\mathbf{z = ax + by + a^2b^2}$, where a and b are arbitrary constants. To find the singular solution, let

$$f(x, y, z, a, b) = z - ax - by - a^2b^2$$

$$\therefore \quad \frac{\partial f}{\partial a} = -x - 2ab^2 \quad \text{and} \quad \frac{\partial f}{\partial b} = -y - 2a^2b$$

$$\therefore \quad f(x, y, z, a, b) = 0 \quad \Rightarrow \quad z - ax - by - a^2b^2 = 0 \qquad ...(2)$$

$$\frac{\partial f}{\partial a} = 0 \quad \Rightarrow \quad -x - 2ab^2 = 0 \qquad ...(3)$$

$$\frac{\partial f}{\partial b} = 0 \quad \Rightarrow \quad -y - 2a^2b = 0 \qquad ...(4)$$

$$\therefore \quad ab^2 = -\frac{x}{2}, a^2b = -\frac{y}{2}, \quad (ab)^3 = \frac{xy}{4}, \quad ab = \left(\frac{xy}{4}\right)^{1/3}$$

$$\therefore \quad (ab)b = -\frac{x}{2} \Rightarrow b = -\frac{x}{2}\left(\frac{4}{xy}\right)^{1/3} = -\frac{x^{2/3}}{2^{1/3}\, y^{1/3}} = -\left(\frac{x^2}{2y}\right)^{1/3}.$$

Similarly, $$a = -\left(\frac{y^2}{2x}\right)^{1/3}$$

$$\therefore \Rightarrow z + \left(\frac{y^2}{2x}\right)^{1/3} x + \left(\frac{x^2}{2y}\right)^{1/3} y - \left(\frac{xy}{4}\right)^{2/3} = 0 \Rightarrow z + x^{2/3}\, y^{2/3}\left(\frac{1}{2^{1/3}} + \frac{1}{2^{1/3}} - \frac{1}{2.2^{1/3}}\right) = 0$$

$$\Rightarrow \mathbf{z = -\frac{3}{2^{4/3}}\, x^{2/3}\, y^{2/3}}.$$

This gives the singular solution, because it also satisfies (1). To find the general solution, let $b = \psi(a)$.

$\therefore$ Using $f(x, y, z, a, \psi(a)) = 0, \dfrac{\partial f}{\partial a} = 0$, the general solution is given by the equations :

$$\mathbf{z - ax - \psi(a)\, y - a^2(\psi(a))^2 = 0,\ - x - \psi'(a)\, y - 2a\, (\psi(a))^2 - 2a^2\psi(a)\, \psi'(a) = 0},$$

where ψ is any arbitrary function.

(*iii*) We have $$z = px + qy + 4\sqrt{1 + p^2 + q^2}\,. \qquad ...(1)$$

This equation is of the form $z = px + qy + g(p, q)$.

$\therefore$ Complete solution of (1) is

$$\mathbf{z = ax + by + 4\sqrt{1 + a^2 + b^2}}\,,$$ where a and b are arbitrary constants.

To find the singular solution, let

$$f(x, y, z, a, b) = z - ax - by - 4\sqrt{1 + a^2 + b^2}$$

$$\therefore \quad \frac{\partial f}{\partial a} = -x - \frac{4a}{\sqrt{1 + a^2 + b^2}} \quad \text{and} \quad \frac{\partial f}{\partial b} = -y - \frac{4b}{\sqrt{1 + a^2 + b^2}}$$

$\therefore \qquad f(x, y, z, a, b) = 0 \quad \Rightarrow \quad z - ax - by - 4\sqrt{1+a^2+b^2} = 0$ ...(2)

$$\frac{\partial f}{\partial a} = 0 \quad \Rightarrow \quad -x - \frac{4a}{\sqrt{1+a^2+b^2}} = 0 \qquad ...(3)$$

$$\frac{\partial f}{\partial b} = 0 \quad \Rightarrow \quad -y - \frac{4b}{\sqrt{1+a^2+b^2}} = 0 \qquad ...(4)$$

Using (3) and (4), we get $x^2 + y^2 = \dfrac{16(a^2+b^2)}{1+a^2+b^2}$

$$\therefore \qquad 16 - x^2 - y^2 = 16 - \frac{16(a^2+b^2)}{1+a^2+b^2} = \frac{16}{1+a^2+b^2}$$

$$\therefore \qquad \sqrt{1+a^2+b^2} = \frac{4}{\sqrt{16-x^2-y^2}}$$

$\therefore$ (3) $\Rightarrow$ $$a = -x\frac{\sqrt{1+a^2+b^2}}{4} = -\frac{x}{4}\cdot\frac{4}{\sqrt{16-x^2-y^2}} = -\frac{x}{\sqrt{16-x^2-y^2}}.$$

Similarly, $$b = -\frac{y}{\sqrt{16-x^2-y^2}}$$

Putting the values of a and b in (2), we get

$$z + \frac{x^2}{\sqrt{16-x^2-y^2}} + \frac{y^2}{\sqrt{16-x^2-y^2}} - \frac{16}{\sqrt{16-x^2-y^2}} = 0$$

or $$z = \frac{16-x^2-y^2}{\sqrt{16-x^2-y^2}} = \sqrt{16-x^2-y^2} \quad \text{or} \quad \mathbf{x^2 + y^2 + z^2 = 16.}$$

This gives the singular solution, because it also satisfies (1). To find the general solution, let $b = \psi(a)$.

Using $f(x, y, z, a, \psi(a)) = 0$, $\dfrac{\partial f}{\partial a} = 0$, the general solution is given by the equations :

$$\mathbf{z - ax - \psi(a)y - 4\sqrt{1 + a^2 + (\psi(a))^2} = 0,\; -x - \psi'(a)y - \frac{4(a + \psi(a)\,\psi'(a))}{\sqrt{1 + a^2 + (\psi(a))^2}} = 0}, \text{ where } \psi$$

is any arbitrary function.

(*iv*) We have $z = px + qy + \log(pq)$. ...(1)

This equation is of the form $z = px + qy + g(p, q)$.

$\therefore$ Complete solution of (1) is

$\mathbf{z = ax + by + \log(ab)}$, where a and b are arbitrary constants.

To find the singular solution, let $f(x, y, z, a, b) = z - ax - by - \log(ab)$

$$\therefore \qquad \frac{\partial f}{\partial a} = -x - \frac{1}{a} \quad \text{and} \quad \frac{\partial f}{\partial b} = -y - \frac{1}{b}$$

$\therefore \quad f(x, y, z, a, b) = 0 \Rightarrow z - ax - by - \log(ab) = 0$ ...(2)

$$\frac{\partial f}{\partial a} = 0 \Rightarrow -x - \frac{1}{a} = 0 \quad ...(3)$$

$$\frac{\partial f}{\partial b} = 0 \Rightarrow -y - \frac{1}{b} = 0 \quad ...(4)$$

$\therefore$ (3) $\Rightarrow$ $a = -\dfrac{1}{x}$ and (4) $\Rightarrow$ $b = -\dfrac{1}{y}$

$\therefore$ (2) $\Rightarrow$ $z + 1 + 1 - \log\dfrac{1}{xy} = 0 \Rightarrow \mathbf{z + 2 + \log xy = 0.}$

This is the singular solution, because it also satisfies (1). To find the general solution, let $b = \psi(a)$.

Using $f(x, y, z, a, \psi(a)) = 0, \dfrac{\partial f}{\partial a} = 0$, the general solution is given by the equations :

$$\mathbf{z - ax - \psi(a)y - \log a - \log \psi(a) = 0, -x - \psi'(a)y - \frac{1}{a} - \frac{\psi'(a)}{\psi(a)} = 0},$$

where ψ is any arbitrary function.

Example 2. *Show that the complete integral of $z = px + qy - 2p - 3q$ represents all possible planes through the point (2, 3, 0). Also find the envelope of all planes represented by the complete integral i.e. find the singular solution.*

Sol. We have $z = px + qy - 2p - 3q.$ ...(1)

This equation is of the form $z = px + qy + g(p, q)$.

$\therefore$ Complete solution of (1) is $z = ax + by - 2a - 3b$, where a and b are arbitrary constants. This represents a family of planes each passing through (2, 3, 0) because $0 = a(2) + b(3) - 2a - 3b$ for all constants a and b.

To find the singular solution, let

$$f(x, y, z, a, b) = z - ax - by - 2a - 3b$$

$$\frac{\partial f}{\partial a} = 0 \Rightarrow -x - 2 = 0, \quad \frac{\partial f}{\partial b} = 0 \Rightarrow -y - 3 = 0$$

$\therefore \quad z - a(-2) - b(-3) - 2a - 3b = 0$ or $z = 0$. It also satisfies (1).

$\therefore$ The singular solution is $\mathbf{z = 0.}$

WORKING RULES FOR SOLVING $z = px + qy + g(p, q)$

Step I. Take complete solution as $z = ax + by + g(a, b)$ where a and b are arbitrary constants.

Step II. For singular solution, take $f(x, y, z, a, b) = z - ax - by - g(a, b)$. Find $\dfrac{\partial f}{\partial a}$ and $\dfrac{\partial f}{\partial b}$

Eliminate a and b from the equations : $f = 0, \dfrac{\partial f}{\partial a} = 0, \dfrac{\partial f}{\partial b} = 0$. This gives the singular solution.

Step III. For general solution, take $b = \psi(a)$, where ψ is any arbitrary function. The equations : $f = 0, \dfrac{\partial f}{\partial a} = 0$ constitute the general solution.

EXERCISE 2

Solve the following partial differential equations (Q. No. 1 — 10) :

1. $z = px + qy + 5pq$
2. $z = px + qy + p^2 + q^2$
3. $z = px + qy + p^2 - q^2$
4. $z = px + qy - 2p - 3q$ *(MDU 2006)*
5. $z = px + qy + 3(pq)^{1/3}$
6. $z = px + qy + p/q$
7. $z = px + qy + 2\sqrt{pq}$
8. $z = px + qy - 2\sqrt{pq}$
9. $z = px + qy + p^2 + pq + q^2$
10. $z = px + qy + \sqrt{\alpha p^2 + \beta q^2 + 1}$.
11. Show that the complete integral of the equation $z = px + qy + \dfrac{pq}{pq - p - q}$ represents a family of planes such that the algebraic sum of the intercepts on the three coordinates axes is unity.
12. Show that the complete integral of the equation $z = px + qy + \sqrt{p^2 + q^2 + 1}$ represents a family of planes each at a unit distance from the origin.

Answers

1. **C.S.** $z = ax + by + 5ab$
   S.S. $5z + xy = 0$
   G.S. $z - ax - \psi(a)\,y - 5a\psi(a) = 0,\ x + 5\psi(a) + (y + 5a)\,\psi'(a) = 0$
2. **C.S.** $z = ax + by + a^2 + b^2$
   S.S. $x^2 + y^2 + 4z = 0$
   G.S. $z - ax - \psi(a)\,y - a^2 - (\psi(a))^2 = 0,\ x + 2a + (y + 2\psi(a))\,\psi'(a) = 0$
3. **C.S.** $z = ax + by + a^2 - b^2$
   S.S. $x^2 - y^2 + 4z = 0$
   G.S. $z - ax - \psi(a)\,y - a^2 + (\psi(a))^2 = 0,\ x + 2a + (y - 2\psi(a))\,\psi'(a) = 0$
4. **C.S.** $z = ax + by - 2a - 3b$
   S.S. $z = 0$
   G.S. $z - ax - \psi(a)\,y + 2a + 3\psi'(a) = 0,\ x + (y - 3)\,\psi'(a) - 2 = 0$
5. **C.S.** $z = ax + by + 3(ab)^{1/3}$
   S.S. $xyz - 1 = 0$
   G.S. $z - ax - \psi(a)\,y - 3(a\,\psi(a))^{1/3} = 0,\ x + \psi'(a)\,y + \dfrac{\psi(a) + a\psi'(a)}{(a\,\psi(a))^{2/3}} = 0$
6. **C.S.** $z = ax + by + a/b$
   S.S. $xz + y = 0$
   G.S. $z - ax - \psi(a)\,y - \dfrac{a}{\psi(a)} = 0,\ x + \psi'(a)\,y + \dfrac{1}{\psi(a)} - \dfrac{a\,\psi'(a)}{(\psi(a))^2} = 0$
7. **C.S.** $z = ax + by + 2\sqrt{ab}$
   S.S. $(x - z)(y - z) = 1$
   G.S. $z - ax - \psi(a)\,y - 2\sqrt{a\psi(a)} = 0,\ x + \psi'(a) + \dfrac{\psi(a) + a\psi'(a)}{\sqrt{a\,\psi(a)}} = 0$

8. C.S. $z = ax + by - 2\sqrt{ab}$

S.S. $(x - z)(y - z) = 1$

G.S. $z - ax - \psi(a)\,y + 2\sqrt{a\psi(a)} = 0,\ x + \psi'(a)\,y - \dfrac{\psi(a) + a\psi'(a)}{\sqrt{a\,\psi(a)}} = 0$

9. C.S. $z = ax + by + a^2 + ab + b^2$

S.S. $x^2 + y^2 - xy + 3z = 0$

G.S. $z - ax - \psi(a)\,y - a^2 - a\psi(a) - (\psi(a))^2 = 0,\ x + (y + a + 2\psi(a))\,\psi'(a) + 2a + \psi(a) = 0$

10. C.S. $z = ax + by + \sqrt{\alpha a^2 + \beta b^2 + 1}$

S.S. $\dfrac{x^2}{\alpha} + \dfrac{y^2}{\beta} + z^2 = 1$

G.S. $z - ax - \psi(a)\,y - \sqrt{\alpha a^2 + \beta(\psi(a))^2 + 1} = 0,\ x + \psi'(a)\,y + \dfrac{a\alpha + \beta\psi(a)\,\psi'(a)}{\sqrt{\alpha a^2 + \beta(\psi(a))^2 + 1}} = 0.$

Hints

7. S.S. We have $z - ax - by - 2\sqrt{ab} = 0,\ x = -\sqrt{\dfrac{b}{a}}$ and $y = -\sqrt{\dfrac{a}{b}}$.

Now $x - z = x - (ax + by + 2\sqrt{ab}\,) = -\sqrt{\dfrac{b}{a}} + a\sqrt{\dfrac{b}{a}} + b\sqrt{\dfrac{a}{b}} - 2\sqrt{ab} = -\sqrt{\dfrac{b}{a}}$

Similarly, $y - z = -\sqrt{\dfrac{a}{b}}$

4. SPECIAL TYPE III : EQUATIONS CONTAINING ONLY z, p AND q

Let $g(z, p, q) = 0$ ...(1)

be a partial differential equation of first order and containing only z, p and q.

Let $z = G(u)$ where $u = x + ay$ be a solution of (1) where a is an arbitrary constant.

$$\therefore \quad p = \frac{dz}{du}\frac{\partial u}{\partial x} = \frac{dz}{du}\,.\,1 = \frac{dz}{du} \quad \text{and} \quad q = \frac{dz}{du}\frac{\partial u}{\partial y} = \frac{dz}{du}\,.\,a = a\,\frac{dz}{du}$$

$$\therefore \quad (1) \Rightarrow g\left(z, \frac{dz}{du}, a\frac{dz}{du}\right) = 0$$

This is an ordinary differential equation of first order. The solution of this equation, say $f(x, y, z, a, b) = 0$ gives the complete solution of (1) where a and b are arbitrary constants. The singular solution is obtained by eliminating a and b from the equations :

$$f(x, y, z, a, b) = 0,\ \frac{\partial f}{\partial a} = 0,\ \frac{\partial f}{\partial b} = 0, \text{ provided it satisfies the given equation.}$$

Let $b = \phi(a)$ where ϕ is an arbitrary function. The general solution is given by the equations :

$$f(x, y, z, a, \phi(a)) = 0,\ \frac{\partial f}{\partial a} = 0.$$

Example 1. *Solve the following partial differential equations :*

(i) $p^2 + q^2 = 4z$ (ii) $z^2 (p^2 + q^2 + 1) = 1$

(iii) $p(1 - q^2) = q(1 - z)$.

Sol. (i) We have $p^2 + q^2 = 4z$. ...(1)

This equation is of the form $g(z, p, q) = 0$.

Let $z = G(u)$, where $u = x + ay$ be a solution of (1).

$$\therefore \quad p = \frac{\partial z}{\partial x} = \frac{dz}{du}\frac{\partial u}{\partial x} = \frac{dz}{du} \text{ and } q = \frac{\partial z}{\partial y} = \frac{dz}{du}\frac{\partial u}{\partial y} = a\frac{dz}{du}.$$

$$\therefore \quad (1) \Rightarrow \left(\frac{dz}{du}\right)^2 + \left(a\frac{dz}{du}\right)^2 = 4z$$

$$\Rightarrow \quad (1 + a^2)\left(\frac{dz}{du}\right)^2 = 4z \Rightarrow \frac{dz}{du} = \frac{2}{\sqrt{1+a^2}} z^{1/2}$$

$$\Rightarrow \quad \frac{dz}{z^{1/2}} = \frac{2}{\sqrt{1+a^2}} du$$

Integrating, we get $2\sqrt{z} = \dfrac{2u}{\sqrt{1+a^2}} + b$

$$\Rightarrow \quad 2\sqrt{1+a^2}\sqrt{z} = 2(x + ay) + b\sqrt{1+a^2}$$

$$\Rightarrow \quad 4(1 + a^2)z = 4(x + ay + c)^2, \text{ where } 2c = b\sqrt{1+a^2}$$

$\Rightarrow$ $\mathbf{(1 + a^2)\, z - (x + ay + c)^2 = 0.}$

This is the complete solution.

Let $f(x, y, z, a, c) = (1 + a^2)\, z - (x + ay + c)^2$

$$\therefore \quad \frac{\partial f}{\partial a} = 2az - 2(x + ay + c)y \text{ and } \frac{\partial f}{\partial c} = -2(x + ay + c)$$

$$\therefore \quad f(x, y, z, a, c) = 0 \Rightarrow (1 + a^2)z - (x + ay + c)^2 = 0 \quad ...(2)$$

$$\frac{\partial f}{\partial a} = 0 \Rightarrow 2az - 2(x + ay + c) = 0 \quad ...(3)$$

$$\frac{\partial f}{\partial c} = 0 \Rightarrow -2(x + ay + c) = 0 \quad ...(4)$$

$(4) \Rightarrow x + ay + c = 0$

$\therefore$ (3) $\Rightarrow 2az - 2(0)y = 0 \Rightarrow 2az = 0 \Rightarrow$ $\mathbf{z = 0.}$

This is the singular solution, because $z = 0$ also satisfies (1).

Let $c = \phi(a)$. Using $f(x, y, z, a, \phi(a)) = 0$, $\dfrac{\partial f}{\partial a} = 0$, the general solution is given by

$$\mathbf{(1 + a^2)\, z - (x + ay + \phi(a))^2 = 0,\ 2az - 2(x + ay + \phi(a))\,(y + \phi'(a)) = 0,}$$

where ϕ is any arbitrary function.

(ii) We have $z^2(p^2 + q^2 + 1) = 1$. ...(1)

This equation is of the form $g(z, p, q) = 0$.

Let $z = G(u)$, where $u = x + ay$ be a solution of (1).

$$\therefore \quad p = \frac{\partial z}{\partial x} = \frac{dz}{du}\frac{\partial u}{\partial x} = \frac{dz}{dx} \text{ and } q = \frac{\partial z}{\partial y} = \frac{dz}{du}\frac{\partial u}{\partial y} = a\frac{dz}{du}.$$

$$\therefore \quad (1) \Rightarrow \quad z^2\left(\left(\frac{dz}{du}\right)^2 + \left(a\frac{dz}{du}\right)^2 + 1\right) = 1$$

$$\Rightarrow \quad (1+a^2)\left(\frac{dz}{du}\right)^2 = \frac{1}{z^2} - 1 \quad \Rightarrow \quad \frac{dz}{du} = \frac{\pm 1}{\sqrt{1+a^2}}\frac{\sqrt{1-z^2}}{z}$$

Let $$\frac{dz}{du} = \frac{1}{\sqrt{1+a^2}}\frac{\sqrt{1-z^2}}{z}.$$

$$\therefore \quad \frac{z}{\sqrt{1-z^2}}\,dz = \frac{du}{\sqrt{1+a^2}}$$

Integrating, we get $-\sqrt{1-z^2} = \dfrac{u}{\sqrt{1+a^2}} + b$

$$\Rightarrow \quad -\sqrt{1+a^2}\,\sqrt{1-z^2} = u + c, \text{ where } c = b\sqrt{1+a^2}$$

$$\Rightarrow \quad \mathbf{(1 + a^2)\,(1 - z^2) = (x + ay + c)^2.}$$

This is the complete solution.

Let $f(x, y, z, a, c) = (1 + a^2)(1 - z^2) - (x + ay + c)^2$

$$\therefore \quad \frac{\partial f}{\partial a} = 2a(1 - z^2) - 2(x + ay + c)y \quad \text{and} \quad \frac{\partial f}{\partial c} = -2(x + ay + c)$$

$$\therefore \quad f(x, y, z, a, c) = 0 \quad \Rightarrow \quad (1 + a^2)(1 - z^2) - (x + ay + c)^2 = 0 \qquad ...(2)$$

$$\frac{\partial f}{\partial a} = 0 \quad \Rightarrow \quad 2a(1 - z^2) - 2(x + ay + c)y = 0 \qquad ...(3)$$

$$\frac{\partial f}{\partial c} = 0 \quad \Rightarrow \quad -2(x + ay + c) = 0 \qquad ...(4)$$

$$(4) \quad \Rightarrow \quad x + ay + c = 0$$

$$\therefore \quad (3) \quad \Rightarrow \quad 2a(1 - z^2) - 2(0)y = 0$$

$$\Rightarrow \quad 2a(1 - z^2) = 0 \quad \Rightarrow \quad 1 - z^2 = 0 \quad \Rightarrow \quad \mathbf{z^2 - 1 = 0.}$$

This is the singular solution, because $z^2 - 1 = 0$ also satisfies (1).

Let $c = \phi(a)$. Using $f(x, y, z, a, c) = 0$, $\dfrac{\partial f}{\partial a} = 0$, the general solution is given by

$$\mathbf{(1 + a^2)(1 - z^2) - (x + ay + \phi(a))^2 = 0,\ 2a(1 - z^2) - 2(x + ay + \phi(a))(y + \phi'(a)) = 0,}$$

where ϕ is any arbitrary function.

(*iii*) We have $\qquad p(1 - q^2) = q(1 - z). \qquad ...(1)$

This equation is of the form $g(z, p, q) = 0$.

Let $z = G(u)$, where $u = x + ay$ be a solution of (1).

$$\therefore \qquad p = \frac{\partial z}{\partial x} = \frac{dz}{du}\cdot\frac{\partial u}{\partial x} = \frac{dz}{dx} \text{ and } q = \frac{\partial z}{\partial y} = \frac{dz}{du}\frac{\partial u}{\partial y} = a\frac{dz}{du}$$

$$\therefore \quad (1) \quad \Rightarrow \quad \frac{dz}{du}\left(1 - a^2\left(\frac{dz}{du}\right)^2\right) = a\frac{dz}{du}(1 - z)$$

$$\Rightarrow \qquad \frac{dz}{du} = 0 \qquad ...(2)$$

or

$$1 - a^2\left(\frac{dz}{du}\right)^2 = a(1 - z) \qquad ...(3)$$

(2) $\Rightarrow$ $z = c$. This is not a complete solution because it does not contain two arbitrary constants.

$$(3) \quad \Rightarrow \qquad \left(\frac{dz}{du}\right)^2 = \frac{1 - a + az}{a^2}.$$

Let

$$\frac{dz}{du} = \frac{\sqrt{1 - a + az}}{a}$$

$$\therefore \qquad (1 - a + az)^{-1/2}\, dz = \frac{du}{a}$$

Integrating, we get

$$\frac{(1 - a + az)^{1/2}}{(1/2)\, a} = \frac{u}{a} + b$$

$$\Rightarrow \qquad 2\sqrt{1 - a + az} = u + ab$$

$$\Rightarrow \qquad \mathbf{4(1 - a + az) = (x + ay + c)^2}, \text{ where } c = ab.$$

This is the complete solution.

Let $\qquad f(x, y, z, a, c) = 4(1 - a + az) - (x + ay + c)^2$

$$\therefore \qquad \frac{\partial f}{\partial a} = 4(-1 + z) - 2(x + ay + c)y \quad \text{and} \quad \frac{\partial f}{\partial c} = -2(x + ay + c)$$

$$\therefore \qquad f(x, y, z, a, c) = 0 \quad \Rightarrow \quad 4(1 - a + az) - (x + ay + c)^2 = 0 \qquad ...(4)$$

$$\frac{\partial f}{\partial a} = 0 \quad \Rightarrow \quad 4(-1 + z) - 2(x + ay + c)y = 0 \qquad ...(5)$$

$$\frac{\partial f}{\partial c} = 0 \quad \Rightarrow \quad -2(x + ay + c) = 0 \qquad ...(6)$$

(6) $\Rightarrow$ $x + ay + c = 0$

$\therefore$ (5) $\Rightarrow$ $4(-1 + z) - 2(0)y = 0 \Rightarrow 4(-1 + z) = 0$

$\Rightarrow$ $-1 + z = 0 \Rightarrow z = 1$

$\therefore$ (4) $\Rightarrow$ $4(1 - a + a(1)) - (0)^2 = 0$

$\Rightarrow$ $4 = 0$, which is impossible.

$\therefore$ There is no singular solution. Let $c = \phi(a)$. Using $f(x, y, z, a, \phi(a)) = 0$ and $\frac{\partial f}{\partial a} = 0$, the general solution is given by $\mathbf{4(1 - a + az) - (x + ay + \phi(a))^2 = 0, - 4 + 4z - 2(x + ay + \phi(a))\ (y + \phi'(a)) = 0}$, where ϕ is any arbitrary function.

WORKING RULES FOR SOLVING g(z, p, q) = 0

Step I. Take $z = G(u)$, where $u = x + ay$.

Step II. By putting $p = \frac{dz}{du}$ and $q = a\frac{dz}{du}$, the given equation reduces to an ordinary differential equation of first order. Let its solution be $f(x, y, z, a, b) = 0$. This gives the complete solution of the given equation.

Step III. For singular solution, eliminate a and b from the equations : $f = 0$, $\frac{\partial f}{\partial a} = 0$, $\frac{\partial f}{\partial b} = 0$.

Step IV. For general solution, take $b = \phi(a)$ where ϕ is any arbitrary function. The equations : $f = 0$, $\frac{\partial f}{\partial a} = 0$ constitute the general solution.

EXERCISE 3

Solve the following partial differential equations :

1. $p^2 + q^2 = z$
2. $z^2(p^2 + q^2 + 2) = 1$
3. $p^2 + pq = 4z$
4. $pz = 1 + q^2$
5. $z = pq$
6. $9(p^2z + q^2) = 4$
7. $p^3 + q^3 = 3pqz, z > 0$
8. $p^3 + q^3 = 27z$
9. $4(1 + z^3) = 9z^4 pq$
10. $q^2 = z^2p^2(1 - p^2)$. *(CDLU 2004)*

Answers

1. **C.S.** $4(1 + a^2) z = (x + ay + c)^2$
   S.S. $z = 0$
   G.S. $4(1 + a^2) z - (x + ay + \phi(a))^2 = 0,\ 8az - 2(x + ay + \phi(a))(y + \phi'(a)) = 0$
2. **C.S.** $(1 + a^2)(1 - 2z^2) = 4(x + ay + c)^2$
   S.S. $1 - 2z^2 = 0$
   G.S. $(1 + a^2)(1 - 2z^2) - 4(x + ay + \phi(a))^2 = 0,\ a(1 - 2z^2) - 4(x + ay + \phi(a))(y + \phi'(a)) = 0$
3. **C.S.** $(1 + a)z = (x + ay + c)^2$
   S.S. $z = 0$
   G.S. $(1 + a)z - (x + ay + \phi(a))^2 = 0,\ z - 2(x + ay + \phi(a))(y + \phi'(a)) = 0$
4. **C.S.** $z^2 - z\sqrt{z^2 - 4a^2} + 4a^2 \log(z + \sqrt{z^2 - 4a^2}) = 4(x + ay + b)$
   S.S. There is no singular solution.
   G.S. $z^2 - z\sqrt{z^2 - 4a^2} + 4a^2 \log(z + \sqrt{z^2 - 4a^2}) - 4(x + ay + \phi(a)) = 0,$

$$\frac{az}{\sqrt{z^2-4a^2}} + 2a\log\left(z+\sqrt{z^2-4a^2}\right) - \frac{4a^3}{(z+\sqrt{z^2-4a^2})\sqrt{z^2-4a^2}} - y - \phi'(a) = 0.$$

5. **C.S.** $4az = (x + ay + b)^2$

   S.S. $z = 0$

   G.S. $4az - (x + ay + \phi(a))^2 = 0,\ 2z - (x + ay + \phi(a))\,(y + \phi'(a)) = 0.$

6. **C.S.** $(z + a^2)^3 = (x + ay + b)^2$

   S.S. No singular solution.

   G.S. $(z + a^2)^3 - (x + ay + \phi(a))^2 = 0,\ 3a(z + a^2)^2 - (x + ay + \phi(a))(y + \phi'(a)) = 0$

7. **C.S.** $(1 + a^3)\log z = 3a(x + ay) + b$

   S.S. No singular solution.

   G.S. $(1 + a^3)\log z - 3a(x + ay) - \phi(a) = 0,\ 3a^2\log z - 3x - 6ay - \phi'(a) = 0.$

8. **C.S.** $(1 + a^3)\,z^2 = 8(x + ay + b)^3$

   S.S. $z = 0$

   G.S. $(1 + a^3)\,z^2 - 8(x + ay + \phi(a))^3 = 0,\ a^2z^2 - 8(x + ay + \phi(a))^2(y + \phi'(a)) = 0.$

9. **C.S.** $a(1 + z^3) = (x + ay + b)^2$

   S.S. $z^3 + 1 = 0$

   G.S. $a(1 + z^3) - (x + ay + \phi(a))^2 = 0,\ 1 + z^3 - 2(x + ay + \phi(a))(y + \phi'(a)) = 0$

10. **C.S.** $z^2 = (x + ay + b)^2 + a^2$

    S.S. $z = 0$

    G.S. $z^2 - (x + ay + \phi(a))^2 - a^2 = 0,\ (x + ay + \phi(a))(y + \phi'(a)) + a = 0.$

---

5. SPECIAL TYPE IV : EQUATIONS OF THE FORM $f_1(x, p) = f_2(y, q)$

Consider the equation $f_1(x, p) = f_2(y, q)$. ...(1)

Let each side of (1) be equal to a.

$\therefore \quad f_1(x, p) = a \quad ...(2) \qquad f_2(y, q) = a$ ...(3)

Solving (2) for p, let $p = F_1(x, a)$

Solving (3) for q, let $q = F_2(y, a)$.

Since z is a function of x and y, we have $dz = \frac{\partial z}{\partial x}dx + \frac{\partial z}{\partial y}dy = p\,dx + q\,dy$

$$\therefore \qquad dz = F_1(x, a)\,dx + F_2(y, a)\,dy$$

Integrating, we get $\mathbf{z = \int F_1(x, a)\,dx + \int F_2(y, a)\,dy + b.}$

This represents the complete solution of the given equation.

To find the singular solution, let $f(x, y, z, a, b) = z - \int F_1(x,a)\,dx - \int F_2(y,a)\,dy - b$.

$\therefore$ Using $f(x, y, z, a, b) = 0,\ \frac{\partial f}{\partial a} = 0,\ \frac{\partial f}{\partial b} = 0$, the singular solution is given by eliminating a and b from the equations :

$$z - \int F_1(x, a)\, dx - \int F_2(y, a)\, dy - b = 0,$$

$$\frac{\partial}{\partial a}\left(\int F_1(x, a)\, dx + \int F_2(y, a)\, dy\right) = 0 \text{ and } -1 = 0.$$

This is impossible, because $-1 \neq 0$.

$\therefore$ There is no singular solution.

To find the general solution, let $b = \phi(a)$, where ϕ is an arbitrary function. Using $f(x, y, z, a, \phi(a)) = 0$, $\dfrac{\partial f}{\partial a} = 0$, the general solution is given by the equations :

$$\mathbf{z - \int F_1(x, a)\, dx - \int F_2(y, a)\, dy - \phi(a) = 0, \quad \frac{\partial}{\partial a}\left(-\int F_1(x, a)\, dx - \int F_2(y, a)\, dy\right) - \phi'(a) = 0.}$$

Example 1. *Solve the following partial differential equations :*

(*i*) $\sqrt{p} - \sqrt{q} + 3x = 0$ (*ii*) $py + qx + pq = 0$ (KU 2004 S)

(*iii*) $p^2 y (1 + x^2) = qx^2$ (*iv*) $px + q = p^2$.

Sol. (*i*) We have $\sqrt{p} + 3x = \sqrt{q}$. ...(1)

This equation is of the form $f_1(x, p) = f_2(y, q)$.

Let each side of (1) be equal to a.

$\therefore$ $\sqrt{p} + 3x = a$ ...(2) $\sqrt{q} = a$ ...(3)

(2) $\Rightarrow$ $p = (a - 3x)^2$ and (3) $\Rightarrow$ $q = a^2$

Now $dz = p\, dx + q\, dy$

$\therefore$ $dz = (a - 3x)^2\, dx + a^2\, dy$

Integrating, we get $z = \int (a - 3x)^2\, dx + \int a^2\, dy + b.$

$$\Rightarrow \qquad \mathbf{z = \frac{(a - 3x)^3}{-9} + a^2 y + b.}$$

This is the complete solution. There is no singular solution.

To find the general solution, let $f(x, y, z, a, b) = z + \dfrac{1}{9}(a - 3x)^3 - a^2 y - b$ and $b = \phi(a)$.

$\therefore$ Using $f(x, y, z, a, \phi(a)) = 0$, $\dfrac{\partial f}{\partial a} = 0$.

The general solution is given by the equations :

$$\mathbf{z + \frac{1}{9}(a - 3x)^3 - a^2 y - \phi(a) = 0, \quad \frac{1}{3}(a - 3x)^2 - 2ay - \phi'(a) = 0,}$$

where ϕ is any arbitrary function.

(*ii*) We have $py + qx + pq = 0$.

$$\Rightarrow \qquad py + q(x + p) = 0 \Rightarrow \frac{p}{x + p} = -\frac{q}{y} \qquad ...(1)$$

This equation is of the form $f_1(x, p) = f_2(y, q)$. Let each side of (1) be equal to a.

$$\therefore \quad \frac{p}{x+p} = a \quad ...(2) \qquad -\frac{q}{y} = a \quad ...(3)$$

$$(2) \Rightarrow \quad p = \frac{ax}{1-a} \quad \text{and} \quad (3) \Rightarrow \quad q = -ay$$

Now $\quad dz = p\,dx + q\,dy$

$$\therefore \quad dz = \frac{ax}{1-a}\,dx - ay\,dy$$

Integrating, we get $\quad z = \int \frac{ax}{1-a}\,dx - \int ay\,dy + \frac{b}{2}$.

$$\Rightarrow \quad z = \frac{a}{1-a}\cdot\frac{x^2}{2} - \frac{ay^2}{2} + \frac{b}{2}$$

$$\Rightarrow \quad \mathbf{2z = \frac{a}{1-a}x^2 - ay^2 + b.}$$

This is the complete solution.
There is no singular solution. To find the general solution, let

$$f(x, y, z, a, b) = 2z - \frac{a}{a-1}x^2 + ay^2 - b \quad \text{and} \quad b = \phi(a).$$

$\therefore$ Using $f(x, y, z, a, \phi(a)) = 0$, $\frac{\partial f}{\partial a} = 0$,

The general solution is given by the equations :

$\mathbf{2z - \frac{a}{1-a}x^2 + ay^2 - \phi(a) = 0, \ -\frac{x^2}{(1-a)^2} + y^2 - \phi'(a) = 0}$, where ϕ is any arbitrary function.

(*iii*) We have $\quad p^2y(1 + x^2) = qx^2$.

$$\Rightarrow \quad \frac{1+x^2}{x^2}p^2 = \frac{q}{y} \qquad ...(1)$$

This equation is of the form $\quad f_1(x, p) = f_2(y, q)$.
Let each side of (1) be equal to a.

$$\therefore \quad \frac{1+x^2}{x^2}p^2 = a \quad ...(2) \qquad \frac{q}{y} = a \quad ...(3)$$

$$(2) \Rightarrow \quad p = \pm\frac{\sqrt{a}\,x}{\sqrt{1+x^2}} \quad \text{and} \quad (3) \Rightarrow \quad q = ay. \qquad \text{(Assuming } a \geq 0\text{)}$$

Let $\quad p = \frac{\sqrt{a}x}{\sqrt{1+x^2}}$

Now $\quad dz = p\,dx + q\,dy$

$$\therefore \quad dz = \frac{\sqrt{a}\,x}{\sqrt{1+x^2}}\,dx + ay\,dy$$

Integrating, we get $z = \frac{\sqrt{a}}{2}\int \frac{2x}{\sqrt{1+x^2}}\,dx + a\int y\,dy + \frac{b}{2}$.

$$\Rightarrow \qquad z = \sqrt{a}\,\sqrt{1+x^2} + \frac{ay^2}{2} + \frac{b}{2} \quad \Rightarrow \quad \mathbf{2z = 2\sqrt{a}\,\sqrt{1+x^2} + ay^2 + b.}$$

This is the complete solution. There is no singular solution.

To find the general solution, let $f(x, y, z, a, b) = 2z - 2\sqrt{a}\sqrt{1+x^2} - ay^2 - b$ and $b = \phi(a)$.

$\therefore$ Using $f(x, y, z, a, \phi(a)) = 0$, $\frac{\partial f}{\partial a} = 0$, the general solution is given by the equations :

$$2z - 2\sqrt{a}\sqrt{1+x^2} - ay^2 - \phi(a) = 0, \quad -2\cdot\frac{1}{2\sqrt{a}}\cdot\sqrt{1+x^2} - y^2 - \phi'(a) = 0$$

or $$\mathbf{2z - 2\sqrt{a}\sqrt{1+x^2} - ay^2 - \phi(a) = 0, \quad \sqrt{1+x^2} + \sqrt{a}y^2 + \sqrt{a}\,\phi'(a) = 0,}$$

where ϕ is any arbitrary function.

(*iv*) We have $px + q = p^2$.

$$\Rightarrow \qquad p^2 - px = q \qquad ...(1)$$

This equation is of the form $f_1(x, p) = f_2(y, q)$.

Let each side of (1) be equal to a.

$$\therefore \qquad p^2 - px = a \quad ...(2) \qquad q = a \qquad ...(3)$$

$$(2) \Rightarrow p^2 - px - a = 0 \Rightarrow p = \frac{1}{2}\left(x \pm \sqrt{x^2 + 4a}\right)$$

Let $$p = \frac{1}{2}\left(x + \sqrt{x^2 + 4a}\right)$$

Now $$dz = p\,dx + q\,dy$$

$$\therefore \qquad dz = \frac{1}{2}\left(x + \sqrt{x^2 + 4a}\right)dx + a\,dy$$

Integrating, we get $$z = \frac{x^2}{4} + \frac{1}{2}\left[\frac{x\sqrt{x^2+4a}}{2} + \frac{4a}{2}\log\left|x + \sqrt{x^2+4a}\right|\right] + ay + b$$

or $$\mathbf{z = \frac{1}{4}\left(x^2 + x\sqrt{x^2+4a}\right) + a\log\left|x + \sqrt{x^2+4a}\right| + ay + b.}$$

This is the complete solution. There is no singular solution.

To find the general solution, let

$$f(x, y, z, a, b) = z - \frac{1}{4}(x^2 + x\sqrt{x^2+4a}) - a\log(x + \sqrt{x^2+4a}) - ay - b \text{ and } b = \phi(a).$$

$\therefore$ Using $f(x, y, z, a, \phi(a)) = 0$, $\frac{\partial f}{\partial a} = 0$, the general solution is given by the equations :

$$z - \frac{1}{4}(x^2 + x\sqrt{x^2+4a}) - a\log(x + \sqrt{x^2+4a}) - ay - \phi(a) = 0,$$

$$-\frac{x}{4}\cdot\frac{4}{2\sqrt{x^2+4a}} - \log(x+\sqrt{x^2+4a}) - a\cdot\frac{1}{x+\sqrt{x^2+4a}}\left(0 + \frac{4}{2\sqrt{x^2+4a}}\right) - y - \phi'(a) = 0$$

or
$$\mathbf{z - \frac{1}{4}(x^2 + x\sqrt{x^2+4a}) - a\log(x+\sqrt{x^2+4a}) - ay - \phi(a) = 0,}$$

$$\mathbf{\frac{x}{2\sqrt{x^2+4a}} + \log(x+\sqrt{x^2+4a}) + \frac{2a}{(x+\sqrt{x^2+4a})\sqrt{x^2+4a}} + y + \phi'(a) = 0,}$$

where ϕ is any arbitrary function.

WORKING RULES FOR SOLVING $f_1(x, p) = f_2(y, q)$

Step I. Take each side of $f_1(x, p) = f_2(y, q)$ equal to a.

Step II. Solve equations for p and q. Let $p = F_1(x, a)$, $q = F_2(y, a)$. Write $z = p\,dx + q\,dy$ and substitute the values of p and q. Integrate this equation to get the complete solution.

Step III. Equation of the form $f_1(x, p) = f_2(y, q)$ has no singular solution.

Step IV. Take the complete solution as $f(x, y, z, a, b) = 0$. Put $b = \phi(a)$. The general solution is given by the equations : $f(x, y, z, a, \phi(a)) = 0$, $\frac{\partial f}{\partial a} = 0$.

EXERCISE 4

Solve the following partial differential equations :

1. $p - q = x^2 + y^2$
2. $x(1+y)p = y(1+x)q$
3. $pq = xy$
4. $q = xyp^2$
5. $x^2p^2 = q^2y$
6. $q(p - \cos x) = \cos y$
7. $yp = 2yx + \log q$
8. $\sqrt{p} + \sqrt{q} = 2x$
9. $p^2 - x = q^2 - y$
10. $p - 3x^2 = q^2 - y$.

Answers

1. **C.S.** $z = \frac{1}{3}(x^3 - y^3) + a(x+y) + b$

   S.S. No singular solution

   G.S. $z - \frac{1}{3}(x^3 - y^3) - a(x+y) - \phi(a) = 0,\ x + y + \phi'(a) = 0$

2. **C.S.** $z = a\log xy + a(x+y) + b$

   S.S. No singular solution

   G.S. $z - a\log xy - a(x+y) - \phi(a) = 0,\ \log xy + x + y + \phi'(a) = 0$

3. **C.S.** $2z = ax^2 + y^2/a + b$

S.S. No singular solution

G.S. $2z - ax^2 - y^2/a - \phi(a) = 0,\ x^2 - y^2/a^2 + \phi'(a) = 0$

4. **C.S.** $2z = 4\sqrt{ax} + ay^2 + b$

S.S. No singular solution

G.S. $2z - 4\sqrt{ax} - ay^2 - \phi(a) = 0,\ 2\sqrt{x/a} + y^2 + \phi'(a) = 0$

5. **C.S.** $z = \sqrt{a}\log x + 2\sqrt{ay} + b$

S.S. No singular solution

G.S. $z - \sqrt{a}\log x - 2\sqrt{ay} - \phi(a) = 0,\ \log x + 2\sqrt{y} + 2\sqrt{a}\,\phi'(a) = 0$

6. **C.S.** $z = ax + \sin x + \dfrac{1}{a}\sin y + b$

S.S. No singular solution

G.S. $z - ax - \sin x - \dfrac{1}{a}\sin y - \phi(a) = 0,\ x - \dfrac{1}{a^2}\sin y + \phi'(a) = 0$

7. **C.S.** $z = x^2 + ax + \dfrac{e^{ay}}{a} + b$

S.S. No singular solution

G.S. $z - x^2 - ax - \dfrac{e^{ay}}{a} - \phi(a) = 0,\ x + \dfrac{e^{ay}(ay-1)}{a^2} + \phi'(a) = 0$

8. **C.S.** $z = \dfrac{1}{6}(2x-a)^3 + a^2y + b$

S.S. No singular solution

G.S. $z - \dfrac{1}{6}(2x-a)^3 - a^2y - \phi(a) = 0,\ 4ay - (2x-a)^2 + 2\phi'(a) = 0$

9. **C.S.** $3z = 2(x+a)^{3/2} + 2(y+a)^{3/2} + b$

S.S. No singular solution

G.S. $3z - 2(x+a)^{3/2} - 2(y+a)^{3/2} - \phi(a) = 0,\ 3\sqrt{x+a} + 3\sqrt{y+a} + \phi'(a) = 0$

10. **C.S.** $z = ax + x^3 + \dfrac{2}{3}(a+y)^{3/2} + b$

S.S. No singular solution

G.S. $z - ax - x^3 - \dfrac{2}{3}(a+y)^{3/2} - \phi(a) = 0,\ x + \sqrt{a+y} + \phi'(a) = 0.$

6. USE OF TRANSFORMATIONS

At times the use of transformations helps a lot in changing a partial differential equation to a much simpler form.

Remark. Keeping in view the scope of the present book, we are restricting ourselves only to the finding of complete solutions of partial differential equations which are reducible to the form $g(P, Q) = 0$, where $P = \dfrac{\partial Z}{\partial X}$, $Q = \dfrac{\partial Z}{\partial Y}$.

Example 1. *Find the complete solution of the following differential equations with the help of transformations :*

(*i*) $x^2p^2 + y^2q^2 = z$ (*ii*) $x^2p^2 + y^2q^2 = 4z^2$

(*iii*) $pq = x^m y^n z^{2l}$ (*iv*) $(1 - x^2)\, yp^2 + x^2q = 0.$

Sol. (*i*) We have $x^2p^2 + y^2q^2 = z.$ ...(1)

$$(1) \Rightarrow \quad \frac{x^2}{z}\left(\frac{\partial z}{\partial x}\right)^2 + \frac{y^2}{z}\left(\frac{\partial z}{\partial y}\right)^2 = 1$$

$$\Rightarrow \quad \left(\frac{z^{-1/2}}{x^{-1}}\frac{\partial z}{\partial x}\right)^2 + \left(\frac{z^{-1/2}}{y^{-1}}\frac{\partial z}{\partial y}\right)^2 = 1 \qquad ...(2)$$

Let X, Y, Z be new variables such that $dX = x^{-1}\,dx$, $dY = y^{-1}\,dy$, $dZ = z^{-1/2}\,dz$.

$\therefore$ By using integration, we have $X = \log x$, $Y = \log y$, $Z = 2\sqrt{z}$

$$\therefore \quad P = \frac{\partial Z}{\partial X} = \frac{dZ}{dz}\cdot\frac{\partial z}{\partial x}\cdot\frac{dx}{dX} = \frac{1}{\sqrt{z}}\cdot\frac{\partial z}{\partial x}\cdot x = \frac{z^{-1/2}}{x^{-1}}\frac{\partial z}{\partial x}$$

and
$$Q = \frac{\partial Z}{\partial Y} = \frac{dZ}{dz}\cdot\frac{\partial z}{\partial y}\cdot\frac{dy}{dY} = \frac{1}{\sqrt{z}}\cdot\frac{\partial z}{\partial y}\cdot y = \frac{z^{-1/2}}{y^{-1}}\frac{\partial z}{\partial y}.$$

$\therefore$ (2) $\Rightarrow$ $P^2 + Q^2 = 1$ ...(3)

This equation is of the form $g(P, Q) = 0$.

Let $Z = aX + \phi(a)Y + c$ ...(4)

be the complete solution of (3), where $\phi(a)$ is some function of a.

$$(4) \Rightarrow \quad P = \frac{\partial Z}{\partial X} = a \quad \text{and} \quad Q = \frac{\partial Z}{\partial Y} = \phi(a)$$

$\therefore$ (3) $\Rightarrow$ $a^2 + (\phi(a))^2 = 1$ or $\phi(a) = \pm\sqrt{1 - a^2}$

Let $\phi(a) = \sqrt{1 - a^2}\,,\ -1 \le a \le 1.$

$\therefore$ The complete solution of (3) is $Z = aX + \sqrt{1 - a^2}\ Y + c.$

$\therefore$ The complete solution of (1) is $\mathbf{2\sqrt{z} = a \log x + \sqrt{1 - a^2}\ \log y + c}$, where a and c are arbitrary constants.

(*ii*) We have $x^2p^2 + y^2q^2 = 4z^2.$ ...(1)

$$(1) \Rightarrow \quad \frac{x^2}{z^2}\left(\frac{\partial z}{\partial x}\right)^2 + \frac{y^2}{z^2}\left(\frac{\partial z}{\partial y}\right)^2 = 4$$

$$\Rightarrow \quad \left(\frac{z^{-1}}{x^{-1}}\frac{\partial z}{\partial x}\right)^2 + \left(\frac{z^{-1}}{y^{-1}}\frac{\partial z}{\partial y}\right)^2 = 4 \qquad ...(2)$$

Let X, Y, Z be new variables such that $dX = x^{-1}\,dx$, $dY = y^{-1}\,dy$, $dZ = z^{-1}\,dz$

$\therefore$ By using integration, we have $X = \log x$, $Y = \log y$, $Z = \log z$

$$\therefore \quad P = \frac{\partial Z}{\partial X} = \frac{dZ}{dz}\cdot\frac{\partial z}{\partial x}\cdot\frac{dx}{dX} = \frac{1}{z}\cdot\frac{\partial z}{\partial x}\cdot x = \frac{z^{-1}}{x^{-1}}\frac{\partial z}{\partial x}$$

and
$$Q = \frac{\partial Z}{\partial Y} = \frac{dZ}{dz}\cdot\frac{\partial z}{\partial y}\cdot\frac{dy}{dY} = \frac{1}{z}\cdot\frac{\partial z}{\partial y}\cdot y = \frac{z^{-1}}{y^{-1}}\frac{\partial z}{\partial y}.$$

$\therefore$ (2) $\Rightarrow$ $P^2 + Q^2 = 4$ ...(3)

This equation is of the form $g(P, Q) = 0$.

Let $Z = aX + \phi(a)Y + c$ ...(4)

be the complete solution of (3), where $\phi(a)$ is some function of a.

(4) $\Rightarrow$ $P = \dfrac{\partial Z}{\partial X} = a$ and $Q = \dfrac{\partial Z}{\partial Y} = \phi(a)$

$\therefore$ (3) $\Rightarrow$ $a^2 + (\phi(a))^2 = 4$ or $\phi(a) = \pm\sqrt{4-a^2}$

Let $\phi(a) = \sqrt{4-a^2}, -2 \le a \le 2$.

$\therefore$ The complete solution of (3) is $Z = aX + \sqrt{4-a^2}\ Y + c$.

$\therefore$ The complete solution of (1) is $\mathbf{\log z = a \log x + \sqrt{4-a^2}\ \log y + c}$, where a and c are arbitrary constants.

(*iii*) We have $pq = x^m y^n z^{2l}$. ...(1)

$\Rightarrow$ $\dfrac{z^{-2l}}{x^m y^n}\,pq = 1$ $\Rightarrow$ $\left(\dfrac{z^{-l}}{x^m}\dfrac{\partial z}{\partial x}\right)\left(\dfrac{z^{-l}}{y^n}\dfrac{\partial z}{\partial y}\right) = 1$ ...(2)

Let X, Y, Z be new variables such that $dX = x^m\,dx,\ dY = y^n\,dy,\ dZ = z^{-l}\,dz$

$\therefore$ By using integration, we have $X = \dfrac{x^{m+1}}{m+1},\quad Y = \dfrac{y^{n+1}}{n+1},\quad Z = \dfrac{z^{1-l}}{1-l}$.

$$\therefore\qquad P = \frac{\partial Z}{\partial X} = \frac{dZ}{dz}\cdot\frac{\partial z}{\partial x}\cdot\frac{dx}{dX} = z^{-l}\cdot\frac{\partial z}{\partial x}\cdot\frac{1}{x^m} = \frac{z^{-l}}{x^m}\frac{\partial z}{\partial x}$$

and
$$Q = \frac{\partial Z}{\partial Y} = \frac{dZ}{dz}\cdot\frac{\partial z}{\partial y}\cdot\frac{dy}{dY} = z^{-l}\,\frac{\partial z}{\partial y}\,\frac{1}{y^n} = \frac{z^{-l}}{y^n}\frac{\partial z}{\partial y}$$

$\therefore$ (2) $\Rightarrow$ $PQ = 1$ ...(3)

This equation is of the form $g(P, Q) = 0$.

Let $Z = aX + \phi(a)\,Y + c$ ...(4)

be the complete solution of (3), where $\phi(a)$ is some function of a.

(4) $\Rightarrow$ $P = \dfrac{\partial Z}{\partial X} = a$ and $Q = \dfrac{\partial Z}{\partial Y} = \phi(a)$

$\therefore$ (3) $\Rightarrow$ $a\,\phi(a) = 1$ or $\phi(a) = 1/a$

$\therefore$ The complete solution of (3) is $Z = aX + \dfrac{1}{a}Y + c$.

$\therefore$ The complete solution of (1) is $\mathbf{\dfrac{z^{1-l}}{1-l} = \dfrac{a}{m+1}x^{m+1} + \dfrac{1}{(n+1)a}y^{n+1} + c}$, where a and c are arbitrary constants and $a \ne 0$.

(*iv*) We have $(1-x^2)\,yp^2 + x^2q = 0$. ...(1)

$$(1) \Rightarrow \qquad \frac{1-x^2}{x^2}\left(\frac{\partial z}{\partial x}\right)^2 + \frac{1}{y}\frac{\partial z}{\partial y} = 0$$

$$\Rightarrow \qquad \left(\frac{1}{x/\sqrt{1-x^2}}\frac{\partial z}{\partial x}\right)^2 + \frac{1}{y}\frac{\partial z}{\partial y} = 0 \qquad \text{...(2)}$$

Let X, Y, Z be new variables such that $dX = \dfrac{x}{\sqrt{1-x^2}}dx$, $dY = y\,dy$, $dZ = dz$

$\therefore$ By using integration, we have

$$X = -\frac{1}{2}.\frac{(1-x^2)^{1/2}}{1/2} = -\sqrt{1-x^2}\,,\quad Y = \frac{y^2}{2},\quad Z = z.$$

$$\therefore \qquad P = \frac{\partial Z}{\partial X} = \frac{dZ}{dz}.\frac{\partial z}{\partial x}.\frac{dx}{dX} = 1.\frac{\partial z}{\partial x}.\frac{\sqrt{1-x^2}}{x} = \frac{1}{x/\sqrt{1-x^2}}\frac{\partial z}{\partial x}$$

and
$$Q = \frac{\partial Z}{\partial Y} = \frac{dZ}{dz}.\frac{\partial z}{\partial y}.\frac{dy}{dY} = 1.\frac{\partial z}{\partial y}.\frac{1}{y} = \frac{1}{y}\frac{\partial z}{\partial y}.$$

$\therefore$ (2) $\Rightarrow$ $P^2 + Q = 0$ ...(3)

This equation is of the form $g(P, Q) = 0$.

Let $\qquad Z = aX + \phi(a)\,Y + c$ ...(4)

be the complete solution of (3), where $\phi(a)$ is some function of a.

(4) $\Rightarrow$ $\qquad P = \dfrac{\partial Z}{\partial X} = a$ and $Q = \dfrac{\partial Z}{\partial Y} = \phi(a)$

$\therefore$ (3) $\Rightarrow$ $\qquad a^2 + \phi(a) = 0$ or $\phi(a) = -a^2$

$\therefore$ The complete solution of (3) is $Z = aX - a^2Y + c$.

$\therefore$ The complete solution (1) is $\mathbf{z = -a\sqrt{1-x^2} - \dfrac{a^2}{2}y^2 + c}$, where a and c are arbitrary constants.

EXERCISE 5

Find the complete solution of the following partial differential equations :

1. $p^2x + q^2y = z$
2. $pq = x^m y^n z^l$
3. $p^2 - q^2 = z$
4. $p^2 + q^2 = z$
5. $p^2y\,(1 + x^2) = qx^2$
6. $zy^2p = x(y^2 + z^2q^2)$
7. $z^2(p^2/x^2 + q^2/y^2) = 1$
8. $x^4p^2 + y^2zq - z^2 = 0$
9. $p^m \sec^{2m} x + z^l q^n \operatorname{cosec}^{2n} y = z^{lm/(m-n)}$
10. $z^2p^2y + 6zpxy + 2zqx^2 + 4x^2y = 0.$

Answers

1. $\sqrt{z} = a\sqrt{x} \pm \sqrt{1-a^2}\,\sqrt{y} + c,\ -1 \le a \le 1$
2. $\dfrac{2z^{1-(l/2)}}{2-l} = \dfrac{a}{m+1}x^{m+1} + \dfrac{1}{(n+1)\,a}y^{n+1} + c,\ a \ne 0$
3. $2\sqrt{z} = ax \pm \sqrt{a^2-1}\,y + c,\ |a| \ge 1$
4. $2\sqrt{z} = ax \pm \sqrt{1-a^2}\,y + c,\ -1 \le a \le 1$
5. $z = a\sqrt{1+x^2} + \dfrac{1}{2}a^2y^2 + c$
6. $z^2 = ax^2 \pm \sqrt{a-1}\,y^2 + c,\ a \ge 1$

7. $z^2 = ax^2 \pm \sqrt{1-a^2}\, y^2 + c, -1 \le a \le 1$

8. $xy \log z + ay = (a^2 - 1)x + cxy$

9. $\dfrac{m-n}{m-n-l} z^{(m-n-l)/(m-n)} = \dfrac{a}{4}(2x + \sin 2x) + \dfrac{(1-a^m)^{1/n}}{4}(2y - \sin 2y) + c$

10. $z^2 = ax^2 - \left(\dfrac{a^2}{2} + 3a + 2\right) y^2 + c.$

7. CHARPIT'S GENERAL METHOD OF SOLUTION

If the given partial differential equation is not of any of the given special types, then the given equation is solved by using Charpit's general method.

Let $f(x, y, z, p, q) = 0$ ...(1)

be the given partial differential equation of first order and non-linear in p and q.

Since z is a function of x and y, we have $dz = p\,dx + q\,dy$ ...(2)

The procedure is to first find an equation involving x, y, z, p, q.

Let $F(x, y, z, p, q) = 0$ ...(3)

be the required equation involving x, y, z, p, q. The equations (1) and (3) are solved to find the values of p and q. The values of p and q are substituted in (2) and is then integrated to get the desired result.

Differentiating (1) and (3) partially w.r.t. x and y, we get

$$\frac{\partial f}{\partial x} + \frac{\partial f}{\partial z} p + \frac{\partial f}{\partial p}\frac{\partial p}{\partial x} + \frac{\partial f}{\partial q}\frac{\partial q}{\partial x} = 0 \quad ...(4)$$

$$\frac{\partial f}{\partial y} + \frac{\partial f}{\partial z} q + \frac{\partial f}{\partial p}\frac{\partial p}{\partial y} + \frac{\partial f}{\partial q}\frac{\partial q}{\partial y} = 0 \quad ...(5)$$

$$\frac{\partial F}{\partial x} + \frac{\partial F}{\partial z} p + \frac{\partial F}{\partial p}\frac{\partial p}{\partial x} + \frac{\partial F}{\partial q}\frac{\partial q}{\partial x} = 0 \quad ...(6)$$

$$\frac{\partial F}{\partial y} + \frac{\partial F}{\partial z} q + \frac{\partial F}{\partial p}\frac{\partial p}{\partial y} + \frac{\partial F}{\partial q}\frac{\partial q}{\partial y} = 0 \quad ...(7)$$

Multiplying (4) by $\dfrac{\partial F}{\partial p}$, (6) by $\dfrac{\partial f}{\partial p}$ and subtracting, we get

$$\frac{\partial f}{\partial x}\frac{\partial F}{\partial p} - \frac{\partial F}{\partial x}\frac{\partial f}{\partial p} + \left(\frac{\partial f}{\partial z}\frac{\partial F}{\partial p} - \frac{\partial F}{\partial z}\frac{\partial f}{\partial p}\right)p + \left(\frac{\partial f}{\partial q}\frac{\partial F}{\partial p} - \frac{\partial F}{\partial q}\frac{\partial f}{\partial p}\right)\frac{\partial q}{\partial x} = 0 \quad ...(8)$$

Multiplying (5) by $\dfrac{\partial F}{\partial q}$, (7) by $\dfrac{\partial F}{\partial q}$ and subtracting, we get

$$\frac{\partial f}{\partial y}\frac{\partial F}{\partial q} - \frac{\partial F}{\partial y}\frac{\partial f}{\partial q} + \left(\frac{\partial f}{\partial z}\frac{\partial F}{\partial q} - \frac{\partial F}{\partial z}\frac{\partial f}{\partial q}\right)q + \left(\frac{\partial f}{\partial p}\frac{\partial F}{\partial q} - \frac{\partial F}{\partial p}\frac{\partial f}{\partial q}\right)\frac{\partial p}{\partial y} = 0 \quad ...(9)$$

Adding (8) and (9), we get

$$\frac{\partial f}{\partial x}\frac{\partial F}{\partial p} - \frac{\partial F}{\partial x}\frac{\partial f}{\partial p} + \left(\frac{\partial f}{\partial z}\frac{\partial F}{\partial p} - \frac{\partial F}{\partial z}\frac{\partial f}{\partial p}\right)p + \frac{\partial f}{\partial y}\frac{\partial F}{\partial q} - \frac{\partial F}{\partial y}\frac{\partial f}{\partial q} + \left(\frac{\partial f}{\partial z}\frac{\partial F}{\partial q} - \frac{\partial F}{\partial z}\frac{\partial f}{\partial q}\right)q = 0$$

$$\left(\because \frac{\partial q}{\partial x} = \frac{\partial^2 z}{\partial x \partial y} = \frac{\partial^2 z}{\partial y \partial x} = \frac{\partial p}{\partial q}\right)$$

$$\Rightarrow \left(\frac{\partial f}{\partial x} + p\frac{\partial f}{\partial z}\right)\frac{\partial F}{\partial p} + \left(\frac{\partial f}{\partial y} + q\frac{\partial f}{\partial z}\right)\frac{\partial F}{\partial q} + \left(-p\frac{\partial f}{\partial p} - q\frac{\partial f}{\partial q}\right)\frac{\partial F}{\partial z}$$

$$+ \left(-\frac{\partial f}{\partial p}\right)\frac{\partial F}{\partial x} + \left(-\frac{\partial f}{\partial q}\right)\frac{\partial F}{\partial y} = 0 \quad ...(10)$$

This is a Lagrange equation of first order with independent variables x, y, z, p, q and dependent variable F. The auxiliary equations of (10) are

$$\frac{dp}{\frac{\partial f}{\partial x} + p\frac{\partial f}{\partial z}} = \frac{dq}{\frac{\partial f}{\partial y} + q\frac{\partial f}{\partial z}} = \frac{dz}{-p\frac{\partial f}{\partial p} - q\frac{\partial f}{\partial q}} = \frac{dx}{-\frac{\partial f}{\partial p}} = \frac{dy}{-\frac{\partial f}{\partial q}} = \frac{dF}{0} \quad ...(11)$$

Any of the integrals of (11) satisfy (10). If any such integral involve p or q or both, it can be taken as the assumed relation (3). Simpler the integral involving p or q or both, that is derived from (11), the easier will be the solution of (1). Substituting these values of p and q in $dz = p\,dx + q\,dy$ and then integrating, we find the required solution.

Example 1. *Find the complete solution of the following partial differential equations by using Charpit's method :*

(*i*) $z = px + qy + p^2 + q^2$ (KU 2005 S) (*ii*) $z^2 = pqxy$

(*iii*) $px + qy = pq$ (KU 2006) (*iv*) $(p^2 + q^2)\,y = qz$ (KU 2004)

(*v*) $p = (qy + z)^2$. (KU 2005)

Sol. (*i*) We have $z = px + qy + p^2 + q^2$. ...(1)

Let $f(x, y, z, p, q) = z - px - qy - p^2 - q^2$.

$$\therefore \quad \frac{\partial f}{\partial x} = -p,\quad \frac{\partial f}{\partial y} = -q,\quad \frac{\partial f}{\partial z} = 1,\quad \frac{\partial f}{\partial p} = -x - 2p,\quad \frac{\partial f}{\partial q} = -y - 2q$$

Charpit's auxiliary equations are

$$\frac{dp}{\frac{\partial f}{\partial x} + p\frac{\partial f}{\partial z}} = \frac{dq}{\frac{\partial f}{\partial y} + q\frac{\partial f}{\partial z}} = \frac{dz}{-p\frac{\partial f}{\partial p} - q\frac{\partial f}{\partial q}} = \frac{dx}{-\frac{\partial f}{\partial p}} = \frac{dy}{-\frac{\partial f}{\partial q}}$$

$$\Rightarrow \quad \frac{dp}{-p + p(1)} = \frac{dq}{-q + q(1)} = \frac{dz}{-p(-x - 2p) - q(-y - 2q)} = \frac{dx}{-x - 2p} = \frac{dy}{-y - 2q}$$

$$\Rightarrow \quad \frac{dp}{0} = \frac{dq}{0} = \frac{dz}{px + qy + 2p^2 + 2q^2} = \frac{dx}{-x - 2p} = \frac{dy}{-y - 2q}$$

First fraction implies $dp = 0$. Let $p = a$.

Similarly, let $q = b$.

Now $dz = p\,dx + q\,dy \quad \therefore \quad dz = a\,dx + b\,dy$

Integrating, we get $z = ax + by + c$.

Putting the value of z in (1), we get $ax + by + c = ax + by + a^2 + b^2$ or $c = a^2 + b^2$.

$$\therefore \quad \mathbf{z = ax + by + a^2 + b^2.}$$

This is the complete solution.

(*ii*) We have $z^2 = pqxy$. ...(1)

Let $f(x, y, z, p, q) = z^2 - pqxy$.

$$\therefore \quad \frac{\partial f}{\partial x} = -pqy,\quad \frac{\partial f}{\partial y} = -pqx,\quad \frac{\partial f}{\partial z} = 2z,\quad \frac{\partial f}{\partial p} = -qxy,\quad \frac{\partial f}{\partial q} = -pxy$$

Charpit's auxiliary equations are

$$\frac{dp}{\frac{\partial f}{\partial x} + p\frac{\partial f}{\partial z}} = \frac{dq}{\frac{\partial f}{\partial y} + q\frac{\partial f}{\partial z}} = \frac{dz}{-p\frac{\partial f}{\partial p} - q\frac{\partial f}{\partial q}} = \frac{dx}{-\frac{\partial f}{\partial p}} = \frac{dy}{-\frac{\partial f}{\partial q}}$$

$$\Rightarrow \quad \frac{dp}{-pqy + p(2z)} = \frac{dq}{-pqx + q(2z)} = \frac{dz}{-p(-qxy) - q(-pxy)} = \frac{dx}{-(-qxy)} = \frac{dy}{-(-pxy)}$$

$$\Rightarrow \quad \frac{dp}{2pz - pqy} = \frac{dq}{2qz - pqx} = \frac{dz}{2pqxy} = \frac{dx}{qxy} = \frac{dy}{pxy} \qquad ...(2)$$

$$(2) \Rightarrow \quad \frac{xdp + pdx}{x(2pz - pqy) + p(qxy)} = \frac{ydq + qdy}{y(2qz - pqx) + q(pxy)}$$

$$\Rightarrow \quad \frac{x\,dp + p\,dx}{2xpz} = \frac{y\,dq + q\,dy}{2yqz} \Rightarrow \frac{d(xp)}{xp} = \frac{d(yq)}{yq}$$

Integrating, we get $\log xp = \log yq + a$

$$\Rightarrow \quad xp = yqb^2 \qquad ...(3) \quad (\text{Putting } a = \log b^2)$$

Solving (1) and (3) for p and q, we get $p = \frac{bz}{x}$ and $q = \frac{z}{by}$.

Now $\quad dz = p\,dx + q\,dy \quad \therefore \quad dz = \frac{bz}{x}dx + \frac{z}{by}dy$

$$\Rightarrow \quad \frac{dz}{z} = \frac{b}{x}dx + \frac{1}{by}dy$$

Integrating, we get $\log z = b \log x + \frac{1}{b} \log y + \log c$.

$$\therefore \quad \mathbf{z = cx^b\, y^{1/b}}$$

This is the complete solution.

(*iii*) We have $\quad px + qy = pq$. ...(1)

Let $\quad f(x, y, z, p, q) = px + qy - pq$.

$$\therefore \quad \frac{\partial f}{\partial x} = p, \quad \frac{\partial f}{\partial y} = q, \quad \frac{\partial f}{\partial z} = 0, \quad \frac{\partial f}{\partial p} = x - q, \quad \frac{\partial f}{\partial q} = y - p$$

Charpit's auxiliary equations are

$$\frac{dp}{\frac{\partial f}{\partial x} + p\frac{\partial f}{\partial z}} = \frac{dq}{\frac{\partial f}{\partial y} + q\frac{\partial f}{\partial z}} = \frac{dz}{-p\frac{\partial f}{\partial p} - q\frac{\partial f}{\partial q}} = \frac{dx}{-\frac{\partial f}{\partial p}} = \frac{dy}{-\frac{\partial f}{\partial q}}$$

$$\Rightarrow \quad \frac{dp}{p + p(0)} = \frac{dq}{q + q(0)} = \frac{dz}{-p(x - q) - q(y - p)} = \frac{dx}{-(x - q)} = \frac{dy}{-(y - p)}$$

$$\Rightarrow \quad \frac{dp}{p} = \frac{dq}{q} = \frac{dz}{-px - qy + 2pq} = \frac{dx}{q - x} = \frac{dy}{p - y} \qquad ...(2)$$

$$(2) \Rightarrow \quad \frac{dp}{p} = \frac{dq}{q} \Rightarrow \log p = \log q + \log a \Rightarrow p = aq \qquad ...(3)$$

Solving (1) and (3), we get $p = 0, q = 0$ or $p = ax + y, q = \frac{ax + y}{a}$.

Case I. $p = 0, q = 0$

$\therefore \quad dz = p\,dx + q\,dy \Rightarrow dz = 0\,dx + 0\,dy = 0 \Rightarrow z = c.$

This is not a complete solution, because it does not contain two arbitrary constants.

Case II. $p = ax + y,\ q = \dfrac{ax+y}{a}$

$$\therefore \quad dz = p\,dx + q\,dy \Rightarrow dz = (ax+y)\,dx + \left(\frac{ax+y}{a}\right)dy$$

$$= \frac{ax+y}{a}(a\,dx + dy) = \frac{ax+y}{a}\,d(ax+y)$$

Integrating we get $\quad z = \dfrac{(\mathbf{ax+y})^2}{\mathbf{2a}} + \mathbf{b}.$

This is the complete solution.

(*iv*) We have $\quad (p^2+q^2)\,y = qz.$ ...(1)

Let $\quad f(x, y, z, p, q) = p^2y + q^2y - qz.$

$$\therefore \quad \frac{\partial f}{\partial x} = 0,\quad \frac{\partial f}{\partial y} = p^2+q^2,\quad \frac{\partial f}{\partial z} = -q,\quad \frac{\partial f}{\partial p} = 2py,\quad \frac{\partial f}{\partial q} = 2qy - z$$

Charpit's auxiliary equations are

$$\frac{dp}{\dfrac{\partial f}{\partial x} + p\dfrac{\partial f}{\partial z}} = \frac{dq}{\dfrac{\partial f}{\partial y} + q\dfrac{\partial f}{\partial z}} = \frac{dz}{-p\dfrac{\partial f}{\partial p} - q\dfrac{\partial f}{\partial q}} = \frac{dx}{-\dfrac{\partial f}{\partial p}} = \frac{dy}{-\dfrac{\partial f}{\partial q}}$$

$$\Rightarrow \quad \frac{dp}{0+p(-q)} = \frac{dq}{p^2+q^2+q(-q)} = \frac{dz}{-p(2py)-q(2qy-z)} = \frac{dx}{-2py} = \frac{dy}{-(2qy-z)}$$

$$\Rightarrow \quad \frac{dp}{-pq} = \frac{dq}{p^2} = \frac{dz}{-2p^2y-2q^2y+qz} = \frac{dx}{-2py} = \frac{dy}{z-2qy} \qquad ...(2)$$

$$(2) \Rightarrow \quad \frac{dp}{-pq} = \frac{dq}{p^2} \Rightarrow \frac{dp}{-q} = \frac{dq}{p} \Rightarrow pdp + qdq = 0$$

Integrating, we get $\quad \dfrac{p^2}{2} + \dfrac{q^2}{2} = \dfrac{a}{2} \quad$ or $\quad p^2+q^2 = a$ ...(3)

Solving (1) and (3), we get $p = \sqrt{a - \dfrac{a^2y^2}{z^2}}$ and $\quad q = \dfrac{ay}{z}$.

$$\therefore \quad dz = p\,dx + q\,dy \Rightarrow dz = \frac{\sqrt{az^2-a^2y^2}}{z}\,dx + \frac{ay}{z}\,dy$$

$$\Rightarrow \quad z\,dz - ay\,dy = \sqrt{az^2-a^2y^2}\;dx \Rightarrow d\left(\frac{z^2}{2}\right) - d\left(\frac{ay^2}{2}\right) = \sqrt{az^2-a^2y^2}\;dx$$

$$\Rightarrow \quad \frac{1}{2a}\,d\,(az^2-a^2y^2) = \sqrt{az^2-a^2y^2}\;dx \Rightarrow \frac{d(az^2-a^2y^2)}{\sqrt{az^2-a^2y^2}} = 2adx$$

Integrating, we get $2\sqrt{az^2-a^2y^2} = 2ax + 2b \Rightarrow \mathbf{az^2 - a^2y^2 = (ax+b)^2}.$

This is the complete solution.

(v) We have $p = (qy + z)^2$. ...(1)

Let $f(x, y, z, p, q) = (qy + z)^2 - p$

$\therefore \quad \frac{\partial f}{\partial x} = 0, \quad \frac{\partial f}{\partial y} = 2(qy + z)q, \quad \frac{\partial f}{\partial z} = 2(qy + z), \quad \frac{\partial f}{\partial p} = -1, \quad \frac{\partial f}{\partial q} = 2(qy + z)\,y$

Charpit's auxiliary equations are

$$\frac{dp}{\frac{\partial f}{\partial x} + p\frac{\partial f}{\partial z}} = \frac{dq}{\frac{\partial f}{\partial y} + q\frac{\partial f}{\partial z}} = \frac{dz}{-p\frac{\partial f}{\partial p} - q\frac{\partial f}{\partial q}} = \frac{dx}{-\frac{\partial f}{\partial p}} = \frac{dy}{-\frac{\partial f}{\partial q}}$$

$$\Rightarrow \quad \frac{dp}{0 + p2(qy + z)} = \frac{dq}{2q(qy + z) + q2(qy + z)} = \frac{dz}{-p(-1) - q2y(qy + z)} = \frac{dx}{-(-1)}$$

$$= \frac{dy}{-2y(qy + z)}$$

$$\Rightarrow \quad \frac{dp}{2p(qy + z)} = \frac{dq}{4q(qy + z)} = \frac{dz}{p - 2yq(qy + z)} = \frac{dx}{1} = \frac{dy}{-2y(qy + z)} \qquad ...(2)$$

$$(2) \Rightarrow \quad \frac{dp}{2p(qy + z)} = \frac{dy}{-2y(qy + z)} \quad \Rightarrow \quad \frac{dp}{p} + \frac{dy}{y} = 0$$

Integrating, we get $\log |p| + \log |y| = \log C$

$\Rightarrow \quad |py| = C \Rightarrow py = \pm C \Rightarrow py = a$ (Putting $a = \pm C$)

$\therefore \quad p = a/y$

Putting the value of p in (1), we get $\frac{a}{y} = (qy + z)^2$.

$$\Rightarrow \quad qy + z = \sqrt{\frac{a}{y}} \quad \Rightarrow \quad qy = \sqrt{\frac{a}{y}} - z \quad \Rightarrow \quad q = \frac{\sqrt{a}}{y^{3/2}} - \frac{z}{y}$$

$$\therefore \quad dz = pdx + qdy \quad \Rightarrow \quad dz = \frac{a}{y}dx + \left(\frac{\sqrt{a}}{y^{3/2}} - \frac{z}{y}\right)dy$$

$$\Rightarrow \quad ydz = adx + \left(\frac{\sqrt{a}}{\sqrt{y}} - z\right)dy \quad \Rightarrow \quad ydz + zdy = adx + \frac{\sqrt{a}}{\sqrt{y}}dy$$

$$\Rightarrow \quad d(yz) = adx + \frac{\sqrt{a}}{\sqrt{y}}dy$$

Integrating, we get $yz = ax + \sqrt{a} \cdot \frac{y^{1/2}}{1/2} + b \Rightarrow$ $\mathbf{yz = ax + 2\sqrt{ay} + b}$.

This is the complete solution.

WORKING RULES FOR USING CHARPIT'S METHOD

Step I. Shift all terms of the given equation to the left side and denote the left side by $f(x, y, z, p, q)$.

Step II. Find $\frac{\partial f}{\partial x}, \frac{\partial f}{\partial y}, \frac{\partial f}{\partial z}, \frac{\partial f}{\partial p}, \frac{\partial f}{\partial q}$.

Step III. Write the Charpit's auxiliary equations and substitute the values of partial derivatives of f and simplify.

Step IV. Select any two fractions so that the resulting integral is the simplest relation involving at least one of p and q. This relation and the given equation are solved to find the values of p and q.

Step V. Put the values of p and q in the equation $dz = p\,dx + q\,dy$ and integrate. This gives the complete solution of the given equation.

EXERCISE 6

Find the complete solution of the following partial differential equations by using Charpit's method :

1. $q = px + q^2$
2. $q = 3p^2$
3. $p^2 - y^2q = y^2 - x^2$ (*MDU 2006*)
4. $pxy + pq + qy = yz$
5. $2(z + px + qy) = yp^2$ (*CDLU 2004*)
6. $2z + p^2 + qy + 2y^2 = 0$ (*MDU 2005*)
7. $q = px + p^2$
8. $2xz - px^2 - 2qxy + pq = 0$ (*MDU 2004*)
9. $p(1 + q^2) + (b - z)q = 0$
10. $(p^2 + q^2)x = pz$.

Answers

1. $z = (a - a^2)\log x + ay + b$
2. $z = ax + 3a^2y + b$
3. $z = \dfrac{x\sqrt{a^2 - x^2}}{2} + \dfrac{a^2}{2}\sin^{-1}\dfrac{x}{a} - \dfrac{a^2}{y} - y + b$
4. $(z - ax)(y + a)^a = be^y$
5. $yz - \dfrac{ax}{y} + \dfrac{a^2}{4y^2} = b$
6. $y^2((a - x)^2 + 2z + y^2) = b$
7. $z = -\dfrac{x^2}{4} \pm \left[\dfrac{x\sqrt{x^2 + 4a}}{4} + a\log\left(x + \sqrt{x^2 + 4a}\right)\right] + ay + b$
8. $z = ay + b(x^2 - a)$
9. $2\sqrt{c(z - b) - 1} = x + cy + a$
10. $az^2 - a^2x^2 = (ay + b)^2$.

Hints

4. $p = a \Rightarrow q = \dfrac{y(z - ax)}{a + y}$

$$\therefore\quad dz = p\,dx + q\,dy \;\Rightarrow\; dz = a\,dx + \frac{y(z - ax)}{a + y}dy \;\Rightarrow\; \frac{dz - a\,dx}{z - ax} = \frac{y}{a + y}dy.$$

5. Charpit's auxiliary equations implies $\dfrac{dp}{4p} = \dfrac{dy}{-2y}$ or $py^2 = a$

Also $dz = \dfrac{a}{y^2}dx + \left(-\dfrac{z}{y} - \dfrac{ax}{y^3} + \dfrac{a^2}{2y^4}\right)dy \;\Rightarrow\; (y\,dz + z\,dy) - a\left(\dfrac{1}{y}dx - \dfrac{x\,dy}{y^2}\right) - \dfrac{a^2}{2y^3}dy = 0$

6. $dz = (a - x)\,dx - \dfrac{1}{y}(2z + 2y^2 + (a - x)^2)\,dy$

Multiplying by $2y^2$, we get $(2y^2\,dz + 4yz\,dy) = (2y^2(a - x)\,dx - 2y(a - x)^2\,dy) - 4y^3\,dy$.

13

Homogeneous Linear Partial Differential Equations with Constant Coefficients

1. INTRODUCTION

Till now we have been discussing the methods of solving partial differential equations of the first order. A partial differential equation of the first order involves, only the first order partial derivatives (p and q) of the dependent variable z. Now we shall consider the solution of partial differential equations of order higher than one.

2. PARTIAL DIFFERENTIAL EQUATIONS OF SECOND AND HIGHER ORDER

We know that the order of a partial differential equation is the order of the highest partial derivative occurring in the given partial differential equation.

For example, $\frac{\partial^3 z}{\partial x^3} + 2\frac{\partial^2 z}{\partial x \partial y} + \frac{\partial z}{\partial y} = x^2 + y$ is a partial differential equation of order 3. For the sake of simplicity, $\frac{\partial}{\partial x}$ and $\frac{\partial}{\partial y}$ are denoted by D(or D_x) and D′(or D_y) respectively. Thus, the above differential equation can also be written as $(D^3 + 2DD' + D')z = x^2 + y$ or as $(D_x^{\ 3} + 2D_x D_y + D_y)z = x^2 + y$.

Remark. DD′z stands for $\frac{\partial^2 z}{\partial x \partial y}$ and not for $\frac{\partial z}{\partial x} \cdot \frac{\partial z}{\partial y}$. The product $\frac{\partial z}{\partial x} \cdot \frac{\partial z}{\partial y}$ is denoted as (Dz)(D′z).

3. HOMOGENEOUS LINEAR PARTIAL DIFFERENTIAL EQUATIONS WITH CONSTANT COEFFICIENTS

We know that a partial differential equation is called linear if the dependent variable and its partial derivatives occur only in the first degree and are not multiplied together. A linear partial differential equation of order n is of the form

$$\left(A_0 \frac{\partial^n z}{\partial x^n} + A_1 \frac{\partial^n z}{\partial x^{n-1} \partial y} + \ldots\ldots + A_n \frac{\partial^n z}{\partial y^n}\right) + \left(B_0 \frac{\partial^{n-1} z}{\partial x^{n-1}} + \ldots\ldots + B_{n-1} \frac{\partial^{n-1} z}{\partial y^{n-1}}\right)$$
$$+ \ldots\ldots + \left(M \frac{\partial z}{\partial x} + N \frac{\partial z}{\partial y}\right) + Pz = F(x, y),$$

where the coefficients $A_0, A_1, \ldots\ldots$ N, P are constants or functions of x and y. If the coefficients $A_0, A_1, \ldots\ldots$, N, P are all constants then such a differential equation is called a **linear partial differential equation with constant coefficients**.

In a linear partial differential equation, the orders of various partial derivatives occurring in the equation may or may not be equal. In case the orders of all partial derivatives involved in the equation are same then it is called a **homogeneous linear partial differential equation** and otherwise it is called a **non-homogeneous linear partial differential equation.**

A homogeneous linear partial differential equation with constant coefficients is of the form $A_0 \dfrac{\partial^n z}{\partial x^n} + A_1 \dfrac{\partial^n z}{\partial x^{n-1}\partial y} + \ldots\ldots + A_n \dfrac{\partial^n z}{\partial y^n} = F(x, y)$,

where $A_0, A_1, \ldots\ldots, A_n$ are all constants.

Consider the following partial differential equations :

(*i*) $4\dfrac{\partial^2 z}{\partial x^2} + 5\dfrac{\partial^2 z}{\partial x \partial y} + \dfrac{\partial^2 z}{\partial y^2} = e^x$

(*ii*) $\dfrac{\partial^2 z}{\partial x^2} - \dfrac{\partial^2 z}{\partial x \partial y} = \cos x \cos 2y$

(*iii*) $(D^3 - 2D^2D' - DD'^2 + 2D'^3)z = \sin x$

(*iv*) $\dfrac{\partial^2 z}{\partial x^2} + \dfrac{\partial^2 z}{\partial x \partial y} + \dfrac{\partial z}{\partial y} - z = e^{-x}$

(*v*) $(2DD' + D'^2 - 3D)z = 3\cos(3x - 2y)$

(*vi*) $r - s + 2q - z = x^2y^2$

(*vii*) $xyr + x^2s - yt = x^3e^y$

(*viii*) $r + (y/x)s = 15xy^2$

(*ix*) $yt + xs + q = 8yx^2 + 9y^2$.

Differential equations (*i*), (*ii*) and (*iii*) are homogeneous linear partial differential equations with constant coefficients.

Differential equations (*iv*), (*v*) and (*vi*) non-homogeneous linear partial differential equation with constant coefficients.

Differential equations (*vii*) and (*viii*) are homogeneous linear partial differential equations with variable coefficients.

Differential equation (*ix*) is a non-homogeneous linear partial differential equation with variable coefficients.

In the present chapter, we shall consider the methods of solving homogeneous linear partial differential equations with constant coefficients.

4. SOME THEOREMS

Let $f(D, D')z = F(x, y)$ be a linear partial differential equation with constant coefficients.

$\therefore$ The function $f(D, D')$ is of the form

$$\left(A_0 \frac{\partial^n z}{\partial x^n} + A_1 \frac{\partial^n z}{\partial x^{n-1}\partial y} + \ldots\ldots + A_n \frac{\partial^n z}{\partial y^n}\right) + \left(B_0 \frac{\partial^{n-1} z}{\partial x^{n-1}} + \ldots\ldots + B_{n-1} \frac{\partial^{n-1} z}{\partial y^{n-1}}\right) + \ldots\ldots + \left(M\frac{\partial z}{\partial x} + N\frac{\partial z}{\partial y}\right) + Pz$$

where $A_0, A_1, \ldots\ldots, N, P$ are all constants.

Theorem 1. Let $f(D, D')z = 0$ be a linear partial differential equation with constant coefficients. If $u_1, u_2, \ldots, u_m$ be m solutions of $f(D, D')z = 0$, then prove that $\sum_{i=1}^{m} c_i u_i$ is also a solution of $f(D, D')z = 0$.

Proof. u_i is a solution of $f(D, D')\, z = 0$ for $1 \le i \le m$.

$\therefore$ $f(D, D')\, u_i = 0$ for $1 \le i \le m$

Now $f(D, D')\left(\sum_{i=1}^{m} c_i u_i\right) = \sum_{i=1}^{m} f(D, D')(c_i u_i) = \sum_{i=1}^{m} c_i f(D, D') u_i = \sum_{i=1}^{m} c_i\,(0) = 0.$

$\therefore$ $\sum_{i=1}^{m} c_i u_i$ is also a solution of the equation $F(D, D')z = 0$.

Theorem 2. Let f(D, D′)z = F(x, y) be a linear partial differential equation with constant coefficients. If u is a solution of f(D, D′)z = 0 and v is a solution of f(D, D′) z = F(x, y), then prove that u + v is a solution of f(D, D′) z = F(x, y).

Proof. u is a solution of $f(D, D')z = 0$.

$\therefore \quad f(D, D')u = 0 \quad \quad ...(1)$

v is a solution of $f(D, D')z = F(x, y)$.

$\therefore \quad f(D, D')v = F(x, y) \quad \quad ...(2)$

Now
$$f(D, D')(u + v) = f(D, D')u + f(D, D')v$$
$$= 0 + F(x, y) \quad \text{(Using (1), (2))}$$
$$= F(x, y).$$

$\therefore \quad u + v$ is a solution of $f(D, D')z = F(x, y)$.

5. GENERAL SOLUTION OF HOMOGENEOUS LINEAR PARTIAL DIFFERENTIAL EQUATION f(D, D′)z = 0 WITH CONSTANT COEFFICIENTS

Let
$$f(D, D')z = A_0 \frac{\partial^n z}{\partial x^n} + A_1 \frac{\partial^n z}{\partial x^{n-1} \partial y} + ... + A_n \frac{\partial^n z}{\partial y^n} = 0 \quad ...(1)$$

be a homogeneous linear partial differential equation with constant coefficients, where $A_0 \neq 0$.

(1) can also be written as $(A_0 D^n + A_1 D^{n-1} D' + ... + A_n D'^n) z = 0 \quad ...(2)$

Let (2) be equivalent to $A_0[(D - m_1 D')(D - m_2 D') ...... (D - m_n D')] z = 0 \quad ...(3)$

Treating D and D′ as variables, the equations (2) and (3) implies

$$A_0 \left(\frac{D}{D'}\right)^n + A_1 \left(\frac{D}{D'}\right)^{n-1} + ... + A_n = A_0 \left(\frac{D}{D'} - m_1\right)\left(\frac{D}{D'} - m_2\right)......\left(\frac{D}{D'} - m_n\right)$$

$\therefore \quad m_1, m_2, ..., m_n$ are roots of the equation

$$A_0 m^n + A_1 m^{n-1} + ... + A_n = 0. \quad ...(4)$$

The equation (4) is called the **auxiliary equation** of (2). This equation can be obtained by putting D equal to m and D′ equal to '1' in the operator of equation (2) and equating it to zero.

The roots $m_1, m_2, ..., m_n$ of the auxiliary equation may or may not be distinct.

Case I. Roots are distinct.

$\therefore \quad m_1 \neq m_2 \neq m_3 \neq ...... \neq m_n$.

Equation (3) shows that for $1 \le i \le n$, the solution of $(D - m_i D') z = 0$ is a solution of (3) and hence of (1).

$$(D - m_i D') z = 0 \quad \Rightarrow \quad p - m_i q = 0$$

$$\Rightarrow \quad \frac{dx}{1} = \frac{dy}{-m_i} = \frac{dz}{0} \quad \Rightarrow \quad dy + m_i dx = 0, \quad dz = 0$$

$$\Rightarrow \quad y + m_i x = c_1, \quad z = c_2$$

$$\Rightarrow \quad z = \phi_i(y + m_i x). \quad \text{(Putting } c_2 = \phi_i(c_1))$$

$\therefore \quad z = \phi_1(y + m_1 x), z = \phi_2(y + m_2 x), ... , z = \phi_n(y + m_n x)$ are solutions of (1).

$\therefore \quad z = \phi_1(y + m_1 x) + \phi_2(y + m_2 x) + ... + \phi_n(y + m_n x)$ is also a solution of (1). Since this solution contains n arbitrary functions $\phi_1, \phi_2, ..., \phi_n$, this solution represents the general solution of the given equation.

Case II. Roots are not distinct.

Let $m_1 = m_2 \neq m_3 \neq \ldots\ldots \neq m_n$. In this case, the solution of (1) can be written as

$$z = (\phi_1 + \phi_2)(y + m_1 x) + \ldots\ldots + \phi_n(y + m_n x). \qquad (\because \quad m_1 = m_2)$$

This solution contains only $n - 1$ arbitrary functions $\phi_1 + \phi_2, \phi_3, \ldots\ldots, \phi_n$.

$\therefore$ This is not a general solution.

Using $m_1 = m_2$ in (3), we get, $A_0\,[(D - m_1 D')^2 (D - m_3 D') \ldots\ldots (D - m_n D')]\, z = 0$ ...(5)

Equation (5) shows that for $3 \le i \le n$, the solution of $(D - m_i D')z = 0$ is also a solution of (5) and hence of (1).

$\therefore$ $z = \phi_i(y + m_i x)$, $3 \le i \le n$ is a solution of (1).

$\therefore$ $z = \phi_3(y + m_3 x) + \ldots\ldots + \phi_n(y + m_n x)$ ...(6)

is a solution of (1).

The solution of $(D - m_1 D')^2 z = 0$ is also a solution of (5) and hence of (1).

$$(D - m_1 D')^2 z = 0 \;\Rightarrow\; (D - m_1 D')(D - m_1 D')\, z = 0 \qquad ...(7)$$

Let $(D - m_1 D')\, z = u$. ...(8)

$\therefore$ (7) $\Rightarrow$ $(D - m_1 D')u = 0$

$\Rightarrow$ $u = \psi_1(y + m_1 x)$, where ψ_1 is arbitrary.

$\therefore$ (7) $\Rightarrow$ $p - m_1 q = \psi_1(y + m_1 x)$

$$\Rightarrow \quad \frac{dx}{1} = \frac{dy}{-m_1} = \frac{dz}{\psi_1(y + m_1 x)} \qquad ...(9)$$

(9) $\Rightarrow$ $dy + m_1 dx = 0 \Rightarrow y + m_1 x = c$

Taking the first and third fractions of (9), we get

$$dx = \frac{dz}{\psi_1(c)} \quad \text{or} \quad dz = \psi_1(c)\, dx$$

$$\Rightarrow \quad z = \psi_1(c)\, x + d$$

$$\Rightarrow \quad z = x\psi_1(y + m_1 x) + \psi_2(y + m_2 x) \qquad ...(10) \quad (\text{Putting } d = \psi_2(c))$$

Combining (6) and (10),

$$z = x\psi_1(y + m_1 x) + \psi_2(y + m_2 x) + \phi_3(y + m_3 x) + \ldots\ldots + \phi_n(y + m_n x)$$

is also a solution of (1).

Since this solution contains n arbitrary functions $\psi_1, \psi_2, \phi_3, \ldots\ldots, \phi_n$, this solution represents the general solution of the given equation.

Remarks 1. If the root m_1 of the auxiliary equation is repeated r times, then the corresponding part of the general solution is $\phi_1(y + m_1 x) + x\phi_2(y + m_1 x) + \ldots\ldots + x^{r-1}\phi_r(y + m_1 x)$, where $\phi_1, \phi_2, \ldots\ldots, \phi_r$ are arbitrary functions.

2. The auxiliary equation of a homogeneous linear partial differential equation with constant coefficients is obtained by putting $D = m$ and $D' = 1$ in the operator of the equation and then equating it to zero.

Exceptional Case.

If $A_0 = 0$, $A_1 \neq 0$, then equation (2) becomes $(A_1 D^{n-1} D' + \ldots\ldots + A_n D'^n)\, z = 0$

or $D'(A_1 D^{n-1} + A_2 D^{n-2} D' + \ldots + A_n D'^{n-1})z = 0$ ...(1)

$\therefore$ The solution of $D'z = 0$ is also a solution of (1).

$$D'z = 0 \;\Rightarrow\; \frac{\partial z}{\partial y} = 0 \;\Rightarrow\; z = \phi(x), \text{ where } \phi \text{ is arbitrary.}$$

Similarly, if D'^r is a factor of the operator of the equation then the corresponding part of the general solution is $z = \phi_1(x) + y\phi_2(x) + \ldots\ldots + y^{r-1}\phi_r(x)$, where $\phi_1, \phi_2, \ldots\ldots, \phi_r$ are arbitrary functions.

Example 1. *Find the general solution of the following partial differential equations :*

(i) $\dfrac{\partial^2 z}{\partial x^2} - 8\dfrac{\partial^2 z}{\partial x \partial y} + 15\dfrac{\partial^2 z}{\partial y^2} = 0$ (ii) $2r + 5s + 2t = 0$

(iii) $(D^3 - 6D^2D' + 11DD'^2 - 6D'^3)\, z = 0$ (iv) $(D^4 + D'^4 - 2D^2D'^2)\, z = 0$

(v) $(D^3D'^2 + D^2D'^3)\, z = 0.$

Sol. (i) We have $\dfrac{\partial^2 z}{\partial x^2} - 8\dfrac{\partial^2 z}{\partial x \partial y} + 15\dfrac{\partial^2 z}{\partial y^2} = 0.$

$\Rightarrow \quad (D^2 - 8DD' + 15D'^2)\, z = 0$ ...(1)

By putting D = m and D′ = 1 in the operator of (1), the auxiliary equation of (1) is

$m^2 - 8m + 15 = 0.$

$\therefore \quad m = 3, 5$

$\therefore$ The general solution of the given equation is $\mathbf{z = \phi_1(y + 3x) + \phi_2(y + 5x)}$, where ϕ_1, ϕ_2 are arbitrary functions.

(ii) We have $2r + 5s + 2t = 0.$

$\therefore \quad (2D^2 + 5DD' + 2D'^2)\, z = 0$ ...(1)

The auxiliary equation of (1) is $2m^2 + 5m + 2 = 0.$

$\therefore \quad m = -1/2, -2$

$\therefore$ The general solution of the given equation is

$$\mathbf{z = \phi_1\left(y - \frac{1}{2}x\right) + \phi_2(y - 2x)}, \text{ where } \phi_1, \phi_2 \text{ are arbitrary functions.}$$

(iii) We have $(D^3 - 6D^2D' + 11DD'^2 - 6D'^3)z = 0.$ ...(1)

The auxiliary equation of (1) is $m^3 - 6m^2 + 11m - 6 = 0.$

$\therefore \quad m = 1, 2, 3$

$\therefore$ The general solution of the given equation is

$\mathbf{z = \phi_1(y + x) + \phi_2(y + 2x) + \phi_3(y + 3x)}$, where ϕ_1, ϕ_2, ϕ_3 are arbitrary functions.

(iv) We have $(D^4 + D'^4 - 2D^2D'^2)z = 0$ ...(1)

The auxiliary equation of (1) is $m^4 + 1 - 2m^2 = 0.$

$\therefore \quad (m^2 - 1)^2 = 0$ or $m = 1, 1, -1, -1.$

$\therefore$ The general solution of the given equation is

$$\mathbf{z = \phi_1(y + x) + x\phi_2(y + x) + \phi_3(y - x) + x\phi_4(y - x)},$$

where $\phi_1, \phi_2, \phi_3, \phi_4$ are arbitrary functions.

(v) We have $(D^3D'^2 + D^2D'^3)z = 0.$ ...(1)

(1) $\Rightarrow \quad D'^2D^2(D + D')z = 0$

The part of general solution corresponding to the factor D'^2 is $\phi_1(x) + y\phi_2(x).$

The auxiliary equation of $D^2(D + D')z = 0$ is $m^2(m + 1) = 0$

$\therefore \quad m = 0, 0, -1$

$\therefore$ The part of general solution corresponding to the factor $D^2(D + D')$ is

$\phi_3(y + 0.x) + x\phi_4(y + 0.x) + \phi_5(y + (-1)x).$

$\therefore$ The general solution of the given equation is

$$\mathbf{z = \phi_1(x) + y\phi_2(x) + \phi_3(y) + x\phi_4(y) + \phi_5(y - x)},$$

where $\phi_1, \phi_2, \phi_3, \phi_4, \phi_5$ are arbitrary.

WORKING RULES FOR SOLVING PROBLEMS

Step I. Express the given equation in terms of D and D′.

Step II. Put D = m and D′ = 1 in the operator of the equation and equate it to zero. This is the auxiliary equation of the given equation. Solve the auxiliary equation.

Step III. If m_i is a distinct root then the corresponding part of the general solution is $\phi(y + m_i x)$. If m_i is a root repeated r times then the corresponding part of the general solution is $\phi_1(y + m_i x) + x\phi_2(y + m_i x) + \ldots\ldots + x^{r-1}\phi_r(y + m_i x)$.

Step IV. If D'^r is a factor of the operator of the equation then we put D = m and D′ = 1 in the other factor of the operator and the part of the general solution corresponding to D'^r is taken as $\phi_1(x) + y\phi_2(x) + \ldots\ldots + y^{r-1}\phi_r(x)$.

EXERCISE 1

Find the general solution of the following partial differential equations :

1. $r = a^2 t$

2. $\dfrac{\partial^2 z}{\partial x^2} - \dfrac{\partial^2 z}{\partial y^2} = 0$

3. $\left(\dfrac{\partial^2 z}{\partial x^2} - 2\dfrac{\partial^2 z}{\partial x \partial y} - \dfrac{\partial^2 z}{\partial y^2}\right) = 0$

4. $(D^2 - 4DD' + 4D'^2)\, z = 0$

5. $25r - 40s + 16t = 0$

6. $(D^3 + 2D^2D' - DD'^2 - 2D'^3)\, z = 0$

7. $(D^3 - 3DD'^2 + 2D'^3)\, z = 0$

8. $(D^3 + D^2D' - 6DD'^2)\, z = 0$

9. $(D^3 - 2D^2D')\, z = 0$

10. $\dfrac{\partial^3 z}{\partial x^3} - 7\dfrac{\partial^3 z}{\partial x \partial y^2} + 6\dfrac{\partial^3 z}{\partial y^3} = 0$

11. $(D^3 - 3D^2D' + 3DD'^2 - D'^3)\, z = 0$

12. $(D^2D' - 3DD'^2 + 2D'^3)\, z = 0$

13. $(D^4 - 2D^3D' + 2DD'^3 - D'^4)\, z = 0$

14. $(D'^3D + D'^4)\, z = 0.$

Answers

1. $z = \phi_1(y + ax) + \phi_2(y - ax)$

2. $z = \phi_1(y + x) + \phi_2(y - x)$

3. $z = \phi_1(y + (1 + \sqrt{2})x) + \phi_2(y + (1 - \sqrt{2})x)$

4. $z = \phi_1(y + 2x) + x\phi_2(y + 2x)$

5. $z = \phi_1\left(y + \dfrac{4}{5}x\right) + x\phi_2\left(y + \dfrac{4}{5}x\right)$

6. $z = \phi_1(y + x) + \phi_2(y - x) + \phi_3(y - 2x)$

7. $z = \phi_1(y + x) + x\phi_2(y + x) + \phi_3(y - 2x)$

8. $z = \phi_1(y) + \phi_2(y + 2x) + \phi_3(y - 3x)$

9. $z = \phi_1(y) + x\phi_2(y) + \phi_3(y + 2x)$

10. $z = \phi_1(y + x) + \phi_2(y + 2x) + \phi_3(y - 3x)$

11. $z = \phi_1(y + x) + x\phi_2(y + x) + x^2\phi_3(y + x)$

12. $z = \phi_1(x) + \phi_2(y + x) + \phi_3(y + 2x)$

13. $z = \phi_1(y - x) + \phi_2(y + x) + x\phi_3(y + x) + x^2\phi_4(y + x)$

14. $z = \phi_1(x) + y\phi_2(x) + y^2\phi_3(x) + \phi_4(y - x)$.

6. GENERAL SOLUTION OF HOMOGENEOUS LINEAR PARTIAL DIFFERENTIAL EQUATION f(D, D′)z = F(x, y) WITH CONSTANT COEFFICIENTS

Let
$$f(D, D')\, z = F(x, y) \qquad \ldots(1)$$
be a homogeneous linear partial differential equation with constant coefficients.

Let u be the general solution of $f(D, D')\, z = 0$.

$$\therefore \quad f(D, D')\, u = 0 \qquad \ldots(2)$$

Let v be a particular integral *i.e.*, a particular solution of $f(D, D')\, z = F(x, y)$.

$$\therefore \quad f(D, D')\, v = F(x, y) \qquad \ldots(3)$$

Now, $f(D, D')(u + v) = f(D, D')u + f(D, D')v = 0 + F(x, y) = F(x, y)$

(Using (2) and (3))

$\therefore$ $u + v$ is a solution of $f(D, D')z = F(x, y)$. Since u is the general solution of the equation $f(D, D')z = 0$, it contains arbitrary functions equal in number to its order.

$\therefore$ The solution $u + v$ of the equation $f(D, D')z = F(x, y)$ also contains as many arbitrary functions as the order of $f(D, D')z = F(x, y)$.

$\therefore$ $u + v$ is the general solution of the equation $f(D, D')z = F(x, y)$.

The general solution u of the equation $f(D, D')z = 0$ is called the **complementary function (C.F.)** of the equation $f(D, D')z = F(x, y)$.

$\therefore$ **The general solution of the equation f(D, D′)z = F(x, y) is obtained by adding the general solution of the equation f(D, D′)z = 0 to any particular integral of the equation f(D, D′)z = F(x, y).**

7. PARTICULAR INTEGRAL OF f(D, D′)z = F(x, y)

Let $$f(D, D')z = F(x, y) \qquad ...(1)$$

be a homogeneous linear partial differential equation with constant coefficients.

The **inverse operator** $\frac{1}{f(D, D')}$ of the operator $f(D, D')$ is defined by the identity

$$f(D, D')\left(\frac{1}{f(D, D')}F(x, y)\right) = F(x, y)$$

$\therefore$ $\frac{1}{f(D, D')}F(x, y)$ is a particular integral of the equation (1) because

$$f(D, D')\left(\frac{1}{f(D, D')}F(x, y)\right) = F(x, y) = \text{R.H.S. of (1).}$$

$\therefore$ $\mathbf{\frac{1}{f(D, D')}F(x, y)}$ **is a particular integral of the equation f(D, D′)z = F(x, y).**

8. PARTICULAR INTEGRAL WHEN F(x, y) IS SUM OR DIFFERENCE OF TERMS OF THE FORM $x^m y^n$.

If $F(x, y)$ is sum or difference of terms of the form $x^m y^n$ then the particular integral $\frac{1}{f(D, D')}F(x, y)$ of the differential equation $f(D, D')z = F(x, y)$ is obtained by expanding $\frac{1}{f(D, D')}$ in an infinite series in ascending powers of either D or D′. The particular integrals obtained in the above mentioned two methods may not be identical. Any of the two particular integrals may be used. If $m < n$, then it is advisible to expand $\frac{1}{f(D, D')}$ in ascending powers of D and in case $n < m$, then we should expand $\frac{1}{f(D, D')}$ in ascending powers of D′.

Example 1. *Find the general solution of the following partial differential equations :*

(i) $(2D^2 - 5DD' + 2D'^2)z = 24(y - x)$

(ii) $r + (a + b)s + abt = xy$.

Sol. *(i)* We have $$(2D^2 - 5DD' + 2D'^2)z = 24(y - x). \qquad ...(1)$$

The A.E. of (1) is $2m^2 - 5m + 2 = 0$.

$\therefore \quad m = 1/2, 2.$

$\therefore \quad \text{C.F.} = \phi_1\left(y + \frac{1}{2}x\right) + \phi_2(y + 2x).$

Now, $\quad \text{P.I.} = \frac{1}{2D^2 - 5DD' + 2D'^2} 24(y - x) = \frac{1}{2D^2}\left(1 - \left(\frac{5D'}{2D} - \frac{D'^2}{D^2}\right)\right)^{-1} 24(y - x)$

$$= \frac{24}{2D^2}\left[1 + \left(\frac{5D'}{2D} - \frac{D'^2}{D^2}\right) + \ldots\ldots\right](y - x)$$

$$= \frac{12}{D^2}\left((y - x) + \frac{5}{2D}(1) + 0\right) = 12\left(\frac{x^2y}{2} - \frac{x^3}{6}\right) + \frac{30}{D^3}(1)$$

$$= 6x^2y - 2x^3 + 30\,\frac{x^3}{6} = 6x^2y + 3x^3.$$

$\therefore$ Using G.S. = C.F. + P.I., the general solution of the given equation is

$$z = \phi_1\left(y + \frac{1}{2}x\right) + \phi_2(y + 2x) + 6x^2y + 3x^3,$$

where ϕ_1 and ϕ_2 are arbitrary functions.

(ii) We have $r + (a + b)s + abt = xy.$

$$\Rightarrow \quad \frac{\partial^2 z}{\partial x^2} + (a + b)\frac{\partial^2 z}{\partial x \partial y} + ab\frac{\partial^2 z}{\partial y^2} = xy$$

$$\Rightarrow \quad (D^2 + (a + b)DD' + abD'^2)z = xy \qquad \ldots(1)$$

The A.E. of (1) is $m^2 + (a + b)m + ab = 0.$

$\therefore \quad m = -a, -b.$

$\therefore \quad \text{C.F.} = \phi_1(y - ax) + \phi_2(y - bx).$

Now, $\quad \text{P.I.} = \frac{1}{D^2 + (a + b)DD' + D'^2}(xy) = \frac{1}{D^2}\left[1 + \left((a + b)\frac{D'}{D} + \frac{D'^2}{D^2}\right)\right]^{-1}(xy)$

$$= \frac{1}{D^2}\left[1 - (a + b)\frac{D'}{D} - \frac{D'^2}{D^2} + \ldots\ldots\right](xy)$$ (MDU 2005)

$$= \frac{1}{D^2}\left[xy - \frac{(a + b)}{D}(x) - 0\right] = y\left(\frac{x^3}{6}\right) - (a + b)\frac{x^4}{24}.$$

$\therefore$ Using G.S. = C.F. + P.I., the general solution of the given equation is

$$z = \phi_1(y - ax) + \phi_2(y - bx) + \frac{1}{6}x^3y - \frac{a + b}{24}x^4,$$

where ϕ_1 and ϕ_2 are arbitrary functions.

EXERCISE 2

Find the general solution of the following partial differential equations :

1. $(D^2 + 3DD' + 2D'^2)z = 2x + 3y$ 2. $(D^2 - 2DD' + D'^2)z = 12xy$
3. $(D^2 - DD' - 6D'^2)z = xy$ 4. $(D^2 - a^2D'^2)z = x^2$
5. $(D^2 - 6DD' + 9D'^2)z = 12x^2 + 36xy$ 6. $(D^2 - 2DD' - 15D'^2)z = 12xy.$ (KU 2004 S)

$$\therefore \quad c_1 = 0, \quad c_2 = \frac{\lambda a^2}{6\mu}, \quad c_3 = 0, \quad c_4 = -\frac{\lambda a^4}{24\mu}$$

$$\therefore \quad (2) \Rightarrow \quad y = -\frac{\lambda x^4}{24\mu} + 0 + \frac{\lambda a^2}{6\mu} \cdot \frac{x^2}{2} + 0 - \frac{\lambda a^4}{24\mu}$$

$$\therefore \quad = -\frac{\lambda}{24\mu}(x^4 - 2a^2x^2 + a^4) = -\frac{\lambda}{24\mu}(x^2 - a^2)^2$$

$$\therefore \quad \mathbf{y = -\frac{\lambda}{24\mu}(x^2 - a^2)^2.}$$

This is the equation of the required extremal.

EXERCISE 2

Find the extremals of the following functionals (Q. No. 1—4) :

1. $\int_{x_1}^{x_2} (16y^2 - y''^2 + x^2)\, dx$ *(KU 2006)*
2. $\int_{x_0}^{x_1} (y''^2 - y^2 + x^2)\, dx$
3. $\int_{x_0}^{x_1} (360x^2y - y''^2)\, dx$
4. $\int_{x_1}^{x_2} (y^2 + 2y'^2 + y''^2)\, dx.$
5. Find the extremal of the functional $\int_0^{\pi/2} (y''^2 - y^2 + x^2)\, dx$ that satisfy the boundary conditions : $y(0) = 1, y(\pi/2) = 0, y'(0) = 0, y'(\pi/2) = -1.$
6. Determine the extremal of the functional $J[y(x)] = \int_{-l}^{l} (\frac{1}{2}\mu y''^2 + ky)\, dx$ subject to $y(-l) = 0$, $y'(-l) = 0, y(l) = 0, y'(l) = 0.$
7. Find the extremals and the stationary function of the functional $\int_0^1 (y'^2 + y''^2)\, dx$ with the boundary conditions : $y(0) = 0, y(1) = \sinh 1, y'(0) = 1, y'(1) = \cosh 1.$ *(MDU 2004)*
8. Find the extremals and the stationary function of the functional $\frac{1}{2}\int_0^1 (y'')^2\, dx$. The boundary conditions are $y(0) = 0, y(1) = \frac{1}{2}, y'(0) = 0, y'(1) = 1.$
9. Find the extremal of the functional $\int_a^b (y + y'')\, dx$ that satisfies the boundary conditions $y(a) = y_0$, $y(b) = y_1, y'(a) = y_0', y'(b) = y_1'.$
10. Find the extremal of the functional $J[y(x)] = \int_{-1}^{0} (240y + y'''^2)\, dx$ subject to the conditions : $y(-1) = 1, y(0) = 0, y'(-1) = -4.5, y'(0) = 0, y''(-1) = 16, y''(0) = 0.$

Answers

1. $y = c_1e^{2x} + c_2e^{-2x} + c_3 \cos 2x + c_4 \sin 2x$
2. $y = c_1e^{x} + c_2e^{-x} + c_3 \cos x + c_4 \sin x$
3. $y = \frac{x^6}{2} + c_1x^3 + c_2x^2 + c_3x + c_4$
4. $y = (c_1 + c_2x)e^{x} + (c_3 + c_4x)e^{-x}$
5. $y = \cos x$
6. $y = -\frac{k}{24\mu}(x^2 - l^2)^2$

The boundary conditions are :

$$y(0) = 0, \quad y(\pi) = 1, \quad z(0) = 0, \quad z(\pi) = 1$$

$y(0) = 0 \Rightarrow (c_1 + c_2.0) \cos 0 + (c_3 + c_4.0) \sin 0 = 0 \Rightarrow c_1 = 0$

$y(\pi) = 1 \Rightarrow (c_1 + \pi c_2) \cos \pi + (c_3 + \pi c_4) \sin \pi = 1$

$\Rightarrow (0 + \pi c_2)(-1) = 1 \Rightarrow c_2 = -1/\pi.$

$z(0) = 0 \Rightarrow (2c_4 + c_1 + c_2.0) \cos 0 + (c_3 - 2c_2 + c_4 . 0) \sin 0 = 0$

$\Rightarrow (2c_4 + 0 + 0) . 1 + \left(c_3 + \frac{2}{\pi} + 0\right) . 0 = 0 \Rightarrow c_4 = 0$

$z(\pi) = 1 \Rightarrow (2(0) + 0 + \pi(-1/\pi)) \cos \pi + (c_3 - 2(-1/\pi) + 0. \pi) \sin \pi = 1$

$\Rightarrow (-1)(-1) = 1$, which is true.

$\therefore \quad c_1 = 0, \quad c_2 = -1/\pi \quad c_4 = 0$

$$\therefore \quad y = \left(0 - \frac{x}{\pi}\right) \cos x + (c_3 + 0.x) \sin x = c_3 \sin x - \frac{x}{\pi} \cos x$$

$$z = \left(2(0) + 0 - \frac{x}{\pi}\right) \cos x + \left(c_3 - 2\left(-\frac{1}{\pi}\right) + 0.x\right) \sin x$$

$$= c_3 \sin x + \frac{1}{\pi} (2 \sin x - x \cos x)$$

$\therefore$ The required extremals are $\mathbf{y = c_3 \sin x - \frac{x}{\pi} \cos x}$

$$\mathbf{z = c_3 \sin x + \frac{1}{\pi} (2 \sin x - x \cos x),}$$

where c_3 is any arbitrary constant.

Example 6. *Find the extremal of the functional* $\int_0^1 \sqrt{1 + y'^2 + z'^2}\, dx$ *that satisfy the boundary conditions* $y(0) = 0, y(1) = 2, z(0) = 0, z(1) = 4$.

Sol. Given functional is $\int_0^1 \sqrt{1 + y'^2 + z'^2}\, dx$.

Let $\quad F(x, y, z, y', z') = \sqrt{1 + y'^2 + z'^2}$

The **Euler's equations** are $F_y - \frac{d}{dx} F_{y'} = 0$ ...(1)

and $$F_z - \frac{d}{dx} F_{z'} = 0 \qquad ...(2)$$

Here $F_y = 0, F_z = 0, F_{y'} = \frac{y'}{\sqrt{1 + y'^2 + z'^2}}, F_{z'} = \frac{z'}{\sqrt{1 + y'^2 + z'^2}}$

$$\therefore \quad (1) \Rightarrow \quad 0 - \frac{d}{dx}\left(\frac{y'}{\sqrt{1 + y'^2 + z'^2}}\right) = 0$$

$$\Rightarrow \quad \frac{y'}{\sqrt{1 + y'^2 + z'^2}} = c_1 \qquad ...(3)$$

Let $\quad z = \dfrac{1}{D - mD'} g(x, y)$

$\therefore \quad (D - mD') z = g(x, y)$

$\Rightarrow \quad p - mq = g(x, y)$

$\therefore$ Lagrange auxiliary equations are $\quad \dfrac{dx}{1} = \dfrac{dy}{-m} = \dfrac{dz}{g(x, y)}$ ...(2)

$(2) \Rightarrow \quad dx = \dfrac{dy}{-m} \Rightarrow dy + mdx = 0 \Rightarrow y + mx = a$

$(2) \Rightarrow \quad dx = \dfrac{dz}{g(x, y)}$

$\Rightarrow \quad dz = g(x, a - mx)\, dx \Rightarrow z = \int g(x, a - mx)\, dx$

$\therefore \quad \dfrac{1}{D - mD'} g(x, y) = \int g(x, a - mx)\, dx$ ...(3)

After evaluation of right side, the constant a is replaced by $y + mx$.

Now we come to the evaluation of a particular integral of (1).

$$\text{P.I. of (1)} = \frac{1}{(D - m_1D')(D - m_2D') \ldots\ldots (D - m_nD')} F(x, y)$$

$$= \frac{1}{D - m_1D'} \frac{1}{D - m_2D'} \ldots\ldots \frac{1}{D - m_nD'} F(x, y)$$

This right side is evaluated by repeated application of the formula (3).

Example 1. *Find the general solution of the following partial differential equations :*

(*i*) $(D^2 + 2DD' + D'^2) z = 2 \cos y - x \sin y$

(*ii*) $\dfrac{\partial^2 z}{\partial x^2} - 4 \dfrac{\partial^2 z}{\partial y^2} = \dfrac{4x}{y^2} - \dfrac{y}{x^2}$

(*iii*) $\dfrac{\partial^2 z}{\partial x^2} - \dfrac{\partial^2 z}{\partial y^2} = \tan^3 x \tan y - \tan x \tan^3 y$

(*iv*) $(D^2 + DD' - 6D'^2) z = x^2 \sin (x + y)$.

Sol. (*i*) We have $\quad (D^2 + 2DD' + D'^2) z = 2 \cos y - x \sin y$. ...(1)

The A.E. of (1) is $\quad m^2 + 2m + 1 = 0$.

$\therefore \quad m = -1, -1$

$\therefore \quad \text{C.F.} = \phi_1(y + (-1)x) + x\phi_2(y + (-1)x) = \phi_1(y - x) + x\phi_2(y - x)$.

$$\text{P.I.} = \frac{1}{D^2 + 2DD' + D'^2}(2 \cos y - x \sin y)$$

$$= \frac{1}{(D + D')(D + D')}(2 \cos y - x \sin y)$$

$$= \frac{1}{D + D'} \int [2 \cos (a + x) - x \sin (a + x)]\, dx$$

$(D + D' = D - mD' \Rightarrow m = -1. \quad \therefore \quad y = a - mx = a + x)$

EXERCISE 3

Find the general solution of the following partial differential equations :

1. $(D^2 + 3DD' + 2D'^2)\,z = 2x + 3y$ *(KU 2005 S)*
2. $(D^2 + 2DD' + D'^2)\,z = e^{2x+3y}$ *(KU 2005)*
3. $(D^2 - 2DD' + D'^2)\,z = e^{x+2y}$
4. $(D^3 - 4D^2D' + 4DD'^2)\,z = \cos(2x + 3y)$
5. $s = e^{x+y}$
6. $4r - 4s + t = 16 \log(x + 2y)$
7. $2r - s - 3t = 5e^x/e^y$
8. $(D^2 - 5DD' + 4D'^2)\,z = \sin(4x + y)$
9. $(D^2 - 2aDD' + a^2D'^2)\,z = g(y + ax)$
10. $(2D^2 - 5DD' + 2D'^2)\,z = 5 \sin(2x + y)$ *(MDU 2005)*
11. $(D^3 - 2D^2D' - DD'^2 + 2D'^3)\,z = e^{x+y}$
12. $(D^3 - 4D^2D' + 4DD'^2)\,z = \sin(y + 2x)$
13. $(D^3 - 4D^2D' + 4DD'^2)\,z = \cos(2x + y)$ *(MDU 2004)*
14. $(D^2 - 3DD' + 2D'^2)\,z = e^{2x-y} + e^{x+y} + \cos(x + 2y)$.

Answers

1. $z = \phi_1(y - x) + \phi_2(y - 2x) + \frac{1}{240}(2x + 3y)^3$
2. $z = \phi_1(y - x) + x\phi_2(y - x) + \frac{e^{2x+3y}}{25}$
3. $z = \phi_1(y + x) + x\phi_2(y + x) + e^{x+2y}$
4. $z = \phi_1(y) + \phi_2(y + 2x) + x\phi_3(y + 2x) - \frac{1}{32}\sin(2x + 3y)$
5. $z = \phi_1(x) + \phi_2(y) + e^{x+y}$
6. $z = \phi_1\left(y + \frac{1}{2}x\right) + x\phi_2\left(y + \frac{1}{2}x\right) + 2x^2 \log(x + 2y)$
7. $z = \phi_1(y - x) + \phi_2\left(y + \frac{3}{2}x\right) + xe^{x-y}$
8. $z = \phi_1(y + x) + \phi_2(y + 4x) - \frac{1}{3}x\cos(4x + y)$
9. $z = \phi_1(y + ax) + x\phi_2(y + ax) + \frac{x^2}{2}g(y + ax)$
10. $z = \phi_1\left(y + \frac{1}{2}x\right) + \phi_2(y + 2x) - \frac{5}{3}x\cos(2x + y)$
11. $z = \phi_1(y - x) + \phi_2(y + x) + \phi_3(y + 2x) - \frac{1}{2}xe^{x+y}$
12. $z = \phi_1(y) + \phi_2(y + 2x) + x\phi_3(y + 2x) - \frac{x^2}{4}\cos(2x + y)$
13. $z = \phi_1(y) + \phi_2(y + 2x) + x\phi_3(y + 2x) + \frac{x^2}{4}\sin(2x + y)$
14. $z = \phi_1(y + x) + \phi_2(y + 2x) + \frac{1}{12}e^{2x-y} - xe^{x+y} - \frac{1}{3}\cos(x + 2y)$.

10. GENERAL METHOD OF FINDING PARTICULAR INTEGRAL

Let $f(D, D')z = E(x, y)$ ...(1)

be a homogeneous linear partial differential equation of order n with constant coefficients.

Let $m_1, m_2, \ldots, m_n$ be the roots of the auxiliary equation of (1). Here some of the roots may be repeated.

$$\text{P.I.} = \frac{1}{f(D, D')}F(x, y) = \frac{1}{(D - m_1D')(D - m_2D')\ldots\ldots(D - m_nD')}F(x, y)$$

We first study the method of evaluating $\frac{1}{D - mD'}g(x, y)$ for some constant m and function $g(x, y)$.

The **Euler's equations** are

$$F_x - \frac{d}{dt} F_{\dot{x}} = 0 \quad ...(1) \qquad \text{and} \qquad F_y - \frac{d}{dt} F_{\dot{y}} = 0 \quad ...(2)$$

We use (1) to find the extremals.

Here $F_x = 0$, $F_{\dot{x}} = y \cdot \dfrac{2\dot{x}}{2\sqrt{\dot{x}^2+\dot{y}^2}} = \dfrac{y\dot{x}}{\sqrt{\dot{x}^2+\dot{y}^2}}$

$$\therefore (1) \Rightarrow 0 - \frac{d}{dt}\left(\frac{y\dot{x}}{\sqrt{\dot{x}^2+\dot{y}^2}}\right) = 0 \Rightarrow \frac{\dot{x}y}{\sqrt{\dot{x}^2+\dot{y}^2}} = c_1 \quad ...(3)$$

Case I. $c_1 = 0$

(3) $\Rightarrow$ $\dot{x}y = 0 \Rightarrow \dot{x} = 0, y = 0 \Rightarrow x = c_2, y = 0.$

Case II. $c_1 \neq 0$

$$(3) \Rightarrow \frac{y}{\sqrt{1+(\dot{y}/\dot{x})^2}} = c_1 \Rightarrow \frac{y}{\sqrt{1+y'^2}} = c_1 \Rightarrow \frac{y^2}{c_1^2} = 1 + y'^2$$

$$\Rightarrow y'^2 = \frac{y^2 - c_1^2}{c_1^2} \Rightarrow \frac{c_1 dy}{\sqrt{y^2 - c_1^2}} = dx \Rightarrow c_1 \cosh^{-1}\frac{y}{c_1} = x + c_3$$

$$\Rightarrow \frac{y}{c_1} = \cosh\frac{x+c_3}{c_1} \Rightarrow y = c_1 \cosh\frac{x+c_3}{c_1}.$$

$\therefore$ The extremals are $\mathbf{x = c_2, y = 0}$ **and** $\mathbf{y = c_1 \cosh \dfrac{x + c_3}{c_1}}$.

Remarks. $(2) \Rightarrow \sqrt{\dot{x}^2+\dot{y}^2} - \dfrac{d}{dt}\left(\dfrac{y\dot{y}}{\sqrt{\dot{x}^2+\dot{y}^2}}\right) = 0 \Rightarrow \dfrac{d}{dt}\left(\dfrac{y\dot{y}}{\sqrt{\dot{x}^2+\dot{y}^2}}\right) = \sqrt{\dot{x}^2+\dot{y}^2}$

$$\Rightarrow \frac{1}{\sqrt{\dot{x}^2+\dot{y}^2}} \frac{d}{dt}\left(\frac{y\dot{y}}{\sqrt{\dot{x}^2+\dot{y}^2}}\right) = 1 \Rightarrow 2\left(\frac{y\dot{y}}{\sqrt{\dot{x}^2+\dot{y}^2}}\right)\frac{d}{dt}\left(\frac{y\dot{y}}{\sqrt{\dot{x}^2+\dot{y}^2}}\right) = (2y)\dot{y}$$

$$\Rightarrow \frac{d}{dt}\left(\frac{(y\dot{y})^2}{\dot{x}^2+\dot{y}^2}\right) = \frac{d}{dt}(y^2) \Rightarrow \frac{y^2\dot{y}^2}{\dot{x}^2+\dot{y}^2} = y^2 + \lambda \Rightarrow \frac{y^2\dot{y}^2}{\dot{x}^2+\dot{y}^2} - y^2 = \lambda$$

$$\Rightarrow \frac{\dot{x}^2y^2}{\dot{x}^2+\dot{y}^2} = \lambda \Rightarrow \frac{\dot{x}y}{\sqrt{\dot{x}^2+\dot{y}^2}} = \sqrt{\lambda} \Rightarrow \frac{\dot{x}y}{\sqrt{\dot{x}^2+\dot{y}^2}} = c_1, \quad \text{where } c_1 = \sqrt{\lambda}.$$

This is same as (3).

$\therefore$ Equations (2) and (1) give the same solution.

12. FUNCTIONALS DEPENDENT ON MORE THAN ONE FUNCTION

Theorem. Let $J[y_1(x), y_2(x), ..., y_n(x)] = \int_{x_1}^{x_2} F(x, y_1(x), y_2(x), ... y_n(x), y_1'(x),$ $y_2'(x), ..., y_n'(x))dx$ be a functional defined on the set of n functions $y_1(x), y_2(x), ...,$ $y_n(x)$ which admits of continuous first order derivative and satisfy the boundary conditions :

$$y_1(x_1) = Y_1, \quad y_2(x_1) = Y_2, \quad ...... ; y_n(x_1) = Y_n,$$
$$y_1(x_2) = Z_1, \quad y_2(x_2) = Z_2, ... y_n(x_2) = Z_n,$$

$$\frac{F_{\dot{x}\dot{x}}}{\dot{y}^2} = \frac{F_{\dot{y}\dot{y}}}{\dot{x}^2} = \frac{F_{\dot{x}\dot{y}}}{-\dot{x}\dot{y}}.$$

Example 2. *Find the extremals of the functional* $\int_{t_1}^{t_2} ((\dot{x}^2 + \dot{y}^2)^{1/2} + a^2 (x\dot{y} - y\dot{x}))\, dt$.

Sol. Given functional is $\int_{t_1}^{t_2} ((\dot{x}^2 + \dot{y}^2)^{1/2} + a^2 (x\dot{y} - y\dot{x}))\, dt$

Let $F(x, y, \dot{x}, \dot{y}) = (\dot{x}^2 + \dot{y}^2)^{1/2} + a^2 (x\dot{y} - y\dot{x})$

$\therefore$

$$\begin{aligned} F(x, y, \lambda\dot{x}, \lambda\dot{y}) &= ((\lambda\dot{x})^2 + (\lambda\dot{y})^2)^{1/2} + a^2 (x(\lambda\dot{y}) - y(\lambda\dot{x})) \\ &= \lambda(\dot{x}^2 + \dot{y}^2)^{1/2} + \lambda a^2(x\dot{y} - y\dot{x}) \qquad (\because \lambda > 0) \\ &= \lambda F(x, y, \dot{x}, \dot{y}). \end{aligned}$$

$\therefore$ F is positive homogeneous function of degree one in $\dot{x}$ and $\dot{y}$.

Weirstrarsian form of Euler's equations is

$$\frac{1}{r} = \frac{F_{x\dot{y}} - F_{y\dot{x}}}{F_1 (\dot{x}^2 + \dot{y}^2)^{3/2}}. \qquad \text{...(1)}$$

Also,

$$F_1 = \frac{F_{\dot{x}\dot{x}}}{\dot{y}^2} = \frac{F_{\dot{y}\dot{y}}}{\dot{x}^2} = \frac{F_{\dot{x}\dot{y}}}{-\dot{x}\dot{y}} \qquad \text{...(2)}$$

Now

$$F_x = a^2\dot{y}, \quad F_y = -a^2\dot{x}, \quad F_{\dot{x}} = \frac{\dot{x}}{\sqrt{\dot{x}^2 + \dot{y}^2}} - a^2 y$$

$\therefore$

$$F_{x\dot{y}} = a^2, \quad F_{y\dot{x}} = -a^2,$$

$$F_{\dot{x}\dot{x}} = \frac{\sqrt{\dot{x}^2 + \dot{y}^2}\,.\,1 - \dot{x}\dfrac{\dot{x}}{\sqrt{\dot{x}^2 + \dot{y}^2}}}{\dot{x}^2 + \dot{y}^2} - 0 = \frac{1}{(\dot{x}^2 + \dot{y}^2)^{3/2}} (\dot{x}^2 + \dot{y}^2 - \dot{x}^2) = \frac{\dot{y}^2}{(\dot{x}^2 + \dot{y}^2)^{3/2}}$$

$\therefore$ (2) $\Rightarrow$

$$F_1 = \frac{F_{\dot{x}\dot{x}}}{\dot{y}^2} = \frac{1}{\dot{y}^2} \cdot \frac{\dot{y}^2}{(\dot{x}^2 + \dot{y}^2)^{3/2}} = \frac{1}{(\dot{x}^2 + \dot{y}^2)^{3/2}}$$

$\therefore$ (1) $\Rightarrow$

$$\frac{1}{r} = \frac{a^2 - (-a^2)}{\dfrac{1}{(\dot{x}^2 + \dot{y}^2)^{3/2}} \cdot (\dot{x}^2 + \dot{y}^2)^{3/2}} = 2a^2$$

$\therefore$ The curvature $(1/r)$ of the extremals is $2a^2$, a constant.

$\therefore$ Extremals are arcs of circles of fixed radius, r, given by $1/2a^2$.

Remark. Extremals are full circles if $x(t_1) = x(t_2)$, $y(t_1) = y(t_2)$.

Example 3. *Find the extremals of the functional* $\int_{t_1}^{t_2} y\sqrt{\dot{x}^2 + \dot{y}^2}\, dt$. (KU 2004 S)

Sol. Given functional is $\int_{t_1}^{t_2} y\sqrt{\dot{x}^2 + \dot{y}^2}\, dt$

Let $F(x, y, \dot{x}, \dot{y}) = y\sqrt{\dot{x}^2 + \dot{y}^2}$.

F is a positive homogeneous function of degree one is $\dot{x}$ and $\dot{y}$

$$D^3 - 4D^2D' + 4DD'^2 = D(D^2 - 4DD' + 4D'^2) = D(D - 2D')^2$$

∴ (2) ⇒ $\text{P.I.} = \dfrac{1}{(D-2D')^2} \cdot \dfrac{1}{D} 4 \sin (2x + y)$ ($\because$ $D = 2, D' = 1 \Rightarrow D - 2D' = 0$)

$$= \frac{1}{(D-2D')^2} \int 4 \sin (2x + y)\, dx^* = \frac{1}{(D-2D')^2} \cdot \frac{4(-\cos(2x+y))}{2}$$

$$= -2 \frac{1}{(D-2D')^2} \cos (2x + y)$$

Again by using the same formula

$$= -2 \cdot \frac{x^2}{(1)^2\, 2!} \cos (2x + y) \qquad (\because\ bD - aD' = (1)D - 2D' = D - 2D')$$

$$= -x^2 \cos (2x + y).$$

∴ Using G.S. = C.F. + P.I., the general solution of the given equation is

$z = \phi_1(y) + \phi_2(y + 2x) + x\phi_3(y + 2x) - x^2 \cos (2x + y)$, where ϕ_1, ϕ_2, ϕ_3 are arbitrary functions.

(*ii*) We have $(D^3 - 7DD'^2 - 6D'^3)z = x^2 + xy^2 + y^3 + \cos (x - y)$. ...(1)

The A.E. of (1) is $m^3 - 7m - 6 = 0$.

⇒ $m = -1, -2, 3$

∴ $\text{C.F.} = \phi_1(y + (-1)x) + \phi_2(y + (-2)x) + \phi_3(y + 3x)$.

$$\text{P.I.} = \frac{1}{D^3 - 7DD'^2 - 6D'^3}(x^2 + xy^2 + y^3 + \cos(x - y))$$

$$= \frac{1}{D^3 - 7DD'^2 - 6D'^3}(x^2 + xy^2 + y^3) + \frac{1}{D^3 - 7DD'^2 - 6D'^3} \cos (x - y).$$

Now, $\dfrac{1}{D^3 - 7DD'^2 - 6D'^3}(x^2 + xy^2 + y^3)$

$$= \frac{1}{D^3}\left[1 - \left(7\frac{D'^2}{D^2} + 6\frac{D'^3}{D^3}\right)\right]^{-1}(x^2 + xy^2 + y^3)$$

$$= \frac{1}{D^3}\left[1 + \left(7\frac{D'^2}{D^2} + 6\frac{D'^3}{D^3}\right) + \ldots\right](x^2 + xy^2 + y^3)$$

$$= \frac{1}{D^3}(x^2 + xy^2 + y^3) + \frac{7}{D^5}(2x + 6y) + \frac{6}{D^6}(6)$$

$$= \left(\frac{x^5}{60} + \frac{x^4y^2}{24} + \frac{x^3y^3}{6}\right) + 7\left(\frac{x^6}{360} + \frac{x^5y}{20}\right) + 36\left(\frac{x^6}{720}\right)$$

$$= \frac{5}{72}x^6 + \frac{1}{60}x^5 + \frac{7}{20}x^5y + \frac{1}{24}x^4y^2 + \frac{1}{6}x^3y^3$$

Also $\dfrac{1}{D^3 - 7DD'^2 - 6D'^3} \cos (x - y)$

$$= \frac{1}{(D + D')(D + 2D')(D - 3D')} \cos (x - y)$$

---

*Alternatively, $\dfrac{1}{D} 4 \sin (2x + y) = \dfrac{1}{2}\displaystyle\int 4 \sin v\, dv$, where $v = 2x + y$

$$= -2 \cos v = -2 \cos (2x + y).$$

$$\text{P.I.} = \frac{1}{D^3 - 4D^2D' + 4DD'^2}\, 6 \sin (3x + 2y) \qquad \ldots(2)$$

and $3x + 2y = ax + by \Rightarrow a = 3,\ b = 2.$

Also, $f(D, D') = D^3 - 4D^2D' + 4DD'^2.$

$\therefore\ f(a, b) = f(3, 2) = (3)^3 - 4(3)^2(2) + 4(3)(2)^2 = 3 \neq 0.$

$$\therefore\ (2) \Rightarrow \text{P.I.} = \frac{1}{f(a, b)} \iiint 6 \sin v \, dv\, dv\, dv, \text{ where } v = 3x + 2y$$

$$= \frac{1}{3} \cdot 6 \iint - \cos v \, dv\, dv = 2 \int (-\sin v)\, dv$$

$$= 2 \cos v = 2 \cos (3x + 2y).$$

$\therefore$ Using G.S. = C.F. + P.I., the general solution of the given equation is

$\mathbf{z = \phi_1(y) + \phi_2(y + 2x) + x\phi_3(y + 2x) + 2 \cos (3x + 2y)}$, where ϕ_1, ϕ_2, ϕ_3 are arbitrary functions.

(*iv*) We have $(D^3 - 6D^2D' + 11DD'^2 - 6D'^3)\, z = e^{5x+6y}.$ ...(1)

The A.E. of (1) is $m^3 - 6m^2 + 11m - 6 = 0$

$\therefore\ m = 1, 2, 3$

$\therefore$ C.F. $= \phi_1(y + x) + \phi_2(y + 2x) + \phi_3(y + 3x).$

$$\text{P.I.} = \frac{1}{D^3 - 6D^2D' + 11DD'^2 - 6D'^3}\, e^{5x+6y} \qquad \ldots(2)$$

$5x + 6y = ax + by \Rightarrow a = 5,\ b = 6.$

Also, $f(D, D') = D^3 - 6D^2D' + 11DD'^2 - 6D'^3$

$\therefore\ f(a, b) = f(5, 6) = (5)^3 - 6(5)^2(6) + 11(5)(6)^2 - 6(6)^3 = -91 \neq 0.$

$$\therefore\ (2) \Rightarrow \text{P.I.} = \frac{1}{f(a, b)} \iiint e^v\, dv\, dv\, dv, \text{ where } v = 5x + 6y$$

$$= \frac{1}{-91} \iint e^v\, dv\, dv = -\frac{1}{91} \int e^v\, dv = -\frac{1}{91} e^v = -\frac{1}{91} e^{5x+6y}.$$

$\therefore$ Using G.S. = C.F. + P.I., the general solution of the given equation is

$\mathbf{z = \phi_1(y + x) + \phi_2(y + 2x) + \phi_3(y + 3x) - \frac{1}{91} e^{5x+6y}}$, where ϕ_1, ϕ_2, ϕ_3 are arbitrary functions.

Example 2. *Find the general solution of the following partial differential equations :*

(*i*) $(D^3 - 4D^2D' + 4DD'^2)z = 4 \sin (2x + y)$

(*ii*) $(D^3 - 7DD'^2 - 6D'^3)z = x^2 + xy^2 + y^3 + \cos (x - y)$ (KU 2004)

(*iii*) $(D^3 - 4D^2D' + 5DD'^2 - 2D'^3)z = e^{y+2x} + (y + x)^{1/2}$

(*iv*) $(D^3 - 7DD'^2 - 6D'^3)z = \sin (x + 2y) + e^{3x+y}$

Sol. (*i*) We have $(D^3 - 4D^2D' + 4DD'^2)z = 4 \sin (2x + y).$ ...(1)

The A.E. of (1) is $m^3 - 4m^2 + 4m = 0.$

$\therefore\ m = 0, 2, 2$

$\therefore$ C.F. $= \phi_1(y + 0.x) + \phi_2(y + 2x) + x\phi_3(y + 2x).$

$$\text{P.I.} = \frac{1}{D^3 - 4D^2D' + 4DD'^2}\, 4 \sin (2x + y) \qquad \ldots(2)$$

$2x + y = ax + by \Rightarrow a = 2,\ b = 1.$

Also, $f(D, D') = D^3 - 4D^2D' + 4DD'^2.$

$f(a, b) = f(2, 1) = (2)^3 - 4(2)^2(1) + 4(2)(1)^2 = 0.$

7. $y = c_1 + c_2x + c_3e^x + c_4e^{-x}$, $y = \sinh x$

8. $y = c_1 + c_2x + c_3x^2 + c_4x^3$, $y = \frac{1}{2}x^2$

9. No extremal

10. $y = \dfrac{x^3}{6}(x^3 + 6x + 1)$.

10. FUNCTIONALS DEPENDENT ON MORE THAN ONE INDEPENDENT VARIABLE

Till now we have been discussing functionals depending on functions of one independent variable *i.e.*, on curves. In the present section we shall consider functionals depending on functions of more than one independent variable *i.e.*, on surfaces. We shall restrict ourselves to only to two independent variables.

Theorem. Let $J[z(x, y)] = \iint_D F(x, y, z, z_x, z_y)\, dx\, dy$ be a functional defined on the set of functions z(x, y) which admits of continuous derivatives upto the second order and assumes given values on the boundary Γ of the region D. Also, F is differentiable three times with respect to all its arguments.

If the functional J[z(x, y)] has an extremum on a function z(x, y) then z(x, y) satisfy the differential equation

$$F_z - \frac{\partial}{\partial x} F_{z_x} - \frac{\partial}{\partial y} F_{z_y} = 0.$$

Proof. We have

$$J[z(x, y) = \iint_D F(x, y, z, z_x, z_y)\, dx\, dy.$$

Let $z = z(x, y)$ be a function which extremise $J[z(x, y)]$ and assumes given values on the boundary Γ of the region D.

Let $\eta(x, y)$ be any arbitrary but fixed function admiting continuous derivatives upto the second order and taking value zero on the boundary of the region D.

Let $\bar{z}(x, y) = z(x, y) + \alpha\eta(x, y)$, where α is a small parameter.

∴ $\bar{z}(x, y)$ admits of continuous derivatives upto the second order and assumes given values on the boundary of the region D.

∴ The functional J is defined at $\bar{z}(x, y)$.

$$\therefore \quad J[\bar{z}(x, y)] = \iint_D F(x, y, \bar{z}, \bar{z}_x, \bar{z}_y)\, dx\, dy$$

$$= \iint_D F(x, y, z + \alpha\eta, z_x + \alpha\eta_x, z_y + \alpha\eta_y)\, dxdy$$

On the regions of the family $z(x, y) + \alpha\eta(x, y)$, the right hand side is a function of α, say $\psi(\alpha)$.

$$\therefore \quad \psi(\alpha) = \iint_D F(x, y, \bar{z}, \bar{z}_x, \bar{z}_y)\, dx\, dy$$

$$= \iint_D F(x, y, z + \alpha\eta, z_x + \alpha\eta_x, z_y + \alpha\eta_y)\, dx\, dy$$

Since the extremising surface $z = z(x, y)$ corresponds to $\alpha = 0$, it follows that $\psi(\alpha)$ is extremised for $\alpha = 0$.

$$\therefore \quad \frac{d\psi}{d\alpha} = 0 \quad \text{at} \quad \alpha = 0.$$

Differentiating $\psi(\alpha)$ under the integral sign, we have

$$\frac{d\psi}{d\alpha} = \iint_D \frac{\partial}{\partial\alpha} F(x, y, \bar{z}, \bar{z}_x, \bar{z}_y)\, dx\, dy$$

(2) $\Rightarrow$ $$0 - \frac{d}{dx}\left(\frac{z'}{\sqrt{1+y'^2+z'^2}}\right) = 0$$

$\Rightarrow$ $$\frac{z'}{\sqrt{1+y'^2+z'^2}} = c_2 \qquad \text{...(4)}$$

Dividing (3) by (4), we get $\frac{y'}{z'} = \frac{c_1}{c_2}, = c_3$ say

$\therefore$ $$y' = c_3 z'$$

Putting the value of y' in (4), we get $$\frac{z'}{\sqrt{1+(1+c_3^2)\,z'^2}} = c_2$$

$\Rightarrow$ $$z'^2 = c_2^2(1+(1+c_3^2)\,z'^2) \Rightarrow z' = \frac{c_2}{\sqrt{1-c_2^2-c_2^2\,c_3^2}} = c_4, \text{ say}$$

$\Rightarrow$ $$z = c_4 x + c_5 \qquad \text{...(5)}$$

$\therefore$ $$y' = c_3 z' \Rightarrow y' = c_3 c_4 = c_6, \text{ say}$$

$\Rightarrow$ $$y = c_6 x + c_7 \qquad \text{...(6)}$$

$\therefore$ The extremals are given by (5) and (6).

The boundary conditions are

$$y(0) = 0, \quad y(1) = 2, \quad z(0) = 0, \quad z(1) = 4$$

$\therefore$ $$c_6(0) + c_7 = 0, \quad c_6(1) + c_7 = 2, c_4(0) + c_5 = 0, \quad c_4(1) + c_5 = 4$$

Solving these equations, we get

$$c_6 = 2, c_7 = 0, c_4 = 4, c_5 = 0$$

(6) $\Rightarrow$ $y = 2.x + 0 \Rightarrow y = 2x$

(5) $\Rightarrow$ $y = 4.x + 0 \Rightarrow z = 4x$

$\therefore$ The required extremals are **y = 2x, z = 4x.**

EXERCISE 3

1. Find the Euler-Ostrogradsky equation for the functional $J[z(x, y)] = \iint_D \left[\left(\frac{\partial z}{\partial x}\right)^2 - \left(\frac{\partial z}{\partial y}\right)^2\right] dx\,dy$, where the values of z are prescribed on the boundary of the domain D.

2. Find the Euler-Ostrogradsky equation for the functional $J[z(x, y)] = \iint_D \left[\left(\frac{\partial z}{\partial x}\right)^4 + \left(\frac{\partial z}{\partial y}\right)^4 + 12z\,f(x, y)\right] dx\,dy$, where the values of z are prescribed on the boundary of the domain D.

3. Find the extremals of the functional $\int_{t_1}^{t_2} \sqrt{\dot{x}^2 + \dot{y}^2}\, dt$. *(MDU 2004, 2005)*

4. Find the stationary function of the functional $\int_{(-1,0)}^{(1,0)} (k\sqrt{\dot{x}^2 + \dot{y}^2} - \dot{x}y)\, dt,\ k > 0$.

Example 3. *Find the inverse Laplace transform of the function* $\frac{1}{(s-1)^5 (s+2)}$ *by using (i) method of partial fractions (ii) convolution theorem.*

Sol. (*i*) $\frac{1}{(s-1)^5 (s+2)} = \frac{1}{z^5 (z+3)}$, where $z = s - 1$.

We divide 1 by $z + 3$ as follows :

$$= \frac{1}{2(D+D')} [\tan y \tan^2 x + \tan x \tan^2 y + \tan y + \tan x]$$

$$= \frac{1}{2(D+D')} [\tan y \sec^2 x + \tan x \sec^2 y]$$

$$= \frac{1}{2} \int [\tan (a+x) \sec^2 x + \tan x \sec^2 (a+x)]\, dx$$

$$(D + D' = D - mD' \Rightarrow m = -1. \quad \therefore \quad y = a - mx = a + x)$$

$$= \frac{1}{2} \left[\tan (a+x) \tan x - \int \sec^2 (a+x) \tan x\, dx + \int \tan x \sec^2 (a+x)\, dx \right]$$

$$= \frac{1}{2} \tan y \tan x.$$

$\therefore$ Using G.S. = C.F. + P.I., the general solution of the given equation is

$$\mathbf{z = \phi_1(y-x) + \phi_2(y+x) + \frac{1}{2} \tan x \tan y}, \text{ where } \phi_1, \phi_2 \text{ are arbitrary functions.}$$

(*iv*) We have $(D^2 + DD' - 6D'^2)\, z = x^2 \sin (x+y)$. ...(1)

The A.E. of (1) is $m^2 + m - 6 = 0$.

$\therefore \quad m = -3, 2$

$\therefore \quad$ C.F. $= \phi_1(y + (-3)x) + \phi_2(y + 2x) = \phi_1(y - 3x) + \phi_2(y + 2x)$.

$$\text{P.I.} = \frac{1}{D^2 + DD' - 6D'^2} x^2 \sin (x+y)$$

$$= \frac{1}{(D+3D')(D-2D')} x^2 \sin (x+y) = \frac{1}{D+3D'} \int x^2 \sin (x + a - 2x)\, dx$$

$$(D - 2D' = D - mD' \Rightarrow m = 2. \quad \therefore \quad y = a - mx = a - 2x)$$

$$= \frac{1}{D+3D'} \int x^2 \sin (a-x)\, dx$$

$$= \frac{1}{D+3D'} \left[x^2 \cos (a-x) - \int 2x \cos (a-x)\, dx \right]$$

$$= \frac{1}{D+3D'} \left[x^2 \cos (a-x) - \left(-2x \sin (a-x) + \int 2 \sin (a-x)\, dx \right) \right]$$

$$= \frac{1}{D+3D'} [x^2 \cos (a-x) + 2x \sin (a-x) - 2 \cos (a-x)]$$

$$= \frac{1}{D+3D'} [(x^2 - 2) \cos (2x + y - x) + 2x \sin (2x + y - x)]$$

$$= \frac{1}{D+3D'} [(x^2 - 2) \cos (x+y) + 2x \sin (x+y)]$$

$$= \int [(x^2 - 2) \cos (x + a + 3x) + 2x \sin (x + a + 3x)]\, dx$$

$$(D + 3D' = D - mD' \Rightarrow m = -3. \quad \therefore \quad y = a - mx = a + 3x)$$

$$= \int [(x^2 - 2) \cos (4x + a) + 2x \sin (4x + a)]\, dx$$

$$= (x^2 - 2)\frac{\sin(4x+a)}{4} - \int 2x \cdot \frac{\sin(4x+a)}{4}\,dx + \int 2x \sin(4x+a)\,dx$$

$$= \frac{1}{4}(x^2 - 2)\sin(4x+a) + \frac{3}{2}\int x \sin(4x+a)\,dx$$

$$= \frac{1}{4}(x^2 - 2)\sin(4x+a) + \frac{3}{2}\left[-x\frac{\cos(4x+a)}{4} - \int 1 \cdot -\frac{\cos(4x+a)}{4}\,dx\right]$$

$$= \frac{1}{4}(x^2 - 2)\sin(4x+a) - \frac{3}{8}x\cos(4x+a) + \frac{3}{32}\sin(4x+a)$$

$$= \left(\frac{x^2}{4} - \frac{13}{32}\right)\sin(4x+y-3x) - \frac{3}{8}x\cos(4x+y-3x)$$

$$= \left(\frac{x^2}{4} - \frac{13}{32}\right)\sin(x+y) - \frac{3}{8}x\cos(x+y).$$

∴ Using G.S. = C.F. + P.I., the general solution of the given equation is

$$\mathbf{z = \phi_1(y-3x) + \phi_2(y+2x) + \left(\frac{x^2}{4} - \frac{13}{32}\right)\sin(x+y) - \frac{3}{8}x\cos(x+y)},$$

where ϕ_1, ϕ_2 are arbitrary functions.

EXERCISE 4

Find the general solution of the following partial differential equations :

1. $r + s - 6t = y \cos x$ 2. $(D^2 + DD' - 6D'^2)\, z = y \sin x$
3. $r + s - 2t = (2x^2 + xy - y^2) \sin xy - \cos xy$ 4. $(D^2 + DD' - 2D'^2)\, z = (y - 1)\, e^x$
5. $(D^3 - 3DD'^2 - 2D'^3)\, z = \cos(x + 2y) - e^y(3 + 2x)$
6. $(D^3 + 2D^2D' - DD'^2 - 2D'^3)\, z = (y + 2)\, e^x$.

Answers

1. $z = \phi_1(y + 2x) + \phi_2(y - 3x) - y \cos x + \sin x$ 2. $z = \phi_1(y + 2x) + \phi_2(y - 3x) - y \sin x - \cos x$
3. $z = \phi_1(y + 2x) + \phi_2(y - x) + \sin xy$ 4. $z = \phi_1(y + 2x) + \phi_2(y - x) + ye^x$
5. $z = \phi_1(y - x) + x\phi_2(y - x) + \phi_3(y + 2x) + \frac{1}{27}\sin(x + 2y) + xe^y$
6. $z = \phi_1(y + x) + \phi_2(y - x) + \phi_3(y - 2x) + ye^x$.

Let $\quad G(x, y, y') = \sqrt{1+y'^2}$

The **Euler's equation** for (1) is $\quad G_y - \dfrac{d}{dx} G_{y'} = 0 \qquad \ldots(2)$

Here $\quad G_y = 0, \quad G_{y'} = \dfrac{y'}{\sqrt{1+y'^2}}$

$$\therefore \quad (1) \Rightarrow \qquad 0 - \frac{d}{dx}\left(\frac{y'}{\sqrt{1+y'^2}}\right) = 0$$

$$\Rightarrow \qquad \frac{y'}{\sqrt{1+y'^2}} = k \;\Rightarrow\; y'^2 = k^2(1+y'^2) \;\Rightarrow\; y' = \frac{k}{\sqrt{1-k^2}} = c_1, \text{ say}$$

$$\Rightarrow \qquad y = c_1 x + c_2$$

$\therefore$ The extremals of the given functional are $\mathbf{r \sin \theta = c_1 r \cos \theta + c_2}$.

Alternative method

We have $\qquad x = r\cos\theta, \quad y = r\sin\theta.$

$$\therefore \quad \frac{dx}{d\theta} = -r\sin\theta + r'\cos\theta, \quad \frac{dy}{d\theta} = r\cos\theta + r'\sin\theta, \quad \text{where} \quad r' = \frac{dr}{d\theta}$$

$$\therefore \quad \left(\frac{dx}{d\theta}\right)^2 + \left(\frac{dy}{d\theta}\right)^2 = (-r\sin\theta + r'\cos\theta)^2 + (r\cos\theta + r'\sin\theta)^2 = r^2 + r'^2$$

$$\therefore \quad \int\sqrt{r^2+r'^2}\,d\theta = \int\sqrt{\left(\frac{dx}{d\theta}\right)^2 + \left(\frac{dy}{d\theta}\right)^2}\,d\theta = \int\sqrt{(dx)^2+(dy)^2}$$

$$= \int\sqrt{1+\left(\frac{dy}{dx}\right)^2}\,dx = \int\sqrt{1+y'^2}\,dx.$$

Remark. The Euler's equation of $J[r(\theta)]$ is

$$\frac{r}{\sqrt{r^2+r'^2}} - \frac{d}{d\theta}\left(\frac{r'}{\sqrt{r^2+r'^2}}\right) = 0,$$

which is difficult to solve.

EXERCISE 4

1. Find the extremals of the functional $J[y(x)] = \int_0^{\log 2} (e^{-x}y'^2 - e^x y^2)\,dx$ by using the transformations :

$$x = \log u, \quad y = v.$$

2. Find the extremals of the functional $\int_{\theta_1}^{\theta_2} r\sin\theta\sqrt{r^2+r'^2}\,d\theta$ by using the transformations :

$$x = r\cos\theta, \quad y = r\sin\theta.$$

Answers

1. $y = c_1 \cos e^x + c_2 \sin e^x$
2. $c_1 \log (r \sin \theta + \sqrt{r^2 \sin^2 \theta - c_1^2}) = r \cos \theta + c_2.$

Hints

1. Use : $y' = \frac{dy}{dx} = \frac{dy}{dv}\frac{dv}{du}\frac{du}{dx} = 1 . \frac{dv}{du} . e^x = u \frac{dv}{du}$.

14. CONDITIONAL EXTREMUM

Theorem. If a curve $y = y(x)$ extremises the functional $\int_{x_1}^{x_2} F(x, y, y')\,dx$ subject to boundary conditions : $y(x_1) = y_1, y(x_2) = y_2$ and one more condition $\int_{x_1}^{x_2} G(x, y, y')\,dx = L$ and if $y = y(x)$ is not an extremal of the functional $\int_{x_1}^{x_2} G(x, y, y')\,dx$, then there exists a constant λ such that the curve $y = y(x)$ satisfy the Euler's equation $F_y - \frac{d}{dx} F_{y'} + \lambda \left(G_y - \frac{d}{dx} G_{y'} \right) = 0.$

Note. The proof of this theorem is beyond the scope of this book.

Example 1. *Find the extremal of the functional $\int_0^1 y'^2\,dx$, $y(0) = 1, y(1) = 6$ subject to the condition $\int_0^1 y dx = 3$.*

Sol. Given functional is $\int_0^1 y'^2\,dx$.

Given condition is $\int_0^1 y dx = 3$ ...(1)

Let $F(x, y, y') = y'^2$ and $G(x, y, y') = y$

The **Euler's equation** is $F_y - \frac{d}{dx} F_{y'} + \lambda \left(G_y - \frac{d}{dx} G_{y'} \right) = 0$ ...(2)

Here $F_y = 0$, $F_{y'} = 2y'$, $G_y = 1$, $G_{y'} = 0$

$\therefore$ (2) $\Rightarrow$ $0 - \frac{d}{dx}(2y') + \lambda \left(1 - \frac{d}{dx}(0) \right) = 0$

$\Rightarrow$ $-2\frac{d^2 y}{dx^2} + \lambda = 0 \Rightarrow \frac{d^2 y}{dx^2} = \frac{\lambda}{2}$

$\Rightarrow$ $\frac{dy}{dx} = \frac{\lambda x}{2} + c_1 \Rightarrow y = \frac{\lambda x^2}{4} + c_1 x + c_2$ ...(3)

The boundary conditions are $y(0) = 1$, $y(1) = 6$

$y(0) = 1 \Rightarrow 0 + c_1(0) + c_2 = 1 \Rightarrow c_2 - 1$

Let $\quad (a_1D + b_1D' + c_1)\, z = u \qquad$ ...(6)

$\therefore$ (5) $\Rightarrow$ $(a_1D + b_1D' + c_1)\, u = 0$

$$\Rightarrow \qquad u = e^{-c_1x/a_1}\ \psi_1(a_1y - b_1x)$$

where ψ_1 is arbitrary. We are assuming that $a_1 \neq 0$.

$$\therefore \quad (6) \Rightarrow \quad a_1p + b_1q + c_1z = e^{-c_1x/a_1}\ \psi_1(a_1y - b_1x)$$

$$\Rightarrow \qquad a_1p + b_1q = e^{-c_1x/a_1}\ \psi_1(a_1y - b_1x) - c_1z$$

$$\Rightarrow \qquad \frac{dx}{a_1} = \frac{dy}{b_1} = \frac{dz}{e^{-c_1x/a_1}\ \psi_1(a_1y - b_1x) - c_1z} \qquad \text{...(7)}$$

$$(7) \Rightarrow \qquad a_1dy - b_1dx = 0 \quad \Rightarrow \quad a_1y - b_1x = c$$

Taking the first and third fractions of (7), we get

$$\frac{dz}{dx} = \frac{1}{a_1}\left(e^{-c_1x/a_1}\ \psi_1(a_1y - b_1x) - c_1z\right)$$

$$\Rightarrow \qquad \frac{dz}{dx} + \frac{c_1}{a_1}z = \frac{1}{a_1}\, e^{-c_1x/a_1}\ \psi_1(a_1y - b_1x) \qquad \text{...(8)}$$

This is a linear equation.

$$\therefore \qquad \text{I.F.} = e^{\int \frac{c_1}{a_1}dx} = e^{c_1x/a_1}$$

$\therefore$ Solution of (8) is

$$z\,.\,e^{c_1x/a_1} = \int \frac{1}{a_1}\, e^{-c_1x/a_1}\ \psi_1(a_1y - b_1x)\,.\,e^{c_1x/a_1}\, dx$$

$$= \frac{1}{a_1}\int \psi_1(c)\, dx = \frac{x\psi_1(c)}{a_1} + d$$

$$\Rightarrow \qquad ze^{c_1x/a_1} = \frac{x}{a_1}\ \psi_1(a_1y - b_1x) + d$$

$$\Rightarrow \qquad ze^{c_1x/a_1} = x\,\phi_1(a_1y - b_1x) + \phi_2(a_1y - b_1x)$$

$$\left[\text{Taking } \phi_1 = \frac{1}{a_1}\psi_1 \text{ and } d = \phi_2(c)\right]$$

$$\therefore \qquad z = e^{-c_1x/a_1}\,(x\,\phi_1(a_1y - b_1x) + \phi_2(a_1y - b_1x)) \qquad \text{...(9)}$$

Combining (4) and (9),

$$\mathbf{z = e^{-c_1x/a_1}\,(x\,\phi_1(a_1y - b_1x) + \phi_2(a_1y - b_1x))}$$

$$\mathbf{+\, e^{-c_3x/a_3}\ \phi_3(a_3y - b_3x) + \ldots\ldots + e^{-c_nx/a_n}\ \phi_n(a_ny - b_nx)}.$$

Since this solution contains n arbitrary functions $\phi_1, \phi_2, \ldots, \phi_n$, this solution represents the general solution of the given equation.

Remark. If the factor $a_1x + b_1y + c_1$ is repeated r times, then the corresponding part of the general solution is $e^{-c_1x/a_1}\,(\phi_1(a_1y - b_1x) + x\,\phi_2(a_1y - b_1x) + \ldots\ldots + x^{r-1}\,\phi_r(a_1y - b_1x))$, where $\phi_1, \phi_2, \ldots\ldots, \phi_r$ are arbitrary functions.

WORKING RULES FOR SOLVING PROBLEMS

Step I. *Express $f(D, D')$ as the product of linear factors in D and D'.*

Step II. *Corresponding to each non-repeated factor $aD + bD' + c$, the part of G.S. is $e^{-cx/a}\,\phi(ay - bx)$, if $a \neq 0$ or $e^{-cy/b}\,\phi(ay - bx)$ if $b \neq 0$.*

Step III. *Corresponding to each repeated factor $aD + bD' + c$, r times, the part of G.S. is*

$$e^{-cx/a} \sum_{i=1}^{r} x^{i-1}\,\phi_i(ay - bx),\ \text{if } a \neq 0 \text{ or } e^{-cy/b} \sum_{i=1}^{r} y^{i-1}\,y_i(ay - bx),\ \text{if } b \neq 0.$$

Example 1. *Find the general solution of following partial differential equations :*

(i) $t + s + q = 0$ (ii) $DD'(D - 2D' - 3)\,z = 0$

(iii) $(DD' + aD + bD' + ab)z = 0$ (iv) $r + 2s + t + 2p + 2q + z = 0.$

Sol. (i) We have $t + s + q = 0.$

$$\Rightarrow \quad (D'^2 + DD' + D')\,z = 0 \quad \Rightarrow \quad (0.D + 1.D' + 0)(D' + D + 1)\,z = 0 \qquad ...(1)$$

$\therefore$ The general solution of (1) is

$$z = e^{-0y/1}\,\phi_1(0y - 1.x) + e^{-1.x/1}\,\phi_2(1.y - 1.x)$$

or $$\mathbf{z = \phi_1(-x) + e^{-x}\,\phi_2(y - x),}$$

where ϕ_1 and ϕ_2 are arbitrary functions.

Remark. $\phi_1(-x)$ is also a function of x and can also be written as $\psi(x)$ for some arbitrary function ψ.

(ii) We have $DD'(D - 2D' - 3)\,z = 0.$ ...(1)

$$\Rightarrow \quad (1.D + 0.D' + 0)(0.D + 1.D' + 0)(D - 2D' - 3)z = 0$$

$\therefore$ The general solution of (1) is

$$z = e^{-0.x/1}\,\phi_1(1.y - 0.x) + e^{-0.y/1}\,\phi_2(0.y - 1.x) + e^{3x/1}\,\phi_3(1.y + 2.x)$$

or $$\mathbf{z = \phi_1(y) + \phi_2(-x) + e^{3x}\,\phi_3(2x + y),}$$

where ϕ_1, ϕ_2, ϕ_3 are arbitrary functions.

(iii) We have $(DD' + aD + bD' + ab)\,z = 0.$

$$\Rightarrow \quad (D + b)(D' + a)\,z = 0 \quad \Rightarrow \quad (1.D + 0.D' + b)(0.D + 1.D' + a)z = 0 \qquad ...(1)$$

$\therefore$ The general solution of (1) is

$$z = e^{-bx/1}\,\phi_1(1.y - 0.x) + e^{-ay/1}\,\phi_2(0.y - 1.x)$$

or $$\mathbf{z = e^{-bx}\,\phi_1(y) + e^{-ay}\,\phi_2(-x),}$$

where ϕ_1 and ϕ_2 are arbitrary functions.

(iv) We have $r + 2s + t + 2p + 2q + z = 0$ ...(1)

$$\Rightarrow \quad (D^2 + 2DD' + D'^2 + 2D + 2D' + 1)\,z = 0$$

$$\Rightarrow \quad [(D + D')^2 + 2(D + D') + 1]\,z = 0$$

$$\Rightarrow \quad (D + D' + 1)^2\,z = 0$$

$\therefore$ The general solution of (1) is

$$z = e^{-1.x/1}\,(\phi_1(1.y - 1.x) + x\,\phi_2(1.y - 1.x))$$

or $$\mathbf{z = e^{-x}\,(\phi_1(y - x) + x\,\phi_2(y - x)),}$$

where ϕ_1, ϕ_2 are arbitrary functions.

5. GENERAL SOLUTION OF IRREDUCIBLE NON-HOMOGENEOUS LINEAR PARTIAL DIFFERENTIAL EQUATION f(D, D′)z = 0 WITH CONSTANT COEFFICIENTS

Let $$f(D, D')\, z = 0 \quad \ldots(1)$$

be an irreducible non-homogeneous linear partial differential equation with constant coefficients.

Let $$z = ce^{ax+by}.$$

$$\therefore \quad D^r D'^s z = D^r D'^s(ce^{ax+by}) = ca^r b^s e^{ax+by} = a^r b^r ce^{ax+by}$$

$$\therefore \quad f(D, D')\, z = f(a, b)\, ce^{ax+by}$$

$\therefore$ $z = ce^{ax+by}$ is a solution of (1) iff $f(a, b) = 0$ and the constant c is arbitrary. Let (a_i, b_i) be one of infinitely many pairs satisfying $f(a_i, b_i) = 0$.

$\therefore$ $z = c_i e^{a_i x + b_i y}$ is a solution of (1) for each i.

$\therefore$ The general solution of (1) is $\mathbf{z = \sum_{i=1}^{\infty} c_i e^{a_i x + b_i y}}$, **where $\mathbf{f(a_i, b_i) = 0}$.**

Remark. For the above irreducible partial differential equation (1), the general solution has been written in terms of arbitrary constants.

> **WORKING RULES FOR SOLVING PROBLEMS**
>
> **Step I.** *Express the given equation in the form f(D, D′) g(D, D′) z = 0, where f(D, D′) is expressible as a product of linear factors in D and D′ and g(D, D′) is irreducible.*
>
> **Step II.** *Write the solution of f(D, D′)z = 0 in terms of arbitrary functions.*
>
> **Step III.** *Write the solution of g(D, D′)z = 0 in terms of arbitrary constants.*
>
> **Step IV.** *Add both general solutions to get the general solution of the given equation.*

Example 2. *Find the general solution of the following partial differential equations :*

(i) $(D^2 + D + D')\, z = 0$ (ii) $(2D^4 - 3D^2D' + D'^2)\, z = 0$

(iii) $(D + 2D' - 3)(D^2 + D')z = 0$ (iv) $(D' + 3D)^2\, (D^2 + 5D + D')\, z = 0.$

Sol. (i) We have $(D^2 + D + D')\, z = 0.$ ...(1)

$D^2 + D + D'$ is irreducible

Let $z = ce^{ax+by}$ be a solution of (1).

$$\therefore \quad (a^2 + a + b)\, ce^{ax+by} = 0$$

$$\Rightarrow \quad a^2 + a + b = 0 \;\Rightarrow\; b = -(a^2 + a)$$

$$\therefore \quad z = ce^{ax - (a^2 + a)y}, \text{ where } a \text{ and } c \text{ are arbitrary constants.}$$

$\therefore$ The general solution of (1) is $\sum_{i=1}^{\infty} \mathbf{c_i e^{a_i - (a_i^2 + a_i)y}}$, where a_i and c_i are arbitrary constants.

(ii) We have $(2D^4 - 3D^2D' + D'^2)\, z = 0.$ ...(1)

$$\Rightarrow \quad (2D^2 - D')(D^2 - D')\, z = 0$$

The factor $2D^2 - D'$ is irreducible.

Let $z = ce^{ax+by}$ be a solution of $(2D^2 - D')\, z = 0.$

$$\therefore \quad (2a^2 - b)\, ce^{ax+by} = 0 \;\Rightarrow\; 2a^2 - b = 0 \quad \text{or} \quad b = 2a^2$$

$\therefore \qquad z = ce^{ax + 2a^2y}$

$\therefore$ Corresponding to $2D^2 - D'$, the part of general solution of (1) is $\sum_{i=1}^{\infty} c_i e^{a_i x + 2a_i^2 y}$.

The factor $D^2 - D'$ is also irreducible.

Let $z = c'e^{a'x+b'y}$ be a solution of $(D^2 - D')z = 0$.

$\therefore \qquad (a'^2 - b')\, c'e^{a'x+b'y} = 0$

$\Rightarrow \qquad a'^2 - b' = 0 \quad \text{or} \quad b' = a'^2$

$\therefore \qquad z = c'e^{a'x + a'^2 y}$

$\therefore$ Corresponding to $D^2 - D'$, the part of general solution of (1) is $\sum_{i=1}^{\infty} c_i' e^{a_i' x + a_i'^2 y}$

$\therefore$ The general solution of (1) is $\mathbf{z} = \sum_{i=1}^{\infty} c_i e^{a_i x + 2a_i^2 y} + \sum_{i=1}^{\infty} c_i' e^{a_i' x + a_i'^2 y}$, where a_i, c_i, a_i', c_i' are arbitrary constants.

(*iii*) We have $\quad (D + 2D' - 3)(D^2 + D')z = 0$. ...(1)

The factor $D + 2D' - 3$ is linear.

$\therefore$ Corresponding to $D + 2D' - 3$, the part of general solution of (1) is

$e^{-(-3)x/1}\phi_1(1.y - 2.x)$ *i.e.* $e^{3x}\phi_1(y - 2x)$.

The factor $D^2 + D'$ is irreducible.

Let $z = ce^{ax+by}$ be a solution of $(D^2 + D')z = 0$.

$\therefore \qquad (a^2 + b)\, ce^{ax+by} = 0.$

$\Rightarrow \qquad a^2 + b = 0 \quad \text{or} \quad b = -a^2$

$\therefore \qquad z = ce^{ax - a^2 y}$

$\therefore$ Corresponding to $D^2 + D'$, the part of general solution of (1) is $\sum_{i=1}^{\infty} c_i e^{a_i x - a_i^2 y}$.

$\therefore$ The general solution of (1) is $\mathbf{z = e^{3x}\,\phi_1(y - 2x)} + \sum_{i=1}^{\infty} c_i e^{a_i x - a_i^2 y}$, where ϕ_1 is arbitrary function and a_i, c_i are arbitrary constants.

(*iv*) We have $\quad (D' + 3D)^2 (D^2 + 5D + D')z = 0$. ...(1)

The factor $(3D + D')^2$ is linear repeated.

$\therefore$ Corresponding to $(3D + D')^2$, the part of general solution of (1) is

$$e^{-0.x/3}(\phi_1(3.y - 1.x) + x\phi_2(3.y - 1.x)) \quad \textit{i.e.} \quad \phi_1(3y - x) + x\phi_2(3y - x).$$

The factor $D^2 + 5D + D'$ is irreducible.

Let $z = ce^{ax+by}$ be a solution of $(D^2 + 5D + D')z = 0$.

$\therefore \qquad (a^2 + 5a + b)\, ce^{ax+by} = 0$

$\Rightarrow \qquad a^2 + 5a + b = 0 \quad \text{or} \quad b = -(a^2 + 5a)$

$\therefore$ $$z = ce^{ax - (a^2 + 5a)y}$$

$\therefore$ Corresponding to $D^2 + 5D + D'$, the part of general solution of (1) is $\sum_{i=1}^{\infty} c_i e^{a_i x - (a_i^2 + 5a_i)y}$.

$\therefore$ The general solution of (1) is $z = \phi_1(3y - x) + x\,\phi_2(3y - x) + \sum_{i=1}^{\infty} c_i e^{a_i x - (a_i^2 + 5a_i)y}$,

where ϕ_1, ϕ_2 are arbitrary functions and a_i, c_i are arbitrary constants.

EXERCISE 1

Find the general solution of the following partial differential equations :

1. $(D + D' - 1)(D + 2D' - 2)z = 0$
2. $(D + 1)(D + D' - 1)z = 0$
3. $(D^2 - DD' - 2D)z = 0$
4. $(D^2 - D'^2 + D - D')z = 0$
5. $(D - D' - 1)(D - D' - 2)\,z = 0$
6. $(D^2 - DD' + D' - 1)z = 0$
7. $s + p - q - z = 0$
8. $(D^2 - DD' - 2D'^2 + 2D + 2D')z = 0$
9. $\dfrac{\partial^2 z}{\partial x^2} + \dfrac{\partial^2 z}{\partial x \partial y} - 6\dfrac{\partial^2 z}{\partial y^2} = 0$
10. $(D - 3D' - 2)^2\, z = 0$
11. $(D - D'^2)\, z = 0$
12. $(2D^2 - D'^2 + D)\, z = 0$
13. $(D^2 + DD' + D + D' + 1)\, z = 0$
14. $(D - 2D' - 1)(D - 2D'^2 - 1)z = 0$
15. $(2D - 3D' + 5)^2\, (D^2 + 3D')\, z = 0$.

Answers

1. $z = e^x\phi_1(y - x) + e^{2x}\phi_2(y - 2x)$
   or $z = e^y\phi_1(y - x) + e^{2y}\phi_2(y - 2x)$
2. $z = e^{-x}\phi_1(y) + e^x\phi_2(y - x)$
3. $z = \phi_1(y) + e^{2x}\phi_2(y + x)$
4. $z = \phi_1(y + x) + e^{-x}\phi_2(y - x)$
5. $z = e^x\phi_1(y + x) + e^{2x}\phi_2(y + x)$
6. $z = e^x\phi_1(y) + e^{-x}\phi_2(y + x)$
7. $z = e^x\phi_1(y) + e^{-y}\phi_2(-x)$
8. $z = \phi_1(y - x) + e^{-2x}\phi_2(y + 2x)$
9. $z = \phi_1(y + 2x) + \phi_2(y - 3x)$
10. $z = e^{2x}\,(\phi_1(y + 3x) + x\phi_2(y + 3x))$
11. $z = \sum_{i=1}^{\infty} c_i e^{b_i^2 x + b_i y}$

$\sum_{i=1}^{\infty} c_i e^{a_i x + b_i y}$, where $2a_i^2 - b_i^2 + a_i = 0$

13. $z = \sum_{i=1}^{\infty} c_i e^{a_i x + b_i y}$, where $a_i^2 + a_i b_i + a_i + b_i = 0$
14. $z = e^x\,\phi(y + 2x) + \sum_{i=1} c_i e^{b_i^2 x + b_i y}$
15. $z = e^{-5x/2}\,(\phi_1(2y + 3x) + x\phi_2(2y + 3x)) + \sum_{i=1}^{\infty} c_i e^{a_i x - a_i^2 y/3}$.

6. GENERAL SOLUTION OF NON-HOMOGENEOUS LINEAR PARTIAL DIFFERENTIAL EQUATION WITH CONSTANT COEFFICIENTS

Let $$f(D, D')\, z = F(x, y) \quad \text{...(1)}$$

be a non-homogeneous linear partial differential equation with constant coefficients.

Let u be the general solution of $f(D, D')\, z = 0$.

$$\therefore \quad f(D, D')\, u = 0 \quad \text{...(2)}$$

Let v be a particular integral of $f(D, D')\, z = F(x, y)$.

$$\therefore \quad f(D, D')\, v = F(x, y) \quad \text{...(3)}$$

Now $$f(D, D')\,(u + v) = f(D, D')\, u + f(D, D')\, v = 0 + F(x, y) = F(x, y).$$

$\therefore$ $u + v$ is a solution of $f(D, D')\, z = F(x, y)$. Since u is the general solution of the equation $f(D, D')\, z = 0$, the solution $u + v$ of the equation $f(D, D')\, z = F(x, y)$ is the general solution of the equation $f(D, D')\, z = F(x, y)$.

The general solution u of the equation $f(D, D')\, z = 0$ is called the **complementary function (C.F.)** of the equation $f(D, D')\, z = F(x, y)$.

$\therefore$ **The general solution of the equation f(D, D′) z = F(x, y) is obtained by adding the general solution of the equation f(D, D′)z = 0 to any particular integral of the equation f(D, D′)z = F(x, y).**

7. PARTICULAR INTEGRAL OF f(D, D′)z = F(x, y)

Let $$f(D, D')\, z = F(x, y) \quad \text{...(1)}$$

be a non-homogeneous linear partial differential equation with constant coefficients.

Since $f(D, D')\left[\dfrac{1}{f(D, D')} F(x, y)\right] = F(x, y)$, the function $\dfrac{1}{f(D, D')} F(x, y)$ is a particular integral of the equation $f(D, D')\, z = F(x, y)$.

8. PARTICULAR INTEGRAL WHEN F(x, y) IS SUM OR DIFFERENCE OF TERMS OF THE FORM $x^m y^n$

If $F(x, y)$ is sum or difference of the terms of the form $x^m y^n$, then the particular integral $\dfrac{1}{f(D, D')} F(x, y)$ of the differential equation $f(D, D')\, z = F(x, y)$ is obtained by expanding $\dfrac{1}{f(D, D')}$ in an infinite series in ascending powers of either D or D′. The particular integrals obtained in the above mentioned two method may not be identical. Any one of the two particular integrals may be used.

Example 1. *Find the general solution of the following partial differential equations :*

(i) $(D^2 - D' - 1)z = x^2 y$ *(ii)* $(D^2 - D'^2 - 3D + 3D')z = xy$.

Sol. *(i)* We have $$(D^2 - D' - 1)\, z = x^2 y. \quad \text{...(1)}$$

$D^2 - D' - 1$ is irreducible.

$$\therefore \quad \text{C.F.} = \sum_{i=1}^{\infty} c_i e^{a_i x + b_i y}, \text{ where } a_i^2 - b_i - 1 = 0 \text{ or } b_i = a_i^2 - 1$$

$$\therefore \quad \text{C.F.} = \sum_{i=1}^{\infty} c_i e^{a_i x + (a_i^2 - 1) y}$$

$$\text{P.I.} = \frac{1}{D^2 - D' - 1} x^2 y = -\frac{1}{1 + (D' - D^2)} x^2 y$$
$$= -(1 + (D' - D^2))^{-1} x^2 y$$
$$= -(1 - (D' - D^2) + (D' - D^2)^2 - \ldots\ldots) x^2 y$$
$$= -(1 - D' + D^2 - 2D'D^2 + \ldots\ldots) x^2 y$$
$$= -(x^2 y - x^2 + 2y - 4 + 0 + \ldots\ldots) = -x^2 y + x^2 - 2y + 8.$$

$\therefore$ Using G.S. = C.F. + P.I., the general solution of (1) is

$$\mathbf{z} = \sum_{i=1}^{\infty} \mathbf{c_i e^{a_i x + (a_i^2 - 1)y}} - \mathbf{x^2 y + x^2 - 2y + 8}, \text{ where } a_i \text{ and } c_i \text{ are arbitrary constants.}$$

(*ii*) We have $(D^2 - D'^2 - 3D + 3D') z = xy.$ ...(1)

$$D^2 - D'^2 - 3D + 3D' = (D - D')(D + D' - 3) = (1.D - 1.D' + 0)(1.D + 1.D' - 3)$$

$\therefore$ $\text{C.F.} = e^{-0x/1} \phi_1(1.y + 1.x) + e^{-(-3)x/1} \phi_2(1.y - 1.x) = \phi_1(y + x) + e^{3x}\phi_2(y - x).$

$$\text{P.I.} = \frac{1}{(D - D')(D + D' - 3)} xy$$
$$= \frac{1}{D}\left(1 - \frac{D'}{D}\right)^{-1} \cdot \frac{1}{-3}\left(1 - \left(\frac{D}{3} + \frac{D'}{3}\right)\right)^{-1} xy$$
$$= -\frac{1}{3D}\left(1 + \frac{D'}{D} + \ldots\ldots\right)\left(1 + \frac{D}{3} + \frac{D'}{3} + \left(\frac{D}{3} + \frac{D'}{3}\right)^2 + \ldots\ldots\right) xy$$
$$= -\frac{1}{3D}\left(1 + \frac{D'}{D} + \ldots\ldots\right)\left(1 + \frac{D}{3} + \frac{D'}{3} + \frac{2DD'}{9} + \ldots\ldots\right) xy$$
$$= -\frac{1}{3D}\left(1 + \frac{D}{3} + \frac{D'}{3} + \frac{2DD'}{9} + \frac{D'}{D} + \frac{D'}{3} + \ldots\ldots\right) xy$$
$$= -\frac{1}{3D}\left(xy + \frac{y}{3} + \frac{x}{3} + \frac{2}{9} + \frac{x^2}{2} + \frac{x}{3} + 0 + \ldots\ldots\right)$$
$$= -\frac{1}{3}\left(\frac{x^2 y}{2} + \frac{xy}{3} + \frac{x^2}{6} + \frac{2x}{9} + \frac{x^3}{6} + \frac{x^2}{6}\right)$$
$$= -\frac{1}{3}\left(\frac{x^2 y}{2} + \frac{xy}{3} + \frac{x^2}{3} + \frac{x^3}{6} + \frac{2}{9} x\right).$$

$\therefore$ Using G.S. = C.F. + P.I., the general solution of (1) is

$$\mathbf{z = \phi_1(y + x) + e^{3x}\phi_2(y - x)} - \frac{1}{3}\left(\frac{\mathbf{x^2 y}}{\mathbf{2}} + \frac{\mathbf{xy}}{\mathbf{3}} + \frac{\mathbf{x^2}}{\mathbf{3}} + \frac{\mathbf{x^3}}{\mathbf{6}} + \frac{\mathbf{2}}{\mathbf{9}}\mathbf{x}\right),$$

where ϕ_1, ϕ_2 are arbitrary functions.

Alternative method of finding P.I.

$$\text{P.I.} = \frac{1}{(D - D')(D + D' - 3)} xy$$

$$= -\frac{1}{3(D-D')}\left(1-\frac{D+D'}{3}\right)^{-1} xy$$

$$= -\frac{1}{3(D-D')}\left(1+\frac{D+D'}{3}+\left(\frac{D+D'}{3}\right)^2+\ldots\right) xy$$

$$= -\frac{1}{3(D-D')}\left(1+\frac{D}{3}+\frac{D'}{3}+\frac{2DD'}{9}+\ldots\right) xy$$

$$= -\frac{1}{3D\left(1-\frac{D'}{D}\right)}\left(xy+\frac{y}{3}+\frac{x}{3}+\frac{2}{9}\right)$$

$$= -\frac{1}{3D}\left(1-\frac{D'}{D}\right)^{-1}\left(xy+\frac{y}{3}+\frac{x}{3}+\frac{2}{9}\right)$$

$$= -\frac{1}{3D}\left(1+\frac{D'}{D}+\frac{D'^2}{D^2}+\ldots\right)\left(xy+\frac{y}{3}+\frac{x}{3}+\frac{2}{9}\right)$$

$$= -\frac{1}{3D}\left(xy+\frac{y}{3}+\frac{x}{3}+\frac{2}{9}+\frac{1}{D}\left(x+\frac{1}{3}\right)+0+\ldots\right)$$

$$= -\frac{1}{3D}\left(xy+\frac{y}{3}+\frac{x}{3}+\frac{2}{9}\right)-\frac{1}{3D^2}\left(x+\frac{1}{3}\right)$$

$$= -\frac{1}{3}\left(\frac{x^2y}{2}+\frac{xy}{3}+\frac{x^2}{6}+\frac{2x}{9}\right)-\frac{1}{3}\left(\frac{x^3}{6}+\frac{x^2}{6}\right)$$

$$= -\frac{1}{3}\left(\frac{x^2y}{2}+\frac{xy}{3}+\frac{x^2}{3}+\frac{x^3}{6}+\frac{2}{9}x\right).$$

Remark. In solving problems, the second method is found comparatively easier and straight forward.

EXERCISE 2

Find the general solution of the following partial differential equations :

1. $r - s + p = 1$
2. $(D - D' - 1)(D - D' - 2)\, z = x$
3. $s + p - q = z + xy$
4. $(D^2 - DD' - 2D'^2 + 2D + 2D')\, z = xy$
5. $(D^2 - D'^2 + D + 3D' - 2)\, z = x^2y$
6. $D(D + D' - 1)(D + 3D' - 2)\, z = x^2 - 4xy + 2y^2$.

Answers

1. $z = \phi_1(y) + e^{-x}\,\phi_2(y + x) + x$
2. $z = e^x\,\phi_1(y + x) + e^{2x}\,\phi_2(y + x) + \frac{x}{2} + \frac{3}{4}$
3. $z = e^x\,\phi_1(y) + e^{-y}\,\phi_2(x) - xy - y + x + 1$
4. $z = \phi_1(y - x) + e^{-2x}\,\phi_2(y + 2x) + \frac{x^2y}{4} - \frac{xy}{4} - \frac{x^3}{12} + \frac{3x^2}{8} - \frac{x}{2}$

5. $z = e^{-2x}\,\phi_1(y + x) + e^x\,\phi_2(y - x) - \frac{1}{2}\left(x^2y + xy + \frac{3}{2}x^2 + \frac{3}{2}y + 3x + \frac{21}{4}\right)$

6. $z = \phi_1(y) + e^x\,\phi_2(y - x) + e^{2x}\,\phi_3(y - 3x) + \frac{1}{12}(2x^3 - 12x^2y + 12xy^2 - 21x^2 + 24xy + 3x)$.

9. PARTICULAR INTEGRAL WHEN F(x, y) IS OF THE FORM e^{ax+by}

Theorem. If f(D, D′) be a function of D and D′ then $\frac{1}{f(D, D')} e^{ax+by} = \frac{1}{f(a, b)} e^{ax+by}$ **provided** $f(a, b) \neq 0$.

Proof. We have $D^r e^{ax+by} = a^r e^{ax+by}$

$$D'^s e^{ax+by} = b^s e^{ax+by}$$

and $$D^r D'^s e^{ax+by} = a^r b^s e^{ax+by}.$$

$$\therefore \quad f(D, D')\, e^{ax+by} = f(a, b)\, e^{ax+by}$$

Dividing both sides by $f(a, b)$, we get $f(D, D') \frac{e^{ax+by}}{f(a, b)} = e^{ax+by}$

$\therefore$ By definition of the inverse operator $\frac{1}{f(D, D')}$, we have $\frac{1}{f(D, D')} e^{ax+by} = \frac{e^{ax+by}}{f(a, b)}$.

Remark 1. The above result is not true for any general function $\phi(ax + by)$ of $ax + by$.

Remark 2. The method $\frac{1}{f(D, D')} e^{ax+by} = \frac{1}{f(a, b)} e^{ax+by}$ is applicable only when $f(a, b) \neq 0$. The case when $f(a, b) = 0$ will be discussed a little later.

Example 1. *Find the general solution of the following partial differential equations :*
(i) $(DD' + aD + bD' + ab)z = e^{mx+ny}$ *(ii)* $(D^2 + D' + 4)z = e^{4x-y}$.

Sol. *(i)* We have $(DD' + aD + bD' + ab)z = e^{mx+ny}$. ...(1)

$$DD' + aD + bD' + ab = (D + b)(D' + a) = (1.D + 0.D' + b)(0.D + 1.D' + a)$$

$$\therefore \quad \text{C.F.} = e^{-bx/1}\,\phi_1(1.y - 0.x) + e^{-ay/1}\,\phi_2(0.y - 1.x) = e^{-bx}\,\phi_1(y) + e^{-ay}\,\phi_2(-x).$$

$$\text{P.I.} = \frac{1}{DD' + aD + bD' + ab} e^{mx+ny} \quad ...(2)$$

$$D = m,\ D' = n \ \Rightarrow\ DD' + aD + bD' + ab = mn + am + bn + ab$$
$$= (m + b)(n + a) \neq 0 \qquad \text{(Assuming } m \neq -b,\ n \neq -a)$$

$$\therefore \quad (2) \Rightarrow \quad \text{P.I.} = \frac{1}{(m + b)(n + a)} e^{mx+ny}$$

$\therefore$ Using G.S. = C.F. + P.I., the general solution of (1) is

$$z = e^{-bx}\,\phi_1(y) + e^{-ay}\,\phi_2(-x) + \frac{e^{mx+ny}}{(m + b)(n + a)},$$

where ϕ_1 and ϕ_2 are arbitrary functions.

(ii) We have $(D^2 + D' + 4)\,z = e^{4x-y}$. ...(1)

$D^2 + D' + 4$ is irreducible.

$$\therefore \quad \text{C.F.} = \sum_{i=1}^{\infty} c_i e^{a_i x + b_i y}, \text{ where } a_i^2 + b_i + 4 = 0$$

$$= \sum_{i=1}^{\infty} c_i e^{a_i x - (a_i^2 + 4)y}.$$

$$\text{P.I.} = \frac{1}{D^2 + D' + 4} e^{4x-y} \quad \text{...(2)}$$

$$D = 4, D' = -1 \Rightarrow D^2 + D' + 4 = (4)^2 + (-1) + 4 = 19 \neq 0$$

$$\therefore \quad (2) \Rightarrow \quad \text{P.I.} = \frac{1}{19} e^{4x-y}$$

$\therefore$ Using G.S. = C.F. + P.I., the general solution of (1) is $\mathbf{z} = \sum_{i=1}^{\infty} c e^{a_i x - (a_i^2 + 4)y} + \frac{1}{19} e^{4x-y}$,

where a_i and c_i are arbitrary constants.

EXERCISE 3

Find the general solution of the following partial differential equations :

1. $(D^2 - DD' - 2D) z = e^{2x+y}$
2. $(D^2 - D'^2 + D - D')z = e^{2x+3y}$
3. $(D^2 - 4DD' + D - 1) z = e^{3x-2y}$
4. $(D^2 - DD' - 2D'^2 + 2D + 2D') z = e^{2x+3y}$
5. $(D^2 - D'^2 + D + 3D' - 2)z = e^{x-y}$
6. $(D^3 - 3DD' + D + 1) z = e^{2x+3y}$.

Answers

1. $z = \phi_1(y) + e^{2x} \phi_2(y + x) - \frac{1}{2} e^{2x+y}$
2. $z = \phi_1(y + x) + e^{-x} \phi_2(y - x) - \frac{1}{6} e^{2x+3y}$
3. $z = \sum_{i=1}^{\infty} c_i e^{a_i x + b_i y} + \frac{1}{35} e^{3x-2y}$, where $a_i^2 - 4a_i b_i + a_i - 1 = 0$
4. $z = \phi_1(y - x) + e^{-2x} \phi_2(y + 2x) - \frac{1}{10} e^{2x+3y}$
5. $z = e^{-2x} \phi_1(y + x) + e^{x} \phi_2(y - x) - \frac{1}{4} e^{x-y}$
6. $z = \sum_{i=1}^{\infty} c e^{a_i x + b_i y} - \frac{1}{7} e^{2x+3y}$, where $a_i^3 - 3a_i b_i + a_i + 1 = 0$.

---

10. PARTICULAR INTEGRAL WHEN F(x, y) IS OF THE FORM sin(ax + by) OR cos(ax + by)

Let the given partial differential equation be

$$f(D, D') z = F(x, y), \text{ where } F(x, y) = \sin(ax + by) \text{ (or } \cos(ax + by)).$$

$$\therefore \quad \text{P.I.} = \frac{1}{f(D, D')} \sin(ax + by) \text{ (or } \cos(ax + by))$$

This is evaluated by putting $D^2 = -a^2$, $DD' = -ab$ and $D'^2 = -b^2$, provided the denominator is not zero.

Example 1. *Find the general solution of the following partial differential equations :*

(*i*) $(D + D')(D + D' - 2)z = \sin (x + 2y)$

(*ii*) $(D^2 - DD' - 2D'^2 + 2D + 2D')z = e^{2x+3y} + \sin (2x + y)$. (KU 2004)

Sol. (*i*) We have $(D + D')(D + D' - 2)\, z = \sin (x + 2y)$. ...(1)

$\Rightarrow \quad (1 \,.\, D + 1 \,.\, D' + 0)(1 \,.\, D + 1 \,.\, D' - 2)z = \sin (x + 2y)$

$\therefore \quad \text{C.F.} = e^{-0x/1}\, \phi_1(1.y - 1.x) + e^{-(-2)x/1}\, \phi_2(1.y - 1.x)$

$\therefore \quad \text{C.F.} = \phi_1(y - x) + e^{2x}\, \phi_2(y - x)$.

$$\text{P.I.} = \frac{1}{(D + D')(D + D' - 2)} \sin (x + 2y) \qquad ...(2)$$

Here $a = 1, b = 2$

$\therefore \quad D^2 = -a^2 = -(1)^2 = -1, \quad DD' = -ab = -(1)(2) = -2,$
$D'^2 = -b^2 = -(2)^2 = -4.$

$$\therefore \quad (2) \Rightarrow \quad \text{P.I.} = \frac{1}{(D + D')^2 - 2(D + D')} \sin (x + 2y)$$

$$= \frac{1}{D^2 + D'^2 + 2DD' - 2D - 2D'} \sin (x + 2y)$$

$$= \frac{1}{-1 - 4 + 2(-2) - 2D - 2D'} \sin (x + 2y)$$

$$= -\frac{1}{2D + 2D' + 9} \sin (x + 2y)$$

$$= -\frac{2D + 2D' - 9}{(2D + 2D')^2 - 81} \sin (x + 2y)$$

$$= -\frac{2D + 2D' - 9}{4D^2 + 8DD' + 4D'^2 - 81} \sin (x + 2y)$$

$$= -\frac{2D + 2D' - 9}{4(-1) - 8(1)(2) - 4(-4) - 81} \sin (x + 2y)$$

$$= \frac{2D + 2D' - 9}{117} \sin (x + 2y)$$

$$= -\frac{1}{117} [2 \cos (x + 2y) + 4 \cos (x + 2y) - 9 \sin (x + 2y)]$$

$$= -\frac{1}{117} [6 \cos (x + 2y) - 9 \sin (x + 2y)]$$

$\therefore$ Using G.S. = C.F. + P.I., the general solution of (1) is

$$\mathbf{z = \phi_1(y - x) + e^{2x}\, \phi_2(y - x) - \frac{1}{117} [6 \cos (x + 2y) - 9 \sin (x + 2y)],}$$

where ϕ_1 and ϕ_2 are arbitrary functions.

(*ii*) We have $(D^2 - DD' - 2D'^2 + 2D + 2D')\, z = e^{2x+3y} + \sin (2x + y)$. ...(1)

$D^2 - DD' - 2D'^2 + 2D + 2D' = (D + D')(D - 2D') + 2(D + D')$

$= (D + D')(D - 2D' + 2) = (1.D + 1.D' + 0)(1.D - 2D' + 2)$

$$\therefore \quad \text{C.F.} = e^{-0x/1}\,\phi_1(1.y - 1.x) + e^{-2x/1}\,\phi_2(1.y - (-2)x)$$

$$\therefore \quad \text{C.F.} = \phi_1(y - x) + e^{-2x}\,\phi_2(y + 2x).$$

$$\text{P.I.} = \frac{1}{D^2 - DD' - 2D'^2 + 2D + 2D'}\,(e^{2x+3y} + \sin(2x + y))$$

$$= \frac{1}{D^2 - DD' - 2D'^2 + 2D + 2D'}\,e^{2x+3y} + \frac{1}{D^2 - DD' - 2D'^2 + 2D + 2D'}\sin(2x + y)$$

$$= \frac{1}{(2)^2 - 2(3) - 2(3)^2 + 2(2) + 2(3)}\,e^{2x+3y} + \frac{1}{(-4) + 2(1) - 2(-1) + 2D + 2D'}\sin(2x + y)$$

$$= -\frac{1}{10}e^{2x+3y} + \frac{1}{2D + 2D'}\sin(2x + y)$$

$$= -\frac{1}{10}e^{2x+3y} + \frac{D - D'}{2(D^2 - D'^2)}\sin(2x + y)$$

$$= -\frac{1}{10}e^{2x+3y} + \frac{D - D'}{2(-4 + 1)}\sin(2x + y)$$

$$= -\frac{1}{10}e^{2x+3y} - \frac{1}{6}(2\cos(2x + y) - \cos(2x + y))$$

$$= -\frac{1}{10}e^{2x+3y} - \frac{1}{6}\cos(2x + y).$$

$\therefore$ Using G.S. = C.F. + P.I., the general solution of (1) is

$$\mathbf{z = \phi_1(y - x) + e^{-2x}\,\phi_2(y + 2x) - \frac{1}{10}e^{2x+3y} - \frac{1}{6}\cos(2x + y)},$$

where ϕ_1, ϕ_2 are arbitrary functions.

EXERCISE 4

Find the general solution of the following partial differential equations :

1. $(D^2 - DD' + D' - 1)z = \cos(x + 2y)$ *(MDU 2004)*
2. $(D - D' - 1)(D - D' - 2)\,z = \sin(2x + 3y)$ *(KU 2005)*
3. $(D^2 - DD' - 2D)\,z = \sin(3x + 4y)$
4. $(2DD' + D'^2 - 3D')\,z = 3\cos(3x - 2y)$ *(MDU 2005)*
5. $(D - D'^2)z = \cos(x - 3y)$
6. $(D^2 + D')(D - D' - D'^2)\,z = \sin(2x + y)$.

Answers

1. $z = e^x\,\phi_1(y) + e^{-x}\,\phi_2(y + x) + \frac{1}{2}\sin(x + 2y)$
2. $z = e^x\,\phi_1(y + x) + e^{2x}\,\phi_2(y + x) + \frac{1}{10}[\sin(2x + 3y) - 3\cos(2x + 3y)]$
3. $z = \phi_1(y) + e^{2x}\,\phi_2(y + x) + \frac{1}{15}[\sin(3x + 4y) + 2\cos(3x + 4y)]$

4. $z = \phi_1(x) + e^{3x/2}\,\phi_2(2y - x) + \frac{3}{50}\,[4\cos(3x - 2y) + 3\sin(3x - 2y)]$

5. $z = \sum_{i=1}^{\infty} c_i e^{b_i^2 x + b_i y} + \frac{1}{82}\,[\sin(x - 3y) + 9\cos(x - 3y)]$

6. $z = \sum_{i=1}^{\infty} c_i e^{a_i x - a_i^2 y} + \sum_{i=1}^{\infty} k_i e^{(b_i + b_i^2)x + b_i y} - \frac{1}{34}\,[5\sin(2x + y) - 3\cos(2x + y)]$.

11. PARTICULAR INTEGRAL WHEN F(x, y) IS OF THE FORM e^{ax+by} V(x, y)

Let the given partial differential equation be

$$f(D, D')z = F(x, y), \text{ where } F(x, y) = e^{ax+by}\,V(x, y).$$

$$\therefore \qquad \text{P.I.} = \frac{1}{f(D, D')}\,e^{ax+by}\,V(x, y)$$

This is evaluated by using the formula :

$$\frac{1}{f(D, D')}\,e^{ax+by}\,V(x, y) = e^{ax+by}\,\frac{1}{f(D + a, D' + b)}\,V(x, y).$$

Remark. If $F(x, y) = e^{ax+by}$ and $f(a, b) = 0$, then we cannot write $\frac{1}{f(D, D')}\,e^{ax+by}$ as $\frac{1}{f(a, b)}\,e^{ax+by}$.

In such a case, we write $\frac{1}{f(D, D')}\,e^{ax+by} = \frac{1}{f(D, D')}\,(e^{ax+by}\,.\,1) = e^{ax+by}\,\frac{1}{f(D + a, D + b)}\,.\,1.$

Example 1. *Find the general solution of the following partial differential equations :*

(i) $(D^2 - 4DD' + 4D'^2 + D - 2D')\,z = e^{x+y}$

(ii) $(D + D' - 1)(D + D' - 3)(D + D')\,z = e^{x+y}\sin(2x + y)$.

Sol. (*i*) We have $(D^2 - 4DD' + 4D'^2 + D - 2D')\,z = e^{x+y}$. ...(1)

$$D^2 - 4DD' + 4D'^2 + D - 2D' = (D - 2D')^2 + (D - 2D')$$

$$= (D - 2D')(D - 2D' + 1) = (1.D - 2D' + 0)(1.D - 2D' + 1)$$

$$\therefore \qquad \text{C.F.} = e^{-0x/1}\,\phi_1(1.y - (-2)x) + e^{-1x/1}\,\phi_2(1.y - (-2)x)$$

$$= \phi_1(y + 2x) + e^{-x}\,\phi_2(y + 2x).$$

$$\text{P.I.} = \frac{1}{(D - 2D')(D - 2D' + 1)}\,e^{x+y} \qquad \text{...(2)}$$

Here $a = 1, b = 1$.

$\therefore \quad D = 1, D' = 1 \;\Rightarrow\; D - 2D' = 1 - 2(1) = -1 \neq 0$ and $D - 2D' + 1 = 1 - 2(1) + 1 = 0$

$$\therefore \qquad \text{P.I.} = \frac{1}{D - 2D' + 1}\left(\frac{1}{D - 2D'}\,e^{x+y}\right) = \frac{1}{D - 2D' + 1}\left(\frac{1}{1 - 2(1)}\,e^{x+y}\right)$$

$$= \frac{1}{D - 2D' + 1}\,.\,\frac{e^{x+y}}{-1} = -\,e^{x+y}\,\frac{1}{(D + 1) - 2(D' + 1) + 1}\,.\,1$$

$$= -\,e^{x+y}\,\frac{1}{D - 2D'}\,1 = -\,e^{x+y}\,.\,\frac{1}{D}\left(1 - 2\frac{D'}{D}\right)^{-1} 1$$

$$= -e^{x+y} \cdot \frac{1}{D}\left(1+2\frac{D'}{D}+\ldots\ldots\right)1 = -e^{x+y} \cdot \frac{1}{D}(1) = -xe^{x+y}.$$

$\therefore$ Using G.S. = C.F. + P.I., the general solution of (1) is

$\mathbf{z = \phi_1(y + 2x) + e^{-x}\, \phi_2(y + 2x) - xe^{x+y}}$, where ϕ_1, ϕ_2 are arbitrary functions.

(*ii*) We have $(D + D' - 1)(D + D' - 3)(D + D')\, z = e^{x+y} \sin (2x + y)$. ...(1)

$\Rightarrow$ $(1.D + 1.D' - 1)(1.D + 1.D' - 3)(1.D + 1.D' + 0)z = e^{x+y} \sin (2x + y)$

$\therefore$ $\text{C.F.} = e^{-(-1)x/1}\, \phi_1(1.y - 1.x) + e^{-(-3)x/1}\, \phi_2(1.y - 1.x) + e^{-0.x/1}\, \phi_3(1.y - 1.x)$

$= e^{x}\, \phi_1(y - x) + e^{3x}\, \phi_2(y - x) + \phi_3(y - x).$

$$\text{P.I.} = \frac{1}{(D + D' - 1)(D + D' - 3)(D + D')}\, e^{x+y} \sin (2x + y)$$

$$= e^{x+y} \frac{1}{(D + 1 + D' + 1 - 1)(D + 1 + D' + 1 - 3)(D + 1 + D' + 1)} \sin (2x + y)$$

$$= e^{x+y} \frac{1}{(D + D' + 1)(D + D' - 1)(D + D' + 2)} \sin (2x + y)$$

$$= e^{x+y} \frac{1.(D + D' - 2)}{((D + D')^2 - 1)((D + D')^2 - 4)} \sin (2x + y)$$

$$= e^{x+y} \frac{D + D' - 2}{(D^2 + D'^2 + 2DD' - 1)(D^2 + D'^2 + 2DD' - 4)} \sin (2x + y)$$

$$= e^{x+y} \frac{D + D' - 2}{(-4 - 1 + 2(-1).2.1 - 1)(-4 - 1 + 2(-1)(2.1) - 4)} \sin (2x + y)$$

$$= e^{x+y} \frac{D + D' - 2}{-130} \sin (2x + y)$$

$$= -\frac{1}{130} e^{x+y} (2 \cos (2x + y) + \cos (2x + y) - 2 \sin (2x + y))$$

$$= -\frac{1}{130} e^{x+y} (3 \cos (2x + y) - 2 \sin (2x + y)).$$

$\therefore$ Using G.S. = C.F. + P.I., the general solution of (1) is

$$\mathbf{z = e^{x}\, \phi_1(y - x) + e^{3x}\, \phi_2(y - x) + \phi_3(y - x) - \frac{1}{130} e^{x+y} (3 \cos (2x + y) - 2 \sin (2x + y))},$$

where ϕ_1, ϕ_2, ϕ_3 are arbitrary functions.

EXERCISE 5

Find the general solution of the following partial differential equations :

1. $(D^2 - DD' + D' - 1)\, z = e^{y}$
2. $(D^2 - DD' + D' - 1)\, z = e^{x}$
3. $(D^2 - D')\, z = e^{x+y}$
4. $(D^2 - D'^2 - 3D + 3D')\, z = xy + e^{x+2y}$ (*KU 2004 S*)
5. $(D^2 + DD' + D + D' - 1)\, z = e^{-2x} (x^2 + y^2)$
6. $D(D - 2D')(D + D')\, z = e^{x+2y} (x^2 + 4y^2)$.

Answers

1. $z = e^{x}\, \phi_1(y) + e^{-x}\, \phi_2(y + x) - xe^{y}$
2. $z = e^{x}\, \phi_1(y) + e^{-x}\, \phi_2(y + x) + \frac{1}{2} xe^{x}$

3. $z = \sum_{i=1}^{\infty} c_i e^{a_i x + a_i^2 y} - y e^{x+y}$

4. $z = \phi_1(y + x) + e^{3x} \phi_2(y - x) - \frac{1}{6} x^2 y - \frac{1}{9} xy - \frac{1}{9} x^2 - \frac{1}{18} x^3 - \frac{2}{27} x - x e^{x+2y}$

5. $z = \sum_{i=1}^{\infty} c_i e^{a_i x + b_i y} + e^{-2x} (x^2 + y^2 + 6x + 2y + 18)$, where $a^2_i + a_i b_i + a_i + b_i - 1 = 0$

6. $z = \phi_1(y) + \phi_2(y + 2x) + \phi_3(y - x) - \frac{1}{81} (9x^2 + 36y^2 - 18x - 72y + 76) e^{x+2y}$

15

Partial Differential Equations Reducible to Equations with Constant Coefficients

1. INTRODUCTION

Till now we have been discussing the solution of linear partial differential equations which are with constant coefficients. Now we shall consider the method of solving a particular type of linear partial differential equations with variable coefficients that are capable of reducing to a linear partial differential equations with constant coefficients.

2. REDUCIBLE LINEAR PARTIAL DIFFERENTIAL EQUATIONS WITH VARIABLE COEFFICIENTS

Let $$f(xD, yD') = F(x, y) \qquad ...(1)$$

be a linear partial differential equation with variable coefficients. Here $f(xD, yD')$ is some function of xD and yD' such that (1) may be a linear partial differential equation. The following are some of the partial differential equations of the form $f(xD, yD') = F(x, y)$:

(*i*) $x^2D^2 - y^2D'^2 = x^2y$

(*ii*) $(x^2D^2 - 2xyDD' + y^2D'^2 - xD + 3yD')\,z = 8(y/x)$

(*iii*) $x^2r - y^2t + px - qy = \log x$.

In general, a reducible linear partial differential equation is of the form :

$$a_0x^n \frac{\partial^n z}{\partial x^n} + a_1x^{n-1}y\frac{\partial^n z}{\partial x^{n-1}\partial y} + ... + a_n y^n \frac{\partial^n z}{\partial y^n} + ... = F(x, y)$$

This equation can also be written as

$$(a_0x^nD^n + a_1x^{n-1}yD^{n-1}D' + ... + a_ny^nD'^n + ...)\,z = F(x, y).$$

3. SOLUTION OF REDUCIBLE LINEAR PARTIAL DIFFERENTIAL EQUATIONS WITH VARIABLE COEFFICIENTS

Let $$f(xD, yD') = (a_0x^nD^n + a_1x^{n-1}yD^{n-1}D' + ... + a_ny^nD'^n + ...)\,z = F(x, y) \qquad ...(1)$$

be a reducible linear partial differential equation with variable coefficients.

Define variables u and v by $u = \log x$ and $v = \log y$.

$\therefore \qquad x = e^u$ and $y = e^v$.

Let $$D_1 = \frac{\partial}{\partial u} \quad \text{and} \quad D'_1 = \frac{\partial}{\partial v}.$$

Now $$x\frac{\partial z}{\partial x} = x\frac{\partial z}{\partial u}\frac{\partial u}{\partial x} = x\frac{\partial z}{\partial u}\frac{1}{x} = \frac{\partial z}{\partial u}$$

$$\therefore \qquad x\frac{\partial}{\partial x}=\frac{\partial}{\partial u} \quad \text{or} \quad xD = D_1 \qquad ...(2)$$

Also, $x\dfrac{\partial}{\partial x}\left(x^{n-1}\dfrac{\partial^{n-1}z}{\partial x^{n-1}}\right)=x\left[x^{n-1}\dfrac{\partial^n z}{\partial x^n}+(n-1)\,x^{n-2}\dfrac{\partial^{n-1}z}{\partial x^{n-1}}\right]$

$$= x^n\frac{\partial^n z}{\partial x^n}+(n-1)\,x^{n-1}\frac{\partial^{n-1}z}{\partial x^{n-1}}$$

$$\therefore \qquad x^n\frac{\partial^n z}{\partial x^n}=\left(x\frac{\partial}{\partial x}-(n-1)\right)x^{n-1}\frac{\partial^{n-1}z}{\partial x^{n-1}}$$

$$\therefore \qquad x^n\frac{\partial^n}{\partial x^n}=\left(x\frac{\partial}{\partial x}-n+1\right)x^{n-1}\frac{\partial^{n-1}}{\partial x^{n-1}}$$

or $$x^nD^n = (xD - n + 1)\,x^{n-1}D^{n-1}$$

or $$x^nD^n = (D_1 - n + 1)\,x^{n-1}D^{n-1}. \qquad ...(3)$$

When $n = 2$, (3) $\Rightarrow$ $x^2D^2 = (D_1 - 1)\,xD = (D_1 - 1)D_1$

$\therefore$ $x^2D^2 = D_1(D_1 - 1)$

When $n = 3$, (3) $\Rightarrow$ $x^3D^3 = (D_1 - 2)\,x^2D^2 = (D_1 - 2)\,D_1(D_1 - 1)$

$\therefore$ $x^3D^3 = D_1(D_1 - 1)(D_1 - 2)$ etc.

Thus, we have $xD = D_1$, $x^2D^2 = D_1(D_1 - 1)$, $x^3D^3 = D_1(D_1 - 1)(D_1 - 2)$, ...

Similarly, we have $yD' = D_1'$, $y^2D'^2 = D_1'(D_1' - 1)$, $y^3D'^3 = D_1'(D_1' - 1)(D_1' - 2)$ ......

Also, $xyDD' = D_1D_1'$,

and $x^ry^sD^rD'^s = D_1(D_1 - 1)$ ...... $(D_1 - r + 1)D_1'(D_1' - 1)$ ...... $(D_1' - s + 1)$.

Substituting these values, the given equation will be reduced to a linear partial differential equation with constant coefficients and with independent variables u and v. This equation is solved by known methods and then the values of u and v are substituted in terms x and y. This represents the general solution of the given equation.

Example 1. *Find the general solution of the following partial differential equations :*

(*i*) $x^2\dfrac{\partial^2 z}{\partial x^2}+2xy\dfrac{\partial^2 z}{\partial x\partial y}+y^2\dfrac{\partial^2 z}{\partial y^2}+x\dfrac{\partial z}{\partial x}+y\dfrac{\partial z}{\partial y}-z=0$

(*ii*) $x^2\dfrac{\partial^2 z}{\partial x^2}-4xy\dfrac{\partial^2 z}{\partial x\partial y}+4y^2\dfrac{\partial^2 z}{\partial y^2}+6y\dfrac{\partial z}{\partial y}=x^3y^4$

(*iii*) $x^2r - y^2t + px - qy = \log x$ (KU 2004)

(*iv*) $x^2\dfrac{\partial^2 z}{\partial x^2}+2xy\dfrac{\partial^2 z}{\partial x\partial y}+y^2\dfrac{\partial^2 z}{\partial y^2}+nz=n\left(x\dfrac{\partial z}{\partial x}+y\dfrac{\partial z}{\partial y}\right)+x^2+y^2+x^3$.

Sol. (*i*) We have $x^2\dfrac{\partial^2 z}{\partial x^2}+2xy\dfrac{\partial^2 z}{\partial x\partial y}+y^2\dfrac{\partial^2 z}{\partial y^2}+x\dfrac{\partial z}{\partial x}+y\dfrac{\partial z}{\partial y}-z=0$.

$$\Rightarrow \qquad (x^2D^2 + 2xyDD' + y^2D'^2 + xD + yD' - 1)\,z = 0 \qquad ...(1)$$

Let $u = \log x$ and $v = \log y$.

$\therefore$ $x = e^u$ and $y = e^v$.

Also, $xD = D_1$, $yD' = D_1'$, $x^2D^2 = D_1(D_1 - 1)$, $xyDD' = D_1D_1'$, $y^2D'^2 = D_1'(D_1' - 1)$,

where $D_1 = \frac{\partial}{\partial u}$ and $D_1' = \frac{\partial}{\partial v}$

$\therefore$ (1) $\Rightarrow$ $(D_1(D_1 - 1) + 2D_1D_1'^2 + D_1'(D_1' - 1) + D_1 + D_1' - 1)z = 0$

$\Rightarrow$ $(D_1' + 2D_1D_1' + D_1' - 1)z = 0$

$\Rightarrow$ $((D_1 + D_1')^2 - 1)z = 0$

$\Rightarrow$ $(D_1 + D_1' - 1)(D_1 + D_1' + 1)z = 0$

$\Rightarrow$ $(1.D_1 + 1.D_1' - 1)(1.D_1 + 1.D_1' + 1)z = 0.$

$\therefore$
$$z = e^{-(-1).u/1}\,\phi_1(1.v - 1.u) + e^{-1.u/1}\,\phi_2(1.v - 1.u)$$
$$= e^u\,\phi_1(v - u) + e^{-u}\,\phi_2(v - u).$$
$$= x\phi_1(\log y - \log x) + \frac{1}{x}\,\phi_2(\log y - \log x)$$
$$= x\phi_1\left(\log\frac{y}{x}\right) + \frac{1}{x}\phi_2\left(\log\frac{y}{x}\right) = x\psi_1\left(\frac{y}{x}\right) + \frac{1}{x}\psi_2\left(\frac{y}{x}\right), \text{ say}$$

$\therefore$ **The general solution is $\mathbf{z = x\psi_1\left(\frac{y}{x}\right) + \frac{1}{x}\psi_2\left(\frac{y}{x}\right)}$, where ψ_1, ψ_2 are arbitrary functions.**

(*ii*) We have $x^2\frac{\partial^2 z}{\partial x^2} - 4xy\frac{\partial^2 z}{\partial x\partial y} + 4y^2\frac{\partial^2 z}{\partial y^2} + 6y\frac{\partial z}{\partial y} = x^3y^4.$

$\Rightarrow$ $(x^2D^2 - 4xyDD' + 4y^2D'^2 + 6yD')z = x^3y^4$ ...(1)

Let $u = \log x$ and $v = \log y$.

$\therefore$ $x = e^u$ and $y = e^v$.

Also, $xD = D_1$, $yD' = D_1'$, $x^2D^2 = D_1(D_1 - 1)$, $xyDD' = D_1D_1'$, $y^2D_1'^2 = D_1'(D_1' - 1)$,

where $D_1 = \frac{\partial}{\partial u}$ and $D_1' = \frac{\partial}{\partial v}$.

$\therefore$ (1) $\Rightarrow$ $(D_1(D_1 - 1) - 4D_1D_1' + 4D_1'(D_1' - 1) + 6D_1')z = e^{3u}e^{4v}$

$\Rightarrow$ $(D_1^2 - 4D_1D_1' + 4D_1'^2 - D_1 + 2D_1')z = e^{3u+4v}$

$\Rightarrow$ $((D_1 - 2D_1')^2 - (D_1 - 2D_1'))z = e^{3u+4v}$

$\Rightarrow$ $(D_1 - 2D_1')(D_1 - 2D_1' - 1)z = e^{3u+4v}$

$(1.D_1 - 2D_1' + 0)(1.D_1 + (-2)D_1' - 1)z = e^{3u+4v}$

$\therefore$
$$\text{C.F.} = e^{0.u/1}\,\phi_1(1.v + 2u) + e^{1.u/1}\,\phi_2(1.v + 2u)$$
$$= \phi_1(2u + v) + e^u\,\phi_2(2u + v) = \phi_1(2\log x + \log y) + x\phi_2(2\log x + \log y)$$
$$= \phi_1(\log x^2y) + x\phi_2(\log x^2y)$$
$$= \psi_1(x^2y) + x\psi_2(x^2y), \text{ say}$$

$$\text{P.I.} = \frac{1}{(D_1 - 2D_1')(D_1 - 2D_1' - 1)}\,e^{3u+4v} \qquad ...(2)$$

Here $a = 3, b = 4$

$$D_1 = 3,\ D_1' = 4 \Rightarrow D_1 - 2D_1' = 3 - 2(4) = -5 \neq 0$$

and $$D_1 - 2D_1' - 1 = 3 - 2(4) - 1 = -6 \neq 0$$

$\therefore$ (2) $\Rightarrow$ $$\text{P.I.} = \frac{1}{(-5)(-6)} e^{3u+4v} = \frac{1}{30} x^3 y^4.$$

$\therefore$ Using G.S. = C.F. + P.I., the general solution of the given equation is

$$\mathbf{z = \psi_1(x^2y) + x\psi_2(x^2y) + \frac{1}{30}x^3y^4}, \text{ where } \psi_1, \psi_2 \text{ are arbitrary functions.}$$

(*iii*) We have $x^2r - y^2t + px - qy = \log x$.

$\Rightarrow$ $(x^2D^2 - y^2D'^2 + xD - yD')z = \log x$ ...(1)

Let $u = \log x$ and $v = \log y$.

$\therefore$ $x = e^u$ and $y = e^v$

Also, $xD = D_1,\ yD' = D_1',\ x^2D^2 = D_1(D_1 - 1),\quad y^2D'^2 = D_1'(D_1' - 1),$

where $D_1 = \frac{\partial}{\partial u}$ and $D_1' = \frac{\partial}{\partial v}$

$\therefore$ (1) $\Rightarrow$ $(D_1(D_1 - 1) - D_1'(D_1' - 1) + D_1 - D_1')z = u$

$\Rightarrow$ $(D_1^2 - D_1'^2)z = u \Rightarrow (D_1 + D_1')(D_1 - D_1')z = u$

$\Rightarrow$ $(1.D_1 + 1.D_1' + 0)(1.D_1 + (-1).D_1' + 0)z = u$

$\therefore$ $$\text{C.F.} = e^{-0.u/1}\phi_1(1.v - 1.u) + e^{-0.u/1}\phi_2(1.v - (-1).u)$$
$$= \phi_1(v - u) + \phi_2(v + u)$$
$$= \phi_1(\log y - \log x) + \phi_2(\log y + \log x)$$
$$= \phi_1\left(\log\frac{y}{x}\right) + \phi_2(\log xy) = \psi_1\left(\frac{y}{x}\right) + \psi_2(xy), \text{ say.}$$

$$\text{P.I.} = \frac{1}{D_1^2 - D_1'^2} u = \frac{1}{D_1^2}\left(1 - \frac{D_1'^2}{D_1^2}\right)^{-1} u$$

$$= \frac{1}{D_1^2}\left(1 + \frac{D_1'^2}{D_1^2} - \ldots\ldots\right)u = \frac{1}{D_1^2}(u + 0) = \frac{u^3}{6} = \frac{1}{6}(\log x)^3.$$

$\therefore$ Using G.S. = C.F. + P.I., the general solution of the given equation is

$$\mathbf{z = \psi_1\left(\frac{y}{x}\right) + \psi_2(yx) + \frac{1}{6}(\log x)^3}, \text{ where } \psi_1, \psi_2 \text{ are arbitrary functions.}$$

(*iv*) We have $$x^2\frac{\partial^2 z}{\partial x^2} + 2xy\frac{\partial^2 z}{\partial x\partial y} + y^2\frac{\partial^2 z}{\partial y^2} + nz = n\left(x\frac{\partial z}{\partial x} + y\frac{\partial z}{\partial y}\right) + x^2 + y^2 + x^3.$$

$\Rightarrow$ $(x^2D^2 + 2xyDD' + y^2D'^2 - nxD - nyD' + n)z = x^2 + y^2 + x^3$ ...(1)

Let $u = \log x$ and $v = \log y$.

$\therefore$ $x = e^u$ and $y = e^v$.

Also, $xD = D_1,\ yD' = D_1',\ x^2D^2 = D_1(D_1 - 1),\ xyDD' = D_1D_1',$

$y^2D'^2 = D_1'(D_1' - 1)$, where $D_1 = \dfrac{\partial}{\partial u}$ and $D_1' = \dfrac{\partial}{\partial v}$.

(1) $\Rightarrow$ $(D_1(D_1 - 1) + 2D_1D_1' + D_1'(D_1' - 1) - nD_1 - nD_1' + n)\, z = e^{2u} + e^{2v} + e^{3u}$

$\Rightarrow$ $(D_1^2 + 2D_1D_1' + D_1'^2 - D_1 - D_1' - nD_1 - nD_1' + n)\, z = e^{2u} + e^{2v} + e^{3u}$

$\Rightarrow$ $((D_1 + D_1')^2 - (n+1)(D_1 + D_1') + n)\, z = e^{2u} + e^{2v} + e^{3u}$

$\Rightarrow$ $(D_1 + D_1' - 1)(D_1 + D_1' - n)\, z = e^{2u} + e^{2v} + e^{3u}$

$\Rightarrow$ $(1.D_1 + 1.D_1' - 1)(1.D_1 + 1.D_1' - n)z = e^{2u} + e^{2v} + e^{3u}$.

$\therefore$ C.F. $= e^{1.u/1}\, \phi_1(1.v - 1.u) + e^{nu/1}\, \phi_2(1.v - 1.u)$

$$= e^u\, \phi_1(v - u) + e^{nu}\, \phi_2(v - u) = x\phi_1\left(\log \frac{y}{x}\right) + x^n\phi_2\left(\log \frac{y}{x}\right)$$

$= x\psi_1(y/x) + x^n\psi_2(y/x)$, say.

$$\text{P.I.} = \frac{1}{(D_1 + D_1' - 1)(D_1 + D_1' - n)}(e^{2u} + e^{2v} + e^{3u})$$

$$= \frac{1}{(D_1 + D_1' - 1)(D_1 + D_1' - n)}e^{2u} + \frac{1}{(D_1 + D_1' - 1)(D_1 + D_1' - n)}e^{2v} + \frac{1}{(D_1 + D_1' - 1)(D_1 + D_1' - n)}e^{3u}$$

$$= \frac{1}{(2 + 0 - 1)(2 - 0 - n)}e^{2u} + \frac{1}{(0 + 2 - 1)(0 + 2 - n)}e^{2v} + \frac{1}{(3 + 0 - 1)(3 + 0 - n)}e^{3u}$$

$$= \frac{1}{2 - n}x^2 + \frac{1}{2 - n}y^2 + \frac{1}{2(3 - n)}x^3$$

$\therefore$ Using G.S. = C.F. + P.I., the general solution of the given equation is

$$\mathbf{z = x\psi_1\left(\frac{y}{x}\right) + x^n\psi_2\left(\frac{y}{x}\right) + \frac{1}{2 - n}(x^2 + y^2) + \frac{1}{2(3 - n)}x^3}$$

where ψ_1 and ψ_2 are arbitrary functions.

WORKING RULES OF SOLVING f(xD, yD′) = F(x, y)

Step I. *Put $u = \log x$ and $v = \log y$.*

Step II. *Change the whole equation in independent variables u and v* by using $x = e^u$ and $y = e^v$. *We shall get a linear partial differential equation with constant coefficients.*

Step III. *Find the general solution of the equation obtained in* **step II.**

Step IV. *In the general solution, put $u = \log x$ and $v = \log y$. This gives the general solution of the given equation.*

EXERCISE 1

Find the general solution of the following partial differential equations :

1. $x^2\dfrac{\partial^2 z}{\partial x^2} + 2xy\dfrac{\partial^2 z}{\partial x \partial y} + y^2\dfrac{\partial^2 z}{\partial y^2} = 0$ *(CDLU2004)* 2. $x^2\dfrac{\partial^2 z}{\partial x^2} - 3xy\dfrac{\partial^2 z}{\partial x \partial y} + 2y^2\dfrac{\partial^2 z}{\partial y^2} + 5y\dfrac{\partial z}{\partial y} - 2z = 0$

3. $x^2 \dfrac{\partial^2 z}{\partial x^2} - y^2 \dfrac{\partial^2 z}{\partial y^2} + x \dfrac{\partial z}{\partial x} - y \dfrac{\partial z}{\partial y} = 0$

4. $x^2 \dfrac{\partial^2 z}{\partial x^2} - y^2 \dfrac{\partial^2 z}{\partial y^2} = xy$

5. $x^2 \dfrac{\partial^2 z}{\partial x^2} - y^2 \dfrac{\partial^2 z}{\partial y^2} = x^2 y$

6. $x^2 \dfrac{\partial^2 z}{\partial x^2} + 2xy \dfrac{\partial^2 z}{\partial x \partial y} + y^2 \dfrac{\partial^2 z}{\partial y^2} = x^m y^n,\ m + n \neq 0, 1$ (*KU 2004 S*)

7. $x^2 r - 3xys + 2y^2 t + px + 2qy = x + 2y$

8. $x^2 r + 2xys - xp = \dfrac{x^3}{y^2}$

9. $yt - q = xy$

10. $x^2 r + 2xys + y^2 t = (x^2 + y^2)^{n/2}$

11. $x^2 r - xys - 2y^2 t + xp - 2yq = \log \dfrac{y}{x} - \dfrac{1}{2}$

12. $x^2 r - 4y^2 t - 4yq - z = x^2 y^2 \log y.$

Answers

1. $z = \psi_1\left(\dfrac{y}{x}\right) + x\psi_2\left(\dfrac{y}{x}\right)$

2. $z = x^2 \psi_1(xy) + \dfrac{1}{x}\psi_2(x^2 y)$

3. $z = \psi_1(xy) + \psi_2\left(\dfrac{y}{x}\right)$

4. $z = \psi_1(xy) + x\psi_2\left(\dfrac{y}{x}\right) + xy \log x$

5. $z = \psi_1(xy) + x\psi_2\left(\dfrac{y}{x}\right) + \dfrac{1}{2} x^2 y$

6. $z = \psi_1\left(\dfrac{y}{x}\right) + x\psi_2\left(\dfrac{y}{x}\right) + \dfrac{x^m y^n}{(m+n)(m+n-1)}$

7. $z = \psi_1(xy) + \psi_2(x^2 y) + x + y$

8. $z = \psi_1(y) + x^2\psi_2\left(\dfrac{y}{x^2}\right) - \dfrac{x^3}{9y^2}$

9. $z = \psi_1(x) + y^2\psi_2(x) + \dfrac{1}{2} xy^2 \log y$

10. $z = \psi_1\left(\dfrac{y}{x}\right) + x\psi_2\left(\dfrac{y}{x}\right) + \dfrac{(x^2 + y^2)^{n/2}}{n(n-1)}$

11. $z = \psi_1(x^2 y) + \psi_2\left(\dfrac{y}{x}\right) + \dfrac{1}{2}(\log x)^2 \log y - \dfrac{1}{4}(\log x)^2$

12. $z = \sum_{i=1}^{\infty} c_i x^{a_i} y^{b_i} + x^2 y^2 \dfrac{(16 - 15 \log y)}{225}$, where $a_i^2 - 4b_i^2 - a_i - 1 = 0.$

16

Monge's Methods

1. INTRODUCTION

In the last chapter we discussed the methods of solving some special type of linear partial differential equations with variable coefficients which were capable of being reduced to linear partial differential equations with constant coefficients by changing the independent variables. Solving any given partial differential equation with variable coefficients is not an easy task. We are moving in this direction step by step.

2. PARTIAL DIFFERENTIAL EQUATION OF SECOND ORDER

A partial differential equation of the second order is of the form $f(x, y, z, p, q, r, s, t) = 0$. It is only in special cases that a partial differential equation of second order can be solved. Monge's methods are used to solve some particular types of equations of second order.

3. INTERMEDIATE INTEGRAL

Let $$f(x, y, z, p, q, r, s, t) = 0 \qquad ...(1)$$
be a partial differential equation of second order. A relation of the form $u = \phi(v)$, where u, v are functions of x, y, z, p, q and ϕ is an arbitrary function, is called an **intermediate integral** of (1) if the given partial differential equation (1) could be derived by eliminating the arbitrary function ϕ.

For example $p - \frac{1}{x}\log y = \phi(x)$ is an intermediate integral of the equation $xys = 1$, because differentiating $p - \frac{1}{x}\log y = \phi(x)$ w.r.t. y, we get $\frac{\partial p}{\partial y} - \frac{1}{x}\cdot\frac{1}{y} = 0$ or $s - \frac{1}{xy} = 0$ or $xys = 1$.

Remark. Finding of one or more intermediate integrals of a partial differential equation of second order is the first step in the direction of finding the general solution of the given partial differential equation of second order.

4. MONGE'S METHODS

Let $$Rr + Ss + Tt + U(rt - s^2) = V \qquad ...(1)$$
be a partial differential equation of second order, where R, S, T, U, V are functions of x, y, z, p, q. An equation of the form (1) may or may not admit of a solution. Monge's methods are used to solve any solvable equation of the form (1).

In particular if $U = 0$, then (1) reduces to $Rr + Ss + Tt = V$. We shall be considering the cases $U = 0$ and $U \neq 0$ separately.

5. MONGE'S METHOD OF SOLVING Rr + Ss + Tt = V (CDLU 2004)

Let $$Rr + Ss + Tt = V \qquad ...(1)$$

be a solvable partial differential equation, where R, S, T, V are functions of x, y, z, p, q.

Since z is a function of x and y, we have

$$dp = \frac{\partial p}{\partial x}dx + \frac{\partial p}{\partial y}dy = \frac{\partial^2 z}{\partial x^2}dx + \frac{\partial^2 z}{\partial y \partial x}dy = r\,dx + s\,dy$$

and $$dq = \frac{\partial q}{\partial x}dx + \frac{\partial q}{\partial y}dy = \frac{\partial^2 z}{\partial x \partial y}dx + \frac{\partial^2 z}{\partial y^2}dy = s\,dx + t\,dy.$$

Solving these equations for r and t, we get $r = \dfrac{dp - sdy}{dx}$ and $t = \dfrac{dq - sdx}{dy}$.

$$\therefore \quad (1) \Rightarrow \quad R\left(\frac{dp - sdy}{dx}\right) + Ss + T\left(\frac{dq - sdx}{dy}\right) = V$$

$$\Rightarrow \quad s[R(dy)^2 - S\,dxdy + T(dx)^2] = R\,dydp + T\,dxdq - V\,dxdy \qquad ...(2)$$

The equations : $R(dy)^2 - S\,dxdy + T(dx)^2 = 0$ ...(3)

and $R\,dydp + T\,dxdq - V\,dxdy = 0$ ...(4)

are called **Monge's equations.** The equation (3) may have either distinct or same factors.

Case I. Let $R(dy)^2 - S\,dxdy + T(dx)^2 = (A_1dy + B_1dx)(A_2dy + B_2dx) = 0.$

In this case we have two distinct systems

$$\left.\begin{aligned} A_1dy + B_1dx = 0 \\ Rdydp + Tdxdq - Vdxdy = 0 \end{aligned}\right] \qquad ...(5)$$

and $$\left.\begin{aligned} A_2dy + B_2dx = 0 \\ Rdydp + Tdxdq - Vdxdy = 0 \end{aligned}\right] \qquad ...(6)$$

Let system (5) be integrable. Let $u = u(x, y, z, p, q) = a$ and $v = v(x, y, z, p, q) = b$ satisfy the system (5).

$\therefore$ $u = \psi(v)$ is an intermediate integral of (1), since $u = a$, $v = b$ satisfy (2) and hence (1). If system (6) is also integrable, we get another intermediate integral. These intermediate integrals are solved to find the values of p and q in terms of x and y. The values of p and q are substituted in $dz = p\,dx + q\,dy$. This is integrated to get the general solution of (1). In case we get only one intermediate integral or we want to use only one intermediate integral then we express it in the form $Pp + Qq = R$ and use Lagrange's method to find the general solution of (1).

Case II. Let $R(dy)^2 - Sdx\,dy + T(dx)^2 = (Ady + Bdx)^2 = 0$

Let $u = u(x, y, z, p, q) = a$, $v = v(x, y, z, p, q) = b$ satisfy the system

$$\left.\begin{aligned} Ady + Bdx = 0 \\ Rdydp + Tdxdq - Vdxdy = 0 \end{aligned}\right]$$

$\therefore$ $u = \psi(v)$ is an intermediate integral of (1), since $u = a$, $v = b$ satisfy (2) and hence (1). We express it in the form $Pp + Qq = R$ and use Lagrange's method to find the general solution of (1).

Type I. Equations giving two distinct intermediate integrals and both are used to find the general solution.

WORKING RULES FOR SOLVING PROBLEMS

Step I. *Write the given equation in the form* $Rr + Ss + Tt = V$.

Step II. *Substitute the values of R, S, T, V in the Monge's equations :*

$$R(dy)^2 - Sdxdy + T(dx)^2 = 0 \qquad ...(1)$$

and $$Rdydp + Tdxdq - Vdxdy = 0 \qquad ...(2)$$

Step III. *Factorise (1) into two distinct factors.*

Step IV. *Find two intermediate integrals. Solve these to find the values of p and q.*

Step V. *Put p and q in* $dz = pdx + qdy$ *and integrate to get the general solution of the given equation.*

Example 1. *Find the general solution of the following partial differential equations :*

(*i*) $r - t\cos^2 x + p\tan x = 0$ (KU 2005) (*ii*) $xy(r - t) - s(x^2 - y^2) = qx - py$. (KU 2005 S)

Sol. (*i*) We have $r - t\cos^2 x + p\tan x = 0$.

$\Rightarrow$ $$r - t\cos^2 x = -p\tan x \qquad ...(1)$$

Comparing (1) with $Rr + Ss + Tt = V$, we get

$$R = 1, S = 0, T = -\cos^2 x, V = -p\tan x.$$

The **Monge's equations** are :

$$R(dy)^2 - Sdxdy + T(dx)^2 = 0 \qquad ...(2)$$

and $$Rdydp + Tdxdq - Vdxdy = 0 \qquad ...(3)$$

(2) $\Rightarrow$ $$(dy)^2 - \cos^2\alpha\,(dx)^2 = 0$$

$\Rightarrow$ $$(dy - \cos\alpha\,dx)(dy + \cos\alpha\,dx) = 0$$

$\Rightarrow$ $$dy - \cos x\,dx = 0 \qquad ...(4)$$

and $$dy + \cos\alpha\,dx = 0 \qquad ...(4')$$

(3) $\Rightarrow$ $$1.dydp + (-\cos^2\alpha)\,dxdq - (-p\tan x)\,dxdy = 0$$

$\Rightarrow$ $$dydp - \cos^2\alpha\,dxdq + p\tan x\,dx\,dy = 0 \qquad ...(5)$$

We consider the system (4) and (5).

Integrating (4), we get $y - \sin x = a$

(4) $\Rightarrow$ $dy = \cos x\,dx$. Putting this value of dy in (5), we get

$$\cos x\,dxdp - \cos^2 x\,dxdq + p\tan x\,dx\cos x\,dx = 0$$

$\Rightarrow$ $$\cos x\,dx\,(dp - \cos x\,dq + p\tan x\,dx) = 0$$

$\Rightarrow$ $$dp - \cos x\,dq + p\tan x\,dx = 0$$

$\Rightarrow$ $$(dp + p\tan x\,dx) - \cos x\,dq = 0$$

$\Rightarrow$ Multiplying by $\sec x$, we get

$$(\sec x\,dp + p\tan x\sec x\,dx) - dq = 0$$

$\Rightarrow$ $$d(p\sec x) - dq = 0$$

Integrating, we get $p\sec x - q = b$

Let $b = \phi(a)$, ϕ arbitrary.

$\therefore$ $$p\sec x - q = \phi(y - \sin x) \qquad ...(6)$$

Similarly by solving (4′) and (5), we get $p\sec x + q = \psi(y + \sin x)$ ...(7)

Solving (6) and (7), we get

$$p = \frac{1}{2 \sec x} (\phi(y - \sin x) + \psi(y + \sin x))$$

and $$q = -\frac{1}{2} (\phi(y - \sin x) - \psi(y + \sin x))$$

Now $dz = pdx + qdy.$

$$\therefore \quad dz = \frac{\cos x}{2} (\phi(y - \sin x) + \psi(y + \sin x)dx - \frac{1}{2} (\phi(y - \sin x) - \psi(y + \sin x)) dy$$

$$\Rightarrow \quad dz = \frac{1}{2} \phi(y - \sin x)(\cos x\, dx - dy) + \frac{1}{2} \psi(y + \sin x)(\cos x\, dx + dy)$$

$$\Rightarrow \quad dz = -\frac{1}{2} \phi(y - \sin x)\, d(y - \sin x) + \frac{1}{2} \psi(y + \sin x)\, d(y + \sin x)$$

Integrating, we get

$$dz = \int -\frac{1}{2} \phi(y - \sin x)\, d(y - \sin x) + \int \frac{1}{2} \psi(y + \sin x)\, d(y + \sin x)$$

$$\Rightarrow \quad \mathbf{dz = \phi_1(y - \sin x) + \phi_2(y + \sin x),} \quad \textbf{say.}$$

This is the general solution of the given equation. Here ϕ_1, ϕ_2 are arbitrary functions.

(*ii*) We have $xy(r - t) - s(x^2 - y^2) = qx - py.$

$$\Rightarrow \quad xyr - (x^2 - y^2)s - xyt = qx - py \quad \text{...(1)}$$

Comparing (1) with $Rr + Ss + Tt = V$, we get

$$R = xy, S = -x^2 + y^2, T = -xy, V = qx - py.$$

The **Monge's equations** are :

$$R(dy)^2 - Sdxdy + T(dx)^2 = 0 \quad \text{...(2)}$$

and $$Rdydp + Tdxdq - Vdxdy = 0 \quad \text{...(3)}$$

$$(2) \Rightarrow \quad xy(dy)^2 + (x^2 - y^2)\, dxdy - xy(dx)^2 = 0$$

$$\Rightarrow \quad (xdy - ydx)(ydy + xdx) = 0$$

$$\Rightarrow \quad xdy - ydx = 0 \quad \text{...(4)}$$

and $$ydy + xdx = 0 \quad \text{...(4')}$$

$$(3) \Rightarrow \quad xydydp - xy\, dxdq - (qx - py)\, dxdy = 0 \quad \text{...(5)}$$

We consider the system (4) and (5)

$$(4) \Rightarrow \quad xdy = ydx \Rightarrow \frac{dy}{y} = \frac{dx}{x}$$

Integrating, we get $\log y = \log x + \log a$

$$\Rightarrow \quad \log \frac{y}{x} = \log a \Rightarrow \frac{y}{x} = a.$$

$$(5) \Rightarrow \quad ydp \,.\, xdy - xdq \,.\, ydx - qdx \,.\, xdy + pdy \,.\, ydx = 0$$

$$\Rightarrow \quad ydp - xdq - qdx + pdy = 0 \quad \text{[By using (4)]}$$

$$\Rightarrow \quad (ydp + pdy) - (xdq + qdx) = 0$$

$$\Rightarrow \quad d(yp - xq) = 0 \Rightarrow yp - xq = b$$

Let $b = \phi(a)$. $\therefore \quad yp - xq = \phi(y/x)$ ...(6)

Now we consider the system (4') and (5).

$$(4') \Rightarrow \quad d(x^2 + y^2) = 0 \Rightarrow x^2 + y^2 = c$$

$$(5) \Rightarrow \quad xdp \,.\, ydy - ydq \,.\, xdx - qdy \,.\, xdx + pdx \,.\, ydy = 0$$

$\Rightarrow \qquad xdp + ydq + qdy + pdx = 0$ [By using (4')]

$\Rightarrow \qquad (xdp + pdx) + (ydq + qdy) = 0$

$\Rightarrow \qquad d(xp) + d(yq) = 0 \Rightarrow d(xp + yq) = 0 \Rightarrow xp + yq = k.$

Let $k = \psi(c)$. $\therefore \quad xp + yq = \psi(x^2 + y^2)$ ...(7)

$\therefore$ We get two intermediate integrals of (1).

Solving (6) and (7) for p and q, we get

$$p = \frac{x\psi(x^2 + y^2) + y\phi(y/x)}{x^2 + y^2} \quad \text{and} \quad q = \frac{y\psi(x^2 + y^2) - x\phi(y/x)}{x^2 + y^2}$$

Now $\qquad dz = pdx + qdy$

$$\therefore \qquad dz = \frac{x\psi(x^2 + y^2) + y\phi(y/x)}{x^2 + y^2}dx + \frac{y\psi(x^2 + y^2) - x\phi(y/x)}{x^2 + y^2}dy.$$

$$\Rightarrow \qquad dz = \frac{\psi(x^2 + y^2)}{x^2 + y^2}(xdx + ydy) + \frac{\phi(y/x)}{x^2 + y^2}(ydx - xdy)$$

$$\Rightarrow \qquad dz = \frac{\psi(x^2 + y^2)}{2(x^2 + y^2)}d(x^2 + y^2) - \frac{\phi(y/x)}{1 + (y/x)^2}\,\frac{xdy - ydx}{x^2}$$

$$\Rightarrow \qquad dz = \frac{\psi(x^2 + y^2)}{2(x^2 + y^2)}d(x^2 + y^2) - \frac{\phi(y/x)}{1 + (y/x)^2}d(y/x)$$

Integrating, we get

$$z = \int \frac{\psi(x^2 + y^2)}{2(x^2 + y^2)}d(x^2 + y^2) + \int -\frac{\phi(y/x)}{1 + (y/x)^2}d(y/x).$$

$$\Rightarrow \qquad \mathbf{z = \phi_1(x^2 + y^2) + \phi_2(y/x),} \quad \textbf{say.}$$

This is the general solution of the given equation. Here ϕ_1, ϕ_2 are arbitrary functions.

Type II. Equations giving two distinct intermediate integral and only one is used to find the general solution.

WORKING RULES FOR SOLVING PROBLEMS

Step I. *Write the given equation in the form* $Rr + Ss + Tt = V$.

Step II. *Substitute the values of R, S, T, V in the Monge's equations :*

$$R(dy)^2 - Sdxdy + T(dy)^2 = 0 \qquad ...(1)$$

and $\quad Rdydp + Tdxdq - Vdxdy = 0 \qquad ...(2)$

Step III. *Factorize (1) into two distinct factors.*

Step IV. *Using any of the factors, find an intermediate integral. Solve this integral by using Lagrange method to get the general solution of the given equation.*

Example 2. *Find the general solution of the following partial differential equations :*

(*i*) $(r - s)y + (s - t)x + q - p = 0$ (*ii*) $(x - y)(xr - xs - ys + yt) = (x + y)(p - q)$.

Sol. (*i*) We have $(r - s)y + (s - t)x + q - p = 0$.

$\Rightarrow \qquad yr + (x - y)s - xt = p - q$ ...(1)

Comparing (1) with $Rr + Ss + Tt = V$, we get

$$R = y, \quad S = x - y, \quad T = -x, \quad V = p - q.$$

The **Monge's equations** are :

$$R(dy)^2 - Sdxdy + T(dx)^2 = 0 \quad ...(2)$$

and

$$Rdydp + Tdxdq - Vdxdy = 0 \quad ...(3)$$

(2) $\Rightarrow$ $y(dy)^2 - (x-y)\,dxdy - x(dx)^2 = 0$

$\Rightarrow$ $(dx + dy)(ydy - xdx) = 0$

$\Rightarrow$ $dx + dy = 0$ ...(4) and $ydx - xdy = 0$ ...(4′)

(3) $\Rightarrow$ $ydydp - xdx\,dq - (p-q)\,dx\,dy = 0$ ...(5)

We consider the system (4) and (5).

Integrating (4), we get $x + y = a$.

(5) $\Rightarrow$ $ydydp - xdxdq - pdxdy + qdxdy = 0$

$\Rightarrow$ $ydpdy + xdq(-dx) + pdy(-dx) + qdxdy = 0$

$\Rightarrow$ $ydp + xdq + pdy + qdx = 0$ $\quad (\because\ dy = -dx)$

$\Rightarrow$ $(ydp + pdy) + (xdq + qdx) = 0$

$\Rightarrow$ $d(py) + d(qx) = 0 \Rightarrow py + qx = b$

Let $b = \psi(a)$. $\quad \therefore\ py + qx = \psi(x+y)$

This is a Lagrange linear equation.

Auxiliary equations are $\dfrac{dx}{y} = \dfrac{dy}{x} = \dfrac{dz}{\psi(x+y)}$ ...(6)

(6) $\Rightarrow$ $\dfrac{dx}{y} = \dfrac{dy}{x} \Rightarrow xdx - ydy = 0 \Rightarrow \dfrac{1}{2}d(x^2 - y^2) = 0$

$\Rightarrow$ $x^2 - y^2 = k$, k arbitrary.

(6) $\Rightarrow$ $\dfrac{dx}{y} = \dfrac{dz}{\psi(x+y)} \Rightarrow \dfrac{dx}{\sqrt{x^2-k}} = \dfrac{dz}{\psi\left(x + \sqrt{x^2-k}\right)}$

$$\Rightarrow \quad dz = \frac{\psi\left(x + \sqrt{x^2-k}\right)}{\sqrt{x^2-k}}\,dx \quad ...(7)$$

$$u = x + \sqrt{x^2-k} \Rightarrow du = \left(1 + \frac{x}{\sqrt{x^2-k}}\right)dx = \frac{u}{\sqrt{x^2-k}}\,dx \Rightarrow \frac{dx}{\sqrt{x^2-k}} = \frac{du}{u}$$

$\therefore$ (7) $\Rightarrow$ $dz = \psi(u)\,.\,\dfrac{du}{u} \Rightarrow dz = \dfrac{\psi(u)}{u}\,du$

Integrating, we get

$$z = \int \frac{\psi(u)}{u}\,du + b\,.$$

$\Rightarrow$ $z = \phi_1(u) + b$, say

$\Rightarrow$ $z = \phi_1(x + \sqrt{x^2-k}) + \phi_2(a)$, say

$\Rightarrow$ $\mathbf{z = \phi_1(x+y) + \phi_2(x^2 - y^2)}$.

This is the general solution of the given equation. Here ϕ_1, ϕ_2 are arbitrary functions.

(*ii*) We have $(x-y)(xr - xs - ys + yt) = (x+y)(p-q)$.

$\Rightarrow$ $(x^2 - xy)\,r - (x^2 - y^2)\,s + (xy - y^2)\,t = (x+y)(p-q)$ ...(1)

Comparing (1) with $Rr + Ss + Tt = V$, we get

$$R = x^2 - xy,\quad S = -(x^2 - y^2),\quad T = xy - y^2,\quad V = (x+y)(p-q).$$

The Monge's equations are :

$$R(dy)^2 - Sdxdy + T(dx)^2 = 0 \quad ...(2)$$

and $$Rdydp + Tdxdq - Vdxdy = 0 \quad ...(3)$$

(2) $\Rightarrow$ $(x^2 - xy)(dy)^2 + (x^2 - y^2)\,dxdy + (xy - y^2)(dx)^2 = 0$

$\Rightarrow$ $x(dy)^2 + (x + y)dxdy + y(dx)^2 = 0$

$\Rightarrow$ $(xdy + ydx)(dx + dy) = 0$

$\Rightarrow$ $xdy + ydx = 0 \quad ...(4)$ and $dx + dy = 0 \quad ...(4')$

(3) $\Rightarrow$ $(x^2 - xy)\,dydp + (xy - y^2)\,dxdq - (x + y)(y + p)\,dxdy = 0$

We consider the system (4) and (5).

(4) $\Rightarrow$ $d(xy) = 0 \Rightarrow xy = a.$

(5) $\Rightarrow$ $(x - y)dp \,.\, xdy + (x - y)dq \,.\, ydx - (p - q)dx \,.\, xdy - (p - q)dy \,.\, ydx = 0$

$\Rightarrow$ $(x - y)dp - (x - y)dq - (p - q)dx + (p - q)dy = 0 \quad (\because \; xdy = -ydx)$

$\Rightarrow$ $(x - y)(dp - dq) - (p - q)(dx - dy) = 0$

$$\Rightarrow \quad \frac{dp - dq}{p - q} = \frac{dx - dy}{x - y} \Rightarrow \frac{d(p - q)}{p - q} = \frac{d\,(x - y)}{x - y}$$

Integrating, let $p - q = b(x - y).$

Let $b = \psi(a).$ $\therefore$ $p - q = (x - y)\,\psi(xy).$

This is a Lagrange linear equation.

Auxiliary equations are $$\frac{dx}{1} = \frac{dy}{-1} = \frac{dz}{(x - y)\,\psi(xy)} \quad ...(6)$$

(6) $\Rightarrow$ $dx = -\,dy \Rightarrow x + y = c.$

Taking $y\psi(xy)$, $x\psi(xy)$, 1 as multipliers, each fraction of (6)

$$= \frac{y\psi(xy)\,dx + x\psi(xy)\,dy + dz}{y\psi(xy) - x\psi(xy) + (x - y)\,\psi(xy)} = \frac{y\psi(xy)\,dx + x\psi(xy)\,dy + dz}{0}.$$

$\therefore$ $y\psi(xy)\,dx + x\psi(xy)\,dy + dz = 0$

$\Rightarrow$ $\psi(xy)(ydx + xdy) + dz = 0 \Rightarrow \psi(xy)\,d(xy) + dz = 0$

Integrating, let $\phi_1(xy) + z = \lambda$

Let $\lambda = \phi_2(c).$ $\therefore$ $\phi_1(xy) + z = \phi_2(x + y)$

$\therefore$ The general solution of the given equation is

$\mathbf{z = \phi_2(x + y) - \phi_1(xy)}$, **where ϕ_1 and ϕ_2 are arbitrary functions.**

Type III. Equations giving two identical intermediate integrals.

WORKING RULES FOR SOLVING PROBLEMS

Step I. *Write the given equation in the form $Rr + Ss + Tt = V$.*

Step II. *Substitute the values of R, S, T, V in the Monge's equations :*

$$R(dy)^2 - Sdxdy + T(dy)^2 = 0 \quad ...(1)$$

and $$Rdydp + Tdxdq - Vdxdy = 0 \quad ...(2)$$

Step III. *Factorize (1) into two identical factors.*

Step IV. *Using one factor, find an intermediate integral. Solve this integral by using Lagrange method to get the general solution of the given equation.*

Example 3. *Find the general solution of the following partial differential equations :*

(*i*) $y^2r - 2ys + t = p + 6y$ (*ii*) $(y - x)(q^2r - 2pqs + p^2t) = (p + q)^2 (p - q)$.

Sol. (*i*) We have $y^2r - 2ys + t = p + 6y$. ...(1)

Comparing (1) with Rr + Ss + Tt = V, we get

$$R = y^2, \quad S = -2y, \quad T = 1, \quad V = p + 6y.$$

The **Monge's equations** are $R(dy)^2 - Sdxdy + T(dx)^2 = 0$ ...(2)

and $Rdydp + Tdxdq - Vdxdy = 0$ ...(3)

(2) $\Rightarrow$ $y^2(dy)^2 + 2y\,dxdy + (dx)^2 = 0$

$\Rightarrow$ $(ydy + dx)^2 = 0 \Rightarrow ydy + dx = 0 \Rightarrow dx = -ydy$ ...(4)

Integrating, let $x = -\dfrac{y^2}{2} + a \Rightarrow y^2 + 2x = b$, where $b = 2a$

(3) $\Rightarrow$ $y^2dydp + 1.dxdq - (p + 6y)\,dxdy = 0$ ...(5)

$\Rightarrow$ $y^2dydp - ydydq + y(p + 6y)(dy)^2 = 0$

$\Rightarrow$ $ydp - dq + (p + 6y)\,dy = 0$

$\Rightarrow$ $(ydp + pdy) - dq + 6ydy = 0$

Integrating, let $py - q + 3y^2 = k$.

Let $k = \psi(b)$. $\therefore$ $py - q + 3y^2 = \psi(y^2 + 2x)$

This is a Lagrange linear equation.

The auxiliary equations are

$$\frac{dx}{y} = \frac{dy}{-1} = \frac{dz}{\psi(y^2 + 2x) - 3y^2} \qquad ...(6)$$

(6) $\Rightarrow$ $\dfrac{dx}{y} = \dfrac{dy}{-1} \Rightarrow ydy + dx = 0 \Rightarrow y^2 + 2x = c$

(6) $\Rightarrow$ $-dy = \dfrac{dz}{\psi(c) - 3y^2} \Rightarrow (3y^2 - \psi(c))\,dy = dz$

Integrating, let $y^3 - y\psi(c) = z + d$.

Let $d = \phi_1(c)$.

$$\therefore \quad \mathbf{y^3 - y\psi(y^2 + 2x) = z + \phi_1(y^2 + 2x).}$$

This is the general solution of (1). Here ψ, ϕ_1 are arbitrary functions.

(*ii*) We have $(y - x)(q^2r - 2pqs + p^2t) = (p + q)^2 (p - q)$.

$\Rightarrow$ $(y - x)q^2r - 2pq(y - x)s + p^2(y - x)t = (p + q)^2 (p - q)$ ...(1)

Comparing (1) with Rr + Ss + Tt = V, we get

$$R = (y - x)q^2, \quad S = -2pq(y - x), \quad T = p^2(y - x), \quad V = (p + q)^2 (p - q).$$

The **Monge's equations** are $R(dy)^2 - Sdxdy + T(dx)^2 = 0$ ...(2)

and $Rdydp + Tdxdq - Vdxdy = 0$ ...(3)

(2) $\Rightarrow$ $(y - x)\,q^2(dy)^2 + 2pq(y - x)dxdy + p^2(y - x)(dx)^2 = 0$

$\Rightarrow$ $(y - x)(qdy + pdx)^2 = 0 \Rightarrow pdx + qdy = 0 \Rightarrow dz = 0 \Rightarrow z = c.$

(3) $\Rightarrow$ $(y - x)\,q^2dydp + p^2(y - x)\,dxdq - (p + q)^2 (p - q)\,dxdy = 0$

$\Rightarrow$ $(y - x)\,[qdp\,.\,qdy + pdq\,.\,pdx] - (p^2 - q^2)\,[pdx\,.\,dy + qdy\,.\,dx] = 0$

$\Rightarrow$ $(y - x)\,(qdp - pdq) - (p^2 - q^2)(-dy + dx) = 0$ $(\because\ pdx + qdy = 0)$

$$\Rightarrow \qquad qdp - pdq - (p^2 - q^2)\frac{d(x-y)}{y-x} = 0$$

$$\Rightarrow \qquad q^2 d\left(\frac{p}{q}\right) + (p^2 - q^2)\frac{d(x-y)}{x-y} = 0$$

$$\Rightarrow \qquad \frac{d(x-y)}{x-y} + \frac{1}{(p/q)^2 - 1} d\left(\frac{p}{q}\right) = 0$$

Integrating, we get $\log(x-y) + \frac{1}{2}\log\frac{p/q - 1}{p/q + 1} = \frac{1}{2}\log b$.

$$\Rightarrow \qquad (x-y)^2 \frac{p-q}{p+q} = b$$

Let $\quad b = \psi(a). \quad \therefore \quad (x-y)^2 \frac{p-q}{p+q} = \psi(z)$

$$\Rightarrow \qquad (x-y)^2 (p-q) - (p+q)\psi(z) = 0$$

$$\Rightarrow \qquad p((x-y)^2 - \phi(z)) - q((x-y)^2 + \psi(z)) = 0 \qquad ...(4)$$

This is a Lagrange linear equation. The auxiliary equations are

$$\frac{dx}{(x-y)^2 - \phi(z)} = \frac{dy}{-((x-y)^2 + \psi(z))} = \frac{dz}{0} \qquad ...(5)$$

(5) $\Rightarrow \qquad dz = 0 \quad \Rightarrow \quad z = c.$

Each fraction of (5) $= \dfrac{dx + dy}{-2\psi(z)} = \dfrac{dx - dy}{2(x-y)^2}$

$$\Rightarrow \qquad d(x+y) = -\psi(c)\frac{d(x-y)}{(x-y)^2}$$

Integrating, we get $\quad x + y = -\psi(c) \,.\, \dfrac{(x-y)^{-1}}{-1} + d.$

$$\Rightarrow \qquad x + y - \frac{\psi(z)}{x-y} = d$$

Let $\qquad d = \phi(c).$

$$\therefore \qquad \mathbf{x + y - \frac{\psi(z)}{x-y} = \phi(z)}.$$

This represents the general solution of (1). Here ψ, ϕ are arbitrary functions.

EXERCISE 1

Find the general solution of the following partial differential equations by using Monge's method :

1. $r = k^2 t$
2. $t - r\sec^4 y = 2q\tan y$
3. $(r - s)x = (t - s)y$ *(MDU 2005)*
4. $pt - qs = q^3$ *(MDU 2004)*
5. $q(1+q)r - (p + q + 2pq)s + p(1+p)t = 0$
6. $xy(t - r) + (x^2 - y^2)(s - 2) = py - qx$
7. $x^2 r - y^2 t - 2xp + 2z = 0$
8. $x^2 r - 2xs + t + q = 0$
9. $y^2 r + 2xys + x^2 t + px + qy = 0$ *(KU 2004)*

Answers

1. $z = \phi_1(y - kx) + \phi_2(y + kx)$
2. $z = \phi_1(\tan y - x) + \phi_2(\tan y + x)$
3. $\dfrac{z}{x + y} = \phi_1(x + y) + \phi_2(y/x)$
4. $y = xz + \phi_1(z) + \phi_2(x)$
5. $x = \phi_1(z) + \phi_2(x + y + z)$
6. $z = xy + \phi_1(x^2 + y^2) + \phi_2(x/y)$
7. $zy = (xy)^{3/2}\, \phi_1(y/x) + \phi_2(xy)$
8. $z = x\phi_1(y + \log x) + \phi_2(y + \log x)$
9. $z = \psi\,(y^2 - x^2) \log (y + x) + \phi\,(y^2 - x^2)$.

Hints

3. The intermediate integrals are $p - q = f(y/x)$ and $xp + yq - z = g(x + y)$.
Solving for p and q, we get

$$p = \frac{1}{x+y}\left[z + g(x+y) + yf\left(\frac{y}{x}\right)\right]$$

and
$$q = \frac{1}{x+y}\left[z + g(x+y) - xf\left(\frac{y}{x}\right)\right].$$

$$\therefore \quad dz = \frac{1}{x+y}\left[z + g(x+y) + yf\left(\frac{y}{x}\right)\right]dx + \frac{1}{x+y}\left[z + g(x+y) - xf\left(\frac{y}{x}\right)\right]dy$$

$$\Rightarrow \quad (x + y)\, dz = zd(x + y) + g(x + y)\, d(x + y) + f\left(\frac{y}{x}\right)(ydx - xdy)$$

$$\Rightarrow \quad \frac{(x+y)\,dz - zd(x+y)}{(x+y)^2} = \frac{g(x+y)}{(x+y)^2}\,d(x+y) + \frac{f(y/x)}{1+(y/x)^2}\,d(y/x)$$

---

6. MONGE'S METHOD OF SOLVING Rr + Ss + Tt + U(rt – s²) = V

Let $\qquad \mathrm{R}r + \mathrm{S}s + \mathrm{T}t + \mathrm{U}(rt - s^2) = \mathrm{V} \qquad$ ...(1)

be a solvable partial differential equation, where R, S, T, U, V are functions of x, y, z, p, q.

Since z is a function of x and y, we have

$$dp = \frac{\partial p}{\partial x}dx + \frac{\partial p}{\partial y}dy = \frac{\partial^2 z}{\partial x^2}dx + \frac{\partial^2 z}{\partial y \partial x}dy = rdx + sdy$$

and
$$dq = \frac{\partial q}{\partial x}dx + \frac{\partial q}{\partial y}dy = \frac{\partial^2 z}{\partial x \partial y}dx + \frac{\partial^2 z}{\partial y^2}dy = sdx + tdy.$$

Solving these equations for r and t, we get $r = \dfrac{dp - sdy}{dx}$ and $t = \dfrac{dq - sdx}{dy}$

$$\therefore \quad (1) \Rightarrow \mathrm{R}\left(\frac{dp - sdy}{dx}\right) + \mathrm{S}s + \mathrm{T}\left(\frac{dq - sdx}{dy}\right) + \mathrm{U}\left(\frac{(dp - sdy)(dq - sdx)}{dxdy} - s^2\right) = \mathrm{V}$$

$$\Rightarrow \quad s[\mathrm{R}(dy)^2 - \mathrm{S}dxdy + \mathrm{T}(dx)^2 + \mathrm{U}(dxdp + dydq)]$$
$$= \mathrm{R}dydp + \mathrm{T}dxdq + \mathrm{U}dpdq - \mathrm{V}dxdy \qquad \text{...(2)}$$

The equations : $\mathrm{R}(dy)^2 - \mathrm{S}dxdy + \mathrm{T}(dx)^2 + \mathrm{U}(dxdp + dydq) = 0 \qquad$ ...(3)

and $\qquad \mathrm{R}dydp + \mathrm{T}dxdq + \mathrm{U}dpdq - \mathrm{V}dxdy = 0 \qquad$ ...(4)

are called **Monge's equations.** Here, the equation (3) cannot be factored.

Let $\lambda = \lambda(x, y, z, p, q)$ be a function such that

$$\lambda\,[\mathrm{R}(dy)^2 - \mathrm{S}dxdy + \mathrm{T}(dx)^2 + \mathrm{U}(dxdp + dydq)] + \mathrm{R}dydp + \mathrm{T}dxdq + \mathrm{U}dpdq - \mathrm{V}dxdy$$

be factorisable.

Let λ $[R(dy)^2 - Sdxdy + T(dx)^2 + U(dxdp + dydq)] + Rdydp + Tdxdq + Udpdq - Vdxdy$

$$= (ady + bdx + cdp)(\alpha dy + \beta dx + \gamma dq)$$
$$= a\alpha(dy)^2 + (a\beta + b\alpha)\, dxdy + b\beta(dx)^2 + c\beta dxdp$$
$$+ a\gamma dydq + c\alpha dydp + b\gamma dxdq + c\gamma dpdq = 0$$

Comparing coefficients, we get

$a\alpha = \lambda R$, $a\beta + b\alpha = -\lambda S - V$, $b\beta = \lambda T$, $c\beta = \lambda U$, $a\gamma = \lambda U$, $c\alpha = R$, $b\gamma = T$, $c\gamma = U$.

Let $\quad a = \lambda, \alpha = R. \quad \therefore \quad a\alpha = \lambda R$

Also $\quad a\gamma = \lambda U \quad \Rightarrow \quad \gamma = U, \quad c\alpha = R \quad \Rightarrow \quad cR = R \quad \Rightarrow \quad c = 1,$

$\quad c\beta = \lambda U \quad \Rightarrow \quad 1\,.\,\beta = \lambda U \quad \Rightarrow \quad \beta = \lambda U, b\gamma = T \quad \Rightarrow \quad bU = T \quad \Rightarrow \quad b = T/U.$

$\therefore \quad a\beta + b\alpha = -\lambda S - V \quad \Rightarrow \quad \lambda(\lambda U) + (T/U)\, R = -\lambda S - V$ ...(5)

$\Rightarrow \quad U^2\lambda^2 + SU\lambda + TR + UV = 0$

Let λ_1, λ_2 be the roots of (5).

We have $(ady + bdx + cdp)(\alpha dy + \beta dx + \gamma dq) = 0$ ...(6)

Taking $\quad \lambda = \lambda_1$, (6) becomes $\left(\lambda_1 dy + \dfrac{T}{U}\, dx + 1\,.\,dp\right)(Rdy + \lambda_1 Udx + Udq) = 0$

$\Rightarrow \quad (\lambda_1 Udy + Tdx + Udp)(Rdy + \lambda_1 Udx + Udq) = 0$ ...(7)

Similarly, taking $\lambda = \lambda_2$, we get $(\lambda_2 Udy + Tdx + Udp)(Rdy + \lambda_2 Udx + Udq) = 0$ ...(8)

Equations (7) and (8) give four systems of equations :

$$\left.\begin{array}{l} \lambda_1 Udy + Tdx + Udp = 0 \\ \lambda_2 Udy + Tdx + Udp = 0 \end{array}\right] \quad ...(9)$$

$$\left.\begin{array}{l} \lambda_1 Udy + Tdx + Udp = 0 \\ Rdy + \lambda_2 Udx + Udq = 0 \end{array}\right] \quad ...(10)$$

$$\left.\begin{array}{l} \lambda_2 Udy + Tdx + Udp = 0 \\ Rdy + \lambda_1 Udx + Udq = 0 \end{array}\right] \quad ...(11)$$

$$\left.\begin{array}{l} Rdy + \lambda_1 Udx + Udq = 0 \\ Rdy + \lambda_2 Udx + Udq = 0 \end{array}\right] \quad ...(12)$$

Subtracting equations of (9), we get $(\lambda_1 - \lambda_2)\, Udy = 0$.

If $\lambda_1 \neq \lambda_2$, then $Udy = 0$ identically, which is not true.

$\therefore$ System (9) does not give intermediate integral.

Similarly, we reject system (12).

$\therefore$ We have only two systems given below :

$$\left.\begin{array}{l} \lambda_1 Udy + Tdx + Udp = 0 \\ Rdy + \lambda_2 Udx + Udq = 0 \end{array}\right] \quad ...(10)$$

$$\left.\begin{array}{l} \lambda_2 Udy + Tdx + Udp = 0 \\ Rdy + \lambda_1 Udx + Udq = 0 \end{array}\right] \quad ...(11)$$

The equation (5) may have either distinct or same roots.

Case I. $\lambda_1 \neq \lambda_2$

In this case we have two distinct systems (10) and (11). Let system (10) be integrable. Let $u = u(x, y, z, p, q) = a$, $v = v(x, y, z, p, q) = b$ satisfy the system (10).

$\therefore \quad u = \psi(v)$ is an intermediate integral of (1).

If system (11) is also integrable, we get another intermediate integral. These intermediate integrals are solved to find the values of p and q in terms of x and y. The values of p and q are substituted in $dz = pdx + qdy$. This is integrated to get the general solution of (1). In case we get only one intermediate integral or we want to use only one intermediate integral then we express it in the form $Pp + Qq = R$ and use Lagrange's method to find the solution of (1).

Case II. $\lambda_1 = \lambda_2$

In this case we have identical systems (10) and (11). Let system (10) be integrable. Let $u = u(x, y, z, p, q) = a$, $v = v(x, y, z, p, q) = b$ satisfy the system (10).

$\therefore$ $u = \psi(v)$ is an intermediate integral of (1). We express it in the form $Pp + Qq = R$ and use Lagrange's method to find the solution of (1).

Remark. In case the computation of finding general solution of an equation is difficult, we restrict ourselves to a solution with arbitrary constants.

Example 1. *Find the solution of the following partial differential equations :*

(*i*) $r + 4s + t + rt - s^2 = 2$ (*ii*) $3r + s + t + rt - s^2 = -9.$ (KU 2004 S)

Sol. (*i*) We have $r + 4s + t + rt - s^2 = 2$ ...(1)

Comparing (1) with $Rr + Ss + Tt + U(rt - s^2) = V$, we get

$$R = 1,\ S = 4,\ T = 1,\ U = 1,\ V = 2.$$

λ-quadratic equation is $U^2\lambda^2 + SU\lambda + TR + UV = 0$.

$\Rightarrow$ $\lambda^2 + 4\lambda + (1 + 2) = 0 \Rightarrow \lambda = -1, -3.$

Let $\lambda_1 = -1,\ \lambda_2 = -3.$

First system of equations giving intermediate integral is

$$\lambda_1 U dy + T dx + U dp = 0 \quad ...(2)$$

$$R dy + \lambda_2 U dx + U dq = 0 \quad ...(3)$$

(2) $\Rightarrow$ $-dy + dx + dp = 0$ ...(4)

(3) $\Rightarrow$ $dy - 3dx + dq = 0$ ...(5)

Integrating (4) and (5), we get $-y + x + p = a$ and $y - 3x + q = b$, where a and b are arbitrary constants.

Let $b = \psi(a)$. $\therefore$ $y - 3x + q = \psi(-y + x + p)$

In particular let $\psi(-y + x + p) = \alpha(-y + x + p) + \beta.$

$\therefore$ $y - 3x + q = \alpha(-y + x + p) + \beta$

$\Rightarrow$ $\alpha p - q = -(\alpha + 3)x + (\alpha + 1)y - \beta$

This is a Lagrange equation.

The auxiliary equations are $\dfrac{dx}{\alpha} = \dfrac{dy}{-1} = \dfrac{dz}{-(\alpha+3)x + (\alpha+1)y - \beta}$ ...(6)

(6) $\Rightarrow$ $\dfrac{dx}{\alpha} = -dy \Rightarrow dx + \alpha dy = 0 \Rightarrow x + \alpha y = \gamma.$ ...(7)

Equating second and third fractions of (6), we get

$$\frac{dy}{-1} = \frac{dz}{-(\alpha+3)(\gamma - \alpha y) + (\alpha+1)y - \beta} \quad \text{(Using (7))}$$

$$\Rightarrow \quad dy = \frac{dz}{-(\alpha^2 + 4\alpha + 1)y + \alpha\gamma + 3\gamma + \beta}$$

$$\Rightarrow \quad ((\alpha^2 + 4\alpha + 1)y - (\alpha\gamma + 3\gamma + \beta))\,dy + dz = 0$$

$$\Rightarrow \quad (\alpha^2 + 4\alpha + 1)\frac{y^2}{2} - (\alpha\gamma + 3\gamma + \beta)\,y + z = k$$

$$\Rightarrow \quad (\alpha^2 + 4\alpha + 1)\frac{y^2}{2} - ((\alpha + 3)(x + \alpha y) + \beta)\,y + z = \phi(\gamma) \qquad [\text{Taking } k = \phi(\gamma)]$$

$$\Rightarrow \quad \left(\frac{\alpha^2}{2} + \alpha - \frac{1}{2}\right)y^2 + (\alpha + 3)\,xy + (\alpha + 3)\,\beta y = z - \phi(x + \alpha y)$$

$$\Rightarrow \quad \mathbf{z = \frac{1}{2}(\alpha^2 + 2\alpha - 1)\,y^2 + (\alpha + 3)\,xy + (\alpha + 3)\,\beta y + \phi(x + \alpha y).}$$

This is the general solution of the given equation.

Here α, β are arbitrary constants and ϕ is an arbitrary function.

Remark. For the above equation, $y - 3x + q = \psi(-y + x + p)$ is an intermediate integral. Since p appears in the argument of the arbitrary function ψ, we cannot find the value of p using this equation and the other intermediate integral of the given equation.

(*ii*) We have $3r + s + t + rt - s^2 = -9$. ...(1)

Comparing (1) with $Rr + Ss + Tt + U(rt - s^2) = V$, we get

$$R = 3,\ S = 1,\ T = 1,\ U = 1,\ V = -9.$$

λ-quadratic equation is $U^2\lambda^2 + SU\lambda + TR + UV = 0$.

$$\Rightarrow \quad \lambda^2 + \lambda - 6 = 0 \quad \Rightarrow \quad \lambda = 2, -3.$$

Let $\lambda_1 = 2,\ \lambda_2 = -3$.

First system of equations giving intermediate integral is

$$\lambda_1 U dy + T dx + U dp = 0 \qquad ...(2)$$

$$R dy + \lambda_2 U dx + U dq = 0 \qquad ...(3)$$

(2) $\Rightarrow$ $2dy + dx + dp = 0 \ \Rightarrow\ 2y + x + p = a$

(3) $\Rightarrow$ $3dy - 3dx + dq = 0 \ \Rightarrow\ 3y - 3x + q = b$

Let $a = \psi(b)$. $\therefore$ $2y + x + p = \psi(3y - 3x + q)$

In particular, let $\psi(3y - 3x + q) = \alpha(3y - 3x + q) + \beta$.

$$\therefore \quad 2y + x + p = \alpha(3y - 3x + q) + \beta$$

$$\Rightarrow \quad p - \alpha q = (3\alpha - 2)y - (3\alpha + 1)x + \beta$$

This is a Lagrange's equation. The auxiliary equations are

$$\frac{dx}{1} = \frac{dy}{-\alpha} = \frac{dz}{(3\alpha - 2)\,y - (3\alpha + 1)\,x + \beta} \qquad ...(4)$$

$$(4) \Rightarrow \quad dx = \frac{dy}{-\alpha} \quad \Rightarrow \quad dy + \alpha dx = 0 \quad \Rightarrow \quad y + \alpha x = \gamma. \qquad ...(5)$$

$$(4) \Rightarrow \quad dx = \frac{dz}{(3\alpha - 2)(\gamma - \alpha x) - (3\alpha + 1)x + \beta} \qquad (\text{Using (5)})$$

$$\Rightarrow \quad (-(3\alpha^2 + \alpha + 1)\,x + 3\alpha\gamma - 2\gamma + \beta)\,dx = dz$$

$$\Rightarrow \quad z = -\frac{1}{2}(3\alpha^2 + \alpha + 1)\,x^2 + (3\alpha\gamma - 2\gamma + \beta)\,x + k$$

$$\Rightarrow \quad z = -\frac{1}{2}(3\alpha^2 + \alpha + 1)\,x^2 + (3\alpha y + 2\alpha^2 x - 2y - 2\alpha x + \beta)x + \phi(\gamma)$$

[(Putting $k = \phi(\gamma)$]

$$\Rightarrow \qquad \mathbf{z = \frac{1}{2}\,(3\alpha^2 - 5\alpha - 1)\,x^2 + (3\alpha - 2)\,xy + \beta x + \phi(y + \alpha x).}$$

This is the general solution of the given equation.

Here α and β are arbitrary constants and ϕ is an arbitrary function.

Example 2. *Find the solution of the following partial differential equations :*

(*i*) $5r + 6s + 3t + 2(rt - s^2) + 3 = 0$

(*ii*) $(q^2 - 1)\,zr - 2pqzs + (p^2 - 1)\,zt + z^2(rt - s^2) = p^2 + q^2 - 1.$

Sol. (*i*) We have $\qquad 5r + 6s + 3t + 2(rt - s^2) = -3. \qquad$ ...(1)

Comparing (1) with $Rr + Ss + Tt + U(rt - s^2) = V$, we get

$$R = 5,\; S = 6,\; T = 3,\; U = 2,\; V = -3.$$

λ-quadratic equation is $U^2\lambda^2 + SU\lambda + TR + UV = 0.$

$\Rightarrow \qquad 4\lambda^2 + 12\lambda + 9 = 0 \;\Rightarrow\; \lambda = -3/2, -3/2.$

Let $\qquad \lambda_1 = -3/2, \quad \lambda_2 = -3/2.$

$\therefore$ The system of equations giving intermediate integral is

$$\lambda_1 U dy + T dx + U dp = 0 \qquad ...(2)$$

$$R dy + \lambda_2 U dx + U dq = 0 \qquad ...(3)$$

(2) $\Rightarrow \quad -3dy + 3dx + 2dp = 0 \;\Rightarrow\; -3y + 3x + 2p = a$

(3) $\Rightarrow \quad 5dy - 3dx + 2dq = 0 \;\Rightarrow\; 5y - 3x + 2q = b$

Let $a = \psi(b)$. $\;\therefore\; -3y + 3x + 2p = \psi(5y - 3x + 2q)$

In particular, let $\psi(5y - 3x + 2q) = \alpha(5y - 3x + 2q) + \beta.$

$\therefore \qquad -3y + 3x + 2p = \alpha(5y - 3x + 2q) + \beta$

$\Rightarrow \qquad 2p - 2\alpha q = 3y - 3x + 5\alpha y - 3\alpha x + \beta.$

This is a Lagrange's equation. The auxiliary equations are

$$\frac{dx}{2} = \frac{dy}{-2\alpha} = \frac{dz}{3y - 3x + 5\alpha y - 3\alpha x + \beta} \qquad ...(4)$$

(4) $\Rightarrow \qquad dx = -\dfrac{dy}{\alpha} \;\Rightarrow\; dy + \alpha dx = 0 \;\Rightarrow\; y + \alpha x = \gamma. \qquad$ ...(5)

(4) $\Rightarrow \qquad \dfrac{dx}{2} = \dfrac{dz}{(3 + 5\alpha)(\gamma - \alpha x) - 3(1 + \alpha)\,x + \beta} \qquad$ (Using (5))

$\Rightarrow \qquad (-(5\alpha^2 + 6\alpha + 3)x + 3\gamma + 5\alpha\gamma + \beta)\,dx = 2dz$

$\Rightarrow \qquad -\dfrac{1}{2}(5\alpha^2 + 6\alpha + 3)x^2 + (3\gamma + 5\alpha\gamma + \beta)\,x = 2z + k$

$\Rightarrow \quad -\dfrac{1}{2}(5\alpha^2 + 6\alpha + 3)x^2 + ((3 + 5\alpha)\,(y + \alpha x) + \beta)\,x = 2z + \phi(\gamma) \qquad$ [Putting $k = \phi(\gamma)$]

$\Rightarrow \quad -\dfrac{1}{2}(5\alpha^2 + 6\alpha + 3)x^2 + (3\alpha x^2 + 5\alpha^2 x^2 + 3xy + 5\alpha xy + \beta x) = 2z + \phi(y + \alpha x)$

$$\Rightarrow \qquad \mathbf{\frac{1}{2}\,(5\alpha^2 - 3)\,x^2 + (3 + 5\alpha)\,xy + \beta x = 2z + \phi(y + \alpha x).}$$

This is the general solution of the given equation.

Here α, β are arbitrary constants and ϕ is an arbitrary function.

(*ii*) We have $\;(q^2 - 1)\,zr - 2pqzs + (p^2 - 1)\,zt + z^2(rt - s^2) = p^2 + q^2 - 1. \qquad$ ...(1)

Comparing (1) with $Rr + Ss + Tt + U(rt - s^2) = V$, we get

$$R = (q^2 - 1)z, S = -2pqz, T = (p^2 - 1)z, U = z^2, V = p^2 + q^2 - 1.$$

λ-quadratic equation is $U^2\lambda^2 + SU\lambda + RT + UV = 0$.

$\Rightarrow \quad z^4\lambda^2 - 2pqz^3\lambda + (q^2-1)(p^2-1)z^2 + z^2(p^2+q^2-1) = 0$

$\Rightarrow \quad z^4\lambda^2 - 2pqz^3\lambda + p^2q^2z^2 = 0 \Rightarrow (z\lambda - pq)^2 = 0 \Rightarrow \lambda = pq/z, pq/z.$

Let $\quad \lambda_1 = pq/z, \lambda_2 = pq/z.$

$\therefore$ The system of equations giving intermediate integral is

$$\lambda_1 U dy + T dx + U dp = 0 \qquad ...(2)$$

$$R dy + \lambda_2 U dx + U dq = 0 \qquad ...(3)$$

$$(2) \Rightarrow \frac{pq}{z} . z^2 dy + (p^2 - 1) z\, dx + z^2 dp = 0 \qquad ...(4)$$

$$(3) \Rightarrow (q^2 - 1) z dy + \frac{pq}{z} . z^2 dx + z^2 dq = 0 \qquad ...(5)$$

$(4) \Rightarrow \quad pqdy + (p^2 - 1)dx + zdp = 0 \Rightarrow p(qdy + pdx) - dx + zdp = 0$

$\Rightarrow \quad pdz + zdp - dx = 0 \Rightarrow d(zp) - dx = 0 \Rightarrow zp - x = a.$

$(5) \Rightarrow \quad (q^2 - 1)dy + pqdx + zdq = 0 \Rightarrow q(qdy + pdx) - dy + zdq = 0$

$\Rightarrow \quad qdz + zdq - dy = 0 \Rightarrow d(zq) - dy = 0 \Rightarrow zq - y = b.$

Let $a = \psi(b)$. $\quad \therefore \quad zp - x = \psi(zq - y)$.

In particular, let $\quad \psi(zq - y) = \alpha(zq - y) + \beta$.

$\therefore \quad zp - x = \alpha(zq - y) + \beta \Rightarrow zp - \alpha zq = x - \alpha y + \beta.$

This is a Lagrange's equation. The auxiliary equations are

$$\frac{dx}{z} = \frac{dy}{-\alpha z} = \frac{dz}{x - \alpha y + \beta} \qquad ...(6)$$

$$(6) \Rightarrow \quad dx = -\frac{dy}{\alpha} \Rightarrow dy + \alpha dx = 0 \Rightarrow y + \alpha x = \gamma \qquad ...(7)$$

$$(6) \Rightarrow \quad \frac{dx}{z} = \frac{dz}{x - \alpha(\gamma - \alpha x) + \beta} \Rightarrow [(1 + \alpha^2)x - \alpha\gamma + \beta]\, dx = zdz \qquad \text{(Using (7))}$$

$$\Rightarrow \quad (1 + \alpha^2)\frac{x^2}{2} - \alpha\gamma x + \beta x = \frac{z^2}{2} + k$$

$\Rightarrow \quad (1 + \alpha^2)x^2 - 2x(y + \alpha x)x + 2\beta x = z^2 + 2k$

$\Rightarrow \quad (1 - \alpha^2)x^2 - 2\alpha xy + 2\beta x = z^2 + \phi(\gamma) \qquad$ [Putting $2k = \phi(\gamma)$]

$\Rightarrow \quad \mathbf{(1 - \alpha^2)x^2 - 2\alpha xy + 2\beta x = z^2 + \phi(y + \alpha x).}$

This is the general solution of the given equation.

Here α, β are arbitrary constants and ϕ is an arbitrary function.

EXERCISE 2

Find the solution of the following partial differential equations by using Monge's method :

1. $3s + (rt - s^2) = 2$
2. $3s - 2(rt - s^2) = 2$
3. $3r + 4s + t + (rt - s^2) = 1$
4. $2r - 6s + 2t + (rt - s^2) = 4.$

Answers

1. $z = \frac{\alpha}{2} y^2 + 2xy + \beta y - \phi(x + \alpha y)$

2. $\alpha z = \frac{5}{2} y^2 - 2\alpha xy - \beta y + \phi(\alpha x - 2y)$

3. $x^2 + 3y^2 + 2z - 4xy - 2\beta x = \phi(y + \alpha x)$

4. $z = (\alpha^2 + \alpha - 1) x^2 + (2\alpha - 2) xy + \beta x + \phi(y + \alpha x)$

SECTION IV

CALCULUS OF VARIATIONS

17

Variational Problems with Fixed Boundaries

1. INTRODUCTION

By a function we mean a correspondence between the elements of sets A and B such that to each element of A there correspond exactly one element of the set B. We have also studied the methods of finding maximum and minimum values of real functions of one or more variables. In calculus of variations, we shall deal with functionals and their maximum and minimum values. A functional associates a unique real number to each function belonging to a certain class of functions.

2. FUNCTIONAL

Let A be a class of functions. A correspondence between the functions of class A and the set of real numbers such that to each function belonging to A, there correspond exactly one real number is called a **functional**. In other words, a functional is a correspondence which assigns a unique real number to each function belonging to some class. Thus a functional is a function, where the independent variable takes functions as values.

A functional is denoted by capital letter I (or J). If $y(x)$ represents a function in the class of functions of a functional J, then we write $J = J[y(x)]$.

The class of functions $y(x)$ on which the functional $J[y(x)]$ is defined is called the **domain** of the functional J.

Illustrations. (*i*) Let $A = C_1[0, 4]$ be the class of functions $y(x)$ having continuous derivatives on $[0, 4]$.

Let $$J[y(x)] = y'(3).$$

$\therefore$ $J[y(x)]$ is a functional defined in the indicated class of functions and to each function of this class there exists a unique number, the value of the derivative of the function at '3'.

Here $$J[x^2] = (x^2)'\Big|_{x=3} = 2x\Big|_{x=3} = 2(3) = 6$$

$$J[x^4 - x + 2] = (x^4 - x + 2)'\Big|_{x=3} = (4x^3 - 1)\Big|_{x=3} = 4(3)^3 - 1 = 107$$

$$J[\log(x+2)] = [\log(x+2)]'\Big|_{x=3} = \frac{1}{x+2}\Big|_{x=3} = \frac{1}{5}$$

(*ii*) Let $A = C[0, 2]$ be the class of functions $y(x)$ continuous on $[0, 2]$.

Let $$J[y(x)] = \frac{1}{3}\int_0^2 y(x)\, dx.$$

$\therefore$ J[$y(x)$] is a functional defined on C[0, 2] and to each function $y(x)$ of this class there exists a unique number given by $\frac{1}{3}\int_0^2 y(x)\,dx$.

Here
$$J[5] = \frac{1}{3}\int_0^2 5\,dx = \frac{1}{3}(5x)\Big|_0^2 = \frac{5}{3}(2-0) = \frac{10}{3}$$

$$J[x^3 + x] = \frac{1}{3}\int_0^2 (x^3 + x)dx = \left(\frac{1}{3}\left(\frac{x^4}{4} + \frac{x^2}{2}\right)\right)\Bigg|_0^2 = 2$$

$$J(\sin x) = \frac{1}{3}\int_0^2 \sin x\,dx = \frac{1}{3}(-\cos x)\Big|_0^2 = \frac{1}{3}(1 - \cos 2).$$

(*iii*) Let A = $C_1[a, b]$ be the class of functions $y(x)$ having a continuous derivative $y'(x)$ on the interval $[a, b]$. Then

$$J[y(x)] = \int_a^b \sqrt{1 + y'^2(x)}\,dx$$

is a functional defined on $C_1[a, b]$. This functional geometrically describes the arc length of the curve $y = y(x)$ with ends at the points $(a, y(a))$ and $(b, y(b))$.

(*iv*) Let A = C[– 1, 1] be the class of functions $y(x)$ continuous on the interval [– 1, 1].

Let $\quad J[y(x)] = \int_{-1}^1 F(x, y(x))\,dx$, where $F(x, y(x)) = \dfrac{x}{1 + (y(x))^2}$.

Here J[$y(x)$] is a functional defined on C [– 1, 1].

For $y(x) = 4x$, we have

$$J[y(x)] = \int_{-1}^1 \frac{x}{1 + (4x)^2}\,dx = \int_{-1}^1 \frac{x}{1 + 16x^2}\,dx = 0.$$

($\because$ The integrand is an odd function)

3. CLOSENESS OF FUNCTIONS

Let $y_1(x)$ and $y_2(x)$ be any two functions.

$y_1(x)$ and $y_2(x)$ are said to be **close in the sense of zero-order proximity** if $|y_1(x) - y_2(x)|$ is small for values of x for which $y_1(x)$ and $y_2(x)$ are defined. Geometrically, this means that the curves of $y = y_1(x)$ and $y = y_2(x)$ are close as to the ordinates.

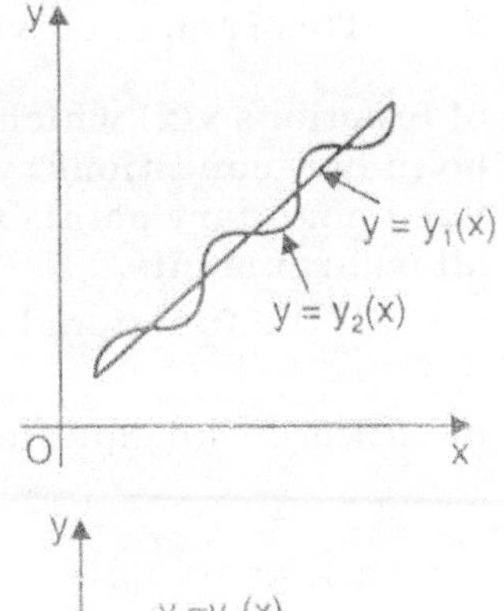

The functions $y_1(x)$ and $y_2(x)$ are said to be **close in the sense of first-order proximity** if $|y_1(x) - y_2(x)|$ and $|y_1'(x) - y_2'(x)|$ are small for values of x for which these functions are defined. Geometrically, this means that the curves of $y = y_1(x)$ and $y = y_2(x)$ are close both as to ordinates and as to directions of the tangents at the appropriate points.

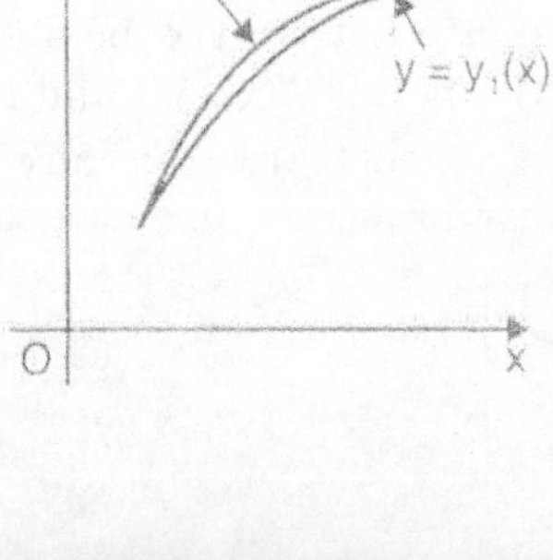

The functions $y_1(x)$ and $y_2(x)$ are said to be **close in the sense of nth-order proximity** if $| y_1(x) - y_2(x) |$, $| y_1'(x) - y_2'(x) |$, ..., $| y_1^{(n)}(x) - y_2^{(n)}(x) |$ are small for values of x for which these functions are defined.

From the above definitions it is clear that if two functions *i.e.*, curves are close in the sense of nth order proximity then they are also close in the sense of proximity of any smaller order.

4. MAXIMUM AND MINIMUM VALUES OF A FUNCTIONAL

A functional $J[y(x)]$ is said to have a **maximum value** on $y = y_0(x)$ if the value of the functional on any curve close to $y = y_0(x)$ is not greater than $J[y_0(x)]$ *i.e.*, $J[y(x)] \le J[y_0(x)]$ for all curves $y(x)$ close to $y_0(x)$.

A functional $J[y(x)]$ is said to have a **minimum value** on $y = y_0(x)$ if the values of the functional on any curve close to $y = y_0(x)$ is not less than $J[y_0(x)]$ *i.e.*, $J[y(x)] \ge J[y_0(x)]$ for all curves $y(x)$ close to $y_0(x)$.

The maximum and minimum values of a functional are called its **extremum values**.

If a functional $J[y(x)]$ attains a maximum (resp. minimum) on $y = y_0(x)$ with respect to all curves $y = y(x)$ in the sense of zero order proximity *i.e.*, $| y(x) - y_0(x) |$ is small, then the maximum (resp. minimum) is said to be **strong.**

Similarly, if a functional $J[y(x)]$ attains a maximum (resp. minimum) on $y = y_0(x)$ with respect to all curves $y = y(x)$ in the sense of first-order proximity *i.e.*, $| y(x) - y_0(x) |$ and $| y'(x) - y'_0(x) |$ are both small, then the maximum (resp. minimum) is said to be **weak.**

Remark. If a strong maximum (resp. minimum) of a functional $J[y(x)]$ is attained on the curve $y = y_0(x)$, then a weak maximum (resp. minimum) is also attained on the same curve. In other words, every strong extremum value is at the same time a weak extremum value. This does not hold conversely.

5. EULER'S EQUATION FOR FUNCTIONALS CONTAINING FIRST ORDER DERIVATIVE AND ONE INDEPENDENT VARIABLE

Theorem. Let $J[y(x)] = \int_{x_1}^{x_2} F(x, y(x), y'(x))\, dx$ be a functional defined on the set of functions y(x) which admits of continuous first order derivative and satisfy the boundary conditions : $y(x_1) = y_1$ and $y(x_2) = y_2$, where y_1 and y_2 are prescribed at the fixed boundary points x_1 and x_2. Also, F is differentiable three times with respect to all its arguments.

If the functional J[y(x)] has an extremum on a function y(x) then y(x) satisfy the differential equation $\dfrac{\partial F}{\partial y} - \dfrac{d}{dx}\left(\dfrac{\partial F}{\partial y'}\right) = 0.$ *(KU 2004, 2004 S ; MDU 2005)*

Proof. We have
$$J[y(x)] = \int_{x_1}^{x_2} F(x, y(x)\, y'(x))\, dx.$$

Let $y = y(x)$ be a function which extremise $J[y(x)]$ and whose curve is passing through the points $A(x_1, y_1)$ and $B(x_2, y_2)$ *i.e.*, $y(x_1) = y_1$ and $y(x_2) = y_2$.

Let $\eta(x)$ be any arbitrary but fixed function such that $\eta''(x)$ is continuous and $\eta(x_1) = \eta(x_2) = 0$.

Let $\bar{y}(x) = y(x) + \alpha\eta(x)$, where α is a small parameter.

$\therefore$ $\bar{y}(x)$ admits of continuous first order derivative.

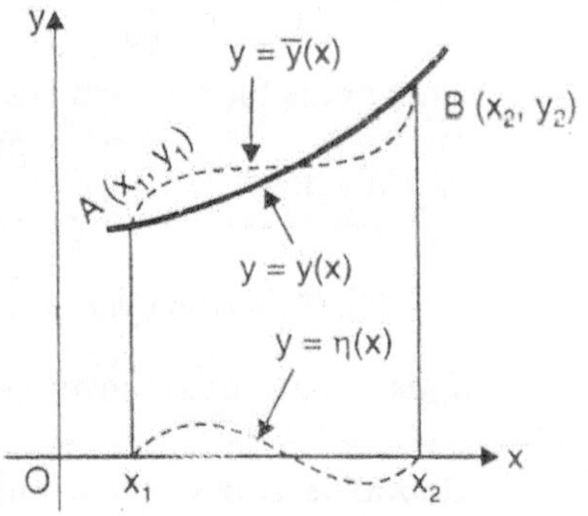

Now $\bar{y}(x_1) = y(x_1) + \alpha\eta(x_1) = y_1 + \alpha(0) = y_1$

and $\bar{y}(x_2) = y(x_2) + \alpha\eta(x_2) = y_2 + \alpha(0) = y_2$.

$\therefore$ $\bar{y}(x)$ also satisfy the boundary conditions.

$\therefore$ The functional J is defined at $\bar{y}(x)$.

$$\therefore \quad J[\bar{y}(x)] = \int_{x_1}^{x_2} F(x, \bar{y}(x), \bar{y}'(x))\, dx$$

$$= \int_{x_1}^{x_2} F(x, y(x) + \alpha\eta(x), y'(x) + \alpha\eta'(x))\, dx$$

On the curves of the family $y(x) + \alpha\eta(x)$, the right hand side is a function of α, say $\psi(\alpha)$.

$$\therefore \quad \psi(\alpha) = \int_{x_1}^{x_2} F(x, \bar{y}(x), \bar{y}'(x))\, dx = \int_{x_1}^{x_2} F(x, y(x) + \alpha\eta(x), y'(x) + \alpha\eta'(x))\, dx$$

Since the extremising curve $y = y(x)$ corresponds to $\alpha = 0$, it follows that $\psi(\alpha)$ is extremised for $\alpha = 0$.

$$\therefore \quad \frac{d\psi}{d\alpha} = 0 \text{ at } \alpha = 0$$

Differentiating $\psi(\alpha)$ under the integral sign, we have

$$\frac{d\psi}{d\alpha} = \int_{x_1}^{x_2} \frac{\partial}{\partial\alpha} F(x, \bar{y}(x), \bar{y}'(x))\, dx$$

$$= \int_{x_1}^{x_2} \left(\frac{\partial F}{\partial x}\frac{\partial x}{\partial\alpha} + \frac{\partial F}{\partial \bar{y}}\frac{\partial \bar{y}}{\partial\alpha} + \frac{\partial F}{\partial \bar{y}'}\frac{\partial \bar{y}'}{\partial\alpha} \right) dx$$

$$= \int_{x_1}^{x_2} \left(\frac{\partial F}{\partial x} . 0 + \frac{\partial F}{\partial y}\eta(x) + \frac{\partial F}{\partial y'}\eta'(x) \right) dx$$

$$\therefore \quad \frac{d\psi}{d\alpha} = \int_{x_1}^{x_2} \left(\frac{\partial F}{\partial y}\eta(x) + \frac{\partial F}{\partial y'}\eta'(x) \right) dx \qquad ...(1)$$

Now $\dfrac{d\psi}{d\alpha} = 0$ at $\alpha = 0$.

$\therefore$ Putting $\alpha = 0$ in (1), we get

$$\int_{x_1}^{x_2} \left(\frac{\partial F}{\partial y}\eta(x) + \frac{\partial F}{\partial y'}\eta'(x) \right) dx = 0$$

$$\Rightarrow \quad \int_{x_1}^{x_2} \frac{\partial F}{\partial y}\eta(x)\, dx + \int_{x_1}^{x_2} \frac{\partial F}{\partial y'}\eta'(x)\, dx = 0$$

$$\Rightarrow \quad \int_{x_1}^{x_2} \frac{\partial F}{\partial y}\eta(x)\, dx + \left[\frac{\partial F}{\partial y'} . \eta(x) \Bigg|_{x_1}^{x_2} - \int_{x_1}^{x_2} \frac{d}{dx}\left(\frac{\partial F}{\partial y'}\right) . \eta(x)\, dx = 0 \right.$$

$$\Rightarrow \quad \int_{x_1}^{x_2} \frac{\partial F}{\partial y}\eta(x)\, dx - \int_{x_1}^{x_2} \frac{d}{dx}\left(\frac{\partial F}{\partial y'}\right)\eta(x)\, dx = 0 \qquad (\because \eta(x_1) = \eta(x_2) = 0)$$

$$\Rightarrow \qquad \int_{x_1}^{x_2} \left[\frac{\partial F}{\partial y} - \frac{d}{dx}\left(\frac{\partial F}{\partial y'}\right)\right] \eta(x)\, dx = 0$$

This holds for any arbitrary continuous function $\eta(x)$.

$\therefore$ We have $\quad \dfrac{\partial F}{\partial y} - \dfrac{d}{dx}\left(\dfrac{\partial F}{\partial y'}\right) = 0.$

$\therefore$ The functions $y(x)$ satisfies the equation $\dfrac{\partial F}{\partial y} - \dfrac{d}{dx}\left(\dfrac{\partial F}{\partial y'}\right) = 0.$

This equation is known as the **Euler's equation.**

Remarks 1. If $y(x)$ is a function extremising the functional $\int_{x_1}^{x_2} F(x, y(x), y'(x))dx$, then $y(x)$ satisfies the Euler's equation. But if a function satisfies the Euler's equation then it may or may not extremise the functional. The solutions of Euler's equation satisfying the boundary conditions are called **stationary functions.** The value of the functional at a stationary function is called a **stationary value** of the functional.

2. In the above theorem, we require the extremum $y(x)$ to be *weak*. Since any strong extremum is at the same time a weak extremum, it follow that any condition necessary for a weak extremum is also necessary for a strong extremum.

6. EXTREMALS

The solutions of Euler's equation which are unrestricted by the boundary conditions are called **extremals.**

The Euler's equation for the functional $\int_{x_1}^{x_2} F(x, y, y')\, dx$ is

$$\frac{\partial F}{\partial y} - \frac{d}{dx}\left(\frac{\partial F}{\partial y'}\right) = 0 \qquad ...(1)$$

$$(1) \Rightarrow \quad \frac{\partial F}{\partial y} - \left[\frac{\partial}{\partial x}\left(\frac{\partial F}{\partial y'}\right) + \frac{\partial}{\partial y}\left(\frac{\partial F}{\partial y'}\right)\frac{dy}{dx} + \frac{\partial}{\partial y'}\left(\frac{\partial F}{\partial y'}\right)\frac{dy'}{dx}\right] = 0$$

$$\Rightarrow \quad F_y - \left[F_{y'x} + F_{y'y}\frac{dy}{dx} + F_{y'y'}\frac{d^2y}{dx^2}\right] = 0$$

$$\Rightarrow \quad F_{y'y'}\frac{d^2y}{dx^2} + F_{y'y}\frac{dy}{dx} + (F_{y'x} - F_y) = 0.$$

$\therefore$ The Euler's equation is a second order differential equation unless, $F_{y'y'} = 0$.

$\therefore$ In general, the extremals constitute a two-parameter family of curves. The extremals which satisfies the given boundary conditions are the stationary functions of the functional $\int_{x_1}^{x_2} F(x, y, y')\, dx$.

7. EXTREMALS IN PARTICULAR CASES

The Euler's equation for the functional $\int_{x_1}^{x_2} F(x, y, y')\, dx$ is $F_y - \dfrac{d}{dx}(F_{y'}) = 0.$

Case I. If x is missing from the function 'F' *i.e.*, the functional is of the form $\int_{x_1}^{x_2} F(y, y')\, dx$, then $F_x = 0$.

We have

$$\frac{d}{dx}\left(F - F_{y'}\frac{dy}{dx}\right) = \frac{d}{dx}(F) - \frac{d}{dx}\left(F_{y'}\frac{dy}{dx}\right)$$

$$= \left(F_x + F_y\frac{dy}{dx} + F_{y'}\frac{dy'}{dx}\right) - \left(F_{y'}\frac{d^2y}{dx^2} + \frac{dy}{dx}\frac{d}{dx}(F_{y'})\right)$$

$$= 0 + F_y\frac{dy}{dx} - \frac{dy}{dx}\frac{d}{dx}(F_{y'}) = \frac{dy}{dx}\left(F_y - \frac{d}{dx}(F_{y'})\right) = \frac{dy}{dx}\,.\,0 = 0.$$

$$\therefore \qquad \frac{d}{dx}\left(F - F_{y'}\frac{dy}{dx}\right) = 0$$

Integrating, we get $F - F_{y'}\dfrac{dy}{dx} = c$.
This is a first order differential equation. This equation is solved to get the extremals.

Case II. If y is missing from the function 'F' *i.e.*, the functional is of the form $\int_{x_1}^{x_2} F(x, y')\,dx$, then $F_y = 0$.

$\therefore$ Euler's equation reduces to $0 - \dfrac{d}{dx}(F_{y'}) = 0$. Integrating, we get $F_{y'} = c$.
On solving this, we get an equation of the form $\mathbf{y' = \phi(x, c)}$.
This differential equation is solved to get the extremals.

Case III. If y' is missing from the function 'F' *i.e.*, the functional is of the form $\int_{x_1}^{x_2} F(x,y)\,dx$, then $F_{y'} = 0$.

$\therefore$ Euler's equation reduces to $F_y - \dfrac{d}{dx}(0) = 0$.

$\Rightarrow$ $F_y = 0$. This is not a differential equation. This finite equation, when solved for y, does not involve any arbitrary constant. Thus, in general, it is not possible to find y satisfying the boundary conditions $y(x_1) = y_1$ and $y(x_2) = y_2$ and as such this variational problem does not, in general, admit of a solution.

Case IV. If x and y are both missing from the function 'F' *i.e.*, the functional is of the form $\int_{x_1}^{x_2} F(y')\,dx$, then, $F_x = 0$ and $F_y = 0$.

$\therefore$ Euler's equation reduces to $0 - \dfrac{d}{dx}(F_{y'}) = 0$.

$$\Rightarrow \qquad \frac{d}{dx}(F_{y'}) = 0 \quad \Rightarrow \quad F_{y'x} + F_{y'y}\frac{dy}{dx} + F_{y'y'}\frac{dy'}{dx} = 0$$

$$\Rightarrow \qquad F_{xy'} + F_{yy'}\frac{dy}{dx} + F_{y'y'}\frac{d^2y}{dx^2} = 0$$

$$\Rightarrow \qquad \frac{\partial}{\partial y'}(F_x) + \frac{\partial}{\partial y'}(F_y)\,.\,\frac{dy}{dx} + F_{y'y'}\frac{d^2y}{dx^2} = 0$$

$$\Rightarrow \quad 0 + 0 \, . \, \frac{dy}{dx} + F_{y'y'} \frac{d^2y}{dx^2} = 0 \;\Rightarrow\; F_{y'y'} \frac{d^2y}{dx^2} = 0.$$

If $F_{y'y'} \neq 0$, then we have $\dfrac{d^2y}{dx^2} = 0.$

$\Rightarrow$ $\mathbf{y = c_1x + c_2}$. $\therefore$ The extremals are all non-vertical straight lines.

WORKING RULES FOR SOLVING PROBLEMS

Step I. *Identify the functional* $\int_{x_1}^{x_2} F(x, y, y')\,dx$ *and the boundary conditions* $y(x_1) = y_1$, $y(x_2) = y_2$ *in the given problem.*

Step II. *Write the Euler's equation* $\dfrac{\partial F}{\partial y} - \dfrac{d}{dx}\left(\dfrac{\partial F}{\partial y'}\right) = 0$ *and solve this equation.*

Step III. *The solutions of this equation are extremals of the given problem.*

Step IV. *Find the extremal that satisfy the given boundary conditions. This particular extremal is the stationary function of the given problem.*

Example 1. *Find the extremals of the functional* $\int_0^{\pi} (y'^2 - y^2 + 4y \cos x)\,dx$. (KU 2005)

Sol. Let $\quad J[y(x)] = \int_0^{\pi} (y'^2 - y^2 + 4y \cos x)\,dx$.

Let $\quad F(x, y, y') = y'^2 - y^2 + 4y \cos x$

The **Euler's equation** is $\dfrac{\partial F}{\partial y} - \dfrac{d}{dx}\left(\dfrac{\partial F}{\partial y'}\right) = 0.$ ...(1)

Here $\quad \dfrac{\partial F}{\partial y} = -2y + 4 \cos x, \quad \dfrac{\partial F}{\partial y'} = 2y'$

$\therefore$ (1) $\Rightarrow$ $-2y + 4\cos x - \dfrac{d}{dx}(2y') = 0$

$$\Rightarrow \quad \frac{d^2y}{dx^2} + y = 2\cos x$$

The A.E. is $D^2 + 1 = 0$. $\therefore$ $D = \pm i$

$$\therefore \quad \text{C.F.} = e^{0x}(c_1 \cos 1.x + c_2 \sin 1.x) = c_1 \cos x + c_2 \sin x$$

$$\text{P.I.} = \frac{1}{D^2 + 1}(2\cos x) = 2x \, . \, \frac{1}{2D} \cos x = x \sin x$$

$$\therefore \quad \mathbf{y = c_1 \cos x + c_2 \sin x + x \sin x.}$$

This is the equation of the extremals.

Example 2. *Find the stationary function of the functional* $\int_0^4 (xy' - y'^2)dx$ *which is determined by the boundary conditions* $y(0) = 0$ *and* $y(4) = 3$. (KU 2005 S)

Sol. Given functional is $\int_0^4 (xy' - y'^2)\,dx$

Let $\quad F(x, y, y') = xy' - y'^2$

The **Euler's equation is** $\frac{\partial F}{\partial y} - \frac{d}{dx}\left(\frac{\partial F}{\partial y'}\right) = 0$ ...(1)

Here $\frac{\partial F}{\partial y} = 0$, $\frac{\partial F}{\partial y'} = x - 2y'$

$\therefore$ (1) $\Rightarrow$ $0 - \frac{d}{dx}(x - 2y') = 0 \Rightarrow -1 + 2\frac{d^2y}{dx^2} = 0$

$\Rightarrow$ $\frac{d^2y}{dx^2} = \frac{1}{2} \Rightarrow \frac{dy}{dx} = \frac{1}{2}x + c_1 \Rightarrow y = \frac{x^2}{4} + c_1x + c_2.$

The boundary conditions are $y(0) = (0)$, $y(4) = 3$.

$y(0) = 0 \Rightarrow 0 + c_1(0) + c_2 = 0 \Rightarrow c_2 = 0$

$y(4) = 3 \Rightarrow 4 + 4c_1 + c_2 = 3 \Rightarrow 4c_1 = -c_2 - 4 = -1 \Rightarrow c_1 = -1/4$

$\therefore$ $y = \frac{x^2}{4} + \left(\frac{-1}{4}\right)x + 0$ *i.e.,* $\mathbf{y = \frac{x^2}{4} - \frac{x}{4}}$.

This is the stationary function of the given functional.

Remark. The extremals of the given functional are given by two-parameter family of curves $y = \frac{x^2}{4} + c_1x + c_2$.

Example 3. *Find the curve on which the functional* $\int_0^1 (y'^2 + 12xy)dx$ *with boundary conditions* $y(0) = 0$ *and* $y(1) = 1$ *can be extremised* (CDLU 2004 ; KU 2006)

Sol. Given functional is $\int_0^1 (y'^2 + 12xy)dx$

Let $F(x, y, y') = y'^2 + 12xy$

The **Euler's equation** is $F_y - \frac{d}{dx}F_{y'} = 0$ ...(1)

Here $F_y = 12x$, $F_{y'} = 2y'$

$\therefore$ (1) $\Rightarrow$ $12x - \frac{d}{dx}(2y') = 0 \Rightarrow \frac{d^2y}{dx^2} = 6x$

$\Rightarrow$ $\frac{dy}{dx} = 3x^2 + c_1 \Rightarrow y = x^3 + c_1x + c_2$ ...(2)

This is the equation of the externals. The boundary conditions are $y(0) = 0$, $y(1) = 1$.

$y(0) = 0 \Rightarrow 0 + c_1(0) + c_2 = 0 \Rightarrow c_2 = 0$

$y(1) = 1 \Rightarrow 1 + c_1(1) + c_2 = 1 \Rightarrow 1 + c_1 + 0 = 1 \Rightarrow c_1 = 0$

$\therefore \Rightarrow$ (2) $\Rightarrow$ $y = x^3 + 0.x + 0$ *i.e.,* $y = x^3$

This is the stationary function of the given variational problem.

$\therefore$ The given functional with given boundary conditions can be extremised on the function $\mathbf{y = x^3}$.

Example 4. *Show that the functional* $\int_0^1 (xy + y^2 - 2y^2y')\,dx$, $y(0) = 1$, $y(1) = 2$ *cannot have any stationary function.* (MDU 2005)

Sol. Given functional is $\int_0^1 (xy + y^2 - 2y^2 y')\,dx$

Let $$F(x, y, y') = xy + y^2 - 2y^2y'$$

The **Euler's equation** is $\dfrac{\partial F}{\partial y} - \dfrac{d}{dx}\left(\dfrac{\partial F}{\partial y'}\right) = 0$ ...(1)

Here $\dfrac{\partial F}{\partial y} = x + 2y - 4yy'$, $\dfrac{\partial F}{\partial y'} = -2y^2$

$\therefore$ (1) $\Rightarrow$ $(x + 2y - 4yy') - \dfrac{d}{dx}(-2y^2) = 0$

$\Rightarrow$ $x + 2y - 4yy' + 4yy' = 0 \Rightarrow x + 2y = 0.$

$\therefore$ There is only one extremal of the given functional.

$y(0) = 1 \Rightarrow 0 + 2(1) = 0$, which is not true.

$\therefore$ There is no stationary function of the given problem.

Example 5. *Find the extremals of the functional* $J[y(x)] = \int_0^{2\pi} (y'^2 - y^2)\,dx$ *that satisfy the boundary conditions* $y(0) = 1$, $y(2\pi) = 1$.

Sol. We have $J[y(x)] = \int_0^{2\pi} (y'^2 - y^2)\,dx$

Let $$F(x, y, y') = y'^2 - y^2$$

The **Euler's equation** is $\dfrac{\partial F}{\partial y} - \dfrac{d}{dx}\left(\dfrac{\partial F}{\partial y'}\right) = 0$ ...(1)

Here $\dfrac{\partial F}{\partial y} = -2y$, $\dfrac{\partial F}{\partial y'} = 2y'$

$\therefore$ (1) $\Rightarrow$ $-2y - \dfrac{d}{dx}(2y') = 0 \Rightarrow \dfrac{d^2y}{dx^2} + y = 0$

The A.E. is $D^2 + 1 = 0$. $\therefore$ $D = 0 \pm i$

$\therefore$ $y = e^{0x}(c_1 \cos 1.x + c_2 \sin 1.x)$ *i.e.*, $y = c_1 \cos x + c_2 \sin x$ ...(2)

This is the equation of the extremals.

The boundary conditions are $y(0) = 1$, $y(2\pi) = 1$.

$y(0) = 1 \Rightarrow c_1 \cos 0 + c_2 \sin 0 = 1 \Rightarrow c_1 = 1$

$y(2\pi) = 1 \Rightarrow c_1 \cos 2\pi + c_2 \sin 2\pi = 1 \Rightarrow c_1 = 1$

$\therefore$ (2) $\Rightarrow$ $y = 1.\cos x + c_2 \sin x$ *i.e.*, $\mathbf{y = \cos x + c_2 \sin x}$.

These are the extremals satisfying given boundary conditions. Here c_2 is arbitrary constant.

Example 6. *Find the extremals and the stationary function of the functional* $\int_1^e (xy'^2 + yy')\,dx$; $y(1) = 0$, $y(e) = 1$.

Sol. Given functional is $\int_1^e (xy'^2 + yy')\,dx$

Let $$F(x, y, y') = xy'^2 + yy'$$

The **Euler's equation** is $\dfrac{\partial F}{\partial y} - \dfrac{d}{dx}\left(\dfrac{\partial F}{\partial y'}\right) = 0$ ...(1)

Here $\dfrac{\partial F}{\partial y} = y'$, $\dfrac{\partial F}{\partial y'} = 2xy' + y$

$\therefore$ (1) $\Rightarrow y' - \dfrac{d}{dx}(2xy' + y) = 0 \Rightarrow y' - 2(xy'' + 1 \,.\, y') - y' = 0 \Rightarrow xy'' + y' = 0$

$\Rightarrow \quad x\dfrac{d^2y}{dx^2} + \dfrac{dy}{dx} = 0 \Rightarrow x\dfrac{dz}{dx} + z = 0$, where $z = \dfrac{dy}{dx}$

$\Rightarrow \quad \dfrac{dz}{z} + \dfrac{dx}{x} = 0 \Rightarrow \log z + \log x = \log c_1$

$\Rightarrow \quad zx = c_1 \Rightarrow x\dfrac{dy}{dx} = c_1 \Rightarrow dy = \dfrac{c_1}{x}dx$

$\Rightarrow \quad \mathbf{y = c_1 \log x + c_2}$. ...(2)

These are the extremals. Here c_1, c_2 are arbitrary constants.

The boundary conditions are $y(1) = 0$, $y(e) = 1$.

$y(1) = 0 \Rightarrow c_1 \log 1 + c_2 = 0 \Rightarrow 0 + c_2 = 0 \Rightarrow c_2 = 0$

$y(e) = 1 \Rightarrow c_1 \log e + c_2 = 1 \Rightarrow c_1 + 0 = 1 \Rightarrow c_1 = 1.$

$\therefore$ (2) $\Rightarrow y = 1 \,.\, \log x + 0$ *i.e.,* $\mathbf{y = \log x}$.

This is the stationary function.

Example 7. *Find the extremal of the functional* $J[y(x)] = \int_0^1 yy'^2\, dx$ *that satisfy the boundary conditions* $y(0) = 1$, $y(1) = \sqrt[3]{4}$.

Sol. We have $J[y(x)] = \int_0^1 yy'^2\, dx$

Let $F(x, y, y') = yy'^2$

The **Euler's equation** is $\dfrac{\partial F}{\partial y} - \dfrac{d}{dx}\left(\dfrac{\partial F}{\partial y'}\right) = 0$ ...(1)

Here $\dfrac{\partial F}{\partial y} = y'^2$, $\dfrac{\partial F}{\partial y'} = 2yy'$

$\therefore$ (1) $\Rightarrow y'^2 - \dfrac{d}{dx}(2yy') = 0 \Rightarrow y'^2 - 2(yy'' + y'y') = 0 \Rightarrow -2yy'' - y'^2 = 0$

$\Rightarrow y'^2 + 2yy'' = 0$

Multiplying by y', we get $y'^3 + 2yy'y'' = 0$.

$\Rightarrow \quad y'(y'^2) + y(2y'y'') = 0 \Rightarrow \dfrac{d}{dx}(yy'^2) = 0$

$\Rightarrow \quad yy'^2 = c_1 \Rightarrow y' = \pm\dfrac{\sqrt{c_1}}{\sqrt{y}} \Rightarrow \dfrac{dy}{dx} = \dfrac{c_2}{\sqrt{y}}$ (Taking $c_2 = \pm\sqrt{c_1}$)

$\Rightarrow \quad \sqrt{y}\, dy = c_2 dx \Rightarrow \dfrac{2y^{3/2}}{3} = c_2 x + c_3$ ...(2)

This is the equation of the extremals. The boundary conditions are $y(0) = 1$, $y(1) = \sqrt[3]{4}$.

$$y(0) = 1 \Rightarrow \frac{2(1)^{3/2}}{3} = c_2(0) + c_3 \Rightarrow c_3 = \frac{2}{3}$$

$$y(1) = 4^{1/3} = \frac{2(4^{1/3})^{3/2}}{3} = c_2(1) + c_3 \Rightarrow c_2 + c_3 = \frac{4}{3} \Rightarrow c_2 + \frac{2}{3} = \frac{4}{3} \Rightarrow c_2 = \frac{2}{3}$$

$$\therefore \quad (2) \Rightarrow \quad \frac{2y^{3/2}}{3} = \frac{2}{3}x + \frac{2}{3}$$

or $$y^{3/2} = x + 1 \quad \text{or} \quad \mathbf{y = (x + 1)^{2/3}}.$$

This is the required extremal.

Alternative method of finding extremals. Since x is missing in $F(x, y, y')$, **the Euler's** equation reduces to $F - F_{y'} \cdot \frac{dy}{dx} = c$.

$$\Rightarrow \quad yy'^2 - (2yy')y' = c$$

$$\Rightarrow \quad yy'^2 = -c \Rightarrow y' = \pm \frac{\sqrt{-c}}{\sqrt{y}} = \frac{k_1}{\sqrt{y}} \qquad \text{(Putting } k_1 = \pm\sqrt{-c}\text{)}$$

$$\Rightarrow \quad \sqrt{y}\, dy = k dx \Rightarrow \frac{2y^{3/2}}{3} = k_1 x + k_2.$$

$\therefore$ We get the same family of curves as extremals.

Example 8. *Find the extremals and the stationary function of the functional* $J[y(x)] = \int_0^1 (y'^2 + 4y^2)\, dx$ *subject to the boundary conditions* $y(0) = e^2$, $y(1) = 1$.

Sol. We have $\quad J[y(x)] = \int_0^1 (y'^2 + 4y^2)\, dx$.

Let $\quad F(x, y, y') = y'^2 + 4y^2$

The **Euler's equation** is $$\frac{\partial F}{\partial y} - \frac{d}{dx}\left(\frac{\partial F}{\partial y'}\right) = 0 \quad \text{...(1)}$$

Here $\frac{\partial F}{\partial y} = 8y, \; \frac{\partial F}{\partial y'} = 2y'$

$$\therefore \quad (1) \Rightarrow \quad 8y - \frac{d}{dx}(2y') = 0 \Rightarrow \frac{d^2y}{dx^2} - 4y = 0$$

$\therefore$ The A.E. is $\quad D^2 - 4 = 0. \quad \therefore \quad D = \pm 2$

$$\therefore \quad \mathbf{y = c_1 e^{2x} + c_2 e^{-2x}} \quad \text{...(2)}$$

This is the equation of the extremals.

The boundary conditions are $y(0) = e^2$ and $y(1) = 1$.

$$y(0) = e^2 \Rightarrow c_1 e^0 + c_2 e^0 = e^2 \Rightarrow c_1 + c_2 = e^2$$

$$y(1) = 1 \Rightarrow c_1 e^2 + c_2 e^{-2} = 1 \Rightarrow c_1 e^2 + c_2 e^{-2} = 1$$

Solving, we get $\quad c_1 = 0, c_2 = e^2$

$$\therefore \quad (2) \Rightarrow \quad y = 0.e^{2x} + e^2.e^{-2x} \quad \textit{i.e.,}\ \mathbf{y = e^{2(1-x)}}.$$

This gives the stationary function.

Example 9. *Show that the general solution of the Euler's equation for the functional*

$$\int_a^b \frac{1}{y}\sqrt{1 + \left(\frac{dy}{dx}\right)^2}\, dx \textit{ is } (x - h)^2 + y^2 = k^2.$$

Sol. Given functional is $\int_a^b \frac{\sqrt{1+y'^2}}{y}\,dx$.

Let $$F(x, y, y') = \frac{\sqrt{1+y'^2}}{y}$$

The **Euler's equation** is $F_y - \frac{d}{dx} F_{y'} = 0$ ...(1)

Since x is missing in $F(x, y, y')$, the Euler's equation reduces to

$$F - F_{y'} \frac{dy}{dx} = c \quad ...(2)$$

Here $F_{y'} = \frac{y'}{y\sqrt{1+y'^2}}$

$$\therefore \quad (2) \Rightarrow \quad \frac{\sqrt{1+y'^2}}{y} - \frac{y'}{y\sqrt{1+y'^2}}\, y' = c$$

$$\Rightarrow \quad \frac{1+y'^2 - y'^2}{y\sqrt{1+y'^2}} = c \quad \Rightarrow \quad \frac{1}{y\sqrt{1+y'^2}} = c$$

$$\Rightarrow \quad y^2(1 + y'^2) = c_1 \quad \Rightarrow \quad y' = \sqrt{\frac{c_1}{y^2} - 1} = \frac{\sqrt{c_1 - y^2}}{y}$$

(Putting $c_1 = \frac{1}{c^2}$ $\therefore$ $c_1 > 0$)

$$\Rightarrow \quad \frac{y}{\sqrt{c_1 - y^2}}\, dy = dx \quad \Rightarrow \quad -\frac{1}{2} \cdot \frac{(c_1 - y^2)^{1/2}}{1/2} = x + c_2$$

$$\Rightarrow \quad -\sqrt{c_1 - y^2} = x + c_2 \quad \Rightarrow \quad c_1 - y^2 = (x + c_2)^2$$

$$\Rightarrow \quad (x + c_2)^2 + y^2 = c_1$$

$\Rightarrow$ $\mathbf{(x - h)^2 + y^2 = k^2}$. (Putting $h = -c_2$, $k^2 = c_1$)

This is the general solution of the Euler's equation of the given functional.

Example 10. *Find the extremals of the functional* $J[y(x)] = \int_{x_1}^{x_2} \frac{\sqrt{1+y'^2}}{x}\,dx$.

(MDU 2004 ; KU 2004 S, 2005 S)

Sol. We have $$J[y(x)] = \int_{x_1}^{x_2} \frac{\sqrt{1+y'^2}}{x}\,dx.$$

Let $$F(x, y, y') = \frac{\sqrt{1+y'^2}}{x}$$

The **Euler's equation** is $\frac{\partial F}{\partial y} - \frac{d}{dx}\left(\frac{\partial F}{\partial y'}\right) = 0$ ...(1)

Here $\frac{\partial F}{\partial y} = 0$, $\frac{\partial F}{\partial y'} = \frac{1}{x} \cdot \frac{2y'}{2\sqrt{1+y'^2}} = \frac{y'}{x\sqrt{1+y'^2}}$

$$\therefore \quad (1) \Rightarrow \quad 0 - \frac{d}{dx}\left(\frac{y'}{x\sqrt{1+y'^2}}\right) = 0 \quad \Rightarrow \quad \frac{y'}{x\sqrt{1+y'^2}} = c_1$$

$$\Rightarrow \quad y'^2 = c_1^2x^2(1+y'^2) \quad \Rightarrow \quad y'^2 = \frac{c_1^2x^2}{1-c_1^2x^2} \quad \Rightarrow \quad y' = \frac{c_1x}{\sqrt{1-c_1^2x^2}}$$

$$\Rightarrow \quad dy = -\frac{1}{2c_1}\cdot\frac{(-2c_1^2x)}{\sqrt{1-c_1^2x^2}}\,dx$$

$$\Rightarrow \quad y = -\frac{1}{2c_1}\cdot\frac{(1-c_1^2x^2)^{1/2}}{1/2} + c_2 \quad \Rightarrow \quad y = -\frac{1}{c_1}\sqrt{1-c_1^2x^2} + c_2$$

$$\Rightarrow \quad (y-c_2)^2 = \frac{1}{c_1^2}(1-c_1^2x^2) = \frac{1}{c_1^2} - x^2$$

$$\Rightarrow \quad \mathbf{x^2 + (y-c_2)^2 = c_3^2.} \qquad \left(\text{Putting } c_3 = \frac{1}{c_1}\right)$$

This family of curves are the required extremals.

Example 11. *From among the curves connecting the points A(1, 3) and B(2, 5), find the curve on which an extremum of the functional*

$$J[y(x)] = \int_1^2 y'(1+x^2y')\,dx \text{ can be attained.}$$

Sol. We have $\quad J[y(x)] = \int_1^2 y'(1+x^2y')\,dx.$

Let $\quad F(x, y, y') = y'(1 + x^2y')$

The **Euler's equation** is $\dfrac{\partial F}{\partial y} - \dfrac{d}{dx}\left(\dfrac{\partial F}{\partial y'}\right) = 0 \qquad \text{...(1)}$

Here $\dfrac{\partial F}{\partial y} = 0, \quad \dfrac{\partial F}{\partial y'} = 1 + 2x^2y'$

$$\therefore \quad (1) \Rightarrow \quad 0 - \frac{d}{dx}(1+2x^2y') = 0 \quad \Rightarrow \quad 1 + 2x^2y' = c_1$$

$$\Rightarrow \quad y' = \frac{c_1-1}{2x^2} \quad \Rightarrow \quad dy = \frac{c_1-1}{2}x^{-2}dx$$

$$\Rightarrow \quad y = \frac{c_1-1}{2}\cdot\frac{x^{-1}}{-1} + c_2 \quad \Rightarrow \quad y = \frac{c_3}{x} + c_2 \qquad \text{...(2)}$$

$$\left(\text{Taking } c_3 = \frac{1-c_1}{2}\right)$$

This is the equation of the extremals.

We are to find that extremal which passes through (1, 3) and (2, 5).

$\therefore$ The boundary conditions are $y(1) = 3$ and $y(2) = 5$.

$$y(1) = 3 \quad \Rightarrow \quad \frac{c_3}{1} + c_2 = 3 \quad \Rightarrow \quad c_2 + c_3 = 3$$

$$y(2) = 5 \quad \Rightarrow \quad \frac{c_3}{2} + c_2 = 5 \quad \Rightarrow \quad c_2 + \frac{c_3}{2} = 5$$

Solving, we get $c_3 = -4$ and $c_2 = 7$.

$$\therefore \quad (2) \Rightarrow \quad y = -\frac{4}{x} + 7$$

This is the stationary function of the given problem.

$\therefore$ The given functional can have an extremum on the curve $y = -\frac{4}{x} + 7$.

8. PRACTICAL VARIATIONAL PROBLEMS

We know that if a function $y(x)$ extremises the functional $\int_{x_1}^{x_2} F(x, y, y')\, dx$, then $y(x)$ satisfies the Euler's equation $\frac{\partial F}{\partial y} - \frac{d}{dx}\left(\frac{\partial F}{\partial y'}\right) = 0$. This does not hold conversely. Thus, if $y(x)$ is a function satisfying the Euler's equation and the boundary conditions then this function may or may not extremise the given functional. In other words, the satisfaction of Euler's equation and boundary conditions is not a sufficient condition for a function to extremise the given functional. Therefore, an extremising function of a functional is a stationary function of the functional but a stationary function may not enjoy the status of an extremising function.

In case of extremising functions of one variable, we use second derivative to give sufficient conditions for deciding whether a particular stationary point is either a maximum point or a minimum point or a point of inflexion. Similar sufficient conditions are also available in the calculus of variations. In actual practice, the geometry or physics of the problem under discussion often makes it possible to determine whether a particular stationary function maximises or minimises the given functional (or neither).

Example 12. *By using Euler's equation find the curve passing through the points* (x_1, y_1) *and* (x_2, y_2) *such that its length between the given points is shortest.* (KU 2005)

Sol. Let $y(x)$ be a function whose curve passes through $A(x_1, y_1)$ and $B(x_2, y_2)$. The length of the arc between A and B is given by $\int_{x_1}^{x_2} \sqrt{1 + y'^2}\, dx$.

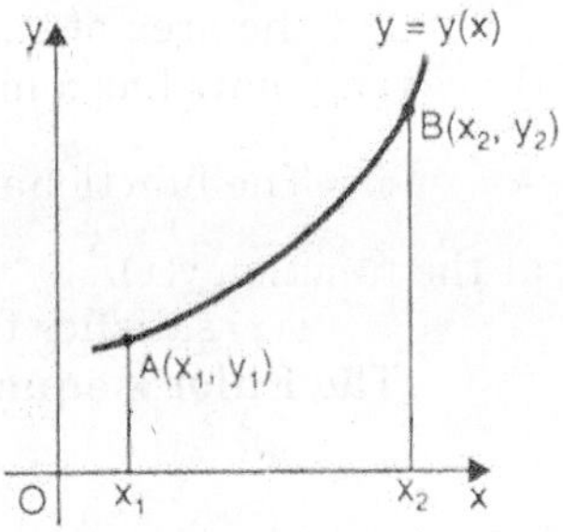

Let $\quad F(x, y, y') = \sqrt{1 + y'^2}$

Let the length of the curve between given points be minimum for the curve $y(x)$.

$\therefore$ The functional $\int_{x_1}^{x_2} F(x, y, y')\, dx$ has a minimum value at the function $y(x)$.

$\therefore$ $y(x)$ satisfies the Euler's equation.

The **Euler's equation** is $\frac{\partial F}{\partial y} - \frac{d}{dx}\left(\frac{\partial F}{\partial y'}\right) = 0.$ ...(1)

Here $\quad \frac{\partial F}{\partial y} = 0, \quad \frac{\partial F}{\partial y'} = \frac{y'}{\sqrt{1 + y'^2}}$

$\therefore$ (1) $\Rightarrow \quad 0 - \frac{d}{dx}\left(\frac{y'}{\sqrt{1 + y'^2}}\right) = 0 \quad \Rightarrow \quad \frac{y'}{\sqrt{1 + y'^2}} = c_1$

$\Rightarrow \quad y'^2 = c_1^2 (1 + y'^2) \quad \Rightarrow \quad y' = \frac{c_1}{\sqrt{1 - c_1^2}} = c_2 \qquad \left(\text{Putting } c_2 = \frac{c_1}{\sqrt{1 - c_1^2}}\right)$

$\Rightarrow \qquad dy = c_2 dx$

$\Rightarrow \qquad y = c_2 x + c_3 \qquad \text{...(2)}$

This is the equation of the extremals. We are to find that extremal which passes through the points (x_1, y_1) and (x_2, y_2).

$\therefore$ The boundary conditions are $y(x_1) = y_1$, $y(x_2) = y_2$.

$$y(x_1) = y_1 \Rightarrow c_2 x_1 + c_3 = y_1$$
$$y(x_2) = y_2 \Rightarrow c_2 x_2 + c_3 = y_2$$

Solving, we get $\quad c_2 = \dfrac{y_2 - y_1}{x_2 - x_1}, \quad c_3 = \dfrac{x_2 y_1 - x_1 y_2}{x_2 - x_1}$

$\therefore$ (2) $\Rightarrow \quad y = \left(\dfrac{y_2 - y_1}{x_2 - x_1}\right) x + \dfrac{x_2 y_1 - x_1 y_2}{x_2 - x_1} \qquad \text{...(2)}$

This is first degree equation.

$\therefore$ This represents a straight line passing through A and B.

$\therefore$ (2) minimises the functional *i.e.*, the length between given points.

$\therefore$ The shortest curve joining (x_1, y_1) and (x_2, y_2) is the straight line joining these points.

Example 13. *Find the curve passing through the points (x_1, y_1) and (x_2, y_2) such that its rotation about the x-axis give rise to a surface of revolution of minimum surface area.*

Sol. Let $y(x)$ be a function whose curve passes through $A(x_1, y_1)$ and $B(x_2, y_2)$. The area of the surface of revolution of the curve between A and B is given by

$$\int_{x_1}^{x_2} 2\pi y \sqrt{1 + y'^2}\, dx.$$

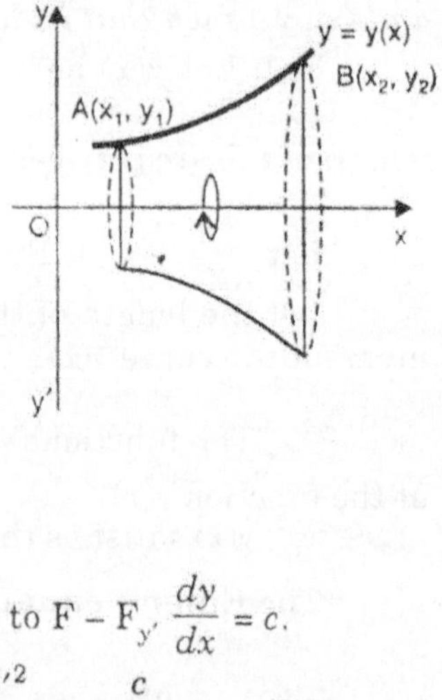

Let $\qquad F(x, y, y') = 2\pi y \sqrt{1 + y'^2}$

Let the area of surface of revolution of the curve between the given points has a minimum value for the curve $y(x)$.

$\therefore$ The functional $\displaystyle\int_{x_1}^{x_2} F(x, y, y')\, dx$ has a minimum value at the function $y(x)$.

$\therefore$ $y(x)$ satisfies the Euler's equation.

The **Euler's equation is**

$$\frac{\partial F}{\partial y} - \frac{d}{dx}\left(\frac{\partial F}{\partial y'}\right) = 0.$$

Since x is missing in $F(x, y, y')$, the Euler's equation reduces to $F - F_{y'} \dfrac{dy}{dx} = c.$

$$\Rightarrow \quad 2\pi y \sqrt{1 + y'^2} - \frac{2\pi y y'}{\sqrt{1 + y'^2}} \cdot y' = c \Rightarrow y\sqrt{1 + y'^2} - \frac{y y'^2}{\sqrt{1 + y'^2}} = \frac{c}{2\pi} = c_1, \text{ say}$$

$$\Rightarrow \quad y = c_1 \sqrt{1 + y'^2} \Rightarrow 1 + y'^2 = \frac{y^2}{c_1^2} \Rightarrow y' = \frac{\sqrt{y^2 - c_1^2}}{c_1}$$

$$\Rightarrow \quad \frac{c_1 dy}{\sqrt{y^2 - c_1^2}} = dx \Rightarrow c_1 \cosh^{-1} \frac{y}{c_1} = x + c_2. \quad \therefore \quad y = c_1 \cosh \frac{x + c_2}{c_1}.$$

The values of c_1 and c_2 (provided they exist) are found by using the boundary conditions. This curve represents a catenary.

$\therefore \quad y = c_1 \cosh \dfrac{x + c_2}{c_1}$ minimises the functional *i.e.*, the area of the surface of revolutions by the curve between the given points.

Example 14. *Show that the geodesics* on a sphere of radius a are its great circles.*

(CDLU 2004 ; MDU 2005, 2006)

Sol. Let A and B be any two points on the given sphere with origin at the centre of the sphere. Let (a, θ_1, ϕ_1) and (a, θ_2, ϕ_2) be their spherical coordinates** respectively. Let $\phi(\theta)$ be a function whose curve passes through A and B and lying itself on the surface of the given sphere.

$\therefore$ The length of the arc between A and B is given by $\int_{\theta_1}^{\theta_2} ds$.

Since, we are dealing with spherical coordinates, we have

$$ds = \sqrt{(dr)^2 + (r\, d\theta)^2 + (r \sin\theta\, d\phi)^2} \qquad \textbf{(Note this step)}$$

$$\Rightarrow \quad ds = \sqrt{0 + a^2 (d\theta)^2 + a^2 \sin^2\theta \,.\, \phi'^2\, (d\theta)^2} \qquad (\because\ r = a \Rightarrow dr = 0)$$

$$= a\sqrt{1 + \phi'^2 \sin^2\theta}\; d\theta$$

$$\therefore \quad \text{Length of arc} = \int_{\theta_1}^{\theta_2} a\sqrt{1 + \phi'^2 \sin^2\theta}\; d\theta$$

Let $\quad F(\theta, \phi, \phi') = a\sqrt{1 + \phi'^2 \sin^2\theta}$

Let the length of the curve between A and B has a minimum value for this curve. In other words, let $\phi(\theta)$ be a geodesic between A and B.

$\therefore$ The functional $\int_{\theta_1}^{\theta_2} F(\theta, \phi, \phi')\, d\theta$ has a minimum value on the function $\phi(\theta)$.

$\therefore$ $\phi(\theta)$ satisfies the Euler's equation.

The **Euler's equation** is $F_\phi - \dfrac{d}{d\theta} F_{\phi'} = 0 \qquad \ldots(1)$

Here $\quad F_\phi = 0, \quad F_{\phi'} = \dfrac{a\phi' \sin^2\theta}{\sqrt{1 + \phi'^2 \sin^2\theta}}$

$$\therefore \quad (1) \Rightarrow \quad 0 - \frac{d}{d\theta}\left(\frac{a\phi' \sin^2\theta}{\sqrt{1 + \phi'^2 \sin^2\theta}}\right) = 0 \Rightarrow \frac{d}{d\theta}\left(\frac{\phi' \sin^2\theta}{\sqrt{1 + \phi'^2 \sin^2\theta}}\right) = 0$$

---

*A *geodesic* is a curve of shortest length lying on a given surface and joining two given points of the surface.

The equations of geodesics may be obtained as Euler's equations corresponding to the variational problem of finding the shortest distance on a surface between two given points.

** **Spherical coordinates.** Let $P(x, y, z)$ be any point in space and let Q be the foot of perpendicular from P on XY- plane.

If $\quad OP = r, \quad \angle ZOP = \theta, \quad \angle XOQ = \phi$, where

$r \geq 0, \quad 0 \leq \theta \leq \pi, \; 0 \leq \phi \leq 2\pi$, then

(r, θ, ϕ) are called the **spherical coordinates** of the point $P(x, y, z)$. Also, $x = r \sin\theta \cos\phi,\ y = r \sin\theta \sin\phi,\ z = r\cos\theta$.

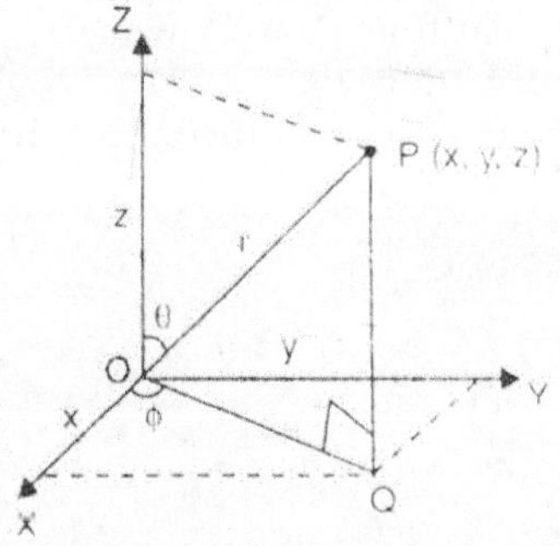

$$\Rightarrow \quad \frac{\phi' \sin^2 \theta}{\sqrt{1+\phi'^2 \sin^2 \theta}} = c_1$$

$$\Rightarrow \quad \phi'^2 \sin^4 \theta = c_1^2 (1 + \phi'^2 \sin^2 \theta)$$

$$\Rightarrow \quad \phi' = \frac{c_1}{\sin\theta \sqrt{\sin^2 \theta - c_1^2}} = \frac{c_1}{\sin^2 \theta \sqrt{1 - c_1^2 \operatorname{cosec}^2 \theta}}$$

$$= \frac{-(-\operatorname{cosec}^2 \theta)\, c_1}{\sqrt{(1-c_1^2) - c_1^2 \cot^2 \theta}} = \frac{-d\,(c_1 \cot\theta)}{\sqrt{(1-c_1^2) - c_1^2 \cot^2 \theta}}$$

Integrating, we get

$$\phi = \cos^{-1} \frac{c_1 \cot \theta}{\sqrt{1 - c_1^2}} + c_2 .$$

$$\Rightarrow \quad \phi(\theta) = \cos^{-1} (c_3 \cot \theta) + c_2, \quad \text{say}$$

$$\Rightarrow \quad c_3 \cot \theta = \cos (\phi(\theta) - c_2)$$

$$\Rightarrow \quad c_3 \cot \theta = \cos \phi(\theta) \cos c_2 + \sin \phi(\theta) \sin c_2$$

$$\Rightarrow \quad \cot \theta = \frac{\cos c_2}{c_3} \cos \phi(\theta) + \frac{\sin c_2}{c_3} \sin \phi(\theta)$$

$$\Rightarrow \quad \cot \theta = c_4 \cos \phi(\theta) + c_5 \sin \phi(\theta), \text{ say}$$

Multiplying by $a \sin \theta$, we get

$$a \cos \theta = c_4(a \cos \phi(\theta) \sin \theta) + c_5(a \sin \phi(\theta) \sin \theta)$$

$$\Rightarrow \quad z = c_4 x + c_5 y \qquad \text{(Using cartesian coordinates)}$$

$z = c_4 x + c_5 y$ represents a plane passing through the centre (0, 0, 0) of the sphere.

The values of c_4 and c_5 are found by using the fact that this plane is to pass through A and B.

∴ The geodesic is the arc of the great circle passing through given points.

Example 15. *Show that the curve of shortest distance between any two points on a circular cylinder of radius a is a helix.* (CDLU 2004)

Sol. Let the axis of the cylinder be taken along the z-axis. Let A and B be any two points on the given cylinder and let (a, ϕ_1, z_1) and (a, ϕ_2, z_2) be their cylindrical coordinates* respectively. Let $z(\phi)$ be a function whose curve passes through A and B and lying itself on the surface of the given cylinder.

---

*__Cylindrical coordinates.__ Let $P(x, y, z)$ be any point in space and let Q be the foot of perpendicular from P on XY-plane.

If $OQ = r$, $\angle XOQ = \phi$, where $r \geq 0$, $0 \leq \phi \leq 2\pi$, $-\infty < z < \infty$, then (r, ϕ, z) are called the **cylindrical coordinates** of the point $P(x, y, z)$.

Also, $x = r \cos \phi$, $y = r \sin \phi$, $z = z$.

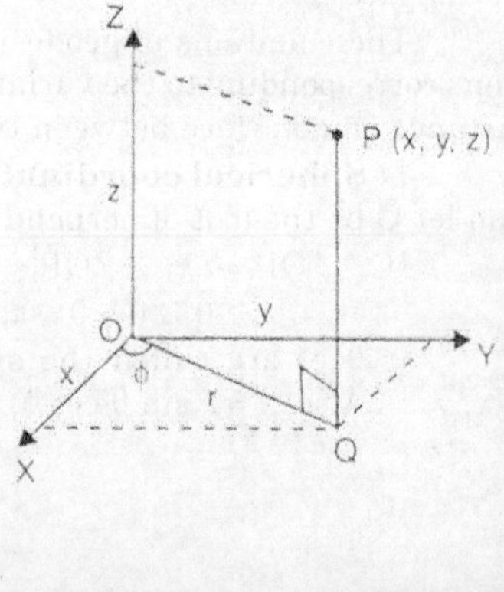

$\therefore$ The length of the arc between A and B is given by $\int_{\phi_1}^{\phi_2} ds$.

Since, we are dealing with cylindrical coordinates, we have

$$ds = \sqrt{(dr)^2 + (rd\phi)^2 + (dz)^2} \qquad \textbf{(Note this step)}$$

$$\Rightarrow \quad ds = \sqrt{0 + a^2(d\phi)^2 + (dz)^2} = \sqrt{a^2 + z'^2}\, d\phi \qquad (\because \; r = a \Rightarrow dr = 0)$$

$\therefore$ Length of arc $= \int_{\phi_1}^{\phi_2} \sqrt{a^2 + z'^2}\, d\phi$

Let $\quad F(\phi, z, z') = \sqrt{a^2 + z'^2}$

Let the length of the curve between A and B has a minimum value for this curve.

$\therefore$ The functional $\int_{\phi_1}^{\phi_2} F(\phi, z, z')\, d\phi$ has a minimum value on the function $z(\phi)$.

$\therefore$ $z(\phi)$ satisfies the Euler's equation.

The **Euler's equation** is $F_z - \dfrac{d}{d\phi} F_{z'} = 0$ ...(1)

Here $F_z = 0, \quad F_{z'} = \dfrac{z'}{\sqrt{a^2 + z'^2}}$

$$\therefore \quad (1) \Rightarrow 0 - \frac{d}{d\phi}\left(\frac{z'}{\sqrt{a^2 + z'^2}}\right) = 0 \Rightarrow \frac{z'}{\sqrt{a^2 + z'^2}} = c_1$$

$$\Rightarrow \quad z'^2 = c_1^2(a^2 + z'^2) \Rightarrow z' = \frac{c_1 a}{\sqrt{1 - c_1^2}} = c_2, \text{ say}$$

$$\Rightarrow \quad \mathbf{z = c_2\phi + c_3.}$$

The values of c_2 and c_3 are found by using the fact that this curve is to pass through A and B. This curve is called a *helix*.

Example 16. *Let A and B be two points in space but not in the same vertical line. Find the curve joining A and B traversed by a particle starting from rest at A and moving under gravity from A to B in the shortest time and ignoring friction along the curve and the resistance of the medium.*

Sol. Fix the origin at A with x-axis horizontal and y-axis vertically downward so that point B is in the xy-plane. Let (h, k) be the coordinates B. Let the particle traversed from A to B along the curve C. Let m be the mass of the particle. Let the velocity of the particle be v when the particle is at the point P (x, y) on C.

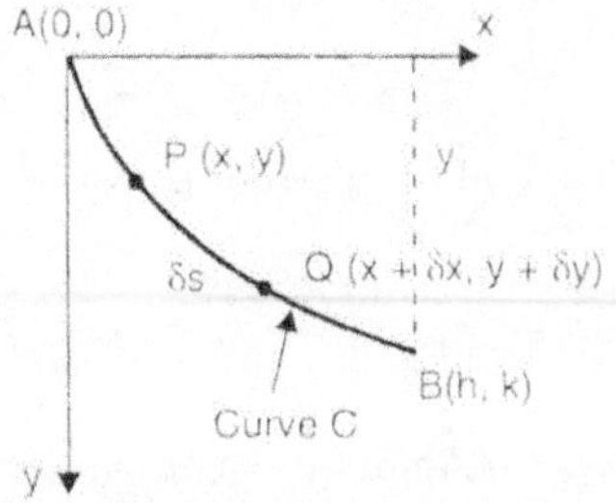

By the **principle of work and energy**,

K.E. at P – K.E. at A

= work done in moving the particle from A to P

$$\Rightarrow \quad \frac{1}{2}mv^2 - \frac{1}{2}m(0)^2 = mgy \Rightarrow v = \sqrt{2gy}.$$

Let $Q(x + \delta x, y + \delta y)$ be a neighbouring point on C such that $\overset{\frown}{PQ} = \delta s$.

$$\therefore \qquad \delta s = \sqrt{(\delta x)^2 + (\delta y)^2} = \sqrt{1+\left(\frac{\delta y}{\delta x}\right)^2}\ \delta x = \sqrt{1+y'^2}\ \delta x\text{, nearly}$$

$\therefore$ Time of descent from P to Q $= \dfrac{\delta s}{v} = \dfrac{\sqrt{1+y'^2}}{\sqrt{2gy}}\ \delta x = \dfrac{1}{\sqrt{2g}} \cdot \dfrac{\sqrt{1+y'^2}}{\sqrt{y}}\ \delta x$

$\therefore$ Total time of transit from A to B

$$= \frac{1}{\sqrt{2g}} \int_0^h \frac{\sqrt{1+y'^2}}{\sqrt{y}}\, dx$$

Also, $y(0) = 0$ and $y(h) = k$.

$\therefore$ **In order to find the shortest time of descent, we have to minimise* the functional** $\displaystyle\int_0^h \frac{\sqrt{1+y'^2}}{\sqrt{y}}\, dx$**, subject to the fixed boundary conditions $y(0) = 0$ and $y(h) = k$.**

Let $$F(x, y, y') = \frac{\sqrt{1+y'^2}}{\sqrt{y}}$$

The **Euler's equation** is $F_y - \dfrac{d}{dx} F_{y'} = 0$.

Since x is missing from $F(x, y, y')$, the Euler's equation reduces to

$$F - F_{y'} \frac{dy}{dx} = c.$$

$$\Rightarrow \qquad \frac{\sqrt{1+y'^2}}{\sqrt{y}} - \left(\frac{1}{\sqrt{y}} \cdot \frac{2y'}{2\sqrt{1+y'^2}}\right) y' = c$$

$$\Rightarrow \qquad \frac{1}{\sqrt{y}\,\sqrt{1+y'^2}}(1 + y'^2 - y'^2) = c$$

$$\Rightarrow \qquad y(1 + y'^2) = \frac{1}{c^2} = c_1, \text{ say} \qquad \ldots(1)$$

Let $y' = \cot u$.

$$\therefore \ (1) \Rightarrow \qquad y = \frac{c_1}{1+\cot^2 u} = c_1 \sin^2 u = \frac{c_1}{2}(1 - \cos 2u)$$

Also $y' = \cot u \Rightarrow dx = \dfrac{dy}{\cot u} = \dfrac{1}{\cot u} \cdot \dfrac{c_1}{2}(0 + 2\sin 2u)du = 2c_1 \sin^2 u\, du$

$$\Rightarrow \qquad \int dx = \int 2c_1 \sin^2 u\, dx + c_2 \Rightarrow x = c_1 \int (1 - \cos 2u)du + c_2$$

---

*From physical considerations, this functional has no maximum value.

$$\Rightarrow \qquad x = c_1\left(u - \frac{\sin 2u}{2}\right) + c_2 \quad \Rightarrow \quad x = \frac{c_1}{2}(2u - \sin 2u) + c_2$$

$\therefore$ The equations of the extremals are

$$x = \frac{c_1}{2}(t - \sin t) + c_2 \text{ and } y = \frac{c_1}{2}(1 - \cos t). \qquad (\text{Putting } t = 2u)$$

The boundary conditions are $y(0) = 0$ and $y(h) = k$.

$$y = 0 \Rightarrow \frac{c_1}{2}(1 - \cos t) = 0 \Rightarrow \cos t = 1 \Rightarrow t = 0$$

$$\Rightarrow \qquad 0 = \frac{c_1}{2}(0 - \sin 0) + c_2 = c_2 \Rightarrow c_2 = 0.$$

$\therefore$ The required curve is

$$\mathbf{x = \frac{c_1}{2}(t - \sin t), \quad y = \frac{c_1}{2}(1 - \cos t).}$$

This represents a cycloid with $c_1/2$ as the radius of the rolling circle.

The value c_1 is to be found by using $y(h) = k$ *i.e.*, by using the fact that the curve passes through B.

Note. This problem is known as **Brachistochrone problem.**

The name 'Brachistochrone is derived from the Greek words 'brachisto' meaning *shortest* and 'chrone' meaning *time*.

EXERCISE 1

1. On what curves can the functional $J[y(x)] = \int_1^2 (y'^2 - 2xy)\, dx$; $y(1) = 0$, $y(2) = -1$ attain an extremum ?
2. Find the stationary function of the functional :

   $J[y(x)] = \int_{-1}^{0} (12xy - y'^2)\, dx$ which is determined by the boundary conditions $y(-1) = 1$, $y(0) = 0$.
3. Find the extremal of the functional $J[y(x)] = \int_{-1}^{1} (y'^2 - 2xy)\, dx$ that satisfy the boundary conditions $y(-1) = -1$, $y(1) = 1$.
4. Find the extremal of the functional $J[y(x)] = \int_1^3 (3x - y)y\, dx$ that satisfy the boundary conditions $y(1) = 1$, $y(3) = 4\frac{1}{2}$.
5. Find the extremal of the functional $J[y(x)] = \int_1^2 \frac{x^3}{y'^2}\, dx$ that satisfy the boundary conditions $y(1) = 0$, $y(2) = 3$.
6. Find the extremals of the following functionals :

   (*i*) $\int_a^b \left(y + \frac{y^3}{3}\right) dx$ (*ii*) $\int_a^b (xy' + y'^2)\, dx.$

7. Find the extremal of the functional $\int_0^1 (2e^y - y^2)\,dx$ that satisfy the boundary conditions $y(0) = 1$, $y(1) = e$.

8. Find the extremals of the functional $\int_a^b (y^2 + y'^2 + 2ye^x)\,dx$.

9. Find the extremal of the functional $\int_0^{\pi/2} (y^2 - y'^2 - 8y \cosh x)\,dx$ that satisfies the boundary conditions $y(0) = 2$, $y\left(\frac{\pi}{2}\right) = 2 \cosh \frac{\pi}{2}$.

10. Find the extremal of the functional $\int_0^1 (x + y'^2)\,dx$ that satisfy the boundary conditions $y(0) = 1$, $y(1) = 2$.

11. Find the extremal of the functional $J[y(x)] = \int_0^\pi (4y \cos x + y'^2 - y^2)\,dx$ that satisfy the boundary conditions $y(0) = 0$, $y(\pi) = 0$. *(KU 2004)*

12. Find the extremal of the functional $J[y(x)] = \int_0^{\pi/2} y(2x - y)\,dx$ that satisfy the boundary conditions $y(0) = 0$, $y(\pi/2) = \pi/2$.

13. Find the extremal of the functional $J[y(x)] = \int_0^1 (e^y + xy')\,dx$ that satisfy the boundary conditions $y(0) = 0$, $y(1) = 0$.

14. Find the extremal of the functional $J[y(x)] = \int_0^{\pi/4} (y'^2 - y^2)\,dx$ that satisfy the boundary conditions $y(0) = 1$, $y\left(\frac{\pi}{4}\right) = \frac{\sqrt{2}}{2}$.

15. Find the extremals and the stationary function of the functional $J[y(x)] = \int_0^\pi (y'^2 - y^2)\,dx$ that satisfy the boundary conditions $y(0) = 1$, $y(\pi) = -1$.

16. Find the stationary function of the functional $\int_0^1 (y^2 + y'^2)\,dx$ subject to the boundary conditions $y(0) = 0$, $y(1) = 1$.

17. Show that the Euler's equation for the functional $\int_{x_1}^{x_2} (a(x)\,y'^2 + 2b(x)\,yy' + c(x)y^2)\,dx$ is a second order linear differential equation. *(MDU 2004)*

18. Find the extremal of the functional $\int_1^2 \frac{\sqrt{1 + y'^2}}{x}\,dx$ which satisfies the boundary conditions $y(1) = 0$, $y(2) = 1$.

19. Find the extremals of the functional $\int_a^b \frac{y'^2}{x^3}\,dx$.

20. By using Euler's equation, find the curve passing through (0, 3) and (4, 11) such that its length between the given points is shortest.

21. Find the geodesics on a right circular cone of semi-vertical angle α. *(KU 2005)*

Answers

1. $y = \frac{x}{6}(1 - x^2)$ 2. $y = -x^3$ 3. $y = \frac{7}{6}x - \frac{1}{6}x^3$ 4. No solution

5. $y = x^2 - 1$ **6.** (*i*) No extremals (*ii*) $y = -\frac{1}{4}x^2 + c_1x + c_2$

7. No solution **8.** $y = c_1e^x + c_2e^{-x} + \frac{1}{2}xe^x$, where c_1 and c_2 are arbitrary constants

9. $y = 2\cosh x$ **10.** $y = x + 1$ **11.** $y = (x + c)\sin x$, where c is an arbitrary constant.

12. $x - y = 0$ **13.** $y = 0$ **14.** $y = \cos x$

15. $y = c_1\cos x + c_2\sin x$, where c_1 and c_2 are arbitrary constants ; $y = \cos x + c_2\sin x$, where c_2 is an arbitrary constant

16. $y = \frac{\sinh x}{\sinh 1}$ **17.** $a(x)y'' + a'(x)y' + (b'(x) - c(x))y = 0$ **18.** $x^2 + (y-2)^2 = 5$

19. $y = c_1x^4 + c_2$ **20.** $y = 2x + 3$ **21.** $c_1r = \sec(\phi\sin\alpha + c_2)$.

9. FUNCTIONALS DEPENDENT ON HIGHER ORDER DERIVATIVES

Theorem 1. Let $J[y(x)] = \int_{x_1}^{x_2} F(x, y(x), y'(x), y''(x))\,dx$ be a functional defined on the set of functions y(x) which are differentiable four times and satisfy the boundary conditions : $y(x_1) = y_1, y'(x_1) = y_1', y(x_2) = y_2, y'(x_2) = y_2'$, where y_1, y_1', y_2, y_2' are prescribed at the fixed boundary points x_1 and x_2. Also, F is differentiable four times with respect to all its arguments.

If the functional J [y(x)] has an extremum on a function y(x) then y(x) satisfy the differential equation

$$F_y - \frac{d}{dx}F_{y'} + \frac{d^2}{dx^2}F_{y''} = 0.$$

Proof. We have $$J[y(x)] = \int_{x_1}^{x_2} F(x, y(x), y'(x), y''(x))\,dx.$$

Let $y = y(x)$ be a function which extremise $J[y(x)]$ and satisfying $y(x_1) = y_1$, $y'(x_1) = y_1'$, $y(x_2) = y_2$, $y'(x_2) = y_2'$.

Let $\eta(x)$ be any arbitrary but fixed function differentiable four times and

$$\eta(x_1) = \eta'(x_1) = \eta(x_2) = \eta'(x_2) = 0.$$

Let $\bar{y}(x) = y(x) + \alpha\eta(x)$, where α is a small parameter.

∴ $\bar{y}(x)$ is differentiable four times.

Now $$\bar{y}(x_1) = y_1,\ \bar{y}'(x_1) = y_1',\ \bar{y}(x_2) = y_2,\ \bar{y}'(x_2) = y_2'.$$

∴ $\bar{y}(x)$ also satisfy the boundary conditions.

∴ The functional J is defined at $\bar{y}(x)$.

$$\therefore \quad J[\bar{y}(x)] = \int_{x_1}^{x_2} F(x, \bar{y}(x), \bar{y}'(x), \bar{y}''(x))\,dx$$

$$= \int_{x_1}^{x_2} F(x, y(x) + \alpha\eta(x), y'(x), \alpha\eta'(x), y''(x) + \alpha\eta''(x))\,dx$$

On the curves of the family $y(x) + \alpha\eta(x)$, the right hand side is a function of α, say $\psi(\alpha)$.

$$\therefore \quad \psi(\alpha) = \int_{x_1}^{x_2} F(x, \bar{y}(x), \bar{y}'(x), \bar{y}''(x))\,dx$$

$$= \int_{x_1}^{x_2} F(x, y(x) + \alpha\eta(x), y'(x) + \alpha\eta'(x), y''(x) + \alpha\eta''(x))\,dx$$

Since the extremising curve $y = y(x)$ corresponds to $\alpha = 0$, it follows that $\psi(\alpha)$ is extremised at $\alpha = 0$.

$$\therefore \qquad \frac{d\psi}{d\alpha} = 0 \quad \text{at} \quad \alpha = 0.$$

Differentiating $\psi(\alpha)$ under the integral sign, we have

$$\frac{d\psi}{d\alpha} = \int_{x_1}^{x_2} \frac{\partial}{\partial\alpha} F(x, \bar{y}(x), \bar{y}'(x), \bar{y}''(x))\, dx$$

$$= \int_{x_1}^{x_2} \left(\frac{\partial F}{\partial x}\frac{\partial x}{\partial \alpha} + \frac{\partial F}{\partial \bar{y}}\frac{\partial \bar{y}}{\partial \alpha} + \frac{\partial F}{\partial \bar{y}'}\frac{\partial \bar{y}'}{\partial \alpha} + \frac{\partial F}{\partial \bar{y}''}\frac{\partial \bar{y}''}{\partial \alpha} \right) dx$$

$$= \int_{x_1}^{x_2} \left(\frac{\partial F}{\partial x}\, 0 + \frac{\partial F}{\partial \bar{y}}\, \eta(x) + \frac{\partial F}{\partial \bar{y}'}\, \eta'(x) + \frac{\partial F}{\partial \bar{y}''}\, \eta''(x) \right) dx$$

$$\therefore \qquad \frac{\partial\psi}{\partial\alpha} = \int_{x_1}^{x_2} \left(\frac{\partial F}{\partial \bar{y}}\, \eta(x) + \frac{\partial F}{\partial \bar{y}'}\, \eta'(x) + \frac{\partial F}{\partial \bar{y}''}\, \eta''(x) \right) dx \qquad \text{...(1)}$$

Now $\qquad \dfrac{\partial\psi}{\partial\alpha} = 0$ at $\alpha = 0$.

$\therefore$ Putting $\alpha = 0$ in (1), we get

$$\int_{x_1}^{x_2} \left(\frac{\partial F}{\partial y}\, \eta(x) + \frac{\partial F}{\partial y'}\, \eta'(x) + \frac{\partial F}{\partial y''}\, \eta''(x) \right) dx = 0 \qquad \text{...(2)}$$

$$\Rightarrow \quad \int_{x_1}^{x_2} \frac{\partial F}{\partial y}\, \eta(x)\, dx + \left[\frac{\partial F}{\partial y'}\, \eta(x) \Big|_{x_1}^{x_2} - \int_{x_1}^{x_2} \frac{d}{dx}\left(\frac{\partial F}{\partial y'}\right) \eta(x)\, dx \right]$$

$$+ \left[\frac{\partial F}{\partial y''}\, \eta'(x) \Big|_{x_1}^{x_2} - \int_{x_1}^{x_2} \frac{d}{dx}\left(\frac{\partial F}{\partial y''}\right) \eta'(x)\, dx \right] = 0$$

$$\Rightarrow \quad \int_{x_1}^{x_2} \frac{\partial F}{\partial y}\, \eta(x)\, dx - \int_{x_1}^{x_2} \frac{d}{dx}\left(\frac{\partial F}{\partial y'}\right) \eta(x)\, dx - \int_{x_1}^{x_2} \frac{d}{dx}\left(\frac{\partial F}{\partial y''}\right) \eta'(x)\, dx = 0$$

$$\Rightarrow \quad \int_{x_1}^{x_2} \left(\frac{\partial F}{\partial y}\, \eta(x) - \frac{d}{dx}\left(\frac{\partial F}{\partial y'}\right) \eta(x) \right) dx - \left[\frac{d}{dx}\left(\frac{\partial F}{\partial y''}\right) \eta(x) \Big|_{x_1}^{x_2} - \int_{x_1}^{x_2} \frac{d^2}{dx^2}\left(\frac{\partial F}{\partial y''}\right) \eta(x)\, dx \right] = 0$$

$$\Rightarrow \quad \int_{x_1}^{x_2} \left(\frac{\partial F}{\partial y} - \frac{d}{dx}\left(\frac{\partial F}{\partial y'}\right) + \frac{d^2}{dx^2}\left(\frac{\partial F}{\partial y''}\right) \right) \eta(x) dx = 0.$$

This holds for any arbitrary continuous function $\eta(x)$.

$\therefore$ We have $\qquad \dfrac{\partial F}{\partial y} - \dfrac{d}{dx}\left(\dfrac{\partial F}{\partial y'}\right) + \dfrac{d^2}{dx^2}\left(\dfrac{\partial F}{\partial y''}\right) = 0.$

$\therefore$ The function $y(x)$ satisfies the equation

$$\mathbf{F_y - \frac{d}{dx} F_{y'} + \frac{d^2}{dx^2} F_{y''} = 0.}$$

This equation is known as the **Euler-Poisson equation.**

In the next theorem, we generalise the above result.

Theorem 2. **Let $J[y(x)] = \int_{x_1}^{x_2} F(x, y(x), y'(x), ..., y^{(n)}(x))\, dx$ be a functional defined on the set of functions $y(x)$ which are differentiable $2n$ times and satisfy the boundary conditions :**

$$y(x_1) = y_1,\ y'(x_1) = y_1',\ ...,\ y^{(n-1)}(x_1) = y_1^{(n-1)},$$
$$y(x_2) = y_2,\ y'(x_2) = y_2',\ ...,\ y^{(n-1)}(x_2) = y_2^{(n-1)},$$

where $y_1, y_1', ...\ y_1^{(n-1)}, y_2, y_2', ..., y_2^{(n-1)}$ are prescribed at the fixed boundary points x_1 and x_2. Also, F is differentiable $n + 2$ times with respect to all its arguments.

If the functional $J[y(x)]$ has an extremum on a function $y(x)$ then $y(x)$ satisfy the differential equation

$$F_y - \frac{d}{dx} F_{y'} + \frac{d^2}{dx^2} F_{y''} - ...... + (-1)^n \frac{d^n}{dx^n} F_{y^{(n)}} = 0.$$

Proof. We have $J[y(x)] = \int_{x_1}^{x_2} F(x, y(x), y'(x), ..., y^{(n)}(x))\, dx.$

Let $y = y(x)$ be a function which extremise $J[y(x)]$ and satisfying

$$y(x_1) = y_1,\ y'(x_1) = y_1', ..., y^{(n-1)}(x_1) = y_1^{(n-1)},$$
$$y(x_2) = y_2,\ y'(x_2) = y_2', ..., y^{(n-1)}(x_2) = y_2^{(n-1)}.$$

Let $\eta(x)$ be any arbitrary but fixed function differentiable $2n$ times and

$$\eta(x_1) = \eta'(x_1) = ... = \eta^{(n-1)}(x_1) = 0$$
$$\eta(x_2) = \eta'(x_2) = ... = \eta^{(n-1)}(x_2) = 0.$$

Let $\bar{y}(x) = y(x) + \alpha\eta(x)$, where α is a small parameter.

$\therefore$ $\bar{y}(x)$ is differentiable $2n$ times.

Now $\bar{y}(x_1) = y_1,\ \bar{y}'(x_1) = y_1', ..., \bar{y}^{(n-1)}(x_1) = y_1^{(n-1)},$

$\bar{y}(x_2) = y_2,\ \bar{y}'(x_2) = y_2', ..., \bar{y}^{(n-1)}(x_2) = y_2^{(n-1)}.$

$\therefore$ $\bar{y}(x)$ also satisfy the boundary conditions.

$\therefore$ The functional J is defined at $\bar{y}(x)$.

$$\therefore \qquad J[\bar{y}(x)] = \int_a^b F(x, \bar{y}(x), \bar{y}'(x), ..., y^{(n)}(x) dx$$

$$= \int_{x_1}^{x_2} F(x, y(x) + \alpha\eta(x), y'(x) + \alpha\eta'(x), ..., y^{(n)}(x) + \alpha\eta^{(n)}(x))\, dx$$

On the curves of the family $y(x) + \alpha\eta(x)$, the right hand side is a function of α, say $\psi(\alpha)$.

$$\therefore \qquad \psi(\alpha) = \int_{x_1}^{x_2} F(x, \bar{y}(x), \bar{y}'(x), ..., \bar{y}^{(n)}(x))\, dx$$

$$= \int_{x_1}^{x_2} F(x, y(x) + \alpha\eta(x), y'(x) + \alpha\eta'(x), ..., y^{(n)}(x) + \alpha\eta^{(n)}(x))\, dx$$

Since the extremising curve $y = y(x)$ corresponds to $\alpha = 0$, it follows that $\psi(\alpha)$ is extremised for $\alpha = 0$.

$$\therefore \qquad \frac{d\psi}{d\alpha} = 0 \text{ at } \alpha = 0.$$

Differentiating $\psi(\alpha)$ under the integral sign, we have

$$\frac{d\psi}{d\alpha} = \int_{x_1}^{x_2} \frac{\partial}{\partial\alpha} F(x, \bar{y}(x), \bar{y}'(x), ..., \bar{y}^{(n)}(x))\, dx$$

$$= \int_{x_1}^{x_2} \left(\frac{\partial F}{\partial x}\frac{\partial x}{\partial \alpha} + \frac{\partial F}{\partial \bar{y}}\frac{\partial \bar{y}}{\partial \alpha} + \frac{\partial F}{\partial \bar{y}'}\frac{\partial \bar{y}'}{\partial \alpha} + \ldots\ldots + \frac{\partial F}{\partial \bar{y}^{(n)}}\frac{\partial \bar{y}^{(n)}}{\partial \alpha} \right) dx$$

$$= \int_{x_1}^{x_2} \left(\frac{\partial F}{\partial x}.0 + \frac{\partial F}{\partial \bar{y}}\eta(x) + \frac{\partial F}{\partial \bar{y}'}\eta'(x) + \ldots + \frac{\partial F}{\partial \bar{y}^{(n)}}\eta^{(n)}(x) \right) dx$$

$$\therefore \quad \frac{\partial \psi}{d\alpha} = \int_{x_1}^{x_2} \left(\frac{\partial F}{\partial \bar{y}}\eta(x) + \frac{\partial F}{\partial \bar{y}'}\eta'(x) + \ldots\ldots + \frac{\partial F}{\partial \bar{y}^{(n)}}\eta^{(n)}(x) \right) dx \qquad \ldots(1)$$

Now $\qquad \dfrac{d\psi}{d\alpha} = 0$ at $\alpha = 0$.

$\therefore$ Putting $\qquad \alpha = 0$ in (1), we get

$$\int_{x_1}^{x_2} \left(\frac{\partial F}{\partial x}\eta(x) + \frac{\partial F}{\partial y'}\eta'(x) + \ldots + \frac{\partial F}{\partial y^{(n)}}\eta^{(n)}(x) \right) dx = 0 \qquad \ldots(2)$$

Integrating by parts the second term once, third term twice and so on and using boundary conditions, we get

$$\int_{x_1}^{x_2} \left(\frac{\partial F}{\partial x} - \frac{d}{dx}\left(\frac{\partial F}{\partial y'}\right) + \frac{d^2}{dx^2}\left(\frac{\partial F}{\partial y''}\right) - \ldots + (-1)^n \frac{d^n}{dx^n}\left(\frac{\partial F}{\partial y^{(n)}}\right) \right) \eta(x)\, dx = 0.$$

This holds for any arbitrary continuous function $\eta(x)$.

$\therefore$ We have $\qquad \dfrac{\partial F}{\partial y} - \dfrac{d}{dx}\left(\dfrac{\partial F}{\partial y'}\right) + \dfrac{d^2}{dx^2}\left(\dfrac{\partial F}{\partial y''}\right) - \ldots + (-1)^n \dfrac{d^n}{dx^n}\left(\dfrac{\partial F}{\partial y^{(n)}}\right) = 0$

$\therefore$ The function $y(x)$ satisfies the equation

$$\mathbf{F_y - \frac{d}{dx}F_{y'} + \frac{d^2}{dx^2}F_{y''} - \ldots + (-1)^n \frac{d^n}{dx^n}F_{y^{(n)}} = 0.}$$

This equation is also known as the **Euler-Poisson equation.**

WORKING RULES FOR SOLVING PROBLEMS

Step I. *Identify the functional* $\int_{x_1}^{x_2} F(x, y, y', ..., y^{(n)})\, dx$ *and the boundary conditions in the given problem.*

Step II. *Write the Euler-Poisson equation*

$$F_y - \frac{d}{dx}F_{y'} + \frac{d^2}{dx^2}F_{y''} - \ldots + (-1)^n \frac{d^n}{dx^n}F_{y^{(n)}} = 0.$$

Step III. *The solutions of this equation are extremals of the given problem.*

Step IV. *Find the extremal that satisfy the given boundary conditions. This particular extremal is the stationary function of the given problem.*

Example 1. *Find the stationary function of the functional* $\int_a^b (y'^2 + yy'')dx$; $y(a) = \lambda_1$, $y'(a) = \lambda_2$, $y(b) = \lambda_3$, $y'(b) = \lambda_4$.

Sol. Given functional is $\int_a^b (y'^2 + yy'')\, dx$.

Let $F(x, y, y', y'') = y'^2 + yy''$

The **Euler-Poisson equation** is

$$F_y - \frac{d}{dx} F_{y'} + \frac{d^2}{dx^2} F_{y''} = 0 \qquad ...(1)$$

Here $F_y = y'', F_{y'} = 2y', F_{y''} = y$

$$\therefore \quad (1) \Rightarrow y'' - \frac{d}{dx}(2y') + \frac{d^2}{dx^2}(y) = 0$$

$$\Rightarrow \quad y'' - 2y'' + y'' = 0 \Rightarrow 0 = 0,$$

which is not a differential equation.

$\therefore$ There is no extremal and hence no stationary function.

Example 2. *Find the extremals of the functional*

$$\int_{x_0}^{x_1} (2xy + y'''^2)\, dx.$$

Sol. Given functional is $\int_x^{x_1} (2xy + y''')^2\, dx$.

Let $F(x, y, y', y'', y''') = 2xy + y'''^2$

The **Euler-Poisson equation** is

$$F_y - \frac{d}{dx} F_{y'} + \frac{d^2}{dx^2} F_{y''} - \frac{d^3}{dx^3} F_{y'''} = 0 \qquad ...(1)$$

Here $F_y = 2x, F_{y'} = 0, F_{y''} = 0, F_{y'''} = 2y'''$

$$\therefore \quad (1) \Rightarrow 2x - \frac{d}{dx}(0) + \frac{d^2}{dx^2}(0) - \frac{d^3}{dx^3}(2y''') = 0$$

$$\Rightarrow \quad \frac{d^6y}{dx^6} = x \Rightarrow \frac{d^5y}{dx^5} = \frac{x^2}{2} + c_1$$

$$\Rightarrow \quad \frac{d^4y}{dx^4} = \frac{x^3}{6} + c_1x + c_2$$

$$\Rightarrow \quad \frac{d^3y}{dx^3} = \frac{x^4}{24} + c_1\frac{x^2}{2} + c_2x + c_3$$

$$\Rightarrow \quad \frac{d^2y}{dx^2} = \frac{x^5}{120} + c_1\frac{x^3}{6} + c_2\frac{x^2}{2} + c_3x + c_4$$

$$\Rightarrow \quad \frac{dy}{dx} = \frac{x^6}{720} + c_1\frac{x^4}{24} + c_2\frac{x^3}{6} + c_3\frac{x^2}{2} + c_4x + c_5$$

$$\Rightarrow \quad y = \frac{x^7}{5040} + c_1\frac{x^5}{120} + c_2\frac{x^4}{24} + c_3\frac{x^3}{6} + c_4\frac{x^2}{2} + c_5x + c_6$$

$$\Rightarrow \quad y = \frac{x^7}{5040} + c_1'x^5 + c_2'x^4 + c_3'x^3 + c_4'x + c_5x + c_6,$$

where $c_1' = \frac{c_1}{120}$, $c_2' = \frac{c_2}{24}$, $c_3' = \frac{c_3}{6}$, $c_4' = \frac{c_2}{2}$

∴ The equation of the extremals is

$$\mathbf{y = \frac{x^7}{5040} + c_1'x^5 + c_2'x^4 + c_3'x^3 + c_4'x^2 + c_5x + c_6,}$$

where $c_1', c_2', c_3', c_4', c_5, c_6$ are arbitrary constants.

Example 3. *Find the curve that extremises the functional* $\int_0^{\pi/4} (y''^2 - y^2 + x^2)\,dx$ *under the boundary conditions* $y(0) = 0, y'(0) = 1, y(\pi/4) = y'(\pi/4) = 1/\sqrt{2}$.

Sol. Given functional is $\int_0^{\pi/4} (y''^2 - y^2 + x^2)\,dx$.

Let $\quad F(x, y, y', y'') = y''^2 - y^2 + x^2$

The **Euler-Poisson equation** is $F_y - \frac{d}{dx}F_{y'} + \frac{d^2}{dx^2}F_{y''} = 0$ ...(1)

Here $F_y = -2y, \quad F_{y'} = 0, \quad F_{y''} = 2y''$

$$\therefore \quad (1) \Rightarrow \quad -2y - \frac{d}{dx}(0) + \frac{d^2}{dx^2}(2y'') = 0 \Rightarrow \frac{d^4y}{dx^4} - y = 0$$

∴ The A.E. is $D^4 - 1 = 0$

$$\Rightarrow \quad D = \pm 1, \ \pm i$$

$$\therefore \quad y = c_1e^{1.x} + c_2e^{-1.x} + e^{0.x}(c_3 \cos 1.x + c_4 \sin 1.x)$$

or $$y = c_1e^x + c_2e^{-x} + c_3 \cos x + c_4 \sin x \quad ...(2)$$

This is the equation of the extremals.

The boundary conditions are $y(0) = 0$, $y'(0) = 1$, $y(\pi/4) = y'(\pi/4) = 1/\sqrt{2}$.

$$(2) \Rightarrow \quad y' = c_1e^x - c_2e^{-x} - c_3 \sin x + c_4 \cos x$$

$$y(0) = 0 \Rightarrow c_1 + c_2 + c_3 = 0 \quad ...(3)$$

$$y'(0) = 1 \Rightarrow c_1 - c_2 + c_4 = 1 \quad ...(4)$$

$$y\left(\frac{\pi}{4}\right) = \frac{1}{\sqrt{2}} \Rightarrow c_1e^{\pi/4} + c_2e^{-\pi/4} + \frac{c_3}{\sqrt{2}} + \frac{c_4}{\sqrt{2}} = \frac{1}{\sqrt{2}}$$

$$\Rightarrow \sqrt{2}\,c_1e^{\pi/4} + \sqrt{2}\,c_2e^{-\pi/4} + c_3 + c_4 = 1 \quad ...(5)$$

$$y'\left(\frac{\pi}{4}\right) = \frac{1}{\sqrt{2}} \Rightarrow c_1e^{\pi/4} - c_2e^{-\pi/4} - \frac{c_3}{\sqrt{2}} + \frac{c_4}{\sqrt{2}} = \frac{1}{\sqrt{2}}$$

$$\Rightarrow \sqrt{2}\,c_1{}^{\pi/4} - \sqrt{2}\,c_2e^{-\pi/4} - c_3 + c_4 = 1 \quad ...(6)$$

Solving (3), (4), (5), (6), we get

$$c_1 = c_2 = c_3 = 0, \quad c_4 = 1$$

∴ **(2)** ⇒ $y = 0.e^x + 0.e^{-x} + 0.\cos x + 1.\sin x$ *i.e.,* $\mathbf{y = \sin x.}$

This is the equation of the required extremal.

Example 4. *Find the extremal of the functional* $\int_{-a}^{a} (\lambda y + \frac{1}{2}\mu y''^2)\,dx$ *which satisfy the boundary conditions* $y(-a) = 0, y'(-a) = 0, y(a) = 0, y'(a) = 0$.

Sol. Given functional is $\int_{-a}^{a} \left(\lambda y + \frac{1}{2}\mu y''^2\right) dx$.

Let $\quad F(x, y, y', y'') = \lambda y + \frac{1}{2}\mu y''^2$

The **Euler-Poisson equation** is $\quad F_y - \frac{d}{dx} F_{y'} + \frac{d^2}{dx^2} F_{y''} = 0 \quad$ ...(1)

Here $F_y = \lambda, \quad F_{y'} = 0, \quad F_{y''} = \mu y''$

$$\therefore \quad (1) \Rightarrow \lambda - \frac{d}{dx}(0) + \frac{d^2}{dx^2}(\mu y'') = 0 \Rightarrow \mu \frac{d^4y}{dx^4} + \lambda = 0 \Rightarrow \frac{d^4y}{dx^4} = -\frac{\lambda}{\mu}$$

$$\Rightarrow \quad \frac{d^3y}{dx^3} = -\frac{\lambda}{\mu}x + c_1$$

$$\Rightarrow \quad \frac{d^2y}{dx^2} = -\frac{\lambda}{\mu}\frac{x^2}{2} + c_1x + c_2$$

$$\Rightarrow \quad \frac{dy}{dx} = -\frac{\lambda}{\mu}\frac{x^3}{6} + c_1\frac{x^2}{2} + c_2x + c_3$$

$$\Rightarrow \quad y = -\frac{\lambda}{\mu}\frac{x^4}{24} + c_1\frac{x^3}{6} + c_2\frac{x^2}{2} + c_3x + c_4 \quad \text{...(2)}$$

This is the equation of the extremals. The boundary conditions are

$$y(-a) = 0, \quad y'(-a) = 0, \quad y(a) = 0, \quad y'(a) = 0$$

$$y(-a) = 0 \Rightarrow -\frac{\lambda a^4}{24\mu} - \frac{c_1a^3}{6} + \frac{c_2a^2}{2} - c_3a + c_4 = 0 \quad \text{...(3)}$$

$$y'(-a) = 0 \Rightarrow \frac{\lambda a^3}{6\mu} + \frac{c_1a^2}{2} - c_2a + c_3 = 0 \quad \text{...(4)}$$

$$y(a) = 0 \Rightarrow -\frac{\lambda a^4}{24\mu} + \frac{c_1a^3}{6} + \frac{c_2a^2}{2} + c_3a + c_4 = 0 \quad \text{...(5)}$$

$$y'(a) = 0 \Rightarrow -\frac{\lambda a^3}{6a} + \frac{c_1a^2}{2} + c_2a + c_3 = 0 \quad \text{...(6)}$$

$$(3) - (5) \Rightarrow -\frac{c_1a^3}{3} - 2c_3a = 0 \Rightarrow c_1a^2 + 6c_3 = 0 \quad \text{...(7)}$$

$$(4) + (6) \Rightarrow c_1a^2 + 2c_3 = 0 \quad \text{...(8)}$$

Solving (7) and (8), we get $c_1 = 0, c_3 = 0$

$$(4) \Rightarrow \frac{\lambda a^3}{6\mu} + 0 - c_2a + 0 = 0 \Rightarrow c_2 = \frac{\lambda a^2}{6\mu}$$

$$(3) \Rightarrow -\frac{\lambda a^4}{24\mu} - 0 + \frac{a^2}{2}\left(\frac{\lambda a^2}{6\mu}\right) - 0 + c_4 = 0 \Rightarrow c_4 = -\frac{\lambda a^4}{24\mu}.$$

$$\therefore \quad c_1 = 0, \quad c_2 = \frac{\lambda a^2}{6\mu}, \quad c_3 = 0, \quad c_4 = -\frac{\lambda a^4}{24\mu}$$

$$\therefore \quad (2) \Rightarrow \quad y = -\frac{\lambda x^4}{24\mu} + 0 + \frac{\lambda a^2}{6\mu} \cdot \frac{x^2}{2} + 0 - \frac{\lambda a^4}{24\mu}$$

$$\therefore \quad = -\frac{\lambda}{24\mu}(x^4 - 2a^2x^2 + a^4) = -\frac{\lambda}{24\mu}(x^2 - a^2)^2$$

$$\therefore \quad \mathbf{y = -\frac{\lambda}{24\mu}(x^2 - a^2)^2.}$$

This is the equation of the required extremal.

EXERCISE 2

Find the extremals of the following functionals (Q. No. 1—4) :

1. $\int_{x_1}^{x_2} (16y^2 - y''^2 + x^2)\, dx$ *(KU 2006)*

2. $\int_{x_0}^{x_1} (y''^2 - y^2 + x^2)\, dx$

3. $\int_{x_0}^{x_1} (360x^2y - y''^2)\, dx$

4. $\int_{x_1}^{x_2} (y^2 + 2y'^2 + y''^2)\, dx.$

5. Find the extremal of the functional $\int_0^{\pi/2} (y''^2 - y^2 + x^2)\, dx$ that satisfy the boundary conditions : $y(0) = 1, y(\pi/2) = 0, y'(0) = 0, y'(\pi/2) = -1.$

6. Determine the extremal of the functional $J[y(x)] = \int_{-l}^{l} (\frac{1}{2}\mu y''^2 + ky)\, dx$ subject to $y(-l) = 0$, $y'(-l) = 0, y(l) = 0, y'(l) = 0.$

7. Find the extremals and the stationary function of the functional $\int_0^1 (y'^2 + y''^2)\, dx$ with the boundary conditions : $y(0) = 0, y(1) = \sinh 1, y'(0) = 1, y'(1) = \cosh 1.$ *(MDU 2004)*

8. Find the extremals and the stationary function of the functional $\frac{1}{2}\int_0^1 (y'')^2\, dx$. The boundary conditions are $y(0) = 0, y(1) = \frac{1}{2}, y'(0) = 0, y'(1) = 1.$

9. Find the extremal of the functional $\int_a^b (y + y'')\, dx$ that satisfies the boundary conditions $y(a) = y_0$, $y(b) = y_1, y'(a) = y_0', y'(b) = y_1'.$

10. Find the extremal of the functional $J[y(x)] = \int_{-1}^{0} (240y + y'''^2)\, dx$ subject to the conditions : $y(-1) = 1, y(0) = 0, y'(-1) = -4.5, y'(0) = 0, y''(-1) = 16, y''(0) = 0.$

Answers

1. $y = c_1e^{2x} + c_2e^{-2x} + c_3 \cos 2x + c_4 \sin 2x$

2. $y = c_1e^x + c_2e^{-x} + c_3 \cos x + c_4 \sin x$

3. $y = \frac{x^6}{2} + c_1x^3 + c_2x^2 + c_3x + c_4$

4. $y = (c_1 + c_2x)e^x + (c_3 + c_4x)e^{-x}$

5. $y = \cos x$

6. $y = -\frac{k}{24\mu}(x^2 - l^2)^2$

7. $y = c_1 + c_2x + c_3e^x + c_4e^{-x}, \quad y = \sinh x$

8. $y = c_1 + c_2x + c_3x^2 + c_4x^3, \quad y = \frac{1}{2}x^2$

9. No extremal

10. $y = \dfrac{x^3}{6}(x^3 + 6x + 1).$

10. FUNCTIONALS DEPENDENT ON MORE THAN ONE INDEPENDENT VARIABLE

Till now we have been discussing functionals depending on functions of one independent variable *i.e.*, on curves. In the present section we shall consider functionals depending on functions of more than one independent variable *i.e.*, on surfaces. We shall restrict ourselves to only to two independent variables.

Theorem. Let $J[z(x, y)] = \iint_D F(x, y, z, z_x, z_y)\, dx\, dy$ be a functional defined on the set of functions z(x, y) which admits of continuous derivatives upto the second order and assumes given values on the boundary Γ of the region D. Also, F is differentiable three times with respect to all its arguments.

If the functional J[z(x, y)] has an extremum on a function z(x, y) then z(x, y) satisfy the differential equation

$$F_z - \frac{\partial}{\partial x} F_{z_x} - \frac{\partial}{\partial y} F_{z_y} = 0.$$

Proof. We have

$$J[z(x, y)) = \iint_D F(x, y, z, z_x, z_y)\, dx\, dy.$$

Let $z = z(x, y)$ be a function which extremise $J[z(x, y)]$ and assumes given values on the boundary Γ of the region D.

Let $\eta(x, y)$ be any arbitrary but fixed function admiting continuous derivatives upto the second order and taking value zero on the boundary of the region D.

Let $\bar{z}(x, y) = z(x, y) + \alpha\eta(x, y)$, where α is a small parameter.

∴ $\bar{z}(x, y)$ admits of continuous derivatives upto the second order and assumes given values on the boundary of the region D.

∴ The functional J is defined at $\bar{z}(x, y)$.

$$\therefore \quad J[\bar{z}(x, y)] = \iint_D F(x, y, \bar{z}, \bar{z}_x, \bar{z}_y)\, dx\, dy$$

$$= \iint_D F(x, y, z + \alpha\eta, z_x + \alpha\eta_x, z_y + \alpha\eta_y)\, dxdy$$

On the regions of the family $z(x, y) + \alpha\eta(x, y)$, the right hand side is a function of α, say $\psi(\alpha)$.

$$\therefore \quad \psi(\alpha) = \iint_D F(x, y, \bar{z}, \bar{z}_x, \bar{z}_y)\, dx\, dy$$

$$= \iint_D F(x, y, z + \alpha\eta, z_x + \alpha\eta_x, z_y + \alpha\eta_y)\, dx\, dy$$

Since the extremising surface $z = z(x, y)$ corresponds to $\alpha = 0$, it follows that $\psi(\alpha)$ is extremised for $\alpha = 0$.

$$\therefore \quad \frac{d\psi}{d\alpha} = 0 \text{ at } \alpha = 0.$$

Differentiating $\psi(\alpha)$ under the integral sign, we have

$$\frac{d\psi}{d\alpha} = \iint_D \frac{\partial}{\partial\alpha} F(x, y, \bar{z}, \bar{z}_x, \bar{z}_y)\, dx\, dy$$

$$= \iint_D \left(\frac{\partial F}{\partial x} \frac{\partial x}{\partial \alpha} + \frac{\partial F}{\partial y} \frac{\partial y}{\partial \alpha} + \frac{\partial F}{\partial \bar{z}} \frac{\partial \bar{z}}{\partial \alpha} + \frac{\partial F}{\partial \bar{z}_x} \frac{\partial \bar{z}_x}{\partial \alpha} + \frac{\partial F}{\partial \bar{z}_y} \frac{\partial \bar{z}_y}{\partial \alpha} \right) dx\, dy$$

$$= \iint_D \left(\frac{\partial F}{\partial x} \cdot 0 + \frac{\partial F}{\partial y} \cdot 0 + \frac{\partial F}{\partial \bar{z}} \eta + \frac{\partial F}{\partial \bar{z}_x} \eta_x + \frac{\partial F}{\partial \bar{z}_y} \eta_y \right) dx\, dy$$

$$\therefore \quad \frac{d\psi}{d\alpha} = \iint_D \left(\frac{\partial F}{\partial \bar{z}} \eta + \frac{\partial F}{\partial \bar{z}_x} \eta_x + \frac{\partial F}{\partial \bar{z}_y} \eta_y \right) dx\, dy \qquad \ldots(1)$$

Now $\dfrac{d\psi}{d\alpha} = 0$ at $\alpha = 0$.

Putting $\alpha = 0$ in (1), we get

$$\iint_D \left(\frac{\partial F}{\partial z} \eta + \frac{\partial F}{\partial z_x} \eta_x + \frac{\partial F}{\partial z_y} \eta_y \right) dx\, dy = 0$$

$$\Rightarrow \quad \iint_D \frac{\partial F}{\partial z} \eta\, dx\, dy + \iint_D \left(\frac{\partial F}{\partial z_x} \eta_x + \frac{\partial F}{\partial z_y} \eta_y \right) dx\, dy = 0$$

$$\Rightarrow \quad \iint_D \frac{\partial F}{\partial z} \eta\, dx\, dy + \int_\Gamma \eta \left(\frac{\partial F}{\partial z_x} dy - \frac{\partial F}{\partial z_y} dx \right) - \iint_D \left(\frac{\partial}{\partial x}\left(\frac{\partial F}{\partial z_x} \right) + \frac{\partial}{\partial y}\left(\frac{\partial F}{\partial z_y} \right) \right) \eta\, dx\, dy = 0$$

(By using Green's theorem)

$$\Rightarrow \quad \iint_D \left(\frac{\partial F}{\partial z} - \frac{\partial}{\partial x}\left(\frac{\partial F}{\partial z_x} \right) - \frac{\partial}{\partial y}\left(\frac{\partial F}{\partial z_y} \right) \right) \eta\, dx\, dy + \int_\Gamma \eta \left(\frac{\partial F}{\partial z_x} dy - \frac{\partial F}{\partial z_y} dx \right) = 0$$

$$\Rightarrow \quad \iint_D \left(\frac{\partial F}{\partial z} - \frac{\partial}{\partial x}\left(\frac{\partial F}{\partial z_x} \right) - \frac{\partial}{\partial y}\left(\frac{\partial F}{\partial z_y} \right) \right) \eta\, dx\, dy = 0 \qquad (\because\ \eta = 0 \text{ on } \Gamma)$$

This holds for any arbitrary continuous function $\eta(x)$.

$$\therefore \quad \text{We have} \quad \frac{\partial F}{\partial z} - \frac{\partial}{\partial x}\left(\frac{\partial F}{\partial z_x} \right) - \frac{\partial}{\partial y}\left(\frac{\partial F}{\partial z_y} \right) = 0.$$

$\therefore$ The function $z(x, y)$ satisfies the equation

$$F_z - \frac{\partial}{\partial x} F_{z_x} - \frac{\partial}{\partial y} F_{z_y} = 0.$$

This equation is known as the **Euler-Ostrogradsky equation.**

In the above equation $\dfrac{\partial}{\partial x} F_{z_x}$ and $\dfrac{\partial}{\partial y} F_{z_y}$ are the total partial derivatives w.r.t. x and y respectively.

If $p = z_x$ and $q = z_y$, then

$$\frac{\partial}{\partial x} F_{z_x} = \frac{\partial}{\partial x} F_p = F_{px} + F_{pz} \frac{\partial z}{\partial x} + F_{pp} \frac{\partial p}{\partial x} + F_{pq} \frac{\partial q}{\partial x}$$

and

$$\frac{\partial}{\partial y} F_{z_y} = \frac{\partial}{\partial y} F_q = F_{qy} + F_{qz} \frac{\partial z}{\partial y} + F_{qp} \frac{\partial p}{\partial y} + F_{qq} \frac{\partial q}{\partial y}.$$

Putting the values of $\frac{\partial}{\partial x} F_{z_x}$ and $\frac{\partial}{\partial y} F_{z_y}$, the Euler-Ostrogradsky equation comes out to be a second order partial differential equation.

Example 1. *Find the Euler-Ostrogradsky equation for the functional* $J[z(x, y)] = \iint_D \left[\left(\frac{\partial z}{\partial x}\right)^2 + \left(\frac{\partial z}{\partial y}\right)^2\right] dxdy$, *where the value of z are prescribed on the boundary of the domain D.*

Sol. We have $J[z(x, y)] = \iint \left[\left(\frac{\partial z}{\partial x}\right)^2 + \left(\frac{\partial z}{\partial y}\right)^2\right] dx\, dy$ *i.e.,* $\iint (z_x{}^2 + z_y{}^2)\, dx\, dy.$

Let $F(x, y, z, z_x, z_y) = z_x{}^2 + z_y{}^2$

The **Euler-Ostrogradsky equation** is

$$F_z - \frac{\partial}{\partial x} F_{z_x} - \frac{\partial}{\partial y} F_{z_y} = 0 \qquad ...(1)$$

Here $F_z = 0$, $F_{z_x} = 2z_x$, $F_{z_y} = 2z_y$

$$\therefore \quad (1) \Rightarrow \quad 0 - \frac{\partial}{\partial x}(2z_x) - \frac{\partial}{\partial y}(2z_y) = 0$$

$$\Rightarrow \quad \frac{\partial}{\partial x} z_x + \frac{\partial}{\partial y} z_y = 0 \Rightarrow \frac{\partial^2 z}{\partial x^2} + \frac{\partial^2 z}{\partial y^2} = 0$$

This is the required equation.

11. VARIATIONAL PROBLEMS IN PARAMETRIC FORM

Theorem. Let $J[x(t), y(t)] = \int_{t_1}^{t_2} F(x(t), y(t), \dot{x}(t), \dot{y}(t))dt$ be a functional defined on the set of parametric functions $x = x(t)$, $y = y(t)$ which admits of continuous first order derivatives and satisfy the boundary conditions : $x(t_1) = x_1$, $y(t_1) = y_1$, $x(t_2) = x_2$, $y(t_2) = y_2$, where x_1, y_1, x_2, y_2 are prescribed at the fixed boundary points t_1 and t_2. Also F is a positive homogeneous function of first degree in $\dot{x}(t)$ and $\dot{y}(t)$ and F is differentiable three times with respect to all its arguments.

If the functional $J[x(t), y(t)]$ has an extremum on a parametric function $x = x(t)$, $y = y(t)$ then the functions $x(t)$ and $y(t)$ satisfy the Euler's equations

$$F_x - \frac{d}{dt} F_{\dot{x}} = 0 \text{ and } F_y - \frac{d}{dt} F_{\dot{y}} = 0 \text{ respectively.}$$

Note. We accept this theorem without proof.

Remarks 1. One of the Euler's equations $F_x - \frac{d}{dt} F_{\dot{x}} = 0$ and $F_y - \frac{d}{dt} F_{\dot{y}} = 0$ is a consequence of the other.

2. The Weierstrarsian form of Euler's equations is

$$\frac{1}{r} = \frac{F_{x\dot{y}} - F_{y\dot{x}}}{F_1(\dot{x}^2 + \dot{y}^2)^{3/2}},$$

where r is the radius of curvature of the extremal and F_1 is the common value of the ratios

$$\frac{F_{xx}}{y^2} = \frac{F_{yy}}{x^2} = \frac{F_{xy}}{-xy}.$$

Example 2. *Find the extremals of the functional* $\int_{t_1}^{t_2} ((\dot{x}^2 + \dot{y}^2)^{1/2} + a^2 (x\dot{y} - y\dot{x}))\, dt$.

Sol. Given functional is $\int_{t_1}^{t_2} ((\dot{x}^2 + \dot{y}^2)^{1/2} + a^2 (x\dot{y} - y\dot{x}))\, dt$

Let $$F(x, y, \dot{x}, \dot{y}) = (\dot{x}^2 + \dot{y}^2)^{1/2} + a^2 (x\dot{y} - y\dot{x})$$

$$\therefore \quad F(x, y, \lambda\dot{x}, \lambda\dot{y}) = ((\lambda\dot{x})^2 + (\lambda\dot{y})^2)^{1/2} + a^2 (x(\lambda\dot{y}) - y(\lambda\dot{x}))$$
$$= \lambda(\dot{x}^2 + \dot{y}^2)^{1/2} + \lambda a^2(x\dot{y} - y\dot{x}) \qquad (\because \lambda > 0)$$
$$= \lambda F(x, y, \dot{x}, \dot{y}).$$

$\therefore$ F is positive homogeneous function of degree one in $\dot{x}$ and $\dot{y}$.

Weirstrarsian form of Euler's equations is

$$\frac{1}{r} = \frac{F_{x\dot{y}} - F_{y\dot{x}}}{F_1 (\dot{x}^2 + \dot{y}^2)^{3/2}}. \qquad \text{...(1)}$$

Also, $$F_1 = \frac{F_{\dot{x}\dot{x}}}{\dot{y}^2} = \frac{F_{\dot{y}\dot{y}}}{\dot{x}^2} = \frac{F_{\dot{x}\dot{y}}}{-\dot{x}\dot{y}} \qquad \text{...(2)}$$

Now $$F_x = a^2\dot{y}, \quad F_y = -a^2\dot{x}, \quad F_{\dot{x}} = \frac{\dot{x}}{\sqrt{\dot{x}^2 + \dot{y}^2}} - a^2 y$$

$$\therefore \quad F_{x\dot{y}} = a^2, \quad F_{y\dot{x}} = -a^2,$$

$$F_{\dot{x}\dot{x}} = \frac{\sqrt{\dot{x}^2 + \dot{y}^2}\,.\,1 - \dot{x}\dfrac{\dot{x}}{\sqrt{\dot{x}^2 + \dot{y}^2}}}{\dot{x}^2 + \dot{y}^2} - 0 = \frac{1}{(\dot{x}^2 + \dot{y}^2)^{3/2}}(\dot{x}^2 + \dot{y}^2 - \dot{x}^2) = \frac{\dot{y}^2}{(\dot{x}^2 + \dot{y}^2)^{3/2}}$$

$$\therefore \ (2) \Rightarrow \quad F_1 = \frac{F_{\dot{x}\dot{x}}}{\dot{y}^2} = \frac{1}{\dot{y}^2}\cdot\frac{\dot{y}^2}{(\dot{x}^2 + \dot{y}^2)^{3/2}} = \frac{1}{(\dot{x}^2 + \dot{y}^2)^{3/2}}$$

$$\therefore \ (1) \Rightarrow \quad \frac{1}{r} = \frac{a^2 - (-a^2)}{\dfrac{1}{(\dot{x}^2 + \dot{y}^2)^{3/2}}\cdot(\dot{x}^2 + \dot{y}^2)^{3/2}} = 2a^2$$

$\therefore$ The curvature $(1/r)$ of the extremals is $2a^2$, a constant.

$\therefore$ Extremals are arcs of circles of fixed radius, r, given by $1/2a^2$.

Remark. Extremals are full circles if $x(t_1) = x(t_2)$, $y(t_1) = y(t_2)$.

Example 3. *Find the extremals of the functional* $\int_{t_1}^{t_2} y\sqrt{\dot{x}^2 + \dot{y}^2}\, dt$. (KU 2004 S)

Sol. Given functional is $\int_{t_1}^{t_2} y\sqrt{\dot{x}^2 + \dot{y}^2}\, dt$

Let $F(x, y, \dot{x}, \dot{y}) = y\sqrt{\dot{x}^2 + \dot{y}^2}$

F is a positive homogeneous function of degree one is $\dot{x}$ and $\dot{y}$

The **Euler's equations** are

$$F_x - \frac{d}{dt} F_{\dot{x}} = 0 \qquad ...(1) \qquad \text{and} \qquad F_y - \frac{d}{dt} F_{\dot{y}} = 0 \qquad ...(2)$$

We use (1) to find the extremals.

Here $F_x = 0,\quad F_{\dot{x}} = y \cdot \frac{2\dot{x}}{2\sqrt{\dot{x}^2 + \dot{y}^2}} = \frac{y\dot{x}}{\sqrt{\dot{x}^2 + \dot{y}^2}}$

$$\therefore\ (1) \Rightarrow \quad 0 - \frac{d}{dt}\left(\frac{y\dot{x}}{\sqrt{\dot{x}^2 + \dot{y}^2}}\right) = 0 \quad \Rightarrow \quad \frac{\dot{x}y}{\sqrt{\dot{x}^2 + \dot{y}^2}} = c_1 \qquad ...(3)$$

Case I. $c_1 = 0$

$$(3) \Rightarrow \quad \dot{x}y = 0 \ \Rightarrow\ \dot{x} = 0, y = 0 \Rightarrow\ x = c_2, y = 0.$$

Case II. $c_1 \neq 0$

$$(3) \Rightarrow \quad \frac{y}{\sqrt{1 + (\dot{y}/\dot{x})^2}} = c_1 \quad \Rightarrow \quad \frac{y}{\sqrt{1 + y'^2}} = c_1 \quad \Rightarrow \quad \frac{y^2}{c_1^2} = 1 + y'^2$$

$$\Rightarrow \quad y'^2 = \frac{y^2 - c_1^2}{c_1^2} \quad \Rightarrow \quad \frac{c_1 dy}{\sqrt{y^2 - c_1^2}} = dx \quad \Rightarrow \quad c_1 \cosh^{-1}\frac{y}{c_1} = x + c_3$$

$$\Rightarrow \quad \frac{y}{c_1} = \cosh\frac{x + c_3}{c_1} \quad \Rightarrow \quad y = c_1 \cosh\frac{x + c_3}{c_1}.$$

$\therefore$ The extremals are $\mathbf{x = c_2,\ y = 0}$ **and** $\mathbf{y = c_1 \cosh\frac{x + c_3}{c_1}}$.

Remarks. $(2) \Rightarrow \quad \sqrt{\dot{x}^2 + \dot{y}^2} - \frac{d}{dt}\left(\frac{y\dot{y}}{\sqrt{\dot{x}^2 + \dot{y}^2}}\right) = 0 \quad \Rightarrow \quad \frac{d}{dt}\left(\frac{y\dot{y}}{\sqrt{\dot{x}^2 + \dot{y}^2}}\right) = \sqrt{\dot{x}^2 + \dot{y}^2}$

$$\Rightarrow \quad \frac{1}{\sqrt{\dot{x}^2 + \dot{y}^2}} \frac{d}{dt}\left(\frac{y\dot{y}}{\sqrt{\dot{x}^2 + \dot{y}^2}}\right) = 1 \quad \Rightarrow \quad 2\left(\frac{y\dot{y}}{\sqrt{\dot{x}^2 + \dot{y}^2}}\right)\frac{d}{dt}\left(\frac{y\dot{y}}{\sqrt{\dot{x}^2 + \dot{y}^2}}\right) = (2y)\,\dot{y}$$

$$\Rightarrow \quad \frac{d}{dt}\left(\frac{(y\dot{y})^2}{\dot{x}^2 + \dot{y}^2}\right) = \frac{d}{dt}(y^2) \quad \Rightarrow \quad \frac{y^2\dot{y}^2}{\dot{x}^2 + \dot{y}^2} = y^2 + \lambda \quad \Rightarrow \quad \frac{y^2\dot{y}^2}{\dot{x}^2 + \dot{y}^2} - y^2 = \lambda$$

$$\Rightarrow \quad \frac{\dot{x}^2 y^2}{\dot{x}^2 + \dot{y}^2} = \lambda \quad \Rightarrow \quad \frac{\dot{x}y}{\sqrt{\dot{x}^2 + \dot{y}^2}} = \sqrt{\lambda} \quad \Rightarrow \quad \frac{\dot{x}y}{\sqrt{\dot{x}^2 + \dot{y}^2}} = c_1, \quad \text{where } c_1 = \sqrt{\lambda}.$$

This is same as (3).

$\therefore$ Equations (2) and (1) give the same solution.

12. FUNCTIONALS DEPENDENT ON MORE THAN ONE FUNCTION

Theorem. Let $J[y_1(x), y_2(x), \ldots\ldots, y_n(x)] = \int_{x_1}^{x_2} F(x, y_1(x), y_2(x), \ldots\ldots y_n(x), y_1'(x),$ $y_2'(x), \ldots\ldots, y_n'(x))dx$ be a functional defined on the set of n functions $y_1(x), y_2(x), \ldots\ldots,$ $y_n(x)$ which admits of continuous first order derivative and satisfy the boundary conditions :

$$y_1(x_1) = Y_1, \quad y_2(x_1) = Y_2, \quad \ldots\ldots ; y_n(x_1) = Y_n,$$
$$y_1(x_2) = Z_1, \quad y_2(x_2) = Z_2, \ldots\ldots y_n(x_2) = Z_n,$$

where $Y_1, Y_2, \ldots\ldots, Y_n, Z_1, Z_2 \ldots\ldots, Z_n$ are prescribed at the fixed boundary points x_1 and x_2. Also, F is differentiable three times with respect to all its arguments.

If the functional $J[y_1(x), y_2(x), \ldots\ldots, y_n(x)]$ has an extremum on functions $y_1(x)$, $y_2(x), \ldots\ldots y_n(x)$, then $y_1(x), y_2(x), \ldots\ldots, y_n(x)$ satisfy the Euler's equations :

$$F_{y_1} - \frac{d}{dx} F_{y_1'} = 0, \quad F_{y_2} - \frac{d}{dx} F_{y_2'} = 0, \ldots\ldots, F_{y_n} - \frac{d}{dx} F_{y_n'} = 0.$$

Note. Proof of this theorem is beyond the scope of this book.

Example 4. *Show that the functional* $\int_0^1 \left(2x + \left(\frac{dx}{dt}\right)^2 + \left(\frac{dy}{dt}\right)^2 \right) dt$ such that $x(0) = 1$, $y(0) = 1$, $x(1) = 1.5$, $y(1) = 1$ *is stationary for* $x = \frac{2+t^2}{2}, y = 1.$ (CDLU 2004)

Sol. Given functional is $\int_0^1 \left(2x + \left(\frac{dx}{dt}\right)^2 + \left(\frac{dy}{dt}\right)^2 \right) dt$ *i.e.,* $\int_0^1 (2x + x'^2 + y'^2)\, dt$

Let $F(t, x, y, x', y') = 2x + x'^2 + y'^2$

The **Euler's equations** are

$$F_x - \frac{d}{dt} F_{x'} = 0 \qquad \ldots(1)$$

and

$$F_y - \frac{d}{dt} F_{y'} = 0 \qquad \ldots(2)$$

Here $F_x = 2, \quad F_y = 0, \quad F_{x'} = 2x', \quad F_{y'} = 2y'$

$$\therefore \quad (1) \Rightarrow \quad 2 - \frac{d}{dt}(2x') = 0 \Rightarrow \frac{d^2x}{dt^2} = 1 \Rightarrow \frac{dx}{dt} = t + c_1$$

$$\Rightarrow \quad x = \frac{t^2}{2} + c_1 t + c_2 \qquad \ldots(3)$$

$$(2) \Rightarrow \quad 0 - \frac{d}{dt}(2y') = 0 \Rightarrow \frac{dy'}{dt} = 0 \Rightarrow y' = c_3$$

$$\Rightarrow \quad y = c_3 t + c_4 \qquad \ldots(4)$$

$\therefore$ (3) and (4) are the equations of the extremals.

The boundary conditions are $x(0) = 1, \quad y(0) = 1, \quad x(1) = 1.5, \quad y(1) = 1$

$$x(0) = 1 \Rightarrow 0 + c_1(0) + c_2 = 1 \Rightarrow c_2 = 1$$

$$y(0) = 1 \Rightarrow c_3(0) + c_4 = 1 \Rightarrow c_4 = 1$$

$$x(1) = 1.5 \Rightarrow \frac{1}{2} + c_1(1) + c_2 = 1.5 \Rightarrow \frac{1}{2} + c_1 + 1 = 1.5 \Rightarrow c_1 = 0$$

$$y(1) = 1 \Rightarrow c_3(1) + c_4 = 1 \Rightarrow c_3 + 1 = 1 \Rightarrow c_3 = 0$$

$$\therefore \quad c_1 = 0, \quad c_2 = 1, \quad c_3 = 0, \quad c_4 = 1$$

$$\therefore \quad (3) \Rightarrow \quad x = \frac{t^2}{2} + 0.t + 1 \quad i.e., \quad x = \frac{2+t^2}{2}$$

$$(4) \Rightarrow \quad y = 0.t + 1 \quad i.e., \quad y = 1$$

$\therefore$ The stationary functions are $\mathbf{x = \frac{2+t^2}{2}, y = 1.}$

Remark. Since, the function $2x + x'^2 + y'^2$ is not a homogeneous functions of x' and y', we have treated the given functional as dependent on two functions.

Example 5. *Find the extremals of the functional* $J[y(x), z(x)] = \int_0^{\pi} (2yz - 2y^2 + y'^2 - z'^2)\, dx$
Also find that extremal which satisfy the boundary conditions :

$$y(0) = 0, \quad y(\pi) = 1, \quad z(0) = 0, \quad z(\pi) = 1.$$

Sol. We have $\quad J[y(x), z(x)] = \int_{x_1}^{x_2} (2yz - 2y^2 + y'^2 - z'^2)\, dx$

Let $\quad F(x, y, z, y', z') = 2yz - 2y^2 + y'^2 - z'^2$

The **Euler's equations** are

$$F_y - \frac{d}{dx} F_{y'} = 0 \qquad ...(1)$$

and

$$F_z - \frac{d}{dx} F_{z'} = 0 \qquad ...(2)$$

Here $\quad F_y = 2z - 4y,\ F_z = 2y,\ F_{y'} = 2y',\ F_{z'} = -2z'$

$$\therefore\ (1) \Rightarrow \quad 2z - 4y - \frac{d}{dx}(2y') = 0 \Rightarrow \frac{d^2y}{dx^2} + 2y - z = 0 \qquad ...(3)$$

$$(2) \Rightarrow \quad 2y - \frac{d}{dx}(-2z') = 0 \Rightarrow \frac{d^2z}{dx^2} + y = 0 \qquad ...(4)$$

$$(3) \Rightarrow \quad (D^2 + 2)y - z = 0 \qquad ...(5)$$

$$(4) \Rightarrow \quad y + D^2 z = 0 \qquad ...(6)$$

Operating (5) by D^2 and adding to (6), we get

$$D^2(D^2 + 2)y + y = 0$$

$$\Rightarrow \quad (D^4 + 2D^2 + 1)y = 0 \Rightarrow (D^2 + 1)^2 y = 0$$

The A.E. is $\quad (D^2 + 1)^2 = 0 \quad \therefore \quad D = \pm i, \ \pm i$

$$\therefore \quad y = e^{0x}((c_1 + c_2 x) \cos 1.x + (c_3 + c_4 x) \sin 1.x)$$

i.e.,

$$y = (c_1 + c_2 x) \cos x + (c_3 + c_4 x) \sin x \qquad ...(7)$$

$$(3) \Rightarrow \quad z = \frac{d^2y}{dx^2} + 2y \qquad ...(8)$$

$$(7) \Rightarrow \quad \frac{dy}{dx} = c_2 \cos x - (c_1 + c_2 x) \sin x + c_4 \sin x + (c_3 + c_4 x) \cos x$$

$$= (c_2 + c_3 + c_4 x) \cos x + (c_4 - c_1 - c_2 x) \sin x$$

$$\therefore \quad \frac{d^2y}{dx^2} = c_4 \cos x - (c_2 + c_3 + c_4 x) \sin x - c_2 \sin x + (c_4 - c_1 - c_2 x) \cos x$$

$$= (2c_4 - c_1 - c_2 x) \cos x - (2c_2 + c_3 + c_4 x) \sin x$$

$$\therefore\ (8) \Rightarrow \quad z = (2c_4 - c_1 - c_2 x) \cos x - (2c_2 + c_3 + c_4 x) \sin x + 2(c_1 + c_2 x) \cos x + 2(c_3 + c_4 x) \sin x$$

$$= (2c_4 + c_1 + c_2 x) \cos x + (c_3 - 2c_2 + c_4 x) \sin x$$

$\therefore$ The family of extremals is

$$\mathbf{y = (c_1 + c_2 x) \cos x + (c_3 + c_4 x) \sin x,}$$

$$\mathbf{z = (2c_4 + c_1 + c_2 x) \cos x + (c_3 - 2c_2 + c_4 x) \sin x,}$$

where $\mathbf{c_1, c_2, c_3, c_4}$ are arbitrary constants.

The boundary conditions are :

$$y(0) = 0, \quad y(\pi) = 1, \quad z(0) = 0, \quad z(\pi) = 1$$

$$y(0) = 0 \quad \Rightarrow (c_1 + c_2.0) \cos 0 + (c_3 + c_4.0) \sin 0 = 0 \quad \Rightarrow c_1 = 0$$

$$y(\pi) = 1 \quad \Rightarrow (c_1 + \pi c_2) \cos \pi + (c_3 + \pi c_4) \sin \pi = 1$$

$$\Rightarrow (0 + \pi c_2)(-1) = 1 \quad \Rightarrow \quad c_2 = -1/\pi.$$

$$z(0) = 0 \quad \Rightarrow (2c_4 + c_1 + c_2.0) \cos 0 + (c_3 - 2c_2 + c_4 . 0) \sin 0 = 0$$

$$\Rightarrow (2c_4 + 0 + 0) . 1 + \left(c_3 + \frac{2}{\pi} + 0\right) . 0 = 0 \quad \Rightarrow \quad c_4 = 0$$

$$z(\pi) = 1 \quad \Rightarrow (2(0) + 0 + \pi(-1/\pi)) \cos \pi \ + (c_3 - 2(-1/\pi) + 0. \pi) \sin \pi = 1$$

$$\Rightarrow (-1)(-1) = 1, \text{ which is true.}$$

$$\therefore \quad c_1 = 0, \quad c_2 = -1/\pi \quad c_4 = 0$$

$$\therefore \quad y = \left(0 - \frac{x}{\pi}\right) \cos x + (c_3 + 0.x) \sin x = c_3 \sin x - \frac{x}{\pi} \cos x$$

$$z = \left(2(0) + 0 - \frac{x}{\pi}\right) \cos x + \left(c_3 - 2\left(-\frac{1}{\pi}\right) + 0.x\right) \sin x$$

$$= c_3 \sin x + \frac{1}{\pi} (2 \sin x - x \cos x)$$

$\therefore$ The required extremals are $\mathbf{y = c_3 \sin x - \frac{x}{\pi} \cos x}$

$$\mathbf{z = c_3 \sin x + \frac{1}{\pi} (2 \sin x - x \cos x),}$$

where c_3 is any arbitrary constant.

Example 6. *Find the extremal of the functional* $\int_0^1 \sqrt{1 + y'^2 + z'^2}\, dx$ *that satisfy the boundary conditions* $y(0) = 0, y(1) = 2, z(0) = 0, z(1) = 4$.

Sol. Given functional is $\int_0^1 \sqrt{1 + y'^2 + z'^2}\, dx$.

Let $\quad F(x, y, z, y', z') = \sqrt{1 + y'^2 + z'^2}$

The **Euler's equations** are $F_y - \frac{d}{dx} F_{y'} = 0$ ...(1)

and $$F_z - \frac{d}{dx} F_{z'} = 0 \quad ...(2)$$

Here $F_y = 0, F_z = 0, F_{y'} = \frac{y'}{\sqrt{1 + y'^2 + z'^2}}, F_{z'} = \frac{z'}{\sqrt{1 + y'^2 + z'^2}}$

$$\therefore \ (1) \quad \Rightarrow \quad 0 - \frac{d}{dx}\left(\frac{y'}{\sqrt{1 + y'^2 + z'^2}}\right) = 0$$

$$\Rightarrow \quad \frac{y'}{\sqrt{1 + y'^2 + z'^2}} = c_1 \quad ...(3)$$

$$(2) \quad \Rightarrow \quad 0 - \frac{d}{dx}\left(\frac{z'}{\sqrt{1+y'^2+z'^2}}\right) = 0$$

$$\Rightarrow \quad \frac{z'}{\sqrt{1+y'^2+z'^2}} = c_2 \qquad \ldots(4)$$

Dividing (3) by (4), we get $\frac{y'}{z'} = \frac{c_1}{c_2}, = c_3$ say

$$\therefore \quad y' = c_3 z'$$

Putting the value of y' in (4), we get $\frac{z'}{\sqrt{1+(1+c_3^2)\,z'^2}} = c_2$

$$\Rightarrow \quad z'^2 = c_2^2(1+(1+c_3^2)\,z'^2) \Rightarrow z' = \frac{c_2}{\sqrt{1-c_2^2-c_2^2\,c_3^2}} = c_4, \text{ say}$$

$$\Rightarrow \quad z = c_4 x + c_5 \qquad \ldots(5)$$

$$\therefore \quad y' = c_3 z' \Rightarrow y' = c_3 c_4 = c_6, \text{ say}$$

$$\Rightarrow \quad y = c_6 x + c_7 \qquad \ldots(6)$$

∴ The extremals are given by (5) and (6).

The boundary conditions are

$$y(0) = 0, \quad y(1) = 2, \quad z(0) = 0, \quad z(1) = 4$$

$$\therefore \quad c_6(0) + c_7 = 0, \quad c_6(1) + c_7 = 2, c_4(0) + c_5 = 0, \quad c_4(1) + c_5 = 4$$

Solving these equations, we get

$$c_6 = 2, c_7 = 0, c_4 = 4, c_5 = 0$$

$$(6) \Rightarrow y = 2.x + 0 \Rightarrow y = 2x$$

$$(5) \Rightarrow y = 4.x + 0 \Rightarrow z = 4x$$

∴ The required extremals are **y = 2x**, **z = 4x.**

EXERCISE 3

1. Find the Euler-Ostrogradsky equation for the functional $J[z(x, y)] = \iint_D \left[\left(\frac{\partial z}{\partial x}\right)^2 - \left(\frac{\partial z}{\partial y}\right)^2\right] dx\,dy$, where the values of z are prescribed on the boundary of the domain D.

2. Find the Euler-Ostrogradsky equation for the functional $J[z(x, y)] = \iint_D \left[\left(\frac{\partial z}{\partial x}\right)^4 + \left(\frac{\partial z}{\partial y}\right)^4 + 12z\,f(x, y)\right] dx\,dy$, where the values of z are prescribed on the boundary of the domain D.

3. Find the extremals of the functional $\int_{t_1}^{t_2} \sqrt{\dot{x}^2 + \dot{y}^2}\, dt$. *(MDU 2004, 2005)*

4. Find the stationary function of the functional $\int_{(-1, 0)}^{(1, 0)} (k\sqrt{\dot{x}^2 + \dot{y}^2} - xy)\, dt,\; k > 0$.

5. Find the extremal of the functional $\int_0^1 (y'^2 + z'^2)\, dx$ that satisfy the boundary conditions $y(0) = 0$, $z(0) = 0$, $y(1) = 1$, $z(1) = 2$.

6. Find the extremal of the functional $\int_0^1 (y'^2 + z'^2 + 4z)\, dx$ that satisfy the boundary conditions $y(0) = 0$, $y(1) = 1$, $z(0) = 0$, $z(1) = 0$.

7. Find the extremal of the functional $\int_0^{\pi/2} (y'^2 + z'^2 + 2yz)\, dx$ that satisfy the boundary conditions $y(0) = 0$, $y(\pi/2) = -1$, $z(0) = 0$, $z(\pi/2) = 1$.

Answers

1. $\dfrac{\partial^2 z}{\partial x^2} - \dfrac{\partial^2 z}{\partial y^2} = 0$

2. $\left(\dfrac{\partial z}{\partial x}\right)^2 \dfrac{\partial^2 z}{\partial x^2} + \left(\dfrac{\partial z}{\partial y}\right)^2 \dfrac{\partial^2 z}{\partial y^2} = f(x, y)$

3. $y = c_1 x + c_2$, $x = c_3$

4. Arc of circle joining $(-1, 0)$ to $(1, 0)$ and of radius k.

5. $y = x$, $z = 2x$

6. $y = x$, $z = x^2 - x$

7. $y = -\sin x$, $z = \sin x$.

13. INVARIANCE OF EULER'S EQUATION UNDER COORDINATES TRANSFORMATION

Let $J[y(x)] = \int_{x_1}^{x_2} F(x, y, y')\, dx$ be a functional to be extremised.

Let u and v be two variables defined by $x = x(u, v)$, $y = y(u, v)$ and $\begin{vmatrix} x_u & x_v \\ y_u & y_v \end{vmatrix} \neq 0$. Then the curve given by the equation $y = y(x)$ in the xy-plane corresponds to the curve given by the equation $v = v(u)$ in the uv-plane.

When we change the variables x and y, the functional

$$J[y(x)] = \int_{x_1}^{x_2} F(x, y, y')\, dx$$

changes into the functional

$$J_1[v(u)] = \int_{u_1}^{u_2} F\left(x(u, v), y(u, v), \frac{y_u + y_v v'}{x_u + x_v v'}\right)(x_u + x_v v')\, du$$

$$\left(\because \frac{dy}{dx} = \frac{dy/du}{dx/du} = \frac{y_u + y_v v'}{x_u + x_v v'}\right)$$

$$= \int_{u_1}^{u_2} G(u, v, v')\, du, \quad \text{(say)}$$

If $y = y(x)$ satisfies the Euler's equation $F_y - \dfrac{d}{dx} F_{y'} = 0$ corresponding to the original functional $J[y(x)]$ then it can be proved that the function $v = v(u)$ satisfies the Euler's equation $G_v - \dfrac{d}{du} G_{v'} = 0$ corresponding to the new functional $J_1[v(u)]$. In other words, $v(u)$ is an extremal of $J_1[v(u)]$ if $y(x)$ is an extremal of $J[y(x)]$. Thus, whether or not a curve is an extremal is a property which is independent of the choice of the coordinate system.

$\therefore$ The extremals of the functional $J[y(x)]$ can be found by solving Euler's equation of the transformed functional $J_1[v(u)]$. This is called the **principle of invariance of Euler's equation under coordinates transformations.**

In solving practical problems, the change of variables is made directly in the integral representing the functional. We then write and solve the Euler's equation for the new integral involving new variables. In the extremals so obtained, the new variables are changed to the original variables to get the desired extremals.

Example 1. *Find the extremals of the functional* $\int_{\theta_1}^{\theta_2} \sqrt{r^2 + r'^2}\, d\theta$, *where* $r = r(\theta)$.

(KU 2004, 2006)

Sol. Let $$J[r(\theta)] = \int_{\theta_1}^{\theta_2} \sqrt{r^2 + r'^2}\, d\theta.$$

Let $$x = r\cos\theta,\quad y = r\sin\theta.$$

$\therefore$ $$r = \sqrt{x^2 + y^2},\quad \theta = \tan^{-1}\frac{y}{x}$$

$$r' = \frac{dr}{d\theta} = \frac{dr/dx}{d\theta/dx} = \frac{r_x + r_y y'}{\theta_x + \theta_y y'} = \frac{\dfrac{x}{\sqrt{x^2+y^2}} + \dfrac{y}{\sqrt{x^2+y^2}}\, y'}{\dfrac{1}{1+\dfrac{y^2}{x^2}}\left(-\dfrac{y}{x^2}\right) + \dfrac{1}{1+\dfrac{y^2}{x^2}}\left(\dfrac{1}{x}\right) y'}$$

$$= \frac{\dfrac{x + yy'}{\sqrt{x^2+y^2}}}{\dfrac{xy' - y}{x^2 + y^2}} = \frac{\sqrt{x^2+y^2}\,(x + yy')}{xy' - y}$$

Also, $$d\theta = \frac{d\theta}{dx}\cdot dx = (\theta_x + \theta_y y')dx = \frac{xy' - y}{x^2 + y^2}\, dx$$

$\therefore$ $$r^2 + r'^2 = x^2 + y^2 + \frac{(x^2+y^2)(x + yy')^2}{(xy' - y)^2}$$

$$= (x^2 + y^2)\left[\frac{(xy' - y)^2 + (x + yy')^2}{(xy' - y)^2}\right] = \frac{(x^2 + y)^2(1 + y'^2)(x^2 + y^2)}{(xy' - y)^2}$$

$\therefore$ $$\sqrt{r^2 + r'^2} = \frac{(x^2 + y^2)\sqrt{1 + y'^2}}{xy' - y}$$

$\therefore$ $$\int \sqrt{r^2 + r'^2}\, d\theta = \int \frac{(x^2+y^2)\sqrt{1+y'^2}}{xy' - y}\cdot\frac{xy' - y}{x^2 + y^2}\, dx = \int \sqrt{1 + y'^2}\, dx$$

Let $\theta = \theta_1 \Rightarrow x = x_1$ and $\theta = \theta_2 \Rightarrow x = x_2$.

Let the transformed functional be denoted by $J_1[y(x)]$

$\therefore$ $$J_1[y(x)] = \int_{x_1}^{x_2} \sqrt{1 + y'^2}\, dx \qquad \ldots(1)$$

Let $\quad G(x, y, y') = \sqrt{1 + y'^2}$

The **Euler's equation** for (1) is $\quad G_y - \dfrac{d}{dx} G_{y'} = 0 \qquad \text{...(2)}$

Here $\quad G_y = 0, \quad G_{y'} = \dfrac{y'}{\sqrt{1 + y'^2}}$

$$\therefore \quad (1) \Rightarrow \quad 0 - \frac{d}{dx}\left(\frac{y'}{\sqrt{1 + y'^2}}\right) = 0$$

$$\Rightarrow \quad \frac{y'}{\sqrt{1 + y'^2}} = k \Rightarrow y'^2 = k^2(1 + y'^2) \Rightarrow y' = \frac{k}{\sqrt{1 - k^2}} = c_1, \text{ say}$$

$$\Rightarrow \quad y = c_1 x + c_2$$

$\therefore$ The extremals of the given functional are $\mathbf{r \sin \theta = c_1 r \cos \theta + c_2}$.

Alternative method

We have $\quad x = r \cos \theta, \quad y = r \sin \theta.$

$$\therefore \quad \frac{dx}{d\theta} = -r \sin \theta + r' \cos \theta, \quad \frac{dy}{d\theta} = r \cos \theta + r' \sin \theta, \quad \text{where} \quad r' = \frac{dr}{d\theta}$$

$$\therefore \quad \left(\frac{dx}{d\theta}\right)^2 + \left(\frac{dy}{d\theta}\right)^2 = (-r \sin \theta + r' \cos \theta)^2 + (r \cos \theta + r' \sin \theta)^2 = r^2 + r'^2$$

$$\therefore \quad \int \sqrt{r^2 + r'^2}\, d\theta = \int \sqrt{\left(\frac{dx}{d\theta}\right)^2 + \left(\frac{dy}{d\theta}\right)^2}\, d\theta = \int \sqrt{(dx)^2 + (dy)^2}$$

$$= \int \sqrt{1 + \left(\frac{dy}{dx}\right)^2}\, dx = \int \sqrt{1 + y'^2}\, dx.$$

Remark. The Euler's equation of $J[r(\theta)]$ is

$$\frac{r}{\sqrt{r^2 + r'^2}} - \frac{d}{d\theta}\left(\frac{r'}{\sqrt{r^2 + r'^2}}\right) = 0,$$

which is difficult to solve.

EXERCISE 4

1. Find the extremals of the functional $J[y(x)] = \displaystyle\int_0^{\log 2} (e^{-x} y'^2 - e^x y^2)\, dx$ by using the transformations : $x = \log u, \quad y = v.$

2. Find the extremals of the functional $\displaystyle\int_{\theta_1}^{\theta_2} r \sin \theta \sqrt{r^2 + r'^2}\, d\theta$ by using the transformations : $x = r \cos \theta, \quad y = r \sin \theta.$

Answers

1. $y = c_1 \cos e^x + c_2 \sin e^x$
2. $c_1 \log (r \sin \theta + \sqrt{r^2 \sin^2 \theta - c_1^2}) = r \cos \theta + c_2.$

Hints

1. Use : $y' = \frac{dy}{dx} = \frac{dy}{dv}\frac{dv}{du}\frac{du}{dx} = 1 . \frac{dv}{du} . e^x = u \frac{dv}{du}$.

14. CONDITIONAL EXTREMUM

Theorem. If a curve $y = y(x)$ extremises the functional $\int_{x_1}^{x_2} F(x, y, y')\, dx$ subject to boundary conditions : $y(x_1) = y_1$, $y(x_2) = y_2$ and one more condition $\int_{x_1}^{x_2} G(x, y, y')\, dx = L$ and if $y = y(x)$ is not an extremal of the functional $\int_{x_1}^{x_2} G(x, y, y')\, dx$, then there exists a constant λ such that the curve $y = y(x)$ satisfy the Euler's equation $F_y - \frac{d}{dx} F_{y'} + \lambda\left(G_y - \frac{d}{dx} G_{y'}\right) = 0.$

Note. The proof of this theorem is beyond the scope of this book.

Example 1. *Find the extremal of the functional* $\int_0^1 y'^2\, dx$, $y(0) = 1, y(1) = 6$ subject to the condition $\int_0^1 y dx = 3$.

Sol. Given functional is $\int_0^1 y'^2\, dx$.

Given condition is $\int_0^1 y dx = 3$ ...(1)

Let $F(x, y, y') = y'^2$ and $G(x, y, y') = y$

The **Euler's equation** is $F_y - \frac{d}{dx} F_{y'} + \lambda\left(G_y - \frac{d}{dx} G_{y'}\right) = 0$ ...(2)

Here $F_y = 0$, $F_{y'} = 2y'$, $G_y = 1$, $G_{y'} = 0$

$\therefore$ (2) $\Rightarrow$ $0 - \frac{d}{dx}(2y') + \lambda\left(1 - \frac{d}{dx}(0)\right) = 0$

$\Rightarrow$ $-2\frac{d^2y}{dx^2} + \lambda = 0 \Rightarrow \frac{d^2y}{dx^2} = \frac{\lambda}{2}$

$\Rightarrow$ $\frac{dy}{dx} = \frac{\lambda x}{2} + c_1 \Rightarrow y = \frac{\lambda x^2}{4} + c_1 x + c_2$ ...(3)

The boundary conditions are $y(0) = 1$, $y(1) = 6$

$y(0) = 1 \Rightarrow 0 + c_1(0) + c_2 = 1 \Rightarrow c_2 = 1$

$$y(1) = 6 \Rightarrow \frac{\lambda}{4} + c_1 + c_2 = 6 \Rightarrow \frac{\lambda}{4} + c_1 + 1 = 6 \Rightarrow c_1 = 5 - \frac{\lambda}{4}$$

$$\therefore \quad (3) \Rightarrow \quad y = \frac{\lambda x^2}{4} + \left(5 - \frac{\lambda}{4}\right)x + 1 \qquad \text{...(4)}$$

Putting the value of y in (1), we get

$$\int_0^1 \left(\frac{\lambda x^2}{4} + \left(5 - \frac{\lambda}{4}\right)x + 1\right) dx = 3$$

$$\Rightarrow \quad \left(\frac{\lambda x^3}{12} + \left(5 - \frac{\lambda}{4}\right)\frac{x^2}{2} + x\right)\Bigg|_0^1 = 3$$

$$\Rightarrow \quad \frac{\lambda}{12}(1-0) + \left(\frac{5}{2} - \frac{\lambda}{8}\right)(1-0) + (1-0) = 3$$

$$\Rightarrow \quad \frac{\lambda}{12} + \frac{5}{2} - \frac{\lambda}{8} + 1 = 3 \Rightarrow \lambda = 12$$

$$\therefore \quad (4) \Rightarrow \quad y = \frac{12x^2}{4} + \left(5 - \frac{12}{4}\right)x + 1 \quad i.e., \quad \mathbf{y = 3x^2 + 2x + 1.}$$

This is the equation of the required extremal.

Example 2. *Find the extremal of the functional* $\int_0^{\pi} (y'^2 - y^2)dx$ *under the boundary conditions* $y(0) = 0, y(\pi) = 1$ *and subject to an additional condition* $\int_0^{\pi} y dx = 1$.

Sol. Given functional is $\int_0^{\pi} (y'^2 - y^2)\, dx$.

Given condition is $\int_0^{\pi} y dx = 1$ ...(1)

Let $F(x, y, y') = y'^2 - y^2$ and $G(x, y, y') = y$

The **Euler's equation** is

$$F_y - \frac{d}{dx}F_{y'} + \lambda\left(G_y - \frac{d}{dx}G_{y'}\right) = 0 \qquad \text{...(2)}$$

Here $F_y = -2y$, $F_{y'} = 2y'$, $G_y = 1$, $G_{y'} = 0$

$$\therefore \quad (2) \Rightarrow \quad -2y - \frac{d}{dx}(2y') + \lambda\left(1 - \frac{d}{dx}(0)\right) = 0$$

$$\Rightarrow \quad -2y - 2\frac{d^2y}{dx^2} + \lambda = 0 \Rightarrow \frac{d^2y}{dx^2} + y = \frac{\lambda}{2}$$

The A.E. is $D^2 + 1 = 0$. $\therefore$ $D = \pm i$

$$\therefore \quad \text{C.F.} = e^{0x}(c_1 \cos 1.x + c_2 \sin 1.x) = c_1 \cos x + c_2 \sin x$$

$$\text{P.I.} = \frac{1}{D^2+1}\left(\frac{\lambda}{2}\right) = (1+D^2)^{-1}\left(\frac{\lambda}{2}\right)$$

$$= (1 - D^2 + \ldots\ldots)\left(\frac{\lambda}{2}\right) = \frac{\lambda}{2} - 0 + \ldots\ldots = \frac{\lambda}{2}$$

$$\Rightarrow \qquad y = c_1 \cos x + c_2 \sin x + \frac{\lambda}{2} \qquad \text{...(3)}$$

The boundary conditions are $y(0) = 0$, $y(\pi) = 1$.

$$y(0) = 0 \;\Rightarrow\; c_1(1) + c_2(0) + \frac{\lambda}{2} = 0 \;\Rightarrow\; c_1 + \frac{\lambda}{2} = 0 \qquad \text{...(4)}$$

$$y(\pi) = 1 \;\Rightarrow\; c_1(-1) + c_2(0) + \frac{\lambda}{2} = 1 \;\Rightarrow\; -c_1 + \frac{\lambda}{2} = 1 \qquad \text{...(5)}$$

Solving (4) and (5), we get $c_1 = -\frac{1}{2}, \lambda = 1$

$$\therefore \quad (3) \Rightarrow \qquad y = -\frac{1}{2}\cos x + c_2 \sin x + \frac{1}{2} \qquad \text{...(6)}$$

Putting the value of y in (1), we get

$$\int_0^\pi \left(-\frac{1}{2}\cos x + c_2 \sin x + \frac{1}{2}\right) dx = 1$$

$$\Rightarrow \qquad \left(-\frac{1}{2}\sin x - c_2 \cos x + \frac{x}{2}\right)\Bigg|_0^\pi = 1$$

$$\Rightarrow \qquad \left(-\frac{1}{2}(0) - c_2(-1) + \frac{\pi}{2}\right) - \left(-\frac{1}{2}(0) - c_2(1) + 0\right) = 1$$

$$\Rightarrow \qquad 0 + c_2 + \frac{\pi}{2} + c_2 = 1 \;\Rightarrow\; c_2 = \frac{2-\pi}{4}$$

$$\therefore \quad (6) \Rightarrow \qquad \mathbf{y = -\frac{1}{2}\cos x + \frac{2-\pi}{4}\sin x + \frac{1}{2}}.$$

This is equation of the required extremal.

Example 3. *Find the extremal of the functional* $\int_0^1 (x^2 + y'^2)\, dx$, $y(0) = 0, y(1) = 0$ *subject to the condition* $\int_0^1 y^2\, dx = 2$.

Sol. Given functional is $\int_0^1 (x^2 + y'^2)\, dx$.

Given condition is $\int_0^1 y^2 dx = 2$ ...(1)

Let $\qquad F(x, y, y') = x^2 + y'^2$ and $G(x, y, y') = y^2$

The **Euler's equation** is

$$F_y - \frac{d}{dx} F_{y'} + \lambda\left(G_y - \frac{d}{dx} G_{y'}\right) = 0 \qquad \text{...(2)}$$

Here $\qquad F_y = 0, \; F_{y'} = 2y', G_y = 2y, G_{y'} = 0$

$$\therefore \quad (2) \Rightarrow \qquad 0 - \frac{d}{dx}(2y') + \lambda\left(2y - \frac{d}{dx}(0)\right) = 0$$

$$\Rightarrow \qquad -2\frac{d^2y}{dx^2} + 2\lambda y = 0 \Rightarrow \frac{d^2y}{dx^2} - \lambda y = 0 \qquad ...(3)$$

The A.E. is $\qquad D^2 - \lambda = 0 \qquad ...(4)$

Case I. $\lambda > 0$ (4) $\Rightarrow$ $D = \pm\sqrt{\lambda}$

$$\therefore \quad (3) \Rightarrow \quad y = c_1 e^{\sqrt{\lambda}x} + c_2 e^{-\sqrt{\lambda}x} \qquad ...(5)$$

The boundary condition are $y(0) = 0, y(1) = 0$.

$$y(0) = 0 \Rightarrow c_1e^0 + c_2e^0 = 0 \Rightarrow c_1 + c_2 = 0 \qquad ...(6)$$

$$y(1) = 0 \Rightarrow c_1e^{\sqrt{\lambda}} + c_2 e^{-\sqrt{\lambda}} = 0 \qquad ...(7)$$

Solving (6) and (7), we get $c_1 = 0, c_2 = 0$.

$$\therefore \qquad y = 0.e^{\sqrt{\lambda}x} + 0.e^{-\sqrt{\lambda}x} \quad i.e., \quad y = 0$$

Now $\qquad \int_0^1 y^2 dx = \int_0^1 0.dx = 0 \neq 2$

$\therefore$ Given condition is not satisfied.

$\therefore$ $\lambda > 0$ is impossible.

Case II. $\lambda = 0$ (3) $\Rightarrow \frac{d^2y}{dx^2} = 0 \Rightarrow \frac{dy}{dx} = c_1 \Rightarrow y = c_1x + c_2$

$$y(0) = 0 \Rightarrow c_1(0) + c_2 = 0 \Rightarrow c_2 = 0$$

$$y(1) = 0 \Rightarrow c_1(1) + c_2 = 0 \Rightarrow c_1 + 0 = 0 \Rightarrow c_1 = 0$$

$$\therefore \qquad y = 0.x + 0 \quad i.e., \quad y = 0$$

Here also $\int_0^\pi y^2 dx = \int_0^\pi 0\, dx = 0 \neq 2$

$\therefore$ $\lambda = 0$ is impossible.

Case III. $\lambda < 0$ (4) $\Rightarrow$ $D = \pm\sqrt{-\lambda}\, i$

$$\therefore \quad (3) \Rightarrow \quad y = e^{0.x}(c_1 \cos\sqrt{-\lambda}\,x + c_2 \sin\sqrt{-\lambda}\,x)$$

i.e.,
$$y = c_1 \cos\sqrt{-\lambda}\,x + c_2 \sin\sqrt{-\lambda}\,x \qquad ...(8)$$

$$y(0) = 0 \Rightarrow c_1 \cos 0 + c_2 \sin 0 = 0 \Rightarrow c_1 = 0$$

$$y(1) = 0 \Rightarrow c_1 \cos\sqrt{-\lambda} + c_2 \sin\sqrt{-\lambda} = 0 \Rightarrow \sin\sqrt{-\lambda} = 0, \text{ for } c_2 \neq 0$$

$$\Rightarrow \sqrt{-\lambda} = n\pi, \quad n \in \mathbf{N}$$

$$\therefore \quad (8) \Rightarrow \quad y = c_2 \sin n\pi x, \quad n \in \mathbf{N}$$

Also, $\qquad \int_0^1 y^2\, dx = c_2^2 \int_0^1 \sin^2 n\pi x\, dx$

$$= \frac{c_2^2}{2}\int_0^1 (1 - \cos 2n\pi x)\, dx = \frac{c_2^2}{2}\left[x - \frac{\sin 2n\pi x}{2n\pi}\right]_0^1$$

$$= \frac{c_2^2}{2}[(1-0)-(0-0)] = \frac{c_2^2}{2}$$

$\therefore \quad \dfrac{c_2^{\ 2}}{2} = 2$ (Using (1))

$\therefore \quad c_2^{\ 2} = 4 \quad \text{or} \quad c_2 = \pm 2$

$\therefore \quad \mathbf{y = \pm 2 \sin n\pi x}, \quad \mathbf{n \in N}.$

This is the equation of the required extremals.

Example 4. *Find the plane curve of fixed perimeter so that the area covered by the curve, ordinates and x-axis is maximum.*

Sol. Let $y = y(x)$ be a curve of given length l between given points $A(x_1, y_1)$ and $B(x_2, y_2)$.

$$\therefore \quad l = \int_{x_1}^{x_2} \sqrt{1+y'^2}\, dx$$

Also, area enclosed by the curve, ordinates and x-axis is $\int_{x_1}^{x_2} y\, dx$. We are to maximise the functional $\int_{x_1}^{x_2} y\, dx$ under the condition $\int_{x_1}^{x_2} \sqrt{1+y'^2}\, dx = l$

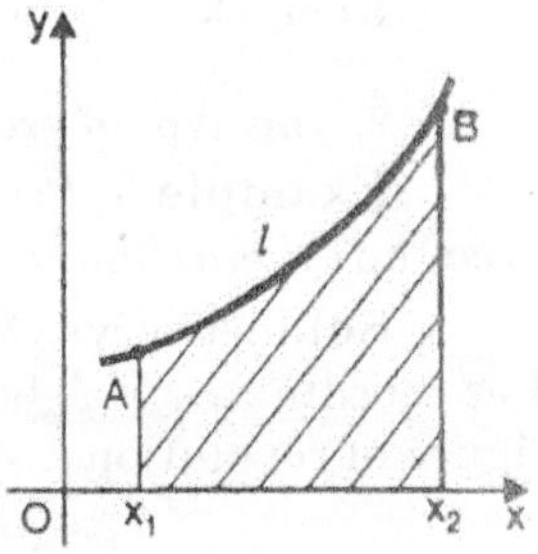

Let $\quad F(x, y, y') = y \quad \text{and} \quad G(x, y, y') = \sqrt{1+y'^2}$.

The **Euler's equation** is

$$F_y - \frac{d}{dx} F_{y'} + \lambda \left(G_y - \frac{d}{dx} G_{y'} \right) = 0 \quad \text{...(1)}$$

Here $\quad F_y = 1,\ F_{y'} = 0,\ G_y = 0,\ G_{y'} = \dfrac{y'}{\sqrt{1+y'^2}}$

$$\therefore \ (1) \Rightarrow \quad 1 - \frac{d}{dx}(0) + \lambda \left(0 - \frac{d}{dx}\left(\frac{y'}{\sqrt{1+y'^2}} \right) \right) = 0$$

$$\Rightarrow \quad \frac{d}{dx}\left(\frac{\lambda y'}{\sqrt{1+y'^2}} \right) = 1 \Rightarrow \frac{\lambda y'}{\sqrt{1+y'^2}} = x + c_1$$

$$\Rightarrow \quad \lambda^2 y'^2 = (x+c_1)^2 (1+y'^2)$$

$$\Rightarrow \quad y'^2 = \frac{(x+c_1)^2}{\lambda^2 - (x+c_1)^2}$$

$$\Rightarrow \quad y' = \frac{x+c_1}{\sqrt{\lambda^2 - (x+c_1)^2}}$$

$$\Rightarrow \quad dy = -\frac{1}{2} \cdot \frac{-2(x+c_1)}{\sqrt{\lambda^2 - (x+c_1)^2}}\, dx$$

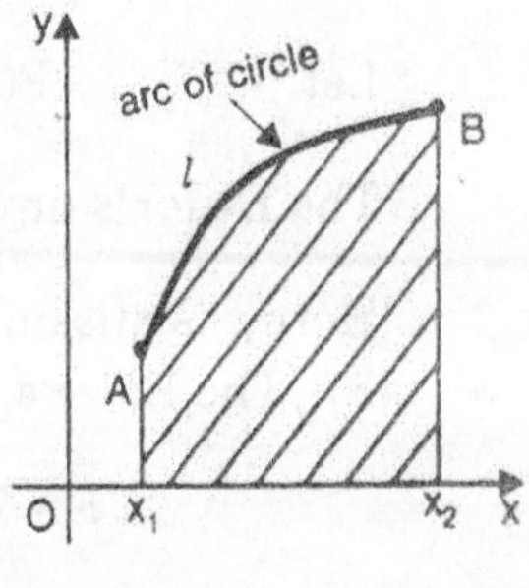

$$\Rightarrow \quad y = -\frac{1}{2} \cdot \frac{(\lambda^2 - (x+c_1)^2)^{1/2}}{1/2} + c_2$$

$$\Rightarrow \quad (y - c_2)^2 = \lambda^2 - (x+c_1)^2$$

$$\Rightarrow \quad (x+c_1)^2 + (y-c_2)^2 = \lambda^2 \quad \text{...(2)}$$

Now $\int_{x_1}^{x_2} \sqrt{1+y'^2}\, dx = \int_{x_1}^{x_2} \sqrt{1+\frac{(x+c_1)^2}{\lambda^2-(x+c_1)^2}}\, dx$

$$= \int_{x_1}^{x_2} \frac{\lambda}{\sqrt{\lambda^2-(x+c_1)^2}}\, dx = \lambda \sin^{-1} \frac{x+c_1}{\lambda}\Bigg|_{x_1}^{x_2}$$

$$\therefore \quad \lambda\left[\sin^{-1}\frac{x_2+c_1}{\lambda} - \sin^{-1}\frac{x_1+c_1}{\lambda}\right] = l \qquad ...(3) \qquad \left(\because \int_{x_1}^{x_2} \sqrt{1+y'^2}\, dx = l\right)$$

(3) is solved to find the value of λ.

$\therefore$ The required curves is an arc of the circle $(x+c_1)^2 + (y-c_2)^2 = \lambda^2$. The values of c_1 and c_2 are found by using the fact that A and B are on this arc. The position of the arc is shown in the adjoining figure.

Remarks 1. In particular, if $l = \pi\left(\frac{AB}{2}\right)$, then AB would be a diameter of the maximising circle.

2. This type of problems are called **isoperimetric problems.**

Example 5. *Prove that sphere is a solid figure of revolution, which for a given surface area, has a maximum volume.* (CDLU 2004)

Sol. Let curve OPA rotates about x-axis as shown in the figure. Let coordinates of A be $(a, 0)$. Let S be the surface area of the solid figure of revolution.

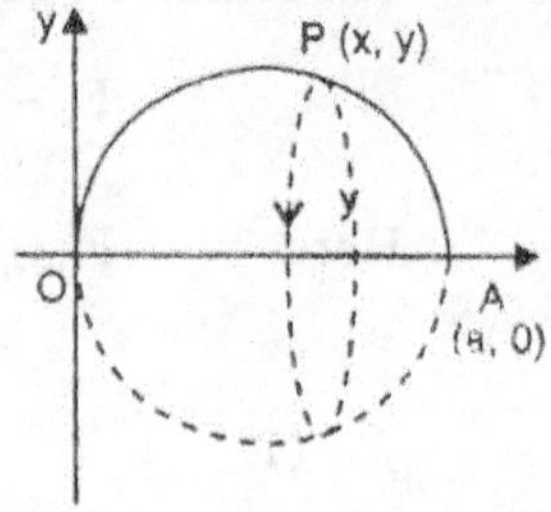

$$\therefore \quad \int_0^a 2\pi y\, ds = S$$

$$\Rightarrow \quad \int_0^a 2\pi y \sqrt{1+y'^2}\, dx = S$$

The volume of the solid figure of revolution is $\int_0^a \pi y^2\, dx$.

$\therefore$ We have to maximise the functional $\int_0^a \pi y^2\, dx$ with boundary conditions $y(0) = 0$, $y(a) = 0$ and under the condition $\int_0^a 2\pi y \sqrt{1+y'^2}\, dx = S$.

Let $F(x, y, y') = \pi y^2$ and $G(x, y, y') = 2\pi y \sqrt{1+y'^2}$.

The **Euler's equation** is $F_y - \frac{d}{dx} F_{y'} + \lambda\left(G_y - \frac{d}{dx} G_{y'}\right) = 0$

Here x is missing from both functions F and G.

$\therefore$ The Euler's equation reduces to

$$F + \lambda G - (F_{y'} + \lambda G_{y'}) \frac{dy}{dx} = c \qquad ...(1)$$

Here $F_{y'} = 0$, $G_{y'} = \frac{2\pi y y'}{\sqrt{1+y'^2}}$

$$\therefore \quad (1) \Rightarrow \quad \pi y^2 + 2\pi\lambda y\sqrt{1+y'^2} - \left(0 + \frac{2\pi\lambda yy'}{\sqrt{1+y'^2}}\right)y' = c$$

$$\Rightarrow \quad \pi y^2 + \left(\frac{2\pi\lambda y(1+y'^2) - 2\pi\lambda yy'^2}{\sqrt{1+y'^2}}\right) = c$$

$$\Rightarrow \quad \pi y^2 + \frac{2\pi\lambda y}{\sqrt{1+y'^2}} = c \qquad ...(2)$$

Since the curve passes through (0, 0), we have $0 + 0 = c$ *i.e.*, $c = 0$

$$\Rightarrow \quad \pi y^2 + \frac{2\pi\lambda y}{\sqrt{1+y^2}} = 0 \Rightarrow y + \frac{2\lambda}{\sqrt{1+y'^2}} = 0$$

$$\Rightarrow \quad \sqrt{1+y'^2} = -\frac{2\lambda}{y} \Rightarrow y'^2 = \frac{4\lambda^2}{y^2} - 1 = \frac{4\lambda^2 - y^2}{y^2}$$

$$\Rightarrow \quad y = \frac{\sqrt{4\lambda^2 - y^2}}{y} \Rightarrow \frac{y}{\sqrt{4\lambda^2 - y^2}}dy = dx$$

$$\Rightarrow \quad -\frac{1}{2}\cdot\frac{(4\lambda^2 - y^2)^{1/2}}{1/2} = x + c_1 \Rightarrow -\sqrt{4\lambda^2 - y^2} = x + c_1 \qquad ...(3)$$

(3) passes through (0, 0) $\therefore \quad -2\lambda = c_1$

$$\therefore \quad -\sqrt{4\lambda^2 - y^2} = x - 2\lambda$$

$$\Rightarrow \quad 4\lambda^2 - y^2 = (x - 2\lambda)^2 \Rightarrow (x - 2\lambda)^2 + y^2 = 4\lambda^2 \qquad ...(4)$$

(4) passes through $(a, 0)$

$$\therefore \quad (a - 2\lambda)^2 + 0 = 4\lambda^2$$

$$\Rightarrow \quad a^2 + 4\lambda^2 - 4a\lambda = 4\lambda^2$$

$$\Rightarrow \quad a^2 - 4a\lambda = 0 \Rightarrow \lambda = a/4$$

$$\therefore \quad (4) \Rightarrow \left(x - \frac{a}{2}\right)^2 + y^2 = \frac{a^2}{4} \qquad ...(5)$$

(5) represents a circle with centre at $(a/2, 0)$ and radius $a/2$.

$\therefore$ The curve OPA is a semi-circle.

$\therefore$ The solved figure revolution is a sphere.

Hence the result holds.

EXERCISE 5

1. Find the extremals of the functional $\int_{x_1}^{x_2} y'^2\, dx$ subject to the condition $\int_{x_1}^{x_2} y\, dx = c$, a constant.

(KU 2006)

2. Show that the extremal of the functional $\int_1^4 y'^2\,dx$ with boundary conditions $y(1) = 3$, $y(4) = 24$ and subject to an additional condition $\int_1^4 y\,dx = 36$ is a parabola.

3. Find the extremal of the functional $\int_0^\pi y'^2\,dx$, $y(0) = 0$, $y(\pi) = 0$ subject to the condition $\int_0^\pi y^2 dx = 1$.

4. Find the extremal of the functional $\int_0^1 y'^2\,dx$, $y(0) = 0$, $y(1) = \frac{1}{4}$ subject to the condition

$$\int_0^1 (y - y'^2)\,dx = \frac{1}{12}.$$

5. Among all curves of length $= l(> 2a)$ in the upper half plane passing through the points $(-a, 0)$ and $(a, 0)$, find the one which together with the segment $-a \le x \le a$ encloses the maximum area.

Answers

1. $y = \dfrac{3}{x_2^3 - x_1^3}(2c - 2c_2(x_2 - x_1) - c_1(x_2^2 - x_1^2))x^2 + c_1 x + c_2.$

3. $y = \pm\sqrt{\dfrac{2}{\pi}}\sin nx, n \in \mathbf{N}$ 4. $y = -\dfrac{x^2}{4} + \dfrac{x}{2}$

5. $x^2 + (y + \sqrt{\lambda_0^2 - a^2})^2 = \lambda_0^2$, where λ_0 is a solution of the equation $\sin\dfrac{l}{2\lambda} = \dfrac{a}{\lambda}$.

18

Variational Problems with Moving Boundaries

1. INTRODUCTION

We know that a functional associates a unique number to each function belonging to a certain class of functions. In the preceding chapter, we studied the methods of finding stationary function of the functional of the form $\int_{x_1}^{x_2} F(x, y(x), y'(x))\, dx$, where the boundary points (x_1, y_1) and (x_2, y_2) were fixed points. In the present chapter, we shall allow one or both boundary points to move. In this case the class of admissible functions is extended because, in addition to the comparison curves with fixed boundary points, we have to admit functions with variable boundary points.

2. FUNCTIONALS DEPENDENT ON ONE FUNCTION

Theorem. Let $J[y(x)] = \int_{x_1}^{x_2} F(x, y(x), y'(x))\, dx$ be a functional defined on the set of functions $y = y(x)$ which admits of continuous first order derivative and the end points of which (x_1, y_1) and (x_2, y_2) lie on the given curves $y = \phi(x)$ and $y = \psi(x)$ respectively so that $y_1 = \phi(x_1)$ and $y_2 = \psi(x_2)$, where $y = \phi(x)$ and $y = \psi(x)$ are functions from the class $C_1[x_1, x_2]$. Also, F is differentiable three times with respect to all its arguments.

If the functional $J[y(x)]$ has an extremum on a function $y = y(x)$ joining two arbitrary points of the given curves $y = \phi(x)$ and $y = \psi(x)$ then $y(x)$ satisfy the Euler's equation

$$F_y - \frac{d}{dx} F_{y'} = 0$$

and the transversality conditions

$$(F + (\phi' - y')\, F_{y'})|_{x = x_1} = 0 \quad \text{and} \quad (F + (\psi' - y')\, F_{y'})|_{x = x_2} = 0.$$

Note. Proof of this theorem is beyond the scope of this book.

Remark. If one of the boundaries say, (x_1, y_1) is fixed, then we need not introduce the function $\phi(x)$. In this case, we shall have only one transversality condition involving the function $\psi(x)$.

WORKING RULES FOR SOLVING PROBLEMS

Step I. *Identify the functions F, ϕ, ψ in the given problem.*

Step II. *Solve the Euler's equation $F_y - \dfrac{d}{dx} F_{y'} = 0$ and obtain a family of extremals $y = f(x, c_1, c_2)$ dependent on parameters c_1 and c_2.*

Step III. *Using $y_1 = \phi(x_1)$ and $y_2 = \psi(x_2)$ form the equations*
$f(x_1, c_1, c_2) = \phi(x_1)$ *and* $f(x_2, c_1, c_2) = \psi(x_2)$.

Step IV. *Simplify the transversality equations.*

Step V. *Solve the equations obtained in the above two steps to find the values of* c_1, c_2, x_1, x_2.

Step VI. *Find the extremum value of the given functional.*

Example 1. *Prove that for a functional of the form* $J[y(x)] = \int_{x_1}^{x_2} h(x, y)\sqrt{1 + y'^2}\, dx$, *where* $h(x, y) \neq 0$ *at the moving boundary points* $(x_1, \phi(x_1))$ *and* $(x_2, \psi(x_2))$, *the transversality conditions are of the form* $y'(x) = -\dfrac{1}{\phi'(x)}$ *at* $x = x_1$ *and* $y'(x) = -\dfrac{1}{\psi'(x)}$ *at* $x = x_2$.

Sol. We have $J[y(x)] = \int_{x_1}^{x_2} h(x, y)\sqrt{1 + y'^2}\, dx$.

Let $F(x, y, y') = h(x, y)\sqrt{1 + y'^2}$

The transversality conditions are :

$$(F + (\phi' - y')F_{y'})|_{x = x_1} = 0 \qquad ...(1)$$

and

$$(F + (\psi' - y')F_{y'})|_{x = x_2} = 0 \qquad ...(2)$$

$$(1) \Rightarrow \left[h(x, y)\sqrt{1 + y'^2} + (\phi' - y')\frac{h(x, y)y'}{\sqrt{1 + y'^2}}\right]\Bigg|_{x = x_1} = 0$$

$$\Rightarrow \quad h(x, y)\,[1 + y'^2 + (\phi' - y')y']|_{x = x_1} = 0$$

$$\Rightarrow \quad h(x, y)(1 + \phi' y')|_{x = x_1} = 0 \Rightarrow (1 + \phi' y')|_{x = x_1} = 0 \qquad (\because\ h(x, y) \neq 0 \text{ at } x = x_1)$$

$$\therefore \quad y'(x) = -\frac{1}{\phi'(x)} \text{ at } x = x_1.$$

Similarly (2) implies $y'(x) = -\dfrac{1}{\psi'(x)}$ at $x = x_2$.

Example 2. *Find the shortest distance between the point A(1, 0) and the ellipse*

$$4x^2 + 9y^2 = 36. \qquad \text{(MDU 2004)}$$

Sol. The given ellipse is

$$\frac{x^2}{9} + \frac{y^2}{4} = 1.$$

$$\Rightarrow \quad y = \pm\frac{2}{3}\sqrt{9 - x^2}$$

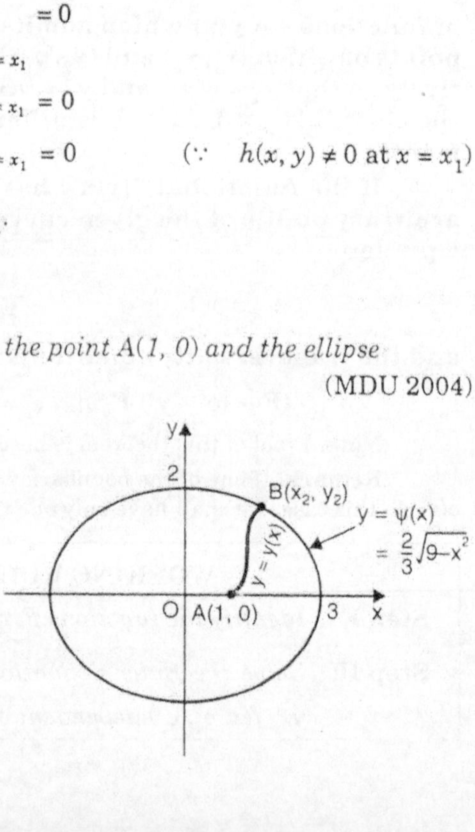

Let $y = \psi(x) = \dfrac{2}{3}\sqrt{9 - x^2}$ for the upper half ellipse. Let $B(x_2, y_2)$ be an arbitrary point on the curve

$y = \psi(x)$. Let $y = y(x)$ be a function whose curve passes through A and B. The length of the arc between A and B is given by the functional $\int_1^{x_2} \sqrt{1+y'^2}\, dx$.

Let $F(x, y, y') = \sqrt{1+y'^2}$

Let the length of the curve between A and B be minimum on the curve of $y = y(x)$.

$\therefore$ The functional $\int_1^{x_2} F(x, y, y')\, dx$ has a minimum value on $y = y(x)$.

$\therefore$ $y(x)$ satisfies the equations :

$$F_y - \frac{d}{dx} F_{y'} = 0 \qquad \text{...(1)}$$

and

$$(F + (\psi' - y')F_{y'})|_{x = x_2} = 0 \qquad \text{...(2)}$$

Here $F_y = 0,\ \ F_{y'} = \dfrac{y'}{\sqrt{1+y'^2}},\ \ \psi' = \dfrac{2}{3}\cdot\dfrac{1}{2}(9 - x^2)^{-1/2}(-2x) = -\dfrac{2x}{3\sqrt{9-x^2}}$

$$(1) \Rightarrow 0 - \frac{d}{dx}\left(\frac{y'}{\sqrt{1+y'^2}}\right) = 0 \Rightarrow \frac{y'}{\sqrt{1+y'^2}} = c_1$$

$$\Rightarrow \quad y'^2 = c_1^2(1 + y'^2) \Rightarrow y' = \frac{c_1}{\sqrt{1-c_1^2}} = c_2, \text{ say}$$

$$\Rightarrow \quad y = c_2x + c_3 \qquad \text{...(3)}$$

This is the equation of the extremals. The boundary conditions are $y(1) = 0$,

$$y(x_2) = y_2 = \psi(x_2) = \frac{2}{3}\sqrt{9-x_2^2}$$

$$y(1) = 0 \quad \Rightarrow \quad c_2(1) + c_3 = 0 \Rightarrow c_2 + c_3 = 0 \qquad \text{...(4)}$$

$$y(x_2) = \frac{2}{3}\sqrt{9-x_2^2} \Rightarrow c_2x_2 + c_3 = \frac{2}{3}\sqrt{9-x_2^2} \qquad \text{...(5)}$$

$$\Rightarrow c_2x_2 - c_2 = \frac{2}{3}\sqrt{9-x_2^2} \qquad \text{(Using (4))}$$

$$\Rightarrow c_2(x_2 - 1) = \frac{2}{3}\sqrt{9-x_2^2} \qquad \text{...(6)}$$

$$(2) \Rightarrow \left.\left(\sqrt{1+y'^2} + \left(-\frac{2x}{3\sqrt{9-x^2}} - y'\right)\frac{y'}{\sqrt{1+y'^2}}\right)\right|_{x=x_2} = 0$$

$$\Rightarrow \left.\frac{1}{\sqrt{1+y'^2}}\left(1 + y'^2 - \left(\frac{2xy'}{3\sqrt{9-x^2}} + y'^2\right)\right)\right|_{x=x_2} = 0$$

$$\Rightarrow \quad 1 - \frac{2x_2c_2}{3\sqrt{9-x_2^2}} = 0 \Rightarrow 2c_2x_2 = 3\sqrt{9-x_2^2} \qquad \text{...(7)}$$

$\therefore$ (6) $\Rightarrow$ $c_2(x_2 - 1) = \frac{2}{3}\left(\frac{2}{3}c_2x_2\right) \Rightarrow x_2 - 1 = \frac{4x_2}{9} \Rightarrow x_2 = \frac{9}{5}$

$\therefore$ (7) $\Rightarrow$ $2c_2\left(\frac{9}{5}\right) = 3\sqrt{9 - \frac{81}{25}} \Rightarrow \frac{18c_2}{5} = \frac{36}{5} \Rightarrow c_2 = 2$

$\therefore$ (4) $\Rightarrow$ $2 + c_3 = 0 \Rightarrow c_3 = -2$

Using (3) the stationary function is $y = 2x - 2$.

$\therefore$ $y = 2x - 2$ minimises the functional *i.e.*, the distance between A and B.

$\therefore$ Shortest distance $= \int_1^{9/5} \sqrt{1+(2)^2}\, dx = \sqrt{5}\left(\frac{9}{5} - 1\right) = \frac{4\sqrt{5}}{5}$ **units.**

Example 3. *Find the snortest distance between the parabola $y = x^2$ and the straight line $x - y = 5$.* (CDLU 2004)

Sol. Let $\phi(x) = x^2$ and $\psi(x) = x - 5$. Let $A(x_1, y_1)$ and $B(x_2, y_2)$ be arbitrary points on the curves $y = \phi(x)$ and $y = \psi(x)$ respectively. Let $y = y(x)$ be a function whose curve passes through A and B. The length of the arc between A and B is given by $\int_{x_1}^{x_2} \sqrt{1+y'^2}\, dx$.

Let $F(x, y, y') = \sqrt{1+y'^2}$

Let the length of the curve between A and B be minimum on the curve of $y = y(x)$.

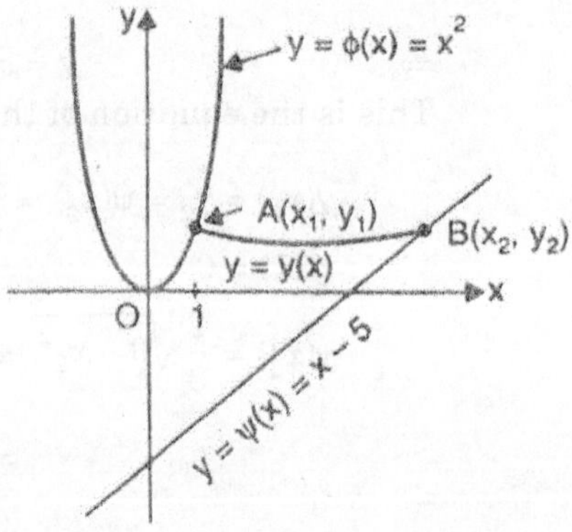

$\therefore$ The functional $\int_{x_1}^{x_2} F(x, y, y')dx$ has a minimum value on $y(x)$.

$\therefore$ $y(x)$ satisfies the equations :

$$F_y - \frac{d}{dx} F_{y'} = 0 \quad \text{...(1)}$$

$$(F + (\phi' - y')F_{y'})|_{x=x_1} = 0 \quad \text{...(2)}$$

and $$(F + (\psi' - y')F_{y'})|_{x=x_2} = 0 \quad \text{...(3)}$$

Here $F_y = 0,\ F_{y'} = \frac{y'}{\sqrt{1+y'^2}},\quad \phi' = 2x,\ \psi' = 1$

(1) $\Rightarrow$ $0 - \frac{d}{dx}\left(\frac{y'}{\sqrt{1+y'^2}}\right) = 0 \Rightarrow \frac{y'}{\sqrt{1+y'^2}} = c_1$

$\Rightarrow$ $y'^2 = c_1^2(1 + y'^2) \Rightarrow y' = \frac{c_1}{\sqrt{1-c_1^2}} = c_2$, say

$\Rightarrow$ $y = c_2x + c_3$ ...(4)

This is the equation of the extremals.

The boundary conditions are :

$$y(x_1) = y_1 = \phi(x_1) = x_1^2, \quad y(x_2) = y_2 = \psi(x_2) = x_2 - 5.$$

$$y(x_1) = x_1^2 \quad \Rightarrow \quad c_2 x_1 + c_3 = x_1^2 \qquad ...(5)$$

$$y(x_2) = x_2 - 5 \quad \Rightarrow \quad c_2 x_2 + c_3 = x_2 - 5 \qquad ...(6)$$

$$(2) \Rightarrow \left.\left(\sqrt{1+y'^2} + (2x - y')\frac{y'}{\sqrt{1+y'^2}}\right)\right|_{x=x_1} = 0$$

$$\Rightarrow \left.\frac{1}{\sqrt{1+y'^2}}(1 + 2xy')\right|_{x=x_1} = 0$$

$$\Rightarrow 1 + 2x_1 c_2 = 0 \qquad ...(7)$$

$$(3) \Rightarrow \left.\left(\sqrt{1+y'^2} + (1 - y')\frac{y'}{\sqrt{1+y'^2}}\right)\right|_{x=x_2} = 0$$

$$\Rightarrow \left.\frac{1}{\sqrt{1+y'^2}}(1 + y')\right|_{x=x_2} = 0$$

$$\Rightarrow 1 + c_2 = 0 \quad \Rightarrow c_2 = -1 \qquad ...(8)$$

$\therefore$ (7) $\Rightarrow 1 + 2x_1(-1) = 0 \quad \Rightarrow x_1 = 1/2$

(5) $\Rightarrow (-1)(1/2) + c_3 = 1/4 \quad \Rightarrow c_3 = 3/4$

(6) $\Rightarrow (-1)x_2 + (3/4) = x_2 - 5 \quad \Rightarrow x_2 = 23/8$

$$\therefore \quad c_2 = -1, \quad c_3 = \frac{3}{4}, \quad x_1 = \frac{1}{2}, \quad x_2 = \frac{23}{8}$$

Using (4), the stationary function is $y = (-1)x + \frac{3}{4}$.

$\therefore$ $y = -x + \frac{3}{4}$ **minimises the functional** *i.e.*, the distance between A and B.

$\therefore$ **Shortest distance** $= \int_{1/2}^{23/8} \sqrt{1+(-1)^2}\, dx = \sqrt{2}\left(\frac{23}{8} - \frac{1}{2}\right) = \frac{19\sqrt{2}}{8}$ **units.**

EXERCISE 1

1. **Find the shortest distance between the point A(– 1, 3) and the straight line $y = 1 - 3x$.**
2. **Find the shortest distance between the point A(0, 0) and the straight line $x + y = \sqrt{2}$.** *(MDU 2005)*
3. **Find the shortest distance from the point A(– 1, 5) to the parabola $y^2 = x$.** *(MDU 2005 ; KU 2006)*
4. **Find the shortest distance between the circle $x^2 + y^2 = 1$ and the straight line $x + y = 4$.**

Answers

1. $\frac{\sqrt{10}}{10}$ units **2.** 1 unit **3.** $2\sqrt{5}$ units **4.** $(2\sqrt{2} - 1)$ units.

3. FUNCTIONALS DEPENDENT ON TWO FUNCTIONS

Theorem. Let $J[y(x), z(x)] = \int_{x_1}^{x_2} F(x, y(x), z(x), y'(x), z'(x))dx$ be a functional defined on the set of functions $y = y(x)$, $z = z(x)$ which admits of continuous first order derivative. Let the point $A(x_1, y_1, z_1)$ corresponding to the lower limit in the above integral be fixed and the other boundary point $B(x_2, y_2, z_2)$ be in motion along a certain curve specified by the equations $y = \phi(x)$, $z = \psi(x)$ so that $y_2 = \phi(x_2)$, $z_2 = \psi(x_2)$, where $y = \phi(x)$ and $z = \psi(x)$ are functions from the class $C_1[x_1, x_2]$. Also, F is differentiable three times with respect to all its arguments.

If the functional $J[y(x), z(x)]$ has an extremum on a curve $y = y(x)$, $z = z(x)$ then $y(x)$ and $z(x)$ satisfy the Euler's equations $F_y - \frac{d}{dx}F_{y'} = 0$, $F_z - \frac{d}{dx}F_{z'} = 0$ and the transversality condition $[F + (\phi' - y')F_{y'} + (\psi' - z')F_{z'}]|_{x = x_2} = 0$.

Note. The proof of this theorem is beyond the scope of this book.

Remark. If the boundary point $A(x_1, y_1, z_1)$ is fixed and the other boundary point $B(x_2, y_2, z_2)$ car move along the surface $z = \psi(x, y)$, then the transversality conditions are :

$$[F - y'F_{y'} + (\psi_x - z')F_{z'}]|_{x = x_2} = 0$$

and
$$[F_{y'} + F_{z'}\,\psi_y]|_{x = x_2} = 0.$$

Example 1. *Find the shortest distance from the point A(0, 2, 1) to the straight line* $\frac{x}{1} = \frac{y}{2} = \frac{z}{3}$. (KU 2005 S)

Sol. The given line is $\frac{x}{1} = \frac{y}{2} = \frac{z}{3}$ or equivalently $y = 2x$, $z = 3x$. Let $y = \phi(x) = 2x$ and $z = \psi(x) = 3x$. Let $B(x_2, y_2, z_2)$ be an arbitrary point on the curve $y = \phi(x)$, $z = \psi(x)$. Let $y = y(x)$, $z = z(x)$ be functions whose curve passes through A and B. The length of the arc between A and B is given by the functional $\int_0^{x_2} \sqrt{1 + y'^2 + z'^2}\, dx$.

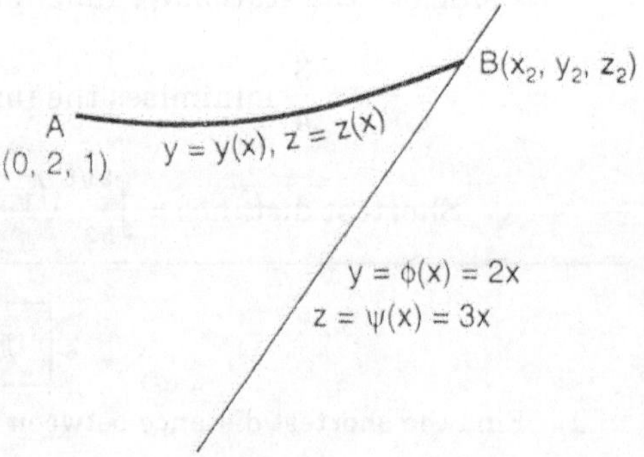

Let $F(x, y, z, y', z') = \sqrt{1 + y'^2 + z'^2}$

Let the length of the curve between A and B be minimum on the curve given by $y = y(x)$, $z = z(x)$.

$\therefore$ The functional $\int_0^{x_2} F(x, y, z, y', z')\, dx$ has a minimum value on the functions $y = y(x)$, $z = z(x)$.

$\therefore$ $y(x)$, $z(x)$ satisfy the equations
$$F_y - \frac{d}{dx}F_{y'} = 0 \quad \text{...(1)}$$
$$F_z - \frac{d}{dx}F_{z'} = 0 \quad \text{...(2)}$$
and
$$[F + (\phi' - y')F_{y'} + (\psi' - z')F_{z'}]|_{x = x_2} = 0. \quad \text{...(3)}$$

Here $F_y = 0$, $F_z = 0$, $F_{y'} = \frac{y'}{\sqrt{1 + y'^2 + z'^2}}$, $F_{z'} = \frac{z'}{\sqrt{1 + y'^2 + z'^2}}$, $\phi' = 2$, $\psi' = 3$.

$\therefore$ (1) $\Rightarrow$ $$0-\frac{d}{dx}\left(\frac{y'}{\sqrt{1+y'^2+z'^2}}\right)=0 \Rightarrow \frac{y'}{\sqrt{1+y'^2+z'^2}}=c_1 \quad ...(4)$$

(2) $\Rightarrow$ $$0-\frac{d}{dx}\left(\frac{z'}{\sqrt{1+y'^2+z'^2}}\right)=0 \Rightarrow \frac{z'}{\sqrt{1+y'^2+z'^2}}=c_2 \quad ...(5)$$

Dividing (4) by (5), we get $\frac{y'}{z'}=\frac{c_1}{c_2}=c_3$, sav

$\therefore$ $y'=c_3z'$

Putting the value of y' in (5), we get $\frac{z'}{\sqrt{1+(1+c_3^2)z'^2}}=c_2$.

$\Rightarrow$ $z'^2=c_2^2(1+(1+c_3^2)z'^2) \Rightarrow z'=\frac{c_2}{\sqrt{1-c_2^2-c_2^2c_3^2}}=c_4$, say

$\Rightarrow$ $z=c_4x+c_5$ ...(6)

$y'=c_3z' \Rightarrow y'=c_3c_4=c_6$, say

$\Rightarrow$ $y=c_6x+c_7$ ...(7)

$\therefore$ The extremals are given by (6) and (7)

The boundary conditions are :

$y(0)=2,\quad z(0)=1, y(x_2)=y_2=\phi(x_2)=2x_2, z(x_2)=z_2=\psi(x_2)=3x_2$

$y(0)=2 \Rightarrow c_6(0)+c_7=2 \Rightarrow c_7=2$

$z(0)=1 \Rightarrow c_4(0)+c_5=1 \Rightarrow c_5=1$

$$y(x_2)=2x_2 \Rightarrow c_6x_2+c_7=2x_2 \Rightarrow c_6x_2+2=2x_2 \Rightarrow c_6=\frac{2x_2-2}{x_2} \quad ...(8)$$

$$z(x_2)=3x_2 \Rightarrow c_4x_2+c_5=3x_2 \Rightarrow c_4x_2+1=3x_2 \Rightarrow c_4=\frac{3x_2-1}{x_2} \quad ...(9)$$

(3) $\Rightarrow$ $$\left(\sqrt{1+y'^2+z'^2}+(2-y')\frac{y'}{\sqrt{1+y'^2+z'^2}}+(3-z')\frac{z'}{\sqrt{1+y'^2+z'^2}}\right)\Bigg|_{x=x_2}=0$$

$\Rightarrow$ $$\frac{1}{\sqrt{1+y'^2+z'^2}}(1+y'^2+z'^2+2y'-y'^2+3z'-z'^2)\Bigg|_{x=x_2}=0$$

$\Rightarrow$ $$1+2c_6+3c_4=0$$

$\Rightarrow$ $$1+2\left(\frac{2x_2-2}{x_2}\right)+3\left(\frac{3x_2-1}{x_2}\right)=0$$

$\Rightarrow$ $$x_2+4x_2-4+9x_2-3=0 \Rightarrow x_2=1/2$$

$\therefore$ (8) $\Rightarrow$ $$c_6=2-\frac{2}{1/2}=-2$$

(9) $\Rightarrow$ $c_4 = 3 - \dfrac{1}{1/2} = 1$

$\therefore$ $c_4 = 1, c_5 = 1, c_6 = -2, c_7 = 2, x_2 = \dfrac{1}{2}$

$\therefore$ (7) $\Rightarrow$ $y = -2x + 2$, (6) $\Rightarrow$ $z = x + 1$

$\therefore$ The stationary functions are $y = -2x + 2, z = x + 1$.

$\therefore$ The curve $y = -2x + 2, z = x + 1$ minimises the functional *i.e.*, the distance between A and B.

$\therefore$ Shortest distance $= \displaystyle\int_0^{1/2} \sqrt{1 + (-2)^2 + (1)^2}\, dx = \sqrt{6}\left(\frac{1}{2} - 0\right) = \frac{\sqrt{6}}{2}$ **units.**

Remark. The minimising curve is a straight line given by the equations :

$$\frac{x-0}{1} = \frac{y-2}{-2} = \frac{z-1}{1}.$$

Example 2. *Find the shortest distance from the point A(1, 1, 1) to the sphere $x^2 + y^2 + z^2 = 1$.* (KU 2004 S)

Sol. The given sphere is $x^2 + y^2 + z^2 = 1$. $\therefore$ $z = \pm\sqrt{1 - x^2 - y^2}$

Let $z = \psi(x, y) = \sqrt{1 - x^2 - y^2}$ for the upper half sphere. Let B (x_2, y_2, z_2) be an arbitrary point on the surface $z = \psi(x, y)$. Let $y = y(x), z = z(x)$ be functions whose curve passes through A and B. The length of the arc between A and B is given by the functional

$$\int_1^{x_2} \sqrt{1 + y'^2 + z'^2}\, dx.$$

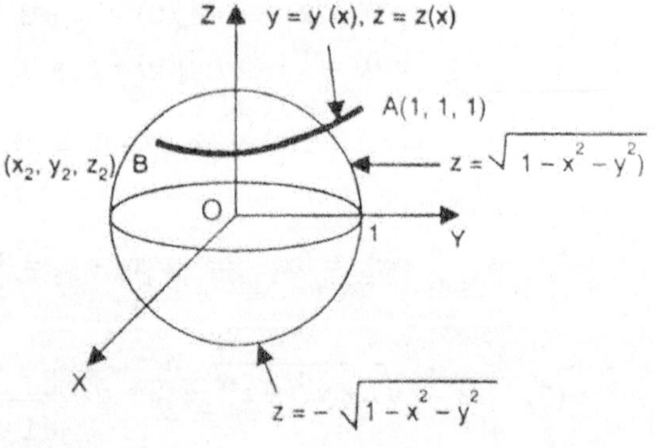

Let $F(x, y, z, y', z') = \sqrt{1 + y'^2 + z'^2}$

Let the length of the curve between A and B be minimum on the curve given by

$$y = y(x), z = z(x).$$

$\therefore$ The functional $\displaystyle\int_1^{x_2} F(x, y, z, y', z')\, dz$ has a minimum value on the functions $y = y(x), z = z(x)$.

$\therefore$ $y(x), z(x)$ satisfy the equations $F_y - \dfrac{d}{dx} F_{y'} = 0$ ...(1)

$$F_z - \frac{d}{dx} F_{z'} = 0 \quad ...(2)$$

$$[F - y'F_{y'} + (\psi_x - z')F_{z'}]\,|_{x = x_2} = 0 \quad ...(3)$$

and $[F_{y'} + F_{z'}\,\psi_y]\,|_{x = x_2} = 0$ ...(4)

Here $F_y = 0, F_z = 0, F_{y'} = \dfrac{y'}{\sqrt{1 + y'^2 + z'^2}}, F_{z'} = \dfrac{z'}{\sqrt{1 + y'^2 + z'^2}}, \quad \psi_x = -\dfrac{x}{\sqrt{1 - x^2 - y^2}},$

$$\psi_y = -\frac{y}{\sqrt{1 - x^2 - y^2}}$$

$$(1) \Rightarrow \quad 0-\frac{d}{dx}\left(\frac{y'}{\sqrt{1+y'^2+z'^2}}\right)=0 \Rightarrow \frac{y'}{\sqrt{1+y'^2+z'^2}}=c_1 \quad \text{...(5)}$$

$$(2) \Rightarrow \quad 0-\frac{d}{dx}\left(\frac{z'}{\sqrt{1+y'^2+z'^2}}\right)=0 \Rightarrow \frac{z'}{\sqrt{1+y'^2+z'^2}}=c_2 \quad \text{...(6)}$$

Dividing (4) by (5), we get $\frac{y'}{z'}=\frac{c_1}{c_2}=c_3$, say $y'=c_3z'$

Putting the value of y' in (6), we get $\frac{z'}{\sqrt{1+(1+c_3^2)\,z'^2}}=c_2$.

$$\Rightarrow \quad z'^2=c_2^2\,(1+(1+c_3^2)\,z'^2) \Rightarrow z'=\frac{c_2}{\sqrt{1-c_2^2-c_2^2\,c_3^2}}=c_4, \text{ say}$$

$$\Rightarrow \quad z=c_4x+c_5 \quad \text{...(7)}$$

$$y'=c_3z' \Rightarrow y'=c_3c_4=c_5, \text{ say}$$

$$\Rightarrow \quad y=c_6x+c_7 \quad \text{...(8)}$$

$\therefore$ **The extremals are given by (7) and (8).**
The boundary conditions are :

$$y(1)=1,\quad z(1)=1,\quad y(x_2)=y_2,\ z(x_2)=z_2 \quad \text{and} \quad z_2=\sqrt{1-x_2^2-y_2^2}.$$

$$y(1)=1 \Rightarrow c_6(1)+c_7=1 \Rightarrow c_6+c_7=1 \quad \text{...(9)}$$

$$z(1)=1 \Rightarrow c_4(1)+c_5=1 \Rightarrow c_4+c_5=1 \quad \text{...(10)}$$

$$y(x_2)=y_2 \Rightarrow c_6x_2+c_7=y_2 \quad \text{...(11)}$$

$$z(x_2)=z_2 \Rightarrow c_4x_2+c_5=z_2 \quad \text{...(12)}$$

$$(3) \Rightarrow \left(\sqrt{1+y'^2+z'^2}-y'.\frac{y'}{\sqrt{1+y'^2+z'^2}}+\left(-\frac{x}{\sqrt{1-x^2-y^2}}-z'\right)\frac{z'}{\sqrt{1+y'^2+z'^2}}\right)\Bigg|_{x=x_2}=0$$

$$\Rightarrow \quad \frac{1}{\sqrt{1+y'^2+z'^2}}\left(1+y'^2+z'^2-y'^2-\frac{xz'}{\sqrt{1-x^2-y^2}}-z'^2\right)\Bigg|_{x=x_2}=0$$

$$\Rightarrow \quad 1-\frac{x_2c_4}{z_2}=0 \Rightarrow z_2=c_4x_2 \quad \text{...(13)}$$

$$(4) \Rightarrow \quad \left(\frac{y'}{\sqrt{1+y'^2+z'^2}}+\frac{z'}{\sqrt{1+y'^2+z'^2}}\left(-\frac{y}{\sqrt{1-x^2-y^2}}\right)\right)\Bigg|_{x=x_2}=0$$

$$\Rightarrow \quad \frac{1}{\sqrt{1+y'^2+z'^2}}\left(y'-\frac{yz'}{\sqrt{1-x^2-y^2}}\right)\Bigg|_{x=x_2}=0$$

$$\Rightarrow \quad c_6-\frac{y_2c_4}{z_2}=0 \Rightarrow c_6z_2=c_4y_2 \quad \text{...(14)}$$

$$(12) \Rightarrow \quad z_2+c_5=z_2 \Rightarrow c_5=0 \quad \text{(Using (13))}$$

$$(10) \Rightarrow \quad c_4+0=1 \Rightarrow c_4=1$$

$(14) \Rightarrow \quad c_6 z_2 = 1 \,.\, y_2 \quad i.e., \quad y_2 = c_6 z_2$

$\Rightarrow \quad y_2 = c_6(c_4 x_2) = c_6 x_2 \qquad (\because\ c_4 = 1)$

$\therefore \quad (11) \Rightarrow \quad y_2 + c_7 = y_2 \Rightarrow c_7 = 0$

$(9) \quad \Rightarrow \quad c_6 + 0 = 1 \quad \Rightarrow \quad c_6 = 1$

$\therefore \quad c_4 = 1, \quad c_5 = 0, \quad c_6 = 1, \quad c_7 = 0$

Also (13) $\Rightarrow \quad z_2 = x_2 \quad (14) \Rightarrow \quad z_2 = y_2$

$\therefore \quad x_2 = y_2 = z_2$

Also $\quad z_2 = \sqrt{1 - x_2^{\,2} - y_2^{\,2}}$

$$\Rightarrow \quad x_2^{\,2} = 1 - x_2^{\,2} - x_2^{\,2} \quad \Rightarrow \quad x_2 = \frac{1}{\sqrt{3}}.$$

$\therefore \quad B = (1/\sqrt{3}, 1/\sqrt{3}, 1/\sqrt{3})$

$\therefore \quad (8) \Rightarrow \quad y = 1.x + 0 \quad i.e., \quad y = x$

$(7) \Rightarrow \quad z = 1.x + 0 \quad i.e., \quad z = x$

$\therefore$ The stationary functions are $y = x, z = x$.

$\therefore$ The curve $y = x, z = x$ minimises the functional *i.e.*, the distance between A and B.

$\therefore$ Shortest distance

$$= \int_1^{1/\sqrt{3}} \sqrt{1 + (1)^2 + (1)^2}\, dx = \sqrt{3}\left(\frac{1}{\sqrt{3}} - 1\right) = \mathbf{(\sqrt{3} - 1)\ units.}$$

Remark. The minimising curve is a straight line given by the equations :

$$\frac{x - 0}{1} = \frac{y - 0}{1} = \frac{z - 0}{1}.$$

EXERCISE 2

1. Find the shortest distance from the point (0, 2, 0) to the straight line $x = y = z$. *(KU 2004)*

2. Find the shortest distance of the point (0, 2, 4) to the straight line $\frac{x - 1}{1} = \frac{y}{3} = \frac{z}{4}$. *(KU 2005)*

Answers

1. $2\sqrt{6}/3$ **units** **2.** $\sqrt{105/26}$ **units.**

19

Sufficient Conditions for an Extremum

1. INTRODUCTION

At an extremum, a functional may have either maximum value or minimum value. In the preceding two chapters, we studied the necessary conditions for an extremum. At a stationary function, a functional may or may not have an extremum. In the present chapter, we shall confine ourselves to the study of sufficient conditions for extremums of variational problems with fixed boundaries only.

2. PROPER FIELD IN A GIVEN DOMAIN

A family of curves $y = y(x, c)$ is called a **proper field in a given domain** D of the xy-plane if through every point of D there passes one and only one curve of the family $y = y(x, c)$.

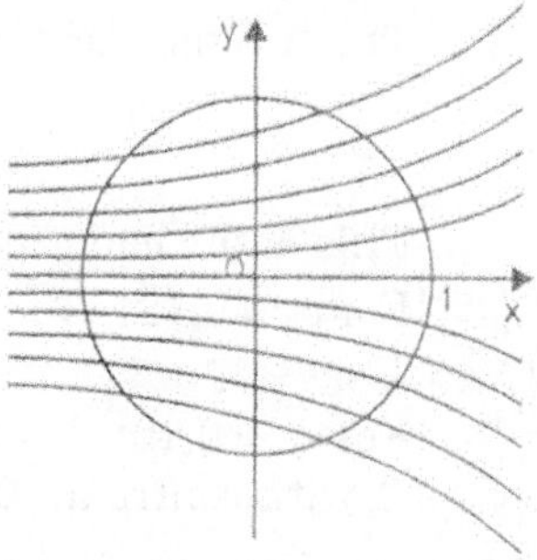

In other words, the curves of the family $y = y(x, c)$ cover the entire domain D without self-intersections.

For example, the family of curves $y = ce^x$, where c is an arbitrary constant, form a proper field inside the circle $x^2 + y^2 = 1$, because through any point inside or on the circle there passes exactly one curve belonging to the family $y = ce^x$.

To take another example, the family of parabolas $y = (x + c)^2$, where c is an arbitrary constant, does not form a proper field inside the circle $x^2 + y^2 = 1$, because through any point inside or on the circle there may pass more than one parabola belonging to the family $y = (x + c)^2$. Moreover, there are infinitily many points inside the circle from where no parabola of the family $y = (x + c)^2$ pass.

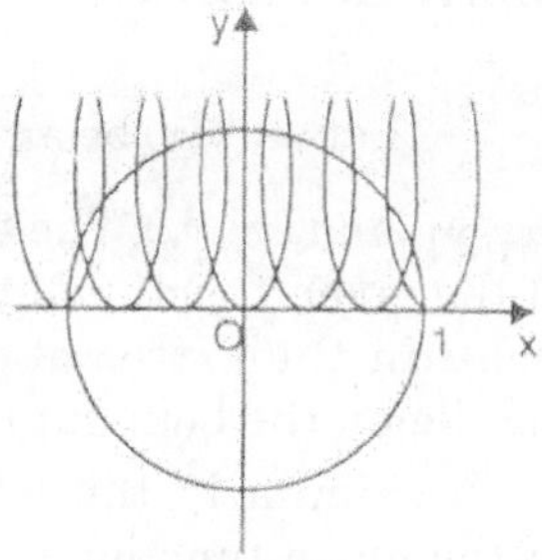

3. CENTRAL FIELD IN A GIVEN DOMAIN

A family of curves $y = y(x, c)$ is called a **central field in a given domain** D of the xy-plane if through every point of D there passes one and only one curve of the family $y = y(x, c)$ and all curves issue from a single point (x_0, y_0) lying outside D. The point (x_0, y_0) is called the **centre of the central field** or **centre of the pencil of curves.**

For example, the family of curves $y = cx$, where c is an arbitrary constant, form a central field with centre (0, 0) in the domain $x > 0$.

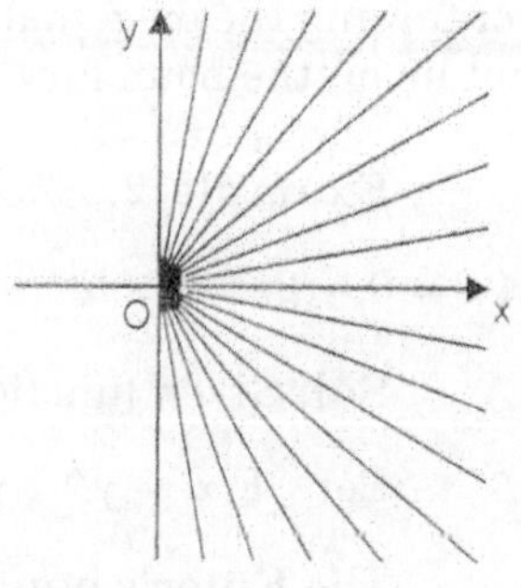

4. EXTREMAL FIELD

A field (proper or central) is called an **extremal field** (or a **field of extremals**) if it is formed by a family of extremals of some variational problem.

Example 1. *Find the proper and central field of extremals for the functional* $\int_0^1 (y^2 - y'^2)\,dx$.

Sol. Given functional is $\int_0^1 (y^2 - y'^2)\,dx$.

Let $F(x, y, y') = y^2 - y'^2$ ...(1)

The **Euler's equation** is

$$F_y - \frac{d}{dx} F_{y'} = 0$$

Here $F_y = 2y$, $F_{y'} = -2y'$

$$\therefore \quad (1) \Rightarrow 2y - \frac{d}{dx}(-2y') = 0 \Rightarrow \frac{d^2y}{dx^2} + y = 0$$

The A.E. is $D^2 + 1 = 0 \quad \therefore \quad D = \pm i$

$$\therefore \qquad y = e^{0.x}(c_1 \cos 1.x + c_2 \sin 1.x)$$

i.e., $$y = c_1 \cos x + c_2 \sin x. \qquad ...(2)$$

This is the equation of the extremals.

For $c_2 = 0$, (2) $\Rightarrow$ $\mathbf{y = c_1 \cos x}$. This forms a proper field of extremals in the domain $0 \le x \le 1$.

For $c_1 = 0$, (2) $\Rightarrow$ $\mathbf{y = c_2 \sin x}$. This forms a central field of extremals in the domain $0 < x \le 1$ with centre at (0, 0).

5. INCLUSION OF AN EXTREMAL IN A FIELD OF EXTREMALS

Let $y = y(x)$ be an extremal of the functional $\int_{x_1}^{x_2} F(x, y, y')\,dx$ with fixed boundary points (x_1, y_1) and (x_2, y_2). The extremal $y = y(x)$ is said to be **included in a proper field of extremals** if the given functional yields a family of extremals $y = y(x, c)$ that forms a proper field and contain the extremal $y = y(x)$ for some particular value of c. Also, this extremal $y = y(x)$ does not lie on the boundary of the domain D in which the family $y = y(x, c)$ form a proper field.

Similarly, the extremal $y = y(x)$ is said to be **included in a central field of extremals** if the given functional yields a family of extremals $y = y(x, c)$ that forms a central field and containing the extremal $y = y(x)$ for some particular value of c. Also, this extremal $y = y(x)$ does not lie on the boundary of the domain D in which the family $y = y(x, c)$ form a central field.

Example 2. *Show that the extremal of the variational problem* $\int_0^2 (y'^3 + \sin^2 x)\,dx$, $y(0) = 0$, $y(2) = 6$ *is included in a central field of extremals of the given functional.*

Sol. Given functional is $\int_0^2 (y'^3 + \sin^2 x)\,dx$.

Let $F(x, y, y') = y'^3 + \sin^2 x$

The **Euler's equation** is $F_y - \frac{d}{dx} F_{y'} = 0$ ...(1)

Here $F_y = 0,\ F_{y'} = 3y'^2$

$$\therefore\ (1)\ \Rightarrow\qquad 0 - \frac{d}{dx}(3y'^2) = 0 \Rightarrow \frac{dy'^2}{dx} = 0$$

$$\Rightarrow\qquad y'^2 = c_1 \Rightarrow y' = \sqrt{c_1} = c_2,\ \text{say}$$

$$\Rightarrow\qquad y = c_2x + c_3 \qquad ...(2)$$

This is the equation of the extremals. The boundary conditions are $y(0) = 0, y(2) = 6$.

$$y(0) = 0 \Rightarrow c_2(0) + c_3 = 0 \Rightarrow c_3 = 0$$

$$y(2) = 6 \Rightarrow c_2(2) + c_3 = 6 \Rightarrow 2c_2 = 6 \Rightarrow c_2 = 3$$

$\therefore$ (2) $\Rightarrow$ $y = 3x + 0$ *i.e.*, $y = 3x$

This is the extremal of the given variational problem.

$$c_3 = 0 \text{ in } (2) \Rightarrow y = c_2x$$

This is a central field of extremals in the domain $0 < x \le 1$ with centre at (0, 0).

For $c_2 = 3,\ y = c_2 x \Rightarrow y = 3x$

$\therefore$ The extremal $y = 3x$ is included in the central field of extremals $y = c_2x$.

EXERCISE 1

1. Show that the family of parabolas $y = (x - c)^2$ is not a proper field inside the circle $x^2 + y^2 = 4$.
2. Find the proper and central fields of extremals for the functional $\int_0^4 y'^2\, dx$.
3. Find the proper and central fields of extremals for the functional $\int_0^{\pi/4} (y'^2 - y^2 + 2x^2 + 4)\, dx$.
4. Show that the extremal of the variational problem $\int_0^2 (y'^3 + \cos^2 x)\, dx, y(0) = 2, y(2) = 2$ is included in a proper field of extremals of the given functional.
5. Show that the extremal of the variational problem $\int_0^1 (y'^2 - 2xy)\, dx$, $y(0) = 0, y(1) = 0$ is included in a central field of extremals of the given functional.
6. Show that the extremal of the variational problem $\int_0^2 (y'^2 + x^2)\, dx$, $y(0) = 1, y(2) = 3$ is included in a proper field of extremals of the given functional.

Answers

2. $y = c_2, 0 \le x \le 4$; $y = c_1x$, (0, 0), $0 < x \le 4$
3. $y = c_1 \cos x, 0 \le x \le \pi/4$; $y = c_2 \sin x$, (0, 0), $0 < x \le \pi/4$.

Hints

5. The extremal $y = -\frac{x^3}{6} + \frac{x}{6}$ is included in the central field of extremals $y = -\frac{x^3}{6} + c_1x$.

6. ENVELOPE OF A FAMILY

Let $\phi(x, y, c) = 0$ be a one parameter family of plane curves. The **envelope** of the family $\phi(x, y, c) = 0$ is a curve, each point of which touches a certain curve of the given family and each portion of which is touched by infinitely many of curves of the family.

7. c-DISCRIMINANT OF THE FAMILY $\phi(x, y, c) = 0$

Let $\phi(x, y, c) = 0$ be a one parameter family of plane curves. The locus of points defined by the equations $\phi(x, y, c) = 0$, $\frac{\partial\phi}{\partial c} = 0$ is called the **c-discriminant** of the given family of plane curves $\phi(x, y, c) = 0$.

In general, the c-discriminant includes the envelopes of the family $\phi(x, y, c) = 0$, the locus of nodal points and the locus of cusps.

For example, if $\phi(x, y, c) = 0$ represents a pencil of curves with centre at the point A, then the centre at A of the pencil belongs to the c-discriminant of the family $\phi(x, y, c) = 0$.

Example 1. *Find the c-discriminant of the family of curves $y(c - x) - c^2 = 0$.* (KU 2005 S)

Sol. Given family is $y(c - x) - c^2 = 0$. ...(1)

Let $\phi(x, y, c) = y(x - c) - c^2$

The equations of c-discriminant are $\phi(x, y, c) = 0$, $\frac{\partial\phi}{\partial c} = 0$.

$$\phi(x, y, c) = 0 \Rightarrow y(c - x) - c^2 = 0 \quad ...(2)$$

$$\frac{\partial\phi}{\partial c} = 0 \Rightarrow y.1 - 0 - 2c = 0 \quad ...(3)$$

(2) $\Rightarrow c = \frac{y}{2}$. Putting the value of c in (1), we get

$$y\left(\frac{y}{2} - x\right) - \frac{y^2}{4} = 0 \quad \text{or} \quad \frac{y^2}{4} - xy = 0 \quad \text{or} \quad \mathbf{y(y - 4x) = 0.}$$

This is the equation of the c-discriminant.

8. CONJUGATE POINT OF A POINT

Let $\phi(x, y, c) = 0$ be a pencil of curves with centre at A and $\psi(x, y) = 0$ represents the c-discriminant of the family $\phi(x, y, c) = 0$. Let $y = y(x)$ be a curve belonging to the pencil of curves $\phi(x, y, c) = 0$. If A* be a point, other than A, on the curve of $y = y(x)$ and also on the c-discriminant $\psi(x, y) = 0$, then the point A* is called a **conjugate point** of the point A.

Example 2. *Given a family of curves $y = c(x + 4)x$, find a point conjugate to the point (0, 0).* (MDU 2004 ; KU 2005 S)

Sol. Given family is $c(x + 4)x - y = 0$.

(1) is a pencil of curves with centre (0, 0).

Let $\phi(x, y, c) = c(x + 4)x - y$

The equations of c-discriminant are $\phi(x, y, c) = 0$, $\frac{\partial\phi}{\partial c} = 0$.

$$\phi(x, y, c) = 0 \Rightarrow c(x + 4)x - y = 0 \quad ...(1)$$

$$\frac{\partial\phi}{\partial c} = 0 \Rightarrow (x + 4)x.1 - 0 = 0 \quad ...(2)$$

(2) $\Rightarrow$ $(x + 4)x = 0$ $\therefore$ (1) $\Rightarrow$ $c.0 - y = 0$ $\Rightarrow$ $y = 0$.

Also, $(x + 4)x = 0$ $\Rightarrow$ $x = -4, 0$

$\therefore$ c-discriminant is the set $\{(-4, 0), (0, 0)\}$.

Let $y = c_0(x + 4)x$ be a curve belonging to the given pencil of curves. The curve of this function passes through $(-4, 0)$ which is also on the c-discriminant of the given family.

$\therefore$ **(– 4, 0)** is a conjugate point of the centre (0, 0).

EXERCISE 2

Find the c-discriminant of the following families of curves (Q. No. 1 – 3) :

1. $y = (x - c)^2$ 2. $y = cx + c^2$ 3. $(x - c)^2 + y^2 = 1$
4. Given a family of curves $y = c(x - 1)x$, find a conjugate point of the point (0, 0).
5. Given a family of curves $y = c \sinh x$, find a conjugate point of the point (0, 0).

Answers

1. $y = 0$ 2. $y = -\dfrac{x^2}{4}$ 3. $y^2 - 1 = 0$ 4. (1,0)
5. No conjugate point.

---

9. JACOBI CONDITION

A given extremal may or may not be included in a central field of extremals. The following is the sufficient condition for an arc of an extremal to be included in a central field of extremals :

For an arc AB of an extremal to be included in a central field of extremals with centre at A, it is sufficient that no conjugate point of A, lie on the arc AB.

This sufficient condition for including an extremal in a central field of extremals is called the **Jacobi condition.**

Let $J[y(x)] = \int_{x_1}^{x_2} F(x, y, y')\, dx$ be a functional with fixed boundaries $A(x_1, y_1)$ and $B(x_2, y_2)$.

The equation $\left(F_{yy} - \dfrac{d}{dx} F_{yy'}\right) u - \dfrac{d}{dx} (F_{y'y'} u') = 0$ is called the **Jacobi equation.** Let $u = u(x)$ be the solution of the Jacobi equation satisfying the condition $u(x_1) = 0$. We have the following results :

(*i*) If $u(x) = 0$ for some $x \in (x_1, x_2)$ then a conjugate point of A lies on the arc AB.

$\therefore$ By the **Jacobi condition,** the arc AB of the extremal of the variational problem is not included in a central field of extremals with centre at A.

(*ii*) If $u(x) \neq 0$ for all $x \in (x_1, x_2]$ then no conjugate point of A lie on the arc AB.

$\therefore$ By the **Jacobi condition,** the arc AB of the extremal of the variational problem is included in a central field of extremals with centre at A.

Remark. In the Jacobi equation if any of F_{yy}, $F_{yy'}$, $F_{y'y'}$, contain y, then the value of y in terms of x is substituted from the extremal of the variational problem.

Example 1. *Show that the Jacobi condition is fulfilled for the extremal of the functional* $\int_0^{\lambda} (x^2 + y^2 + y'^2)\, dx$ *with fixed boundaries A(0, 0) and B (λ, 0).* (KU 2004)

Sol. Given functional is $\int_0^{\lambda} (x^2 + y^2 + y'^2)\, dx$.

Let $F(x, y, y') = x^2 + y^2 + y'^2$

The **Euler's equation** is $F_y - \frac{d}{dx} F_{y'} = 0$ ...(1)

Here $F_y = 2y, \quad F_{y'} = 2y'$

$\therefore$ (1) $\Rightarrow$ $2y - \frac{d}{dx}(2y') = 0 \Rightarrow \frac{d^2y}{dx^2} - y = 0$

The A.E. is $D^2 - 1 = 0 \quad \therefore \quad D = \pm 1$

$\therefore$ $y = c_1e^x + c_2e^{-x}$ ...(2)

This is the equation of the extremals. The boundary conditions are $y(0) = 0, y(\lambda) = 0$.

$y(0) = 0 \Rightarrow c_1e^0 + c_2e^0 = 0 \Rightarrow c_1 + c_2 = 0 \Rightarrow c_2 = -c_1$

$y(\lambda) = 0 \Rightarrow c_1e^{\lambda} + c_2e^{-\lambda} = 0 \Rightarrow c_1(e^{\lambda} - e^{-\lambda}) = 0 \Rightarrow c_1 = 0$

$\therefore$ $c_2 = -(0) = 0$

$\therefore$ (2) $\Rightarrow$ $y = 0.e^x + 0.e^{-x}$ *i.e.*, $y = 0$. ...(3)

This is the extremal of the given variational problem.

The **Jacobi equation** is

$$\left(F_{yy} - \frac{d}{dx} F_{yy'}\right) u - \frac{d}{dx}(F_{y'y'}\, u') = 0 \quad ...(4)$$

Here $F_{yy} = 2, F_{yy'} = 0, \quad F_{y'y'} = 2$

$\therefore$ (4) $\Rightarrow$ $\left(2 - \frac{d}{dx}(0)\right) u - \frac{d}{dx}(2u') = 0 \Rightarrow \frac{d^2u}{dx^2} - u = 0$

The A.E. is $D^2 - 1 = 0 \quad \therefore \quad D = \pm 1$

$\therefore$ $u = k_1e^x + k_2e^{-x}$

Also, $u(0) = 0 \Rightarrow k_1e^0 + k_2e^0 = 0 \Rightarrow k_1 + k_2 = 0 \Rightarrow k_2 = -k_1$

Let $u(x) = k_1e^x - k_1e^{-x} = k_1(e^x - e^{-x}), k_1 \neq 0$

Here $u(x) \neq 0$ for $x \in (0, \lambda]$

$\therefore$ No conjugate point of A(0, 0) lie on the arc AB *i.e.*, on the curve of $y = 0$.

$\therefore$ By the Jacobi condition, the curve of the extremal $y = 0$ is included in a central field of extremals with centre at A(0, 0).

Verification. The family of extremals is $y = c_1e^x + c_2e^{-x}$.

$$c_2 = -c_1 \Rightarrow y = c_1e^x - c_1e^{-x} = 2c_1\left(\frac{e^x - e^{-x}}{2}\right) = 2c_1 \sinh x.$$

This is a central field of extremals with centre at A(0, 0) in the domain $0 < x \leq \lambda$.

For $c_1 = 0$, $y = 2(0) \sinh x \Rightarrow y = 0$.

$\therefore$ The extremal $y = 0$ is included in the central field of extremals $y = 2c_1 \sinh x$ with centre at A(0, 0).

Example 2. *Show that the Jacobi condition is fulfilled for the extremal of the functional* $\int_0^a (y'^2 - 4y^2 + e^{-x^2})\, dx$, $a \neq \frac{n\pi}{2}$ *with fixed boundaries A(0, 0) and B(a, 0).*

Sol. Given functional is $\int_0^a (y'^2 - 4y^2 + e^{-x^2}) dx$.

Let $F(x, y, y') = y'^2 - 4y^2 + e^{-x^2}$

The **Euler's equation** is $F_y - \frac{d}{dx} F_{y'} = 0$ ...(1)

Here $F_y = -8y,\ F_{y'} = 2y'$

$\therefore$ (1) $\Rightarrow$ $-8y - \frac{d}{dx}(2y') = 0 \Rightarrow \frac{d^2y}{dx^2} + 4y = 0$

The A.E. is $D^2 + 4 = 0 \quad \therefore \quad D = \pm 2i$

$\therefore$ $y = e^{0.x}(c_1 \cos 2x + c_2 \sin 2x)$

i.e., $y = c_1 \cos 2x + c_2 \sin 2x$ ...(2)

This is the equation of the extremals. The boundary conditions are $y(0) = 0, y(a) = 0$.

$y(0) = 0 \Rightarrow c_1 \cos 0 + c_2 \sin 0 = 0 \Rightarrow c_1 = 0$

$y(a) = 0 \Rightarrow c_1 \cos 2a + c_2 \sin 2a = 0 \Rightarrow 0.\cos 2a + c_2 \sin 2a = 0 \Rightarrow c_2 = 0$

$\left(\because a \neq \frac{n\pi}{2}\right)$

$\therefore$ (2) $\Rightarrow$ $y = 0.\cos 2x + 0.\sin 2x$ *i.e.,* $y = 0$. ...(3)

This is the extremal of the given variational problem.

The **Jacobi equation** is

$$\left(F_{yy} - \frac{d}{dx} F_{yy'}\right) u - \frac{d}{dx}(F_{y'y'}\, u') = 0 \quad \text{...(4)}$$

Here $F_{yy} = -8,\quad F_{yy'} = 0,\quad F_{y'y'} = 2$

$\therefore$ (4) $\Rightarrow$ $\left(-8 - \frac{d}{dx}(0)\right) u - \frac{d}{dx}(2u') = 0 \Rightarrow \frac{d^2u}{dx^2} + 4u = 0$

$\therefore$ $u = k_1 \cos 2x + k_2 \sin 2x$

Also, $u(0) = 0 \Rightarrow k_1 \cos 0 + k_2 \sin 0 = 0 \Rightarrow k_1 = 0$

Let $u(x) = k_2 \sin 2x,\ k_2 \neq 0$.

For a, there are two possibilities.

Case I. $a < \pi/2$

Here $u(x) = k_2 \sin 2x \neq 0\ \forall\ x \in (0, a]$ $\left(\because 0 < a < \frac{\pi}{2} \Rightarrow 0 < 2a < \pi \Rightarrow \sin 2x \neq 0\right)$

$\therefore$ No conjugate point of A(0, 0) lie on the arc AB *i.e.,* on the curve of $y = 0$.

$\therefore$ By the Jacobi condition, the curve of the extremal $y = 0$ is included in a central field of extremals with centre at A(0, 0).

Case II. $a > \pi/2$

Here $u(x) = k_2 \sin 2x = 0$ for $x = \frac{\pi}{2}$, because $\frac{\pi}{2} \in (0, a)$

$\therefore$ A conjugate point of A(0, 0) lies on the arc AB *i.e.,* on the curve of $y = 0$.

$\therefore$ By the Jacobi condition, the curve of the extremal $y = 0$ is not included in a central field of extremals with centre at A(0, 0).

Verification. Case I. a < π/2.

The family of extremals is $y = c_1 \cos 2x + c_2 \sin 2x$.

$c_1 = 0 \Rightarrow y = c_2 \sin 2x$. This is a central field of extremals in the domain $0 < x \le a$ with centre at A(0, 0). $\left(\because 0 < a < \dfrac{\pi}{2} \Rightarrow 0 < 2a < \pi \Rightarrow \sin 2x \ne 0\right)$

For $c_2 = 0, y = c_2 \sin 2x \Rightarrow y = 0$.

∴ The extremal $y = 0$ is included in the central field of extremals $y = c_2 \sin 2x$ with centre at A(0, 0).

Case II. a > π/2. The family of extremals is $y = c_1 \cos 2x + c_2 \sin 2x$.

$c_1 = 0 \Rightarrow y = c_2 \sin 2x$. This is not a central field of extremals because each curve in this family passes through the points (0, 0) and (π/2, 0)

$c_2 = 0 \Rightarrow y = c_1 \cos 2x$. This is also not a central field of extremals because there is no centre of this family of curve.

∴ The extremal $y = 0$ is not included in a central field of extremals.

EXERCISE 3

1. Show that the Jacobi condition is fulfilled for the functional $\int_0^a (x^2 + y'^2)\, dx, a > 0$ with fixed boundaries A(0, 0) and B(a, 2). *(KU 2005 S)*

2. Show that the Jacobi condition is fulfilled for the functional $\int_0^5 (9y^2 + y'^2 - 3x)\, dx$ with fixed boundaries A(0, 0) and B(5, 0). *(KU 2004 S)*

3. Show that the Jacobi condition is fulfilled for the functional $\int_{-1}^1 (12xy + y'^2 + x^2)\, dx$ with fixed boundaries A(– 1, – 2) and B(1, 0). *(KU 2006)*

4. Show that the Jacobi condition is fulfilled for the functional $\int_0^1 (1 + y'^2)\, dx$ with fixed boundaries A(0, 0) and B(1, 0).

Hints

1. The extremal is $y = \dfrac{2}{a} x$.

$u(x) = k_1 x, (k_1 \ne 0)$ and $u(x) \ne 0 \;\forall\; x \in (0, a]$.

Also $y = c_1 x$ is a central field of extremals with centre at (0, 0) and containing $y = \dfrac{2}{a} x$.

10. LEGENDRE CONDITION

A given extremal may or may not give a maximum or minimum value of the functional under consideration. The following is the sufficient condition for an extremal of a functional to give a maximum or minimum value of the functional.

Let $J[y(x)] = \int_{x_1}^{x_2} F(x, y, y')\, dx$ be a functional with fixed boundaries $A(x_1, y_1)$ and $B(x_2, y_2)$. Let $F(x, y, y')$ has a continuous partial derivative $F_{y'y'}(x, y, y')$. Let C be the curve of the extremal of the given functional which passes through A and B. Also, let the extremal of the curve C be included in a field of extremals.

(*i*) **For a strong maximum (resp. minimum) to be attained on the curve C, it is sufficient to have $F_{y'y'} \le 0$ (resp. $F_{y'y'} \ge 0$) at the points close to the curve C and also for arbitrary values of y′.**

(*ii*) **For a weak maximum (resp. minimum) to be attained on the curve C, it is sufficient to have $F_{y'y'} < 0$ (resp. $F_{y'y'} > 0$) on the curve C.**

This sufficient condition for an extremal to give a maximum or minimum value of the corresponding functional is called the **Legendre condition.**

Remark. It may be recalled that every strong extremum is at the same time a weak extrəmum but not conversely.

Example 1. *Using Legendre condition, test the functional*

$$I[y(x)] = \int_0^2 (4 - e^{y'})\, dx,\ y(0) = 0,\ y(2) = 1 \text{ for extremal.} \qquad \text{(MDU 2005)}$$

Sol. We have $\quad I[y(x)] = \int_0^2 (4 - e^{y'})\, dx.$

Let $\quad F(x, y, y') = 4 - e^{y'}$

The **Euler's equation** is

$$F_y - \frac{d}{dx} F_{y'} = 0 \qquad ...(1)$$

Here $\quad F_y = 0,\ F_{y'} = -e^{y'}$

$$\therefore\ (1) \Rightarrow 0 - \frac{d}{dx}(-e^{y'}) = 0 \Rightarrow \frac{de^{y'}}{dx} = 0 \Rightarrow e^{y'} = e^{c_1}$$

$$\Rightarrow y' = c_1 \Rightarrow y = c_1 x + c_2 \qquad ...(2)$$

This is the equation of the extremals.

The boundary conditions are $\quad y(0) = 0,\ y(2) = 1$

$$y(0) = 0 \Rightarrow c_1(0) + c_2 = 0 \Rightarrow c_2 = 0$$

$$y(2) = 1 \Rightarrow c_1(2) + c_2 = 1 \Rightarrow 2c_1 + 0 = 1 \Rightarrow c_1 = \frac{1}{2}$$

$$\therefore\ (2) \Rightarrow y = \frac{1}{2}x + 0 \quad i.e.,\ y = \frac{x}{2}$$

This is the extremal of the given variational problem.

$c_2 = 0$ in (2) $\Rightarrow$ $y = c_1 x$. This is a central field of extremals with centre (0, 0) and domain $0 < x \le 2$.

For $\quad c_1 = \frac{1}{2},\ y = c_1 x \Rightarrow y = \frac{x}{2}$

$\therefore$ The extremal $y = \frac{x}{2}$ is included in the central field of extremals $y = c_1 x$.

Now, $$F_{y'y'} = \frac{\partial}{\partial y'}\left(\frac{\partial}{\partial y'} F\right) = \frac{\partial}{\partial y'}\left(\frac{\partial}{\partial y'}(4 - e^{y'})\right) = \frac{\partial}{\partial y'}(-e^{y'}) = -e^{y'}$$

The function '$-e^{y'}$' is continuous.

Also $F_{y'y'} = -e^{y'} \le 0$ for all values of y'.

$\therefore$ By Legendre condition, the given functional has a strong maximum on the function $y = x/2$.

Example 2. *Using Legendre condition, test the following functional for extrema :*

$$J[y(x)] = \int_2^3 \frac{x^3}{y'^2}\,dx\,,\ y(2) = 4\,,\ y(3) = 9.$$

Sol. We have $\quad J[y(x)] = \int_2^3 \frac{x^3}{y'^2}\,dx.$

Let $\quad F(x, y, y') = \frac{x^3}{y'^2}$

The **Euler's equation** is $\quad F_y - \frac{d}{dx} F_{y'} = 0$ ...(1)

Here $\quad F_y = 0, F_{y'} = -\frac{2x^3}{y'^3}$

$\therefore$ (1) $\quad 0 - \frac{d}{dx}\left(-\frac{2x^3}{y'^3}\right) = 0 \Rightarrow \frac{d}{dx}\left(\frac{x^3}{y'^3}\right) = 0$

$\Rightarrow \quad \frac{x^3}{y'^3} = c_1 \Rightarrow y' = \left(\frac{1}{c_1}\right)^{1/3} x$

$\Rightarrow \quad y = \left(\frac{1}{c_1}\right)^{1/3} \frac{x^2}{2} + c_2 \Rightarrow y = c_3 x^2 + c_2$, say ...(2)

This is the equation of the extremals. The boundary conditions are $y(2) = 4, y(3) = 9$.

$y(2) = 4 \Rightarrow c_3(2)^2 + c_2 = 4 \Rightarrow 4c_3 + c_2 = 4$ ...(3)

$y(3) = 9 \Rightarrow c_3(3)^2 + c_2 = 9 \Rightarrow 9c_3 + c_2 = 9$ ...(4)

Solving, we get $c_2 = 0, c_3 = 1$

$\therefore$ (2) $\Rightarrow \quad y = 1x^2 + 0$ *i.e.,* $y = x^2$. ...(5)

This is the extremal of the given variational problem.

$c_2 = 0$ in (2) $\Rightarrow y = c_3 x^2$.

This is a central field of extremals with centre at (0, 0) and domain $2 \le x \le 3$.

For $c_3 = 1$, $y = c_3 x^2 \Rightarrow y = x^2$

$\therefore$ The extremal $y = x^2$ is included in the central field of extremals $y = c_3 x^2$.

Now $\quad F_{y'y'} = \frac{\partial}{\partial y'} F_{y'} = \frac{\partial}{\partial y'}\left(-\frac{2x^3}{y'^3}\right) = \frac{6x^3}{y'^4}$

The function $\frac{6x^3}{y'^4}$ is continuous.

For $y' = 0$, the quantity $\frac{6x^3}{y'^4}$ is not defined.

$\therefore$ The function $y = x^2$ is neither a strong maximum nor a strong minimum.

$$y = x^2 \Rightarrow y' = 2x.$$

$\therefore$ On the extremal $y = x^2$,

$$F_{y'y'} = \frac{6x^3}{(2x)^4} = \frac{3}{8x}$$

Also, on [2, 3], $\frac{3}{8x} > 0$

$\therefore$ $F_{y'y'} > 0$ on the extremal $y = x^2$.

$\therefore$ By **Legendre condition,** the given functional has a weak minimum on the function $y = x^2$.

EXERCISE 4

Using Legendre condition, test the following functionals for extrema :

1. $J[y(x)] = \int_0^1 (x^2 + y'^2)\, dx$, $y(0) = -1$, $y(1) = 1$ *(KU 2004 S)*
2. $J[y(x)] = \int_0^2 (4 + e^{y'})\, dx$, $y(0) = 0$, $y(2) = 1$ *(KU 2004)*
3. $J[y(x)] = \int_0^2 (e^{y'} + 3)\, dx$, $y(0) = 0$, $y(2) = 1$. *(KU 2005)*
4. $J[y(x)] = \int_0^1 yy'^2\, dx$, $y(0) = 4$, $y(1) = 4$
5. $J[y(x)] = \int_1^2 (xy'^4 - 2yy'^3)\, dx$, $y(1) = 0$, $y(2) = 1$.

Answers

1. Strong minimum on the function $y = 2x - 1$
2. Strong minimum on the function $y = \frac{x}{2}$
3. Strong minimum on the function $y = \frac{x}{2}$
4. Strong minimum on the function $y = 4$
5. Weak minimum on the function $y = x - 1$.

Hints

1. The extremal $y = 2x - 1$ is included in the central field of extremals $y = cx - 1$ with centre at $(0, -1)$.
2. The extremal $y = x/2$ is included in the central field of extremal $y = cx$ with centre at $(0, 0)$.

11. VARIATION OF A FUNCTIONAL

Let $J[y(x)]$ be a functional defined on a class A of functions $y(x)$. The increment of the argument $y(x)$ of the functional $J[y(x)]$ is given by the difference $y_1(x) - y(x)$ for some function $y_1(x)$ in A. This increment is denoted by $\delta y(x)$. The **variation of the functional** $J[y(x)]$ at the point $y(x)$ is defined as the value of the derivative of the functional $J[y(x) + \alpha\delta y(x)]$ with respect to the parameter α when $\alpha = 0$. The variation $J[y(x)]$ is denoted by δJ.

$$\therefore \qquad \delta J = \frac{\partial}{\partial \alpha} J[y(x) + \alpha \delta y(x)] \Big|_{\alpha=0}$$

If the variation of a functional exists, then the functional is said to **differentiable.**

Example 1. *Find the variation of the functional* $J[y(x)] = \int_{x_1}^{x_2} y(x)\,dx$.

Sol. We have $\quad J[y(x)] = \int_{x_1}^{x_2} y(x)\,dx$.

Let $\delta y(x)$ be an increment of $y(x)$.

$$\therefore \quad J[y(x) + \alpha\delta y(x)] = \int_{x_1}^{x_2} (y(x) + \alpha\delta y(x))\,dx$$

$$\therefore \quad \frac{\partial}{\partial\alpha} J[y(x) + \alpha\delta y(x)] = \frac{\partial}{\partial\alpha}\int_{x_1}^{x_2} (y(x) + \alpha\delta y(x))\,dx$$

$$= \int_{x_1}^{x_2} \frac{\partial}{\partial\alpha}(y(x) + \alpha\delta y(x))\,dx$$

$$= \int_{x_1}^{x_2} (0 + 1\,.\,\delta y(x))\,dx = \int_{x_1}^{x_2} \delta y(x)\,dx$$

$$\therefore \quad \frac{\partial}{\partial\alpha} J[y(x) + \alpha\delta y(x)]\Bigg|_{\alpha=0} = \int_{x_1}^{x_2} \delta y(x)\,dx$$

$\therefore$ Variation of $\quad J[y(x)] = \int_{x_1}^{x_2} \boldsymbol{\delta y(x)\,dx}$.

Example 2. *Find the variation of the functional*

$$J[y(x)] = y^2(0) + \int_0^1 (x\,.\,y(x) + (y'(x))^2)\,dx.$$

Sol. We have $\quad J[y(x)] = y^2(0) + \int_0^1 (x\,.\,y(x) + (y'(x))^2)\,dx$

Let $\delta y(x)$ be an increment of $y(x)$.

$$\therefore \quad J[y(x) + \alpha\delta y(x)] = (y(0) + \alpha\delta y(0))^2 + \int_0^1 (x(y(x) + \alpha\delta y(x)) + (y'(x) + \alpha(\delta y)'(x))^2)\,dx$$

$$\therefore \quad \frac{\partial}{\partial\alpha} J[y(x) + \alpha\delta y(x)] = 2(y(0) + \alpha\delta y(0))\,\delta y(0)$$

$$+ \int_0^1 (0 + x\delta y(x) + 2(y'(x) + \alpha(\delta y)'(x))\,(\delta y)'(x))\,dx$$

$$\therefore \quad \frac{\partial}{\partial\alpha} J[y(x) + \alpha\delta y(x)]\Bigg|_{\alpha=0} = 2(y(0) + 0)\,\delta y(0) + \int_0^1 (x\delta y(x) + 2(y'(x) + 0)\,(\delta y)'(x))\,dx$$

$$= 2y(0)\,\delta y(0) + \int_0^1 (x\delta y(x) + 2y'(x)\,(\delta y)'(x))\,dx$$

$\therefore$ Variation of $\;J[y(x)] = \boldsymbol{2y(0)\delta y(0) + \int_0^1 (x\delta y(x) + 2y'(x)\,(\delta y)'(x))\,dx}$.

12. SECOND VARIATION OF A FUNCTIONAL

Let $J[y(x)]$ be a functional defined on a class A of functions $y(x)$. The **second variation of the functional** $J[y(x)]$ is defined as the value of the second derivative of the functional $J[y(x) + \alpha\delta y(x)]$ with respect to the parameter α when $\alpha = 0$. The second variation of $J[y(x)]$ is denoted by $\delta^2 J$.

$$\therefore \quad \delta^2 \mathbf{J} = \frac{\partial^2}{\partial \alpha^2} \mathbf{J}\,[\mathbf{y(x)} + \alpha \delta \mathbf{y(x)}]\Big|_{\alpha=0}.$$

Example 3. *Find the second variation of the functional* $J[y(x)] = \int_{x_1}^{x_2} y(x)\,dx$.

Sol. We have $\quad J[y(x)] = \int_{x_1}^{x_2} y\,dx$

Let δy be an increment of y

$$\therefore \quad J[y + \alpha\delta y] = \int_{x_1}^{x_2} (y + \alpha\delta y)\,dx$$

$$\therefore \quad \frac{\partial}{\partial\alpha} J\,[y + \alpha\delta y] = \frac{\partial}{\partial\alpha}\int_{x_1}^{x_2} (y + \alpha\delta y)\,dx = \int_{x_1}^{x_2} \frac{\partial}{\partial\alpha}(y + \alpha\delta y)\,dx = \int_{x_1}^{x_2} (0 + \delta y)\,dx$$

$$\therefore \quad \frac{\partial^2}{\partial\alpha^2} J\,[y + \alpha\delta y] = \frac{\partial}{\partial\alpha}\int_{x_1}^{x_2} \delta y\,dx = \int_{x_1}^{x_2} \frac{\partial}{\partial\alpha}(\delta y)\,dx = \int_{x_1}^{x_2} 0\,dx = 0$$

$$\therefore \quad \frac{\partial^2}{\partial\alpha^2} J[y + \alpha\delta y]\Big|_{\alpha=0} = 0$$

$$\therefore \quad \delta^2 J = \mathbf{0}.$$

Remark. For the sake of simplicity, the function $y(x)$ has been written as 'y'.

Example 4. *Find the second variation of the functional* $e^{F(y)}$, *where* $F(y)$ *is a twice differentiable function.*

Sol. Let $\quad J[y] = e^{F(y)}$

Let δy be an increment of y.

$$\therefore \quad J[y + \alpha\delta y] = e^{F(y + \alpha\delta y)}$$

$$\therefore \quad \frac{\partial}{\partial\alpha} J[y + \alpha\delta y] = e^{F(y + \alpha\delta y)}.F'(y + \alpha\delta y).\delta y$$

$$\therefore \quad \frac{\partial^2}{\partial\alpha^2} J[y + \alpha\delta y] = \delta y[e^{F(y + \alpha\delta y)}\,F'(y + \alpha\delta y)\delta y\,.\,F'(y + \alpha\delta y) + e^{F(y + \alpha\delta y)}.F''(y + \alpha\delta y)\delta y]$$

$$= (\delta y)^2\, e^{F(y + \alpha\delta y)}[(F'(y + \alpha\delta y))^2 + F''(y + \alpha\delta y)]$$

$$\therefore \quad \frac{\partial^2}{\partial\alpha^2} J\,[y + \alpha\delta y]\Big|_{\alpha=0} = (\delta y)^2 e^{F(y + 0)}\,[(F'(y + 0))^2 + F''(y + 0)]$$

$$= (\delta y)^2\, e^{F(y)}[(F'(y))^2 + F''(y)] \qquad ...(1)$$

Let $\quad I[y] = F(y)$

$$\therefore \quad I[y + \alpha\delta y] = F(y + \alpha\delta y)$$

$$\therefore \quad \frac{\partial}{\partial\alpha} I[y + \alpha\delta y] = F'(y + \alpha\delta y).\delta y$$

and $$\frac{\partial^2}{\partial\alpha^2} I[y + \alpha\delta y] = \delta y.F''(y + \alpha\delta y)\,.\,\delta y = F''(y + \alpha\delta y)\,.\,(\delta y)^2$$

$$\therefore \quad \frac{\partial}{\partial\alpha} I[y + \alpha\delta y]\Big|_{\alpha=0} = F'(y).\delta y \quad \text{and} \quad \frac{\partial^2}{\partial\alpha^2} I[y + \alpha\delta y]\Big|_{\alpha=0} = F''(y).(\delta y)^2$$

$\therefore$ $\delta F = F'(y).\delta y$ and $\delta^2 F = F''(y).(\delta y)^2$

$$\therefore \quad (1) \Rightarrow \quad \frac{\partial^2}{\partial \alpha^2} J[y + \alpha \delta y]\bigg|_{\alpha=0} = e^{F(y)}[F'(y)\delta y)^2 + F''(y).(\delta y)^2] = e^{F(y)}[(\delta F)^2 + \delta^2 F]$$

$$\therefore \quad \delta^2 J = e^{F(y)}[(\delta F)^2 + \delta^2 F].$$

EXERCISE 5

1. Show that the functional $J[y(x)] = y(4)$, $y(x) \in C\ [4, 10]$ is differentiable.
2. Find the variation of the functional $\int_{x_1}^{x_2} (6y(x) + 7)\, dx$.
3. Find the variation of the functional $\int_3^5 y^2(x)\, dx$.
4. Find the variation of the functional $\int_{x_1}^{x_2} (x + y)\, dx$.
5. Find the variation of the functional $\int_a^b (y^2 - y'^2)\, dx$.
6. Find the variation of the functional $\int_0^\pi y' \sin y\, dx$.
7. Find the second variation of the functional $\int_a^b y^2(x) dx$.
8. Find the second variation of the functional $\int_0^1 (xy^2 + y'^3)\, dx$.

Answers

2. $6\int_{x_1}^{x_2} \delta y(x)\, dx$
3. $2\int_3^5 y(x)\, \delta y(x)\, dx$
4. $\int_{x_1}^{x_2} \delta y(x)\, dx$
5. $2\int_a^b (y\delta y - y'(\delta y)')\, dx$
6. $\int_0^\pi (\delta y)' \sin y + y' \delta y \cos y)$
7. $2\int_a^b (\delta y)^2\, dx$
8. $2\int_0^1 [x(\delta y)^2 + 3y'(\delta y)'^2]\, dx$.

EXAMINATION PAPERS

KU KURUKSHETRA

B.A./B.Sc. II EXAMINATION, Sept. 2005

Paper II

Differential Equations

Time : Three Hours] [*Maximum Marks : B.Sc.—45*
B.A.—30

Note : Attempt *five* questions, selecting atleast *one* from each Section.

SECTION I

1. (*a*) Find the power series solution of the differential equation

$$x\frac{d^2y}{dx^2}+\frac{dy}{dx}+2y=0 \text{ in powers of } (x-1).$$

(*b*) Show that $n\,P_n = x\,.\,P'_n - P'_{n-1}$.

2. (*a*) Show that

$$\cos(x\,.\,\sin\phi) = J_0 + 2J_2\cos 2\phi + 2J_4\cos 4\phi + \ldots$$

(*b*) Show that $\int J_3(x)\,dx = -J_2(x) - \frac{2}{x}J_0(x) + c$.

SECTION II

3. (*a*) Evaluate

(*i*) $L(\sin^2 2t)$ (*ii*) $L(\sin 3t.\cos 2t)$

(*b*) Using $L(\sin bt) = \frac{b}{s^2+b^2}$, find $L(\cos bt)$.

4. (*a*) Find $L^{-1}\left[\frac{1}{(s+3)(s-2)}\right]$.

(*b*) Solve the integral equation using Laplace transforms

$$y(t) = t + \int_0^t y(u)\sin(t-u)\,du.$$

SECTION III

5. (*a*) Find the general solution of the Lagrange's linear equation

$$(x^2 + 2y^2)\,p - xy\,q = xz.$$

(*b*) Find complete solution using Charpit's method

$$z = px + qy + p^2 + q^2.$$

6. (*a*) Solve $(2D^2 - 5DD' + 2D'^2)\,z = 5(y - x)$.

(*b*) Solve $(3D^2D' + D'^2)\,z = 0$.

7. (*a*) Use Monge's method to solve :

$$xy\,(r - t) - s\,(x^2 - y^2) = qx - py.$$

(*b*) Find general solution of

$$(D^2 + 3DD' + 2D'^2)\,z = 2x + 3y.$$

SECTION IV

8. (*a*) Find the extremals of the functional

$$J[y(x)] = \int_{x_1}^{x_2} \frac{\sqrt{1+y'^2}}{x}\,dx.$$

(*b*) Find the stationary function of the functional $\int_0^4 (xy' - y'^2)\,dx$,

determined by the boundary conditions $y(0) = 0$ and $y(4) = 3$.

9. (*a*) Find the shortest distance from the point A (0, 2, 1) to the straight line $\frac{x}{1} = \frac{y}{2} = \frac{z}{3}$.

(*b*) Given a family of curves $y = c\,(x + 4)\,x$. Find a point conjugate to the point (0, 0).

10. (*a*) Find the *c*-discriminant of the family of curves $y(c - x) = c^2$.

(*b*) Show that Jacobi condition is fulfilled for the functional $\int_0^a (x^2 + y^2)\,dx$,

$a > o$ with fixed boundaries A(0, 0) and B(*a*, 2).

HINTS/SOLUTIONS OF QUESTIONS NOT ALREADY COVERED IN THE BOOK

Sol. 6. (*b*) We have $(3D^2\,D' + D'^2)\,z = 0$ ...(1)

$\Rightarrow$ $D'\,(3D^2 + D')\,z = 0$

The factor D' is linear.

Also, $D' = 0.D + 1.D' + 0$

$\therefore$ Corresponding to D', the part of general solution of (1) is

$$e^{0.y/1}\,\phi_1\,(0.y - 1.x) = \phi_1\,(-x) = \phi_2\,(x), \text{ say}$$

The factor $3D^2 + D'$ is irreducible.

Let $z = ce^{ax + by}$ be a solution of $(3D^2 + D')z = 0$

$\Rightarrow \quad (3a^2 + b)\,ce^{ax + by} = 0.$

$\Rightarrow \quad 3a^2 + b = 0 \quad \text{or} \quad b = -3a^2$

$\therefore$ Corresponding to $3D^2 + D'$, the part of general solution of (1) is $\sum_{i=1}^{\infty} c_i e^{a_i x - 3a_i^2 y}$

$\therefore$ The general solution of (1) is

$$z = \phi_2(x) + \sum_{i=1}^{\infty} c_i e^{a_i x - 3a_i^2 y}$$

KU KURUKSHETRA

B.A./B.Sc. II EXAMINATION, APRIL 2006

Paper II

Differential Equations

Time : Three Hours] [*Maximum Marks : B.Sc.—45*
B.A.—30

Note : Attempt *five* questions, selecting atleast *one* from each Section.

SECTION I

1. (*a*) Show that the Bessel function

$$J_{5/2}(x) = \sqrt{\frac{2}{\pi x}}\left(\frac{3-x^2}{x^2}\sin x - \frac{3}{x}\cos x\right).$$

(*b*) Show that :

$$\sin(x\sin\theta) = 2[J_1(x)\sin\theta + J_3(x)\sin 3\theta + \ldots\ldots].$$

2. (*a*) Prove that : $(n+1)P_{n+1}(x) + nP_{n-1}(x) = (2n+1)xP_n(x)$, where $P_n(x)$ denotes Legendre polynomial of oder n.

(*b*) Show that : $\frac{d}{dx}F(\alpha, \beta; \gamma; x) = \frac{\alpha\beta}{\gamma}F(\alpha+1, \beta+1; \gamma+1; x)$,

where $F(\alpha, \beta; \gamma; x)$ denotes hypergeometric function.

SECTION II

3. (*a*) Evaluate $L(t^2\cos at)$.

(*b*) Find the Laplace transform of $\int_0^t \frac{\sin x}{x}\,dx$.

4. (*a*) Find the inverse Laplace transform of $\frac{1}{s(s+2)^3}$.

(*b*) Solve $f'(t) = t + \int_0^t f(t-u)\cos u\,du$; given $f(0) = 4$.

SECTION III

5. (a) Solve : $(z^2 - 2yz - y^2)\,p + (xy + zx)\,q = xy - zx$.
Here p, q have their usual meanings.
(b) Find the singular integral of :
$$z = px + qy + \log pq.$$

6. (a) Apply Charpit's method to find the complete integral of
$$px + qy = pq.$$
(b) Solve : $\dfrac{\partial^3 z}{\partial x^3} - \dfrac{4\partial^3 z}{\partial x^2\,\partial y} + \dfrac{4\partial^3 z}{\partial x \partial y^2} = 2\sin(3x + 2y)$.

7. (a) Solve $r + (a + b)\,s + abt = xy$ using Monge's method. Here r, s, t have their usual meanings.

(b) Find the general solution of the partial differential equation :
$$(D^2 - D'^2 + D + 3D' - 2)\,z = e^{x-y} - x^2y,$$
where D and D′ stand for $\dfrac{\partial}{\partial x}$ and $\dfrac{\partial}{\partial y}$ respectively.

SECTION IV

8. (a) Find the curve on which the functional $\int_0^1 [(y')^2 + 12xy]\,dx$ with boundary conditions $y(0) = 0$ and $y(1) = 1$ can be extremized.

(b) Determine the extremal of the functional :
$$I\,[y(x)] = \int_{x_0}^{x_1} (16y^2 - y'^2 + x^2)\,dx.$$

9. (a) Find the extremals of the isoperimetric problem :
$$v[y(x)] = \int_{x_0}^{x_1} y'^2\,dx \text{ given that } \int_{x_0}^{x_1} y\,dx = c, \text{ a constant.}$$

(b) Find the extremals of the functional $\int_{\theta_1}^{\theta_2} \sqrt{(r^2 + r'^2)}\,d\theta$, where $r = r(\theta)$.

10. (a) Find the shortest distance from the point (– 1, 5) to the parabola $y^2 = x$.

(b) Show that the Jaçobi's condition is fulfilled for the functional $\int_{-1}^{1} (12\,xy + y'^2 + x^2)\,dx$ with fixed boundaries A (–1, 2) and B (1, 0).

HINTS/SOLUTIONS OF QUESTIONS NOT ALREADY COVERED IN THE BOOK

Sol. 3. (*a*) $L(\cos at) = \frac{s}{s^2 + a^2}$

By differentiating of Laplace transform,

$$L(t\,.\,\cos at) = -\frac{d}{ds}\left(\frac{s}{s^2 + a^2}\right)$$

$$= -\left[\frac{(s^2 + a^2).1 - s.2s}{(s^2 + a^2)^2}\right] = \frac{s^2 - a^2}{(s^2 + a^2)^2}$$

Again by using the same formula,

$$L(t\,.\,t\cos at) = -\frac{d}{ds}\left(\frac{s^2 - a^2}{(s^2 + a^2)^2}\right)$$

$$= -\frac{(s^2 + a^2)^2\,.\,2s - (s^2 - a^2)\,.\,2(s^2 + a^2)\,2s}{(s^2 + a^2)^4} = \frac{\mathbf{2s\,(s^2 - 3a^2)}}{\mathbf{(s^2 + a^2)^3}}.$$

Sol. 4. (*a*) $\frac{1}{s(s+2)^3} = \frac{1}{s}\,.\,\frac{1}{(s+2)^3} = F(s)\,.\,G(s)$, where $F(s) = \frac{1}{s}$ and $G(s) = \frac{1}{(s+2)^3}$.

$$L^{-1}(F(s)) = L^{-1}\left(\frac{1}{s}\right) = 1 = f(t), \text{ say}$$

and

$$L^{-1}(G(s)) = L^{-1}\left(\frac{1}{(s+2)^3}\right) = e^{-2t}L^{-1}\left(\frac{1}{s^3}\right)$$

$$= \frac{e^{-2t}}{2}L^{-1}\left(\frac{2!}{s^3}\right) = \frac{e^{-2t}}{2}t^2 = \frac{1}{2}t^2e^{-2t} = g(t), \text{ say}$$

By **Convolution Theorem,**

$$L^{-1}(F(s)\,.\,G(s)) = f * g = g * f = \int_0^t g(T)f(t-T)\,dT$$

$$\Rightarrow \quad L^{-1}\left(\frac{1}{s(s+2)^3}\right) = \int_0^t \frac{1}{2}T^2e^{-2T}\,.\,1\,dT$$

$$= \frac{1}{2}\left[T^2\,.\,\frac{e^{-2T}}{-2}\Big|_0^t - \int_0^t 2T\frac{e^{-2T}}{-2}dT\right]$$

$$= \frac{1}{2}\left[-\frac{1}{2}(t^2e^{-2t} - 0) + T\,.\,\frac{e^{-2T}}{-2}\Big|_0^t - \int_0^t 1\,.\,\frac{e^{-2T}}{-2}dT\right]$$

$$= -\frac{1}{4}t^2e^{-2t} - \frac{1}{4}(te^{-2t} - 0) + \frac{1}{4}\,.\,\frac{e^{-2T}}{-2}\Big|_0^t$$

$$= -\frac{1}{4}t^2e^{-2t} - \frac{1}{4}te^{-2t} - \frac{1}{8}[e^{-2t} - 1]$$

$$= -\frac{1}{4}t^2e^{-2t} - \frac{1}{4}te^{-2t} - \frac{1}{8}e^{-2t} + \frac{1}{8}$$

$$= -\frac{1}{8}e^{-2t}(2t^2 + 2t + 1) + \frac{1}{8}.$$

Sol. 5. (*a*) We have $(z^2 - 2yz - y^2)p + (xy + zx)q = xy - zx$

$\therefore$ Auxiliary equations are

$$\frac{dx}{z^2 - 2yz - y^2} = \frac{dy}{xy + zx} = \frac{dz}{xy - zx} \quad ...(1)$$

Taking the last two fractions of (1), we get

$$\frac{dy}{x(y + z)} = \frac{dz}{x(y - z)}$$

$$\Rightarrow \quad \frac{dy}{y + z} = \frac{dz}{y - z}$$

$$\Rightarrow \quad (y - z)\,dy = (y + z)\,dz$$

$$\Rightarrow \quad y\,dy - z\,dz - (z\,dy + y\,dz) = 0$$

$$\Rightarrow \quad \frac{y^2}{2} - \frac{z^2}{2} - yz = c_1$$

$$\Rightarrow \quad y^2 - z^2 - 2yz = c_2 \quad \text{(Putting } c_2 = 2c_1\text{)}$$

Taking x, y, z as multipliers,

$$\text{each fraction of (1)} = \frac{x\,dx + y\,dy + z\,dz}{x(z^2 - 2yz - y^2) + y(xy + zx) + z(xy - zx)} = \frac{x\,dx + y\,dy + z\,dz}{0}$$

$$\therefore \quad x\,dx + y\,dy + z\,dz = 0$$

$$\Rightarrow \quad 2x\,dx + 2y\,dy + 2z\,dz = 0$$

$$\Rightarrow \quad x^2 + y^2 + z^2 = c_3$$

$\therefore$ The general solution of the given equation is

$$\mathbf{f(y^2 - z^2 - 2yz,\ x^2 + y^2 + z^2) = 0.}$$

Sol. 6. (*b*) See solved question 1.(*iii*) on page 292.

Sol. 7. (*a*) We have $r + (a + b)s + abt = xy \quad ...(1)$

Comparing (1) with $R_r + S_s + T_t = V$, we get

$$R = 1,\ S = a + b,\ T = ab,\ V = xy$$

The **Monge's equations** are

$$R(dy)^2 - S\,dx\,dy + T(dx)^2 = 0 \quad ...(2)$$

and

$$R\,dy\,dp + T\,dx\,dq - V\,dx\,dy = 0 \quad ...(3)$$

$$(2) \Rightarrow \quad (dy)^2 - (a + b)\,dx\,dy + ab\,(dx)^2 = 0$$

$$\Rightarrow \quad (dy - a\,dx)(dy - b\,dx) = 0$$

$$dy - a\,dx = 0$$

and $$dy - bdx = 0 \quad ...(4')$$

(3) $\Rightarrow$ $$dy\,dp + ab\,dx\,dq - xy\,dx\,dy = 0 \quad ...(5)$$

We consider the system (4) and (5).

Integrating (4), we get

$$y - ax = c_1$$

Putting $dy = a\,dx$ in (5), we get

$$a\,dx\,dp + ab\,dx\,dq - axy\,dx\,dx = 0$$

$$\Rightarrow \quad adx\,(dp + bdq - xy\,dx) = 0$$

$$\Rightarrow \quad dp + bdq - x(ax + c_1)\,dx = 0$$

Integrating we get $$p + bq - \frac{ax^3}{3} - \frac{c_1x^2}{2} = c_2$$

$$\Rightarrow \quad p + bq - \frac{a}{3}x^3 - \frac{(y - ax)x^2}{2} = c_2$$

$$\Rightarrow \quad p + bq - \frac{1}{2}x^2y + \frac{1}{6}a\,x^3 = c_2$$

$$\Rightarrow \quad p + bq - \frac{1}{2}x^2y + \frac{1}{6}ax^3 = \phi_1(c_1) \text{ say}$$

$$\Rightarrow \quad p + bq - \frac{1}{2}x^2y + \frac{1}{6}ax^3 = \phi_1(y - ax) \quad ...(6)$$

Similarly, the other intermediate integral corresponding to (4′) is

$$p + aq - \frac{1}{2}x^2y + \frac{1}{6}bx^3 = \phi_2(y - bx) \quad ...(7)$$

Solving (6) and (7), we get the values of p and q.

These values of p and q are put in the equation $dz = p\,dx + y\,dy$. This equations is solved to get the required solution.

(*b*) Given question is combination of Q. No. 5 (page 313) and Q. No. 5 (page 315).

M.D.U. Rohtak

B.Sc. II EXAMINATION, APRIL 2006

Paper II

Differential Equations and Calculus of Variations

Time : Three Hours] [*Maximum Marks : 50*

Note : Attempt *five* questions in all, selecting at least *one* question from each Unit.

UNIT I

1. (*a*) Find the power series solution of :

$$(x^2-1)\frac{d^2y}{dx^2}+3x\frac{dy}{dx}+xy=0,$$

$$y(0)=2 \quad \text{and} \quad y'(0)=3.$$

(*b*) (*i*) Solve the equation :

$$x^2\frac{d^2y}{dx^2}+x\frac{dy}{dx}+(x^2-25)\,y=0$$

in terms of Bessel's functions.

(*ii*) Verify that $J_{1/2}(x)=\sqrt{\frac{2}{\pi x}}\sin x$ satisfies the Bessel's equation of order 1/2.

2 (*a*) show that :

$$\frac{1}{\sqrt{1-2xt+t^2}}=\sum_{n=0}^{\infty}t^n\,P_n(x)$$

where $|x|\le 1$ and $-1<t<1$.

(*b*) If $-1<x<1$ and $-1<\frac{x}{1-x}<1$, then show that :

$$F(a,b,c,x)=\frac{1}{(1-x)^a}\,F\left(a,c-b,c,\frac{x}{x-1}\right).$$

UNIT II

3. (a) Find the Laplace transform of the following :
(i) $te^{-2t} \sin 3t$ (ii) $e^{-2t} \sin t \cos 3t$.
(b) Apply convolution theorem to evaluate :
$$L^{-1}\left[\frac{s}{(s^2+2s)^2}\right].$$
4. Solve the following differential equations by transform method :
(i) $\frac{d^2y}{dt^2} + y = 3 \cos 2t$ (ii) $\frac{dx}{dt} - y = e^{2t},\ \frac{dy}{dt} + x \sin t$.

UNIT III

5. (a) Form the partial differential equation by eliminating a, b, c from :
$$b^2x^2 + a^2y^2 = 2a^2b^2z.$$
(b) Solve the partial differential equation :
$$p + 3q = z + \cot(y - 3x).$$
6. (a) Find the complete solution of differential equation :
$$z = px + qy - 2p - 3q.$$
(b) Solve the differential equation :
$$p^2 - qy^2 = y^2 - x^2 \text{ by Charpit's method.}$$
7. Solve the following partial differential equations :
(i) $\frac{\partial^3 z}{\partial x^3} - 4\frac{\partial^3 z}{\partial x^2 \partial y} + 5\frac{\partial^3 z}{\partial x \partial y^2} - 2\frac{\partial^3 z}{\partial y^3} = 3e^{3x-2y}$.
(ii) $x^2\frac{\partial^2 z}{\partial x^2} + 2xy\frac{\partial^2 z}{\partial x \partial y} + y^2\frac{\partial^2 z}{\partial y^2} - nx\frac{\partial z}{\partial x} - ny\frac{\partial z}{\partial y} + nz = x^2 + y^2$.

UNIT IV

8. (a) Find extremal of the functional :
$$I[y(x)] = \int_0^4 \frac{(y')^{-2}}{x^{-3}}\, dx,\ y(0) = 0,\ y(4) = 4.$$
(b) Find extremal of functional :
$$I[y(x)] = \int_a^b [4y^2 - (y'')^2 + 2x^2]\, dx$$
9. (a) Find the geodesics on a sphere of radius r.
(b) Show that the extremal of functional :
$$\int_{t_1}^{t_2}\left[5\left(\frac{dx}{dt}\right)^2 + 7\left(\frac{dy}{dt}\right)^2\right]^{1/2} dt \text{ is a straight line.}$$

10. (*a*) Find the shortest distance from the point $(-1, 5)$ to the curve $\frac{y^2}{x} = 1, x \neq 0$.

(*b*) Find the necessary condition for the extremum of a function :

$$\int_a^b f(x, y(x), y'(x), \ldots\ldots, y^n(x))\, dx.$$

HINTS/SOLUTIONS OF QUESTIONS NOT ALREADY COVERED IN THE BOOK

Sol. 1. (*a*) Let the solution of given equation be

$$y = \sum_{m=0}^{\infty} a_m x^m .$$

$$y' = \sum_{m=0}^{\infty} m\, a_m x^{m-1}$$

$$y(0) = 2 \Rightarrow a_0 = 2$$

$$y'(0) = 3 \Rightarrow a_1 = 3$$

Substituting, the values of y, y' and y'' in the given equation, we shall get

$$a_2 = 0,\ a_3 = \frac{a_0 + 3a_1}{6} = \frac{2 + 3(3)}{5} = \frac{11}{5}$$

and
$$a_{m+2} = \frac{(m^2 + 2m)\, a_m + a_{m-1}}{(m+2)(m+1)} \quad \forall\, m \geq 2$$

(compare the given question with Q. No. 15 on page 25)

$$m = 2 \Rightarrow a_4 = \frac{(4+4)a_2 + a_1}{(2+2)(2+1)} = \frac{8(0) + 3}{12} = \frac{1}{4}$$

$\therefore$ The solution is $\mathbf{y = 2 + 3x + \frac{11}{5}x^3 + \frac{1}{4}x^4 + \ldots.}$

Sol. 2. (*b*) We know that

$$F(a, b, c\,; x) = \frac{1}{B(b, c-b)} \int_0^1 t^{b-1} (1-t)^{c-b-1} (1-xt)^{-a}\, dt \qquad \ldots(1)$$

Let $z = 1 - t \quad \therefore \quad dz = -dt$

$$\therefore \quad (1) \Rightarrow F(a, b, c\,; x) = \frac{1}{B(b, c-b)} \int_1^0 (1-z)^{b-1} z^{c-b-1} (1 - x(1-z))^{-a} (-dz)$$

$$= \frac{1}{B(b, c-b)} \int_0^1 (1-z)^{b-1} z^{c-b-1} (1 - x + xz)^{-a}\, dz$$

$$= \frac{1}{B(b, c-b)} \int_0^1 (1-z)^{b-1} z^{c-b-1} (1-x)^{-a} \left[1 + \frac{xz}{1-x}\right]^{-a} dz$$

$$= \frac{(1-x)^{-a}\, \Gamma(b + c - b)}{\Gamma(b)\, \Gamma(c-b)} \int_0^1 z^{c-b-1} (1-z)^{b-1} \left(1 + \frac{xz}{1-x}\right)^{-a} dz$$

$$= \frac{(1-x)^{-a}\,\Gamma(c)}{\Gamma(c-b)\,\Gamma(c-(c-b))}\int_0^1 z^{(c-b)-1}(1-z)^{b-1}\left(1+\frac{xz}{1-x}\right)^{-a} dz$$

$$= \frac{1}{(1-x)^a}\cdot\frac{1}{\mathrm{B}(c-b,c)}\int_0^1 z^{(c-b)-1}(1-z)^{c-(c-b)-1}\left(1-\frac{x}{x-1}z\right)dz$$

$$= \frac{1}{(1-x)^a}\,\mathrm{F}\left(a, c-b, c, \frac{x}{x-1}\right).$$

Sol. 3. (*a*) (*i*) $\mathrm{L}(\sin 3t) = \dfrac{3}{s^2+9} \Rightarrow \mathrm{L}(t\sin 3t) = -\dfrac{d}{ds}\left(\dfrac{3}{s^2+9}\right) = \dfrac{6s}{(s^2+9)^2}$

∴ By **first shifting theorem,**

$$\mathrm{L}(e^{-2t}\,t\sin 3t) = \frac{6(s-(-2))}{((s-(-2))^2+9)^2} = \frac{6(s+2)}{(s^2+4s+13)^2}.$$

(*ii*) $\mathrm{L}(\sin t\cos 3t) = \dfrac{1}{2}\mathrm{L}(2\cos 3t\sin t) = \dfrac{1}{2}\mathrm{L}(\sin 4t - \sin 2t)$

$$= \frac{1}{2}\left[\frac{4}{s^2+16} - \frac{2}{s^2+4}\right] = \frac{2}{s^2+16} - \frac{1}{s^2+4}$$

∴ By **first shifting theorem,**

$$\mathrm{L}(e^{-2t}\sin t\cos 3t) = \frac{2}{(s-(-2))^2+16} - \frac{1}{(s-(-2))^2+4} = \frac{2}{s^2+4s+20} - \frac{1}{s^2+4s+8}.$$

(*b*) $\dfrac{s}{(s^2+2s)^2} = \dfrac{s}{s^2(s+2)^2} = \dfrac{1}{s(s+2)^2} = \mathrm{F}(s)\ \mathrm{G}(s),$

where, $\mathrm{F}(s) = \dfrac{1}{s}$ and $\mathrm{G}(s) = \dfrac{1}{(s+2)^2}$

∴ $\mathrm{L}^{-1}(\mathrm{F}(s)) = \mathrm{L}^{-1}\left(\dfrac{1}{s}\right) = 1 = f(t)$, say

and $\mathrm{L}^{-1}(\mathrm{G}(s)) = \mathrm{L}^{-1}\left(\dfrac{1}{(s+2)^2}\right) = e^{-2t}\,\mathrm{L}^{-1}\left(\dfrac{1}{s^2}\right) = e^{-2t}\,t = g(t)$, say

By **Convolution Theorem,**

$$\mathrm{L}^{-1}(\mathrm{F}(s)\,\mathrm{G}(s)) = f * g$$

$$= \int_0^t \mathrm{T}e^{-2\mathrm{T}}\,d\mathrm{T} = \mathrm{T}\,.\,\frac{e^{-2\mathrm{T}}}{-2}\Bigg|_0^t - \int_0^t 1.\frac{e^{-2\mathrm{T}}}{-2}\,d\mathrm{T}$$

$$= -\frac{1}{2}[te^{-2t} - 0] + \frac{1}{2}.\frac{e^{-2\mathrm{T}}}{-2}\Bigg|_0^t = -\frac{1}{2}te^{-2t} - \frac{1}{4}[e^{-2t} - 1]$$

$$= -\frac{1}{2}te^{-2t} - \frac{1}{4}e^{-2t} + \frac{1}{4} = -\frac{1}{4}[2te^{-2t} + e^{-2t} - 1].$$

Sol. 4. The statements are apparently incomplete because boundary conditions are not given.

Sol. 7. (*i*) We have $(D^3 - 4D^2D' + 5DD'^2 - 2D'^3)z = 3e^{3x-2y}$ ...(1)

The A.E. of (1) is

$$m^3 - 4m^2 + 5m - 2 = 0 \quad \therefore \quad m = 1, 1, 2$$

$$\therefore \quad \text{C.F.} = \phi_1(y+x) + x\,\phi_2(y+x) = \phi_3(y+2x)$$

$$\text{P.I.} = \frac{1}{D^3 - 4D^2D' + 5DD'^2 - 2D'^3}\, 3e^{3x-2y}$$

$$= 3\,\frac{1}{(D-D')^2(D-2D')}\, e^{3x-2y}$$

$$= 3\,\frac{1}{(D-D')^2} \cdot \frac{1}{3-2(-2)} \int e^v\, dv, \text{ where } v = 3x - 2y$$

$$= \frac{3}{7} \cdot \frac{1}{(D-D')^2}\, e^v = \frac{3}{7} \cdot \frac{1}{(D-D')^2}\, e^{3x-2y}$$

$$= \frac{3}{7} \cdot \frac{1}{(3-(-2))^2} \iint e^v\, dv \text{ where } v = 3x - 2y$$

$$= \frac{3}{175}\, e^v = \frac{3}{175}\, e^{3x-2y}$$

$$\therefore \quad \textbf{G.S.} = \boldsymbol{\phi_1(y+x) + x\,\phi_2(y+x) + \phi_3(y+2x) + \frac{3}{175}\, e^{3x-2y}}.$$

7. (*ii*) We have $(x^2D^2 + 2xy\,DD' + y^2D'^2 - nx\,D - ny\,D' + n)z = x^2 + y^2$ ...(1)

Let $u = \log x$ and $v = \log y$

$\therefore$ $x = e^u$ and $y = e^v$

Also $xD = D_1,\ yD' = D'_1,\ x^2D^2 = D_1(D_1 - 1),$

$$xy\,DD' = D_1D_1',\ y^2D'^2 = D_1'(D_1' - 1), \text{ where } D_1 = \frac{\partial}{\partial u} \text{ and } D_1' = \frac{\partial}{\partial v}.$$

$$\therefore \ (i) \Rightarrow (D_1(D_1-1) + 2D_1D_1' + D_1'(D_1'-1) - n\,D_1 - n\,D_1' + n)z = e^{2u} + e^{2v}$$

$$\Rightarrow \quad (D_1^2 - D_1 + 2D_1D_1' + D_1'^2 - D_1' - nD_1 - nD_1' + n)z = e^{2u} + e^{2v}$$

$$= (D_1^2 + 2D_1D_1' + D_1'^2 - (n+1)D_1 - (n+1)D_1' + n)z = e^{2u} + e^{2v}$$

$$= ((D_1 + D_1')^2 - (n+1)(D_1 + D_1') + n)z = e^{2u} + e^{2v}$$

$$(D_1 + D_1' - 1)(D_1 + D_1' - n)z = e^{2u} + e^{2v}$$

$$\Rightarrow \quad (1.D_1 + 1.D_1' - 1)(1.D_1 + 1.D_1' - n)z = e^{2u} + e^{2v}$$

$$\therefore \quad \text{C.F.} = e^{1.u/1}\,\phi_1(1.v - 1.u) + e^{nu/1}\,\phi_2(1.v - 1.u)$$

$$= e^u\,\phi_1(v-u) + e^{nu}\,\phi_2(v-x)$$

$$= x\,\phi_1(\log y - \log x) + x^n\,\phi_2(\log y - \log x)$$

$$= x\,\phi_1(\log y/x) + x^n\,\phi_2(\log y/x)$$

$$= x\,\psi_1(y/x) + x^n\,\psi(y/x), \text{ say}.$$

$$\text{P.I} = \frac{1}{(D_1 + D_1' - 1)(D_1 + D_1' - n)} (e^{2u} + e^{2v})$$

$$= \frac{1}{(D_1 + D_1' - 1)(D_1 + D_1' - n)} e^{2u} + \frac{1}{(D_1 + D_1' - 1)(D_1 + D_1' - n)} e^{2v}$$

$$= \frac{1}{(2+0-1)(2+0-n)} e^{2u} + \frac{1}{(0+2-1)(0+2-n)} e^{2v}$$

$$= \frac{1}{2-n} x^2 + \frac{1}{2-n} y^2 = \frac{1}{2-n} (x^2 + y^2)$$

$\therefore$ $$\textbf{G.S.} = \mathbf{x\, \psi_1 (y/x) + x^n\, \psi_2 (y/x) + \frac{1}{2-n} (x^2 + y^2)}.$$

Sol. 8. (*a*) We have $I[y(x)] = \int_0^4 \frac{(y')^{-2}}{x^{-3}}\, dx.$

Let $$F(x, y, y') = \frac{(y')^{-2}}{x^{-3}} = \frac{x^3}{y'^2}$$

The **Euler's equation** is $$\frac{\partial F}{\partial y} - \frac{d}{dx}\left(\frac{\partial F}{\partial y'}\right) = 0 \quad \ldots(1)$$

Here, $$\frac{\partial F}{\partial y} = 0, \quad \frac{\partial F}{\partial y'} = -\frac{2x^3}{y'^3}$$

$\therefore$ (1) $\Rightarrow$ $$0 - \frac{d}{dx}\left(-\frac{2x^3}{y'^3}\right) = 0$$

$\Rightarrow$ $$\frac{d}{dx}\left(\frac{x^3}{y'^3}\right) = 0 \Rightarrow \frac{x^3}{y'^3} = c_1 \Rightarrow y' = \frac{x}{\sqrt[3]{c_1}}$$

Integrating, we get $$y = \frac{x^2}{2\sqrt[3]{c_1}} + c_2$$

$\Rightarrow$ $$y = kx^2 + c_2 \quad \left(\text{Putting } k = \frac{1}{2\sqrt[3]{c_1}}\right)$$

The boundary conditions are $y(0) = 0$ and $y(4) = 4$.

$$y(0) = 0 \Rightarrow k(0)^2 + c_2 = 0 \Rightarrow c_2 = 0$$

$$y(4) = 4 \Rightarrow k(4)^2 + c_2 = 4 \Rightarrow 16k + 0 = 4 \Rightarrow k = \frac{1}{4}$$

$\therefore$ The required extremal is

$$y = \frac{1}{4} x^2 + 0 \quad i.e., \quad \mathbf{y = \frac{1}{4} x^2}.$$

(*b*) We have $I[y(x)] = \int_a^b (4y^2 - (y'')^2 + 2x^2)\, dx$

Let $F(x, y, y', y'') = 4y^2 - (y'')^2 + 2x^2$

The **Eular-Poisson equation** is

$$F_y - \frac{d}{dx} F_{y'} + \frac{d^2}{dx^2} F_{y''} = 0 \qquad ...(1)$$

Here, $F_y = 8y, F_{y'} = 0, F_{y''} = -2y''$

$\therefore$ (1) $\Rightarrow$ $8y - \frac{d}{dx}(0) + \frac{d^2}{dx^2}(-2y'') = 0$

$\Rightarrow$ $\frac{dy^4}{dx^4} - 4y = 0 \Rightarrow (D^4 - 4)y = 0$

The A.E. is $D^4 - 4 = 0$

$\Rightarrow$ $(D - \sqrt{2})(D + \sqrt{2})(D - \sqrt{2}i)(D + \sqrt{2}i) = 0$

$\Rightarrow$ $D = \pm \sqrt{2}, \pm \sqrt{2}i$

$\therefore$ $y = c_1 e^{\sqrt{2}x} + c_2 e^{-\sqrt{2}x} + e^{0.x}(c_3 \cos \sqrt{2}\, x + c_4 \sin \sqrt{2} x)$

$\therefore$ $\mathbf{y = c_1 e^{\sqrt{2}x} + c_2 e^{-\sqrt{2}x} + c_3 \cos \sqrt{2} x + c_4 \sin \sqrt{2}\, x.}$

(*b*) Let $J = \int_{t_1}^{t_2} \left[5\left(\frac{dx}{dt}\right)^2 + 7\left(\frac{dy}{dt}\right)^2 \right]^{1/2} dt$

$\therefore$ $J = \int_{t_1}^{t_2} \sqrt{5\dot{x}^2 + 7\dot{y}^2}\, dt$

Let $F(x, y, \dot{x}, \dot{y}) = \sqrt{5\dot{x}^2 + 7\dot{y}^2}$

F is a positive homogeneous function of degree one in $\dot{x}$ and $\dot{y}$.

The **Euler's equations** are

$$F_x - \frac{d}{dt} F_{\dot{x}} = 0 \qquad ...(1)$$

$$F_y - \frac{d}{dt} F_{\dot{y}} = 0 \qquad ...(2)$$

We use (1) to find the extremals.

Here, $F_x = 0, F_{\dot{x}} = \frac{5\dot{x}}{\sqrt{5\dot{x}^2 + 7\dot{y}^2}}$

$\therefore$ (1) $\Rightarrow$ $0 - \frac{d}{dt}\left(\frac{5\dot{x}}{\sqrt{5\dot{x}^2 + 7\dot{y}^2}}\right) = 0$

$\Rightarrow$ $$\frac{\dot{x}}{\sqrt{5\dot{x}^2 + 7\dot{y}^2}} = c_1 \qquad ...(3)$$

Case I. $c_1 = 0$ $\therefore$ (3) $\Rightarrow$ $\dot{x} = 0 \Rightarrow x = c_2$

Case II. $c_1 \neq 0$ $\therefore$ (3) $\Rightarrow$ $\dot{x}^2 = c_1^2(5\dot{x}^2 + 7\dot{y}^2)$

$\Rightarrow$ $1 = c_1^2\left(5 + 7\left(\frac{\dot{y}}{\dot{x}}\right)^2\right) \Rightarrow 1 = c_1^2\,(5 + 7y'^2)$

$$\Rightarrow \qquad y' = \sqrt{\frac{5(1-5c_1^2)}{7c_1^2}} = \lambda, \text{ say}$$

$$\Rightarrow \qquad y = \lambda x + \mu$$

∴ The extremals are given by the equations $\mathbf{x = c_2}$, $\mathbf{y = \lambda x + \mu}$,

∴ The extremals are straight lines.